THE PAPERS OF

WOODROW WILSON

VOLUME 68

APRIL 8, 1922 - FEBRUARY 6, 1924

SPONSORED BY THE WOODROW WILSON
FOUNDATION
AND PRINCETON UNIVERSITY

THE PAPERS OF

WOODROW WILSON

ARTHUR S. LINK, *EDITOR*

JOHN E. LITTLE, *ASSOCIATE EDITOR*

L. KATHLEEN AMON, *ASSISTANT EDITOR*

PHYLLIS MARCHAND, *INDEXER*

Volume 68
April 8, 1922 - February 6, 1924

PRINCETON, NEW JERSEY

PRINCETON UNIVERSITY PRESS

1993

INTRODUCTION

THE opening of this volume, April 8, 1922, finds Wilson still recovering from the aftermath of his stroke of October 2, 1919. Although still crippled on his left side, largely housebound, and depressed by his failure to make a fast recovery, he grows increasingly interested in the affairs of his party and the political situation of the country at large. He continues to work with Colby, Brandeis, Davis, Houston, and Baruch on "The Document," which he intends to use as the Democratic platform when he runs for a third term in 1924. After many conferences with his collaborators and revisions of and additions to "The Document," Wilson produces what is the final version about January 20, 1924. Although strong for American membership in the League of Nations, it reveals the difficulties of preparing a new progressive manifesto in the changing contemporary political scene. It remains a confidential document, known only to its authors; moreover, Wilson steadfastly resists all suggestions that he give interviews or make pronouncements on current politics. He says that he will speak out only when the time is ripe to do so.

Still, it is impossible for the old warrior to sit mute on the sidelines. He welcomes the election of Cordell Hull as the new chairman of the Democratic National Committee and bombards him with advice, some of it very acerbic, about possible candidates and about the need to gentrify the Democratic party. He plunges into the Democratic senatorial primary contest in Missouri in 1922 between his loyal friend, Breckinridge Long, and the Democratic apostate, James A. Reed, with several public denunciations of what he calls the Missouri marplot. Reed wins renomination narrowly, but Wilson helps to prevent the come back of his old foe, James K. Vardaman, for senator from Mississippi. Buoyed up by the success of Democrats and insurgents in wresting control of Congress from the Harding administration in the congressional election of 1922, Wilson looks forward confidently to the presidential election two years hence. He tells his friends privately that he is now the acknowledged leader of his party, and that the Democrats will win in 1924 if they stand firm for national honor and leadership abroad.

During these same months, the business of Wilson & Colby continues to languish, mainly because Wilson will not accept any case that might raise even the shadow of a conflict of interest on account of his earlier administration of the foreign affairs of the United States. One case does excite Wilson's interest and elicit his approval. The government of the putative Western Ukraine Republic (eastern Galicia) asks Wilson & Colby to represent it in its

pleading for recognition from the Council of the League of Nations. Colby goes to London to investigate and finds that nothing
effective can be done. A short time before, Colby is eager to represent the Sinclair Oil Company in the Teapot Dome hearings in
Congress; Wilson promptly vetoes this initiative. Wilson realizes
the burden he is imposing on Colby and, in the summer of 1922,
suggests a dissolution of the partnership. Colby agrees, and the
two part company in a friendly way on December 13, 1922.

All the while, there are numerous evidences of a groundswell of
support among church and peace groups and other makers of elite
public opinion for American membership in or some kind of close
association with the League of Nations. Hamilton Holt organizes
the Woodrow Wilson Democracy to make membership in the
League the leading issue in the election of 1922, but this organization does not prosper in a milieu of preoccupation with the lingering effects of the recession of 1921, particularly among farmers.
But, in the winter of 1922-1923, Holt and former Supreme Court
Justice John H. Clarke found the Non-Partisan Association for the
League of Nations, and organization begins with much fanfare
and support. Its chief problem is the lack of Wilson's endorsement.
He tries to turn Holt and Clarke aside from their campaign with
soft words, but in the end he has to say that he will have nothing
to do with fair-weather friends, the pro-League Republicans. Non-
partisanship is a blind alley, Wilson says; Republicans cannot be
trusted; only the Democratic party can be trusted to uphold the
nation's honor.

The Non-Partisan Association never becomes more than a gorup
centered in New York; Wilson remains the most forthright and
uncompromising champion of American membership in the
League of Nations. Crowds come constantly to his home to pay
him homage and praise him for his steadfastness. Addressing the
nation over radio on November 10, 1923, he lashes out at "deeply
ignoble," "cowardly and dishonorable" isolation. On the next day—
the fifth anniversary of the Armistice, Carter Glass leads 20,000
persons in a pilgrimage to S Street. Wilson is overcome with emotion as he struggles to reply to Glass' salutation. Looking at the
disabled veterans before him, Wilson is unable to speak, and the
band begins the strains of *How Firm a Foundation*. Wilson inter-
rupts by raising his right arm. He thanks Glass for his encomium
and says that he is proud to have been the commander in chief of
"the most ideal army that was ever thrown together." Then he
chokes up, and the band starts again. But Wilson rallies, raises his
arm, and throws out a defy in the last words that he utters to the
American people:

"I am not one of those that have the least anxiety about the triumph of the principles I have stood for. I have seen fools resist Providence before and I have seen the destruction, as will come upon these again—utter destruction and contempt. That we shall prevail is as sure as that God reigns. Thank you."

There are other signs that Wilson is steadily gaining strength and hope during 1923. He had tried in 1922 to begin a book on the impact of the founding of the United States on the monarchies and despotisms of the Old World but did not have the strength to write more than a few paragraphs. However, in the spring of 1923 he is able to dictate a brief article, which he entitles "The Road Away From Revolution." Pointing to the Bolshevik Revolution as an example of what happens when people are exploited, oppressed, and denied opportunities for a better life, he indicts capitalism for its failure to place people above material things and calls for the Christianization of the capitalistic system.

Meanwhile, Wilson continues his routine of daily rides with his constant companion and devoted nurse, Mrs. Wilson. He maintains a voluminous correspondence and welcomes old friends and colleagues to his home. The family circle is partially broken when the McAdoos move to California and the Sayre family go to Siam for a year. But Wilson's spirits rise when a group of friends, led by Cleve Dodge, covenant to pay Wilson a pension of $10,000 a year in honor of his services to his country and the world and present him with a specially designed Rolls-Royce touring automobile. Wilson is in good heart when he greets the members of the Democratic National Committee and a host of friends at his home on January 16, 1924. There is now serious talk in the newspapers about a Wilson candidacy in 1924, and Wilson begins work on an acceptance speech and a third inaugural address.

On January 27 and 28, 1924, Wilson feels terribly tired and languid. The next two days, he is troubled by attacks of indigestion and can take only little nourishment. Death now moves rapidly to claim a new victim. Uremic poisoning and cardiac arrests set in. Crowds gather outside the house and women keep a prayer vigil while life ebbs. The end comes peacefully at 11:55 in the morning of February 3, and a new star swings into the historical firmament. Wilson's former pastor in Princeton, his pastor in Washington, and the Protestant Episcopal Bishop of Washington conduct simple services in the home and before the interment in the vault of the Bethlehem Chapel of the unfinished Washington Cathedral. The strife is over, the battle done; Woodrow Wilson is at peace.

Although this is the last narrative volume in this series, it is not the last volume of *The Papers of Woodrow Wilson*. The last volume, Volume 69, will be a cumulative contents-index volume for

Volumes 53-68, the most recent of which is Volume 52. Volume 69 will appear soon after the publication of Volume 68 and will include a retrospective essay by the Editor and a list of all persons and organizations which have helped us to bring this series to a conclusion.

We extend our heartfelt thanks to the many persons who have given invaluable assistance in the preparation of this volume, Volume 68: James Gordon Grayson and Cary T. Grayson, Jr., for making available documents from their father's papers; Timothy Connelly, Archivist of the National Historical and Publications Commission, for his assistance to the Editors in research in the National Archives and Library of Congress; John Milton Cooper, Jr., William H. Harbaugh, August Heckscher, Richard W. Leopold, Bert E. Park, and Betty Miller Unterberger of our Editorial Advisory Committee, for carefully reviewing the manuscript of this volume; and Alice Calaprice, our editor at Princeton University Press, for keeping things on track.

THE EDITORS

Princeton, New Jersey
May 1, 1992

CONTENTS

CONTENTS

ILLUSTRATIONS

Following page 264

ABBREVIATIONS

ALI	autograph letter initialed
ALS	autograph letter signed
ASB	Albert Sidney Burleson
BC	Bainbridge Colby
BMB	Bernard Mannes Baruch
CC	carbon copy
CCL	carbon copy of letter
CHD	Cleveland Hoadley Dodge
DFH	David Franklin Houston
EAW	Ellen Axson Wilson
EBW	Edith Bolling Galt Wilson
EBWhw	Edith Bolling Galt Wilson handwriting, handwritten
EMH	Edward Mandell House
FDR	Franklin Delano Roosevelt
FLP	Frank Lyon Polk
FR	*Papers Relating to the Foreign Relations of the United States*
HSC	Homer Stillé Cummings
Hw, hw	handwriting, handwritten
JPT	Joseph Patrick Tumulty
JRB	John Randolph Bolling
LDB	Louis Dembitz Brandeis
MS, MSS	manuscript, manuscripts
NDB	Newton Diehl Baker
NHD	Norman Hezekiah Davis
PPC	*Papers Relating to the Foreign Relations of the United States, The Paris Peace Conference, 1919*
RSB	Ray Stannard Baker
T	typed
TC	typed copy
TCL	typed copy of letter
TL	typed letter
TLI	typed letter initialed
TLS	typed letter signed
WGM	William Gibbs McAdoo
WW	Woodrow Wilson
WWhw	Woodrow Wilson handwriting, handwritten
WWsh	Woodrow Wilson shorthand
WWT	Woodrow Wilson typed
WWTLS	Woodrow Wilson typed letter signed

ABBREVIATIONS FOR COLLECTIONS AND REPOSITORIES

Following the National Union Catalog of the
Library of Congress

CtY-D	Yale University Divinity School
DLC	Library of Congress
G-Ar	Georgia State Department of Archives
IEN	Northwestern University

KyLoU	University of Louisville
MoHi-MoU	Missouri State Historical Society, University of Missouri
MHi	Massachusetts Historical Society
MNF	Forbes Library, Northampton, Massachusetts
NcD	Duke University
NjP	Princeton University
NjP-Ar	Princeton University Archives
NjR	Rutgers University
NHpR	Franklin D. Roosevelt Library
NRU	University of Rochester
OClW-Ar	Case Western Reserve University Archives
PMA	Allegheny College
PRO	Public Record Office
RSB Coll., DLC	Ray Stannard Baker Collection of Wilsoniana, Library of Congress
TxHR	Rice University
TxU	University of Texas
ViU	University of Virginia
WC, NjP	Woodrow Wilson Collection, Princeton University
WHi	State Historical Society of Wisconsin
WP, DLC	Woodrow Wilson Papers, Library of Congress

SYMBOLS

[May 1, 1922]	publication date of published writing; also date of document when date is not part of text
[*Nov. 11, 1922*]	composition date when publication date differs
[[Dec. 1, 1923]]	delivery date of speech when publication date differs
**** ***	text deleted by author of document

THE PAPERS OF

WOODROW WILSON

VOLUME 68

APRIL 8, 1922 - FEBRUARY 6, 1924

THE PAPERS OF
WOODROW WILSON

A News Report

[*April 8, 1922*]

COX BOOM LAUNCHED ON WILSON KEYNOTE OF
JUSTICE FOR ALL
Ex-President Sends Greetings

Attributing our "business adversity" to the failure of the United States to enter the League of Nations, ex-Governor James M. Cox of Ohio, Democratic nominee for President in 1920, urged a continuation of the fight to have this country join the League in an address at the annual Jefferson Day dinner of the National Democratic Club at the Hotel Commodore last night.

Mr. Cox said that the League furnished the only hope for "a stable prosperity," and attacked the national Administration for its failure to co-operate with other nations in humanitarian movements merely because these movements had been started by the League.

The impression prevailed as the dinner proceeded that it was the beginning of a Cox boom for the Democratic Presidential nomination in 1924. This impression was increased when the following message from Woodrow Wilson was read:

"Say to the Democrats of New York that I am ready to support any man who stands for the salvation of America, and the salvation of America is justice to all classes."

The enthusiasm which greeted every mention of Mr. Wilson's name was particularly noticeable, the more so that many of those present were members of Tammany, which never supported him strongly. Mr. Cox lauded the ex-President, and United States Senator Pat Harrison of Mississippi praised him as a "wounded soldier" to whom ultimately would be raised monuments throughout the country sufficiently high and broad to obscure his critics. . . .

Printed in the *New York Times*, April 9, 1922.

To Bainbridge Colby

My dear Colby: Washington D C 8th April 1922

I have gone over and assembled the material of the document which you put into such convenient shape for my examination and believe that you will find the enclosed document to contain our materials in a natural order and in a sufficiently clear form.[1]

My mind found both your suggestions and those of Justice Brandeis most acceptable, and I think you will see in this document a mosaic of the work of all three of us. It reads to me now like a very impressive declaration of clear and definite purpose.

With affectionate regard,

Faithfully yours,   Woodrow Wilson

TLS (B. Colby Papers, DLC).

[1] It is printed as an Enclosure with the following letter. Readers will recall that Wilson, Colby, and Brandeis had been collaborating upon what came to be known as "The Document," which, as it was added to, became in Wilson's mind a platform upon which he would run for the presidency in 1924.

To Louis Dembitz Brandeis, with Enclosure

My dear Mr. Justice: Washington D C 9th April 1922

Colby was kind enough to send me the materials for our document upon which you and he have been generously engaged, and the enclosed is the result of my efforts to assemble the several pieces into a single document. I hope you will think the result satisfactory. It seems to me a very clear and self-consistent document.

The question is now whether there is any wise immediate use that can be made of it. I had thought of handing it to Chairman Hull[1] with the suggestion that he send copies of it confidentially to Democratic candidates for election to the House or Senate this autumn with permission to select from it the issues for their own local campaigns. But my friend Baruch, to whom I mentioned the matter, has convinced me that such a course would not be wise. It is not likely that the confidential character of the document would be respected by ambitious gentlemen for more than a few minutes after it came into their hands, and it is quite possible that some one of them would put forth the whole thing as his own, which would of course kill it as a suggestion to the committee on resolutions of the Convention of 1924.

Do you think there is any immediate use that could wisely be made of the document that would not militate against the realization of our hope that it can be made the official Party declaration two years hence? Or shall we wait for that mysterious thing, "the psychological moment," to promulgate it as a whole and trust to the inspiration of that moment to suggest the best channel and method of promulgation? I shall await with a great deal of interest your views on this subject, my own being a good deal in doubt.

With the warmest regard and genuine gratitude for the invaluable aid you have given in this critical and important work,

Cordially and faithfully yours,   Woodrow Wilson

TLS (photostat in WP, DLC).
¹ That is, Cordell Hull, chairman of the Democratic National Committee since November 1, 1921.

E N C L O S U R E
CONFIDENTIAL DOCUMENT

1. We recognize the fact that the complex, disturbing and for the most part destructive results of the great war have made it necessary that the progressive countries of the world should supply for the reconstruction of its life a programme of law and reform which shall bring it back to health and effective order; and that it lies with the political party which best understands existing conditions, is in most sympathetic touch with the mass of the people, and is ready and best qualified to carry a constructive programme through to take the initiative in making and pressing affirmative proposals of remedy and reform.

2. In this spirit and with this great purpose, the Democratic party of the United States puts forth, in deep earnestness, the following platform of principle and purpose and seeks to serve America and, through America, liberal men throughout the world who seek to serve their people.

3. "AMERICA FIRST" is a slogan which does not belong to any one political party; it is merely a concise expression of what is in the heart of every patriotic American. We enthusiastically incorporate it into this our declaration of principles and purposes. But it means different things in different mouths and requires definition. When uttered by the present leaders of the Republican party it means that America must render no service to any other nation or people which she can reserve for her own selfish aggrandizement.

4. When we use it we mean that in every international action or organization for the benefit of mankind America must be foremost; that America, by developing within her own citizenship a sensitive regard for justice in all the relations of men, must lead the world in applying the broadest conceptions of justice and of peace, of am-

ity and respect, to the mutual relations of other peoples, and in rendering them material aid in the realization of those ideals.

5. We are suffering in common with the other nations of the world from the industrial and commercial prostration which succeeded the great war. Bound up with world conditions from which we cannot extricate ourselves, the Republican administration nevertheless prates of isolation. Unwilling to use our accumulated strength, our savings and our matchless resources in the rescue of our sister nations, from which alone our own recovery can arise, we have not only failed to display the generosity of a great nation to a world stricken with calamities which it could neither foresee nor avoid, but we have persisted in the ignorant delusion that we are untouched and unaffected by these all-encompassing conditions. Unwarned of our dwindling foreign commerce, our tied up shipping, and the helplessness of our debtors among the nations, we only brandish our contracts and clamour for payment, indifferent to the fact that we hold the gold of the world in our chests and will not receive the goods of our debtors, with which alone their debts can be discharged.

6. We demand the immediate resumption of our international obligations and leadership,—obligations which were shamelessly repudiated and a leadership which was incontinently thrown away by the failure of the Senate to ratify the Treaty of Versailles and the negotiation of separate treaties with the central powers.

7. We condemn the group of men who brought about these evil results as the most partisan, prejudiced, ignorant and unpatriotic group that every [ever] misled the Senate of the United States.

8. We call attention to the lamentable record of incompetence, evasion and political truckling of the present Congress, dominated in both the Senate and House of Representatives by a commanding Republican majority. No step has been taken toward the redemption of the pledges made by the Republican party. Despite the crying needs of the hour and the hopes of the people, it has not enacted a single piece of constructive or ameliorative legislation, although for the last three years it has controlled both houses of Congress.

9. The demand for a revision of the tax laws, made three years ago by a Democratic President upon the conclusion of the armistice, is still unheeded, and the burdensome and unequal war taxes, born of and justified only by a great emergency, still persist, thwarting the normal processes of post-war recovery, and robbing the frugality and industry of the people of their just rewards.

10. A budget still unbalanced, and distended beyond the requirements of efficient and economical administration in time of peace,

shows no sign of contraction, and every day brings the report of some fresh conspiracy against the public treasury. We promise studious and disinterested approach to the problems of national relief and rehabilitation and condemn the callousness and levity with which the Republican party has subordinated the duty of intelligent attention to these vital problems to the petty considerations of partisan politics.

11. We shall use every legitimate means to advance to the utmost the industrial and commercial development of the United States. That development has already made the people of the United States the greatest economic force in the world. It is as convincing proof of their practical genius as their free institutions are proof of their political genius. It is their manifest opportunity and destiny to lead the world in these great fields of endeavour and achievement. Our opponents have sought to promote the accumulation of wealth as an instrument of power in the hands of individuals and corporations. It is our object to promote it as a means of diffused prosperity and happiness and of physical and spiritual well being on the part of the great working masses of our people.

12. Without the systematic coordination, cooperation and interchange of services by the railroads the expanding, varying and changeable commerce and industry of the country cannot be properly served. All of these conditions are now lacking because our present laws deal with the railroads without system and altogether by way of interference and restriction. The result is a confusion which is constantly made worse almost to the point of paralysis by the multiplicity and intermittent conflict of regulative authorities, local and national.

13. We need a Secretary of Transportation who shall rank with the heads of other great federal cabinet departments and who shall be charged with the formulation and execution of plans for the coordinated use and full development of the transportation systems of the country. He should be associated with a federal Transportation Board which should be invested with all the powers now lodged with the Interstate Commerce Commission and, in addition, with the authority to determine the occasions and the conditions of all loans floated and of all securities issued by the several railway and steamship lines. This Board should have the same powers of supervision and regulation over the steamship lines of the United States that are now exercised by the Interstate Commerce Commission over the railways.

14. The present menace to political liberty and peaceful economic prosperity lies, not in the power of kings or irresponsible governments, but in hasty, passionate and irrational programmes

I am sorry this delicate throat of mine deprived me of the pleasure of seeing you while you were here, but I shall look forward to that pleasure on the occasion of your visit in May.

With highest regard;

Cordially yours,   John Randolph Bolling.

TLS (W. E. Dodd Papers, DLC).
   [1] W. E. Dodd to JRB, March 31, 1922, ALS (WP, DLC).

To Joseph Patrick Tumulty

My dear Tumulty: [Washington] 10th April 1922

I am deeply distressed to find in all the papers that contain an account of the dinner in New York last Saturday night a statement that a telegram was read that was said to be from me. This is particularly annoying to me because I understand that the dinner was interpreted as a boom for the re-nomination of Cox whose renomination would in my judgment be an act of deliberate suicide. I shall do everything that I honourably can to prevent it.

Since you were present at the dinner it is possible that you may have had some means of judging, or may have been able to guess, what the real source of the alleged message [was]. If you are able to throw any light on the matter for me I would be very grateful. It is obviously my duty as well as my privilege to probe the incident to the bottom.

In haste,   Affectionately yours,   [Woodrow Wilson]

CCL (WP, DLC).

From Bainbridge Colby

My dear Mr President: New York City April 10, 1922

I am in receipt of your letter of the 8th with the finished document, in connection with which Justice Brandeis and I have had the privilege of collaborating with you. I have read it over with care, noting each point where your magic touch is revealed. You have made it live. It now has form as well as substance and I think it is a very impressive declaration.

Will you or shall I send a copy of it to Justice Brandeis? I am sure he will be very much gratified to see your adoption of his ideas, as we were both very anxious to help you and only regretted that we could do so little and not more.

You have not told me just what use you purpose making of the material. Can I be of assistance to you in this aspect of the matter?

Affectionately always   Colby

TLS (WP, DLC).

John Randolph Bolling to Louis Wiley[1]

Dear Mr. Wiley: Washington D C 10th April 1922

Mr. Wilson was greatly distressed to note in your paper[2] of yesterday a copy of telegram purporting to have been sent by him, and read at the annual dinner of the Democratic National Club on Saturday evening. The message was an absolute fabrication.

Knowing the care with which your paper prints any matter of this kind, Mr. Wilson will be greatly obliged if you will try to run the message to earth and find where it originated.

With kind regards;

Cordially yours,   John Randolph Bolling

TLS (L. Wiley Papers, NRU).
    [1] The carbon copy of this letter in WP, DLC, bears a notation to the effect that Wilson dictated it.
    [2] That is, the *New York Times*.

A News Report

[*April 11, 1922*]

DOUBT IS CAST ON WILSON 'MESSAGE'
TO THE COX DINNER
Not a Direct Telegram, but a Typewritten Slip Presented
by His Former Secretary.

TUMULTY'S EXPLANATION

Washington, April 11.—Joseph P. Tumulty, former Secretary to ex-President Wilson, returned to Washington tonight from New York, where he had gone to attend the Jefferson Day dinner of the National Democratic Club, at which ex-Governor James M. Cox of Ohio, defeated Democratic candidate for President, was the principal speaker.

Mr. Tumulty made a short statement explanatory of the circumstances under which he gave to the club a message from ex-President Wilson, which was read at the dinner, but he declined to go into details concerning its presentation there.

In his statement Mr. Tumulty said that Mr. Wilson's message

had nothing to do with any individual or any particular political situation.

Mr. Tumulty's statement was as follows:

"The message read at the banquet came merely in a casual conversation with me at Mr. Wilson's home on Friday last, when he remarked that he would support any candidate who stood for justice for all. There was nothing unusual in this, and it was not significant in any way from a political standpoint. He sent no telegram. He simply gave a casual message to me in casual manner. It had nothing to do with any individual or any particular political situation." . . .

No statement for publication was obtained at the Wilson residence. . . .

Printed in the *New York Times*, April 12, 1922.

To Breckinridge Long

My dear Long: Washington D C 11th April 1922

I daresay that Reed[1] would evade in a public meeting as you suggest, but the evasion in itself would be significant and instructive. Moreover your letter of April eighth[2] leads me to think that I did not make my suggestion perfectly clear. It was not that Reed should be publicly asked if he had or deemed himself likely to have my support or approval, but that he should be asked if he would be willing that the questioner should ask me if I were willing to endorse him. The method you suggest of waiting for an opportunity to contradict some obscure newspaper seems to me a very slow one and one not likely to come to a head. It moreover leaves the whole matter to the initiative of our opponents, and I do not think that is the way to fight. We ought to take the initiative ourselves and force them to accept the issue.

You say nothing about it in your last letter but am I not right in detecting in that letter a tone of discouragement? There is no use in being afraid of Reed, and if he is gone after without gloves he will do the fearing.

Let me know from time to time how things seem to be going.

With cordial best wishes,

Faithfully yours,   Woodrow Wilson

TLS (B. Long Papers, DLC).
    [1] The reader will recall that Long was engaged in a bitter battle with Senator James Alexander Reed for the Democratic nomination for senator from Missouri, and that Wilson had publicly entered the contest on Long's side.
    [2] B. Long to WW, April 8, 1922, TLS (WP, DLC).

To Bainbridge Colby

My dear Colby: Washington D C 11th April 1922

I myself sent a copy of the document to Justice Brandeis and asked his advice, as I now beg for yours, as to what immediate use if any might wisely be made of it. I had had the idea of suggesting to Chairman Hull that he send copies of it to our candidates for House or Senate in the Fall elections in order that they might select from it such issues and declarations as they thought might be made most effective use of in their local contests. But when I discussed the matter with Baruch the other day he convinced me that such a course would not be wise and I now think with him that such candidates would not be likely to respect the confidential character of the document for more than a few minutes after they had read it, and that it would not be surprising if some one of them put the whole document forth as his own which I suppose would make it violently improbable that the Committee on Resolutions in the Convention of 1924 would seriously consider its promulgation by themselves as the official proposal of a platform. Please think the whole matter over and let me know the result of your cogitations.

Do you think I should send a copy also to Chadbourne,[1] or would that seem like closing the document before receiving his suggestions as to what it would contain? (Please answer this question by telegraph, saying "Think copy should be sent" or "Think copy should not be sent").

With affectionate regard,

                                     Faithfully yours,   Woodrow Wilson

P.S. I have not said, but no doubt it is unnecessary for me to say, how greatly pleased I am that you like the document as now formulated.   W.W.

TLS (B. Colby Papers, DLC).
   [1] That is, Thomas Lincoln Chadbourne, Jr., of New York.

From Louis Dembitz Brandeis

My dear Mr Wilson: Washington, D. C. April 11/22

I agree entirely with Mr. Baruch. Ammunition so potent should not be dissipated.

You have taught us the lesson of watchful waiting.

                                     Most Cordially   Louis D Brandeis

ALS (WP, DLC).

To the Editor of the *New York Times*

My dear sir: Washington D C 12th April 1922

I notice in the issue of the Times this morning an article headed "DOUBT IS CAST ON WILSON 'MESSAGE' TO THE COX DINNER."

I write to say there need be no doubt about the matter. I did not send any message whatever to that dinner nor authorize anyone to convey a message.

I hope that you will be kind enough to publish this letter.

Very truly yours,   Woodrow Wilson[1]

TLS (*New York Times* Archives).
[1] A facsimile of this letter was printed on the first page of the *New York Times*, April 14, 1922.

To Arthur Bernard Krock

My dear Krock: [Washington] 12th April 1922

I was sorry to disappoint you about the message.[1] I should have been happy to send greetings to the Kentucky Democrats but frankly the circumstance that our defeated candidate was to be the guest of honor was the reason I did n[ot].

There is a fatuous movement on foot to induce the party to commit suicide by nominating him again, and I do not feel that any one of us should lend the slightest countenance to the effort.

I know that I can always be perfectly open and frank with a true friend like yourself and that you would rather know my real mind.

With warm regard, in unavoidable haste,

Cordially and sincerely yours,   [Woodrow Wilson]

CCL (WP, DLC).
[1] A. Krock to WW, April 11, 1922, T telegram (WP, DLC).

From Joseph Patrick Tumulty

My dear Governor: Washington, D. C. 12 April 1922.

While I was in New York my secretary, Mr. Johnson,[1] read to me over the telephone your letter of the tenth of April in which you showed distress at an alleged telegram that was read at the banquet given last Saturday in New York City by the National Democratic Club, purporting to come from you. I am very sorry, indeed, my dear Governor, that there has been any misunderstanding as a result of the message read at the banquet. In the newspaper dispatches, containing accounts of the dinner, it was erroneously stated that you had sent a telegram and unwarranted significance was unfortunately given to it by reason of the presence at the banquet of Governor Cox of Ohio. There was no telegram read at the banquet purporting to come from you. I accept full responsibility for the message of greeting to the Democrats assembled—a message which was handed by me to Mr. Rush and which was read to those in attendance by Mrs. Montgomery Hare.[2]

On Friday, last, when I visited you, after discussing the matter which brought me to your home, I expressed a desire to have you send a telegram to the President of the National Democratic Club. You replied that you could not see your way clear to do so, saying that it was your desire to maintain a policy of absolute silence. After discussing other matters, we again came to the subject of the banquet and my trip to New York to attend it, a fact that I apprised you of. I told you with what warmth any message from you, no matter how inconsequential or insignificant, would be greeted by your admirers there. As I stood up to go, you took hold of my arm and in substance said what was contained in the message read by Mrs. Hare. It is only fair to you to say that there was no express direction on your part that I should convey any message but I think I was justified by every fair implication from what you said to me, in conveying a word of greeting to the Democrats of New York. Of course, your remarks were casual.

When I returned to my office immediately after the visit, I dictated to my secretary in substance what you said to me and upon my arrival in New York, handed the message to Mr. Rush. There was nothing significant in the message which you addressed but unfortunately the newspapers "played it up" and placed what, in my opinion, was an unwarranted interpretation upon it.

No one regrets this more deeply than do I, and that any act of mine should cause you the least uneasiness is of the deepest concern to me. While I am responsible for the delivery of this message, I think you will hold me blameless for the unjust interpretations put upon it.   Cordially and sincerely yours,   J P Tumulty

TLS (WP, DLC).
   [1] Warren Forman Johnson.
   [2] Thomas Edward Rush, lawyer of New York, Surveyor of the Customs for the Port of New York, 1914-1920, and chairman of the committee on arrangements for the Jefferson Day Dinner; Constance Parsons (Mrs. Montgomery) Hare, "chairman" of the New York City Women's Committee of the Woodrow Wilson Foundation.

A Telegram and Two Letters from Bainbridge Colby

New York Apr 12 22

Think copy should not be sent pending receipt of my letter which will give you fuller back-ground for your final decision either way   Colby

T telegram (WP, DLC).

My dear Mr President: New York City April 12, 1922

I think Chadbourne would be very much interested in the document and would appreciate receiving a copy of it from you. But I sent you a telegram this morning in answer to your specific inquiry, saying that I thought a copy should not be sent until you had this letter before you with a fuller statement of the background, so that you might be in a position to decide just what you wish to do.

Your considerate unwillingness to seem like closing the document before receiving his suggestions need not deter you, in my opinion. Chadbourne was very explicit in his request to be relieved altogether from the consideration of the subject. He is doubtless greatly preoccupied with a situation about which you may have read in the papers, in which his conduct as an attorney has been called into question.[1] I not only feel great sympathy for him, but I believe, from the facts as disclosed, that his position is unassailable and that he will come out of the incident completely exonerated. I have taken occasion to express this opinion to him. It is a very nettling and disturbing thing, however, and I can readily conceive that he has little room in his mind for any other subject, until the matter is disposed of.

Always most cordially   Bainbridge Colby

[1] The *New York Times*, in front-page articles on March 6 and 7, 1922, had revealed that a committee of the New York Bar Association was about to begin disbarment proceedings against Chadbourne. The charges against him grew out of his long-term relationship with his client, George Jay Gould, the son of the late financier, Jay Gould, and the chief executor of his estate. It was alleged that Chadbourne had had guilty knowledge of Gould's profiteering on the sale of stock held by the estate and that he had also participated in a corrupt financial transaction involving the Missouri Pacific Railroad, during the period when the younger Gould had been its president. The Appellate Division of the New York Supreme Court dismissed the charges against Chadbourne on March 2, 1923. *Ibid.*, March 3, 1923.

My dear Mr President: New York City April 12, 1922

Just how the document should be used to achieve the best effect, is quite a question. My first impulse on receiving your letter of yesterday was to telegraph you that I would run down to Washington to confer with you. It is rather a big and many sided subject for satisfactory treatment by letter.

I think it should be issued now or at least soon, and the way that occurs to me as best calculated to give it official character as the Party's programme would be to have it adopted by the National Committee. It is about time for the National Committee to hold a meeting and I assume that Mr Hull would like to convene his committee with something so definite and important to consider as a thought-out and effective expression of party purposes. It would strengthen his position as Chairman, hearten the rank and file of the party and have a tonic effect on the eve of the Congressional primaries. Any other course is exposed to the danger you speak of, that someone would appropriate the document in its entirety and prejudice its chances later of official adoption and general acceptance.

I know how little you care for the small currents of party gossip. I don't care much for them myself and am not in a position to catch all the whispers and murmurs. But there are some things that I would probably mention to you if I were sitting with you, and I will stretch my letter a little to refer to them, as they may have some bearing upon the strategy of the document.

There were a good many Democrats in New York to attend the Jefferson Day dinner last Saturday night. Although I was mentioned among those present, I did not attend the dinner, because I learned that there was a likelihood that I would be called on to speak despite my declination of the formal invitation. This might have presented its embarrassments.

I have heard a good deal about the dinner from various persons who were there. The only genuine enthusiasm was aroused by the references made to you. It was unmistakable and very great. Governor Cox's speech was disappointing to his friends and there was a visible waning of interest and enthusiasm as he proceeded toward its conclusion. Senator Harrison's speech was well received and there were many signs that he has a very real popularity within the party. The other speakers, including Senator Hitchcock, were not considered to have been very effective. Of course a New York audience is a strange conglomerate, and the success of any big dinner is a matter of luck. A banquet has its own temperament, which is often embodied in the toastmaster. On this occasion the toastmaster was Mr C. B. Alexander,[1] who I am told never got control of the audience, and found great difficulty in making himself heard. The general tone of comment is one of disappointment. The speeches were regarded as having little that was new in them, and nothing that was affirmative.

If I am correctly informed and am giving you a true impression of the atmosphere of the dinner, it would seem that the time is ripe for launching an aggressive programme such as the document sets forth.

Some of the regulars in the party do not want ideas injected into the campaign. It is their thought that the Republicans have made a complete fizzle; that all that the Democrats need do is to ride comfortably upon the widespread and growing disgust and resentment felt toward the Republicans. Among these men there is a good deal of talk about the importance of favoring a bonus for the soldiers, and a growing but still timid notion that it may be good politics to assail the Volstead law.

The statement was made to me yesterday by Scott Ferris of Oklahoma that no man in the Southwest could be elected to Congress who was opposed to a soldier's bonus. Ferris furthermore expressed the opinion, which I merely repeat to you because it is the opinion of a man who runs pretty close to the ground politically, that the party should avoid affirmative proposals of every nature, and fasten the hard times of the farmers and the wage-earners upon the Republican party as the cause of the diminished value of farm products and of industrial unemployment.

Expressions such as this reveal the rather stagnant condition of party thinking. They also indicate that a clean-cut and courageous declaration such as the document contains, may encounter some opposition from the men who prefer to slide into power rather than to stride into it.

I understand that a factional contest within the party is brewing in Ohio. I am told that Mr Ed Moore, who was so vigorous and effective in promoting the nomination of Governor Cox, is now active in Senator Pomerene's candidacy for re-election and believes that if Pomerene is elected he will be a formidable candidate for the Democratic nomination in 1924. This prospect is not pleasing to the Cox men in Ohio and I have been told that a dangerous rift is opening up there.

This chatter amounts only to this,—that some of the party's active managers are peering around corners and looking at political conditions in a very narrow personal way. The old choice seems to stand squarely in the party's pathway,—whether we shall fritter our energies in little struggles waged in a little way, or stand out to sea for the big destinations. And in my endeavor to answer your letter helpfully it seems to me that there is but one course to pursue, i.e.—to commit the forceful and enlightened men in the National Committee to the view that a genuine programme is the only salvation of the party, and the only thing that makes its existence worth while.

Specifically, I think that Mr Hull should be taken into conference on the subject. I should like to talk it over with Homer Cummings, but will not do so until authorized by you. The fact that the document bears the unmistakable marks of your authorship will give it great strength in the National Committee. I fear that you cannot keep its authorship secret, and my belief is that it would greatly enthuse the members of the Committee to feel that you were out in front and doing the party's thinking.

Yours ever   Colby

TLS (WP, DLC).
¹ Charles Beatty Alexander, lawyer of New York, long active in Democratic party politics, graduate (1870) and former trustee of Princeton University. See the index references to him in Vols. 13 and 26.

To Bainbridge Colby

Dear Colby: Washington D C 13th April 1922

Thank you for your opinion about the way to handle the document.

So soon as the proper people are within reach I will call a little council and we shall then have all the light we can get.

With affectionate regard,

Faithfully yours,   Woodrow Wilson

TLS (B. Colby Papers, DLC).

To Thomas Lincoln Chadbourne, Jr.

My dear Chadbourne: [Washington] 13th April 1922

I am taking pleasure in enclosing for your perusal, and if you choose for your comment, a copy of a document which will explain itself. As you know, Justice Brandeis, Colby and I have been occupying ourselves in formulating in pieces a statement of principles and purposes for the use of the party if it should choose to use it. This is the process in which I urged you to take part and concerning which you kindly conferred with Justice Brandeis and Colby at one time.

The document enclosed is the result of my attempt to assemble the several pieces which have resulted from the thinking of the collaborators into a consecutive document whose several parts are meant to constitute a consistent who[le.]

I shall be very much obligated in any comments you may care to make upon the document and should value any suggestions you may care to make as to its alteration or improvement.

I am also asking myself this question; is there any immediate use that could wisely be made of the document or are there any steps that could wisely be taken to recommend its use to members of the party who are likely to play an influential part in framing the programme of the party at its next national convention. I should greatly value your own answers to these questions.

I hope that the years ahead of us will disclose many opportunities of collaboration between us for I have always felt the benefit of having your counsel and the stimulation of being associated with you.

Before I close may I not take the liberty (which I hope is not presumptuous) of saying that I hope you know, as I do, that your friends and all who really know you will be able to fully understand and discount the recent malevolent attacks upon you. You can absolutely count upon that.

With warm regard,

Faithfully and sincerely yours,   [Woodrow Wilson]

CCL (WP, DLC).

From Joseph Patrick Tumulty

My dear Governor: Washington, D. C. 13 April 1922.

In my letter to you, of yesterday's date, I sought to make clear all of the facts and circumstances surrounding our discussion of Friday last with reference to the message which I delivered to Mr. Rush on Saturday evening, a message for which I accept full responsibility, regardless of the unhappy circumstances that have grown out of its publication and the unfair interpretation put upon it by the newspapers. My memory is very clear on every detail of our discussion of Friday last. I recall, for instance, that we discussed the present plight of America by reason of our failure to enter the League of Nations and when you asked me how I thought America felt about it, I said that there was only one thing that symbolized the grief of America and that was the statue of "Grief" by St. Gaudens in Rock Creek Cemetery.[1] You took issue with me on this and, pointing to a statue on the mantlepiece of your home, said that you would rather believe that that statue typified the real feelings of America. It was the statue of a beautiful young girl holding a child by the hand; pointing to it you said, "That, Tumulty, represents to me the feeling of America,—a picture of America leading the way of salvation for the small nations of the world."

We then turned to a discussion of the domestic problems of America and I recall that you used an unusual phrase in describing your feelings. You spoke of America having reached the limit of what you characterized as a "quantitative democracy" and that the business of the statesmen of the future was to discover processes to make the democracies throughout the world "qualitative." The sentence in the greeting to the National Democratic Club was not original with me. When I got into my car, immediately after leaving your home, I took an envelope out of my pocket and jotted down in shorthand the message you gave me. When I arrived at my office, a few minutes later, I called my secretary and dictated this message which, as I recall it, was as follows: "Former-President Wilson through a friend conveyed a word of greeting to the Democrats assembled at the National Democratic Club's banquet in New York in the following words, 'Former-President Wilson says that he will support any man who will stand for the salvation of America, and the salvation of America is justice to all classes.'" So certain was I that you intended to have this message conveyed through me, and being apprised of the fact that I was to be in attendance at the banquet, it was my intention to ask the privilege of the toastmaster personally to present it. But upon considering the matter, I drew away from this resolve, becoming convinced that some unkind critics of mine would say that "Tumulty was seeking to put himself forward as Woodrow Wilson's spokesman." It was then that I resolved to deliver the message to Mr. Rush. There was nothing mysterious about the way the message was handed to Mr. Rush. I frankly told him of my talk with you and of your desire that the words of greeting be delivered. There was nothing concealed or secretive about my conduct in any way. The only hypothesis upon which I could be condemned in this matter is the one that I was seeking to fabricate a message at your expense for the purpose of attaching your name to the proceedings of the banquet and to any presidential boom that might be discussed there. This, of course, is tantamount to saying that I would be guilty of an act of base treachery to you. I think you will at least give me credit for having more political sense than to propose so foolish a scheme as this of seeking at this early day, three years before a national convention, to attach your name to any move that had as its objective the advancement of the interests of a particular man. My own feeling is that no Democrat who wishes to serve his party in an unselfish way ought to be devoted to any particular man at this time, and to propose the name of Mr. Cox or Mr. McAdoo or anyone else, would be only to hurt and injure them.

The message could not be construed, under any of the circumstances of its handling at the banquet, by any sane, sensible person as an endorsement of anybody. In the first place it was read two hours before Governor Cox took the floor and was read in connection with telegrams from Mr. McAdoo and Senator Underwood. Not a single individual at the banquet, in my opinion, attributed any importance to it, as bearing upon the present political fortunes of anyone.

When I first heard of your distress at the alleged telegram, I sought the opportunity personally and frankly to lay the facts before you so that you might have from my own lips a description of the whole affair. I felt certain, from the tone of your letter to me where you stated that you wished the incident probed to the bottom, that this meant that you would appreciate it if you could be put in possession of all the facts. Feeling that this was your desire, I sought an interview with you but for some reason or other, you did not feel free to grant it to me. As I have told you I am very sorry about this whole incident. Certainly it was no desire of mine to compromise your prestige in the least and I am sure that Governor Cox and his friends deprecate the incident as much as I do. I sincerely trust that you will not be swayed by the stories appearing in some of the newspapers that some foolish friends of Mr. McAdoo think that this was an attempt on my part to attach your name to Governor Cox's political future.

Since the earliest days of my association with you, I have had but one thought, but one ambition, and that was to serve you and the great purposes which I know lay close to your heart. Since you left office and power, that loyalty, affection and admiration, which I trust I gave you in unstinted fashion, have in no way been changed. No matter what the temptation may be, not [no] matter how keenly I may feel the injustice of any public action you may take in this matter, you may rest assured that I will never engage in a controversy with you. No slight bruise nor public rebuke from you can in any way lessen my devotion to and affection for you. You will find me as a mere private in the ranks, deferring to your unselfish leadership and defending your policies at every turn of the long road which lies ahead of us. I think you know me well enough to believe that if you decide that this message of greeting which I delivered, has embarrassed you in any way and that I must be rebuked, I shall not complain. You will find, my dear Governor, that I will not wince under the blow nor shall I grow in the least faint-hearted or dispirited.

Cordially and sincerely yours,   J P Tumulty

TLS (WP, DLC).
[1] That is, the bronze figure commissioned by Henry Adams as a memorial to his wife, Marion Hooper Adams. For the deep impression made on Wilson by this statue, see the extract from the Diary of Colonel House printed at April 1, 1913, Vol. 27.

To Eleutherios Kyrios Vénisélos

My dear Friend: [Washington] 14th April 1922

I am gratified to learn through your secretary's letter of today to my secretary[1] that I may have the pleasure of another call from you.

The routine of my convalescence is unhappily somewhat rigorous, but it would give me great pleasure to see you on Monday next, the seventeenth,[2] at three in the afternoon if you can make it convenient to call at my home at that time.

I am sorry to have to remind you that there is no language which we speak in common and that it will be necessa[ry] for you to bring an interpreter with you. I wish that it were possible for us to get at each other's ideas more simpl[y] and directly but unhappily like most Americans I am uni-ling[ual] and cannot have the freedom of expression I so much covet and should so much enjoy.

With warm regard and most cordial greetings of welcome [to] America,

Cordially and sincerely your friend,   [Woodrow Wilson]

CCL (WP, DLC).
[1] C. Michalopoulos to JRB, April 14, 1922, TLS (WP, DLC).
[2] Because of Vénisélos's indisposition, the appointment was later changed to Wednesday, April 19, at 3 p.m.

A Memorandum by Dr. Grayson

[Washington] April 15, 1922.

Mr. Wilson, in referring to the practice of designating certain weeks for specific movements—such as Be Kind to Animals Week, Clean-UP Week, Music Week, National Air Week, Better Homes Week—said there should be a week designated for people to mind their own business.

T MS (received from James Gordon Grayson and Cary T. Grayson, Jr.).

To the Editor of the *Washington Post*[1]

My dear sir: [Washington, c. April 15, 1922]

May I take the liberty of making a suggestion through your columns:

Since we are having a "week" for this, and a "week" for that and "week" for the other, I suggest we have a Mind Your Own Business week; and that each one of us accept the title of the week as an admonition to himself as well as to the rest of the community.

Very truly yours,   [Woodrow Wilson]

TL (WP, DLC).
[1] This letter bears the following typed notation at the top: "Dict. but not sent—deciding later it was better not to do so."

To the Editor of the *St. Louis Daily Globe-Democrat*

My dear sir: [Washington] 15th April 1922

I note in your issue of April 12th that one Lee Meriwether[1] is quoted as saying he had seen a letter from me to Senator Reed "warmly thanking him for the great service the Senator rendered in perfecting and passing the federal reserve bill."[2] I have no recollection of ever having written any such letter. On the contrary I clearly remember that Mr. Reed, as a member of the Committee on Banking and Currency, interposed every possible objection to the completion and adoption of the bill. His objections indeed were so many, so varied and so inconsistent with one another that I recall speaking to him about them in conversation. Having spoken of reading a certain parody on a well known novel, I told him that his course in the committee reminded me of the conduct of the hero in that parody who, when rejected by the heroine, rushed from the house, mounted several horses and rode off in every direction.

Statements such as the one quoted from Mr. Meriwether appear to be intended to create the impression that Mr. Reed and I have held the same principles and advanced the same policies and that he is entitled to and may be assumed to have my endorsement as a candidate for re-election to the Senate. This is far from being the case. To those who have closely observed Mr. Reed's career in Washington he has shown himself incapable of sustained allegiance to any person or any cause. He has repeatedly forfeited any claim to my confidence that he may ever have been supposed to have, and I shall never willingly consent to any further association with him.

I beg that you will do me the courtesy to publish this letter.

Very truly yours,   [Woodrow Wilson][3]

CCL (WP, DLC).
    [1] Lawyer and author of St. Louis, an active campaigner for Reed.
    [2] See WW to J. A. Reed, Oct. 23, 1913, Vol. 28.
    [3] This letter was printed, e.g., in the *New York Times*, April 18, 1922.

To Ellen Duane Davis

My dear Friend: [Washington] 16th April 1922

It distresses us to hear that you have been really ill,[1] and I am sorry to notice you do not expressly say you are better.

It is delightful to know that we shall have an opportunity to see E.P. again soon. Please ask him for me to come and lunch with us at half past one on May first, and instruct him to reach the house at quarter before one when I shall be having my separate meal and can gossip with him.

It interests me deeply that you are really running for Congress, and you may be sure I shall hope most earnestly for your success.

Tumulty is already in the depths of humiliation, and I think you will agree with me that if after what has happened I should send a message to Philadelphia he would feel that it was rather rubbing it in. Moreover every political situation in Pennsylvania is sure to be a delicate one, and I should not know in what tone to cast the message.

It heartens me to learn that there is a good prospect for getting a Democratic Governor for Pennsylvania, and I trust you to assess truly the quality of the candidate. I am sorry to say I do not know him.[2]

Please take care of yourself most studiously and get entirely well and strong.

With love to E.P.,
                    Affectionately yours,   [Woodrow Wilson]

CCL (WP, DLC).
    [1] Wilson was replying to Ellen D. Davis to WW, April 15, 1922, TLS (WP, DLC).
    [2] John Aldus McSparran. He was defeated by Gifford Pinchot in the general election.

To Cleveland Hoadley Dodge

My dear Cleve.:   Washington D C 16th April 1922

The enclosed is a modest contribution to the Near East Relief. If I had the money you may be sure I would make the check several times larger, but I felt I should not hold back altogether because I can do so little.

We unite in the most affectionate messages to Mrs. Dodge[1] and you, and the hope that every aspect of the present Easter is bright and happy for you all.

> Affectionately yours,   Woodrow Wilson

TLS (received from Phyllis Boushall Dodge).
  [1] That is, Grace Parish Dodge.

To Bainbridge Colby

My dear Colby: Washington D C 16th April 1922

Yes, I think it would be safe to make an exception of the luncheon to Marshal Joffre.[1] As a commander he won my thorough admiration, and as a man my affectionate regard. I cannot see that any political slant can be successfully given to anything you might say on such an occasion; but may I suggest that you go it mild in eulogizing France. She is the present marplot of the world.

I shall be amused to learn when I see you of what you think of the dinner episode at the "National" Democratic Club.

With affectionate regard,

> Faithfully yours,   Woodrow Wilson

TLS (B. Colby Papers, DLC).
  [1] Wilson was replying to BC to WW, April 15, 1922, TLS (WP, DLC).

John Franklin Jameson to Helen Jameson[1]

Dear H.,   [Washington] Apr. 16 [1922].

We went, and found him as cheerful and entertaining as of old, and Mrs. Wilson quite charming and hospitable, but physically it was sad to see an old friend so disabled. He may have gained a great deal, and of course has his ups and downs, but that he could not get up from his chair nor move his left arm, and his head seemed inclined to droop to one side, though his speech was not affected, except that it is a little weak.

With much love,   Your J.

ALI (J. F. Jameson Papers, DLC).
  [1] Jameson's sister.

To Louis Dembitz Brandeis

My dear Mr. Justice: Washington D C 17th April 1922

Things are ready now for a brief conference on the matters you, Chadbourne, Colby and I have been discussing, and I will greatly appreciate it if you could make it convenient to be at my house here on Monday afternoon next, the twenty-fourth, at three o'clock to help round the matter out.

        Cordially and faithfully yours,   Woodrow Wilson[1]

TLS (L. D. Brandeis Papers, KyLoU).
   [1] Wilson sent the same letter, *mutatis mutandis*: WW to BC, April 17, 1922, TLS (B. Colby Papers); WW to BMB, April 17, 1922, TLS (B. M. Baruch Papers, NjP); WW to T. L. Chadbourne, Jr., April 17, 1922, CCL (WP, DLC); and WW to H. S. Cummings, April 17, 1922, TLS (H. S. Cummings Papers, ViU). Wilson sent a different letter of invitation to D. F. Houston on April 19, 1922: draft Hw telegram (WP, DLC). See also WW to NHD, April 18, 1922.

To Thornwell Jacobs

My dear Dr. Jacobs: [Washington] 17th April 1922

I am sorry to disappoint you[1] but frankly my relations with Mr. Lloyd George are not such as to warrant me in giving a letter of introduction to him. He is a very singular and incalculable person and I do not think that a letter of introduction would be needed to smooth your way.

    In haste,   Sincerely yours,   [Woodrow Wilson]

CCL (WP, DLC).
   [1] Wilson was replying to T. Jacobs to WW, April 14, 1922, TLS (WP, DLC).

To Norman Hezekiah Davis

My dear Davis: [Washington] 18th April 1922

I hope that you can make it convenient to come down and have a talk with me here on Monday afternoon next, the twenty-fourth, at three o'clock. I am asking a few others whom we both trust to come at the same time because it seems to me that it is high time we should hold common counsel as to what the party ought to do for the country in these times of disappointment and reaction brought on by the stupidity, faithlessness and bad principles of the Republicans. It is obviously a time of opportunity of which it is our duty to take advantage to the fullest extent, and only the united judgment of men of the same spirit and purpose, such as I am about to assemble, can determine the wisest way to do this. May I not expect you? You are indispensable.

    With affectionate regard,
           Faithfully yours,   [Woodrow Wilson]

CCL (WP, DLC).

From Bainbridge Colby

My dear Mr President: New York City April 18, 1922

I observe that you are moving with your customary despatch in arranging so promptly a conference for Monday afternoon next at 3 o'clock. I appreciate your invitation to attend it and will of course be there.

I am in receipt also of your letter in relation to the luncheon to be given to Marshal Joffre. I thank you for your wise little word of caution and will rigidly observe it.

The dinner episode is a subject of widespread interest and comment. Everybody seems to think it was an intolerable thing to inject you into a situation like that without your consent and in a form not authorized by you. And it is also the general opinion that you could hardly have done less than you did in correcting the matter. I know only what I have read in the press, but I hope the incident is susceptible of an amiable termination. I should find it hard to alter my belief in Tumulty's sincere attachment to you, although his blunder, if that is what it was, seems quite inexplicable.

I know the incident is very painful to you and I am sorry you should have been subjected to it.

With affectionate regard,   Ever yours   Bainbridge Colby

TLS (WP, DLC).

Two Letters from Thomas Lincoln Chadbourne, Jr.

Dear Mr. Wilson: New York April 19, 1922.

Your letters of the 13th and 17th have remained unanswered only because of my absence from the city. I regret very much indeed that it is impossible for me to be in Washington Monday, April 24th. That is a day which has been set for some time for a conference in this city of the independent steel manufacturers, who have engaged my services in an effort to effect their consolidation, and the entire week will be taken up with continuous conferences respecting their negotiations. I want to assure you that nothing but a most important meeting of this kind would keep me from complying with your invitation to come to Washington.

I will try between now and Sunday afternoon to mail you my views upon the document you so kindly enclosed me, so that you will have these views for what they are worth before you on Monday.

You are very kind to assure me of your continued confidence

notwithstanding this ugly attack which has been made upon me, the outcome of which I do not in the least fear.

The time will never come when I shall be unresponsive to any call you may make upon my time and services; and the predicament I found myself in with respect to helping you upon this work which you now have in hand was a cause of real sorrow to me, and was brought about by this attack, which has been pending for a year, coupled with my commitment in the Steel situation, which antedated your suggestion that I take part with Messrs. Brandeis and Colby in this work.

Sincerely yours,   Thomas L Chadbourne

Dear Mr. Wilson: New York April 23, 1922.

I find myself, at noon today, in my office, over my ears in work, and am reminded that I have not made any effort to discuss the confidential document you enclosed me in your letter of April 13th, which I will do by paragraphs.

I am in hearty accord with the first four paragraphs, but doubt the political wisdom at this time of giving publicity, if publicity is intended, to the fifth paragraph in its present form. Not because I disagree with its spirit, but because it is my judgment, and has been for six months past, that this country is entering upon another era of, I will not say prosperity, but of a secondary inflation which will look so much like prosperity as to make the charge "from which alone our own recovery can arise," seem to be an exaggeration, although, in fact, the truth, upon a permanent basis. I predicted six months ago, and persisted continuously in the belief, that the emptiness of our shelves and the enormous amount of gold in this country would bring about an inflation, and I believe this opinion is now shared by many, although I was severely alone when I first advanced it.

Such an inflation when it comes, as it seems to be coming now, is rarely over in a short time. The probability of it lasting a year or two or even three is good; and it is going to lead while it does last, the public to believe that the selfish policy of the Republican party in isolating this country has been a successful policy, and they will continue to believe this until the bubble bursts, which it will unless it is overtaken by a commercial recovery from the other side worked out by themselves without our help; and if that is so, which seems to me almost impossible, the inflation will become a real prosperity. If not so overtaken we will be in much worse case at some period in the not very distant future than we were in 1921, and then our public will be awakened to the fact that our export trade is not simply the Maraschino cherry in their financial cocktail which they now believe it to be. At present they think the cocktail will taste well without the Maraschino cherry, and this inflation is going to be its test; and in my judgment the dregs are going to be very bitter. But if I am right, that we are going into something that is going to look to the public like prosperity, it would be a political mistake to advance a proposition that the evidence, or apparent evidence, all about us in the near future is going to contradict.

I do not think that paragraphs 6, 7, 8, 9, 10, and 11 can be much improved upon.

With respect to paragraphs 12 and 13, we are approaching a big subject, and I doubt greatly the advisability of generalizing upon it without establishing the kind of foundation for it I shall suggest at the conclusion of my letter. I have long thought that when the Government delegated to private individuals the right to build (carrying with it as it does the privilege of eminent domain), and the right to operate railroads, it was delegating one of its sovereign powers, and one not much less in the gravity of the consequences following upon its delegation than, for instance, farming out its taxing power. In brief, I am convinced that government ownership is a prime essential to diffusing "prosperity and happiness and * * * physical and spiritual well-being" to the great working masses of our people. I do not believe that a Secretary of Transportation and a Federal Transportation Board invested with the powers of the Interstate Commerce Commission and with further authority, can deal with the question while private ownership remains. And this conclusion has not been lightly arrived at, but comes after having been for years general counsel of 17,000 miles of railroad in this country. I will mention but one instance, as my time is so limited, which I know to be a fact. No independent coal operator has a chance to compete with railroad-owned coal unless he has interested with him one or more officials of the railroad upon whose car supply he is dependent. Think of this for a moment and apply it to the business of the country generally, and tell me the answer so long as human beings remain as they are.

I am heartily in accord with paragraph 14; but in regard to paragraph 15, I believe the substance of that also should receive the most careful study before put out by our party, in accordance with the suggestion of my last paragraph.

I am in accord with paragraph 16, and was tremendously interested in following the vicissitudes of the Non-Partisan League in attempting to secure the things, and more than these, advocated in this paragraph.

I am not in sympathy with paragraph 17, because in my opinion even the possibility of an American merchant marine under present conditions is doubtful; and that also should be studied with greater care before we commit ourselves. I am in accord, however, with the scientific study of this question, which offers very serious problems, which study you advocate together with the Inland Waterway study in paragraph 18.

Some of the propositions which I refer to above presented by your memorandum require, and should have, intensive and exhaustive study by competent men, whose whole time would be devoted to them. This can only be attained by financing such a study; and I would be willing to be one of a group to contribute heavily to such a project if you initiated it. It is unfortunate that there are so few rich men among the Democrats who have a liberal instinct, and so many rich men among the Republicans who don't care to investigate anything for the public good; but the answer probably is that the Democrats perhaps would not be poor and the Republicans rich if the possession of that instinct were reversed. But such a project is so much more worthy and vital than any charity can possibly be, that it seems to me, under your leadership, the necessary sum could be gotten to go into the railroad situation and the participation of labor in enterprise, on a real scale. What I suggest will, I realize, require a large fund,—I should think a half a million dollars to do it well—; and of this sum you may put me down for $50,000 if you think well of it and conclude to go ahead, or 10% of whatever sum not less than $300,000 and not more than $500,000, that you and Judge Brandeis and Mr. Colby conclude might be necessary. That the first sum I mention is probably not too large is well illustrated by the fact that my investigation of the Steel situation in my effort to make this consolidation of independents has only been going on six months, and has already cost in excess of one hundred thousand dollars.

I regret more than I can tell you that I cannot be with you tomorrow, and that this letter has had to be written with a mind so full of other things.

With regards to Justice Brandeis and Mr. Colby, I beg to remain,
          Very sincerely yours,   Thomas L Chadbourne.

TLS (WP, DLC).

To David Franklin Houston

My dear Houston: [Washington] 25th April 1922

It seems clear to me that every Democratic candidate in the approaching autumn elections should be supplied with just such a recital as you outlined yesterday of the liberal and progressive policies inaugurated by the Democratic Administration and of the way in which the Republicans have destroyed and distorted them, and I hope will all my heart that you will prepare such a paper. No one else could do it so well. I am sure it would be a great contribution towards our success this year. Will you not undertake it? It would be very serviceable to publish it in a magazine of high standing. If you will send it to me I will see to its distribution among the candidates by the National Committee.

I find my practical thinking very much aided by our little conference of yesterday, and I am so glad you were able to come and take part. This letter is the first fruit of my clarified practical thinking.

With warm regards,

Faithfully yours,   [Woodrow Wilson]

CCL (WP, DLC).

To Norman Hezekiah Davis

My dear Davis: Washington D C 25th April 1922

As I promised (or threatened?) yesterday I am enclosing a copy of paragraph five of the document[1] in the hope that you and Houston will put your heads together over it and re-ph[r]ase it so that it will conform with the facts and existing circumstance. I am personally very grateful to you and Houston for your willingness to undertake this.

I do not think it is too much to say that we are engaged just now in concerting the measures and perfecting the means for emancipating the world by leadership on the part of this country and our party.

It was delightful to have you here yesterday and you made your characteristic contribution of clear thinking and clear statement to the little conference which I believe clarified the views of all of us with regard to personal and party action.

With affectionate regard,

Faithfully yours,   Woodrow Wilson

TLS (N. H. Davis Papers, DLC).
[1] Printed as the Enclosure with WW to L. D. Brandeis, April 9, 1922.

To Thomas Lincoln Chadbourne, Jr.

My dear Mr. Chadbourne:　　　　　[Washington] 25th April 1922

I am very much obliged to you for the comments in your letter of April twenty-third on the confidential document of which I sent you a copy.

Our little conference was held yesterday very successfully indeed and I read to the men who were present your comments on paragraph five. I think that we all clarified our thinking by our interchange of views.

I greatly appreciated your offer to contribute to the expenses of certain studies which you thought ought to be made, but my own experience has been that such studies in the preparation of a document like this lead to very little beyond the accentuation of rivalries and jealousies among the men who participate. There is no pride quite so sensitive or suspicious as the pride of authorship.

I am going to take the liberty of suggesting that you contribute as liberally as possible to the expenses which the National Committee must undertake in connection with the approaching autumn campaign. There will not in my judgment be any time when their activity is more likely to be serviceable to the party and to the country. I myself have some very practical ideas with regard to this particular campaign and am in sufficient close touch with the Committee to feel confident that they can be acted upon.

It is exceedingly heartening at this critical turning point in the affairs of the world to feel that there is a man like yourself behind the instrumentalities which must be used (I am sure I speak without exaggeration) for the emancipation of mankind.

With warm regard and grateful appreciation, and the hope that I shall have many opportunities to consult with you,

　　　　　　　　　Faithfully yours,　[Woodrow Wilson]

CCL (WP, DLC).

To Emily Jane Newell Blair[1]

My dear Mrs. Blair:　　　　　　[Washington] 25th April 1922

I need not assure you that our hearts will be with you all at the dinner on Saturday evening,[2] but unhappily my body is still so lame that I cannot venture to promise to be present and crave your indulgence of my selfishness in keeping Mrs. Wilson at home also with m[e.]

I need not assure you and the ladies associated with you of my keen interest in what they are undertaking and my earnest hope and belief that they will succeed. This is undoubtedly a critical turning point in the affairs of mankind, and it clearly falls to the Democrats of the United States to lead the way to the light. Women such as those who are to gather at the dinner on Saturday evening are sure to contribute to this great purpose the invaluable stimulation of their enthusiasm and devotion.

With warm regard,   Sincerely yours,   [Woodrow Wilson]

CCL (WP, DLC).
  ¹ Mrs. Harry Wallace Blair, of Joplin, Mo. Long active in the woman suffrage movement, she was at this time a member of and "vice-chairman" of the Democratic National Committee.
  ² A dinner of the women members of the Democratic National Committee in honor of Cordell Hull in Washington on April 29, 1922. Hull and Senator Thomas J. Walsh of Montana were among the speakers. Wilson's letter, read to the diners, elicited cheers. *New York Times*, April 30, 1922, which printed Wilson's letter in full.

From Bainbridge Colby

My dear Mr President: New York City April 25, 1922

We were all so happy to find ourselves seated about you yesterday and conferring upon questions of interest and great importance. You were quite your old self throughout the long discussion and it gave us all great pleasure to note your vigor of mind and voice.

I did not stay after the conference adjourned, although I had a few matters that I wanted to speak to you about, because I felt that you had done a full day's work and furthermore my matters will keep until I see you again, which will be within a few days. I rode home on the 5 o'clock train with Baruch and Davis and they were both of the opinion that the conference had been most fruitful.

I think it would be very well to get the suggestions of Baruch and Davis and Senator Swanson, so that they can be examined in comparison with the original text of the document and, to the extent that you deem advisable, incorporated in the document.

With affectionate regard,   Cordially always   Colby

TLS (WP, DLC).

From Raymond Blaine Fosdick

Dear Mr. Wilson: New York April 25, 1922.

I am sending you herewith a summary of the work of the League of Nations during its first two years, published by the Information Section of the Secretariat. It is possible that you have already seen it, but as it came to me from Geneva only the other day, I am venturing to forward the copy to you.

I know that it must be with keen satisfaction that you are watching the growing prestige and authority of the League. It is steadily winning for itself a place from which it can never be dislodged, and is establishing itself as the only possible agency for maintaining the world's peace. To it the nations will inevitably turn for an answer to their difficulties when the hopes of the Washington and Genoa Conferences have turned to ashes, and all the other substitutes have failed.

I think of you in these hours of vindication with an increasing affection. The point of view which you gave us in the classroom at Princeton I have never forgotten, and I know with what a serene and smiling faith you are facing the future, confident of the foundations of your work and of its lasting place in the life of men. God is on our side in this business and the future is secure.

Ever faithfully yours,   Raymond B. Fosdick

TLS (WP, DLC).

To Lawrence Vest Stephens[1]

My dear Governor Stephens,   Washington D C 27th April 1922

Your letter of April twenty-second has gratified me.[2] I am glad to be sustained in my own judgment of Reed by your own closer knowledge of him, and I shall hope and confidently expect to see him repudiated by the Democrats at the primaries. Certainly Missouri cannot afford to be represented by such a marplot, and it might check the enthusiasm of Democrats throughout the country if their comrades in Missouri should not redeem the reputation of the party by substituting for Reed a man of the true breed of Democratic principle. I am sure your own great influence will contribute to the desired and expected redemption.

Please accept assurances of my entire confidence in the Missouri Democrats and believe me, with best wishes,

Sincerely yours,   Woodrow Wilson[3]

TLS (W. E. Dodd Papers, DLC).
  [1] Of St. Louis, Governor of Missouri, 1897-1901.
  [2] L. V. Stephens to WW, April 22, 1922, TLS (WP, DLC).
  [3] This letter was printed, e.g., in the *New York Times*, May 9, 1922.

To Raymond Blaine Fosdick

My dear Fosdick,   Washington D C 27th April 1922

Thank you for sending me the summary of the League's work for the first two years. I shall examine it with the greatest interest. The League has indeed become a vital and commanding force and will more and more dominate international relationships. I am thankful that I had something to do with its institution and I am also thankful, my dear fellow, that it has drawn to its service men like yourself in whose ideals and purposes I have perfect confidence.

I hope that the future will afford us many opportunities of counsel and cooperation.

With warm regard,   Faithfully yours,   Woodrow Wilson

TLS (WP, DLC).

From Franklin Delano Roosevelt

My dear Mr. President: New York April 27, 1922.

I am sending you a letter with inclosure received from Mr. Kathrens which explains itself.[1] Mr. Kathrens is somewhat cryptic as to whom he wishes the letter forwarded to, but I assume that he means it for your eyes.

I am delighted to hear such good reports of your improvement, and I know you will be pleased to learn that I am getting along famously myself.

Always sincerely yours,   Franklin D Roosevelt

TLS (WP, DLC).
[1] Richard Donland Kathrens, journalist of Kansas City. His letter is missing, but see WW to FDR, April 30, 1922.

A News Report

[April 28, 1922]
1,000 WOMEN CHEER AT WILSON'S HOME
Delegates to Baltimore Convention Sing Hymns and Acclaim League of Nations.
HE RECITES A LIMERICK
His Frail Appearance, Leaning on a Cane and Helped by an Attendant, Is Shock to Many.

Washington, April 28.—Former President Wilson greeted about 1,000 of the delegates to the Women's Pan-American Conference[1] and their guests at his home in S Street, N.W., this afternoon and after acknowledging the demonstration and explaining that he was not strong enough to make an address, recited a favorite limerick which he frequently quoted during his first campaign for the Presidency.

The limerick ran:

> For beauty I am not a star;
> There are others more handsome by far.
> But my face, I don't mind it,
> For I am behind it;
> It's the people in front that I jar.

Mr. Wilson's frail appearance and the fact that he had to be assisted to the door and back into the house by an attendant deeply affected many of the women, but the humorous twist which the former President gave to the proceedings by his recitation relieved the tension and caused laughter. He got a hearty cheer and the women joined in singing "My Country 'Tis of Thee," and "Onward, Christian Soldiers." As Mr. Wilson finally withdrew, after appearing first in the doorway and later in a balcony window of the second floor, a delegate called for three cheers for the League of Nations. They were given lustily.

There was nothing political in the demonstration and Mr. Wilson avoided any reference to such topics. It had been reported also that Lady Astor,[2] who was in Washington, would be present, but that, it developed, was due to a misunderstanding. The meeting had been arranged by Mrs. George B. Sevey of Chicago[3] of the National League of Women Voters, who asked, through Mrs. Wilson, if several of the groups of women who have been attending the Women's Pan-American Congress in Baltimore might pay their respects and hope for a word of greeting. Lady Astor happened to be a guest of the women, but other engagements had been made for her.

There were in the assemblage, which turned out to pay a tribute to Mr. Wilson, women from many of the Latin-American countries who have been attending the Women's Pan-American Congress, as well as delegations from the National League of Women's Voters and the League of American Pen Women. Many had understood that the reception was to be held at 3:30 o'clock. Mr. Wilson appeared at 3 o'clock and the demonstration continued only fifteen minutes, and as a result there were hundreds who were on their way to the Wilson home when the reception was ended.

A few minutes before 3 o'clock a burly police Captain caused some excitement by shouting that Mr. Wilson refused to appear until a dozen cameras and moving picture machines were taken away. The entrance door had been opened and the crowd was waiting in an awed silence.

"Mr. Wilson will not come out and face that battery of cameras," shouted the Captain.

The cameras were quickly removed and Mr. Wilson stepped out. The former President was dressed in a frock coat and silk hat and supported himself with a cane. An attendant helped him to turn as he faced the women. He smiled and raised his hat. A little group of women began singing "Onward, Christian Soldiers." As the hymn was concluded Mr. Wilson smiled again and spoke in a voice so low that only those within a few yards of him could hear.

"I thank you very much for the compliment," he said. "I appreciate it very deeply. I am sorry that I am not strong enough to make an address."

There were calls for Mrs. Wilson and she appeared in the doorway for a moment and stood beside her husband. She was smiling brightly and recognized a few of her women friends. Then the attendant assisted Mr. Wilson to turn slowly and re-enter the house. As he disappeared there was a hushed applause which turned into a demonstration that was continued intermittently until the former President, a few minutes later, came to the front balcony window. He looked down at the gathering until there was silence, and indicated again that he would not make an address.

"I'm not much to look at," Mr. Wilson then said. It was an expression which he frequently used in the early campaigning days when he had joked with his audience about the fact that no one could accuse him of being good to look upon. He then said in a low voice which a few nearby caught that he would repeat a favorite limerick. His voice was faint at first, but gained strength as he proceeded and the words of the limerick could be heard distinctly by those directly in front of the window.

There was a ripple of laughter among the women clustered beneath the window and then there were calls for Mrs. Wilson. As she stepped beside him again, Mr. Wilson took his silk hat from an attendant, placed it on his head and removed it quickly and waved it to the assemblage. Mrs. Wilson and Miss Margaret Wilson came to the window for a moment and acknowledged the greetings. Then the window curtains were dropped. Half the delegates remained singing until the former President and Mrs. Wilson appeared in their automobile to go for a ride. Cheers followed the automobile and it slipped away on S Street.

There was much comment afterward about the appearance of the former President. Few who have seen him frequently during his rides about the city or at the theatre noted much change in him. Mr. Wilson's apparent weakness affected many of those who had come to pay their tribute. There were others who felt that he had gained slightly since his last public appearance.

Today's reception was an entirely informal affair and the women got a general invitation to participate without regard to political affiliations.

Printed in the *New York Times*, April 29, 1922.
[1] The Pan-American Conference of Women, held in Baltimore at the invitation of the National League of Women Voters, April 20-22, 1922. Thirty-one official delegates from twenty-two nations of the western hemisphere met before an audience of over two thousand persons to discuss problems of world peace and social and political reform. See John Barrett, "Women's Big Conference," *New York Times*, April 16, 1922, Sect. VII, 6, and the reports of the conference sessions in *ibid.*, April 21-23, 1922.
[2] Nancy Witcher Langhorne, Lady Astor, Virginia-born wife of Waldorf, Viscount Astor; M.P., 1919-1945, the first woman to sit in Parliament.
[3] The Editors have not been able to discover her given names.

To Franklin Delano Roosevelt

My dear Roosevelt,   Washington D C 30th April 1922

I am indeed delighted to hear you are getting well so fast and so confidently, and I shall try and be generous enough not to envy you.

Mr. Kathrens meaning in the letters you thoughtfully enclosed is not always luminous, but he is evidently bent on helping to handle Reed without gloves and that I heartily applaud.

I hope that your generous labours in behalf of the Foundation have not overtaxed you, and you are certainly to be congratulated on your successful leadership in the complicated and difficult undertaking.

Mrs. Wilson joins me in warm greetings to Mrs. Roosevelt and you and sincere congratulations on your recovered health.

With warm regard,
        Cordially and faithfully yours,   Woodrow Wilson

TLS (F. D. Roosevelt Papers, NHpR).

Plans and Notes for Books

[c. May 1, 1922]

DEDICATION.

To my incomparable wife, Edith Bolling Wilson, whose gentle benefits to me are beyond all estimation, this book, which is meant

to contain what is best in me, is, with deep admiration and gratitude, lovingly dedicated.

◊

PREFACE

In the following pages I have set forth as clearly and truly as I
could the ideals and principles which have governed my life, and
whihch have also (such is my faith)governed the life of the nation,
although they have. not always been articulately avowed or always
audibly uttered amidst the niose [noise] of events

◊

FOREWORD

I have tried in this articleand in one or two articles which are to
follow the following pages to set dorth as fullyand faithfully as possible the ideals and principles which have governed my life. They
are the same (such is my assured faith) that have governed the
action and deve,opment of the nation itself.

◊

THE DESTINY OF THE REPUBLIC.
I.

The Vision and Purpose of the Fathers (Founders)
II.
III
"he Great Opportunity.
III.
Afterwards.

◊

I.

THE PLAN
II.

THE OPPORTUNITY.
III.

AFTERWARDS.
IV.

LOOKING FORWARD.

◊

The Vision and Purpose of the Founders.
Unlike the government of every other great state, ancient or
modern, the government of the United Stateswas set up for the

benefit of mankind as well as for the benefit of its own people,—a most ambitious enterprise, no doubt, but undertaken with high purpose, with clear vision, and with thoughtful and deliberate unselfishness, and undertaken by men who were no amateurs but acquainted with the world they lived in, practiced in the conduct of affairs, who set the new government up with an ordiliness and self-possession which marked them as men who were proud to serve liberty with the dignity and restraint of true devotees of a great ideal.

But their experiment was not welcomed by their contemporaries. Seasoned observers and sophisticated politicians must have marvelled at the profound sensation which this event in distant America occasioned in Europe. The new state had no material power that any European government need have feared. And yet it was almost everywhere looked upon with dislike and suspicion. Mankind were, of course, everywhere. under e established governments; and established g governments looked with deep concern upon this new thing in the West, heard with unconcealed alarm this new and confident voice of liberty

◇

To follow opening sentence:

Mem.

But mankind were everywhere under governments and established governments looked with deep concern upon this new thing in the West, heard with unconcealed alarm this new and confident voice of liberty

Note how Europe looked on and pondered (de Tocqueville.)

The Holy Alliance

The Monroe Doctrine, hated and feared ever since.

American influence everywhere the yeast.

◇

III.

AFTERWARDS.

Effects on the world politically and economicelly

Effects on the United States,

Its influence internationally

Its financial and commercial power

"o recover?

Show that America, knows how to lead the world in the solution of modern political and industrial problems, and thus vindicate democracy.

◇

It was not the possible physical power of the new republicthat was feared. Statesmen oversea feared the effect, rather, which its principles and example would have on their own people. No old government felt confident that it could justify itself in the midst of a public opinion aroused and free to ask questions.

France, the while, caught in a luminous fog of political theory, was groping her way from revolution to revolution in bewildered search of firm ground upon which to build a permanent government.

◇

France, the while, was groping her way through irridescent mists of politilal theory from revolution to revolution in bewildered search of firm ground upon which to build a permanent government

◇

France the while was groping her way through a luminous fog of political theory from revolution to revolution in bewildered search of firm ground upon which to build a permanent government.   W.W.
                                                                         per EBW

April 26, 1922

WWT and EBWhw MSS (WP, DLC).

From David Franklin Houston

Dear Mr. Wilson: New York May 1, 1922.

I shall be glad to try my hand at a statement along the line you suggest in your letter,[1] and to see if I can prepare something which will be helpful. Norman Davis is my neighbor and it will be easy for me to confer with him. I always find it helpful to get his views on important matters.

It was a great pleasure to see you and Mrs. Wilson last Monday, and particularly to note how much you have improved since I saw you last Spring.

Mrs. Houston[2] joins me in cordial messages to both of you.
                                    Faithfully yours,   D. F. Houston.

TLS (WP, DLC).
  [1] WW to DFH, April 25, 1922.
  [2] That is, Helen Beall Houston.

To David Franklin Houston

My dear Houston: [Washington] 3rd May 1922

Thank you for your letter of May first. I am heartily glad to know you can and will undertake the statement I suggested and I am sure when it appears there will be hundreds of Democrats besides myself who will be deeply grateful to you.

It was a real pleasure to see you and to catch a glimpse not long ago of Mrs. Houston.

Mrs. Wilson joins me in kind regards to you both and the hope that the future will bring us more frequent meetings with you both than circumstances have vouchsafed us in the recent past.

With warm regards,

Faithfully yours,   [Woodrow Wilson]

CCL (WP, DLC).

To Fred W. Bentley[1]

My dear Mr. Bentley: [Washington] 3rd May 1922

I value your letter of May second and thank you for it sincerely. It is such sincere expressions of opinion and sentiment that keep a man's thinking straight, and I am glad to feel myself your comrade in the very straight thinking you are evidently doing.

There is little wonder that men like yourself who lost sons in the great struggle for the emancipation of the world (for it was nothing less) should feel as you do about those who are seeking in every way possible to belittle and nullify the objects for which your boy and other men's boys so heroically offered their lives. I, for one, believe that a great reaction will presently manifest itself in public opinion which will serve to re-establish on lasting foundations of national self-respect our moral primacy among the nations. I have the most confident faith in the essential principles and permanent purposes of the great people to whom we belong. You will understand, I am sure, how such letters as yours serve to keep me steady in that faith.

Allow me to thank you also for giving me the privilege and pleasure of seeing the verses which you enclosed in your letter. I comprehend and share the feelings which prompted them.

With warm personal good wishes,

Cordially and sincerely yours,   [Woodrow Wilson]

CCL (WP, DLC).
[1] Wilson was replying to F. W. Bentley to WW, May 2, 1922, TLS (WP, DLC). Bentley was from Chicago and was corresponding secretary of the Gold Star Fathers' Association.

To Cordell Hull, with Enclosure

My dear Mr. Chairman: Washington, D C 4th May 1922

I take the liberty of enclosing for your consideration a telegram from Mr. Hamilton Holt which I am sure you will regard, as I do, as deserving the most serious consideration. You will know how far the judgment expressed can be used in advising candidates for the House and Senate in the coming election.

The Woodrow Wilson Democracy[1] is made up, so far as I can learn, of very serious people who are really devoted to the principles they profess, and their *unanimous* judgment is an impressive thing.

I shall be interested to learn whether you regard the recent Reoublican [Republican] primaries in Indiana[2] as having any particular significance for us. Beveridge will of course add nothing to the intellectual force of the Senate but New is, so far as I can judge, a happy riddance as a disreputable person. What Democrat will contest the seat with Beveridge?

Please command me for any service I can render.

Cordially and sincerely yours,   Woodrow Wilson

TLS (C. Hull Papers, DLC).

[1] Founded by Holt in May 1921, this organization was intended to promote Wilsonian ideas and objectives within the Democratic party and to make the League of Nations a leading issue in the campaign of 1922. *New York Times*, Oct. 13, 1921; Warren F. Kuehl, *Hamilton Holt: Journalist, Internationalist, Educator* (Gainesville, Fla., 1960), pp. 158-60.

Holt had discussed the proposal set forth in the Enclosure with Wilson and with Hull in separate meetings in Washington on April 29. Wilson was enthusiastic about the idea; Hull, less so. Holt then had the proposal put to a vote at the annual meeting of the Woodrow Wilson Democracy in New York on May 3. *New York Times*, May 4, 1922.

[2] Former Senator Albert Jeremiah Beveridge had defeated incumbent Senator Harry Stewart New in the Republican primary held on May 2. Samuel Moffett Ralston, Governor of Indiana, 1913-1917, easily won over four opponents in the Democratic primary and was to defeat Beveridge in the November election. See John Braeman, *Albert J. Beveridge: American Nationalist* (Chicago, 1971), pp. 280-88.

E N C L O S U R E

New York City May 4 1922

It is the unanimous opinion of the Woodrow Wilson Democracy assembled at its annual meeting that if the great moral cause, the League of Nations, for which you have labored so faithfully and at such personal sacrifice, is made the chief issue by the Democratic Party it is certain eventually to bring victory.

Hamilton Holt.

T telegram (C. Hull Papers, DLC).

A Memorandum by Ida Minerva Tarbell

Mem. Visit to Woodrow Wilson—May 5, 1922

An invitation to "drink tea" with Mr. and Mrs. Wilson at half past five, May 5, 1922. My first visit to 2340 S Street. Mrs. Wilson came to the drawing room for me. Fine impression of sweetness, self-control and elegance—never was more taken with her. Very cordial, took me into the library where, at the right of the fireplace, Mr. Wilson was sitting. Startled by a sense that he was a very sick man. My first conscious thought was that this was no time to push the idea that I had in mind of persuading him about a series of conversations. The impropriety, if not cruelty of it, came on me at the first glimpse of him. His hand clasp was strong and warm, but there was an almost pathetic look in his face when he said, "You will forgive my not getting up, I cannot rise." And his voice had a fatigure [fatigue] in it which was heart-breaking. All the way through the conversation I noticed this fatigue of voice—a bad sign, in my judgment.

The weather was terrible, floods of rain, and I said, "I suppose you could not go out this afternoon." "On the contrary," they both exclaimed, "we always go." Mrs. Wilson added, "I never let him miss a day." He spoke of the pleasure he took in his drive. I found it difficult to make conversation. There was a restraint on his part, quite unlike his old self.

The library, which is a beautiful room, offered a subject. We had already talked about the house. Mrs. Wilson had shown me her garden and commented on how lucky they were to step into so beautiful a place and it is really a delightful place. The books at the further end of the room rup [run] to the top, and he spoke of them as being marooned, and said he didn't like it. Mrs. Wilson said that she had been trying to find a ladder that was not ugly, and he said "There ain't no such animal." She told of a political admirer—a lady from Baltimore, who had visited her and who had told her of a really beautiful ladder in a Baltimore house and promised to get the design for her, but she never heard from her.

We spoke of Sprunt, and MacRae,[1] whom I had just seen in Wilmington. He warmly approved of MacRae's work of colonization. I spoke of how wamr [warm] their loyalty to him was and of their interest in any of his expressions, making this an opening to the idea I had in mind. Mrs. Wilson spoke of my having been in Washington through the Conference and asked me if I found the foreigners interesting. I said, I did, that the whole thing had interested me very much—Mr. Harding especially. She spoke of feeling sorry for him, but it is obvious that W.W. is not sorry, rather contemptuous. I said, Of course he doesn't know anything, and did not know how to think. He said, "no, he has nothing to think with." But, I added, he is very likeable. He went on to say that when he (W.W.) went before the Senate Committee in regard to the League of Nations,[2] Harding was one of the Committee and that nobody asked such unintelligent questions—which I can quite believe.

Wilson thinks little of the Four Power Pact, says that in entering such a pact as that, we have more need of the navy than ever, that it will be nothing but a navy that can enforce such a pact.

I said that of course Harding never understood anything about the League of Nations, that in my judgment it was the bewilderment of the country and not any conscious rejection of the League that was the trouble in 1920—spoke of my experience in the North-west. Mrs. Wilson said that Mrs. Barnes[3] had recently been there and that she thought, from intelligently analyizing [analyzing] the causes that were behind the overwhelming defeat were: the German vote, the Irish vote, the Negro vote, etc. Mr. Wilson says that he doesn't think it was a referendum in any sense—though he didn't use that word. I took this chance to get in my suggestion that he could call—particularly the women of the country back to basic ideals—perhaps write a primer of democracy. That is, that it looks to me that they don't quite know where they are going, and that they try to satisfy their ideals by fidelity to the political machine, that they will accept things that otherwise they would disdain to have anything to do with, out of loyalty—that loyalty to party is being put before principle—and this is seen in the Newberry case,[4] which worries me greatly.

Wilson says that the Newberry case is the most dangerous thing of its kind that has ever happened in the Republic, that Newberry was used to pack the Senate against the League of Nations, that if it had not been for him it would not have been rejected, that now the party having used him, has to sustain him. I said that this had disturbed me more than anything that has happened for a long time in regard to women, that I have found that women who are entirely committed to the League of Nations were standing by their party in this, and that was one reason why I felt so strongly that we need this basic instruction in democratic idealism.

Wilson says he sympathizes with party loaylty [loyalty], that you cannot have democratic government unless leadership is accepted and followed. He says that certain Senators came to him recently and talked over a program for the party. He said that he would lay out the program if they would put it before the democratic caucus, and, having accepted it, would agree to follow it; that they would

not do it. He said, "They have their petty, willful notions of independence, apart from party—will not follow a program."

I take it that here what he is talking about is a program quite
apart from political immorality like the Newberry case. The Newberry case was introduced, as I remember now, by his taking up a
copy of a little evening paper and saying to Mrs. Wilson, "My dear,
here is a new mot—New-bury—very good is it not?" Then we were
off as above. This of course is accepting the explanation that the
Newberry case buried New. I said, I am glad that he was defeated.
He says, "Yes, there are worse men, in many respects, in the
United States than Beveridge." Well, I say, he is better than New
anyway. He says, "Yes."

One of his expressions in this discussion was, "We have made
the world safe for democracy. The world would not permit today
that any small nation should be seized, agree that it has the right
to work out its destiny; but democracy is in danger from interior
revolution, it must learn to preserve itself." He says that the danger
to the League of Nations today is from the Supreme Council, that
it is an unauthorized body, made up of the worst elements in Europe. (whether he refers to Lloyd George here or not I do not
know.)

Am much interested in Mrs. Wilson's attitude—perfectly charming, kindly, literary, interested, watching him every moment—
most delightful to look at.

Wilson speaks of the fact that there are many common people,
working men, who have written, expressing their loyalty to the
league. She says that the mail is very interesting. For a time, in the
illness of his secretary, Mr. Bolling, she read the mail to Mr. Wilson
and became so interested in it that now she takes her knitting and
goes in while the mail is being read to him. Evidently he follows it
with keen interest, it is his communication with the country and a
measure of the country's interest in him.

At the end of half an hour I think and feeling that I had staid as
long as I ought, that he was beginning to be tired, I rose to go. Mr.
Wilson said, "You will come again. Let us know in advance." Mrs.
Wilson said, "He is allowed to see only one person a day, so we
have to arrange ahead."

When I go away I say to him, "Don't forget the primer of democracy, Mr. Wilson, we need it very much." He quite surprised me by
a droop of his head and a very humble, "I don't know enough to do
it."

My whole impression is of a broken man but of a spirit as un-
yielding, as capable of contempt for those he reagrds [regards] as

contemptible, of outspoken repudiations of those he regards as "marplots" as he calls Reid [Reed] and others, as ever. His mind is clear and strong, but there is a bitterness of spirit which I fear will make it incapable of rendering the very great service that I believe he might do today; and that is, putting aside all contemporary questions and policies, to recall the country constantly to the big fundamental principles and ideals. To carry out J.S.P.'s[5] idea I am going to try and get the suggestion in a letter. It should be a discussion in which one would ask, What is out [our] situation today? What are its tendencies? its dangers? What is the citizen's attitude today? What are we working for anyway in a democracy? How can we realize it, etc.? It is not as a leader of the democratic party but as the leader of democracy that Mr. Wilson can render his great service today. But I don't know whether I dare put that to him. I think he still clings to party leadership, but I don't believe he will ever have the physical force to take it on.

In speaking of Harding, Mr. Wilson said he was entirely right not to see the women and children who had presented themselves the day before to plead for the release of their fathers and husbands, the political prisoners.[6]

"There [They] do not deserve release," he said severely. "Debs never should have been released.[7] Debs was one of the worst men in the country. He should have staid in the penetentiary."

When you run up against this side of Mr. Wilson's mind you are touching one of the reasons why so many people who came in contact with him, hated him. He is inflexible in his judgments.

T MS (Ida M. Tarbell Coll., PMA).
    [1] James Sprunt, cotton broker, philanthropist, and historian of Wilmington, N. C., frequently mentioned in earlier volumes of this series. Hugh MacRae, wealthy public utilities magnate of Wilmington. About his farm colonies, see n. 2 to the remarks at a press conference printed at Jan. 12, 1915, Vol. 32.
    [2] That is, the conference with the Senate Foreign Relations Committee at the White House on August 19, 1919, about which, see the reports of that affair printed at that date in Vol. 62.
    [3] Unidentified.
    [4] About which, see n. 2 to the Enclosure printed with ASB to EBW, March 23, 1920, Vol. 65.
    [5] John Sanburn Phillips, long-time manager of *McClure's Magazine* and, later, editor of the *American Magazine*; at this time a consulting editor of the latter.
    [6] Harding, on April 29, had refused to meet a delegation of wives and children of prisoners imprisoned under the Espionage Act. The President's Secretary, George Busby Christian, Jr., had explained to Kate Richards (Mrs. Frank Patrick) O'Hare, Theresa Hirschl (Mrs. Charles Edward) Russell, and two other leaders of the group that requests for pardons had to be considered by Attorney General Harry Micajah Daugherty on a case-by-case basis, and he arranged an appointment for them with him. *New York Times*, April 30, 1922.
    [7] Harding, on December 25, 1921, had commuted the sentences of Debs and twenty-three other persons to time served.

From Norman Hezekiah Davis

Dear Mr. Wilson: New York May 5, 1922.

I have delayed acknowledging receipt of your letter of April 25th expecting from day to day to get in touch with Houston and to agree upon the re-phrasing of paragraph five.

I have made an effort on this and have sent it to Houston but find that he will be absent until Monday, at which time we are to lunch together and go over it.

I enjoyed very much the conference with you. It was an excellent opportunity to clarify our minds and direct our attention in the same direction. There is certainly great need of concerted action and it is most satisfying that you are able and willing to take the lead.

With warmest regards to Mrs. Wilson and yourself, I am
Affectionately yours,   Norman H. Davis

TLS (WP, DLC).

From Cordell Hull

My dear Mr. President: Washington D C May 5th 1922.

I thank you for your letter of the 4th instant with enclosure from Honorable Hamilton Holt. I may say that I had a lengthy conference with Mr. Holt on last Saturday, with the promise of further conferences from time to time in order that the wisest policies may be developed with respect to keeping the most essential and important issues properly and effectively before the country. While I cannot speak for Mr. Holt, I am of opinion that he was reasonably well satisfied with the outcome of our first and preliminary conference.

As you are aware, I am striving to keep myself familiar with all important angles and legitimate viewpoints as they relate to the party situation during this year with the idea of getting the best possible Congressional results for the party in the November election. I shall be only too glad to go over any and all phases of these problems with you with such reasonable frequency as you think advisable.

The Indiana primary results undoubtedly offered the most severe jolt to the administration it has received thus far. While we could probably have defeated New more easily than Beveridge, yet the beneficial party effects of what is generally accepted as a repudiation of the administration by the Indiana Republicans, will be very great for the Democrats throughout the country. Ex-Governor

Samuel M. Ralston made a runaway race for the Democratic Senatorial nomination. He is thoroughly sound on all the fundamentals of the domestic and foreign policies of your administration and
at this stage I think he has an excellent chance to win. We should
be able to elect six or seven Democrats out of the thirteen Districts
in Indiana. We have none at present.

I had an exceptionally fine State-wide conference of Democratic
officials, editors, and leaders in Connecticut on yesterday, and an
unusually large attended banquet at New Haven last evening. If
we are able to avoid complications within the party, as I think we
shall be, we should elect a Senator, Governor and three or four
Congressmen in Connecticut. I believe I gave you a general account of my recent Western visit to some ten States.

Conditions, fundamentally, have been worse for the Republicans
each month since the November election, 1920, and correspondingly better for the Democrats. If the Democrats of the country can
only be induced to become active and to increase their activities as
the election approaches, and at the same time make no serious tac-
tical blunders, we should carry the House next fall and make satisfactory gains in the Senate. This, of course, is my impression
based on conditions at the present stage.

I shall be out of the City during next week. I shall thank you to
let me hear from you at any time with such suggestions as you may
have in mind.   Very sincerely,   Cordell Hull

TLS (WP, DLC).

To Cordell Hull

My dear Mr. Chairman,   Washington D C 6th May 1922

In a letter which Mr. Bolling has just received from Mr. Schuyler
Warren, Jr.,¹ of the Woodrow Wilson Democracy, appears the following:

> "A resolution was approved and sent to Mr. Hull calling for a
> conference of the Party in some form to shape a program for the
> election."

May I volunteer the opinion, which I daresay is also your own,
that such a conference would lead to nothing but talk and outside
rumors about it which would be misleading and hurtful to the
party. My knowledge of you convinces me that you are not in need
of comment of that sort.

Thank you very much for your letter of May fifth and its comments on the situation in Indiana and elsewhere. Certainly what
you say is most encouraging and therefore most cheering to me.

With the most agreeable anticipations of our association, and assurances of my confidence and warm regard,

Faithfully Yours,   Woodrow Wilson

TLS (C. Hull Papers, DLC).
¹ Schuyler Neilson Warren, Jr., to JRB, May 4, 1922, ALS (WP, DLC). Warren, from New York, was treasurer of the Woodrow Wilson Democracy.

John Randolph Bolling to Norman Hezekiah Davis

Dear Mr. Davis,   [Washington] 7th May 1922

Mr. Wilson wishes me to say that your letter to him of May fifth has given him very great pleasure, and that he is happy to know you have been generous enough to start the revision of paragraph five.

He also wishes me to inform you that Mr. Houston has agreed to write an article pointing out the liberal policies that were initiated and substantially advanced by the Democratic administration, and the way in which those policies have one after another been distorted or absolutely nullified by the party now in power. That he has asked Mr. Houston to publish the article in a magazine, but that it seems to him it will also serve in any form (in which Mr. Houston can early supply it) as valuable material for all Democratic speakers in the Congressional campaign this year.

With warm regards from us all;

Cordially yours,   [John Randolph Bolling]

CCL (WP, DLC).

A Memorandum by Dr. Grayson

[Washington] May 10, 1922.

The President seemed much distressed and pained to write the letter to the New York TIMES about the Tumulty incident, but he said it was a question of personal privilege; that he could not let it go unanswered. He felt that it had to be answered through the papers to correct the wrong impression which had been given out through the papers. He said that he hated to do this to Tumulty, but if it had been his son he would have had to act in the same manner.

T MS (received from James Gordon Grayson and Cary T. Grayson, Jr.).

To John Franklin Jameson

My dear Jameson,   Washington, D C 11th May 1922

I am thinking of devoting a part of my (enforced and uncomfortable) leisure to a closer study than I have ever made before of the effects wrought upon European politics by the establishment of our present national government, and I would be greatly indebted to you if you would direct me to the books which are likely to be of the most service to me in carrying out that purpose.

My only hesitation in preferring this request is that I know you are so generous in your helpfulness that you would not refuse even if you knew to comply would cost you an unreasonable amount of labour.

With warm regard and many apologies,
                    Faithfully yours,   Woodrow Wilson

TLS (J. F. Jameson Papers, DLC).

John Randolph Bolling to Albert Kelsey,[1] with Enclosure

Dear sir: [Washington] 11th May 1922

Mr. Wilson asks me to say that—in accordance with the suggestion contained in your letter of May ninth—he sends herewith the inscription to be placed upon the tablet. The dates of his Father's pastorate can be secured, he is sure, from the Church records.

At your convenience, Mr. Wilson will be glad to receive the design which you have so kindly offered to make.
                    Yours very truly,   [John Randolph Bolling]

CCL (WP, DLC).
   [1] An architect of Philadelphia. His letter was A. Kelsey to WW, May 9, 1922, TLS (WP, DLC). Kelsey wrote in regard to a memorial tablet in honor of Wilson's father, which Woodrow Wilson wished to present to the Presbyterian Church of Staunton, Virginia, which Dr. Wilson had served as pastor from 1855 to 1857 or 1858. Kelsey asked Wilson to forward his inscription so that he could begin work on the design of the tablet.

E N C L O S U R E[1]

IN MEMORY
of
JOSEPH R. WILSON

Who was pastor of this Church (insert dates). In all his work and intercourse with his people there shone the singular genius of a man who served God with an ardent devotion and drew his fellow men towards himself by genial and lovable gifts of every kind which attested his kinship to the divine Master whom he served.

CC MS (WP, DLC).
  ¹ There are WWsh and WWT drafts of this inscription in WP, DLC.

From John Franklin Jameson

My dear Wilson: Washington, D. C. May 12, 1922.

I am delighted with the thought of being able to be in any way useful to you. That is what I am for, to help real historians—an historical powder-monkey, to pass forward ammunition to historical gunners (or gunmen). But I shall be obliged, Yankee fashion, to reply to your question by asking another. When you speak of the effects wrought upon European politics by the establishment of our present national government, am I right in supposing that what you have in mind are the effects produced by the substitution in 1789 of an effective government for an effective one previously existing? That is to say, effects produced by the bringing into existence of an American power that must be reckoned with, rather than, in a more general sense, the effects produced by the creation, a few years earlier, of an independent American republic, *i.e.,* by the American Revolution and its consequences.

In either case it will not take me long to provide you with a certain number of references to the "literature" that has come out since you graduated from our professorial class—given the difficulty of proving such inferences as you are seeking and the consequent effect that most of the books one would mention would be books from which conclusions would be gathered by inference rather than directly.

With best wishes,   Very truly yours,   J. F. Jameson

TLS (WP, DLC).

From Norman Hezekiah Davis, with Enclosure

My dear Mr. Wilson: New York May 12, 1922.

Enclosed you will please find the result of the efforts on the part of Houston and myself to draft the substitute for the proposed Article Five.

Houston thought it well to inject in condensed form a statement of the inconsistencies of the Republicans, and as you will notice, this has been attempted. I think it would be well for him some time to enlarge upon these aspects, probably in an article for some magazine.

Mrs. Davis[1] and I are considering a trip to Europe and if I can arrange to get away, I think we will sail within a week or ten days. This will be a good way to get a rest and at the same time it should be interesting to get some first-hand information about conditions over there. Frankly, I am more concerned about conditions here, because the Republicans are showing more stupidity than the Governments of Europe.

With affectionate regards to Mrs. Wilson and yourself, I am, as ever   Faithfully yours,   Norman H. Davis

TLS (WP, DLC).
  [1] That is, Mackie Paschall Davis.

E N C L O S U R E[1]

We are suffering in common with other nations of the world from the industrial and commercial prostration which followed the great war. Bound up with world conditions from which we could not extricate ourselves, the Republican Administration nevertheless committed itself to a policy of isolation. It blindly persisted in the delusion that we are unaffected by the world's all-encompassing perils and calamities and that, although we have great accumulated strength and matchless resources, we have no responsibility and need not interest ourselves in efforts to discover and apply safeguards and remedies. It still refuses to take the lead or to cooperate with the Governments of other nations in the adoption of measures which would improve our own situation or that of our customers and debtors.

The Republican Administration has no economic policy, domestic or foreign. In economic matters, it is trying to go in a number of opposite directions at the same time. It declares its desire to stimulate foreign trade and to revive shipping and then, under pressure of special interests and for their benefit, it erects a high tariff barrier to lessen imports and therefore to limit or destroy foreign trade. It recklessly ignores the fact that we have more than half of the gold of the world; that other nations cannot pay us in gold, that it would not benefit us to receive it if ⟨we⟩ *they* could, and that we cannot sell our surplus products of the farm and factory and collect our debts unless our customers and debtors can produce and sell their goods.

That it would be worse than stupid to try to maintain a merchant fleet by direct and indirect subsidies to carry freight and then to

ۏ

destroy trade by excluding commodities, does not enter the minds of the Old Guard Republican leaders *who are* in charge of the Government. They assert their eagerness to reduce taxes and the cost of living and yet *ought to* know, in their hearts, *if they had any intelligent conception of the situation*, that they add to both by their tariff program, based on greed. They preach economy and *yet* press legislation for new undertakings *and obligations* involving hundreds of millions of dollars. They profess to be concerned about the *laborers'* standard of living, ⟨of the laborers⟩ and at a time when the beneficiaries of their tariff policy are omitting nothing to reduce wages, they are devising measures to increase the laborers' cost of living. They clamour for the stabilization of trade and exchange and by their course contribute to the conditions which render stabilization impossible. They are blind to the fact that the protection which the American farmer and manufacturer need is that which would be afforded by a great foreign market, and that this can be secured only by measures which will bring peace to the world, stimulate the forces of production everywhere and make possible through legitimate business ventures this nation's assistance to Europe through loans and investments.

T MS (WP, DLC).
[1] Words in angle brackets deleted by Wilson; words in italics added by him.

To John Franklin Jameson

My dear Jameson,   Washington D C 13th May 1922

Thank you for your reply to my letter. What I want is as clear a picture as I can get of the effect on the minds and actions of European public men of the establishment of an independent government in America of a form likely to last and gather power to itself and more than that likely to have a very material effect upon the thinking and political sympathies of their own people who were already beginning to look critically at the forms of government under which they were living. If this is not a clear enough form of the question, please let me try again.

With warm appreciation of your kind willingness to help me,
          Cordially and Faithfully Yours,   Woodrow Wilson

TLS (J. F. Jameson Papers, DLC).

To Norman Hezekiah Davis

My dear Davis,   [Washington] 13th May 1922

Thank you very gratefully for the paper enclosed in yours of May twelfth. I shall proceed at the earliest possible moment to give it very careful study.

I think that probably the article I wrote you about a short while ago, which Houston is going to undertake, will inferentially if not explicitly cover the ground of the article which you suggest he should write.

I am heartily glad that there is the prospect of a real vacation before Mrs. Davis and you. I hope that it will all come true and that you will both greatly enjoy and profit by it. Our affectionate good wishes will follow you and render us impatient for your return. You will no doubt come back with a mind better furnished than ever with the particulars of the present distresses of the world, and particularly of our own misguided country.

With affectionate regard,

Faithfully Yours,   [Woodrow Wilson]

CCL (WP, DLC).

From Bainbridge Colby

My dear Mr President: New York City May 19, 1922

I beg to enclose a memorandum setting forth the salient facts regarding the Ecuadorian loan upon which I have been very actively engaged for some time.[1] I do not wish to speak with undue hopefulness about it, but there is a strong promise that it will go through. I have it up with a group of important bankers who display genuine interest in it. It would be a very fine piece of business, with several legitimate and interesting ramifications.

I have many things I wish to talk to you about, but none of sufficient importance to invade the peace and continuity of your days, by a special visit. The success of Beveridge in Indiana and Pinchot in Pennsylvania[2] interests me. I know each of them well. We were thrown much together during the early Progressive days. They belonged to the misguided contingent that went back to the Republican Party when Colonel Roosevelt applied the extinguisher to the Progressive party, and I haven't seen much of them since, but their success in the recent primaries is a pretty fair index of popular dissatisfaction with the present Administration in Washington.

There is a languid revival of local political interest in New York, pivoting for the present upon speculation as to whether William

Randolph Hearst will be a candidate for Governor or Senator. The local organization seems to be hiding under the chairs, to see which way the situation develops.

I enclose a clipping from a recent issue of the "Evening Post,"[3] commenting upon the adoption by the Harding Administration of your foreign policies, notwithstanding the announced intention of Mr Harding to reverse all of them.

I read with much interest the account in the "Times" the other day of your visit to the theater.[4] I wish I had been with you to enjoy the demonstration and to hear the cheering.

Always with affectionate regard,

Sincerely yours,   Bainbridge Colby

TLS (WP, DLC).

[1] "MEMORANDUM. PROPOSED LOAN TO EQUADOR," T MS (WP, DLC).

[2] In the primary election held on May 16, Gifford Pinchot had narrowly defeated George Elias Alter, the Pennsylvania Attorney General and the hand-picked candidate of the remnants of the Penrose machine, in the contest for the Republican nomination for Governor. He was to win easily over John Aldus McSparran, the Democratic nominee, in the general election in November.

[3] It is missing but it was an anonymous letter to the editor printed in the New York *Evening Post*, May 12, 1922, under the heading "Policies at Washington." The writer cited a long list of foreign policies of the Wilson administration, including those toward Russia, Mexico, and the Open Door, which, he asserted, remained unchanged by the Harding administration. "One of the most striking declarations," he concluded, "made by President Harding in his campaign for election was that he would reverse every foreign policy of his predecessor. Even more striking is his adoption without deviation of every policy that he included in his blanket denunciation, urged, it is true, often upon weaker grounds, and stated with less power and convincing effect than by the Wilson Administration, but nevertheless, followed in every detail."

[4] "WASHINGTON SEES A GENTLER WILSON," *New York Times*, May 15, 1922.

To Carter Glass

My dear Glass: Washington D C 21st May 1922

I assume that you read Vanderlip's views on the present economic situation in Europe and the world which appeared in this morning's Washington Star.[1] I read between the lines that his mind is tending towards the suggestion of a reserve system and organization for the world similar to ours in the United States. I should feel very much instructed if you would tell me whether you think such a thing practicable, and if practicable, wise and desirable.

If you feel disinclined to tackle this big question right now please say so and I shall understand and shall feel none the less indebted to you for many wise counsels in the field of finance. I am merely trying to get as much light into my own mind in these troubled times as possible.

Cordially and Faithfully Yours,   Woodrow Wilson

TLS (C. Glass Papers, ViU).

¹ Frank Arthur Vanderlip's article appeared as "VANDERLIP REVIEWS GENOA," in the New York *World*, May 21, 1922, and was syndicated to other newspapers such as the *Washington Star*. It was also printed in the *Cong. Record*, 67th Cong., 2d sess., pp. 7363-66. Vanderlip, who had been in Genoa during the international conference held there from April 10 to May 19, 1922, provided a lengthy summary of the successes and failures of the conference and made extensive suggestions as to what should be done in the future, both by the European nations involved and by the United States. He believed that the conferees, by negotiating a temporary pact of peace, had provided themselves with a vital breathing space before tackling the enormous economic and political problems of Europe, but that they had made no progress at all toward solving those problems. He discussed in particular the necessities of the readjustment of German reparation payments to a reasonable level, reduction of armaments, the readjustment and determination of national boundaries to achieve some degree of political security, the rearrangement of international indebtedness to make the burdens of individual nations bearable, and reconstruction of the European transportation system.

On the subject mentioned by Wilson in the second sentence of the above letter, Vanderlip made the following remarks:

"The essential part of the central bank program [of the nations represented at Genoa] is to induce the United States to cooperate in its discount and gold policy to help Europe regain currency stability.

"I have heretofore pointed out the danger of involving the Federal reserve bank, created to hold the reserves of 10,000 banks, in too close relation with European central banks. The European central banks present varying degrees of insolvency and will find great difficulty reaching an effective working entente.

"I am convinced our huge gold stock presents a dangerous invitation to inflation in the United States; and diversion of a portion of that gold into a sound plan for helping stabilize European currencies would be not only extremely useful to all parties but tend to avoid the danger of a period of wild inflation in America.

"The method of cooperation should not be such as to involve in alien entanglements the reserves of the American banking system. There should be considered a plan for creating an institution with a great gold capital, formed for the special purpose of cooperating with European central banks in their effort to stabilize currency.

"There is no need of actual exportation of gold to Europe. The gold itself may much better remain in America. All that is necessary is that European central banks be put in a position to clear obligations between themselves through American gold funds, just as the Federal reserve banks clear mutual obligations through the gold fund deposited at Washington." *Ibid.*, p. 7365.

Two Memoranda by Dr. Grayson

May 22, 1922.

I had a long visit with Mr. Wilson today. I made a thorough physical examination of him, after which he discussed with me a number of questions. One of them was whether I thought he should go away for the summer or remain here.¹ My advice was that a change would be good for him if it could be had in the proper circumstances. The question of traveling, the problem of servants and securing a suitable house were gone over. I felt that it would be out of the question for him to live at a hotel. I said that if the nights were cool he should have an open-fire place (since he is very sensitive to cold), and that a house with an elevator in it would be preferable, as it is difficult for him on some days to get up the steps. In other words, if he could have all the conveniences and all the privacy of his home on S Street and could get to the place selected in an automobile without undue fatigue, I would advise him to go away for the summer. He said: "Your requirements cannot be complied with," to which I replied: "Then I would advise you not to go." He said: "I think you are right: but I would like to get away on account of Mrs. Wilson. Personally, I would rather stay where I am. I have stood the Washington heat during my entire time in the White House and it has done me all the harm that I imagine it could do. I shall follow your advice." He added: "I would like to be in Washington during the summer in order to keep in touch with what is going on politically. This is a Congressional election, and, in case my advice was needed, I would be near at hand. I want to keep an eye on the situation."

¹ Wilson was at this time in a rather heavy correspondence with Fred L. Seely, proprietor of the Grove Park Inn in Asheville, N. C., about the prospects of the Wilsons occupying a cottage on the grounds of the inn for the summer of 1922. We have not printed any of this correspondence since nothing ever came of the invitation except that Wilson was persuaded that he should not accept it.

May 22, 1922.

On April 5th Mr. Tumulty wrote a letter to Mr. Wilson asking that he give him a statement to take to New York to be read at the Jefferson Day Banquet. Mr. Wilson replied the following day that he thought it would be unwise for him to give out a statement to be read at this dinner, especially since it was his present policy not to give out statements on public questions. A few days later Mr. Tumulty wrote Mr. Wilson a long letter begging him to reconsider and give him this statement to take to the New York Banquet, giving as his reasons that James M. Cox would be one of the principal speakers; that he (Mr. Cox) had loyally advocated the League of Nations, and that he thought it was due Mr. Cox that Mr. Wilson endorse the stand that Mr. Cox had taken; also that there would be many prominent persons present, among them Frank Polk, Henry Morgenthau, Abram I. Elkus, and others, and if no message were read from Mr. Wilson on this occasion it would be misunderstood and misconstrued by those present at the dinner.

Mr. Wilson replied to this letter saying that he could not, in the circumstances, change the opinion previously formed by him on this subject; that for him to give a letter that would appear to endorse Cox would be construed as an endorsement of his renomination in 1924, and he would consider Cox's renomination as the suicide of the Democratic Party. He addressed Mr. Tumulty substantially in these words: "My dear Tumulty: I would like to do this to accommodate you, but this must be considered as final. I cannot do it."

After receiving Mr. Wilson's letter, Mr. Tumulty telephoned several times to Mrs. Wilson saying what a pity it would be and how it would be misunderstood if Mr. Wilson would not give this message. He begged Mrs. Wilson to try to get Mr. Wilson to change his mind.

A day or two before the Jefferson Day Banquet Mr. Tumulty called at the Wilson residence and had a visit with Mr. Wilson. Mrs. Wilson was absent. She came in, however, just as Mr. Tumulty was leaving. She went up to Mr. Wilson's room and asked him if Mr. Tumulty had bothered him any more about the Jefferson Day Dinner, to which Mr. Wilson replied: "No, the subject was not mentioned. That is like Tumulty. When I write him and tell him anything is final, he never mentions the subject again."

Several days afterwards I cautioned Mr. Wilson not to worry, as worry would interfere with his sleep, and I asked him whether he had had a good night. He said: "No, not very good." And then he emphasized the point that he was not worrying; that that was not the cause of his loss of sleep. He said: "I am not worrying about the Tumulty incident. If Tumulty had been my son and had acted as he did, I would have done the same thing."

A few days after the publication of this whole matter, the question of Tumulty came up and I expressed regret that he had broken with him, as his enemies would be sure to say that he could not get along with any one. He abruptly told me that I did not know what I was talking about; that it was none of my business. Several days after this conversation, while in bed, he asked Mrs. Wilson and his colored attendant to please step out of the room, as he wanted to talk over some private matters with me. After they had left the room, he said: "I want to apologize for the way in which I spoke to you the other day. I want you to read these letters, which will explain the whole situation." He then showed me the letters to which I have referred to above.

T MSS (received from James Gordon Grayson and Cary T. Grayson, Jr.).

To Cordell Hull

My dear Mr. Chairman,   Washington D C 23rd May 1922

I am warmly obliged to you for your letter of May twenty-second.[1] It satisfies my great desire to be kept informed as to the political conditions developing in the country.

May I venture a suggestion: I am sure that there is a great deal of faking in the repeated statements recently emanating from the Administration as to economy and savings. Would it not be well to have some one of our experts (a man trained in the work of the

Ways and Means Committee or formerly connected with the Treasury and thoroughly acquainted with its processes) look into these figures with the closest scrutiny in order to discover where the deception lies,—for deception I am sure there must be. A brief on the subject could be prepared by him which would be of the utmost service to our candidates in the approaching elections.

Since you speak of Tennessee in your letter, may I not advise that an eye of distrust be kept on Senator McKellar. I have found him false and untrustworthy. The genuine article is indeed hard to find.

I get letters from Missouri which encourage me to believe that Reed's day of reckoning has come and that he will be convinced of the consequences of disloyalty.

I admire the work you are doing and shall be happy to help in any way in my power.

With warm regard,

Cordially and Faithfully Yours,   Woodrow Wilson

TLS (C. Hull Papers, DLC).
   [1] C. Hull to WW, May 22, 1922, TLS (WP, DLC).

From Carter Glass

My dear Mr. President: Washington, D. C. May 23, 1922.

I am genuinely glad to note that you have a keener sense of important current events than I, for this betokens a return to your real splendid self.

The Sunday papers usually are so interminable in their array of special articles that I make it a point to confine myself to The New York Times on Sundays; hence I did not see, and have not read, Mr. Vanderlip's contribution to The Washington Star of the 21st. However, I observe that it was inserted in the Congressional Record of Monday and I shall endeavor to get a chance to read it tonight, having done which I shall be glad to tell you what I think of it.

I am always wanting to see you and talk with you briefly about more or less important happenings; but I so much fear that I may be a bother that I refrain from making the effort. Nevertheless my personal affection is so constant that I never permit a week to go by without communicating with Dr. Grayson to find out whether or not things are well with you.

With cordial regards,

Always your devoted friend,   Carter Glass.

TLS (WP, DLC).

From David Franklin Houston

Dear Mr. Wilson: New York May 24, 1922.

I am delighted to try to be of service to you in your thinking about international banking and currency.[1] I have been called upon to express opinions before different groups on such suggestions as Vanderlip's. I have been in conference with bankers and economists who were discussing stabilizing exchanges and money.

I have taken this position: There are no such things as stable exchanges or currencies. There can be no such things. These things can no more be fixed absolutely than can the quantity of goods whose prices they measure or reflect. Present exchanges and currencies are highly abnormal. They are symptoms. There is no superficial treatment, and this is what most people are trying to give them. The disease must be overcome. When I think about trying to get exchanges and currencies back to their normal condition, I ask myself what caused them to become abnormal. The answer is, of course, the great explosion and all the courses of action which it set up, mostly unwise actions on the Continent of Europe. To bring exchanges and currencies back to a somewhat normal condition, the steps will have to be retraced. Europe must establish firm peace. Armies must be disbanded and government expenditures greatly curtailed. Printing presses will have to be shut down. Artificial barriers must be removed. People must set to work under better conditions and work as they have never worked before. Of course federation should be established in Europe, but Europe is far away from such things. If these things were done, we should have no problem of stabilizing exchanges and currencies. The result would be attained.

We can do very little until Europe does its part, unless we are ready to aid promptly and in large ways in establishing peace in the world, and to assert our leadership again in this direction and give such legitimate economic aid as we may be able to render if the European nations will take the wise course. The principal nations of Europe are insolvent or very nearly so beginning with Russia, and the others in the following order: Germany, Austria, Poland, Hungary, Roumania, Czecho-Slovakia, Bulgaria, Jugo-Slavia, Italy and France. They must perform very major surgical operations before treatment will do them much good.

I have read Mr. Vanderlip's suggestions. I have come to attach little or no importance to anything he says. He has a sloppy mind. Perhaps you may prefer to call it a sentimental mind. I think he is doing more harm than good by what he is saying. Incidentally, he is misleading European people.

This afternoon there came into my hands a bulletin prepared by Mr. Anderson,[2] economist of the Chase National Bank. In this bulletin he refers to various schemes for stabilizing exchanges and for reforming currencies. He specifically discusses Mr. Vanderlip's suggestions. I agree with his main positions. I have marked the paragraphs in which I think you will be most interested.[3] At the top of the front cover, I have indicated the pages which you may wish to look at if you do not have time to read the entire document.

If I can be of any further help, please command me.

Faithfully yours,   D. F. Houston

TLS (WP, DLC).
  [1] Houston was replying to WW to DFH, May 21, 1922, CCL (WP, DLC). Wilson's letter was, *mutatis mutandis*, the same as WW to C. Glass, May 21, 1922.
  [2] Benjamin McAlester Anderson.
  [3] This "bulletin" is missing in WP, DLC.

From Cordell Hull

My dear Mr. President: Washington, D. C. May 24th, 1922.

I am real glad to get your letter of the 23rd instant. I am in the most hearty accord with your timely suggestion relative to the advisability of having a thorough analysis of the Treasury condition made, and the true facts relative to alleged economy gotten before the country. I may say that some five of the regular annual appropriation bills have not yet passed through Congress.

I have had many conferences with Congressman Byrns of Tennessee and Byrnes of South Carolina,[1] two ranking and most capable Democrats on the Appropriations Committee, relative to the extreme importance of their making just such study and analysis as you suggest. I shall closely follow up this matter because I fully share your views as to its great importance.

I am very thankful for the benefit of the other observations contained in your letter.   Very sincerely,   Cordell Hull

TLS (WP, DLC).
  [1] Joseph Wellington Byrns and James Francis Byrnes.

To Cordell Hull

My dear Mr. Chairman,   Washington D C 25th May 1922

Your kind letter of May twenty-fourth emboldens me to discourse upon another subject. I think that we ought, in advising our friends about the choice of candidates for this autumn, to dwell upon the necessity of disregarding all the ordinary considerations of "availability" and of considering only ability and suitability.

North of Mason and Dickson's line particularly the Republicans have been able to build up the fiction that citizens of the first class in every community are the natural supporters of their party; in brief, that high social standing, moral elevation and wide practical influence belong chiefly if not only to men and women who vote the Republican ticket. We must break down that impression and this is the time to do it, because it is just people of that sort who are now everywhere turning to us. Take a case:

Mr. John F. Moors of Massachusetts is a man who belongs to the very highest class of citizens. He is of the highest social standing and devotes his unusual abilities to civic services of the most useful and elevating sort. Whenever I mention him to the self-styled "practical" men of his State they doubt his "vote-getting" power and his ability to "appeal to the people," but it is clear to my mind that just such objections ought at this particular time to be contemptuously ignored. In the first place they are not true, and in the second they mean in brief that the man will not wear the same harness with the scheming politicians. If that is true, he is the very man we are looking for and ought to be nominated for the Senate. We must fill our seats with gentlemen and men of honour and let the politicians get used to good company.

I do not think that these considerations can be too earnestly or too *imperatively* pressed upon our party men everywhere. I am not afraid of making ours a "high brow" party, for high brows at least think and comprehend the standards of high conduct.

I know that you will indulge me in these reflections.
Cordially and Faithfully Yours,   Woodrow Wilson

TLS (C. Hull Papers, DLC).

From Cleveland Hoadley Dodge

My dear Woodrow: New York May 25, 1922.

I have had a pretty mean time of it for the past two months, and a pretty close call, but have at last been moved to the country, and for the first time, have been allowed to see my mail and do a little dictating. Cleveland[1] wrote you in reply to your delightful letter of April 16th, with the generous check, and I just want to add my thanks

Now that I have to go through a little invalidism, I can sympathize with you, as I hobble around with a walking stick, and go up a few steps of the stairs sidewise, like a crab.

Hoping you will get into the country soon and have a good change, with warm regards to Mrs. Wilson,
Yours affectionately,   C H Dodge

TLS (WP, DLC).
¹ His son, Cleveland Earl Dodge. His letter was C. E. Dodge to WW, April 18, 1922, TLS (WP, DLC).

From Edward Parker Davis

My dear Woodrow,   [Philadelphia] May 25th 1922

I have gone over the situation with Dr. Dercum, and we feel that it is best for you to stay in your home in Washington. You are gaining steadily there, and you can command the situation as you could not elsewhere. So we would avoid risk, and go on gaining at home.

It was such a pleasure to see you and Mrs. Wilson: she looked much better than for some time before. The Representative joins me in "Hail to our Chief." Our best wishes and affectionate regard to Mrs. Wilson.   Affectionately Yours,   E P Davis.

ALS (WP, DLC).

To Edward Parker Davis

My dear E.P.:   [Washington] 26th May 1922

Thank you warmly for your report of your conference with Durcum. You have carried out the programme in your usual kind and thorough fashion, and I am very grateful.

Your visits not only always give me a great deal of pleasure but always cheer and strengthen me. I cannot tell you how I value and am benefited by your friendship.

Mrs. Wilson joins me in warm regards to you both and I am,

As always,   Affectionately Yours,   [Woodrow Wilson]

CCL (WP, DLC).

From John Franklin Jameson

My dear Wilson: Washington, D. C. May 26, 1922.

When you asked me to mention what materials there might be that would show the effect exerted upon the minds of European public men by the institution of the new system of government in the United States in 1789, it appeared to me that not many such indications could be found, and after some search I am obliged to continue in that opinion. It most certainly must be that public men whose positions required them to deal with the government of the United States appreciated that now there was a government with which one could do business, more easily and more effectually, but I do not find that these men anywhere said so, and other men seem to have been little impressed by the significance of the change. If anywhere, one would expect to find such evidences of interest and appreciation in England, France, and Spain, but of course the French were intensely preoccupied with their own affairs in 1789 and 1790, and in the case of Spain, I do not remember to have seen any evidence of interest in the matter. Our first minister there was so extraordinarily inactive, hardly writing more than two or three letters a year, that one gets nothing through that channel; and in Dr. W. R. Manning's elaborate monograph on the Nootka Sound affair of 1790,—in the course of which one would think that such appreciation of the changed value of the United States would come out if it existed,—while it would seem that some of these powers would have been glad to draw the United States into certain of their endeavors, I do not see any evidence that they thought much more of that country and its government than they previously had. What light there is, at this point, can be got by reading chapter X. of Manning's "Nootka Sound Controversy" in the *Annual Report* of the American Historical Association for 1904, pages 412 to 423.

In the preceding volume of that series, volume II. of the *Annual Report* for 1903, are the despatches of the French ministers in Philadelphia, edited by Turner, beginning with those of Ternant in the latter part of 1791. They do not show anything of such appreciation as we are seeking; perhaps they are too late for this, and those of Otto, the chargé d'affaires in the two preceding years, have, I think, never been published.

As for Great Britain, I myself have transcripts of all Grenville's instructions and letters to George Hammond, first minister, 1791-1795, acquired during the past winter for the purposes of my proposed volumes of the *Correspondence of the British Ministers to the United States*, and have not found in them any evidence of a heightening appreciation of the United States government under its new form, other than such as is to be found from the very fact that now for the first time, eight years after recognizing the independence of the United States, the British government sends over a minister. A curious trait is, by the way, that in all the correspondence of those four years there is hardly a mention of the president of the United States. It is, "you are to represent to the American Ministers," or "if you find the American Ministers averse to this," or "in my conversations with the American Ministers." All that sounds very much as if Grenville and Hammond underestimated the actual power of President Washington in the conduct of the government, but I do not lay too much stress upon this, for Hammond was a very intelligent young man, and Grenville was extraordinarily well-informed as a rule. However, in the three volumes of

his correspondence for these years 1789-1795 (Historical Manuscripts Commission, Report on the Manuscripts of Mr. H. B. For-
tescue of Dropmore, I.-III.) I do not think that anyone can see any
evidence of any concern about America until the troubles arise
about neutrality in the war against France.

Really, I think I can point you to only three places where you
will find discussion by European public men of the results of the
establishment of the new government in America. These are:

1. Report of a Committee of the Privy Council on Trade and
Commerce of the United States of America, January, 1791, pages
52-69 of the original edition (which, a rare book, and one not easy
to find from the catalogue, is marked in the Library of Congress,
HF 3025 G 78). This report, which I imagine was prepared mostly
by Hawkesbury (Charles Jenkinson), was reprinted in a volume
put forth in 1807 by the Society of Ship Owners, entitled *Collection
of Interesting and Important Papers on Navigation*, HF 3025 S 72
and the passage to which I have adverted may be found on pages
94-110, if that volume of the original happens to be out.

2. In the *Windham Papers*, edited by Lord Rosebury, volume I.,
pages 121 to 134, is an interesting anonymous memorandum on
the United States, and especially its government, written in English, in 1793, by a Frenchman in Philadelphia, whom the editor
does not identify, but who is clearly the Vicomte de Noailles.

3. In the *Correspondance Diplomatique de Talleyrand: Mission
de 1792*, ed. Pallain, on pages 421 to 444, there is a long letter of
Talleyrand to Lansdowne, 1795, in which he sets forth results of
his observations on America, with such fullness as makes it sort of
Vorschrift to his Memoirs on America and the Colonial System
which he read to the Institut National in 1797, and which are to
be found in its *Mémoires*, and also as pamphlets in English translation.

I ought to add that, since coming away from the Library yesterday afternoon, it has occurred to me that I ought to have looked
also at the *Political Memoranda of Francis Fifth Duke of Leeds*,
published by the Royal Historical Society in 1884, since Leeds preceded Grenville as foreign secretary, holding that office from 1783
to 1791; also that in an indirect manner something might be derived from the Diary and Letters of Gouverneur Morris.

I am sorry to have been unable to do better with the inquiry, but
the matter is somewhat elusive.

Very sincerely yours,   J. F. Jameson.

P.S.—I hope that "My dear Wilson" does not sound cheeky; for
on the other hand "Mr. Wilson" seems more cool and distant than

I like to be to one who is now a neighbor at about the same distance that he was on McCulloh street in 1883-1885![1]

TLS (WP, DLC).
    [1] When Wilson had been a graduate student and Jameson an Associate in History at The Johns Hopkins University in Baltimore. At this time, Jameson lived at 2231 Q Street in Washington.
    Jameson later sent what he called a postscript to his letter of May 26. In it he cited *The Political Memoranda of Francis Fifth Duke of Leeds* and the *Diary and Letters of Gouverneur Morris.* "They show," he wrote, "the British official mind (Pitt, Leeds, et al.) hardly at all affected by anything occurring in the United States in 1788-1792." Hw MS dated May 30, 1922 (WP, DLC). Bolling acknowledged the postscript for Wilson in JRB to J. F. Jameson, May 31, 1922, TLS (J. F. Jameson Papers, DLC).

John Randolph Bolling to William Edward Dodd

My dear Professor Dodd: 2340 S Street N W 26th May 1922

Your charming letter of May 21st[1] gave both Mr. Wilson and me the greatest pleasure.

I have been in touch with Dr. Jameson and find that your meeting will be on June 1st. Mr. Wilson will be most happy to see you, and the other members of the Board of Editors of the American Historical Review, at three o'clock on Thursday afternoon, June first. Dr. Jameson assures me that this hour will be satisfactory to all of you.

In this mail I am writing Prof. Ford[2] to the Cosmos Club, and Dr. Jameson has kindly offered to communicate with Profs. Becker and Coolidge.[3]

Looking forward with the greatest pleasure to seeing you,
          Cordially yours,   John Randolph Bolling.

TLS (W. E. Dodd Papers, DLC).
    [1] W. E. Dodd to JRB, May 21, 1922, TLS (WP, DLC).
    [2] Guy Stanton Ford, Professor of History and Dean of the Graduate School, University of Minnesota.
    [3] Carl Lotus Becker, Professor of History, Cornell University, and Archibald Cary Coolidge, Professor of History and Director of the Library, Harvard University.

To Philip Henry Kerr

My dear Kerr,   [Washington] 27th May 1922

I deeply appreciate the spirit and purpose of your letter of May twenty-second[1] and unaffectedly thank you for it. I sincerely rejoice to hear what Christian Science did for you but I must frankly say that I am too long and too deeply grounded in another view of religion to be able to open my mind just now to a consideration of Christian Science as a substitute for that view.

I know that you will understand and will believe that I am grateful to you even if I cannot accept the kind of help you so generously offer.

It was a real pleasure to see you again, for you long ago won my affectionate confidence and I am sure you will always retain it.

Cordially and Faithfully Yours,   [Woodrow Wilson]

CCL (WP, DLC).
¹ P. H. Kerr to WW, May 22, 1922, ALS (WP, DLC), a long dissertation on Christian Science which, Kerr said, saved him from being a "mental & nervous wreck." Kerr was in New York when he wrote this letter. He had recently visited Wilson.

To Cleveland Hoadley Dodge

My dear Cleve.,   Washington D C 27th May 1922

Thank you for your letter of May twenty-fifth. There is a touch of the old spirit in it, and its tone,—more than what it really says,—assures me of your returning strength, and that makes me very happy. Please be sure to omit nothing which will complete your recovery for the happiness of your friends as well as for a great many other things which depend on that.

Mrs. Wilson joins me in warm regards to you all and I am always,   Yours Most Affectionately,   Woodrow Wilson

TLS (WC, NjP).

To Josephus Daniels

My dear Daniels,   Washington D C 27th May 1922

I am mighty glad to have a copy of your "Our Navy at War."¹ It was exceedingly kind of you to think of sending it, and I thank you most warmly. I shall look forward with real pleasure to a time when I can give it the careful perusal which I am sure it deserves.

I hope that I made you feel throughout the war how completely I approved and supported your administration of the Navy which was, on the whole, the most difficult part of our warring activities.

I hope that Mrs. Daniels² and all your dear ones are very well. Mrs. Wilson and I join in sending to you all our warmest greetings.

With affectionate regard,

Cordially and Faithfully Yours,   Woodrow Wilson

TLS (J. Daniels Papers, DLC).
¹ Josephus Daniels, *Our Navy at War* (Washington, 1922).
² That is, Addie Worth Bagley Daniels.

From Cordell Hull

My dear Mr. President: Washington, D. C. May 27th, 1922.

It is refreshing to get your letter of the 25th instant and have the benefit of the highly important, timely and valuable suggestions and comment contained therein.

I may say that during the winter I inaugurated a campaign through the mails and by sending personal representatives here and there, as well as by making visits myself, to urge most strenuously on the disinterested, wide awake and patriotic local Democrats in each State and Congressional District the extreme importance of inaugurating movements in each instance to bring about the candidacy and the nomination of the cleanest, ablest and most suitable person possible to select. I think we have accomplished much good in this respect in many States and localities. I earnestly preached and stressed this doctrine in all my conferences in the eighteen States I visited.

I, of course, have exercised all possible efforts to stamp out and minimize factionalism wherever the same existed. I went so far in each instance as to insist that no Democrat had a right to put forward his personal ambition during this year, so critical for the party, where to do so might to any substantial extent jeopardize the success of the party in the November election. Naturally, we have had more success with this character of work in some States and localities than in others. As I see the situation, we can only do our level best with respect to this important phase with the knowledge that we will succeed in many instances, only partially succeed in others, and possibly fail in still others.

Since November, when I had a talk with Mr. Baruch about Massachusetts conditions, I have in all my conversations with representatives of the various groups and elements of Democrats in Massachusetts brought up for discussion in the most favorable light possible the person whose name you mention in your letter. I am, of course, most vitally concerned about the Massachusetts situation, as much so as I think any Democrat or good citizen could be. The primaries in Massachusetts are in September. It may therefore be some weeks before conditions will clarify there. I shall lose no opportunity to make every contribution within my power, at all consistent with my present situation, to the wisest solution there.

Speaking in strict confidence, I am striving most earnestly to develop a plan under which some of our Democratic leaders in the House and myself, as an official of the National Committee, will announce a policy, to the extent that we can bring about its success, of giving to each section of the country their reasonable representation with respect to committee chairmanships in the House in the event the Democrats should control in the elections of 1922 and 1924. This is an extremely difficult task, as you know, but it would be a wonderful step towards thoroughly nationalizing the Democratic party.   Very sincerely,   Cordell Hull

TLS (WP, DLC).

To Cordell Hull

My dear Mr. Chairman,   Washington D C 29th May 1922

Your letter of May twenty-seventh cheers me. I can see that you are pushing,—and will continue to push,—the policy I took the liberty of suggesting in regard to candidates, and I believe that policy—if carried out—will alter the whole aspect of national politics for us.

Perhaps a useful line of comment would be this: There are many signs from every part of the country that the class of people,—professional and business men and the leaders of social effort of every kind upon whom the Republicans used to count for cooperation,—are turning to us. It is manifestly good politics therefore to meet them half way and to choose our candidates from their ranks so as to bring over to our forces the social leaders (in the wide sense of that term) in every community. Even men of hitherto limited experience and narrow impulse ought to be able to see the practical expediency of such a course.

With warm regard and congratulations on the grounds for encouragement,
          Cordially and Faithfully Yours,   Woodrow Wilson

TLS (C. Hull Papers, DLC).

To David Franklin Houston

My dear Houston,   [Washington] 30th May 1922

Thank you for your letter of May twenty-fourth. In it you are always frank and lucid and what you say gives my thinking just the right sort of assistance. It is delightful to have such a counsellor to whom I can turn with perfect confidence.

I liked very much the revised section of our declaration of principles which you and Norman Davis so kindly drew up, and I have embodied it with much satisfaction in the document. The more I think of the approaching contest of '24 the more confident I feel that the fight will be best sustained by such a declaration of principles and purposes.

It was a pleasure and privilege to see Mrs. Houston the other day when she came in for tea with Mrs. Wilson, and I hope that everything is going well and happily with you all.

Mrs. Wilson joins me in warm regards to you both and I am, my dear Houston, always,

With affectionate regard,

Faithfully Yours,   [Woodrow Wilson]

CCL (WP, DLC).

To John Franklin Jameson

My dear Jameson,   Washington D C 30th May 1922

I am as much obliged to you as if you had cited me a whole library. I am sorry I gave you so blind a task. You have, I am sure, got more out of it for me than could have been got by anybody else.

With warm appreciation,

Cordially and Faithfully Yours,   Woodrow Wilson

TLS (J. F. Jameson Papers, DLC).

From William Gibbs McAdoo

Dear Governor: Los Angeles, Cal. June 2, 1922.

Ever since we arrived here I have been wanting to write you, but I have been under such extraordinary pressure that I have had no opportunity until today. Between finding a space for a law office and organizing it, and then finding a house to live in, we have had a very busy time. We have bought a modest and charming house here, and Nell is at last to realize her dream of a home of her own. The lot is 160 x 250 feet, so that we have a nice lawn and garden for the children. We expect to move into it about the 18th of this month. Nell is having a delightful time fixing it up to suit her own ideas and, as she has excellent taste and is quite artistic, I know that she will make a wonderful place of it.

We wish with all our hearts that you and Edith could come out and see us. We believe you would like California immensely if you could see it in favorable circumstances. Maybe that good luck is in store for us in the not far distant future.

Ellen and the baby[1] are wonderful. Ellen was thrilled with your birthday telegram, and did not fail to crow over the fact that Faith had not been honored in the same way on her birthday. I wish you could see these children now. Faith is at the most delightfully entertaining age.

I am getting well started with my law practice here, and feel that the outlook is very promising. Nell and I have always liked the West. We find the people congenial and the climate is certainly most satisfactory. It is a relief to get away from the over-crowded and intense life of New York. Certainly one gets a larger satisfaction out of life in this part of the world.

I suppose you have heard of the innuendoes and insinuations which malevolent Republicans have been directing at me in connection with the so-called Morse case.[2] These political desperadoes seem to stop at nothing to injure anyone who was prominent in your administration. My New York firm never represented Morse. We represented the Virginia Shipbuilding Company in one matter before the Shipping Board, and it is needless to say that there was no impropriety in our acting as Counsel for the Company in that case, and that what we did is above just criticism. Republican leaders, in their efforts to smirch me, are trying to distract attention from their own crookedness. It is difficult to restrain my indignation, but thus far I have been able, after violent efforts, to do it.

I think the Republicans are digging their political graves with unusual clarity. I recently went to Hutchinson, Kansas, and Kansas City, Missouri, and found everywhere discontent and great dissatisfaction with the administration. If our side is managed intelligently, we ought to capture the House, and perhaps the Senate in the coming elections.

We are rejoiced at the good news we hear about your health. We miss you and Edith more than I can tell you. The only unhappy feature of life out here is the separation from those we love most.

Nell joins me in dearest love to you and Edith. I hope that she is well. Remember us also warmly to Randolph. Please send us a line when you can.   Affectionately yours,   W G McAdoo

TLS (WP, DLC).
[1] Ellen Wilson McAdoo and Mary Faith McAdoo.
[2] Charles Wyman Morse, a New York financier who had already served a prison term for misapplication of funds of a bank he controlled, and several of his associates had been indicted on February 27, 1922, by a federal grand jury on charges of conspiring to defraud the United States Shipping Board and the Emergency Fleet Corporation in connection with contracts to build ships during the war. One of the indictments specifically mentioned McAdoo and Stuart Gatewood Gibboney, alleging that they had conveyed to officials of the Shipping Board statements indicating that the financial condition of the Virginia Shipbuilding Corporation, one of the companies in which Morse was concerned, was excellent. The indictment said that McAdoo and Gibboney were acting as lawyers for the corporation but did not charge them with having knowledge of the alleged falsity of the statements. *New York Times*, Feb. 28, 1922.
    A brief news report in *ibid.*, May 25, 1922, stated that "Washington dispatches" had suggested that McAdoo, while Secretary of the Treasury, had accepted a fee from Morse's organization to intercede in a case pending before the United States Shipping

Board. The report then quoted McAdoo's statement in response: "Any insinuation or suggestion that I represented professionally anybody, while I was Secretary of the Treasury, is false and unworthy of notice."

After much delay, the Morse case went to trial in April 1923. McAdoo testified for the defense on July 17 of that year, at which time he admitted that he had represented the Morse interests *after* his retirement as Secretary of the Treasury. No one at that time raised any question about the propriety of his conduct in regard to the affair. *Ibid.*, July 18, 1923. Morse and the other defendants were acquitted by the jury on August 4, 1923.

For voluminous news reports on the Morse case and other aspects of Morse's incredibly tangled affairs, see the references under "Morse, Chas. W.," in the *New York Times Index*, Oct. 1921-Sept. 1923; see also his obituary in the *New York Times*, Jan. 13, 1933.

To Bainbridge Colby

My dear Colby,   Washington D C 10th June 1922

I have given a very thoughtful reading to the Ecquador memorandum which you sent me and must say that the thoughts are not comfortable thoughts. I should feel very unhappy to have any part in fixing on the people of Ecquador the proposed monopolies, and a glimpse or two which I had in the past of the dealings of our financiers with regard to the Guayaquil and Quito railways make me unwilling to give them any further control in that quarter. It seems to me moreover highly dangerous and undesirable to give any of our bankers the practical unlimited control over the financial administration of the country which the Ecquadorian Government foolishly proposes to offer them.

This memorandum reminds me of the many instances of similar dealings with Latin America to which my attention was called while I was in office. In the memorandum the Ecquadorian Government anticipates and offers to yield to the usual demands. The picture is this:

The bankers consent to make a loan which they represent as extra hazardous on condition that an extravagant rate of interest be paid and guarantees given which remove the risk. Then when the inevitable pinch comes and the consequences ensue which were certainly to have been anticipated the bankers resort to the State Department to have the screws put upon the hapless government. In this case Ecquador does not even wait to have the unreasonable demands made but says, "Don't shoot, Mr. Crockett, I'll come down."

Frankly, my dear Colby, I am not willing to have my name associated with this transaction. I am sure you will comprehend my feelings and indulge my scruple.

With affectionate regard,

Faithfully Yours,   Woodrow Wilson

TLS (received from Mrs. A. Harrison Reynolds).

Two Letters to William Gibbs McAdoo

My dear Mac,   [Washington] 11th June 1922

Thank you for your letter of June second. We are always hungry for news of you all and hope you will find it possible to repeat your kindness frequently and keep us posted as to what is happening to you. It is particularly delightful to realize how comfortable and happy you all evidently are because,—say what you will,—you and Nell are not at home in the west and a certain period of adjustment is inevitable. Fortunately that period promises to lack the trying features which usually attend such adjustments. Both of you are very adaptable and with children such changes do not count.

Pray let us know nevertheless as many of the circumstances and incidents of the process as you can find time to tell me of, for we shall wish, since we cannot literally be with you, to be with you in thought as much as possible.

Things are going about as usual with us. I suppose and believe that I am getting better but not in a way that would startle you with its rapidity or at all excite you with a sense of haste. Patience has never been my long suit but it now contains evidently all of the winning cards, and I must do the best I can to simulate it at least. The real burden of course, both of the waiting and the planning, falls on dear Edith and that is of course for me an element of very great distress. She carries everything off so wonderfully that you never could tell by watching her that there was any strain, but that alas does not alter the fact.

Edith joins me in loving messages to you all. I wish that Nell and you and the children could realize how often and with what solicitous love I think of you and hope for frequent reunions not too long delayed. After all the continent is not too wide or too broad to be bridged by our thoughts and affections, and there is no danger that our section of the bridge will fall into disrepair. Our thoughts are constantly sending you loving messages and we shall make you aware of it as often as possible. If I ever get strong again I am sure that I can find many means of making our intercourse more conscious and vital.

I congratulate you, my dear fellow, on the promising beginnings of your law practice.

Affectionately Yours,   [Woodrow Wilson]

My dear Mac,   [Washington] 14th June 1922

Thank you for letting me see a copy of your Kansas speech.[1] I looked it over sufficiently to make sure you are uttering sound doctrine and preaching the gospel in its integrity. I hope that you found the Kansas Democrats in a more equable frame of mind than they sometimes were when they were trying to support the Administration. Kansas has always abounded in eccentricity.

We have just had the pleasure of a brief call from Elliott[2] and were delighted to get from him direct news of yourselves, of the new house and of all that he could tell us affecting you.

We join in the heartiest love messages to you all, and shall always be grateful for any direct news of yourselves which you have a chance to send us,—including news even of your political indiscretions.

With deep affection,

                    Faithfully Yours,   [Woodrow Wilson]

CCL (WP, DLC).
   [1] It is missing in WP, DLC.
   [2] Edward Graham Elliott, husband of Margaret Randolph Axson Elliott, sister of Ellen Axson Wilson. Elliott, former Professor of Politics and first Dean of the College at Princeton, was at this time vice-president of the Security Trust and Savings Bank of Los Angeles.

To Calvin Coolidge

My dear Mr. Vice President,   [Washington] 14th June 1922

Someone the other day had the kindness to call my attention to a recent speech of yours in which there occurs what seems to me a very public spirited and open minded reference to the League of Nations.[1] It is on account of that passage in the speech that I give myself the privilege of wishing to pay to you my tribute of respect and admiration for your independence and courage and predilection for what is right and for the general benefit.

I remember with the greatest gratification your public endorsement of the work of the Versailles Conference on the occasion of my very generous reception in Boston when I paid a visit home during an interval in the sessions at Paris.[2]

I beg, my dear Mr. Vice President, that you will accept this as the simple and unaffected tribute it is intended to be from

                    Yours Most Sincerely,   [Woodrow Wilson]

CCL (WP, DLC).
   [1] Coolidge's remarks were part of a commencement address at The American University in Washington on June 7. The relevant portion reads as follows: "The lessons of the great conflict have not gone unlearned. . . . There is a general admission throughout the earth of a mutual relationship and a mutual responsibility. There is the League of Nations which, whether successful or not, whatever imperfections may be contained within its terms, is at least the attempted expression of a noble aspiration for world association and understanding." *New York Times*, June 8, 1922.
   [2] See the extract from the Grayson Diary and Wilson's address in Boston, both printed at Feb. 24, 1919, Vol. 55.

To Royal Meeker

My dear Meeker,   [Washington] 14th June 1922

Thank you very much for sending me[1] a copy of the German-Polish convention with regard to Upper Silesia. I do not know that I shall ever read it for I agree with you that a convention of this sort which attempts every detail is likely to be a source of trouble rather than of settlement, but the fundamental characteristics of European public men is that they have no practical sense in politics. We must give them all the time they need to learn "sense" by the painful process of running their heads against stone walls. Heads as soft as theirs ought after while to be beaten into some shape.

A friend of mine here speaks of "attending Benjamin Franklin's academy," referring to a remark of Franklin's: "Experience is a hard school but fools will learn in no other." Europe has at least set up for itself a great school of experience. Perhaps it will some day become a tractable pupil.

I hope that your own work goes smoothly and satisfactor[ily,] and that the days may brighten rather than darken as the League gets accustomed to the mastery which it must presently exercise.

With warm regard,

Faithfully Yours,   [Woodrow Wilson]

CCL (WP, DLC).
[1] Wilson was replying to R. Meeker to WW [c. June 1, 1922], TLS (WP, DLC).

To Francis Bowes Sayre, Jr.

My dear Francis,   Washington D C 14th June 1922

It made me very happy to see the bags of love and the stars of kisses which you sent me in your letter.[1] I think very often indeed of Eleanor, Woodrow and you and wish with all my heart that I might often have you all with me as playmates and companions.

Give a great deal of love to your Father and Mother from Grandma Edith and me and keep as much for your little selves as you can possibly want.   Lovingly,   Grandfather

TLS (received from Francis B. Sayre).
[1] F. B. Sayre, Jr., to WW [c. June 12, 1922], ALS (WP, DLC).

From Carter Glass

My dear Mr. President: [Washington] June 16, 1922.

As occasion would permit, I have snatched a little time from the harassments of routine legislative work on the appropriations committees of the Senate to examine Mr. Vanderlip's international reserve bank scheme, if it may accurately be said to have reached the point of a real scheme. I approached the examination with some misgivings, because I was long ago convinced of Mr. Vanderlip's lack of continuity of judgment and purpose. You will recall how, after trying to scuttle our federal reserve legislation, he projected a central government bank scheme which contained the very outstanding features of the federal reserve bill which Mr. Vanderlip had bitterly assailed before the Senate Committee.[1]

The impression that I get of his suggested international reserve bank is that he is proposing a banking mechanism which is not needed in Europe. In short, the various countries of Continental Europe, in addition to Great Britain, have excellent banking mechanism; what these countries really lack is credits and capital and not machinery. And the only way to get either credits or capital is to go to work, which they have been prevented from doing by the failure of the United States to go into the League of Nations and thereby consolidate all the great nations of the world in a firm determination to compel peace by putting an end to war.

But this aside, I am afraid there are inherent obstacles of an almost insuperable nature to the formation of an international reserve banking system. The various nations which might be expected to contribute to the establishment of such a bank and become stockholding factors are so different of race, temperament and habits as to make complete cooperation exceedingly difficult. Their systems of taxation, having such intimate essential relation to commerce and industry, both foreign and domestic, are so widely at variance one with another as to produce a state of inequality which would prove troublesome in the administration of a common banking system. An incorrigible trouble with some of the European nations today is their unwillingness to assess taxes and exact from the substance of the people the wherewithal to discharge their indebtedness. They prefer the inflationary printing press process which, in the end, exacts a greater toll. This depraves their currency systems and would make it almost a hopeless task readily to relate their currencies and exchanges to our gold basis.

With the possible exception of Great Britain, the United States would be the only country whose contribution to Mr. Vanderlip's reserve bank would be in gold. Mr. Vanderlip thinks, assuming that all the countries could make their contribution to the capital stock in gold, that all transactions thereafter would be in the terms of dollars and thus would be created a new world currency, providing a stable standard of value for international trade. While this seems fair enough on its face, when we get down to the practical aspect of it, we must assume that the people who borrow must be able to command dollars.

For example, if a producer of or tradesman in potash in Germany, with a large quantity in hand, desires to sell and ship to the United States, he would have a definite dollar value in his movable property. Having that, he would not require any new European banking mechanism; he would experience no trouble in borrowing at the great European banks. If he should, he could easily borrow from the already established agencies in Europe of the larger American banks. The Irving National Bank of New York, for instance, has a correspondent in Belgium, who may negotiate advances to a Belgian manufacturer of plate glass; the Irving National Bank is eager to get such business, because when the plate glass comes to the United States and is sold, the bill is liquidated in dollars and the proceeds of the transaction are remitted to the Belgian shipper, less the bank's commission. Hence I say Mr. Vanderlip's plan proposes new banking machinery when what is really needed in Europe is *new investment capital.*

I note that Mr. Vanderlip also suggests that, when our former allies shall pay interest on their debts, the United States should leave money thus paid on deposit in the respective countries instead of receiving it here in terms of dollars, the argument being that it would then be reloaned over there instead of being drawn to this country. Leaving out of the question the many other uses to which it is proposed to put these interest payments, such as reducing our own bonded indebtedness or paying a soldiers' bonus or doing something else, the thing would not work. If Great Britain should pay us fifty million pounds in annual interest, in order that Mr. Vanderlip's plan should work the money would have to be invested not in Great Britain, but in Germany or Eastern Europe. That wouldn't help Great Britain, for the latter would as well pay the money to the United States as to Germany. On the contrary, reinvesting in Great Britain would be of no special service because British concerns can now borrow in the United States on favorable terms through established banks and the government of Great Britain can borrow in the United States on terms more favorable than accorded by English banks. In those European countries

which cannot now pay us interest there would, of course, be no
funds to invest.

I must confess that it is difficult for me to follow Mr. Vanderlip's
reasoning, particularly as he does not long stick to his original proposal. His dispatches from Genoa, printed in The World, seem to
modify his earlier suggestions. I do not exactly understand how he
can expect European countries to establish large credits in the
United States while the balance of trade is running so severely
against them. Indeed, Mr. President, I do not think I have sense
enough to be of much help in considering the various schemes of
as agile a financial juggler as I conceive Mr. Vanderlip to be.

Regretting that I can not be of actual service in the discussion
of this problem, believe me, with renewed expressions of affection
and good wishes,   Sincerely yours,   Carter Glass.

TLS (WP, DLC).
    [1] See Arthur S. Link, *Wilson: The New Freedom* (Princeton, N. J., 1956), pp. 231-35,
237.

To Carter Glass

My dear Glass,   Washington D C 18th June 1922

Thank you for your letter of June sixteenth. It comes near to
doing the impossible, namely, to clearing away the fogs which
hang so heavily throughout the atmosphere of Vanderlip's mind. I
ought to have seen that there is really no use in discussing a thing
which its own author cannot elucidate.

You are quite right that there is no use in creating machinery
where there is no material, or insufficient material, of energy and
industry for the machinery to work upon.

With affectionate regard,
                    Sincerely Yours,   Woodrow Wilson

TLS (C. Glass Papers, ViU).

From Calvin Coolidge

My dear Mr. Wilson: Washington. June 19 1922

It was very kind of you to write referring to my address at the
American University.

I was speaking of the advance I believe society is making the
world over, of the power of good in spite of evil, and of the duty of
educated men to recognize the high privilege they have to work

with the Eternal Purpose instead of feeling that the affairs of the earth are unworthy of them.

Thanking you for your words of appreciation, I am

Sincerely yours,   Calvin Coolidge

ALS (WP, DLC).

From Bainbridge Colby

My dear Mr President: New York City June 19, 1922

I duly received your letter of June 13th[1] enclosing a letter dated June 9th from Mrs R. B. Flatt of Clinton, Kentucky, setting forth her experience with Mr Richard G. Badger, a publisher, of Boston. It gave me pleasure to comply with your suggestion to have a personal interview with Badger, and I left for Boston the day after the receipt of your letter.

Your characterizations of him, I found to be entirely borne out by his reputation in Boston. Before calling at his office at 194 Boylston Street I called on Mr Sherman Whipple[2] to ascertain if he knew him. He did not, but he called up a prominent publisher, an officer of the University Press, who stated that Badger's reputation in the business was very bad; that he operated on a small scale, turned sharp corners and took mean advantages. He does business under the name of The Gorham Press. His office is of modest size, in an old building, and his staff consists of two or three young women in the outer rooms who seem to be folding papers and addressing envelopes. Badger is a man of about forty-five, shifty, nervous and unprepossessing. I remarked that I assumed he had a contract with Mrs Flatt, and he said, "Of course." Men of Badger's stamp usually have artfully drawn contracts, and from the copy which I procured, it is apparent that Badger has fortified himself with a contract of this description.

Clause "7" of the contract is the one under which Badger gives Mrs Flatt the alternative of paying him $465 in addition to the money she has already paid him, or submitting to the destruction of the plates and the unbound sheets. The clause is as follows:

"7. If, at any time after publication, Richard G. Badger shall be satisfied that the public demand does not justify the continued publication of the work, or if for any other cause he shall deem its further publication improper or inexpedient, then he may offer in writing to said Flatt, her heirs or assigns, any plates and engravings used in said work at cost, all bound copies then on hand at forty cents per copy, and all unbound copies then on hand at twenty cents per copy; and said Flatt, her heirs or assigns, shall have the right to take and pay for the same, and shall thereupon become sole owner of the copyright herein named; and Richard G. Badger shall thereupon transfer said copyright; but if said offer be not accepted within thirty days and such payment made, then Richard G. Badger may destroy all plates and sell all copies, bound or unbound, then on hand free of any percentage to said Flatt, her heirs or assigns, and this agreement shall thereupon terminate, the copyright reverting to said Flatt, her heirs or assigns."

Badger's purpose, according to his statement, is to "job" the copies of the books and the unbound sheets that remain unsold. He means by this, sell them for 35 or 40 cents a copy. He has a clause in this contract which exempts him from the payment of any royalties on copies of the book which are "sold at or below cost."

I told him I thought the contract was a very unfair and one-sided contract; that it was apparent that Mrs Flatt had paid the entire cost of the making of the book, both plates and printing, and that the threat to destroy the plates and sell the remaining copies of the book without royalty returns to Mrs Flatt was in my opinion a very harsh way to treat Mrs Flatt, not to characterize it more severely. I strongly urged him to return the plates and the unbound sheets to Mrs Flatt, intimating that if he did not do so we would see what could be done notwithstanding his contract. He told me that he thought he would do it, but he wanted to give the matter a little reflection and said he would write me early this week.

I tried to impress upon him that Mrs Flatt had succeeded in interesting some powerful friends in her behalf, but at the same time I was too much impressed by the terms of the contract to indulge in any provocative talk.

It is a very unfortunate contract, and yet its provisions are clear and courts are chary about upsetting contracts which are free from ambiguity. I think Mrs Flatt was probably so eager to obtain the publication of her book that she didn't scrutinize the contract closely and was probably willing to pay anything within reason and to sign any sort of agreement if she could only achieve publication.

I tried to see Judge Grant as you suggested, but was unable to find him. He is the Judge of Probate in Boston. I learned from Badger that Judge Grant's son had already called upon him in connection with the matter.

If I do not hear from Badger by the middle of the week I think I will ask Whipple to threaten him with a suit to set aside the agreement, and an examination as to the actual cost of the publication of the book. I think it could be shown that the property he threatens to destroy, belongs to Mrs Flatt, equitably at least.

Would you like me to summarize these facts in a letter to Mrs Flatt?   Cordially always   Bainbridge Colby

TLS (B. Colby Papers, DLC).
    [1] WW to BC, June 13, 1922, CCL (B. Colby Papers, DLC).
    [2] Sherman Leland Whipple, lawyer of Boston, who had served as general counsel of the United States Shipping Board and the Emergency Fleet Corporation from August 1918 to March 1919.

To Bainbridge Colby

My dear Colby,   Washington D C 20th June 1922

Thank you for your letter about the Flatt matter and the rascal Badger. I daresay you are right, that the rascally contract would stand in the way in the courts of upsetting him as he should be upset.

Just a word in your ear: I think I should be chary about doing anything through Sherman Whipple. He is about as narrow as a knife blade and is not the kind of human being to take real interest in the hard case of another human being. At least so I judge him from the little I know of him. I have been trying incidentally to make the leading Democrats in Massachusetts understand that Whipple would be a most unfortunate choice as a Democratic candidate for the Senate. He is not of our intellectual breed and is, I should judge, just about as much interested in human progress broadly and concretely conceived as a hog is in grand opera.[1] If I have misjudged him I shall put myself in the hands of the reparations commission,—with the more cheerfulness since that commission does not seem ever to do anything.

In haste,
With affectionate regard,
                    Faithfully Yours,   Woodrow Wilson

P.S. I do not think it will be worth while to summarize in a letter to Mrs. Flatt the facts set forth in your letter to me of yesterday.
                                W.W.

TLS (B. Colby Papers, DLC).
    [1] Actually, insofar as we know, Wilson had always thought well of Whipple. For example, Wilson seriously considered him for appointment as Attorney General in February 1919. See WW to JPT, Feb. 21, 1919 (first radiogram of that date), Vol. 55. Wilson undoubtedly said these hard things about Whipple in his letter because he had set his heart upon Moors' nomination for the Senate.

From Norman Hezekiah Davis

My dear Mr. Wilson: New York June 23, 1922.

I am enclosing a draft of my proposed article for the "Rask Orsted Foundation."[1] Frankly, I am not very well satisfied with my effort, but as I am leaving for Stockbridge today, where I hope to be uninterrupted, it may be possible for me to go over it again and make some improvement. However, as the time is now limited in which the article should be forwarded, I am sending this draft[2] to you in order to give you a general idea of the direction in which it is headed, so that you may, if you feel so inclined, head me off and give me the benefit of your valuable advice. I notice on reading over my draft that I have used the word "principles" until it is worn out, and hope to be able to eliminate it in several places, or to find some substitute.

If you think the question should be tackled from an entirely different angle, please do not hesitate to say so. I dislike bothering you with this, but feel that it is of considerable importance that this matter should be handled wisely and effectively.

It may be just as well to eliminate entirely that portion of the article which purports to answer some of the stupid arguments which have been advanced to the effect that Covenant of the League should not have be made a part of the Treaty, because since it has been done, it is practically an academic question.

I had hoped to stop by Washington on my way back from Tennessee, but found that it was impossible to do so. Hoping that you are continuing to improve, and with affectionate regards to Mrs. Wilson and yourself,

I am, as ever,   Faithfully yours,   Norman H. Davis

P.S.: Please address my mail to me at Stockbridge, Massachusetts, where I will be for most of the summer.   N.H.D.

TLS (WP, DLC).
 [1] The Rask-Ørsted Fondet, founded by the Danish government in 1919 to advance Danish and international science. In 1921, the executive committee of the foundation decided to publish a study of the origins and work of the League of Nations. It was to consist of essays by experts on the subject from many countries. The work was published as Peter Munch, ed., *Les Origines et l'Oeuvre de la Société des Nations* (2 vols., Copenhagen, 1923-24). The final version of Davis's essay appeared as "The Necessity for the League of Nations: The Past and Probable Future Attitude of the United States," I, 252-66.
 [2] This draft is missing in both the Wilson and Davis Papers, DLC.

To Norman Hezekiah Davis

My dear Davis,   [Washington] 25th June 1922

I have such confidence in your skill and judgment in handling the matter which your article discusses that I am not going to undertake any revision.

I will only answer the one or two questions which your letter seems to put. I do not think that the word "principles" can be used too often or can be worn out. After all there is no adequate substitute for it. I agree with you that it is hardly necessary to reply to the argument to the effect that the Covenant of the League should not have been made a part of the Treaty. To answer it at all only lends dignity to them and does not penetrate the stupidity in which they originated. As you say there is no longer any practical importance in the question.

I hope that the air and freedom of Stockbridge will greatly refresh you all. We all need to be in our best fighting form, and you are one of the most valuable of our fighters.

We are disappointed that we did not catch a glimpse of you on your way back from Tennessee, but I feel sure that you were right in making straight for Stockbridge.

Mrs. Wilson joins me in affectionate messages to you all, and in the hope that your summer vacation will be full of enjoyment and of genuine rest.

With affectionate regard,
                    Faithfully yours,   [Woodrow Wilson]

CCL (WP, DLC).

From Cordell Hull

My dear Mr. President: Washington, D. C. June 26th, 1922.

May I report a few detailed party conditions to you as I see them since last writing you.

According to my best information, the strong trend away from the National administration continues unabated. The farmers, the laborers and the legitimate business men are greatly dissatisfied and desirous of a change. We should carry the House of Representatives in the event of an election at the present time. Our problem is to organize, educate and hold the favorable sentiment now existing.

I recently had a splendid State-wide meeting and conference in Maine. Our people could win up there for the entire ticket, with the exception of one or two Congressmen, provided the Republicans, as they so generally do, do not dump a large amount of money for the effect on the November election. Conditions in other respects are ripe for Democratic success. I cannot make definite predictions as to Maine, however, in view of the money factor.

In Massachusetts I am satisfied the sentiment now favors the Democratic party. The great problem is to get a suitable candidate for Senator, who can command the support of the various elements and groups of Democrats, without which the defeat of Senator Lodge is not possible. I had an extended conference with the Democratic State Committee in Boston on last Friday, and in the most strenuous manner I insisted that it was the duty of unselfish, patriotic, Democratic leaders and others to have a series of conferences and work out a situation which would give us a clean, able, and in other essential respects, suitable candidate who could command the maximum number of Democratic votes in November. I insisted that factionalism, group antagonism, and personal ambitions must be suppressed until after the November election. In other words, I could not have impressed this line of talk on them in stronger terms.

I am obliged to leave for Tennessee and Kentucky tonight, returning seven or eight days hence. With all good wishes,

Very sincerely,   Cordell Hull

TLS (WP, DLC).

To Cordell Hull

My dear Mr. Chairman,   Washington D C 27th June 1922

Thank you for your letter of June twenty-sixth. I am sincerely obliged to you for so thoughtfully keeping me in touch with the situation as it slowly develops. Every indication that reaches me of what is coming increases my confidence that our party will be presently returned to power and will have the greatest opportunity for service that has ever been accorded it.

I daresay these lines will not reach you before your return from Tennessee and Kentucky. I hope that they will find you encouraged by what you heard and saw there.

With sincere appreciation of the earnest work you are doing, and very warm regard,   Faithfully Yours,   Woodrow Wilson

TLS (C. Hull Papers, DLC).

From Stephen Samuel Wise

Dear Mr. Wilson,   [London] 28th June, 1922.

Your name is so often on my lips as I speak to Englishmen, and particularly to English statesmen, in London that I feel I must write to you a line to tell you something of what I find here,—a feeling of deep unhappiness over America's position respecting the League of Nations. It is really sorrow rather than anger, and the feeling that nothing that is attempted can be done aright as long as we touch Europe and European relations only occasionally and fitfully instead of doing so in orderly and consistent fashion. I have had the chance of some good talks with supporters of the League, including particularly, Lord Robert Cecil and Professor Gilbert Murray. The latter almost justified the position of Senator Borah in objecting to indefinite commitments such as America is asked to make, outside of the League of Nations, and his argument was so sound that I asked him to put it to paper and to let me have it for Borah to whom I am sending it for his illumination,—if such a thing be possible. You might care to glance over Gilbert Murray's statement, which I think puts the thing admirably, though I hardly believe that you will agree to the plan of entering into the League of Nations by the back-stairs. Perhaps "back-stairs" is not a fair term, seeing that the suggestion is that we work with the League for definite and limited ends, even though *not yet* a member.

My English friends rejoice to hear that things are very much more hopeful in America in 1922 than in 1920, i.e. just because they are so very much worse and because the commitments of the Administration from one point of view make just and equitable dealing with the industrial situation all but impossible. I am promising them that the election of 1922 will show that America is on the way to sanity even though that boon shall not completely have come quite so soon.

I trust that you are well and gaining strength every day so that when we shall most need your counsel and leadership we shall have it.

With warmest greeting to you and Mrs. Wilson in which Mrs. Wise[1] joins me,

Believe me, *my* dear Mr. President,

Faithfully yours,   Stephen S. Wise

TLS (WP, DLC).
[1] Louise Waterman Wise.

A Memorandum by Homer Stillé Cummings[1]

Memorandum of Interview with Woodrow Wilson
June 28—1922 at 3:30 P.M.
at his house 2340 S Street Washington.

The appointment was made through Mr. Bolling and when I arrived, I was shown into the library where I found Mr. Wilson awaiting me. From remarks which I had heard about his condition, I had rather expected to find him in feeble health. He was, however, fully dressed and received me cordially. His hand clasp was firm and strong and he looked better than I had seen him at any time since his illness began. He seemed to have gained in weight, he was more cheerful and the general impression created was one of distinct improvement. I expressed my pleasure at seeing him so much better and he said that it was hard for him to realize that he was improving but that looking back over a long period of time, he could not help but be persuaded that there had been a slow but steady gain.

He motioned me to a chair which had evidently been placed directly in front of him. It was a rather formidable looking chair made entirely of wood but comfortable when one was once seated in it. I remarked upon the formidable appearance of the chair and he said that from that chair he had rendered very many unwelcome decisions. He then informed me that it was a chair which he had used when he was President of Princeton and he spoke in a pleasant and reminiscing sort of way of some of his experiences during that period.

We then drifted into a discussion of matters politically. He asked me how I thought Cordell Hull was doing as Chairman. I told him that I thought Mr. Hull was doing remarkably well under very apparent difficulties and that he was a man who could be relied upon and would make no mistakes and was a man of fine character and dependable in every way. Mr. Wilson said that he thought that my comments were entirely correct, and that he thought very highly of Mr. Hull and had a very high opinion of him. He expressed the hope that I would do everything I could to aid Mr. Hull in his work.

We then spoke of the present administration and of the general mess in which it found itself. Mr. Wilson expressed the view that the chief difficulty was that the President seemed to have no distinct capacity for leadership. He said that whatever else might be said, of the Roosevelt Administration [and] of his own administration, that both these administrations had accustomed the people to

---

[1] As will become apparent, Cummings did not write or dictate this memorandum on June 28, 1922. We assume that he wrote or dictated it soon after his talk with Wilson.

the idea of leadership and that it was better for a President to make mistakes than it was to do nothing and permit things to drift. He expressed the view that there was a revival of faith in Democratic ideals and that the country was coming back very rapidly to the Democratic viewpoint. I told him that this was undoubtedly true and that there was a tremendous change in public sentiment but that the only question in my mind was whether this change was coming rapidly enough to cause an overturn in the present control of Congress. Mr. Wilson expressed the view that if an election were held now, that the next Congress would be Democratic and if that were true, that the next President of the United States would be a Democrat. I made no rejoinder to this as I did not quite agree with his conclusions. It was merely a matter of opinion, and he was at least as likely to be right about it as I was.

He said that the next President should have a distinct program and should assume a firm leadership in public affairs and that it would not do merely for us to get in power on the mistakes of the opposition without a definite program of our own. He expressed a view that we ought to begin formulating our program. I ventured the suggestion that the San Francisco program[2] was still extant and was a party law on the subject up to date at least. He said the trouble was that no one seemed to have read the platform. He went on to say that the world had been made safe for democracy, that was an accomplished fact, that there was no sort of possibility that military government or autocratic power or hereditary dynasties would ever again control the destinies of the human race. But he said Democracy itself had not yet been made an instrument of justice and the difficulty with the present situation is that it contains the elements of popular upheaval sweeping and even revolutionary in character, and that the need of the present moment was men in public life who sensed this situation and who had the character and the vision to apply the proper remedies. He said that this could not be accomplished by merely drifting or waiting for the mistakes of the opposition or capitalizing discontent or in any other way relying upon a mere party struggle for control.

He spoke of the disputes between labor and capital and he said that his experience was, while in the White House, that in all controversies between the representatives of capital and the representatives of labor, that the former seemed interested only in maintaining their position rather than in doing justice while the latter always knew what they wanted and why they wanted it. In fact, he said that the representatives of labor seemed to know their case

[2] That is, the platform adopted by the Democratic National Convention on July 2, 1920.

whereas the representatives of capital talked in a language of a decade ago. He said this was a dangerous situation. He said that if you tell men that they shall not improve their condition in the only way in which they know how to improve it, that you make them crazy and that when that happens, it is the beginning of the end of orderly government. I told him that I had observed amongst the representatives of capital a disposition as soon as the war was over to "put labor in its place," that this was a common phrase on their lips and that it seemed to me that the trouble with them was, not that they lacked intelligence, because many of them were men of extraordinary ability but that they lacked a sympathetic understanding of classes other than their own. He said that this was precisely the point that he had in mind.

He said that the present Administration was now engaged in an attempt to reestablish all the injustices of the past. He said that they talked about getting back to normalcy whereas in this country the only normal thing was orderly progress. He spoke again of the need of the right kind of men in public office and then looking at me very quickly, he said "I hope you are going to run for the Senate this Fall." I told him that "the salary would not compensate me for the humiliation that I should feel." This seemed to amuse him and he then added it is quite true that the Senate is lower in public esteem to-day than ever before in its history. I told him that I was somewhat weary of politics and that the holding of public office had no charm for me. I said that when I ran for the Senate in 1916 and came reasonably close to an election, I would have been greatly pleased to have been elected, that nothing would have afforded me greater pleasure than to have a part in an intimate way with all the great constructive work that went on as well as during the period of the War, and especially would I have prized the opportunity to have held up his hands in the struggle over the League of Nations. I presume I stated this rather earnestly for he seemed moved by it but then recovering himself, he said that the issues of the future were as important as those of the past and that it was highly important that the right kind of men should be in public office. I told him that one of our difficulties was that the type of men needed was such as to impose a rather exacting standard upon ordinary humanity, that there were so many essentials that there were very few left who could pass scrutiny because you had to have not only intelligence and character but you had to have men of a sympathetic viewpoint and who were able to vizualize conditions from which they themselves did not suffer, and that therefore it required men who were willing to make sacrifices and that a democracy itself, as I understood it, was a sort or [of] religion for which people made sacrifices, that there was nothing in it for the individual and that those who devoted themselves to it were engaged in an altruistic enterprise, and to get men of that type and to find them also free to render service unhampered by lack of means or family or business ties was limiting the number, that it was a constant struggle to keep together even a nucleus of the right sort of leadership. He listened very attentively to all this and was evidently not very much impressed by it because he said if the call were issued, that the right kind of men would respond just as they did in the time of the war. I said "Yes, the response during the period of the war was really a beautiful illustration of what humanity could do at its best but in that situation, the whole country recognized a common peril and the people were responding to one of the most primal of instincts—the instinct of patriotism whereas a matter of mere public service was not so well understood." He said nevertheless if the call were issued the right kind of men would respond. I told him they would not respond if I called them. It would depend upon who called them and I thought that if he called them, they might respond. This aspect of our conversation evidently made some impression upon him because a few days later I received a letter from him dealing with this very subject.[3]

During our conversation he spoke of his presence in the Armistice Day Parade in Washington when the ceremonies were held in connection with the burial of the unknown soldier.[4] He said I wanted to be in that procession and I wanted to go to the cemetery but of course—I could not walk and I wanted to use a horse drawn vehicle. Imagine my surprise, he said, that I was informed that I would have to make formal application to the War Department for permission. He said I did so and permission was denied. He said I was somewhat irritated and concluded not to let the matter rest until I took it up with Mr. Harding. I wrote Mr. Harding calling his attention to the situation and stating in substance that I could not believe that this order was final until he himself said so. He said, in due course, I received a letter written in Mr. Harding's mixed English which explained everything and nothing but ultimately sustaining the ruling of the War Department. He said the result was that I was unable to go to the cemetery but I was in the procession and dropped out before it went to the cemetery. I told him that the general understanding was that he had not gone to the ceme-

[3] WW to HSC, June 29, 1922.
[4] About this incident, see the index references to "Wilson, Woodrow" and "Harding, Warren Gamaliel" in Vol. 67.

tery on account of ill health. He said he thought of publishing the correspondence but after all, it was more or less a personal matter and I let it drop.

I spoke of the ovation he received and he seemed pleased at this but expressed regret that there had not been greater acclaim for General Pershing who was in the party and I believe rode with President Harding. Somewhat maliciously I suggested that perhaps the reason that the people did not cheer for Pershing was because they feared that their applause might be mistaken and [as] intended for Mr. Harding. He laughed a little at this but made no comment.

I then related to him several incidents I had witnessed in theatres and moving picture houses and told him of the comedian in a certain skit telling what [a] great man Columbus was because he had proved the world to be round and the other comedian then suggested that Wilson was a great man because he had taught the people in the whole world that they ought to be square. It was a silly little story but afforded the audience an opportunity for a demonstration.

Altogether we had a very pleasant and amiable interview. It lasted for the greater part of an hour. I attempted to withdraw on several occasions as I feared he might be getting tired but he kept calling me back and saying something new.

T MS (H. S. Cummings Papers, ViU).

To Homer Stillé Cummings

My dear Cummings,   Washington D C 29th June 1922

I have been thinking of our conversation of yesterday so much, and with so much interest, that I am now prompted to send you a postscript to it.

You will remember that we spoke of the need of the party for what I may term a team of leaders. I expressed the opinion that when the occasion arose the men we called to service would respond as they did during the war. You were gracious enough to say, as you left the room, that they would come at *my* call. I respond to your challenge and send this letter to you as my call to you to seek and obtain a seat in the Senate. You are really needed there and the war is now on with all the forces of injustice and corruption. Shall we not combine to win?

I write in the confidence that you will understand and believe that this call is not meant to impose a burden upon you but to express my admiration and confidence in you and my conviction that men like yourself must now come to the front to do the great service for the country and mankind which we are unmistakably called upon now to undertake.

With affectionate regard,

Faithfully Yours,   Woodrow Wilson

TLS (H. S. Cummings Papers, ViU).

To Lucian Lamar Knight

My dear Dr. Knight,   Washington D C 1st July 1922

I have your letter of June twenty-seventh[1] and do not hesitate to say that if your present Governor should succeed in impairing or destroying the State Department of Archives and History he would be putting upon the State a most undeserved disgrace. I am sorry to say that I can think of no way in which I can be of service to you in the matter. I have no influence with Mr. Hardwick and do not desire to have any. I have found that my principles and his are utterly different. He constantly showed while he was in Washington an antagonism that was all but malignant to the things I believed in and advocated, and I am consequently not surprised that as Governor of the State he is proving unworthy of the traditions of the great Commonwealth with which I am happy to think I was once for a time associated.

Hoping that your fears for the Department of History will not, after all, be realized,   Sincerely Yours,   Woodrow Wilson

TLS (L. L. Knight Coll., G-Ar).
  [1] L. L. Knight to WW, June 27, 1922, TLS (WP, DLC). Knight, the State Historian and Director of the Department of Archives and History of Georgia, informed Wilson that Governor Thomas William Hardwick was "trying to abolish" his department. He asserted that this was Hardwick's way of seeking revenge for his (Knight's) attack on Hardwick's allegedly pro-German stance as a United States senator during the war. He asked that Wilson write him a letter commending the importance of his department and stating that Hardwick had not supported the administration during the war. Hardwick did not succeed in his designs.

To James F. McCaleb[1]

My dear Dr. McCaleb: [Washington] 8th July 1922

I have your letter of July fifth.[2] In reply let me say that I am not in a position to review Mr. Vardaman's record in Washington in detail, but I can sum up my impression of him in a single sentence:

I think that he is thoroughly false and untrustworthy and that it would be a great detriment to Mississippi and the nation if he should be returned to the Senate.

With deep interest in the outcome of the contest of which you speak,[3]   Sincerely Yours,   [Woodrow Wilson][4]

CCL (WP, DLC).
    [1] Physician of Carlisle, Miss.
    [2] J. F. McCaleb to WW, July 5, 1922, ALS (WP, DLC). He informed Wilson that James K. Vardaman was running for the Senate seat being vacated by John Sharp Williams. He urged Wilson to denounce Vardaman for his allegedly unpatriotic conduct during the war.
    [3] In a primary election held on August 15, Vardaman won a plurality of 74,573 votes to 65,980 votes for former Representative Hubert Durrett Stephens, and 18,285 votes for Belle Kearney, the first woman in Mississippi to run for the Senate. In the run-off primary held on September 5, Stephens defeated Vardaman by a vote of 95,351 to 86,285. William F. Holmes, *The White Chief: James Kimble Vardaman* (Baton Route, La., 1970), pp. 378-79.
    [4] This letter was printed, e.g., in the *New York Times*, July 27, 1922.

To Stephen Samuel Wise

My dear Rabbi Wise,   [Washington] 11th July 1922

I am grateful to you for your letter of twenty-eighth June and I value anything from Gilbert Murray whom I have had the great advantage of knowing and whom I admire with a touch of real affection.

I think that to encourage the idea that the United States should cooperate with the League in any way but as a full member would be a fatal mistake, and I confidently believe that opinion here will force the Government to become a member.

I am making discouragingly slow progress towards health but still I am making some and am exceedingly eager to fit myself physically as well as in every other way for the great battles that are just ahead of us.

Hoping that you will presently be safe on this side of the water and that your trip has proved in every way profitable and beneficial,
    With warm regard,
                    Faithfully Yours,   [Woodrow Wilson]

CCL (WP, DLC).

To David John Lewis[1]

My dear Lewis,   Washington D C 12th July 1922

I need hardly say that my cordial best wishes attend you in your contest for a seat in the Senate.[2] I shall rejoice to see you there for you have come up to every test to which I have seen you subjected. Just such men as yourself are greatly needed in the Senate.[3]

I shall be glad to have a few words with you (you are one of the

few men I know who can limit themselves to a few words) and will
be glad if you will come to see me next Monday afternoon at three-
thirty o'clock.

    With best wishes,   Faithfully Yours,   Woodrow Wilson

TLS (D. J. Lewis Papers, NcD).
    [1] Democratic representative from Maryland, 1911-1917; member of the Tariff Com-
mission since 1917.
    [2] Wilson was replying to D. J. Lewis to WW, July 11, 1922, TLS (WP, DLC). Lewis
told Wilson that he was entering the Maryland Democratic primary as a senatorial candidate and asked for an interview with Wilson.
    [3] William Cabell Bruce defeated Lewis in the primary held on September 11.

To Cordell Hull

My dear Mr. Chairman,   Washington D C 13th July 1922

    The enclosed letter[1] has impressed me and I hope you will not
think it an imposition upon you if I suggest that you seek an interview with the writer of the letter and form your own conclusions
as to his serviceability and the practicability of his plans. What he
suggests is undoubtedly just the sort of thing that our opponents
do, and it may be that we can outdo them at their own methods.
You will be very much better able to judge the merits of the whole
matter than I will be, and I am confident that you will come to the
right conclusion about it in conference with Mr. D'Amico.

    Cordially and Faithfully Yours,   Woodrow Wilson

TLS (C. Hull Papers, DLC).
    [1] John B. D'Amico to WW, July 11, 1922, TLS (C. Hull Papers, DLC). D'Amico, an
accountant of New York, informed Wilson that he had organized the "National Italian
Democratic League" in 1912 to further the interests of the Democratic party among
Italian-American voters. He said that since that time he had repeatedly tried to convince
successive Democratic national chairmen of the potential importance of Italian Americans to the party, but with little success. He warned that the Republican party, which
had formed a "National Italian Republican League," modeled on his organization, in
1919, was taking a strong, if belated, interest in organizing the Italian vote.

From Cordell Hull

My dear Mr. President: Washington, D. C. July 14th, 1922.

    I am very thankful indeed for your letter of the 13th instant with
enclosures relative to methods of organizing the Italian and other
foreign voters.

    I thoroughly agree with you and with the writer as to the very
great importance and value of the suggested method of organization of these classes of voters. Not being able thus far to employ a
foreign language organizer, I sometime ago effected arrangements
with a very capable foreign language man in New York to furnish

me a synopsis of the comment and utterances of the foreign language press every two weeks. I am desperately striving to raise a sufficient amount of money real soon to enable me to install in our office a suitable person to deal with the work of organizing and educating the foreign voters. I am hopeful I may accomplish this within a few days. I am writing to the writer of the letter you enclosed, requesting a conference with him.

While it is true that the country is experiencing a period of some inflation in certain industries, with the result that a sprinkling of persons at the head of some large financial, commercial and industrial concerns are less vocal in their criticisms of the present National administration than a few months ago, nevertheless all the information reaching me from County Chairmen, precinct committeemen, and others in contact with the masses of the voters, is to the effect that the trend of sentiment against the National administration continues to grow stronger each month thus far in every part of the country.

I, of course, do not know how long this rising tide will continue, but every indication now is that any changes that may occur between now and November cannot seriously affect our election chances. I prefer, however, to be conservative rather than over-optimistic in making predictions, especially during this period of abnormal conditions and sometimes unexpected shifts and changes in sentiment.

My best information is that if Whipple should be nominated in Massachusetts,[1] he has a good chance to win in the November election. Our candidate for Senator in North Dakota, Mr. F. J. T. O'Connor,[2] came within 5,000 votes of being elected Governor in 1920, while Cox lost the State by 54,000. He feels confident at present that he can win next fall. Conditions in other Western States, such as Utah, Montana, and others, have perceptibly improved during the past two months according to a variety of reports I have received.

I am keeping in close touch with each of our nominees for Senator, Representative, etc., and aiding each in developing and putting into operation the most effective detailed methods and plans of organization and education possible for us to devise.

Apart from direct contact and conference with State Chairmen, candidates and other leading Democrats in each State, I am urging that the candidates and party officials begin to hold regional conferences from time to time at the most central points in each locality, and it is also planned to hold regional conferences of National Committeemen and women and State party officials representing certain groups of States at central points most accessible to all.

There are two possible outcomes of the tariff situation in Congress, as I see it: one might be that Republicans may go to pieces and let the Bill[3] fail of passage. Should this occur it would probably be the most desirable thing that could happen from the standpoint of the Democratic party and the country. I am warning our Democratic friends in Congress, on the other hand, that if, in their judgment, the Republicans will finally pass the Tariff Bill, it is better now to let them pass it with as many vicious features retained as possible, rather than for the Democrats to contest all the items and possibly secure the elimination of many bad features, with the result that the measure would be correspondingly more acceptable to the Republican party. In other words, the best way to get rid of a bad measure is to let it pass without undertaking such improvements as would mollify vast numbers of voters who would otherwise aid the Democratic party in making a fight to get in power and repeal it.

I shall be more than delighted to send you memoranda in case of any important developments, pro or con, or to call in person whenever you may desire. Trusting your health continues to improve.   Very sincerely,   Cordell Hull

TLS (WP, DLC).
[1] Whipple had announced on July 7 that he was a candidate for the Democratic senatorial nomination in Massachusetts. However, he lost in the primary held on September 12 to William Alexander Gaston, a lawyer and banker of Boston. Gaston was defeated by Henry Cabot Lodge in a close contest in the general election on November 7.
[2] James Francis Thaddeus O'Connor. As it turned out, he lost the senatorship to former Governor Lynn Joseph Frazier, the candidate of the Nonpartisan League.
[3] Joseph W. Fordney, chairman of the House Ways and Means Committee, had introduced a comprehensive tariff bill, H.R. 7456, on June 29, 1921. This bill passed the House on July 21, 1921. It was not until April 11, 1922, that Porter J. McCumber, chairman of the Senate Finance Committee, reported out a greatly revised version which called for mostly increased rates on a wide variety of farm products, raw materials, and manufactured goods. The Senate debates on the measure were long and bitter. The bill finally passed the Senate on August 19, 1922. A conference committee revised the measure once again and, after further acrimonious discussion, the two houses finally agreed to the bill and Harding signed the so-called Fordney-McCumber Tariff Act on September 21, 1922. Estimates of the significance and impact of this act vary greatly. For general discussions, see Robert K. Murray, *The Harding Era: Warren G. Harding and His Administration* (Minneapolis, Minn., 1969), pp. 271-80, and Frank W. Taussig, *The Tariff History of the United States*, 7th edn. (New York and London, 1923), pp. 447-89. The text of the act is printed in 42 *Statutes at Large* 858.

From Homer Stillé Cummings

Dear Mr. Wilson: Stamford, Connecticut 15 July 1922.

Your compelling summons stirred me deeply. Every impulse of my being moves me to respond affirmatively. The personal reluctance which I cannot help but feel and the need to serve the interests of my family, when perhaps I can best do so, I could put aside or postpone; but there are other considerations which I am not at liberty to deal with in this way.

My political friends and associates in this State have known for many months that I did not desire to be considered in connection with the Senatorial nomination. I think, for the most part, they regretted this decision—but they have accepted it. Under these circumstances, others have entered the field and are open and avowed candidates for the nomination.

Mr. Spellacy,[1] who was United States District Attorney and later an Assistant Attorney General under your Administration and whose loyalty and service were quite above reproach, is one of these candidates. Former Congressman Lonergan,[2] whose capable service in the House is widely recognized, is also a candidate. These men are able, conscientious, loyal and deservedly popular. They are both personal friends of mine though, in the event of a contest between them, my voice would be for Spellacy. Either one would make a capable, dependable and progressive Senator, fully in sympathy with the larger purposes of our party. They have gone so far in the matter and are so fully committed to their present purposes, and, at least in the case of Mr. Spellacy, have so fully relied upon my being out of the field, that I could not, if I would, enter the lists at this late date.

So, my dear Mr. Wilson, you see how the matter stands, and I trust that you will think that I have decided aright. In any event, I shall hope to have many opportunities to serve, even though unofficially, in that forward movement which is so imperatively required if democracy is to be made the servant of justice.

I am, my dear Mr. Wilson,

Most sincerely yours,   Homer S. Cummings

TLS (WP, DLC).
  [1] Thomas Joseph Spellacy.
  [2] Augustine Lonergan.

To Louisa Patterson Henderson[1]

My dear Mrs. Henderson,   [Washington] 20th July 1922

It gives me pleasure to reply to your letter of July nineteenth because it is always a pleasure to testify to the character and attainments of such a man as Mr. David J. Lewis. My observation of him and my association with him in public matters have led me to entertain a very high opinion of his integrity, his ability and his equipment to deal with public questions. I have been very much interested to learn of his candidacy for the United States Senate

and do not hesitate to say that I regard him as in every way qualified to fill the position of Senator. He is most conscientious in all
his dealings with public questions and has moreover a legal insight
into their merits and extraordinary industry in familiarizing himself with their details. I was often glad to be guided by his knowledge and judgment in dealing with legislative matters and should
deem the State of Maryland fortunate in having such a representative in the United States Senate.

Mrs. Wilson joins me in warm regard and most cordial good
wishes and I am,

As always,   Your Sincere Friend,   [Woodrow Wilson][2]

CCL (WP, DLC).
    [1] Widow of Wilson's classmate at Princeton, Robert Randolph Henderson. Wilson was
replying to Louisa P. Henderson to WW, July 19, 1922, ALS (WP, DLC).
    [2] This letter was published in the Baltimore *Sun*, July 24, 1922.

From Frank Irving Cobb

Dear Mr. Wilson: New York July 20th, 1922.

Apropos of Hughes' feeble and evasive reply to Hamilton Holt in
regard to The League of Nations,[1] it occurred to me that no treaty
would be necessary in the case of the United States. The United
States could join the League by a joint resolution of Congress
whenever the Democrats obtained a majority, and a two-thirds vote
of the Senate would be unnecessary. Is that your opinion too? I
have had it in mind as something that might be taken up after the
Fall election, but I should like to know, in confidence, what your
personal judgment is, if you feel free to express it.

I hope you are withstanding this erratic Summer, and that it is
not impairing your strength. Please give my best regards to Mrs.
Wilson.   Most sincerely yours,   Frank I Cobb.

TLS (WP, DLC).
    [1] Holt had addressed an open letter to Charles E. Hughes on July 7, 1922. He accused
the Secretary of State of having repudiated the League of Nations, reiterated the charge
that the State Department did not answer communications from the League except in
a formal or indirect manner, and asserted that Hughes had deliberately blocked programs put forward by the League. Holt demanded answers to specific questions. Where
was the "association of nations" that the administration had earlier spoken of? Did
Hughes currently favor United States entry into the League? Did he plan such entry
during the current presidential term of office?
    Hughes replied to Holt on July 13. He said that the State Department was corre-
sponding with the League "courteously and appropriately." "The fact is," he pointed out,
"that the United States is not a member of the League and I have no authority to act as
if it were." He did not answer Holt's questions.
    Holt wrote a second letter to Hughes on July 18 in which he sought to refute the
latter's statements. Hughes replied on July 19 that he had no blanket authority as Secretary of State to take the United States into the League. Any such action depended
upon the Senate, and the resubmission of the Treaty of Versailles, even with reservations, to that body would only pointlessly reopen the original controversy. After quoting

extensively from Harding's statements on the League since taking office, Hughes declared that the correspondence with Holt was closed.

Holt's letters are summarized in the *New York Times*, July 8 and 19, 1922. Hughes's replies are printed in full in *ibid.*, July 15 and 20, 1922. See also the summary of the correspondence in Kuehl, *Hamilton Holt*, pp. 160-61.

To Frank Irving Cobb

My dear Cobb,   [Washington] 21st July 1922

The idea of a joint resolution broached in your letter of July twentieth is entirely novel to me and I should not feel prepared to express a judgment about it without expert advice. Lets keep it for thorough examination after the autumn elections when we can consult impartial experts in international law like James Brown Scott. There will be much else to talk over also for we should have a comprehensive programme and should carry it out in thoroughgoing fashion.

Thank you for your letter and for keeping these great questions before you. I should naturally resort to you for suggestion and advice in any case.

With warm regard,
                Cordially and Faithfully Yours,   [Woodrow Wilson]

CCL (WP, DLC).

To Louis Lipsky[1]

[Washington] July 25 1922

Thank you warmly for your telegram.[2] I am proud that it should be thought that I have been of service to the Jewish people.
                                Woodrow Wilson.

TC telegram (WP, DLC).
    [1] Journalist of New York; chairman of the executive committee of the Zionist Organization of America.
    [2] L. Lipsky to WW, July 24, 1922, T telegram (WP, DLC). It reads as follows: "At this hour of our celebration of great triumph of a just cause in the registration of Palestine Mandate Zionist Executive Committee in session assembled remembers with gratitude your distinguished and unselfish cooperation in behalf of the Zionist cause."
    The mandate of Palestine to Great Britain was confirmed by the Council of the League of Nations on July 22, 1922. *New York Times*, July 23, 1922.

From Frank Irving Cobb

Dear Mr. Wilson: New York July 25th, 1922.

You are wholly right in urging a comprehensive programme, but who will prepare it if you do not? Certainly there is nothing to be expected from the Democrats in Congress. They have shown themselves hopelessly incompetent to carry on an intelligent opposition. Not one of them has presented a constructive idea in the course of all this turmoil. Nothing saves them from universal public contempt except the horrible blunders of the Republican majority.

If the Democratic party is to have a programme, somebody will have to frame it, and unless you assume that burden, I am afraid the party will continue to drift.

Sincerely yours,   Frank I Cobb.

TLS (WP, DLC).

To Frank Irving Cobb

My dear Cobb,   Washington D C 26th July 1922

Thank you warmly for your letter of July twenty-fifth. You may be sure that I shall be ready to use all the brains I have in the preparation of the comprehensive programme when the right time comes for putting such a programme out. You may be sure that I have been thinking the matter over not sometimes but very often.

With warm regard,   Faithfully Yours,   Woodrow Wilson

TLS (IEN).

To Duane Reed Stuart

My dear Professor Stuart,   Washington D C 27th July 1922

I hope that you will not think I am presuming overmuch on your courtesy and kindness by asking you again to help me out with my depleted Greek vocabulary. Will you not be kind enough to tell me the Greek word for court,—not a tribunal but the space in an enclosed building,—like the court at Holder Hall.[1]

By the way, is there a trustworthy English-Greek dictionary which I could consult for answers to such questions?

I hope that all goes happily with you and yours and beg that you will accept my most cordial greetings.

With warm regard,   Faithfully Yours,   Woodrow Wilson

TLS (received from D. R. Stuart, Jr.).
[1] A dormitory complex on the Princeton University campus.

To Henry Burchard Fine

My dear Harry,   Washington D C 27th July 1922

It distresses me most deeply to learn of your loss of Jack.[1] I can easily understand what your grief must be and my heart goes out to you in warmest sympathy. I hope that Jack was at least in his last days spared acute suffering.

I shall always remember him with affectionate regard.

Mrs. Wilson joins me in assurances of deep sympathy, and I hope that it is some comfort to you to know of the deep affection of such friends as   Yours, Most Faithfully,   Woodrow Wilson

TLS (WC, NjP).
   [1] His son, John Fine. For details of his career and death, see H. B. Fine to WW, July 31, 1922.

John Randolph Bolling to Thomas H. Lyon[1]

[Washington]

My dear Mr. Commonwealth's Attorney: 27th July 1922

Mr. Wilson asks me to say that he has recently learned of the praiseworthy manner in which you fulfilled your duties in saving a man from violence at the hands of a mob,[2] and he desires me to extend to you his thanks as an America[n] citizen and a native of Virginia for your service in the matter.

With every good wish;

Cordially yours,   [John Randolph Bolling]

CCL (WP, DLC).
   [1] Of Manassas, Va.
   [2] The *New York Times*, July 30, 1922, carried a brief report of this incident and mentioned Wilson's letter. Lyon had saved a black man accused of killing a law officer from possible lynching in Manassas by spiriting him to jail in Alexandria in his own automobile. Wilson first dictated the following letter:
   "Having recently learned of the highly honourable and praiseworthy manner in which you fulfilled your duties in saving Alvin Harris from violence at the hands of a mob, I take the liberty of extending to you my thanks as an American citizen and a native of Virginia. There is, it seems to me, no better way to advance the honour and preserve the civilization of the country we love than to absolutely prevent and discredit the barbarous practice of lynching, and it seems to me that in the course you have recently pursued you have not only performed your duty in a distinguished manner but also vindicated the honour and safeguarded the institutions of the great Commonwealth of Virginia and of all her sister States of the Union.
   "Pray accept my personal thanks and admiration and believe me, With much regard, Cordially yours, Woodrow Wilson." WW to T. H. Lyon, July 25, 1922, TLS (WP, DLC).
   It is entirely possible that Bolling and Mrs. Wilson decided to substitute Bolling's letter for Wilson's.

From Henry Burchard Fine

My dear Tommy   Mt. Pocono, Pa. July 31, 1922

I am very grateful to you and Mrs. Wilson for your kind words of sympathy.

As you know, ever since his return from the War Jack had been ill with a severe type of diabetes, the result, his physician Dr. Allen of N. Y., said, of the strain of his war service. He was unwilling to live the life of an invalid to any greater extent than necessary, and therefore until Christmas of this year continued, when he had the strength, his work at the U. S. District Attorney's Office in New York. But it was then discovered that tuberculosis had also developed. He steadily lost ground and finally breathed his last on July 12th.

I have never known a braver man than dear Jack. His friends at the front tell me that he met danger there with a laugh. He fought his long hard fight with illness without a word of repining, cheerful and dauntless to the very end. Mingled with our grief is a deep pride that such a son was ours and thankfulness that God granted us so many years of his sweet companionship.

I hope with all my heart, my dear Tommy, that you are steadily gaining in health and strength, and that you are now able to enjoy the rest which is yours after your great service for the nation and the world. It is a great gratification to us your friends, and how much greater it must be yours, that there are so many signs that the cause for which you stood so ably and so bravely and at such heavy cost to your health will ultimately prevail.

Mrs. Fine and Philena[1] join me in messages of love to you and Mrs. Wilson.   Affectionately yours,   Henry B. Fine

ALS (WP, DLC).
[1] Philena Fobes Fine and their daughter, also Philena Fobes Fine.

From Duane Reed Stuart

My dear Mr. Wilson: Greensboro, Vermont. August 1, 1922.

I hope that you will never feel hesitant about asking any question of me that you may think I may be able to answer. It is nothing but a pleasure to me to serve you in any way in my power.

The Greek word for court or quadrangle—just such an enclosure as Holder Court—is αʼυλή, *anglicè* = aulé. In capitals we should write the word thus: ΑΥΛΗ, without accent or breathing. If you wish to say "the court," you would prefix the article and write ʻηαʼυλή or in caps.: Η ΑΥΛΗ.

I am sorry that I have not my typewriter with me in this rustic spot in which I am summering with my family but perhaps you will find it not impossible to read my freehand efforts at Greek characters.

The other day, at a small place called Barton, a few miles distant, I met in the friendly rivalry of a golf match the village banker. Needless to say, Vermont being Vermont, he is a Republican. But if you had heard the eulogy which he pronounced on you as we pursued our balls over the green hillsides, you would have respected his intellect—perhaps more than his golf.

This reminds me of another adventure of mine in this state. Some years since we were picnicing near here with the Bliss Perrys. I was deputed to stop at a wayside farm for drinking water. In the course of a gossip with the housewife, something I said must have aroused her suspicions for she asked: "Be you a Democrat?" On my admission of the soft impeachment, she gasped out: "Well! All I can say is, you dont *look* it!"

In my loquacity, I find I have almost forgotten to answer your question as to a good English-Greek dictionary. The best one with which I am familiar is White's but I cannot at the moment recall the publisher and my book lists are far away. I will look up the various possibilities at the earliest moment I am able and give you a more explicit reply. In the meantime let me, please, try to help you out so far as I can.

With all friendly messages and deep regard, I am

Yours ever faithfully,   Duane Reed Stuart.

ALS (WP, DLC).

From Frank Irving Cobb

Dear Mr. Wilson: New York August 1st, 1922.

Fine; you are the only man who can do that job. We are going to have nothing but political chaos in this country until we get two parties to deal with definite issues. As it is now, we really have four parties, two democratic parties and two republican parties.

I am watching the outcome of the Missouri primaries today with intense interest. If Reed wins, he will win with the republican vote, particularly the German and Irish. Therein lies the weakness of most of these primary laws. It is impossible to obtain an honest expression of party opinion, because any primary can be raided from the outside.

With sincerest regards,   As ever yours,   Frank I Cobb.

TLS (WP, DLC).

From Ewing Young Mitchell[1]

St. Louis Mo Aug 5 1922

On face of unofficial returns Reed has five thousand plurality The returns in Kansas City and St Louis are wreaking [reeking] with fraud In many precincts where Long was given only one or two votes by election judges it has been proven that he received many more The laws of the state provide that he may have a re-count by the Boards of Election Commissioners by simply filing an affidavit alleging fraud Reeds friends are urging him not to do this and Long is wavering There is every reason to believe that a re-count would show that at least twenty five hundred votes were un-lawfully counted for Reed instead of Long This would be enough to give Long the nomination Please wire him immediately urging him to resort to every measure provided by law to demonstrate that he is legally nominated and the Democrats of the nation realize the life of the party in this state and perhaps the nation for some years to come depends upon his action Please consider this confi-dential   Ewing Y Mitchell

T telegram (WP, DLC).
   [1] Lawyer of Springfield, Missouri; active in Democratic party politics.

To Breckinridge Long

[Washington, Aug. 6, 1922]

I earnestly advise the use of every legal means to test the validity and good faith of Tuesday's votes.[1]   [Woodrow Wilson]

TC telegram (WP, DLC).
   [1] Long issued a statement on August 8 in which he said that he would not ask for a recount and that he would not officially challenge the results of the election. He as-serted that 40,000 to 50,000 Republicans had voted for Reed in the primary but that, due to a defective primary law, he had no legal recourse in the premises. *New York Times*, Aug. 9, 1922. The final official vote count was Reed, 195,955; Long, 190,013.

An Addition to the Document[1]

[Aug. 7, 1922]

We believe that the President and the members of his cabinet should be accorded the right to places on the floor of the Senate and the House of Representatives whenever those bodies have un-der discussion affairs which are entrusted by the Constitution or the laws to the executive branch of the Government; that they should also be accorded the right to take part in such discussions; and that they should be required to answer upon the floor all proper questions addressed to them concerning matters dealt with by the Executive.

T MS (WP, DLC).
    [1] There is a WWsh draft of the following document and a WWT draft dated August 3, 1922, in WP, DLC. The revised draft printed below bears the notation: "Revised copy Aug. 7th 1922."

From Schuyler Nielson Warren, Jr.

Dear Mr. Wilson: 111 Broadway, N. Y. C. August 7th, 1922.

I am taking the liberty of writing to you on a matter on which I am very anxious to get your advice.

The reaction from Lord Balfour's note on the question of Inter-Allied Indebtedness[1] seems to have produced the opinion in this Country, that Europe can expect little from us in the way of cancellation or diminuation of debts or of political relationship until she puts her house in order, disarms, etc.

I feel that this attitude is wrong in view of our past record, and that it would be timely and beneficial to issue a Statement pointing out that this political instability and resultant militarism is very largely due to the denial by the United States of the principles which govern World cooperation, and second, by its refusal to enter the League of Nations and finally, that the political and economic problems of Europe can not be separated into watertight compartments, they must be considered one and the same.

There does not seem to be any leadership on the subject and while there is no one who can express this sentiment with greater justice and strength than you, I realize that there may be reasons why you would not be willing to do it. For this reason I am very anxious that the Woodrow Wilson Democracy should issue such a statement and in the event of your approving of this idea, I will be glad to submit a Statement which could be issued subject to your approval.

I am enclosing a copy of a speech delivered by my brother-in-law, Robert Wilberforce (who is the Director of the British Library of Information) before the students of Wilberforce University, Ohio, which I thought would be of interest to you.

              Very sincerely yours,   Schuyler N. Warren Jr

TLS (WP, DLC).
    [1] Balfour had been ennobled as the Earl of Balfour in May 1922. In his capacity as Acting Secretary of State for Foreign Affairs, he had sent to the French government on August 1 a diplomatic note discussing in detail the subject of interallied indebtedness. The same note, *mutatis mutandis*, was sent to the governments of Italy, Yugoslavia, Rumania, Portugal, and Greece. The gravamen of the note was that, since the United States Government continued to demand that Great Britain fund, and ultimately pay,

its debt to the United States, the British government, most reluctantly in view of the European financial situation, would have to request that France and the other nations pay at least a portion of their debts to Britain. However, the note continued, these nations would have to pay only enough of their indebtedness to Great Britain to allow that nation to meet its obligations to the United States. The note also reiterated the British government's preference for a general cancellation of intergovernmental indebtedness. The text of this note is printed in the London *Times* and the *New York Times*, both Aug. 2, 1922. It attracted much adverse comment in the United States. See, e.g., the selection of comment from the press and from political figures in the *New York Times*, Aug. 3, 1922.

John Randolph Bolling to Schuyler Nielson Warren, Jr.

Dear Mr. Warren: [Washington] 8th August 1922

In reply to your letter of August 7th, Mr. Wilson requests me to say that he doubts the wisdom of any statement on the subject to which you refer. For your information, and in the strictest confidence, he bids me add that he is totally opposed to the cancellation of debts due by our former allies to the United States.

Mr. Wilson appreciates your thoughtfulness in sending copy of speech delivered by your brother-in-law, Mr. Wilberforce, and will be interested in looking over it.

With kindest regard;

Cordially yours,   [John Randolph Bolling]

CCL (WP, DLC).

Frederick Ingate Thompson[1] to Cary Travers Grayson

My dear Admiral: Washington Aug 10 [1922]

I know where this is from so won't you convey it with all good wishes. The label is missing, from storage, though the cap is intact. It's what I call Republican & Democratic brand—Black & White!

Sorry not to have seen you before sailing but we will have the deferred luncheon upon my return about September 10th.

With all good wishes

Sincerely yours,   Frederick I. Thompson.

ALS (WP, DLC).
    [1] Chief owner and publisher of the *Mobile Register, Mobile News-Item, Montgomery Journal,* and *Birmingham Age-Herald*; member of the United States Shipping Board since November 1920.

From Ray Stannard Baker

My dear Mr. Wilson: Amherst Massachusetts August 11, 1922.

You may possibly have seen Lloyd George's remark in the Commons the other day to the effect that he was the "first man to propose to the Council of Ten at Paris that the League of Nations should be an essential part of the treaty."[1] This has called out quite a number of editorials like the enclosed,[2] and several people have written me about it.

Of course I just send them the record as we have it in one of the chapters. There I have shown how, again and again, you spoke of the League as the "key of the whole settlement," how you wanted it first, how the attempt was made to sidetrack it while you were away and how you brought things up with a round turn upon your arrival at Paris March 15.

Of course the resolution itself—of January 15[3]—was prepared by the British and introduced by Lloyd George in the way the British had of printing ideas, often American ideas, into the form of resolutions (like the mandate resolutions). The original copy of these League resolutions in your file (copy enclosed) contains two corrections or changes, one in your handwriting, and one in type-writing—the important words "an integral" and "general treaty of," which I think is also yours, for it expresses exactly your idea. I should be glad for any enlightenment upon this document you can give me, or any other facts regarding the incident—not to quote, but to guide me when I read proofs for the book, which will be in a few days now.

Of course, there is no putting your finger on Lloyd George: he is as nimble as a flea: if he said one thing yesterday the probability is that he will be saying quite the contrary to-day: yet I should like some ammunition!   Cordially yours,   Ray Stannard Baker

I greatly enjoyed having my son[4] meet you.

ALS (WP, DLC).
   [1] Actually, Lloyd George had made this remark in a speech before a luncheon of the National Free Church Council in London on July 28. *New York Times* and London *Times*, both July 29, 1922.
   [2] This clipping is missing in WP, DLC.
   [3] For this resolution, see the notes of the meeting of the Council of Ten printed at Jan. 22, 1919, and n. 2 thereto, Vol. 54.
   [4] Either James Stannard Baker or Roger Denio Baker.

John Randolph Bolling to Ray Stannard Baker

My dear Mr. Baker: [Washington] 13th August 1922

Mr. Wilson requests me to reply to your letter of August 11th and say that your version of the transaction, as outlined in your letter, is exactly right; that the change in pen and ink is, of course, in his handwriting—and that he thinks the change made in typewriter is also his—though the re-print which you enclose is so small that he is not absolutely sure about this.

I am returning the editorial which you sent, and the reproduction thinking you can use them.

It was a pleasure to see you again the other day, and to meet your son. We will look for you again sometime next month.

Cordially yours,   [John Randolph Bolling]

CCL (WP, DLC).

From Bernard Mannes Baruch

My dear Mr. Wilson: Saratoga Springs, N. Y., August 13, 1922.

It was my original intention to come immediately to report to my commander-in-chief. But, as I was so thoroughly disgusted with myself because I was not at all up to the mark, I decided to come up here to get absolute rest and quiet, which, I am glad to say, I am doing by having a cottage all to myself. I haven't even the pleasure of having Dr. Grayson, who, with Mrs. Grayson,[1] is stopping with some friends; but I am in hopes of having him later in the season.

My object in coming to see you was not that I had any matter of importance to discuss, but because of the pleasure it always gives me to see you and Mrs. Wilson. Soon I shall telegraph and ask of you the privilege of coming down. Everyone I saw wherever I went inquired most solicitously after you.

In the strictest confidence: M. Clemenceau intends coming to America. There have been rumors regarding this; but he told me definitely he would do so. He is not coming under the auspices of anyone; nor is any organization over there or here to make arrangements for him. He is coming quite as himself and as a private individual.

With very best wishes to Mrs. Wilson, and most affectionate regards to yourself, I remain, as ever,

Devotedly yours,   Bernard M Baruch

TLS (WP, DLC).
[1] Alice Gertrude Gordon Grayson.

From Bainbridge Colby

My dear Mr President: New York City August 14, 1922

I have a proffer of employment which presents some questions to be weighed carefully and I should be very grateful for your judgment. Here are the facts, which I will summarize as briefly as I can.

The Western Ukraine Republic is the name of a provisional government as yet unrecognized but functioning after a fashion in the territory of Eastern Galicia. Eastern Galicia was a crown province of Austria. It lies to the north of the Carpathian mountains and has an area of 22,000 square miles. The determination of its status was expressly reserved in the Treaty of Versailles for future determination. The decision of the question probably lies with the Supreme Council, which in turn has shown an inclination to remit the decision of such questions to the League of Nations. In the meantime Poland is exercising a mandate over the territory and from all accounts exercising it badly, oppressing the native Ukrainian element which numbers about 70 per cent of the whole population, colonizing with her own nationals and in general acting as if the disputed territory was a part of her domain.

The Council of the League of Nations is already on record as favoring the recognition of the Republic and according it full autonomy. It has requested the Supreme Council to give the subject its earliest consideration. I am informed that the nations assembled at the recent Genoa conference adopted a resolution of the same purport.

The provisional government has a representative named F. A. Boyer[1] whose credentials I have seen. They seem to be in good form and carry the signature of the President of the National Council of the provisional government.

Mr Boyer, claiming to be acting with the full authorization of the provisional government, has requested me to attend the meeting of the Council of the League of Nations in Geneva in September and urge action looking to the recognition of the provisional government. I received today a check for $10,000 to cover the expenses of my journey and am told that a fee commensurate with the work and the time involved will be paid as soon as the provisional government is in easier circumstances financially. I have not deposited the check, and in acknowledging its receipt I have said that I am not yet resolved to accept it or to undertake the case without further reflection.

This is all clear and straight enough as far as it goes. The aspirations of the Western Ukrainian Republic are legitimate enough and have had a very impressive measure of moral recognition, as I have indicated above. The fact that its government should come to America for an advocate and spokesman has a degree of compliment. I also confess that a participation in the activities of the League just at this moment would be agreeable to me and I think the effect of appearing as counsel and spokesman of a provisional government which turns to the League to establish its national position might please the friends of the League all over the world.

Now,—the other side of the picture. Eastern Galicia is one of the great oil-producing areas of the world. Mr Boyer who represents the provisional government has received prospective concessions contingent upon recognition by Great Britain, covering oil, banks and railroads. He tells me he could have obtained additional concessions for the asking; that the purpose of giving the concessions was to supply him with persuasive negotiating material, so that he could assist the struggling republic to recognition and overcome the machinations of powerful and greedy neighbors, such as Poland and, behind Poland, of course France. In this connection I might say that I recently heard it stated without qualification and by a responsible man that M. Viviani[2] represents Standard Oil interests.

I do not vouch for this statement. I have no means of verifying it, and only mention it to show the subtle and complex struggle for commercial advantage, which hides near the surface of almost every situation.

Mr Boyer professes, and I think with sincerity, that he isn't primarily interested in the concessions, and would toss them all in a hat if he could thereby advance the interests of the Ukrainians, who have put their trust in him.

This may or may not be so. It is my duty of course to mention to you the fact that the plagued question of concessions is a feature of the picture, and that the concessions depend for their validity and value upon recognition by the British, it being assumed that recognition by the other Powers would follow in the course of time. The action of the United States is in no way involved.

Is my pathway in this matter broad enough to walk upon?

It would be a somewhat notable case and as such interesting. And furthermore there is hardly any employment that comes to a lawyer which hasn't a good deal to do with commerce and values and the aims and strivings of merchants and bankers.

There is a brief and informing discussion of the problem of Eastern Galicia in the enclosed pamphlet,[3] pp. 912 to 923.

Regarding the Ecuador loan, I have practically done nothing since the receipt of your letter indicating your distaste for the business. I have in mind your suggestion that the bankers might possibly enter into the business in a public-spirited and more constructive way than is usual with bankers. Of this I have some doubts, however. The credit of Ecuador is bad and she can hardly obtain loans that she needs, even upon severe terms,—the terms which she herself offers, and urges the none too willing bankers to accept.

I received the enclosed letter a few days ago from Sir William Wiseman who has an influentail [influential] position (not a partner) with Kuhn, Loeb & Company. In view of their interest in the matter I shall probably turn the business over to them if it cannot be handled in a way that is agreeable to you.

The enclosed letter came from former Attorney-General Pattengall[4] of Maine asking me to help the Democrats in their State campaign.

Do you think the time has yet come for me to do these things?

I have not been out of town this summer. Matters at the office continue to be very quiet. I hope the days are passing comfortably with you. I should have been down to see you several times if I had not felt that I should not bother you unless some genuine occasion required me to see you.

With sincere and affectionate regard always,

Faithfully yours   Bainbridge Colby

TLS (WP, DLC).

[1] A brief news report in the *New York Times*, Dec. 17, 1920, identified F. A. Boyer as a businessman of Montreal. He was at that time involved in organizing trade with Soviet Russia. Another news report in *ibid.*, Sept. 30, 1926, identified him as a "French capitalist" who was then organizing a French-Italian-English syndicate to exploit Mexican oil fields. The Editors have been unable further to identify him.

[2] René Raphaël Viviani, former Premier of France.

[3] It is missing in WP, DLC, as are the two letters mentioned below.

[4] William Robinson Pattangall.

To Cleveland Hoadley Dodge

My dear Cleve,   [Washington] 15th August 1922

I am rendered uneasy by the fact that I have not heard anything about your health for a long time, either directly or indirectly. Will you not relieve me by dropping me a line to say how you are faring these days? I would appreciate it very much if you would.

For myself I am still emulating the snail in my progress, but even the snail does move a little and so do I, and I am managing not to lose heart.

Our thoughts frequently turn to you, and we are eager to hear as much as possible about all the Dodges.

It is heart-breaking to be so near as we are to a fool of a President for, though he is often ridiculous, there is nothing in his conduct that the country can laugh at with the slightest degree of enjoyment, and we seem to be passing through an endless desert. Apparently hopeless circumstances however are the very sort which should stimulate us to the most energetic action, and I am hoping and believing that that will be the effect upon the country.

We unite in the most affectionate messages to Mrs. Dodge and you and all the Dodges, and I am,

You may be sure,

Always Your Devoted Friend,   [Woodrow Wilson]

CCL (WP, DLC).

To Bainbridge Colby

My dear Colby,   [Washington] 15th August 1922

The Ukrainian question would seem to be simple enough if it were not for that sinister monster, the oil interests, who seems now to play a part in every international matter. However, the advocacy of the recognition of the independence of the Ukrainian Republic is certainly most legitimate and is in the interest of the application of the principles we have conspicuously stood for. I am sure that you will have the discretion to keep free from all association with commercial and pecuniary interests of any kind, and therefore I feel that it would be as safe as it would be honourable for you to appear before the Council of the League of Nations in behalf of the inchoate republic.

I must admit that I am somewhat at a loss to advise you about the invitation to Maine, but I can assure you that I shall be perfectly content to accept your own judgment and conclusions in the matter. Our hopes have never been fulfilled, so far as I can remember, in the case of Maine, but that is no reason for giving up or ceasing to put forth every possible effort.

I hope that in spite of the way you have been tying yourself to work this summer that you are well and that Mrs. Colby and your daughters[1] are in the best of shape.

Do not feel too strong a scruple about coming down to see me, because you will always be welcome, and the discussion of most things face to face is sure to be more satisfactory than writing letters about them.

I am sorry to hear that the Ecuadorian matter is stalled. I find it hard to give up the hope that American bankers can be found who will take a broad and public-spirited view of their duty in the matter. I suggest (at a venture) that you have a talk with my Princeton classmate, Edward Sheldon, now president of the United States Trust Company, in the hope that he may be able to give you suggestive advince [advice]. I can promise that you will get nothing from him that is not honourable and of the highest intention. You are quite at liberty, if you choose, to tell him that I suggested your calling on him.

With affectionate regard,

Faithfully Yours,   [Woodrow Wilson]

P.S. Before sailing, drop Kriz[2] a word telling him that you are going abroad—and about how long you expect to be away. This will be of help to him in handling inquiries.

CCL (WP, DLC).
    [1] Nathalie Sedgwick Washburn Colby and their daughters, Katherine Sedgwick Colby, Nathalie Sedgwick Colby, and Frances Bainbridge Colby.
    [2] Edward C. Kriz, John Randolph Bolling's stenographer.

John Randolph Bolling to Bainbridge Colby

Dear Mr. Colby: [Washington] 15th August 1922

May I be permitted a word, in very strict confidence, on the matters touched upon in your letter of yesterday to Mr. Wilson? I am sure you will understand the spirit in which I write.

Mr. W. is much pleased at the idea of your taking up the Ukrainian matter, and his letter to you of today seems to clear the way for your going into it.

In regard to the Ecuadorian matter; I think he has somewhat changed his views—since he expressed himself so forcibly about it a few weeks ago; and that he would be inclined to accept Mr. Sheldon's view of the situation. In other words, if you can get from Mr. Sheldon an opinion that the terms are fair—in view of the rather doubtful credit conditions—that he would be entirely willing for you to go ahead with it. Try and do this, as it seems a pity to pass the business up.

May I strongly advise that you have nothing to do with the Maine matter? I base this advice upon the very unkind and vicious criticism that has been levelled against Mr. W. (none of which of course I have let him see). It occurs to me that your prospective trip to the other side may offer a most valid excuse for your keeping clear of this matter.

I have rather hesitated to write you upon these matters, but I am quite sure that you will appreciate the genuinely helpful spirit in which I do so.

Everything seems to be moving along nicely here, and Kriz continues on the job. Unless you have something about which you wish to see Mr. W. before you go, I don't think it is at all necessary to take the time—and undergo the fatigue—of a trip down here. When you get back of course you will come—and then I am sure he will be most interested to hear from you your experience before the Council of the League of Nations.

This letter is for your eyes only.

With warm regard;

Faithfully yours,   [John Randolph Bolling]

CCL (WP, DLC).

From Cleveland Hoadley Dodge

Riverdale-on-Hudson

My dear Woodrow   New York August 16th 1922

Great is telepathy—only yester-evening Grace and I were talking of you & wondering how you were getting on, & now comes your wonderful letter, rejoicing our hearts—"mil gracias"

Even a snail goes ahead and I am very glad that you are not retrograding. Washington must be trying this hot weather & I long to get you off on Corona. Couldn't you manage it? She has been a life saver for me this summer. I keep her at City Island only 1/2 hour distance by motor and we go off two or three times a week for day sails & have had one good cruise of ten days & are starting tomorrow for another little cruise of five days. She is full of delightful memories of you

My progress is that of the tortoise who you remember got there finally. For the first time in my life I have had to learn how to be idle, & I assure you it is hard work. Someone once said that "ennui is a great force" & it must be so. My forced inaction is making me long to get to work & I hope that in a few more weeks I will be able to get to my office & do a little work, though I never can be as active as I once was.

We expect Elizabeth & her husband[1] back from Constantinople the end of next week & later Julia[2] & her children all of which & whom will keep us very lively

You must have a lot of grim enjoyment out of the troubles of your successor. He is a pretty weak brother but your old friends in the Senate are just the same old stick-in-the-muds. I should think you would bring out a new edition of "Constitutional Government"

I hope that all the McAdoos & Sayres and Margaret keep well & that you & Mrs Wilson will get through the hot Summer all right.

Perhaps I may be able to get to Washington again in December for the Carnegie[3] meeting & I shall go if I can in hopes of seeing you once more again

Grace joins me in much love to both you and Mrs Wilson

Ever faithfully & affectionately yours

Cleveland H Dodge

ALS (WP, DLC).

[1] That is, his daughter Elizabeth Wainwright Dodge Huntington, and her husband, the Rev. George Herbert Huntington.

[2] That is, Julia Parish Dodge (Mrs. James Childs) Rea.

[3] The Carnegie Institution of Washington, of which he was a trustee.

To Bernard Mannes Baruch

My dear Baruch,   2340 S Street N W 17th August 1922

I am glad you let me hear from you at Saratoga and gladder still that you give us the prospect of seeing you soon again. I shall expect with the greatest pleasure the receipt of the telegram of which you speak.

I am pegging along at the usual pace and wish I could borrow some of the vigour and speed of some of the horses you are watching at Saratoga.

I am heartily sorry that you yourself have not been well. Your first duty to yourself and all of us is to get and keep fit, and I am glad that there is intimation in your letter that you realize that.

I am greatly interested in the news you give me of Clemenceau's plans. It will be hard to know what to do with him when he gets here, but he is in the habit of determining for himself where to go and how to conduct himself and probably will not be asking us for suggestions.

First, second and all the time take care of yourself.

Mrs. Wilson joins me in the kindest messages and is glad, as I am, that we are to see you again soon.

Affectionately Yours,   Woodrow Wilson

TLS (B. M. Baruch Papers, NjP).

To Frederick Ingate Thompson

My dear Mr. Thompson,   [Washington] 18th August 1922

Admiral Grayson kindly fulfilled the delicate mission you were so kind and thoughtful as to assign to him, and I am your debtor for what you very appositely designate as a symbol of Republicanism and Democracy. Please accept my heartfelt thanks for this additional evidence of your generous friendship.

I hope that the trip I understand you are to take to the other side of the water will prove in every way beneficial and enjoyable. My sincere best wishes will follow you and I shall hope to learn of your return in fine shape for the work which lies ahead of all of us and which is as serious as it is necessary and challenging to all that is best in us.

With warm appreciation,

Cordially Yours,   [Woodrow Wilson]

CCL (WP, DLC).

To Cleveland Hoadley Dodge

My dear Cleve,   [Washington] 18th August 1922

Your delightful letter cheered and strengthened me. Bless you for it.

You speak of "telepathy." I have not once but often this summer thought of that delightful boat Corona, and your invitation is a tug at my heart. But alas, my dear fellow, I have been on boats enough to know that I could not enjoy even your delightful yacht so long as my present lameness hampers and limits my movements.

I am grateful to learn that you are improving and shall treasure your promise that we shall see you if you can get down here to the next Carnegie meeting.

Happily the summer here has been very pleasant indeed,—not at all like the summers for which Washington has gained a reputation. Even August has been less truculent than usual, and pleasant airs are almost always stirring; so that my daily motor rides keep me sufficiently refreshed and I am doing remarkably well considering the circumstances.

Your affection helps more than any sort of weather or tonic could help, and I bless you for it.

Mrs. Wilson joins me in most affectionate messages to Mrs. Dodge and you, in congratulations that your daughters and their little ones are so soon expected and in affectionate messages to them when they arrive.

Your Devoted Friend,   Woodrow Wilson

TLS (WC, NjP).

From Bainbridge Colby

My dear Mr President: New York City August 18, 1922

I was very much pleased to receive your letter of the 15th and to see, in connection with the Ukrainian business, that I was not proceeding on lines that did not have your approval.

I think your suggestion to submit the terms of the Ecuadorian loan to Mr Sheldon for his opinion is excellent, and before I resume activity in this matter I will make a point of doing so and writing you what he says.

Thank you very much for your kind references to Mrs Colby and my daughters. The fact that you speak of them is always a source of pleasure to them, and I never fail to report your gracious inquiries about them.

There are some details to be straightened out before I depart on the Ukrainian business. It will be a week or ten days before I go, and I will write you again unless I should luckily have an opportunity of seeing you before I go.

I have written General Pattengall of Maine a letter of which I enclose a copy.[1] There are a lot of good Democrats up there,— Democrats on principle, who have nothing but defeat as their perennial portion. I have been in almost every part of the State in former campaigns, and if it were not for the trip to Europe I am planning, I think I should be unable to resist the temptation to get back in the trenches.

With affectionate regard,
Cordially always   Bainbridge Colby

TLS (WP, DLC).
    [1] BC to W. R. Pattangall, Aug. 16, 1922, TCL (WP, DLC).

To Bainbridge Colby

My dear Colby,   [Washington] 20th August 1922

I was glad to get your letter of August eighteenth and to see your reply to Pattengall which, by the way, pleased me very much.

I am sure that when you see Sheldon you will not only be glad I assisted you to good counsel in the Ecuadorian matter but also grateful that I brought you into the circle of so interesting a man. Besides being an eminent man of business he is also a man of letters and has one of the best private libraries in the country. He was one of the chief literary ornaments of our class in the University (for we were classmates). When you see him please give him my affectionate regards.

By all means let me have a glimpse of you in person if it is possible before you get off to Europe.

With affectionate regard,

Faithfully Yours,   Woodrow Wilson

TLS (B. Colby Papers, DLC).

From Bainbridge Colby

My dear Mr President: New York City August 22, 1922

I had an important interview today with one of the officers of the Sinclair Consolidated Oil Corporation. The Corporation wishes me to represent it in two investigations that are soon to open up under two separate resolutions which have passed the Senate. I should be associated with ex-Senator Sutherland,[1] who is as you know a lawyer of very unusual ability.

The investigations involve:

(1) The recent acquisition under lease of the so-called Teapot Dome property in Wyoming,[2] and

(2) A general investigation of the manufacture and distribution of gasolene, with a view to determining the causes of its fluctuating price and the reasonableness of its price to the public.[3]

I have not seen the text of either resolution and am stating the facts as they are stated to me.

From a lawyer's point of view, this is a very substantial and important employment. It would involve attendance from day to day before the Committees charged with the conduct of the investigations, a very thorough study of the facts, and compensation that would be in keeping with the importance of the subject and interests involved and the expenditure of time and energy which would be required.

Do you see any objection to accepting this employment?

It is not to be confused with appearing before a Congressional committee in advocacy of special relief or favorable legislative action. I should be representing a defendant in an important tribunal, seeking to uphold his practices against criticism and vindicating his reputation against ugly charges.

From a business point of view, this would swamp the inadequate financial returns that are involved in the Ukrainian business. I might be able to arrange for my appearance before the League at a subsequent meeting, so that I would not have to disappoint the people interested in the Ukrainian matter, and I think I could do so.

If you would like to confer with me I will come down at once. My first feeling is in favor of taking the employment. From a strictly lawyer point of view it is interesting. I have not given the subject extended reflection, however, as the moment the interview with the Sinclair caller was over I rang for my stenographer and began the dictation of this letter.

Cordially always   Bainbridge Colby

TLS (WP, DLC).

[1] That is, George Sutherland, former representative and senator from Utah.

[2] Albert B. Fall, soon after taking office as Secretary of the Interior, had arranged a transfer of jurisdiction over the naval oil reserve lands in California and Wyoming from the Navy Department to the Interior Department. Harding had signed an Executive Order formalizing the transfer on May 31, 1921. Fall's maneuver immediately aroused the suspicions of many conservationists, who feared that he intended to lease all the naval oil reserves to private interests for development. Fall in fact did firmly believe in such a policy and intended to implement it as soon as possible. However, it was not until April 14, 1922, that a report appeared in the *Wall Street Journal* that Fall had leased the entire Teapot Dome oil field in Wyoming to Harry Ford Sinclair's Mammoth Oil Company. The Interior Department confirmed the lease on April 18. In response, Senator Robert M. LaFollette, on April 21, introduced S. Res. 282, which directed the Secretary of the Interior to send to the Senate full information on all leases involving the naval oil reserves in California and Wyoming, together with all documents in the department's files relating to this subject. One week later, La Follette proposed that a new section be added to his resolution calling upon the Senate Committee on Public Lands and Surveys to make a full investigation of the entire subject of leases upon the naval oil reserve. He accompanied his revised resolution with a scathing attack upon the oil-leasing policy of Fall and the Interior Department. The Senate approved La Follette's resolution, with many abstentions but without a single dissenting vote, on April 29.

The passage of La Follette's resolution marked the beginning of the Senate investigation which was to make the so-called Teapot Dome scandal famous in American history. La Follette urged Senator Thomas J. Walsh, Democrat of Montana, to lead the investigation. Walsh reluctantly agreed but was in no hurry to begin the hearings. Indeed, he and other investigators spent more than sixteen months examining a mountain of documents which Fall sent to the Senate in early June 1922 in response to La Follette's resolution. Fall resigned as Secretary of the Interior on January 2, 1923. Hearings before the Committee on Public Lands and Surveys finally began on October 22, 1923. See Burl Noggle, *Teapot Dome: Oil and Politics in the 1920's* (Baton Rouge, La., 1962), pp. 15-63 *passim*; J. Leonard Bates, *The Origins of Teapot Dome: Progressives, Parties, and Petroleum, 1909-1921* (Urbana, Ill., 1963), pp. 232-44; *Cong. Record*, 67th Cong., 2d sess., pp. 5792, 6041-50, 6097.

[3] La Follette had submitted S. Res. 295, which called upon the Senate Committee on Manufacturers to investigate the price of gasoline, on May 15, 1922. The Senate passed the resolution on June 5. La Follette himself headed the subcommittee which carried out an extensive investigation in 1922 and 1923. *Ibid.*, pp. 6932, 8140; Noggle, pp. 49-50.

An Unsent Letter to Bainbridge Colby[1]

My dear Colby,   [Washington] 23rd August 1922

I have your letter of yesterday about the proposal of the Sinclair Consolidated Oil Corporation. It puzzles me a little because I do not know just what the present situation is in the country as to the oil companies and their many machinations. I only know the newspapers give the impression that some ugly business is going on in respect to the Teapot Dome, and inasmuch as it is known as part of the Naval Reserve I can testify that the oil companies are constantly attempting to invade that Reserve with or without right.

My second impression from your letter is that it would not look well to postpone your appearance before the Council of the League of Nations in regard to the Ukrainian business, and that it would be better to conclude that business before going into the other matter. I think the Ukrainian business very much more worth while than the other, and hope that if it is possible you will give it precedence.

You speak of Senator Sutherland as a lawyer. I know only this of him,—that he has seemed to me one of the most thick headed and impenetrable of the Senate partisans. I have not been able to make anything else of him.

If you are coming down this way soon we can talk over this and any other matter that needs conference.

Since you are silent about yourself and your family I hope I may take it for granted that you are all well and that things are going well with you.

In haste,

With affectionate regard,

Faithfully Yours,   [Woodrow Wilson]

CCL (WP, DLC).
[1] Typed at the top of this letter: "Not sent—as decided after dictating to wire for Mr. Colby to come down. See telegram this date."

To Bainbridge Colby

Washington D C Aug 23 1922

It would be most satisfactory to answer your letter in person Stop Could you come down[1]   Woodrow Wilson

T telegram (B. Colby Papers, DLC).
[1] Colby had dinner with Wilson on August 25.

To Winterton Conway Curtis[1]

My dear Professor Curtis,   [Washington] 29th August 1922

May it not suffice for me to say, in reply to your letter of August twenty-fifth,[2] that of course like every other man of intelligence and education that I do believe in organic evolution. It surprises me that at this late date such questions should be raised.

Sincerely Yours,   Woodrow Wilson

TLS (MoHi-MoU).
    [1] Professor of Zoology at the University of Missouri.
    [2] W. C. Curtis to WW, Aug. 25, 1922, TLS (WP, DLC). Curtis called attention to the case of one F. E. Dean, a former student of his, who had been dismissed as superinten- dent of schools at Fort Sumner, New Mexico, by the local school board because he had questioned its decision to prohibit the teaching of evolution. Wilson's name had come up in the discussion of the case because a minister of the Fort Sumner area had as- serted that Wilson did not believe that "man came from the beast." Curtis asked Wilson to send "some statement" in regard to his opinion of "organic evolution."

To Jessie Woodrow Wilson Sayre

My darling Jessie,   [Washington] 30th August 1922

I forgot the other day, when I telegraphed on your birthday, that I could not send you by wire the usual little birthday present I have been accustomed to send. I am sending it now and hope it will prove useful.

We unite in love to you all and the hope that Marthas Vineyard has yielded you all the usual refreshment and invigoration.

Lovingly Yours,   [Father]

P.S. I was so glad to get your recent letter[1] for I am always hungry for every item of news I can get about you, and it made me happy that all the news was good.

CCL (WC, NjP).
    [1] We have not found this letter.

From William Gibbs McAdoo

Dear Governor: Los Angeles, Cal. Sept. 1, 1922.

Nell and I feel enriched by your delightful letters recently re- ceived. I had intended writing sooner but every conceivable thing has gotten in the way.

We are at last comfortably established in our house, and my of- fice is now fairly well organized, so that we hope for a less stren- uous and more comfortable time in the future.

Sally[1] was here in the early part of August and Nell and I took her on a trip to the Yosemite, which she had never seen. The In- dian Games were in progress under the supervision of Chief Ranger Townsley of the Park, so we took a hand and had a fine time. I enclose a picture which appeared recently in the New York Times[2] and which is extremely good of Sally and fairly good of Nell.*

In going out of the Yosemite we took horses and went over a wonderful but very precipitous trail over the mountains to Lake Tenaya, which is at an altitude of about six thousand feet above sea level. There our motor met us and we proceeded eastwardly over the high Sierras through the famous Tioga Pass, where the scenery is indescribably grand and beautiful, to a remarkable lake in the desert of Eastern California called Mono Lake. We spent the night there in tents and proceeded the next day to Lake Tahoe, which I think you visited and which, I think, is one of the most beautiful lakes in California. We spent the night there and motored over very hot and dusty roads the next day to Sacramento, where we took one of the paddle-wheel river boats, putting the motor on board, and found ourselves the next morning in San Francisco.

I attended the Convention of the American Bar Association for two days there. It looked more like a Republican national convention than anything else, but it was an interesting occasion, although I could not help being impressed with the conservative and reactionary atmosphere which seems to surround such a large part of the legal profession. I was called on unexpectedly to make a speech along with Chief Justice Taft at one of the sessions over which your old friend and admirer, Judge Goodwin[3] of Chicago, presided. Sometime before the Convention Newt Baker wrote me that the report of the Committee on International Relations contained a gratuitous statement that the Versailles Treaty had failed of ratification because you would not accept the reservations, and suggested that some of your friends ought to see that this was eliminated from the report. I took the matter up with several of our friends and Judge Goodwin, when the report was presented to the Convention, called attention to it as injecting controversial matter which was wholly immaterial to the discussion and said that, unless Mr. Scott,[4] Chairman of the Committee, would consent to the deletion of the objectionable matter, he would carry the fight to the floor of the Convention. This was wildly applauded. Mr. Scott, the Chairman, seeing the timbre of the Convention, very promptly and wisely consented to eliminate the objectionable statement.

After two days at the Convention we ran down to Del Monte Lodge on Monterey Bay where we spent five quiet days in delightfully cool climate. I brushed up on my golf again and Nell practiced hers and we had the most restful time that I have enjoyed in many years, it seemed to me. Unhappily, Sally had to leave us there, as she was conditioned in Physics and had to go to a camp at Port Henry, New York, to be tutored for a re-examination in this subject when she enters Bryn Mawr the 20th of September. She is now eighteen and is a most charming, original and attractive girl. Nell and she are so fond of each other that it is really delightful. We hated to see her go, and I hated particularly to think of her in a Pennsylvania Republican environment. The only thing that reconciles me to it is the fact that her eldest sister, Mrs. Platt,[5] lives at Chestnut Hill and that will make it pleasant for Sally.

We are delighted with our new house. We have a lovely garden and we both wish more than we can tell you that you and Edith could come out and see us and enjoy this delightful climate. Of course, September is the worst month of the year because it is the warmest and the dryest. Temporarily Nell and the babies are spending two weeks at Santa Barbara while I am leaving today for an exciting trip down the Snake River in Idaho, which we navigate for 110 miles on a raft, fishing for trout in the day time, and camping on the shore at night. We shall take our guns and probably have an opportunity to get some small game.

This is the first time for many years that I have been in an environment that I really enjoy. This western life is delightful, not only because of the climate, but because of the variety of scenery and interests which one can enjoy without making any particular effort, because it is all practically at ones door.

The babies are wonderfully well. This is certainly the right climate for them. It is also a most healthful climate for older people too. I tell Nell facetiously that, unfortunately for her, it will probably prolong my life and that she will therefore have me on her hands many years longer than would otherwise have been the case! I wish that you could see the children. They are perfectly lovely. I have never seen them so well or happy, nor have I ever seen Nell looking more beautiful than she is now. I am going to have some pictures taken of them and the house as soon as I get back from the fishing trip, and shall send them to you.

We think of you and Edith constantly and with the tenderest affection and solicitude. I hope you have had a pleasant summer and that you continue to improve. Nell joins me in warmest love to you and Edith. Please write to us when you can. You don't know how happy it makes us to get letters from you and Edith.

Devotedly yours,   W G McAdoo

* P.S. I cannot find the picture, but will get another one and send it in another letter.   W.G.M.

TLS (WP, DLC).

[1] His daughter, Sarah Fleming McAdoo.

[2] The photograph, which also included McAdoo himself and "Chief Ranger" Townsley, appeared in the Rotogravure Picture Section, pt. 2, p. 1, *New York Times*, Aug. 20, 1922.

[3] Clarence Norton Goodwin, lawyer of Chicago, former judge of the Superior Court of Cook County and of the Illinois Appellate Court.

[4] James Brown Scott, chairman of the Committee on International Law. The exchange between Goodwin and Scott, which took place on August 10, is printed in *Report of the Forty-fifth Annual Meeting of the American Bar Association Held at San Francisco, California, August 9, 10 and 11, 1922* (Baltimore, 1922), pp. 55-57.

[5] His daughter, Harriet Floyd McAdoo Martin (Mrs. Clayton) Platt.

From Bainbridge Colby

My dear Mr President: New York City September 2, 1922

I received a couple of days ago the enclosed cablegram from Sir Eric Drummond,[1] the Secretary of the League of Nations, from which you will see that I am left in some confusion as to whether the Western Ukrainian case can be heard at the September meeting of the Council of the League. He says, "Letter will follow," and it has seemed best to await the receipt of his letter before sailing. Mr Boyer sails today on the "Olympic" for London and will meet the President of the Provisional Government in London. I will not start until a week from Tuesday at the earliest, reserving final decision until I see Drummond's letter.

I had a long and friendly talk this week with the president of the Sinclair Company[2] and did my best to explain, in as considerate a way as I could, our decision with reference to the case we discussed last week. He took my explanation, outwardly at least, in a very friendly and understanding way, and the incident, which in its nature was a little difficult, seemed to pass off as well as could be expected.

I thoroughly appreciate and assent to your thought in this matter. I left you last Friday night with a deepened sense of admiration and respect. To a man who has spent his life in the rough and tumble of the legal profession, as I have done, it makes one a little dizzy at times to toss away business which one's professional brethren are bending every energy and resource to get. But it's a fine game and worth the candle as long as we can hold out.

The other day I wrote two letters, of which I enclose copies for your information.[3] The decisions were easy. It was impossible to take the business.

I am sending you an article on "America and Russia" by Mr A. J. Sack,[4] whom you may recall as the Secretary for a number of years of the Russian Bureau of Information in New York. Mr Sack is a cultivated, earnest, Russian democrat, a warm admirer of yours as his letter shows, and an ardent believer in your Russian policy. He sent me his article some days ago for my opinion of it, and I asked him to let me have a copy so that you might have an opportunity to read it. It is to be published soon, I believe, in what periodical I do not know. May I ask you to return it at your earliest convenience after you have read it.

With affectionate regard,

Sincerely always   Bainbridge Colby

TLS (WP, DLC).
[1] It is missing.

² Earle Westwood Sinclair, president of the Sinclair Consolidated Oil Corp.; brother of Harry Ford Sinclair, who was chairman of the board of this firm.
³ BC to William H. Wadhams, Aug. 30, 1922, and BC to Louis S. Levy, Aug. 30, 1922, both TCL (WP, DLC).
⁴ Arkady Joseph Sack. We have not been able to locate the article.

From William Edward Dodd

My dear Mr. Wilson: Round Hill, Virginia, September 3, 1922.

We were glad indeed to share with you and Mrs. Wilson a little of our crop of peaches. It is a part of the year's academic task for me to harvest a crop of peaches. It is my golf and right lively golf it sometimes turns out to be. Two or three months here in the sun and hot climate (not so warm as in Washington) generally suffices to equip me for the other ten months of the year, spent in Chicago, engaged in the useless task, it sometimes seems, of teaching what I regard as the true history of this country. Useless, it seems, because knowledge and high purpose so seldom form any part of the stock in trade of the men who act for us in Washington. Think of all that Sumner[1] at Yale taught Taft about political economy and how completely Taft reversed it all as President. I sometimes think a teacher's business is to show what should not be done in the hope that students, grown to politicians, may do the contrary.

One thing yet, was it not a stupid thing for Democrats to re-nominate Reed in face of all they knew? Yet I can not help thinking that the result is largely due to the way the primary campaign was managed by Long and his friends. If they had made the issue clearly one of pursuing the only possible foreign policy and then shown the absurdity of trying to get on in any party with the executive going one way and senators of the same party going another way, the voters would have reacted more sensibly. As it was Reed's plurality was very small. There certainly was great enthusiasm both in Saint Louis and in Saint Joseph, not to claim too much for the saints, for the ideals and the leadership you had set up both for the country and for the Democratic party. That enthusiasm was somehow frittered away. But to expect too much of politics is like expecting too much from intelligent teaching. For the sake of a great cause and a great leader, so clearly embodying that cause, I was greatly disappointed at the nomination of such a character as Reed is commonly known to be.

More than once I have had a vague thought of entering the public service and offering for election and there have been several suggestions looking that way. But such outcomes as that in Missouri discourage even where one's physical strength might offer promise of holding out. I am doubtful whether I could make the kind of appeal that would win the complex electorate of a great Northern state. Yet it is clear some men who have a little knowledge of the nation's affairs ought to offer themselves.

Now this letter has taken a quite different turn from what was intended. I leave it as it is, however, in the hope that you will understand. I only wish you were well enough to be a more active leader of those who do try to think straight and that in these days of doubts and distress we might all turn to you.

As ever yours sincerely and with high regards to Mrs. Wilson,

William E. Dodd

If you can pardon the perversity of this poor typewriter.

TLS (WP, DLC).
¹ That is, William Graham Sumner, Professor of Political and Social Science at Yale University, 1872-1909.

To John Hessin Clarke

My dear Friend,   [Washington] 5th September 1922

It has deeply grieved me to learn of your retirement from the Supreme Court.¹ I have not the least inclination to criticise the action because I know that you would have taken it from none but the highest motives. I am only sorry,—deeply sorry. Like thousands of other liberals throughout the country, I have been counting on the influence of you and Justice Brandeis to restrain the Court in some measure from the extreme reactionary course which it seems inclined to follow.

In my few dealings with Mr. Sutherland I have seen no reason to suspect him of either principles or brains, and the substitution is most deplorable.

The most obvious and immediate danger to which we are exposed is that the courts will more and more outrage the common peoples sense of justice and cause a revulsion against judicial authority which may seriously disturb the equilibrium of our institutions, and I see nothing which can save us from this danger if the Supreme Court is to repudiate liberal courses of thought and action.

But I did not mean to write you a homily; I meant only to express my heartfelt regret at your withdrawal from the Court and to express in that way my confidence, friendship and admiration.

I hope with all my heart that you may find a new sort of happiness in your freedom, and I am sure you will find many means for public service.

With warm regard,

Faithfully Yours,   [Woodrow Wilson]

CCL (WP, DLC).
 ¹ Harding, on September 4, had announced Clarke's resignation from the Supreme Court and his own decision to nominate George Sutherland to fill his place. *New York Times*, Sept. 5, 1922.

To William Edward Dodd

My dear Dodd,   Washington D C 6th September 1922

Of course I understand your letter perfectly and hasten to say in reply that I wish with all my heart that you would enter public life. I think it is getting to be plain that only by such sacrifices can the men who think straight effectively assist in turning the country's face in the right direction.

We have greatly enjoyed the peaches, and it adds to their flavour to know you have benefited in producing them.

With warm regards, in which Mrs. Wilson joins me,

Cordially and Faithfully Yours,   Woodrow Wilson

TLS (W. E. Dodd Papers, DLC).

To W. A. Cole¹

[Washington] Sept. 6th 1922

W. A. Cole: Please convey my congratulations to Mr. Stephens upon a result which cannot but prove beneficial to the whole country. The Democrats of Miss. are certainly of the right stuff, and I rejoice in being their comrade in the party ranks. Cordial best wishes to you and all my fellow Democrats in the faithful State of Mississippi.   Woodrow Wilson.

T MS (WP, DLC).
 ¹ Of Lambert, Mississippi. We have not been able to identify him further. Wilson was replying to W. A. Cole and I. L. Singleton to WW, Sept. 5, 1922, T telegram (WP, DLC), which informed him that Stephens had defeated Vardaman for the Mississippi Democratic senatorial nomination in the run-off primary election held on that date.

To William Gibbs McAdoo

My dear Mac,   [Washington] 7th September 1922

It was delightful to get your newsy letter of September first particularly because the news was so good and gave a picture of such happiness. Our thoughts and affections constantly search you all out and dwell with you, and it makes us very happy to know how delightfully things are going with you all.

I think I can say (though with doubt) that I continue to improve at the old snail's pace. Fortunately a snail's pace is better than no pace at all.

We have had a really delightful summer in the matter of weather. It has been cool and refreshing, and for my own part I have very much enjoyed the rest it has given me.

I have attended meetings of the American Bar Association and think that you put it very mildly indeed when you speak of a "conservative and reactionary atmosphere." The members of the Association constitute the most reactionary and pig-headed group in the nation, in my opinion, and are likely to hasten the peril which damned fools like Judge Wilkerson of Chicago[1] are bringing upon us through the medium of what they choose to designate as "the administration of justice." I fear a universal revulsion of feeling against the courts. The people of America are no more in a humor to be trifled with than are the people of the older countries.

We are delighted to hear of the blooming health of the dear little ones, and Edith joins me in loving messages and congratulations to you all.   Affectionately Yours,   [Woodrow Wilson]

CCL (WP, DLC).
    [1] James Herbert Wilkerson, United States district judge for the northern district of Illinois, on September 1, had issued a temporary injunction which prohibited striking railroad shopcraft workers and all the officers of their unions and affiliated organizations in the American Federation of Labor from interfering in any way with the operation of the railroads of the nation. Attorney General Daugherty had appeared personally in Wilkerson's court in Chicago to petition for the injunction. He declared that the government would defend the principle of the open shop and virtually admitted that its intent was to break the shopmen's strike which had begun on July 1 as a protest against wage reductions proposed by the Railroad Labor Board. The injunction set off a firestorm of protest by union organizations and their sympathizers. Even some members of Harding's cabinet, such as Hoover, Hughes, and Fall, denounced the severity of the injunction. Despite the furor, Wilkerson extended the temporary injunction on September 11 and converted it into a preliminary injunction on September 23. *New York Times*, Sept. 2, 12, and 24, 1922. A virtually complete text of the temporary injunction is printed in *ibid.*, Sept. 2, 1922. For the background of the railroad strike and its dénouement, see Murray, *The Harding Era*, pp. 244-45, 248-58, 260-61.

From John Hessin Clarke

My dear Friend: Atlantic City, N. J. Sept. 9th 1922

I rejoice in the new proof which your good note brings me of your improving health and strength.

I must write my reply with my own hand for I cannot trust it to a public stenographer.

Unless you have much more intimate knowledge of the character of work which a Supreme Judge must do than I had before going to Washington you little realize the amount of grinding, uninteresting, bone labor there is in writing more than half the cases decided by the Supreme Court. Much more than 1/2 the cases are of no considerable importance whether considered from the point of view of the principles or of the property involved in them, but, nevertheless, a conscientious judge writing them must master their details with the utmost care. My theory of writing opinions has always been that if clearly stated 9 cases out of 10 will decide themselves,—what the decision should be will emerge from the statement of the facts as certainly as the issues will. In this spirit I wrote always, and a recent re-reading of my more important opinions gives me a modest degree of confidence that they will stand fairly well the test of "the wise years."

I protested often, but in vain, that too many trifling cases were being written, that our strength should be conserved for better things, and that no amount of care could avoid hopeless confusion and conflict in the decisions.

It resulted from all this and from court conditions which I cannot describe in writing that for 2 or 3 years the work kept growing more & more irksome to me. Still I supposed I would have continued, uncomfortable though I was, for a few more years had it not been for the death last year of my two sisters,[1] the only near relations I had in the world. This so changed my outlook on life that the prospect of continuing the work became simply insupportable. Of course I could not state this to the public as a cause for resigning. It may be I can interest myself in other studies & work—but I am by no means sure that I can. I shall try.

Of one, and by no means the least distressing of the conditions I must write in answer to a suggestion in your note.

Judge Brandeis and I were agreeing less & less frequently in the decision of cases involving what we call, for want of a better designation, liberal principles. It is for you to judge which was falling away from the correct standards. During the last year in the Hardwood anti-trust case[2] which I wrote B and Holmes dissented B writing an opinion: It is one of the most important anti-trust cases ever decided by that court for it involved for the first time there "The Open Competitive Plan" which was devised with all the cunning astute lawyers & conscienceless business men could command to defeat or circumvent the law.

It seemed to me me [*sic*] and to six others that it was a most flagrant case of law breaking. It may interest you some time to read the two opinions but in doing so please note that my quotations from the record show my statement of the facts to be scrupulously accurate.

In the last child labor case I alone dissented.[3] Unfortunately the case was considered and decided when one of my sisters was dying and I could not write a dissenting opinion. I am sure a dissent based on the decisions from the Oleomargarine to the Narcotic Drug Cases[4] could have been made very convincing.

In a personal injury case involving the doctrine of attractive nuisance[5] the Chief Justice[6] & Justice Day[7] joined in an opinion which I wrote dissenting from the rule that contributory negligence of a trespassing child of tender years barred recovery in a case of flagrant poisoning of the water in a pool in an unfenced common in which two children perished when bathing. The decision involved overruling two Supreme Court decisions in order to substitute the Mass rule. In a wall crane case and in several safety appliance cases we differed. You doubtless noted how we differed with respect to war legislation.[8]

There is much more, but this will suffice, to show that in leaving the court I did not withdraw any support from Judge Brandeis. One or the other of us was shifting or had shifted his standards so that in critical or crucial cases we were seldom in agreement. Our personal relations, of course, continued entirely cordial.

McReynolds[9] as you know is the most reactionary Judge on the Court. There were many other things which had better not be set down in black & white which made the situation to me deplorable & harassing to such a degree that I thought myself not called on to sacrifice what of health & strength I may have left in a futile struggle against constantly increasing odds. Sometime I should like to tell you of it all. It was in some respects as disillusioning a chapter as Washington could afford—I am sure I need not say more than this to one who has suffered as you have in the recent past. So much for what is past. Now as to the future.

I need not say to you that personal ambitions did not have any part in inducing my action. If my strength permits I intend to do what I can to promote the entrance of our govt into the League of Nations.[10] To me it is the indispensable as well as the noblest political conception of our time and, very certainly, to have launched it as you did makes secure for you one of the highest places in history.

When your illness withdrew you from active leadership there was no other to even approximately fill your place and the result is that the great public opinion favorable to the League is leaderless and little is being accomplished for "the great cause." I have been profoundly impressed as to the truth of this by my correspondence of the past week. The N. Y. Times & World, the Balt Sun & two important news agencies have written or sent men to me urging that something be done & offering every aid. While I am too old to think of accepting leadership of the cause even were I fitted for it, which I am not, it may be possible for me to do something toward getting the "true believers" together & coordinating their efforts. If I am strong enough I shall try. The fact is your illness prevented a really adequate & comprehensive presentation of the case from being made to the country. I have urged this on Baker[11]—after you the most competent man in the country to make it—but he smiles indulgently and contents himself with making desultory "remarks" about it. Will you not be strong enough soon to do it? All the country would rise up to answer such a call from you. Personally I shall do all that careful study and unstinted effort will enable me to do to press the subject on the attention of the country. I can do no more & my sense of duty to my country will not permit me to do less. And so I may sink into the grave but not into an old mans corner and if I am given health & strength I may be of unofficial service greater than I could have rendered hampered as I was on the bench.

I am sure you know, my dear Friend, without my writing it, that there is not anything in this world within my power that I would not do to serve you or to advance the cause which I know is nearest to your heart. God bless you! Believe me always

Your Sincere friend   John H. Clarke

P.S. I leave tonight for Youngstown, Ohio, where I will have a secretary & a typewriter.   J.H.C.

ALS (WP, DLC).

[1] Alice Clarke, of Youngstown, Ohio, had died on March 28, 1921; Ida Clarke, a physician of Youngstown, had died on March 3, 1922.

[2] American Column and Lumber Co. *et al. v.* United States, 257 U.S. 377. For further discussion of this case, see Hoyt Landon Warner, *The Life of Mr. Justice Clarke: A Testament to the Power of Liberal Dissent in America* (Cleveland, Ohio, 1959), pp. 84-86.

[3] Child Labor Tax Case, 259 U.S. 20, decided May 15, 1922.

[4] The "oleomargarine case" was McCray *v.* United States, 195 U.S. 27. The "narcotic drug" case was United States *v.* Doremus, 249 U.S. 86.

[5] United Zinc & Chemical Co. *v.* Britt *et al.*, 258 U.S. 268.

[6] William Howard Taft.

[7] William Rufus Day.

[8] Cases arising out of wartime legislation in which Clarke and Brandeis differed included Abrams *et al. v.* United States, 250 U.S. 616; Schafer *v.* United States, 251 U.S. 466; and Milwaukee Social Democratic Publishing Co. *v.* Burleson, 255 U.S. 407. For further discussion of these cases, see Warner, pp. 96-105.

[9] James Clark McReynolds.

[10] About Clarke's thoughts about the need for a great nationwide movement on behalf of American membership in the League of Nations, see *ibid.*, pp. 124-25.

[11] Newton D. Baker.

To Newton Diehl Baker

My dear Friend,   [Washington] 11th September 1922

I was very much grieved to see in this morning's paper that the editors of the Encyclopaedia Britannica have permitted statement to be printed in their latest supplement which must have been distressing to you.[1] Too many people are familiar with the high quality of your splendid work during the war to make such an attack of the least consequence, but it is nevertheless a pleasure to take the liberty of saying how indignant the attack has made me, and of expressing again my unqualified admiration of your administration of the office of Secretary of War during the great conflict.

Mrs. Wilson joins me in messages of warm regard to Mrs. Baker[2] and you, and I hope that we may again soon have the privilege of seeing you. It is always a privilege to swap views with you and to renew our delightful friendship.

With affectionate regard,

Faithfully Yours,   [Woodrow Wilson]

CCL (WP, DLC).

[1] Wilson had probably read "SLANDER OF BAKER IN ENCYCLOPAEDIA ROUSES AMERICANS," New York *World*, Sept. 11, 1922. This news report described what it termed a "scathing biographical article" on Baker in a new supplementary volume of the *Encyclopaedia Britannica*. The report quoted the paragraphs relating to Baker's wartime activities as follows:

"After the outbreak of the World War he indorsed the Administration's peace policy, supported the League to Enforce Peace, and urged that the National Guard be tried fully before compulsory service be decided upon. After America entered the war he recommended moderation toward conscientious objectors and forbade men in uniform to interfere with anti-conscription meetings.

"The charge of pacificism was often brought against him, and his career generally as Secretary was widely condemned throughout the United States as lacking in energy, foresight and ability, and especially for his failure to prepare adequately in the months immediately preceding the American declaration of war."

The *World's* news report went on to quote many American military leaders, including John J. Pershing, Hugh L. Scott, and Tasker H. Bliss, who had publicly defended Baker in response to the article. It also noted that the editors of the encyclopaedia were standing behind the article.

The offending biographical sketch of Baker appeared in Vol. XXX of the so-called 12th edition of the *Encyclopaedia Britannica*, published in 1922. Actually, this edition was simply a reprinting of the twenty-nine volumes of the 11th edition (1910-1911), with three new volumes added to cover the period 1910 to 1921. It should perhaps be mentioned that Vol. XXIX of the 13th edition, published in 1926, contained a considerably revised, and somewhat less critical, sketch of Baker.

[2] That is, Elizabeth Leopold Baker.

From Bainbridge Colby

My dear Mr President: New York City September 11, 1922

While waiting for Sir Eric Drummond's letter I sent a cable to Lord Robert Cecil under date of September 6th of which I enclose you a copy and his reply of September 8th.[1] This morning I have the enclosed letter from Drummond dated August 31st and a memorandum in French, of which I enclose a translation, showing the action heretofore taken by the Council of the League in reference to the question of Eastern Galicia's (another name for Western Ukrainia) independence.

I would be very grateful if you will examine this memorandum carefully and give me the benefit of your judgment as to what should be done. It looks to me as if the point of approach to the recognition of the Western Ukrainian Republic is the British Foreign Office.

Our clients are anxious to see action and are not particular as to what the action is, or in what direction it proceeds. Their psychology is that of baffled and disappointed men, to whom even ill-considered action is better than none. They are very anxious that I should go to London or Geneva or anywhere, so long as I seem to be going in their interest.

I consider the memorandum of the League Council's action as practically precluding the possibility of favorable action beyond that which has already been taken.

As I have a temperamental aversion to embarking under a full head of sail for nowhere, will you let me have the benefit of your clear counsel?   Cordially always   Colby

TLS (WP, DLC).
   [1] Bolling returned all the enclosures mentioned in this letter. They are missing in the B. Colby Papers, DLC.

To Cordell Hull

My dear Mr. Chairman,   Washington D C 12th September 1922

I see by my Baltimore paper this morning that the Democrats of Maryland have nominated William Cabell Bruce[1] for the Senate, and I deem it my conscientious duty to write you a line of respectful warning (respectful to you—not to him) about him. I have known him since he was a young man and feel it my duty to say that it would not be wise to admit him in any way to intimate party counsel. He is incapable of loyalty in any manner which he does not think likely to directly advance his own personal interests. He is by nature envious and intensely jealous, and cannot take part in disinterested service of any kind.

But counsel with Maryland advisors will no doubt have sufficiently acquainted you already with the character of the man, and my impression of him may be entirely unnecessary in the formation of your judgment. My thought was simply that in the campaign of this year, and the campaign of '24, it would be very dangerous to entrust him with any function which might affect the result.

But I must not grow prolix, and have written only because I was afraid to run any risk of your being uninformed with regard to the real character of this man.

With deep appreciation of your constant thought of me, and the hope that I may be of assistance to you in every possible way,

With cordial regard,

Faithfully Yours,   Woodrow Wilson

TLS (C. Hull Papers, DLC).

[1] Bruce had been Wilson's debating opponent at the University of Virginia (see the index references to him in Vol. 1). Bruce defeated incumbent Senator Joseph Irwin France in the general election held on November 7.

This letter, better than any other in this volume, illustrates the state of Wilson's mind when commenting on persons he did not for some reason like. Wilson had been very wounded and offended when the judges at the annual debate of the Jefferson Society at the University of Virginia in 1880 had given a slight edge to Bruce. Since that time, to our knowledge, he had neither seen nor written to Bruce, in fact had rarely thought of him until he ran for the Senate.

Bruce, meantime, had had a distinguished career as a lawyer in Baltimore and a reform Democrat in Maryland and Baltimore politics. He had supported Wilson's candidacy for the Democratic presidential nomination in 1912 and was a strong supporter of American entry into the League of Nations. During his single term in the Senate, he opposed prohibition and was an outspoken foe of the Ku Klux Klan, of lynching, and of bigotry of all kinds. James B. Crooks, "William Cabell Bruce," *Dictionary of American Biography*, Supp. Four (New York, 1974), pp. 116-17.

Bruce had a sentence in his entry in *Who's Who in America* during this period about his besting of Wilson at the University of Virginia, but it does not seem likely that Wilson ever read it.

To Bainbridge Colby

My dear Colby: Washington D C 13th September 1922

Thank you for your letter of September eleventh and its enclosures, which I have read. My first comment is that the socalled "Conference of Ambassadors" is in my judgment an entirely irregular body[1] with only the powers of conversation and of persuading the several Governments they represent to adopt their opinions.

I suggest that the best course for us to pursue is for you to proceed to Geneva; there consult with Sir Eric Drummond and anyone else it may seem wise to talk with as to the best way in which we can assist the Ukrainians to obtain what they desire; and then to work out the most effective course of persuasive action feasible in the circumstances. Inasmuch as we no longer have any official authority, the best we can do is to feel our way to the discovery of channels of influence, and I feel some confidence that by frank conference with Drummond and Cecil you can get an opportunity to present the Ukrainian case to the Council. At any rate I think this ought to be attempted and that the way I have suggested is perhaps the most promising way.

I am sorry to give counsel which, if followed, will take you out of the country at an early date, but I am anxious to have the men on the other side of the water realize that they cannot deal with the legitimate claims of the small nacent nations negligently or indifferently, and that such peoples have friends who will make their voices heard throughout the world when necessary. We must make the authorities of the League very uncomfortable until they do the right thing and give the socalled "Conference of Ambassadors" the impression that we do not regard them as anybody in particular. Things will have come to a pretty pass if European statesmen are to be given the impression that George Harvey represents the opinions of upright and thoughtful Americans.[2]

I hope that you can read this advice more clearly than I have written it, and that it will conform with the thoughts you yourself have on the subject by this time.

With affectionate regard,

Faithfully Yours,   Woodrow Wilson

TLS (B. Colby Papers, DLC).
   [1] Legally, the Conference of Ambassadors (known also as the Committee of Ambassadors and the Council of the Heads of Delegations when the heads of government were present) was the successor to the Council of Four, which of course ceased to exist once Wilson left Paris on June 28, 1919. Wilson and the State Department participated in the conference through Ambassador Hugh Campbell Wallace until Wilson broke relations with it after the Senate's defeat of the Versailles Treaty on March 19, 1920. However, the Conference of Ambassadors (or the group called Heads of Government) continued to function as the body responsible for the execution of the various peace treaties.
   [2] George B. M. Harvey, United States Ambassador to the Court of St. James's, was not a member of the Conference of Ambassadors.

From Newton Diehl Baker

My dear Mr President—:   Cleveland September 13, 1922

If I have any grief about the article in the Encyclopaedia Britannica it is in the chance it gives your partisan enemies to question your wisdom in entrusting me with your confidence and with responsibilities of such tragic might and importance. The facts recited in the article are, with singular consistency, exact opposites of the facts shown by official data and records on the several subjects. Upon the opinions expressed by the writer of the article I am prejudiced and disqualified, but I am receiving letters from every corner of the country which are very generous and gracious in their reassurance, and I would be glad to have you know that Pershing, Scott, Bliss, Graves[1] and a host of others, military and civil, say that they felt the War Department a firm support in the work they had to do.

After all it is a mere personal incident which will soon be forgotten both ways and ought in all conscience to make way for the vital things which are not personal but involve the peace of the world and the happiness of mankind. If I can but have some hope of renewed discussion of that sort of thing I shall not stop to grieve over what may be said about me personally by men who did not see and cannot know. At any rate I shall not grieve while I still have your confidence and you can still express so generous a judgment as you have in your letter of yesterday. Mrs Baker joins me in sending deep and respectful regards to you and Mrs Wilson

Gratefully yours,   Newton D. Baker

ALS (WP, DLC).
  [1] That is, Gen. William S. Graves.

To Charles H. Leichliter[1]

My dear Mr. Leichliter,   [Washington] 15th September 1922

I do not regard your letter of September twelfth as presumptuous in any respect.[2] The question you discuss in it is of very high importance.

My own opinion is that a newspaper published here which was not a party organ but an organ of principle and truth would be of very great value, and my suggestion is that you draw together somewhere a small group of men, who you know to be devoted to the same ideals, to discuss the enterprise in all its aspects. Among others the following occur to me:

B. M. Baruch, 598 Madison Ave., New York City.
Cleveland H. Dodge, 99 John Street, New York City.
Robert Bridges, c/o Scribner's Magazine, New York City.
Norman H. Davis, 14 Wall Street, New York City.
Joseph P. Tumulty, Southern Bldg., Washington, D. C.
Such a group could of course widen itself by adding others.
I am very much interested in the idea, and you and your associ-

ates would of course be welcome to any advice I might be able to give from time to time.

With cordial interest in your high purposes,

Sincerely Yours,   [Woodrow Wilson]

CCL (WP, DLC).
    [1] A journalist of Chicago.
    [2] C. H. Leichliter to WW, Sept. 12, 1922, TLS (WP, DLC). Leichliter informed Wilson that Richard Linthicum, head of the Publicity Bureau of the Democratic National Committee, and others had suggested that he (Leichliter) establish in Washington a "Weekly Democratic newspaper." He wanted the publication to be "Democratic in plan and purpose" but did not want it to be financed by any single wealthy politician or clique, or even by the Democratic National Committee. He estimated that he personally could contribute about $25,000 toward the establishment of the paper; enough, he thought to carry it until it had "demonstrated its possibilities" and consequently could attract other financing. He asked Wilson to advise him on the proposal.

To John Hessin Clarke

My dear Friend,   Washington D C 21th [21st] September 1922

Your letter from Atlantic City has done a great deal to relieving [relieve] the sickness of heart which I felt at your retirement from the bench.

Your plans and hopes for the future are those of a genuine patriot and of a man who sees the real needs of the nation and of the world. May God speed you in their realization.

You will be amazed when I tell you that your letter brings me the first news I have had of the death of your two sisters. I am sure you will not think that my sympathy is any less deep or sincere because I have been so long delayed in expressing it.

I hope and believe that in the new work you have projected for yourself you will find a source of very great consolation and inspiration.

With warmest regard,

Your Sincere Friend,   Woodrow Wilson

TLS (J. H. Clarke Papers, OClW-Ar).

To Francis Xavier Dercum

My dear Dr. Dercum: Washington D C 21st September 1922

It distressed me yesterday to be obliged to say that I could not speak by radio, and I am writing to ask if you will not—when the Pasteur dinner is tolerably near at hand—write me a letter expressing your desire that I should speak at the dinner, and allow me to write a reply which can be read at the dinner if you choose. I should like to have an opportunity to pay my (ignorant) tribute to Pasteur, and I should particularly like to please you if such a correspondence will please you.

It was a great pleasure to see you yesterday, and I was truly grateful to you for the visit. It has done me good.

With affectionate regard,

Faithfully Yours,   Woodrow Wilson

TLS (received from Steven Lomazow).

From John Hessin Clarke

My dear Friend: Youngstown, Ohio, September 21, 1922.

I thank you sincerely for your kind expression of sympathy for me in the loss of my sisters. My younger sister, the last to die, was an extraordinary woman. After thirty years of the practice of medicine she retired, but instead of letting the years wear her out, she increased, if possible, her interest in the public library, of which she was president for twenty-one years, and in charities, which her medical training and experience enabled her to serve as others could not. It was, and still is, a great comfort to me to have all that is best in this little city agree that, from a community point of view, she was the most useful woman of her generation to Youngstown.

I thank you also for your approval of the use I propose making of what may remain to me of health and strength. It will interest you to know that many letters—as many from Republicans as from Democrats—welcome my coming to the ranks of the League advocates as likely to promote a renewed interest in "The Great Cause."

I hope you will approve my disposition, as it will be published soon, to try and bring about some sort of a program of cooperation, on an independent basis, between the endowed peace organizations of our country and the churches, schools and women's clubs favorable to the League. Governor Cox very certainly will do all within his power within the party lines, and I am convinced the most useful services I can render will be in trying to find some common ground of union for other than active partisan believers in the cause. I am wondering if in your large acquaintance you may have chanced upon a man who impresses you as fitted to take charge of the details of organization, if a program can be agreed upon.

Of course, my dear friend, yours will be the controlling voice and spirit in this great movement, always, and I shall hope to have the benefit of your counsel in everything that I may do with respect to it. I am enlisted for the war. Even though I shall fail utterly, I shall be happier for having done what I could.

Please remember me very cordially to Mrs. Wilson, and believe me always   Sincerely your friend   John H. Clarke

TLS (WP, DLC).

To John Hessin Clarke

My dear Friend,   Washington D C 23rd September 1922

I am greatly interested in your projected effort to bring about cooperation between the various organizations that are striving, or ought to be striving, for organized peace; and in reply to your question as to a man who could superintend the coordination let me say I think you could find no better adviser than George Creel (No. 104 East 39th Street, New York City). At any rate I suggest that you get hold of him and have a talk with him which will enable you to see whether your minds can pull in harness together in this great matter.

I need not say that I shall be happy at any time to cooperate (or advise if you wish) in any way or degree that may be within my power.

Mrs. Wilson joins me in most cordial regards and I am always, my dear Clarke,

With affectionate regard,
                    Your Sincere Friend,   Woodrow Wilson

TLS (J. H. Clarke Papers, OClW-Ar).

From Bainbridge Colby

My dear Mr President: New York City September 23, 1922

That was a splendid letter of yours, giving me your opinion as to procedure in the Ukrainian matter,—wise and practical and incidentally of immeasurable value to our clients. I was struck particularly by your phrase, "The best we can do is to feel our way to the discovery of channels of influence, etc." This is a precise statement of our professional duty to the Committee of the Provisional Government.

You may have noticed in the newspapers a despatch to the effect that the Canadian representatives at the meeting of the League Assembly last week for the second time brought up the question of determining the status of Eastern Galicia, and on their motion a resolution was adopted by the Assembly reiterating its request of a year ago that proper action be taken by the Principal Allied and Associated Powers. This is undoubtedly the result of our cablegrams to Sir Eric Drummond and to Lord Robert Cecil. The latter evidently took the matter up promptly and effectively with the Canadian representatives, with the result stated.

This is all that could be done at the present time with the Assembly of the League, and the next step is to bring the matter as forcibly as possible to the attention of the representatives of the Principal Allied Powers.

I have been in active cable communication with Mr Boyer in London this week, and a cable received from Mr Boyer this morning requests me to come to London within a few days, stating that he thinks the situation there is favorable for the presentation of our appeal. I think I will not sail until there is some indication that the crisis in the Near East[1] has been solved or is on the way to solution, because I can readily imagine, and in fact I am confirmed in this by cablegrams received, that British official attention is very much preoccupied at the moment with the situation in the Near East.

What a situation that is, and how clearly foreseen by you. And what a majestic vindication, my dear Mr President, you are receiving from the procession of events.

I was talking to Frank Cobb the other day and he said the only thing left in this country, and in fact the only thing left in the world today, is Wilsonism. He was discussing the record of the Congress just closed and remarking the utter disappearance from our public life of conscience, courage and intelligence. I entirely agreed with him. The meeting was unanimous. And now comes the collapse of all the old conjuror's tricks of the European Foreign Offices, with a serious war not only threatened but in progress.

I feel that great things are coming to pass, and I just want you to know that your men are thinking of you with a thrilling sense of the immeasurable significance of your work in the world.

With affectionate regard,

Sincerely always   Bainbridge Colby

TLS (WP, DLC).
[1] Turkish forces under the command of Mustapha Kemal had routed the Greek army in Asia Minor in early September and had seized Smyrna on September 9. The Turkish army continued its advance, and by September 23 appeared to be about to attack British forces occupying a neutral zone near the town of Chanak on the Asiatic side of the Dardanelles. Although France and most of the British dominions refused to support him, Lloyd George was determined to risk even war with Turkey in order to defend the Dardanelles and Constantinople. The British cabinet, on September 29, sent a telegram to Lt. Gen. Sir Charles Harington, the British commander in the neutral zone, instructing him to give the Turkish army an ultimatum to withdraw. Harington chose to delay

doing so pending a meeting between British, French, and Turkish emissaries at Mudania, which began on October 3. This meeting resulted in a convention signed at Mudania on October 11, by which, among other terms, the Turkish forces agreed to respect the neutral zone. Lloyd George's precipitate handling of this crisis was the proximate cause of the downfall of his coalition government. He resigned on October 19. See Briton Cooper Busch, *Mudros to Lausanne: Britain's Frontier in West Asia, 1918-1923* (Albany, N. Y., 1976), pp. 340-58, and Peter Rowland, *Lloyd George* (London, 1975), pp. 579-84.

To Bainbridge Colby

My dear Colby,   [Washington] 25th September 1922

With the utmost respect I differ with you on the question as to the time you ought to sail. The socalled "Principal Allied and Associated Powers" are not going to come to any real agreement as to this Eastern matter, and if you wait until they have patched up some sort of compromise you will find them in so ill a humor with each other and themselves that they will not be in a condition of mind to listen to liberal and rational views with regard to any question which they can find an excuse for postponing or dodging, whereas now they may be relieved to find some pending question which they can settle honourably and on principle. I think that this is the psychology of the moment, and that the sooner you invite them into another atmosphere the better the prospect of success.

Thank you will all my heart for your generous views about my own past policy and my former judgment upon matters still unsettled and vexatious.

I need not tell you that my heart goes with you on your great errand, and that I am heartened to think of being myself even indirectly engaged in such business.

Please give my affectionate regards to Lord Robert when you see him and tell him it makes my very happy to think of our old association.

God speed you and bring you safely and successfully through.

Mrs. Wilson joins me as always in messages of warmest regard to Mrs. Colby and your daughters.

With affectionate regard,

Faithfully Yours,   [Woodrow Wilson]

CCL (WP, DLC).

To Claude Augustus Swanson

My dear Senator,   [Washington] 25th September 1922

It was exceedingly good of you to bring the bottle of whiskey which Mrs. Wilson received from you last night. I was mighty sorry that I was not up to "company" when you came. The routine of convalescence which I maintain is decidedly one of undress and I stick to it only because I am improving and do not wish to check the improvement. But I know I need not explain; I can count upon you to understand.

It gave me the greatest satisfaction that your primary test went so happily in Virginia,[1] and I shall look forward with the greatest satisfaction to our keeping up the habit of intercourse and consultation which I have hitherto enjoyed and profited by.

Thank you again for the whiskey; I really need it now and it is only the kindness of friends like yourself that enables me to get it.

I understand that you are going down into the Ninth District of Virginia to campaign. I wish you the utmost success. That District ought certainly to be reclaimed and this seems a favourable opportunity to reclaim it.[2]

As ever,
With warm regard,
                    Faithfully Yours,   [Woodrow Wilson]

CCL (WP, DLC).
    [1] Swanson had easily defeated former Governor Westmoreland Davis in the Democratic senatorial primary election held on August 1.
    [2] Campbell Bascom Slemp, a Republican, had been the representative from the ninth district of Virginia since 1907. He declined to run again in 1922. George Campbell Peery, a Democrat, defeated John H. Hassinger, Republican, in the general election.

From John Hessin Clarke

My dear Friend: Youngstown, Ohio September 25, 1922.

I thank you cordially for your good note of September 23rd, and for the suggestion as to Mr. Creel. I intend to go East to meet friends of the "Great Cause" as soon as I can possibly arrange to do so, and you may be sure that I will talk with Mr. Creel.

It will interest you to know that my statement to the public is bringing me so many letters, from all parts of the country, that I am encouraged to believe that it will be possible to accomplish more promptly than I had thought, something really substantial.

It grows increasingly clear to me that success, in time to be of value to the country, must be accomplished through an independent rather than a partisan movement. Of course I realize fully how difficult it is to persuade important men to act independently of their party organizations, but the feeling on this subject is very deep and if we can develop a cooperation, on a definite program, on the part of churches, women's clubs and schools and colleges— these with the great newspapers which are enthusiastic in its support, should be sufficient to produce the desired impression upon the country.

Ah, my dear friend, if you were only strong enough to take active lead, all would soon be well.

Later on, when I can determine whether anything substantial is to come out of it all, I shall be eager to accept your suggestion of a conference, but until I can be sure that the prospects are sufficiently encouraging, I will not permit myself to disturb you.

Hoping that you may soon be restored to health and strength, and that you will remember me cordially to Mrs. Wilson, I am

Sincerely your friend,   John H. Clarke

TLS (WP, DLC).

John Randolph Bolling to John Hessin Clarke

My dear Mr. Clarke: [Washington] 27th September 1922

Mr. Wilson asks me to thank you very warmly for your letter of September twenty-fifth, and say he is most happy to note the encouragement which you are receiving in the materialization of your plans.

May I be permitted to say that your letters give Mr. Wilson the greatest pleasure, and that I feel confident it will really be of great benefit to him if you can find the time to keep him fully posted as to your progress.

Cordially yours,   [John Randolph Bolling]

CCL (WP, DLC).

To John William Frazer[1]

My dear Mr. Frazer,   [Washington] 28th September 1922

I very much value your letter of September twenty-fifth.[2] Undoubtedly it is the opportunity and duty of the clergymen of the United States to preach in favour of America in the League. To tell the truth, I was amazed at the moral failure of the church in this regard when the question was definitely before the public, and I have felt with no little sadness the church failed in a great duty.

No more definite service could be rendered the nation than to lead it back to the path of duty in this great matter upon which the happiness of mankind so directly depends.

It happens that a valued friend of mine, Honorable John H. Clarke, is about to make an effort to stimulate the very sort of effort which you yourself suggest, and I respectfully hope that you will put yourself in correspondence with him on the subject. His address is No. 746 Bryson Street, Youngstown, Ohio.

It heartens me that you should have thought of this supremely useful service, and I hope with all my heart that you may both succeed in it yourself and draw the other ministers of the country into a like patriotic service. I believe that it would clarify and purify the whole atmosphere of public discussion, and I devoutly wish you Godspeed.

Cordially and Faithfully Yours,   [Woodrow Wilson]

CCL (WP, DLC).
¹ Pastor of the First Methodist Episcopal Church, South, of Pensacola, Fla.
² J. W. Frazer to WW, Sept. 25, 1922, TCL (WP, DLC).

From William Gibbs McAdoo

Dear Governor: Los Angeles, Cal. Sept. 28, 1922

I have just returned from a most interesting and somewhat thrilling trip in Idaho where we floated on a raft down the Snake River for a hundred miles, shooting all kinds of rapids and catching trout on the way, but I did not catch a seventeen-pound rainbow trout, as some foolish reporter telegraphed to the newspapers! That reporter was certainly "some liar" or he could not have told such a whopper of a fish story! We camped on the shore each night, hunting for small game, and, while the trip was a very crude and rough one, and the work was hard, we had a most enjoyable time.

We had a moving picture man with us on a part of the trip, and I hope to send you later an interesting film which you can put on your machine and get a very excellent idea of the adventure. I am also going to have a moving picture made of Nell and the children at our new house, as soon as the children get back from Santa Barbara, which will be within the next ten days, and I shall send you one so that you can see how your daughter and granddaughters look at this time. You never saw more lovely or beautiful children. They are most interesting, and both Nell and I regret that we are not near enough to you so that you could enjoy at least an occasional visit from them.

We are delighted to hear that you are getting better, even though you say you are progressing only at a snail's pace. As you say, this is better than making no progress at all. Nell had a letter recently from Edith and was made very happy by the encouraging news she gave of your progress.

On my return I find myself swamped with urgent appeals from sixteen states west of the Mississippi River for speeches in behalf of Democratic candidates. In ten of these states senators are to be elected, and our chance of success is excellent in all of them with the possible exception of California.[1] We have a hot and close fight everywhere. Our most formidable dangers are Republican money and organization. I am told that, if I will speak in these various states, I can, in some instances at least, practically assure Democratic success. I do not attach this much importance to it, but this is the way the case is put to me. I should like immensely to avoid making political speeches this year because of the fatigue and inconveniences one must endure on a hard and long trip of this character, but my friends will say that I am a shirker if I don't do it. Democrats throughout this section of the country are already saying that Democratic leaders are making no affirmative effort, whereas the Republicans are sending out their very best speakers and spending money prodigally to retain control of the Congress.

It is, in my opinion, most important to gain control of the Congress in November. It will strengthen the Democratic position in every way if we can succeed in doing this. It is absolutely necessary to hold not only the seats we now have in the Senate, but to gain a number of new ones in November, if we are to stand any chance of capturing the Senate in 1924. Again, it is conceivable that the next Presidential election may be thrown into the House. There is every prospect now that a new Party will be organized and that it will secure the electoral vote of some of the middle western states,[2] in which event no one of the candidates may have a majority in the electoral college. In the House of Representatives, the vote will have to be by states, so that Nevada, Wyoming and New Mexico, for instance, each of which have but one Congressman, will be as potential in the selection of a President as New York or any other highly populous state. We ought, therefore, to concentrate our efforts on gaining not only a majority of the House at this time, but also a majority of the states represented in the House.

Among the states the Democrats have asked me to speak in is

[1] Hiram Warren Johnson was overwhelmingly re-elected in California.
[2] For a discussion of this situation, caused primarily by the emergence of Farmer-Labor parties in the upper Middle West and the Plains states, see Theodore Saloutos and John D. Hicks, *Agricultural Discontent in the Middle West, 1900-1939* (Madison, Wisc., 1951), pp. 342-50.

Missouri. Of course they want me to speak for the ticket *generally*, and, in that case, I should be obliged to advocate the election of the state officers as well as the candidates for Congress and the Democratic nominee for the Senate—Reed. If I speak in the states west of the Mississippi River only, my itinerary will inevitably carry me across the State of Missouri, and it will be very difficult for me to avoid making a speech there. I need not tell you of the embarrassment this invitation causes me, and yet I do feel that it is of the highest importance to prevent the Republicans from carrying Missouri again this year, because it will almost certainly make Missouri a Republican state in 1924. I should discuss national issues largely, reaffirm my belief in the League of Nations, and say that, while I do not at all agree with Senator Reed's position about this matter, nevertheless, as he is the nominee of the Party, he ought to be supported, along with the rest of the ticket.

This, in substance, is what I should have to say if I went into the State at all. Will you not kindly write me candidly what you think about it, as I should be glad to have the benefit of your views. In no event would I be willing to do anything that would embarrass you. Every inclination of mine is to stay out of Missouri.

Isn't it the very irony of fate that the Harding administration has been obliged to say that it is concerned in the Turkish situation and is disposed to take a hand in the solution of the Turkish problem? The papers out here state that we are rushing warships to Turkey.[3] I am quite sure that, if your plans for the League of Nations had not been thwarted by the Republicans, the present crisis in Turkey would have been prevented. I find that belief to be receiving rather general acceptance among those with whom I have talked. Even Oscar Straus admits it in an interview just published in the Scripps papers. No administration in our history has been so weak and vacillating, nor so hypocritical and incompetent, nor so subservient to special interests, as the present one. It is entangling us more in European and Oriental affairs by its policies than we ever could have been through membership in the League of Nations. The thirty-one gentlemen—"eminent Republicans"—who

[3] The administration had ordered several destroyers from Constantinople to Smyrna in early September to protect American lives and property. The White House announced on September 19 that in no circumstances would the United States intervene militarily in the Greco-Turkish conflict. The American warships presently in the area, it continued, were there solely to defend American lives and property. Edwin Denby, the Secretary of the Navy, revealed on September 27 that twelve destroyers would be rushed from Norfolk to Constantinople to reinforce the naval force under the command of Rear Adm. Mark L. Bristol, the American High Commissioner at Constantinople. The objective of the augmented force, Denby reiterated, would be to "protect American interests." *New York Times*, Sept. 7, 20, and 28, 1922.

advised the American people to vote for Harding as the best means of getting into the League,[4] ought to feel like convicted criminals now.

I agree with you fully about the damn-fool injunction granted by Judge Wilkerson upon the application of the Attorney General. There is a great revulsion of feeling against the Federal courts among the great masses of our fellow-countrymen, who believe that the Federal courts, including the Supreme Court, have become the very citadels of vested and predatory interests and that human rights are of second importance if they are considered at all. If the prosecution of William Allen White by the State of Kansas,[5] and the injunction granted by Judge Wilkerson in Chicago are sustained by the higher courts, I cannot see that anything is left of the Bill of Rights in the Federal Constitution. A very dangerous situation is being created by these decisions, and by the avowed policy of the administration to destroy the unions in spite of the Clayton Act and all of the enlightened legislation for which you were responsible during your administration. I have never seen such bitter feeling among the laboring classes and the farmers as that now existing. It is a fruitful field for any kind of radical propaganda.

It is quite clear that Henry Ford is going to be a candidate in 1924 for the Presidency. He has a strong hold upon the radical labor and farmer element, and if he should enter the primaries in the various states, running on both Democratic and Republican tickets, where that is permissible, he will demoralize both parties to a very great extent. I doubt if he could capture either the Republican or Democratic nomination, although I am not sure, since he has an extraordinary organization through his agencies in every town and city of consequence in the United States, has unlimited

[4] About the thirty-one Republicans and their statement during the campaign of 1920, see JPT to WW, Oct. 19, 1920 (first letter of that date), n. 2, Vol. 66.

[5] White had supported the nationwide strike of the railroad shopworkers. However, his old friend and political ally, Henry Justin Allen, at this time Governor of Kansas, had invoked the terms of a state law to prohibit the strikers from picketing within the state. The unionists resorted to the posting of placards in support of their strike. The Kansas Attorney General, Richard Joseph Hopkins, then ruled that the placards represented another form of picketing, and Governor Allen ordered them removed. White denounced this as a violation of freedom of speech and, about July 19, placed one of the posters in a window of the office of the *Emporia Gazette*. Allen most reluctantly had White arrested on July 22. This gave White the occasion to write one of his most famous editorials, "To an Anxious Friend," published in the *Emporia Gazette* on July 27, which became a classic defense of freedom of speech and the press. The case and White's editorial attracted nationwide attention, and White received offers of assistance from such well-known lawyers as Felix Frankfurter, William E. Borah, Albert J. Beveridge, and McAdoo himself. As it turned out, much to White's chagrin, the case never came to trial. It was dismissed on December 8, 1922, at the behest of Hopkins, who had opposed White's arrest. Walter Johnson, *William Allen White's America* (New York, 1947), pp. 361-69.

means at his disposal, is an extraordinary advertiser and is circulating his personal organ, "The Dearborn Independent," throughout the country regardless of cost. The present tendencies inevitably indicate, I think, the formation of a third Party in 1924, and Ford might become its candidate, if he cannot get either of the old line nominations. I am informed by people who know that this is a well-laid plan and that it is being quietly and effectively prosecuted throughout the country. Ford is an excellent manufacturer, but I cannot take him seriously as a statesman or as President of the United States. The enclosed clipping from this morning's Los Angeles Times about Ford is quite significant.

I see also that Pomerene is being played up as a candidate in 1924 if he is reelected. If the Democrats should nominate such a reactionary, the future of the Party would be hopeless.

I have been taking very little hand in the political situation—in fact, my disinclination to get back into public life is so great that I cannot get up any enthusiasm about politics except to the extent that I can help the cause of liberal democracy. I would make any sacrifice in that direction, when I would not do anything for myself.

Dixon Williams[6] is here and begs me to send you his warmest regards.

Nell joins me, as always, in devoted love to you and Edith.

W G McAdoo

TLS (WP, DLC).
  [6] Dixon C. Williams, president of the Chicago Nipple Manufacturing Co. and long active in Democratic party politics. See the index references to him in Vols. 36, 38, and 47.

From Jessie Woodrow Wilson Sayre

Darling, darling Father,　　　　　[Cambridge, Mass.] Sept. 29, 1922

Your dear letter and telegram reached us when we were away on a little camping trip up into the Vermont Hills that we love so much.

Thank you so, so much, dearest Father. It is so wonderful to be remembered and I feel your love always around us. Our hearts are always pouring love in your direction, we think of you constantly and are with you in spirit all the time.

Our camping trip was a great success. Frank was very tired and seedy after working all summer on his case book,[1] even sleeping badly and dreaming nightmares—and the out of door life was just what he needed with a complete change of scene and thought. We took a little Ford and wandered along whither we would, sampling lakes and streams and "spring pastures" for camping spots. Then we made a sudden dash for Montreal and Quebec, where I had never been, and that was great fun for Quebec gives you the feeling that you have been in a foreign land more than any place on this side of the ocean, except Bermuda, that I know of.

We got home just in time to pack up and come up here. I started this down in Vineyard Haven but the processes of packing, house cleaning unpacking and settling in up here proved too absorbing to allow of finishing it. But now we are pretty much in order for the long stretch of winter ahead. School outfits, and so forth, are still to be secured but they are more or less routine things and not *extra*, like house-cleaning.

Eleanor's school has opened and Francis' begins on Tuesday. In the meantime he wavers between dread and dislike of changing and a feeling of superiority over having an extra week of holiday. We are hoping that the school will give him the fresh air he needs. After the summer of out of doors he is a perfect joy, so well and vigorous and reasonable and after the winter of indoors he gets so high strung and excitable and sleeps so poorly that we feel we must try a fresh air school for him.

Eleanor is in fine form, so lovable and generous and sweet that she is a joy every minute of the day. The minute she came home all the little satellites in the neighborhood were appearing to ask her to play with them. All the *little* children, two and three, etc., prefer Francis. He seems to them such a big boy and yet is so gentle with them.

Eleanor and Francis and Woodrow all send love to dear grandfather, and as for Frank and me, we just can't tell how much we love and adore you. With dearest love to Edith,

Ever your devoted little daughter   Jessie.

ALS (WC, NjP).
    [1] Francis Bowes Sayre, *A Selection of Cases and Other Authorities on Labor Law* (Cambridge, Mass., 1922).

Edith Bolling Galt Wilson to Ray Stannard Baker

[Washington] Oct. 1st 1922

Heartiest Congratulations and all happy wishes, my dear Mr. Baker, that your great task is done, and that the results will be more than equal to the conscientious labor and unselfish devotion it represents. As I told you—when you were last here—my only regret is that we will not see you so often I fear, but we are all touched by your glowing tribute to us, and I can only add that it has been the very happiest association, and proven a cement to a warm admiration and lasting friendship.

We will look for you soon, and I will prize more than I can say the "first book from the press."

Mr Wilson wants me to thank you for him for the splendid spirit that prompted, and carried on your work, and say he is profoundly touched by the way you are helping the world to a new height.

My brother joins in congratulatory and warmest assurances

Faithfully yours   Edith Bolling Wilson

ALS (R. S. Baker Papers, DLC).

To William Gibbs McAdoo

My dear Mac,   Washington D C 4th October 1922

I have just read your letter of September twenty-eighth and hasten to comply with your request for advice about going into Missouri. I am clear it would be a mistake to go. I do not agree with you in thinking that if Missouri goes Republican now it will necessarily go Republican in '24. Since it is well known that the Republicans nominated Reed his defeat, even by a Republican, would indicate a revival of conscience and good faith on the part of the average voters of the State and clear the air where it most needs to be cleared. It seems to me out of the question for anyone who cares for the standards of honour to aid even indirectly the return of Reed to the Senate. His bad character is known to the whole country now, and we have found out that he is not to be counted on as part of the Democratic majority in the Senate. I hope most sincerely that you will not compromise yourself by even seeming to lend him aid.

These are times of confused counsel when it is difficult to see just what ought to be done, but we know a bad man from a good one and no circumstances can justify the support of a bad egg.

I think that I take Henry Ford a little more seriously than you do as a public character, but I cannot share your apprehensions about his becoming a candidate for the Presidency. However nothing can confidently be predicted about '24 except an overthrow of the present incompetency,—when we shall see.

I am glad you are going to send me the films you speak of; I shall await them with impatience.

Things are going with us as usual; severe colds have for the present taken their grip upon us.

Edith unites with me in loving messages to you all. We are delighted that all the personal news about you, Nell and the children is so good. It gives our hearts great content.

Affectionately Yours,   Woodrow Wilson

TLS (W. G. McAdoo Papers, DLC).

From Bainbridge Colby

My Dear Mr President.   On Board S.S. *Majestic* Oct 7, 1922

At last I am off. Everything seemed to conspire to hold and delay me—a mortgage of $260,000 to replace, provision to be made for payments to be made in my absence, on a building operation that I am embarked on, for better or for worse—I wish I knew which—and countless other things, too wearisome to recall, much less to rehearse.

If I meet with any measure of success in this business I am starting upon, it will all be due to you,—to your high confidence in a good cause and a sound principle. I have a polite cable from Lord Robert Cecil, expressing anticipations of my coming etc.

My address will be the Ritz Hotel London, and I will keep you advised of any change.

Mrs Colby whom I have just bade good-bye to, asked me to include her warmest regards with mine to you and Mrs Wilson, and I hope, My Dear Mr President, to find you happy and thriving on my return, which will not be long delayed.

With affectionate regard   Colby

ALS (WP, DLC).

From Warren Gamaliel Harding

My Dear Mr. Wilson: The White House October 9, 1922

At the time Mrs. Harding's illness[1] gave us very great concern you and Mrs. Wilson were so thoughtful as to call and express your sympathetic interest and good wishes. Mrs. Harding, now slowly improving, has been informed of your thoughtfulness and asks me to include her grateful acknowledgment with my own.

Permit me to express the hope that your own health is mending encouragingly. After an opportunity of eighteen months in which to appraise the weight of burdens which I know to have been yours, there is a sincerity in that kindly wish which could be written by no one without personally knowing something of the task, no matter how it is met.   Sincerely   Warren G. Harding

ALS (WP, DLC).

¹ Florence Mabel Kling DeWolf Harding had been critically ill with hydronephritis and a kidney blockage in early September 1922. Dr. John Miller Turpin Finney of the Johns Hopkins Medical School and Dr. Charles Horace Mayo were called in on the case. By September 13, the crisis was past, and Dr. Mayo returned home to Minnesota. Murray, *The Harding Era*, pp. 418-19.

From William Gibbs McAdoo

Dear Governor,   Los Angeles, California Oct. 10. 1922

Many thanks for your letters and for your opinion—I shall keep out of Missouri. In fact I had decided on this course before your letter came and had rearranged my itinerary to avoid crossing the State. It was difficult but I have managed it. I agree fully with you about the necessity of preserving high standards. Unfortunately in Missouri—the Republican candidate[1] is, I am told, worse than Reed—violent anti-League and otherwise narrow and hard boiled. I always reach the conclusion now, in view of the events of 1920 & since, that any democrat almost is better than a hide-bound hard boiled republican—especially of the Lodge type. I hope Gaston[2] will beat him although he is by no means all that he should be. Am leaving on the 12th. I fear the pictures will have to await my return. I'm sorry.

Hope your colds are gone and that you are all well now. I have had a dreadful one and am just recovering. Too bad as it has sadly interfered with my preparation of my speeches for the trip. I shall have to "go it" on notes.

Nell & the babies are lovely and all wish we could see you & Edith. Devoted love from us to you both. In great haste and
                    Most affectionately   Mac

P.S. I have tried my best to keep out of this campaign but they will not let me escape. I go most reluctantly.

ALS (WP, DLC).

¹ Reginald R. Brewster, like Reed, a lawyer of Kansas City.
² That is, William Alexander Gaston.

To George Foster Peabody

My dear Friend,   Washington D C 11th October 1922

When you write and send me the little document you so generously promised yesterday, it would complete my obligation if you would accompany it with a statement of the reasons for it drawn out of your own observation and experience. What I myself see is this, that there is no use fighting the control of the money power unless we take out of the hands of those who wield it the chief instrument by which they work their will on the economic life of the nation, and if I were writing the reasons I am asking for I would point out with some particularity how the instrument is used. You can do that much better than I could, but you will not need any suggestion as to how the reasons can be made clear and convincing.

It was a great pleasure to see you and Miss Pardee[1] on yesterday. As I write, Mrs. Wilson is out in the motor taking Miss Pardee for a short drive about the city.

Hoping that our association in public affairs will be constant, and that the near future will afford us an opportunity to be of real service to the nation and the world,

With warm regard,   Faithfully Yours,   Woodrow Wilson

TLS (G. F. Peabody Papers, DLC).
[1] Allena Gilbert Pardee, who had been for many years a companion and household staff person for Kate Nichols Trask Peabody.

From Cordell Hull

My dear Mr. President: Washington, D. C. Oct. 12th, 1922.

This is to thank you in unmeasured terms for the fine party spirit which every citizen in America knows you possess in sending check for $200.00, as contribution to the Democratic National Committee.[1] I hope you will not think that I was soliciting a contribution from you in any sense in any reference made to our lack of funds in recent memorandum on election conditions which I sent you.

I am supplementing what I said in last memorandum[2] by calling attention to reports from New Jersey, which indicate a very hard fight between Edwards and Frelinghuysen.[3] The opinion is we have no real chance for Senator in New York,[4] but the situation is about 50-50 between Smith and Governor Miller. In Massachusetts the Democrats are putting up a real fight, notwithstanding the odds and the complicated conditions within the party. It is possible that they may make a better showing there than would naturally be expected in the circumstances.

It may appear a little strange also that I am able to say that all our correspondence up to this hour is uniformly optimistic.

Very sincerely,   Cordell Hull

TLS (WP, DLC).
[1] Hull was replying to WW to C. Hull, Oct. 10, 1922, TLS (C. Hull Papers, DLC).

² C. Hull to WW, Oct. 9, 1922, TLS (WP, DLC), in which Hull reported on Democratic prospects in the impending elections.
³ That is, Edward Irving Edwards and Joseph Sherman Frelinghuysen, who were
contesting the Senate seat currently held by the latter.
⁴ As will be seen, Hull was unduly pessimistic concerning this contest.

Schuyler Nielson Warren, Jr., to John Randolph Bolling

Dear Mr. Bolling: Baltusrol New Jersey October 12, 1922

I only arrived from Europe last week after having had a most interesting experience observing the League of Nations at Geneva. Mr. Holt and Mr. Marburg¹ were also there and together we met most of the important leaders, and have returned with some ideas for developing a campaign for the League. Mr. Holt and myself would very much like to see Mr. Wilson and I wonder whether the interview could be arranged for some day at the end of this month.

I hope that you have been well and that I shall have the pleasure of seeing you soon.

Sincerely Yours   Schuyler N. Warren Jr

ALS (WP, DLC).
¹ Theodore Marburg, civic leader and publicist of Baltimore, long active in the movement for international organization.

To Cordell Hull

My dear Mr. Chairman,   Washington D C 13th October 1922

Thank you very much for your gracious letter of October twelfth.

If it is true as "The Washington Post" said the other day (I always doubt anything I see in "The Post") that the women of the country are taking an active and unusual interest in the present campaign, surely that should be greatly to our advantage since our ideals are assuredly nearer their standard than are the ideals (if there are any such) of the Republicans. I shall be interested to learn whether you find that the women are rallying to our cause. I shall be very much disappointed in them if they do not and think that they have forgotten that they are chiefly indebted to me for the suffrage.

With warm regard and sincere felicitations on the character of the reports you are receiving,

Faithfully Yours,   Woodrow Wilson

TLS (C. Hull Papers, DLC).

John Randolph Bolling to Schuyler Nielson Warren, Jr.

Dear Mr. Warren: [Washington] 14th October 1922

Your very interesting letter of October twelfth came this morning, and I took the liberty of reading it to Mr. Wilson.

If you and Mr. Holt can be here at three thirty on the afternoon of Monday, October 30th, Mr. Wilson will be glad to see you for a few minutes. Please find out if this time is agreeable to Mr. Holt, and drop me a line about it, so I can arrange Mr. Wilson's other appointments accordingly.

Looking forward with much pleasure to seeing you both again so soon;   Cordially yours,   [John Randolph Bolling]

CCL (WP, DLC).

From Emily Jane Newell Blair

My dear Mr. President: Washington, D. C. October 17th, 1922.

The Chairman[1] has given me the privilege of reading your recent letter to him.

It encourages me to write you what I said to Mrs. Wilson at Mrs. Harriman's[2] one evening,—that it was because of the debt the American women owe you, not only for the suffrage but for the fight you made for ideals, that I undertook this work of organizing the Democratic women. And may I say to you that wherever we are able to state those ideals clearly to the American woman, she does respond. She fails to rally to our cause only where our candidates do not stand by those ideals.

In many states the Democratic women are working valiantly. In New York they have thrown themselves with vigor into "Al" Smith's fight. In Ohio, Indiana, Nebraska, New Mexico,—they are reported as working harder than the men. In Republican states like Pennsylvania and Iowa, they have an excellent working organization, while in so-called hopeless states like Minnesota they are working as hard for their principles as for a victory.

In some states we work against the handicap that the men do not appreciate the necessity of making an appeal to the women on principles, and attempt to gather in what I call the wife-vote, without making any effort to organize the women.

May I also call your attention to the valiant fight that little Mrs. Olesen[3] is making for the Democratic Party in Minnesota. She is speaking daily to thousands, and whatever the result of her personal fortunes in this campaign, she will have done a big piece of work for our party and brought back hundreds of the liberal-minded to its fold ready to join us in the 1924 campaign.

On the whole, however, I think I may report to you that the Democratic women are alive to their advantage over the Republican women and are carrying their message to the independent women with missionary zeal.

Sincerely,   Emily Newell Blair

TLS (WP, DLC).
  [1] That is, Cordell Hull.
  [2] That is, Florence Jaffray Hurst (Mrs. Jefferson Borden) Harriman.
  [3] Anna Dickie (Mrs. Peter) Olesen, member for Minnesota of the Democratic National Committee. She was the Democratic candidate for the Senate in Minnesota, running against Henrik Shipstead, the Farmer-Labor party candidate, and Frank B. Kellogg, the Republican incumbent. Shipstead won the election.

To Emily Jane Newell Blair

My dear Mrs. Blair,   Washington D C 18th October 1922

Thank you very warmly for your letter of October seventeenth. It gives me just the kind of information I desire, and what it says cheers me not a little.

If you have the opportunity, please convey my cordial greetings and best wishes to Mrs. Olesen.

You are doing fine work and the Party must assuredly recognize some day how much it is indebted to you for your self-sacrificing labours.

With admiration and warm regard,

Faithfully Yours,   Woodrow Wilson

TLS (received from Emily Forsythe Warren).

Schuyler Nielson Warren, Jr., to John Randolph Bolling

Dear Mr. Bolling: New York City. Oct. 22 1922

With reference to the appointment which Mr. Wilson was good enough to grant to me and Mr. Holt for Monday, October 30th; I am sorry to say that Mr. Holt is in the west and finds it will be impossible for him to get back much before November 20th.

Mr. Ex-Justice Clarke was here this past week, and I went over with him a plan which Mr. Holt, Mr. Charles Bauer[1] and I have worked out—respecting the consolidation of certain forces to forward the League of Nations movement. Mr. Clarke was very much impressed with the plan, and I am wondering if it would be agreeable to Mr. Wilson to let Mr. Bauer come to Washington with me, in place of Mr. Holt. Mr. Bauer is a man of about forty, an ardent Wilsonian, and heart and soul for the League of Nations. If Mr. Wilson prefers, however, to see Mr. Holt instead of Mr. Bauer, we

can of course wait; though we would like to set the plan in motion
as soon as possible. Mr. Bauer has a very easy and delightful manner, and I am sure would not tire Mr. Wilson.

I will be obliged if you will drop me a line to 12 West 53rd St.,
New York, and let me know Mr. Wilson's wishes—remembering
always that we do not want to do anything that will interfere with
his convenience.

Cordially yours,   Schuyler N. Warren, Jr.

TL (WP, DLC).
   [1] Charles Christian Bauer, an associate of Hamilton Holt, secretary of the Woodrow
Wilson Democracy.

John Randolph Bolling to Schuyler Nielson Warren, Jr.

Dear Mr. Warren: [Washington] Oct. 23 1922

I related to Mr. Wilson this morning the substance of our telephone talk of yesterday, and he wishes me to say that as he has
several provisional engagements for the end of this week and the
first of next, it would really suit him better to have you and Mr.
Holt come down later on.

While I have no idea, of course, what it is that you wish to discuss with Mr. Wilson—let me say that if the matter could be put
before him in a letter I believe it would be even more satisfactory
than a personal conference. This would also save considerable
time, as I understood you to say that Mr. Holt could not come down
until the end of November. I merely mention this plan, with the
idea of expediting matters.

With warm regard;
Cordially yours,   [John Randolph Bolling]

CCL (WP, DLC).

John Hessin Clarke to John Randolph Bolling

My dear Mr. Bolling—   Youngstown, Ohio October 23, 1922

I spent the whole of last week in New York and was almost constantly in conference with men deeply interested in cultivating a
public opinion favorable to our Government entering the League
of Nations. I find, as a result of my visit, that there is a distinct
difference of opinion as to the method most likely to prove successful in advancing "The Great Cause."

One group, which I think finds its chief advocate in Professor

Hudson of Harvard[1] who has greatly influenced Mr. Fosdick,[2] believes that we should organize an association similar to the League of Nations Union in England which should devote itself chiefly to informing the people as to the things which the League is actually accomplishing, and as to the manner in which it is operating. They feel that any emphasis laid upon the value of either the boycott or the reliance upon force of arms as sanction for the decisions of the League will lead us back into the party conflict of 1920, to a legalistic discussion of the terms of the Covenant with the result that the progress which they think is now being made, would cease and "The Cause" fail.

I said to them, frankly, that I did not share in such opinion as to policy and that if upon reflection I concluded it to be sound, I would take up a reservation which I have for a voyage around the world and would sail early in January.

There is another group, led, so far as I could make out, chiefly by Hamilton Holt and in a measure by Herbert Houston,[3] who share my point of view that it is worth while to attempt to secure an agreement upon amendments or modifications to the Covenant which would be satisfactory to us all, but that failing in this, we should inaugurate an aggressive movement in favor of our Government entering the League of Nations even though we can not formulate the terms of entry. It seemed to be the conviction of this group, and it is especially strong among leading women of New York, that I should attempt a re-statement of the case for the League fundamentally and in the light of what it has been doing, and that perhaps an organization approximating that which the other group favors might also be organized and be useful.

Dr. Faunce[4] of Brown University, after a conference with me, said that he would sound out the Thirty-One and see what their disposition would be toward joining in such action as I purposed, assuming that it could be kept entirely non-partisan.

It is interesting to know that a letter which I have from Ex-Senator Root comes pretty nearly agreeing with the approach plan I have indicated. I wrote to him not as one of the Thirty-One but as an influential member of the Carnegie Endowment organization. His letter is, as I expected it would be, non-committal, but he expresses a desire to meet me in conference in New York and it is plain enough that in his way he is anxious to see our Government

[1] Manley Ottmer Hudson, at this time Professor of Law at the Harvard University Law School.
[2] That is, Raymond Blaine Fosdick.
[3] That is, Herbert Sherman Houston.
[4] That is, William Herbert Perry Faunce.

enter the League. His notion, however, is that the approach must be first through the International Court.

It may be said as the result of my visit that even the small degree of confidence which I had in the possibility of securing union on a program of reservations is distinctly lessened. I fear it is not possible, although as a matter of fact, so far as I can learn the attempt to arrive at such an agreement has never gone beyond the talking stage—I mean no one has sat down with pen and paper and tried in large outline to express reservations which it was thought might satisfy all concerned.

I find that the party line of division continues distinctly clear. The Democrats with whom I talked are willing to go in on almost any terms and all the reports are that our country would be accepted on any terms we might state. But, the Republicans, naturally perhaps, are not disposed to do anything which could prove embarras[s]ing to the administration, and quite certainly there is sharp division in the councils at Washington, although it is now reported that Mr. Hoover says, rather vaguely, that he has changed his mind and thinks our country is better out of the League than in it. Hughes adheres to his theoretical friendliness to the League, but his recent letter to Hamilton Holt[5] shows that party considerations are dominating with him.

The effect of all these conferences on me personally is that I am all but convinced that it will not be possible to get more than a half dozen, if indeed that many, of the Thirty-One to agree upon any kind of a movement pressing the administration to adopt s [a] program for international action. On the other hand, I am clear that there is a great feeling among business men, especially since the Bankers' Convention, favorable to our joining the League on some terms.

The pastoral letter of the House of Bishops, which you sent me and which I have read with great interest, confirms what I had heard from laymen who attended the convention.

The statement in the morning papers that the Federated Council of Churches is inaugurating a referendum to determine whether concerted action shall be taken in urging the administration to formulate a Near East policy is especially interesting in view of what I learned, somewhat confidentially, last week, that the Church Peace Union with its large Carnegie endowment (I am not sure of the title) has agreed to the principle and referred it to a committee to formulate and circulate a declaration that it is the duty of the churches to press the administration to either enter the League on

5 See F. I. Cobb to WW, July 20, 1922, n. 1.

some terms or establish its equivalent. I was promised a copy of this resolution, but learned later that it had not yet been formulated. There can be no doubt that there is a great unrest among the church people of the country which has been stimulated by the recent Near East experiences.

I met several of the leading women of New York and they are enthusiastic for prompt and aggressive action. I have no doubt that an effective appeal can be made to them, and it is entirely possible that our chief reliance must ultimately be made upon the women to carry us into the League.

The cowardice of Democratic politicians, growing out of their fear of losing the Irish and German vote, is general, and unless a new spirit can be aroused, it will result in defeating any action until after the next war.

I declined all suggestion of a dinner to be given in my honor in New York at which I should make my principal speech in favor of the League of Nations, and at present my disposition is to make it in Cleveland about Christmas time, with perhaps discussion of particular phases of it in speeches to be made at bar dinners and perhaps one on Armistice Day.

I believe that after the election, the attention of the country can be arrested and a distinctly favorable movement inaugurated by a few speeches which it ought to be possible for us to procure to be made.

Unfortunately, everywhere I go, the disposition is to turn to me to lead "The Cause" and I feel such misgiving as to my capacity for such a task and as to my having health and strength to go through with it if I should attempt it, that I am almost dismayed.

My first conclusion holds that the feeling in favor of our joining the League is deep seated and widespread, and that it lacks only leadership and definiteness of program to become successful, but I must confess that as yet I do not see the leader and that the difficulty of uniting on a program is very great. I should greatly appreciate the opinion of Mr. Wilson as to what he thinks the most promising course of action would be.

I tried in every way to get into communication with George Creel, first through Mr. Fosdick who found that he was a member of the Players' Club, and then through the Club through which I learned his house number. Telephone Information said that he had a telephone, but that they were forbidden to give it to any person except on his order. Finally, as a last resort, I addressed a note to him at his residence address which was given me by the Players' Club. I sent the note on Thursday, asking him to get into communication with me by telephone, but no call came up to my leaving

Saturday night. It is possible that he was out of the city. At all events, I did everything I could to secure conference with him.

Hoping that I have stated sufficient of my experience to enable Mr. Wilson to give me the benefit of his views, I am

Sincerely yours, John H. Clarke

TLS (WP, DLC).

Schuyler Nielson Warren, Jr., to John Randolph Bolling

Dear Mr. Bolling: [New York] October 24, 1922

I quite understand regarding the interview on October 30, and hope that it may be possible for Mr. Holt and myself to see Mr. Wilson at the end of November.

This is what Mr. Holt wanted me to submit to Mr. Wilson namely that a national non-partisan organization be formed for the promotion of the entry by the United States into the Legue [League] of Nations at the earliest opportunity.

Ex Justice Clarke who has been in New York is willing to head it and Mr. Everett Colby of New Jersey[1] is willing as a Republican to back Mr. Clarke in every way. Mr. Colby wrote a stinging letter to Mr Wickersham[2] which was published in the press on his failure as one of the 31 Republicans to press the administration on its attitude towards the League. I will send you a copy of the letter tomorrow.

The movement would be sponsored by a committee of representative people and would by means of propaganda and education focus the issue before the country. Plans are now under way for the organization of the society which would resemble in some respects the League of Nations Union in England.

Mr. Holt thought that Mr. Wilson would be interested to know of this and will send him the definite program as soon as it is drawn up.

Thanking you again for the trouble which you have taken in the matter and with kind regards.

Sincerely yours   Schuyler N Warren Jr

ALS (WP, DLC).

[1] Lawyer of New York, progressive Republican leader of New Jersey (his state of residence), member for New Jersey of the Republican National Committee.

[2] George Woodward Wickersham, former Attorney General of the United States, 1909-1913, at this time member of the New York law firm of Cadwalader, Wickersham & Taft.

To Andrew Bonar Law

[Washington, Oct. 25, 1922]

Accept my congratulations.[1] Permit me to wish for the new cabinet success of the highest and noblest kind and to hope that it will give whole-hearted support to the League of Nations

Woodrow Wilson

WWhw telegram (WP, DLC).
[1] Bonar Law organized a new Conservative cabinet and formally took office as Prime Minister on October 23.

From Andrew Bonar Law

London Oct 25 22

Am deeply grateful for your congratulations and good wishes and hope that the new government during its term of office may be able to help forward work of the League of Nations

Prime Minister

T telegram (WP, DLC).

To Schuyler Nielson Warren, Jr.

My dear Mr. Warren, [Washington] 26th October 1922

Mr. Bolling has shown me your letter of October twenty-fourth and I am sorry to find that my judgment does not accord with that of men whom I so much honour and trust. The work of organizations in the field of politics proper is going to be so relatively important from now until the Presidential election two years hence that there would be serious danger that the organization of an independent body like that suggested (important and useful as such a body might prove) would be likely to divert energy which it would be more effective to devote to a great political achiev[e]ment which would win the country back to the mood and purpose which made us the leading nation of the world during the great war. As I view the political contests of the immediate future they will inevitably turn upon and determine the relation of the country to international affairs which unavoidably means the League of Nations.

I feel it my duty (though it is a very unpleasant one) to warn you and Mr. Holt to beware of Everett Colby. As a Jerseyman I am familiar with his career and am bound to pronounce him a fake. He always thunders in the index but fails in the performance.

With much regard and very great admiration for what you and Mr. Holt and Mr. Clarke are doing in a great cause,

Cordially and Faithfully Yours,   [Woodrow Wilson]

CCL (WP, DLC).

From Newton Diehl Baker

My dear Mr. President: Cleveland October 26, 1922.

I have seen only so much of Lane's letters as are quoted in the newspapers advertising the book,[1] but I have had several telegraphic requests for interviews and statements on the subject. I confess it has been difficult for me to keep quiet. So far as criticism of myself is concerned, I have long followed the practice of paying no attention to it, and where you are concerned I have felt that at least sometimes your friends made a mistake by permitting themselves to be drawn into controversies when the obvious answer to all criticism is to point to achievements quite without parallel in American history, and in some ways without parallel in human history anywhere. As you know, I was very deeply attached to Lane, yet I am obliged to say that the publication of these letters shocks me inexpressably. The gods who write history will forgive mistakes, but not disloyalty, and I find myself earnestly hoping that these letters when we see them all, will have less of that taint.

At the first cabinet meeting I attended after I became Secretary of War, I suggested for discussion an exceedingly confidential matter. When the cabinet meeting was over and the other members were leaving the room, you drew me into one of the windows and said kindly but earnestly: "Baker, whenever you have that kind of a matter, take it up with me personally; do not bring it up here for discussion." You then hesitated as though uncertain whether you should finish your thought, but finally added: "I regret to say that the matters discussed in cabinet meetings are not held confidentially." I was amazed, as it seemed to me that no obligation could be more sacred than the confidential character of cabinet discussions. Twice, later, I saw in newspapers in Washington, disclosures of things discussed in the cabinet, and realized that the disclosure must have been made by a member of the cabinet. On the first of these occasions I spoke to Burleson about it feeling that, as the latest addition to the cabinet, I might naturally be thought to be inexperienced and therefore indiscrete [indiscreet]. Burleson's comment was: "Hell, Baker, don't you bother about it. The Old Man knows who the leaks are." On the second occasion, since the matters about which the leak occurred affected the War Department, I wrote to you an earnest assurance that no thoughtlessness or indiscretion of mine was responsible. From these instances, and others, I came to realize that with the life of the nation in your hands and an international situation so infinitely delicate that an indiscretion might be a calamity, it was impossible for you to bring up for general disclosure and discussion, many things which under other conditions you might well have desired to try out with your confidential advisers, and I have a thousand times thought of the unutterable loneliness of the presidential responsibility when even the cabinet could not be trusted to be discrete and silent. Lane's letters as published are a clear instance. Apparently, he left the cabinet meetings and contemporaneously wrote letters to his brother and others, divulging discussions which had gone on there and trusting others to preserve a confidence which he himself was breaching.

I am sure you will understand that I am not judging Lane to have been consciously disloyal, but clearly he was not silent and safe in a situation where torture ought not to have been able to wring a syllable from him.

I have no sort of idea what the newspaper reaction of these letters is going to be. The first impression created will obviously be unfortunate, as serious men here have already commented to me upon the bad light in which they put Lane himself. The purpose of this letter, however, is to say to you that if you wish it now, or at any time, I will be very happy to write a statement and give it publicity on my own responsibility on this subject. I know, of course, that you will not, and should not, dignify these letters by any comment, and my only concern is lest my unwillingness to make you a subject of controversy should have the effect of creating an impression that others who were admitted to your confidence are in some part sharers in these critical opinions, and therefore hesitate to comment on them.

This letter, my dear Mr. President, needs no answer unless you would prefer to have me depart in this instance from the rule which I have set of refraining from participating in these absurd controversies. Of course, Lane's letters, and all other like tattlings and gossip by people who saw but did not understand, will not count the weight of the foot of a fly in the permanent estimate which will be made, and is in large part already made upon your services to mankind.

Affectionately yours,   Newton D. Baker

TLS (WP, DLC).
    [1] Anne Wintermute Lane and Louise Herrick Wall, eds., *The Letters of Franklin K. Lane* (Boston and New York, 1922).

To Lawrence Vest Stephens

My dear Governor Stephens,   [Washington] 27th October 1922

I am sincerely obliged to you for your letter of October twenty-first.[1] I know how entirely competent you are to assess the true situation in Missouri, and I value accordingly the carefully considered information conveyed in your letter.

I do not think that I ought to attempt any advice as to the election. I am too far away from what I may call the interior conditions of the situation. I feel, besides, that leaders like yourself can be confidently counted upon to guide the loyal Democrats of Missouri to the right course of action.

If Reed is returned to the Senate he will of course be there a man without a party, repudiated by Democrats and elected above their own man by Republican votes. I should think that the usual organization of the Senate would be rendered quite impossible.

With cordial greetings to all true Democrats who, like yourself, uphold the real interests and best ideals of the party and of mankind; and with sincere personal regard,

Faithfully Yours,   [Woodrow Wilson][2]

CCL (WP, DLC).

[1] L. V. Stephens to WW, Oct. 21, 1922, TLS (WP, DLC). He discussed the reasons for Reed's victory in the Missouri senatorial primary. Breckinridge Long, he said, had carried ninety of the 114 counties in the state. However, Reed had won Kansas City and St. Louis by a combined majority of 50,000 votes, made up, as Stephens put it, of "pro-Germans, life-long Republicans, and Wets." The anti-Reed Democrats, he declared, were now working to defeat Reed in the general election by supporting the Republican candidate, Reginald R. Brewster. But Reed would probably still get 50,000 Republican votes in St. Louis alone. Stephens concluded with the suggestion that a statement by Wilson, over his signature, opposing Reed's election would greatly assist the anti-Reed forces.

[2] This letter, along with an excerpt from Governor Stephen's letter, was printed, e.g., in the *New York Times*, Nov. 9, 1922.

To John Hessin Clarke

My dear Friend,   [Washington] 27th October 1922

Thank you for your letter of October twenty-third with its full expression of views and impressions.

I am taking the liberty of sending you copy of a letter I wrote the other day to Mr. Schuyler N. Warren, Jr. which will show you that I am wholly of your group in the difference of opinion of which you speak in the first part of your letter.

I am very happy to exchange views with you in the most candid fashion. In the first place I would not consent to any agreement or association with any of the discredited Thirty-One. They are not sincere and Dr. Faunce by the way,—as I found out when I was also a college president,—is a thick head. Believe me, no sort of influence can bring the present administration or its backers to do anything sincere or intelligent.

As for reservations, I am sure that none can be formulated and agreed upon which will not in effect alter the Covenant beyond recognition and amount to a nullification.

Personally I am clear as to the effective course of action: I believe that we should concentrate our influence upon active Democratic workers; make a distinct and aggressive declaration of purpose in favor of the League in the 1924 platform, and nominate a man whom the country will follow in retrieving the gross and criminal blunder of failing to ratify the Treaty of Versailles. I believe that all this can be done, and that because it is so worth doing we can do it with enthusiasm. I should have not the slightest misgiving as to the result, for you are undoubtedly right in believing that the thought and purpose of the country are turning towards the League. We have only to do a clean cut piece of party work to put our party in the most enviable and influential position in the world.

I daresay you have noted that the new Prime Minister of Great Britain declares the purpose of his party to "give the League of Nations wholehearted and practical support."

The moral forces of the world will presently prove too strong even for the moss-backs.

Pray let me know whenever I can be of any assistance, and believe me always,

With warm regard,

Your Sincere Friend,   [Woodrow Wilson]

CCL (WP, DLC).

To Frederick Ingate Thompson

My dear Friend,   [Washington] 28th October 1922

I have received through the courtesy of Dr. Grayson the bottle of "Black & White" you were so kind and thoughtful as to send me. I am greatly indebted to you and thank you most warmly. I really need the stuff as medicine to keep me toned up from day to day in my slow convalescence. It is therefore a most kindly service that you have rendered me.

I was glad to see in the paper the other day that Lasker had had the descency [decency] to speak in high terms of praise of your disinterested service to the Shipping Board,[1] and I know the praise was deserved. I hope that your plans are developing to your entire satisfaction and that complete success will crown your work in the newspaper field. I am interested to learn (if it be true) that you have acquired another important newspaper property.

I don't know of a more important field than the South for the promotion of borad [broad]-minded views for domestic and foreign affairs. As a Southerner I am eager to see the South dispel all the prejudice against Southern leadership by exhibiting a breadth and catholicity of national and international purpose, which would put such prejudice entirely out of countenance. Would it not be a great thing to see all of the public men of the South unite to lift the country to the high levels of leadership and ideal purpose to which it attained in the war time.

With most cordial personal good wishes,

Faithfully Yours,   [Woodrow Wilson]

CCL (WP, DLC).
    [1] Albert Davis Lasker, advertising executive of Chicago, at this time Chairman of the United States Shipping Board.

To Newton Diehl Baker

My dear Baker,   [Washington] 29th October 1922

Of course I was very much distressed and wounded by the extracts from Mrs. Lane's publication which I have seen in the newspapers, but a letter like yours of October twenty-sixth goes far to remove the sting.

You are as generous as usual in offering to say something publicly, but I agree with what is evidently your main judgment that it is best to ignore the book altogether and let it sink of its own weight.

I cannot tell you what cheer it gives me to have you think of me as you do, and I am profoundly grateful and deeply proud of your friendship. I am confident that we shall yet have an opportunity to work together for the things to which we have devoted our lives,— and that in happier circumstances.

With affectionate regard,

Faithfully Yours,   [Woodrow Wilson]

CCL (WP, DLC).

John Randolph Bolling to Schuyler Nielson Warren, Jr.[1]

[Washington] Oct 30 1922

Mr. Wilson will expect you and Mr. Holt five thirty Thursday afternoon.[2]   John Randolph Bolling

T telegram (WP, DLC).

¹ Bolling was replying to S. N. Warren, Jr., to JRB, Oct. 29, 1922, T telegram (WP, DLC). Holt and Warren talked to Wilson on November 2 about the plan for a nonpartisan movement for American membership in the League. Wilson tried to persuade Holt to drop the idea in favor of a partisan movement, but he seemed to indicate that he would not publicly oppose the nonpartisan plan. Warner, *The Life of Mr. Justice Clarke*, p. 128.

² November 2, 1922.

From Edward William Bok

Philadelphia
November first
My dear Mr. Wilson: Nineteen hundred and twenty-two

I have been asked to lead a group of forty or fifty of the most distinguished men in the East who propose to form themselves into a Committee, with headquarters in New York. These men are Republicans and Democrats in politics, but their main idea is to realize in a sense the League of Nations. They propose to borrow your idea when America entered the war and you designated us not as an ally, but as an associated power. The idea now is, through this Committee, to awaken public sentiment to a point of crystallization of getting the United States to enter the League of Nations as an associate power through the appointment by the President of a delegation of three or five, which shall sit in at all meetings of the League of Nations. There would be no question of reservations or modifications. Of course, this would not fully realize your hope of making the United States an integral part of the League, but it would give to the League the moral support of having the United States present and taking part only in those questions where the United States is concerned. In other words, it would be a first step.

I understand that this group of men have sounded out others, as well as important media of publicity, and they feel encouraged that this could be put over. Of course, the Committee would be a national one, and active. They now ask me to lead them.

What I want to know is your reaction, and I hope you may feel that you can write to me fully and confidentially. Naturally, if I went into this matter it would take a great deal of my time, and I would do it very largely on your account.

Believe me, with every good wish to Mrs. Wilson and yourself,
Very sincerely yours,   Edward W. Bok

TLS (WP, DLC).

To Edward William Bok

My dear Mr. Bok,   Washington D C 2nd November 1922

I am very much complimented to be consulted as has been done in your letter to me of November first, and since it is evident from your letter that you have faith in the project outlined I am sorry to have to say in candor that it would not in my opinion be of the least service in the world, and would obscure the sense of responsibility on the part of our Government and people if such a project were to be realized.

Nothing can restore to us the international leadership which we lost by failure to ratify the Treaty of Versailles, or put us in the rightful attitude of frank cooperation and joint responsibility with the rest of the world, except our entrance into the League on the same footing and terms with all the other members. This is my settled conviction and this is what I shall fight for so soon as Providence vouchsafes me additional physical strength.

With sincere appreciation of your frankness,
          Cordially and Sincerely Yours,   Woodrow Wilson

TLS (WP, DLC).

From Frederick Ingate Thompson

My dear Mr. Wilson: Washington November 2, 1922.

You said in your very kind note of the 15th of August, when generously expressing the hope my vacation would prove of benefit, that I would return "in fine shape for the work that lies ahead of all of us and which is as serious as it is necessary and challenging to all that which is best in us."

I think, my dear Mr. Wilson, that this expression helped to focus a growing thought that here, in an environment not always pleasant, real opportunity for public service was lacking. When, therefore, chance was given to purchase control of the "Birmingham Age-Herald," in which acquirement you manifest interest in your note of last Saturday, it was conceived that the journalistic linking of the "Age-Herald" and the "Mobile Register" did offer a field of service in my native section. These two newspapers are regarded as most important in the life of Alabama and geographically permit of statewide distribution. It always will be my effort to use their influence for the promotion of those ideals personified in your life and character and which, if I may presume intimacy of expression, I conceive to represent that which is best in citizenship and public morality in the life of our nation. As in answer to your sentiment with respect to our domestic and international policies I hope it will not tax you to read the enclosed copy of a letter I addressed to Dr. Erwin Craighead, the chief editorial writer of the "Register,"[1] nearly a year ago, at the time the Woodrow Wilson Foundation was inaugurated. What was stated then is impressed upon me more deeply now, and I shall be rewarded if the additional journalistic opportunity now afforded me can result in inculcating the sentiments conveyed therein into the hearts and conscience of the citizenship of my State.

It is worth very much to me, and most inspiring, to know that I have your good wishes. I shall treasure always the commission you gave me—my first and, I think, my last public office—and the interest in my future you now so generously manifest.

With great respect and high regard, I am,

Faithfully yours,   Frederick I. Thompson.

TLS (WP, DLC).
  [1] LL.D., University of Alabama, 1906. About his earlier career with the *Mobile Register*, see Tennant S. McWilliams, *The New South Faces the World: Foreign Affairs and the Southern Sense of Self, 1877-1950* (Baton Rouge, La., and London, 1988), pp. 51-67. Wilson returned Thompson's letter to Craighead.

To John Hessin Clarke

My dear Friend,   Washington D C 3rd November 1922

I was very much distressed to hear yesterday that you have not been well. I write to beg that you will be much more obedient to the doctors than I have ever been, and I pray very heartily that your recovery may be steady and rapid.

I had a call on yesterday from Mr. Hamilton Holt and Mr. Schuyler N. Warren, Jr. who spoke very warmly of you, and with whom I discussed all the pending suggestions as to plans for promoting public interest in the League of Nations. We all wished that you might have been present to take part in the discussion and throw light upon it with your own views.

But the main thing for both of us is to get well. There is too much work of the highest importance to do now to spare workers who really put their heart into the work, and the signs of the times lead me to believe that work for the things you and I believe in will, in the near future, be more and more richly rewarded by success. So take care of yourself in every possible way and get ready to come again to the bat. I promise for my part to try and do the same thing.

With affectionate regard,

Faithfully Yours,   Woodrow Wilson

TLS (J. H. Clarke Papers, OClW-Ar).

To Norman Hezekiah Davis

My dear Davis,   Washington D C 3rd November 1922

I was so very much interested the other day in what you repeated of your outline of the history of the Democratic Party that I am writing to express the hope that you either have it already in writing or can write it out while it is fresh in your mind. Somewhat elaborated it would be of high interest and importance. I hope you can reproduce it.

And for fear that you have not enough to do, I am going to take the liberty of begging that you get hold of Houston and you two together formulate a paragraph about tariff policy for our next national platform. I think that before 1924 comes around the public mind will be thoroughly aroused on that subject, and will be ready by the time the campaign opens for sound doctrine very plainly and vigorously stated. Please tell me that you can do this without too greatly burdening yourself.

With affectionate regard,

Faithfully Yours,   Woodrow Wilson

TLS (N. H. Davis Papers, DLC).

From Edward William Bok

Philadelphia
November third

My dear Mr. Wilson: Nineteen hundred and twenty-two

I thank you very much for your letter, and if I seem to have indicated a faith in the project outlined it was not intended. From the moment it was suggested to me it failed to reach my conviction, but I was afraid I might be wrong, and I wanted to get your reaction. You now say to me exactly what I thought you would say.

I trust your hopes for greater physical strength will soon be realized.

With every good regard, believe me,

Very sincerely yours,   Edward W. Bok

TLS (WP, DLC).

From Hamilton Holt

Dear Mr. Wilson: New York November 3, 1922

On my return to New York I am writing you with regard to our conversation of yesterday in respect to the League of Nations.

Briefly, this is my position:

I have done everything I could personally and as President of the Woodrow Wilson Democracy for the past year and a half to make the League an issue in the present campaign. But these are off years, and since, as you say, miscellaneous local issues naturally come more to the fore, we find the League issue more or less ignored.

While at Geneva this Summer I found the unanimous opinion of friends of the League was that the time was now at hand when a great non-partisan movement could wisely be launched in America, along the lines of the English-Speaking Union—not to do as the friends of Mr. Bok proposed, namely, to make the United States an associate member of the League—but definitely to bring the United States into the League at the earliest possible moment.

When I arrived in town a month ago, I found Judge Clarke was on the point of deciding to head such a movement provided it was properly financed and a large representative non-partisan committee acceptable to him could be formed. So a few of us, not to let Judge Clarke's leadership slip away, started in to see what could be done. Already a preliminary committee has got together. Mr. Cleveland Dodge has agreed to underwrite the first $10,000 of expenses and Judge Clarke has said he is ready to co-operate if the movement is strictly non-partisan.

I was so greatly impressed, however, by your views yesterday, which I understand to be that the best and quickest way to get the United States into the League of Nations is by making the issue a straight out and out party fight to the finish, that I am writing you to ask your further advice.

Personally, I never thought for a moment that one and the same person should stand before the public as the simultaneous leader of both a partisan and a non-partisan movement, but as immediately after election there will follow the inevitable lull in national politics for at least six months, I thought I might lend a hand in some appropriate way in this non-partisan movement until party politics began to boil again.

At all events, for me to withdraw from this non-partisan movement would be probably unwise, unless I was convinced that I could do better work in helping the Democratic Party make the League the dominant issue in the forthcoming presidential campaign.

I ask you, therefore, what assurances you think could be obtained from the National Democratic Committee for the necessary backing for this activity thru the Woodrow Wilson Democracy or otherwise with sufficient funds properly to carry on the work. With such assurances I would seriously consider withdrawing from the non-partisan movement to throw all my efforts in party politics.

I await your reply with interest.

Very sincerely yours   Hamilton Holt

TLS (WP, DLC).

John Hessin Clarke to John Randolph Bolling

My dear Mr. Bolling—   Youngstown, Ohio November 3, 1922

I thank you very much for the letter of Mr. Pierce[1] and the attached circulars. I wish I could agree with Mr. Pierce that it is wise to insist upon acceptance by the Administration of the League Covenant without reservations. I, however, do not know of any friends of the League who think that such a forward movement could be successful.

The enemies of the Covenant so succeeded in misrepresenting it that I am sure the feeling is very general that to insist upon unconditional acceptance would revive all the bitterness of the 1920 campaign, and would render futile any attempted progress, at least until 1924. The belief is very general that if we can get the country into the League, necessities of international conditions will gradually give such form to the Covenant as may be found desirable and that, therefore, nothing will be lost by conditional entry and perhaps much gained.

I cannot doubt that the movement among the church people of the country is having its effect upon the Administration and it may be that the election next Tuesday will prove of value.

I am sorry to be obliged to write that I am far from well. I had noticed an irregularity of heart action for some months, but as I had had heart disturbance some years ago without serious interruption of my work I decided to ignore it. However, it recurred in such form last week that an examination by specialists resulted in an imperative order that I take a month's rest and I am trying more or less successfully to obey. I am quite confidently assured that rest will restore me, but for the present it has become necessary for me to cancel a good many League engagements which I was anxious to keep.

However, the friends in New York, acting through Mr. Holt, chiefly, are attempting to organize a committee of one hundred, of Democrats, Republicans and Independents pledged to aid with their names and influence a forward movement which it is desired that I shall undertake to lead. I have not yet consented to accept the leadership but have promised to co-operate with the movement in every way in my power.

I am also in receipt of your letter from Mr. Dickinson[2] which you sent, and beg to say that he must have mailed a copy of this same letter to me at the time he mailed the one to Mr. Wilson as they are in identical terms. I have considered his program for education in behalf of the League of Nations, and while it is no doubt excellent if it could be realized even in part, yet, as I have said to him, I think the first thing for us to do is to try to arrest the attention of the country anew to the subject in such a way that an educational process such as he suggested would be of value. His plan is impracticable also because of the expense involved.

Please remember me very cordially to Mr. and Mrs. Wilson, and believe me,   Sincerely yours,   John H. Clarke

TLS (WP, DLC).
    [1] Robert Morris Pierce. The Editors have been unable further to identify him. Bolling had enclosed his letter in JRB to J. H. Clarke, Oct. 29, 1922, CCL (WP, DLC).
    [2] Thomas Herbert Dickinson, Associate Professor of English at the University of Wisconsin, 1909-1916; at this time an independent author, anthologist, and playwright living in Wilton, Conn. He was soon to publish *The United States and the League* (New York, 1923). Bolling enclosed his letter in JRB to J. H. Clarke, Nov. 1, 1922, CCL (WP, DLC).

To Frederick Ingate Thompson

My dear Friend,   [Washington] 4th November 1922

I have examined carefully the letter to Dr. Craighead, of which you were kind enough to send me copy, and want to tell you how deeply and warmly I appreciate the whole tone and purpose of the editorial you speak of. It is very delightful to be so thought of and seconded.

Permit me however a comment on one sentence in the letter. You speak in it of my getting well enough to make a "re-statement of his international and domestic ideas." I believe such a re-statement to be absolutely unnecessary now and likely to remain unnecessary for a considerable time to come. I have evidence which convinces me of the extraordinary fact that my principles and purposes are known and sympathetically interpreted in every part of the world,—particularly I may say by the plainer and simpler kind of people. The selfish conspiracy against the realization of my ideals is confined to a few highbrows who have their own ends to seek and whom it would be impossible to awaken out of their selfishness except by a sound threshing [thrashing] (metaphorically speaking) in the form of a thorough-going political defeat.

I think I am justified in saying that I am perhaps the only public man in the world who does not need to be interpreted to anybody. I do not know how this has come about (I might form plausible theories on the subject) but I think I have abundant evidence of it.

The fact does not so much minister to my satisfaction as it serves to increase the sense of my responsibility. It gives me an opportunity of influence which I must be the more careful to take advantage of with sober and elevated purpose.

I am writing to you in great frankness as to a confidential friend and under the conviction that we must speak the truth even when it affects ourselves and may seem to violate the canons of good taste. The world is in too critical a state politically to justify giving good taste precedence to the facts of the case.

I am interested to see that you have enlisted Dr. Craighead, whom I knew as the president of Tulane,[1] on your editorial staff, and I hope sincerely that the association will be mutually advantageous. Perhaps you will be kind enough to give him my regards when you see him next.

I hope that your newspaper enterprises will prosper in the highest degree, and wish to express my sincere admiration of the purposes with which you have undertaken them. The part of the South in which you work is undoubtedly the seed bed of much of the thinking of the great party by means of which we must set the country in the right ways again and render an immortal service to mankind.

With warm regard and appreciation,

Faithfully Yours,   [Woodrow Wilson]

CCL (WP, DLC).

[1] Wilson was confusing Erwin Craighead with Edwin Boone Craighead, President of Tulane University, 1904-1912.

Ray Stannard Baker to Edith Bolling Galt Wilson

Dear Mrs. Wilson: New York November 4 '22

The great BOOK goes on to you to-day. I do hope you and Mr. Wilson will like it—more than almost anything else I want that. I hope and believe it will give a juster view of Woodrow Wilson and of the very great struggle he made at Paris.

I think Doubleday has done a pretty good job of bookmaking, and he seems determined now to let the country know about the book. Whether it has a wide circulation, of course, no one can tell. That is on the lap of the gods. The book is cast into a pot bubbling with controversy and must make its own way.

With warm regards to Mr. Wilson and yourself,

Sincerely,   Ray Stannard Baker

ALS (EBW Papers, DLC).

To Michael Kwapiszewski[1]

Washington D C

My dear Mr. Kwapiszewski,   5th November 1922

It is a matter of peculiar pleasure and gratification to me to learn in any way of the approbation and friendship of the Polish people and their Government.

It will afford me peculiar pleasure therefore to receive at your hands the symbol of the order of the "White Eagle," and I am hoping that it will be convenient to you to come to my residence for that purpose on the afternoon of Thursday, the ninth of November, at five-thirty o'clock. I assure you that I shall be very proud of the honour your Government has so generously conferred upon me.

Pray accept, sir, from Mrs. Wilson and me, assurances of our best wishes for yourself and believe me,

With high respect,   Sincerely Yours,   Woodrow Wilson

TLS (Wilson Library, DLC).
    [1] Polish Chargé d'Affaires in Washington. Wilson was replying to M. Kwapiszewski to WW, Nov. 2, 1922, TLS (WP, DLC).

To Hamilton Holt

My dear Mr. Holt,   Washington D C 5th November 1922

Thank you for your frank letter of November third.

I do not think we need any assurances of any kind from the Democratic National Committee to enable us to see our way. So soon as the new Congress gets to work and shows its quality of one kind or another, men's minds will begin to turn to the Presidential contest of 1924. That will be the time for all of us to do what I intend myself to do, namely, bring every legitimate influence to bear to make our entrance into the League the dominant issue of the campaign, and my personal opinion is that we shall find abundant fuel for the fire, and presently thereafter a candidate who will keep the fire hot and will make it dangerous for anyone whose metal will not stand the fire to venture to stir it or in any way touch it.

It is like Dodge to do the generous and disinterested thing you tell me of, and it is with unaffected reluctance that I express an opinion which may run athwart his judgment and desire. But now of all times we must speak our real opinions to each other and make our convictions realities of the most effective kind.

You are approaching the whole question with admirable frankness and freedom from personal motive, and it will always be a pleasure to cooperate with you.[1] I see clearly that when the time to which I am looking forward comes you will find it the most effective and therefore the most satisfactory thing you can do to turn away from non-partisan lines and action and put on the full harness of aggressive party action; and I feel confident that as circumstances mature this will be your own judgment and impulse.

With warmest regard and the most assured hopes for the near future,   Sincerely and Faithfully Yours,   Woodrow Wilson

TLS (Woodrow Wilson Coll., NjR).
  [1] Reassured by this comment that Wilson would not openly oppose a nonpartisan movement, Holt now proceeded to organize one. His first objective—to persuade Clarke to head the movement—was easily attained. On December 15, 1922, Holt made public the names of 112 "sponsors" of the League of Nations Non-Partisan Committee. The list included a number of prominent Republicans and many leaders in all walks of life, but particularly persons prominent in the peace movement and in religious denominations and organizations. *New York Times*, Dec. 16, 1922. Thus, on January 10, 1923, came the announcement of the formal organization of the League of Nations Non-Partisan Association at a banquet at the Hotel Biltmore in New York, at which Clarke gave the principal address. Clarke was president; Everett Colby was chairman of the executive committee; and George W. Wickersham was "President of the Council." As Holt's biographer has said, "The list of members, with only a few conspicuous omissions, contained the names of all who had been active in the pro-League movement in the previous decade. It was a veritable who's who of notable Americans." Kuehl, *Hamilton Holt*, pp. 167-68; *New York Times*, Jan. 11, 1923.
  The League of Nations Non-Partisan Association soon became a large and well-funded organization. It was very active in 1923 and 1924 to achieve its announced objective: "to secure the insertion in both the Republican and Democratic party platforms, in 1924, of a plank favoring entrance of the United States into the League of Nations." The organization ceased to exist as a national one after the Republicans ignored the League in their platform and the Democrats only referred to it in theirs. The association survived as a group composed largely of New Yorkers, which issued occasional papers and reprints of speeches. The organization changed its name to the League of Nations Association in 1929 and to the American Association for the United Nations in 1945. See Kuehl, pp. 168-70, and Warner, *The Life of Mr. Justice Clarke*, pp. 124-78, for a detailed history of the association through 1928.

From Norman Hezekiah Davis

My dear Mr. Wilson: New York City. November 6, 1922.

I feel flattered that you were interested and that you should think there may be some merit in the short history of the Democratic Party which I gave in my speech at Philadelphia,[1] and which I outlined very briefly to you last Tuesday. Before going to Philadelphia I dictated the speech which I proposed to make. I will go over this and send you a corrected copy. For the purpose which you have in mind it may be well to cut out a portion of my speech and cover a little more carefully the basic principles for which the Democratic Party has stood in its long and useful life. If you have any suggestions to make after "wading through" my effort, I hope you will do so.

In obedience to your suggestion I will get hold of Houston some time in the near future, and collaborate with him in the formulation of the paragraph on our Tariff Policy. It is astonishing that the people are not taking more interest in, or showing more hostility to the recent Tariff Bill.[2] This may be because it was passed so recently that its iniquities have not been fully demonstrated. It is strange how continuous the struggle for privilege has always been, and that whenever political privilege is done away with, the struggle shifts to one for economic privileges.

With affectionate regards, I am,

Very sincerely yours,   Norman H. Davis

TLS (WP, DLC).
  [1] Davis delivered an address on the history of the Democratic party to the Democratic Women's Luncheon Club of Philadelphia on October 30, 1922. This thoughtful and scholarly address was published by the Democratic Women's Luncheon Club of Philadelphia under the title of *The Principles of the Democratic Party, An Address by the Hon. Norman H. Davis* . . . [Philadelphia, 1922 (?)].
  [2] That is, the Fordney-McCumber Tariff Act, about which, see C. Hull to WW, July 14, 1922, n. 3.

John Randolph Bolling to John Hessin Clarke

My dear Mr. Clarke: [Washington] 6th November 1922

First of all let me say how sorry I was to learn the other day of your illness; and I hope that Mr. Wilson's letter to you was interpreted as an expression of my own regret. As he so wisely pointed out, it is imperative that you take things easy until you are entirely restored; and I hope you will not attempt to acknowledge this, or any other letters I may send in the interim.

I read your letter of November third to Mr. Wilson and he directs me to say that "No one has proposed to urge the unconditional acceptance of the League Covenant on the present Administration; that he thinks that indeed would be futile."

With very warm regard, and the sincere hope that this will find you rapidly improving;

Cordially yours,   [John Randolph Bolling]

CCL (WP, DLC).

From Daniel Calhoun Roper

Washington D C Nov 8th 1922

Hearty congratulations to you and to the country on election[1]

Daniel C Roper

T telegram (WP, DLC).

[1] Agrarian unrest in the Middle West on account of low farm prices, an aggressive campaign by the American Federation of Labor and the railroad brotherhoods, lingering unemployment, and resentment against the Fordney-McCumber Tariff Act resulted in what was in fact a repudiation of the Harding administration in the off-year elections of 1922. In the new Congress there would be 225 Republicans, 205 Democrats, and one Socialist in the House of Representatives and fifty-one Republicans, forty-three Democrats, and two Farmer-Laborites in the Senate, but the administration lost control of Congress because of the alienation from it of many midwestern and western Republican insurgents. Perhaps most significant was the shift of big cities with immigrant populations toward the Democratic party. Lodge won narrowly in Massachusetts, and Alfred E. Smith won the governorship of New York. Edward I. Edwards of New Jersey and Royal S. Copeland were elected to the Senate, and Gifford Pinchot won the governorship of Pennsylvania on a reform Republican ticket. See John D. Hicks, *Republican Ascendancy, 1921-1933* (New York, 1960), pp. 84-89, and David Burner, *The Politics of Provincialism: The Democratic Party in Transition, 1918-1932* (New York, 1968), pp. 103-106.

To Daniel Calhoun Roper

[Washington] Nov 8 1922

Election results are indeed most gratifying and encouraging stop We must now gird our loins to carry out the great work which they so clearly indicate we shall have an opportunity to do stop Twenty four will complete the result which twenty two has begun

Woodrow Wilson

CC telegram (WP, DLC).

To Jessie Woodrow Wilson Sayre

My dearest Jessie,   Washington D C 9th November 1922

Unhappily it turns out that the defeat of Lodge forecast in your telegraphic message of Tuesday[1] was not verified by the event. But I hope that his reduced majority gave him a jolt which may make even him comprehend the new temper of the voters.

We now have the serious duty of making the best use of our victories.

I am getting along about as usual, and we are looking forward with much satisfaction to seeing you at Thanksgiving.

Edith joins me in warmest love to you all and I am,

With a heart full of love,   Your Devoted   Father

TLS (photostat in RSB Coll., DLC).
[1] Jessie W. W. Sayre to WW, Nov. 7, 1922, T telegram (WC, NjP).

To Cordell Hull

My dear Mr. Chairman,   [Washington] 9th November 1922

I feel that I speak only the sentiment of the whole party when I convey to you my heartfelt congratulations on the results of Tuesday. I am sure that the fine work you and the Committee did by way of preparation will be universally recognized.

It is now all the more clearly our duty to offer the nation exactly the right kind of service and the right kind of candidate in 1924.

I shall hope to have an early talk with you about the immediate use we ought to make of victory, on the assumption that the leading Democrats of the new Congress will wish my advice.

Cordially and Faithfully Yours,   [Woodrow Wilson]

CCL (WP, DLC).

Two Letters from Norman Hezekiah Davis

My dear Mr. Wilson: New York November 9, 1922.

In a brief conversation with Col. House the other day he advanced the idea that the United States become an associate member of the League of Nations, pending a change of Administration, and asked for my opinion. I told him I would prefer that the United States stay out rather than go in to an emasculated League, but that I would like to think over his suggestion before expressing a definite opinion about it. He then said he would write a letter to me stating clearly what he had in mind. He has done that and the letter is herewith enclosed.[1]

If Col. House has diagnosed the situation correctly, the question to decide is whether or not it is better to go in as an associate member of the League without any change of the Covenant, or to go into an emasculated League, or wait until we can go in as a full fledged member. It seems to me that of the two first alternatives, it would be better to go in as an associate member. However, I have become so irritated at the unsportsmanlike attitude of the Administration and the policy of trying to get something for nothing that I would regret to see us do something which is not courageous, or which shows an indication that we are shrinking from assuming our full share of responsibility. I do not quite understand how we could enter as an associate member unless it should be under a special resolution of the League, permitting us to join as an associate member, agreeing to adhere to the principles in the Covenant, but not binding us to their enforcement in respect of other nations. After all, if we should enter in that way, we could not very well escape the same moral obligation which we would have if we were an active member because in the latter case we are only obliged to act where in the unanimous opinion of the Council a situation had arisen which requires united action.

As I understand from Col. House, he is seeking the views of some of the principal Party members, and in case there should be a general concurrence in the view which he holds, a Resolution would be introduced in Congress by some Democrat, which would only require a majority vote to put us in, and not a two-thirds vote since it does not involve the ratification of the Treaty. There is no doubt in my mind that it would be more dignified and sensible for the United States to enter the League as an associate member than to be sending "observers" to the various conferences, and to get the League to make changes which would enable us to participate in the International Court, etc. The question, however, is whether the Democrats in order to avoid that and get something better, should advocate something which is not entirely perfect.

If you feel so inclined, I should like very much to have your reaction and suggestions for my guidance.

With affectionate regards, I am,

Faithfully yours,   Norman H. Davis

[1] EMH to NHD, Nov. 6, 1922, TLS (N. H. Davis Papers, DLC).

My dear Mr. Wilson: New York City, November 9, 1922.

I am enclosing corrected copy of the speech which I made in Philadelphia.[1] There are a few paragraphs in this which were only applicable to the audience which I was addressing, but which can easily be eliminated if you think there is anything in the speech with enough merit to be used for some general purpose.

I am returning the letter from Miss Hood[2] which you kindly sent to me which I have read with considerable interest. My observation is that the women are making a more thorough and conscientious effort to understand public questions than the men are. In New York I know several intelligent women, wives of Republicans, who are now confirmed Democrats.

I expect to get in touch with Houston in the near future on the Tariff plank.

With affectionate regards, I am,

Sincerely yours,   Norman H. Davis

TLS (WP, DLC).
[1] As will soon be seen, Wilson returned this copy to Davis. We have not found a copy of it in the Davis Papers, DLC, but see NHD to WW, Nov. 6, 1922, n. 1.

² This was Ellen Gowen Hood to WW, Nov. 6, 1922, receipt of which Bolling acknowledged on November 7. Miss Hood's letter is missing in WP, DLC. She was "Chairman" of the Democratic Women's Luncheon Club of Philadelphia.

To Michael Kwapiszewski

                                                    Washington D C
My dear Mr. Kwapiszewski,   10th November 1922

I was so much flattered and touched by the little ceremony of yesterday that I find myself deeply interested to learn something of the origin and history of the Order of the White Eagle. Could you, in your kindness, refer me to some authority from which I could learn about it.¹

I hope you will let your Government know that I shall always feel very proud of the distinguished honour it has conferred upon me, and I greatly appreciate the courtesy and sincerity with which you presented the decoration of the Order to me on yesterday.

Allow me to express to you my sincere personal good wishes and to request that you will present my respectful compliments to your chief² when he returns.

    Cordially and Sincerely Yours,   Woodrow Wilson

TLS (Wilson Library, DLC).
¹ M. Kwapiszewski to WW, Jan. 8, 1923, TLS (WP, DLC), records the history of the order, which August II, Elector of Saxony and King of Poland, created in 1705.
² That is, Prince Kazimierz Lubomirski. As it turned out, Lubomirski did not return to the United States and was replaced in November 1922 by Wladyslaw Wroblewski.

From Cordell Hull

My dear Mr. President: Washington, D. C. Nov. 10th, 1922.

I deeply appreciate your letter of the 9th instant and most sincerely thank you for your kind expressions relative to the work of our Democratic National organization.

To use a hackneyed expression, it was "in my system" throughout the year that a great overturn was due in the recent election and I could not escape that firm belief. I know you entertained a similar feeling.

Without going into details, however, I shall avail myself of your kind invitation to call on you, at which time we can discuss in person the lessons to be derived from the election and some of the important phases of a proposed party programme during the next two years.

I shall be delighted to call at any time you may suggest. I may say that it may be necessary for me to leave the City for three or four days after next Monday.

With all good wishes,   Very sincerely,   Cordell Hull

TLS (WP, DLC).

From John Hessin Clarke

My dear Friend—   Youngstown, Ohio November 10, 1922

Your generous note of sympathy touches my heart.[1] Some days ago I wrote Mr. Bolling of my condition.[2] The doctors think I am improving but, more to the purpose, I feel myself growing stronger and the heart disturbance growing less.

Frankly, I am skeptical of medical opinion. Perhaps in part because not very long ago I paid two liberal fees for two examinations in one day which were flatly conflicting.—But when I suggested something of this kind to my family physician, he retorted, rather pertinently, "Mr. Justice, have you never heard of lawyers or even Supreme Judges differing about a case?"

It is very certainly true that rest reduces the disturbance and as no drugs are given and rest alone prescribed, I have decided to submit to the doctors' orders and am doing so with as good grace as I can command.

But how can a man remain quiet and calm with such news coming as I have been reading since midnight of the seventh? While the League was not an issue in many states, the result affords an opportunity for the forward movement we are trying to inaugurate. I had hoped to restate the case for the League early in December in the light of the experience of the past two years, and to put into the statement my most earnest effort. This must now be delayed, but I hope not beyond the first of the year. I am entirely willing to take the risk now which the doctors say there may be in delivering such an address, but of course a delay of some weeks may not prove serious.

It seems to me, however, of great importance to do all that we can to direct the attention of the country anew to the League in as arresting a manner as possible while the churches and the women are so interested as they are just now in international affairs and when the Republicans, chastened in spirit, may perhaps be disposed to see the light.

When I think how heroically you are submitting to discipline, my duty seems plain and my burden light. If only we were both strong enough to press "The Great Cause" as we could have done in our prime!

Believe me always,

Sincerely and affectionately yours,   John H. Clarke

TLS (WP, DLC).
[1] WW to J. H. Clarke, Nov. 3, 1922.
[2] J. H. Clarke to JRB, Nov. 3, 1922.

A News Report

[*Nov. 11, 1922*]

WILSON SEES NATION MOVING FORWARD; HITS AT HIS FOES
Declares Men Who Beat the Treaty Did Not Represent the United States.

SAYS THEY ARE SLIPPING

Washington, Nov. 11.—Woodrow Wilson, the invalid ex-President, speaking today to more than 5,000 of his friends and admirers who had assembled in front of his home to honor him on Armistice Day, declared that the men who prevented the ratification of the Treaty of Versailles and kept the United States out of the League of Nations did not represent the United States "because the United States is moving forward and they are slipping backward."

"Where their slipping will end," he added, "God only will determine."

Reed, Moses, La Follette, Brandegee, McCormick, Norris, Poindexter[1] and other Senators who had battled to defeat the work of the Paris conference the ex-President described as "a group in the United States Senate who preferred personal motives to the honor of their country and the peace of the world."

The occasion was the annual Armistice Day pilgrimage to the S Street home of Mr. Wilson. It was a crowd that jammed every inch of space for a block on either side of the mansion, a crowd of citizens who had followed Wilson in his days of triumph and who have remained loyal to him in his retirement. There were not more than a dozen nationally known persons in the throng, among them being Henry Morgenthau, who was Ambassador to Turkey in the second Wilson term; President Edwin A. Alderman of the Univer-

[1] That is, Senators James A. Reed of Missouri, George H. Moses of New Hampshire, Robert M. La Follette of Wisconsin, Frank Brandegee of Connecticut, Medill McCormick of Illinois, George W. Norris of Nebraska, and Miles Poindexter of Washington.

sity of Virginia, and ex-Secretary of Agriculture Edwin T. Meredith.

The greeting on behalf of the crowd was delivered by Mr. Morgenthau, who was the first person to be welcomed by Mr. Wilson. Once when Mr. Morgenthau referred to the election last Tuesday the crowd interrupted with a cheer, while from all parts of it came the shout that Mr. Wilson was himself largely responsible for the great overturn.

When Mr. Morgenthau said that Tuesday had demonstrated the country was escaping from "materialism and selfishness," Mr. Wilson exclaimed, but not in a loud voice, "Hear, hear!" The crowd, for the most part, failed to catch this little exclamation.

Immediately Mr. Morgenthau had concluded Mr. Wilson began his speech. It was extemporaneous, and was as follows:

"Mr. Morgenthau, ladies and gentlemen:

"I am very much moved by this wonderful exhibition of your friendship and approval, and I have been reflecting today that Armistice Day has a particular significance for the United States because the United States has remained contented with the armistice and has not moved forward to peace.

"It is a very serious reflection that the United States, the great originative nation, should remain contented with a negation. Armistice is a negation; it is a standstill of arms; it is a cessation of fighting, and we are so bent on a cessation of fighting that we are even throwing our arms away.

"It is a singular circumstance to which Mr. Morgenthau has in part adverted that while we prescribed the conditions of the armistice we will not concur in the establishment of permanent peace. That, of course, was brought about by a group in the United States Senate who preferred personal partisan motives to the honor of their country and the peace of the world. (Applause.)

"They do not represent the United States, because the United States is moving forward and they are slipping backward. Where the slipping will end, God only will determine.

"And I have also been reflecting upon the radical difference between armistice and peace. Armistice, as I have said, is a mere negation; it is refraining from force. But peace is a very positive and constructive thing as the world stands nowadays, because it must be brought about by the systematic maintenance of common understanding and by cultivation—not by amiable phrases, but the active co-operation for justice; and justice is a greater thing than any kind of expediency. (Applause.)

"America has always stood for justice and always will stand for it. Puny persons who are now standing in the way will presently find that their weakness is no match for the strength of a moving Providence.[2]

"If you will pardon an invalid for putting on his hat, I will promise not to talk through it. (Laughter and applause.)

"I think, then, we may renew today our faith in the future though we are celebrating the past. The future is in our hands, and if we are not equal to it the shame will be ours and none others.

"I thank you from a very full heart, my friends, for this demonstration of kindness by you, and bid you and the nation godspeed."
. . .

The exercises in front of the Wilson home began at 3 o'clock, and lasted for about three-quarters of an hour. It started with the singing of "The Swanee River," "My Old Kentucky Home," and other Southern songs, and came to an end with "Take Me Back to Old Virginia." The crowd began to assemble an hour before the time set for the demonstration and so great was the rush that the street car lines had to put on extra cars to handle it.

The chairman of the committee in charge of the pilgrimage was Mrs. Kate Trenholm Abrams, the other members being Mrs. Huston Thompson, Mrs. Oliver P. Newman, Mrs. Stephen Bonsal and Mrs. James William Copeland.[3]

Mr. Wilson was very happy. There could be no question about that. His friends maintained that physically he appeared to be in better condition than he was a year ago. The old ring of his voice was missing, but his enunciation was clear and distinct and reached to most parts of the crowd.

He was assisted to his position on the stoop by his colored attendant,[4] but stood without support while he was making his speech, by far the longest he has made since he was stricken in the Fall of 1919. For a while he remained with head uncovered. Then with a smile he placed his hat on his head.

On one occasion, as if to emphasize that he could stand without assistance, he lifted his big malacca cane and placed the crook of it in the upper pocket of his coat and there it remained until he ended his talk with a "god-speed" to the nation and his friends. This act occasioned another of the many demonstrations that marked the delivery of his speech.

Mr. Wilson's complexion was clear, his eyes were bright and

---

[2] A T transcript of this speech in WP, DLC, renders this paragraph as follows:

"America has always stood for justice and always will stand for it. Puny persons who are now standing in the way will presently find a rude awakening when they experience the strength of the movement of Providence."

[3] Caroline Margaret Cordes Thompson, Jennie E. Bixby Newman, Henrietta Fairfax Morris Bonsal, Mrs. Copeland unidentified.

[4] Isaac Scott.

continually surveying the great crowd, and he looked to have put on considerable weight. His posture, however, occasioned some comment. He was not able to hold himself erect, and in this respect he did not seem to have improved to any considerable extent.

When he had concluded his speech and had received three huge baskets of flowers, one from little Helen Sue Trinkle, the daughter of the Governor of Virginia;[5] another from Miss Julia Edwards, a daughter of Senator-elect Edward I. Edwards of New Jersey, and one from Miss Olive Chase of Washington, Mr. Wilson retired to reappear a few moments later at a window in the second story of his home. For ten minutes he remained there facing the crowd which cheered and cheered. With him were Mrs. Wilson, and she, too, came in for a hearty greeting. . . .

When the demonstration at the Wilson home had ended the great crowd formed in two lines on either side of S Street, the lines extending for two blocks beyond Connecticut Avenue. Through these cheering lines, the ex-President left his home for his daily automobile ride. He lifted his hat time and again and smiled his deep appreciation of the tribute accorded him.

Printed in the *New York Times*, Nov. 12, 1922.
  [5] Elbert Lee Trinkle.

To Edward Irving Edwards

My dear Governor,   [Washington] 12th November 1922

Your generous note[1] gave me a great deal of pleasure. I was hoping to have a chance to take you by the hand and congratulate you on the new honours that have come to you. But we shall after while both be Washingtonians and we can then collogue on events old and new to our hearts content.

With warmest appreciation and most cordial greetings,
                    Faithfully Yours,   [Woodrow Wilson][2]

CCL (WP, DLC).
  [1] E. I. Edwards to WW, Nov. 8, 1922, TLS (WP, DLC).
  [2] This letter, lacking the first sentence, was printed in the *New York Times*, Nov. 17, 1922.

To John Hessin Clarke

My dear Friend,   Washington D C 13th November 1922

Your letter of November tenth reassures me, and I am very much relieved to hear you are already feeling better and beginning to feel the tide of returning strength. Allow me to counsel prudence and to say that I think the delay you speak of as probably necessary for you to deliver your address ought not to be begrudged as a measure of safety.

I believe with you that Tuesday's elections make it easier to turn the thoughts of the country in the right direction and to make ready for the great duty of 1924.

With warm regard and sincere felicitations on your already improved condition,   Faithfully Yours,   Woodrow Wilson

TLS (J. H. Clarke Papers, OClW-Ar).

To Norman Hezekiah Davis

My dear Davis,   Washington D C 13th November 1922

The suggestion that we become "associate members" of the League has come to me before from another quarter, and it is clear to me that it emanates from minds that haven't the metal [mettle] for an out and out fight. We must work for full accession to the League under its present Covenant. I have opposed and shall continue to oppose everything of this sort and even to the discountenance of all attempts at "non-partisan" advocacy of the League. It must be made a party issue and fought out to a finish if we are the men of courage and principle we believe ourselves to be.

I believe that the business can be done and thoroughly done in 1924, and that only by making our great party the instrument of national service in this matter will it be possible to accomplish anything worth while.

The suggestion is one of the many insidious proposals of compromise against which we must harden our hearts and double our fists. These are the things that eat away all principle like a corroding acid, and they will disappear if we are only steadfast.

I am heartily glad to have the copy of the speech to the women in Philadelphia and am looking forward with pleasure to giving it a careful perusal this evening. If any suggestions from me seem worth while I shall make them with alacrity because I believe that a general and clear setting forth of what the party is and stands for may be of great service, and that this is a peculiarly happy time at which to catch the ear of the public on that subject.

Mrs. Wilson joins me in very warm regards, and I am,

As always,   Affectionately Yours,   Woodrow Wilson

TLS (N. H. Davis Papers, DLC).

From Hamilton Holt

My dear Mr. Wilson: Wake Forest. N. Ca. Nov. 13. 1922

My secretary has forwarded your kind letter of Nov. 5th to me here, where I am giving a course of four lectures on the League.

It is needless to say that I find myself in accord with it, & that I shall hope to be permitted to take part in the fight to make the Democratic Party the great instrument by which the country will be brought into the League.

The election shows that the American people are beginning to turn away from false gods, and I believe we can win if we have have [sic] your spirit. It is all very heartening to feel that you will be able to take some part in the endeavor.

Very respectfully yours   Hamilton Holt

ALS (WP, DLC).

From Bernard Mannes Baruch

My dear Mr. Wilson: New York November 14, 1922.

Your speech the other day was simply wonderful. You have the happy faculty somehow of always saying the things we have in mind but can't express.

I think you ought to feel gratified at the election. I myself was genuinely disappointed in Lodge's reelection; but the people of Massachusetts had no choice. If Whipple or anyone other than Gaston had been nominated Lodge would have been badly beaten.

It may interest you to know that Dr. Copeland[1] is a very strong League man. He said that if the information regarding hygiene was all that the League ever did it would have justified its existence. Frank Cobb has been talking with him on the subject.

I know that Bruce, Neely and Ralston are strong League men. I think Bayard[2] is also.

I have been anticipating coming down to see you in reference to the subject we discussed the last time I was there. But I think your Armistice Day talk has done more in that direction than anything else.

I am wondering whether it would be possible at an early date for you and Mrs. Wilson to come to New York for a day or two. I could arrange to have a car for you and give you a whole floor of my house with a private elevator. I thought that perhaps you might like to go to the theatre. However, we can discuss this on my next trip which I expect to make in a very few days. I am waiting now for Mr. Clemenceau;[3] after that I shall be free.

I presume you have seen the editorials and comments in the newspapers which all agree that you have come back into the leadership of the Democratic party. They evidently overlooked the fact that you have always been its leader.

I congratulate you upon the election, and I congratulate you particularly upon your speech. I also want to thank you for it.

With affectionate regards to Mrs. Wilson and the same to yourself, I am,   Ever devotedly yours,   Baruch

TLS (WP, DLC).
¹ Royal Samuel Copeland, M.D., Democrat, distinguished ophthalmologist and medical educator and a writer, who had just been elected United States senator from New York.
² William Cabell Bruce of Maryland, Matthew Mansfield Neely of West Virginia, Samuel Moffett Ralston of Indiana, and Thomas Francis Bayard, Jr., of Delaware, all Democrats recently elected for the first time to the United States Senate.
³ Georges Clemenceau was to arrive in New York on November 18 to begin a lecture tour in the Northeast, about which, see Jean-Baptiste Duroselle, *Clemenceau* (Paris, 1988), pp. 888-91. Baruch was a member of the committee to greet him upon his landing.

To Bernard Mannes Baruch

My dear Baruch,   Washington D C 15th November 1922

I cannot tell you what pleasure it affords me that you liked my little speech of last Saturday. I by no means felt proud of it, but the approval of a friend like yourself redeems it even in my own eyes. Thank you with all my heart for cheering me with such praise.

I pray that I may give the party the right sort of leadership in these days when the nations of the world are so perturbed and confused and so sadly in need of the guidance we once gave them.

We are delighted to know that you may come down soon. Let me know as usual a little in advance. I shall look forward to seeing you as always with the greatest pleasure.

With affectionate regards from us both,
                    Faithfully Yours,   Woodrow Wilson

TLS (B. M. Baruch Papers, NjP).

To Frank Irving Cobb

My dear Cobb: [Washington] 15th November 1922

I am proud that you like the little speech of last Saturday.¹ I did not feel I was at my best by any means, but hoped that the simplicity and sincerity of its utterance would redeem it. I do not know anyone whose approval of the little effort I would rather have than yours.

My own feeling is that not merely must the Republicans be put on one side but that the Democrats must offer the country in 1924 a constructive programme which will clear the air of the mists and doubts and ineptitudes of the last two years, and also a candidate who can be counted on with reasonable confidence to carry such a programme out.

My present formula is: The world has been made safe for democracy but democracy has not yet made the world safe from irrational radicalism and revolution, and our task is to remove by rational and enlightened reform the soil in which such weeds grow. God send that we may have the intelligence and steadfastness to do it. If the United States does not serve the world in this matter I know of no other democracy that can.

With very warm regard, and heartfelt thanks for your cheering letter,   Faithfully Yours,   [Woodrow Wilson]

CCL (WP, DLC).
    [1] Wilson was replying to F. I. Cobb to WW, Nov. 14, 1922, TLS (WP, DLC).

From Cleveland Hoadley Dodge

                                          Riverdale-on-Hudson
My dear Woodrow   New York Nov. 15th 1922

I have delayed writing to congratulate you on the result of the elections in order to get a better perspective, but I can't wait any longer to tell you how happy we all are

I never believed that the 1920 election was a complete repudiation of you & your policies & probably the last election was not a complete vindication of you but it undoubtedly was to a very great extent & we ought to thank God & take courage.

The millions of Christian people in the U. S. who are giving such enormous sums for relief in the Near East realize what our abstention from the League of Nations means & they want us to get in as never before. It is humiliating to have America represented at Lausanne[1] simply on the side lines, or it is nearer to the truth to say on the bleachers.

Hamilton Holt has a fairly good plan for education if it is well handled, & later it can be decided how far the Democratic party should make the League the big issue in 1924.

The sad thing is that our party seems to be sadly lacking in big leaders, but the Republicans are in the same boat and old Harding, as a prominent Republican said to me the other day, is too flabby.

I am very glad that you were well enough to make such a good talk on Election night[2] & didn't talk through your hat.

We are all well & still at Riverdale & I sincerely trust that Mrs Wilson is well & that you are steadily gaining

With much love to you both from us all

Ever affectionately   Cleveland H Dodge

ALS (WP, DLC).
¹ He referred to the forthcoming (November 20) conference between the Allies and Turkey to conclude a treaty of peace.
² He meant Armistice Day.

From Norman Hezekiah Davis

My dear Mr. Wilson: New York City, November 15, 1922.

I am in hearty accord with your views on "associate member-ships," and also with the necessity of making our entrance into the League a straight-out party issue. The so-called non-partisan pro-Leaguers have done more harm to the cause than have the straight-out anti-Leaguers. It will not be possible to prevent strad-dling on this question or to prevent the so-called non-partisan pro-Leaguers, whose primary interest is to save the face of the Repub-lican Party, from confusing the issue unless it is made a party question. As you know, I myself am not very much on compromis-ing, but I wrote you because I felt that you should know about the suggestion, and also because I was afraid a situation might be cre-ated which would make it more difficult later on to have a clean-cut issue. Since writing you I have heard that the Administration has been considering an Associate Membership but don't know what they have decided. I have also seen a dispatch from England stating that Austin [Austen] Chamberl[a]in had just said in a speech that there was hardly any alteration in the statutes of the League of Nations to which he would not gladly consent if by that America could be induced to join.

Several days ago I wrote a letter to Mr. Bonar Law, with whom I became very well acquainted when he was Chancellor of the Ex-chequer, in which I told him in substance that every move which Europe has made to get us into the League has been in the wrong direction; that America will never play an active or proper part in European or world affairs except through the League of Nations, and that all the statements to the effect that Europe is willing to emasculate the League in order to get the United States in damp-ens the ardor of the pro-Leaguers and plays into the hands of the anti-Leaguers who offer this as a proof that Europe cares nothing about the League and merely wishes to get the United States en-tangled.

Your Armistice Day speech could not have been better or more to the point. I am enclosing an editorial from the Newark Evening News[1] which I think you may find of some interest.

With affectionate regards, I am, As ever,

Faithfully yours,   Norman H. Davis

TLS (WP, DLC).
    [1] It is missing in WP, DLC.

Ray Stannard Baker to John Randolph Bolling

Dear Mr. Bolling: Amherst Massachusetts November 15 1922

I have just received the first royalty reports on the book publication: that is, on the advance sales. They are as follows:

Volumes I and II	1310.00
Volume III	478.00
	1788.00
One half	894.00

I therefore enclose a check of $894.

The advance sale was not quite as much as I expected: but this was in part due to the lateness in getting the book ready. If we could have had it in hand a month sooner, before the book-sellers were so fully stocked up, there is no doubt that the advance would have been greater. However, this is a small consideration, for if the book *moves*, as we hope, the sales will come later. And this movement depends largely upon the discussion and publicity the book receives.

I am deeply interested, of course, in seeing the book sell, but still more in having Woodrow Wilson's body of principles, his fundamental political philosophy, which is set forth in this book again widely discussed. The country *must* come back to Woodrow Wilson: there was never such a need of leadership and of clear and high moral principles. If only we can get people to reading and discussing our book, even though they attack it, we shall be helping greatly the common cause of bringing the American people back to reality. The speech on Armistice day gave us a breath of new hope. I wish I had been with you on that day!

I am doing my best,—as are the publishers also—in having the book reviewed by the best people we can get, and there will be all the advertising the book will stand: but the great thing is to get it somehow into men's minds that this record of Woodrow Wilson at Paris is the true handbook of American foreign policy as it ought to be and must be, if we are to redeem ourselves.

Mrs. Wilson's letter to me the other day acknowledging the

books[1] was the source of much satisfaction and pleasure: it was a real reward.

Please remember me to Mr. Wilson. I only wish there were other ways for me to advance the great things he stands for.

Cordially yours,   Ray Stannard Baker

Kindly return the royalty statements

ALS (WP, DLC).
[1] It is missing in the R. S. Baker Papers and the EBW Papers, DLC.

To Cleveland Hoadley Dodge

My dear Cleve,   Washington D C 16th November 1922

It was delightful and refreshing to get your letter of November fifteenth. I do indeed "thank God and take courage" because of the elections. I believe that they mean that the Democratic Party must make ready to obtain and deserve a great triumph in 1924 with a constructive programme which shall remove from this beloved country the provocations to revolution which seem to be operating in every other country in the world.

It cheers me to think that when the time for action comes you and I shall have new grounds for comradeship and mutual trust and confidence. I pray God I may have the physical strength to play my full part in the contest and victory.

With ever growing affection,

Faithfully Yours,   Woodrow Wilson

TLS (WC, NjP).

From Frank Irving Cobb

Dear Mr. Wilson: New York November 16th, 1922.

Your letter encourages me to offer a suggestion which may not be worth anything, but it is something I have had in mind for several weeks. The Democratic party needs the essentials of a constructive programme at once if it is to consolidate the gains it made in the election. The only man who can present a programme that will attract nation-wide discussion is yourself. What I had in mind was this: If one of the newly elected Senators were to write to you asking what, in your opinion, the policies of the Democratic party should be in the light of existing conditions, you could make a concrete presentation that is essential if we are to make any headway. This matter, I am sure, could easily be arranged by Baruch, whose enthusiasm is equalled only by his abilily [ability] and loyalty.

My vanity will not be wounded if you throw this suggestion into the waste basket. On close examination it may turn out to be quite inexpedient. I trust your own judgment in this matter much further than I would my own.

With sincerest regards,   As ever yours,   Frank I. Cobb.

TLS (WP, DLC).

John Hessin Clarke to John Randolph Bolling

My dear Mr. Bolling—   Youngstown, Ohio November 16, 1922

I thank you for sending me a copy of the letter and circular letter of Mr. Jones of Atlanta.[1] Very certainly there can be no doubt now that the churches are thoroughly aroused.

I am happy to say that I am improving every day and am quite confident that I shall be able to go to New York within a couple of weeks to confer with a group which is organizing the forward movement.

Please remember me to Mr. Wilson.

Sincerely yours,   John H. Clarke

TLS (WP, DLC).
[1] It is missing. "Mr. Jones" was (Meredith) Ashby Jones, pastor of the Ponce de Leon Avenue Baptist Church in Atlanta.

To Norman Hezekiah Davis

My dear Davis,   Washington D C 17th November 1922

I have been very much heartened by your letter of November fifteenth because it is so full of your true spirit and of useful counsel.

I am heartily glad that you wrote to Bonar Law as you did. Austin Chamberlin is an even more slippery customer than his father[1] was, and is probably up to some deliberate mischief.

I have read your address on the Democratic Party with real pleasure. It seems to me it would be very useful indeed to have it in the hands of every stump speaker in our behalf in the campaign of 1924, and I hope we can think out some means by which that end can be accomplished. I shall be glad to suggest anything you may wish to the National Committee about it.

May I respectfully venture a single criticism: You speak of the makers of the Constitution as having designed to create an oligarchy. I suggest that it would be a truer interpretation of their purpose to say that they wished to create a carefully concentrated rather than a vaguely dispersed responsibility, and since they succeeded it is all the sadder to have that responsibility in the hands of such persons as now exercise it.

Thank you very much for taking the trouble to send me a full copy of the address. Mrs. Wilson read it aloud to me and we both enjoyed it very much.

It strengthens me to feel in close touch with you, and I hope that our opportunity to cooperate may constantly widen.

With affectionate regard,

Faithfully Yours,   Woodrow Wilson

P.S. For fear what you sent me is the original of the Address, I feel obliged to return it.   W.W.

TLS (N. H. Davis Papers, DLC).
    [1] That is, Joseph Chamberlain. "Austin Chamberlin" was of course (Joseph) Austen Chamberlain.

To Frank Irving Cobb

My dear Cobb,   [Washington] 17th November 1922

You may be sure that any suggestion from you makes a great impression on me, and I dare say that some manifesto, such as that suggested in your letter of November sixteenth, would be not only timely but of great service in drawing together the forces of liberalism and sane reform. But I am not yet sure what will be the best method of origination and promulgation.

I am hoping to see Baruch down here soon. My opinion of him is just the same as yours, and I shall discuss your suggestion with him as I am sure you will wish.

It steadies me to feel in touch with you on great matters, and I hope that opportunities for our conference and cooperation will multiply.

With warm regard and deep confidence,

Faithfully Yours,   [Woodrow Wilson]

CCL (WP, DLC).

To Georges Clemenceau

[Washington] 18th Novr 1922

Allow me to bid you affectionate welcome to America where you will find none but friends   Woodrow Wilson

T telegram (WP, DLC).

From Georges Clemenceau

New York Nov 18 1922

Deeply touched by your kind message Accept my kindest regards and best wishes Am looking forward with great pleasure seeing you in Washington   Georges Clemenceau

T telegram (WP, DLC).

John Randolph Bolling to John Hessin Clarke

Dear Mr. Clarke: [Washington] 18th November 1922

It is delightful to know from your letter of the 16th inst. that your health is improving. Mr. Wilson joins me in hoping, however, that you will take things easy for a while—and not resume work until you feel confident the recent trouble has passed.

I note what you say about going to New York, and I am hopeful that much will come out of the conferences you will doubtless hold there. Mr. Hamilton Holt will, I am sure, have much to tell you of his recent talk here.

With high regard;

Cordially yours,   [John Randolph Bolling]

CCL (WP, DLC).

To Charles Dana Gibson[1]

My dear Mr. Gibson,   [Washington] 19th November 1922

I hope you will permit me to yield to the impulse to write and tell you how much pleasure I derived from your cartoon, "The Straphanger."[2] It seems to me extraordinarily fine.

May I also venture very respectfully to hope that "Life" will return to its editorial policy of supporting the League of Nations. I have been deeply disappointed to see it reverse that policy, for it seems to me that all enlightened forces of the nation ought now to pull together and pull in the same direction. I am sure you will understand that this suggestion is made in the most sincerely friendly spirit and because I value highly the influence that "Life" can exert.

Mrs. Wilson joins me in warmest regards to Mrs. Gibson[3] and you, and I beg that you will give my affectionate regards to your distinguished foreign guest whom I am happy to claim as my friend.

With sincere regard,

Faithfully Yours,   [Woodrow Wilson]

CCL (WP, DLC).
  ¹ The artist and illustrator. He had purchased the controlling interest in *Life* in 1920 and was chairman of its board.
  ² "The Straphanger," *Life*, LXXX (Nov. 16, 1922), 16-17. It is reproduced in the illustrations section of this volume.
  ³ Irene Langhorne Gibson.

From Bainbridge Colby

My dear Mr President: New York City November 20, 1922

I have made inquiries about Mr Mahaffy. His full name is Charles A. Mahaffy and he now holds the position of Director of Finance with the Interstate Commerce Commission, drawing I am told an annual salary of eight or ten thousand dollars.

I fear he is out of our reach. His present duties are important and undoubtedly interesting to him, and the position in our Washington office would hardly justify paying him a sum that would attract him.

Until we get this matter ironed out Mr Kriz, I am informed, is willing to resume his old position and we will not be exposed to unfriendly newspaper remark, as would be the case I think if we abruptly closed the Washington office without intimation of the reason.

I have been reverting to a thought you expressed some time ago that it might be well to consider closing the Washington office and to see such clients as were worth while by appointment in your study. I can see the appeal which this idea might have for you and I am ready cheerfully to second it, if it should prove to be your real wish.

Sometimes these little curves in the track give one a broader glance at the course of the journey, and I am conscious of a deepening of certain thoughts which have lately been in my mind. I have not sought to conceal from you my disappointment that my efforts have not been more successful. While it is true that we have with complete accord imposed upon ourselves some severe restrictions in the acceptance of proffered business, I cannot but feel that despite these limitations, from which I can see no escape, I should have been able with the great prestige of your name and the powerful aid of your constant interest and accessibility to conference, to have done more. I sometimes feel very strongly that the arrangement must be irksome to you, at least at times. It could hardly be otherwise, with its negligible results, and the recurrence of more or less harassing decisions. I should hate to feel deficient in a promptness of perception that the time had possibly arrived to offer, without waiting for you to ask, the opportunity to re-examine your position with reference to the firm.

Sometimes the littlest kind of a change or shift brings improvement, and the thought has occurred to me that possibly you would feel more comfortable if you were to accept such matters as were referred to you for your opinion or guidance, and I were to fare forth alone. I feel quite certain that I could be instrumental in bringing to you employments worthy of your attention and suitable in their returns. And I have an idea that some little rearrangement, of no greater significance than what I am here discussing, might enable me to change the whole current of things so far as they affect you.

I am relying, my dear Mr President, upon your perceptive and understanding mind to rescue this letter from any misconstruction that my halting words, written with such difficulty and depression, may expose me to. You must know in what intense admiration and deep affection I hold you. The honor of being your professional partner has filled me with pride and happiness, and you have been a perfect partner, infinitely helpful, generous and true.

I submit my reflections to you in the candour which has guided all our intercourse.

Affectionately always   Bainbridge Colby

TLS (WP, DLC).

From Ray Stannard Baker

Dear Mr. Wilson: Amherst Massachusetts November 20, 1922.

As you may know, Jean Longuet, Editor of *L'Humanité*, the Socialist paper of Paris, is here in America lecturing. He is a grandson of Karl Marx. I saw quite a good deal of him in Paris during 1918, and he helped me in numerous ways. Whatever his radicalism, he was a far truer supporter of your policies than Clemenceau or the other official French leaders. He represents as well as anyone today the opposition in France, what little there is of it and unenlightened as it may be. He expects to be in Washington December twelfth and is very anxious to call upon you. I have felt bound to suggest it to you and even to hope that you will let him come. In these days one feels that almost any sort of opposition ought to be encouraged in France.

How the election must have pleased and gratified you! The country is sick and tired of Harding and all that he represents and thousands read your words of Armistice Day with reviving hope.

Our book seems to be starting off well and to be getting some good notices. If only we can get it really discussed I feel certain that it will change opinion fundamentally in this country. People must get back to your principles, Mr. President, for they are the fundamental principles which must govern American policies if we are not to disgrace ourselves everlastingly.

With warm and deep personal regard,

Ray Stannard Baker

TLS (WP, DLC).

To Ray Stannard Baker

My dear Baker,   [Washington] 22nd November 1922

Thank you for your letter of twentieth November.

There is this embarrassment about my seeing Longuet: He is, I believe, openly antagonistic to Clemenceau, and Clemenceau is likely to be in Washington and to call upon me at about the time you think Longuet's visit to Washington probable. I think therefore that I had better keep the two calls as far apart as possible and not commit myself at present on the subject of receiving a call from Longuet. I am sure you will approve of such prudence and forgive me for saying I know of no man who has more perverted the thinking of the world than Karl Marx, his grandfather.

Let me congratulate you again on the completion and publication of the book. I feel confident it will fulfill the high mission to which you have so generously dedicated it. It contains the truth, and the truth will prevail.

Mrs. Wilson joins me in warm regard, and I beg that you will realize that I always think of you with affectionate regard.

Faithfully and Sincere[ly] Yours,   [Woodrow Wilson]

CCL (WP, DLC).

To James Michael Curley

My dear Mr. Mayor,   [Washington] 23rd November 1922

Unhappily it is not true that I have been planning a visit to Boston.[1] The conditions of my convalescence make it necessary I should remain at home.

But I am none the less warmly obliged to you for the cordial invitation brought to me by your letter of November twenty-first. It would be a pleasure to renew our old acquaintance and to confer informally upon the means which our party is to employ for the redemption of the nation, and through the nation for the redemption of civilization. As I see it the opportunity and duty of the party are nothing less than that, and we should all steady our spirits for the great enterprise.

I hope that everything goes fortunately with you and that Boston prospers notwithstanding its stupid failure to repudiate Lodge. Surely Massachusetts is enlightened enough to discern his real character. Though I am of course not a Massachusetts man, it mortifies me that the State of Daniel Webster should have such a representative in the Senate.

Thank you very much for your kind wishes about my health and believe me, with the most cordial personal greetings,

Sincerely and Faithfully Yours,   [Woodrow Wilson]

CCL (WP, DLC).
    [1] Wilson was replying to J. M. Curley to WW, Nov. 21, 1922, TLS (WP, DLC). Curley was of course Mayor of Boston.

To Bainbridge Colby

My dear Colby,   Washington D C 24th November 1922

I have been thinking very seriously over the matter we have occasionally discussed and feel that I must, in justice to you, renew the suggestion I made to you in the summer, namely, that we dissolve our partnership so as to leave you free individually to take business such as has frequently come to us but with which I,— because of my years of public service and conduct of national affairs,—cannot associate myself as counsel.

It is a matter of deep and sincere regret to me to sever our professional relations, but I cannot consistently with my affectionate regard for you in conscience go on putting my personal limitations upon your activities.

We understand each other too well not to feel that a frank avowal will strengthen our friendship even though it sever our formal relationship. Please feel that you can count on my comprehension of your generous position, but believe that this decision has not been arrived at hastily and that I am sure I am right in the matter. We shall, I am confident, continue to bear to one another the same confidential relationship that has been to me a source of strength and comfort throughout our association.

With loyal affection,

Faithfully Yours,   Woodrow Wilson

TLS (B. Colby Papers, DLC).

From George Foster Peabody, with Enclosures

Saratoga Springs New York

My great and good Friend: Nov. 25, 1922.

I am sending herewith the letter and the memorandum of my thought respecting the next Democratic platform. You were kind enough to intimate that you would be hospitable to this. I rather vainly hoped that I might condense my thought as to the railroad matter and am quite certain you had no expectation that I would so greatly trespass upon your time and attention.

I am reminded of my continual admiration for your marvelous power of condensing. I was gratified yesterday in riding with a geologist of 77 with forty years' experience and a young business man of New York to find them so enthusiastic over your recent Armistice day speech because of its effective putting of much in little. I find my heart continually warmed by the references to your good self.

There is much I have omitted respecting my observation of railroad methods and lack of efficiency, but I could not bring myself to make the letter longer. I shall, however, be most glad to elaborate any particular aspect if you desire.

I must again express my deep sense of the honor you do me in letting me put before you this thought. I concluded that as the achievement of the end I desire was so great an accomplishment, it would doubtless be wise to approach it more gradually with reference to the thorough understanding necessary to a settled result. I have therefore suggested a pledge to a specific study and publication of facts. I am not clear but that it would be well to embody at the same time a similar pledge as to the coal situation. I am firmly of the opinion from my considerable experience in the coal business and from the receipt of the unearned increment in the profits of that business that no settlement of that vital issue can come excepting through Federal ownership. It is, of course, wise to await the results of President Harding's fact finding commission. It is to be hoped that they will do better than the "best minds" have done in other directions.

I am, with high respect and regard,

Faithfully yours,   George Foster Peabody

E N C L O S U R E   I

From George Foster Peabody

Saratoga Springs, N. Y.

Dear President Wilson: November 25th 1922

   I fear I shall be rather long in stating my reasons for such strong convictions respecting the operation of the railroads. It is, however, a long history and a complicated question. It is not yet a hundred years since the first railroads were built yet the relation of those railroads to the officials and functioning of government has been constant and on the whole thoroughly demoralizing. Is it not necessarily so? The transpor[t]ation of passengers and freight relates itself to every citizen, young and old. Any lack of courtesy or consideration is bound to make friction because of the quasi public character of the railroad corporation. We, therefore, get much of the evil with less of the good that should go with an established public operation. The first railroads were all built by public aid which showed the recognition of the public obligation to transportation. Even now new railroads are built by private concession of rights of way oftentimes.

   The present status evolved out of continual friction between the public, the railroads and lawmakers is illogical. The essential element of economic efficiency is a single-minded administration. The dual obligation residing in boards of directors responsibility and State and Federal commission over-ruling is of necessity uneconomic. The state of mind of the operating official is constantly antagonistic to the supervising official and this necessarily carries on to the public whom he represents. The private owner is not really considered. The directors and back of them the single-minded banking interests or group in control of the officials through power of the purse for new capital is the only bit of real loyalty. This pertains with reference to the individual railroad system considered as an economic unit. As a matter of fact, however, no present system can live to itself: its operation is largely related to its connections and its competitors. If its connections control terminals it is in effect dominated by them. The measure of competition that exists is necessarily limited by the regulations of the governmental commissions. The unity of feeling and opposition to these commissions make the final loyalty to the group and operating officials, owners ignored and, in antagonism to the government—the people. Such competition as there is, therefore, is based upon the greater natural advantage of terminals or gradients and capacity of the equipment with efficiency in management. This last element which should be the important one as regards the public interest with reference to low cost is the least powerful, of necessity.

The competition of a generation ago, which was so active and violent that it necessitated first, gentlemen's agreements to maintain rates and thereafter compelled regulation of rates, was to a large degree legitimate commercial competition, but was in effect the manifestation of a state of war between rival batallions directed by generals seeking, not for railroad efficiency and success but for domination of wide tracts of country. It was not merely figuratively the modern succession to the warring feudal barons of the early generations,—Vanderbilt, the Pennsylvanis [Pennsylvania] railroad group, Daniel Drew, Jay Gould, Huntington, Henry Villard, James J. Hill, E. H. Harriman were in effect commanders of armies battling for control of the transportation of vast sections of the country and the varied profits personally resultant. They succeeded in directing the accumulated surplus of wealth into their banking and personal treasuries to a large extent, their banking associates being sharers of this very great proportion of the products of the labor on the farms, mines and in the factories.

I have tried to sketch briefly this outline of what has been my own experience in personal relations as banker and railroad executive for forty years past during which period I have had responsibility in construction of railroads in Canada, Illinois, Utah and Mexico specifically. I am convinced it is impossible to carry on without continual demoralization of governmental representatives and to an extent the people concerned the private ownership and operation of transportation facilities. The country has paid an incalculable price during these ninety years of railroad experimentation and development. I suppose if it were possible to calculate it would prove that a good percentage of all the coal ever mined in the United States had been consumed in transporting it longer distances to compete with mines nearer the consumer which under a properly developed system of transpor[t]ation would have supplied cheap coal to a community more intensively and, therefore, more economically developed. I believe the damage to the last two generations of the Unites [United] States growing up in small communities spread abroad by competitive railroad construction so that only one teacher school houses could be afforded and the most valuable education, that of environment and intercommunication by reason of moderately concentrated population, being entirely lost, is quite incalculable. The greenback, populist, free silver and other such waves of perfectly honest effort to right wrongs being instances of the results of such sparsely settled lands. For many years there were five railroads from the Mississippi to Missouri where two would have been ample for all the available excess population. This resulted in careless culture of new land and reckless and wasteful habits of farming and neglect of farming machinery resulting in farm mortgage, foreclosures, also chattel mortgages and the steady tendency to tenant farming, which is so injurious to the upbuilding of a self-respecting, rightly informed and trained democratic citizenship.

I could go on with many details that my experience and observation in the Western and Southern States have afforded me but these are perhaps more than necessary for suggestion. I regret to have felt obliged to cite so many. It may be said that the country has paid this price for experimentation in the construction of railroads to bind together the East and West and the North and South. Therefore, why go into the change which will involve paying a price to educate the people and the officials to operation for public welfare and not for profit. Why not take advantage of the efficiency gained by the experience which has brought the railroads to the point where comparison with Europe is so frequently claimed to be in favor of private operation. I reply the present efficiency is not thorough, not all genuine and will not be maintained. The recent labor struggles are sufficient proof of this but much more could be found by careful and thorough analysis. My chief reason, however, for such insistence upon government operation as well as governmental ownership is that the welfare of a democratic government is dependent upon constant knowledge of and familiarity with the functioning of government by the citizens. The early efficiency of the simpler government activities was due to the interest of the farmer and the storekeeper and the small manufacturer of that day in the administration of each office and particularly his knowledge as to how much money was raised and where it was expended. It is no longer possible in our complicated life of today, even the farmer is unable to keep track of things in his own neighborhood because so much of his own activity is related to what he delivers and receives from the railroads and the postoffice.

Our Hampton motto "Learning by doing" is I think most pertinent to the education necessary for a democracy responsible for government—twenty five years of political experimentation in operating railroads will be a small price to pay for a public conscience demanding efficient civil service and understanding of true enlightened leadership.

I am with high respect

Faithfully Yours   George Foster Peabody

TLS (WP, DLC).

Suggestion for consideration in 1924

The Democratic party recognizes that the functions of government should adjust themselves from time to time to the conditions of life which the progress of civilization and industrial development produce. The profound changes in human relations which have resulted from the world war call for even more careful consideration than is usually given in party councils. These changes have brought to the front economic issues that are fundamental in human relations. This situation calls for the earnest thought of every citizen as to whether the party of his previous affiliations is frankly and openly dealing with the major issues that are really uppermost in the daily thought of the citizens.

The Democratic party in National convention assembled deems the situation so critical that it presents a platform less extensive because the conditions call for action which is radical in the sense that it shall go to the root of the evils from which the country now realizes it is suffering. The necessity for reaching a decision as to these major issues makes it desirable to confine the thought of the voters to these few fundamental questions. When they shall be settled rightly, the more full programs which in their functioning relate themselves to the basic policy can be more effectively considered.

It seems worth while to restate the fact that in this Republic of the United States the people are the government and not the officials whom they choose from time to time to carry out their will. These, whether legislative, executive or judicial, are merely representatives of the people. They must have knowledge of the people's judgment and will. They are entitled to have definite expression of public opinion, which is the only supreme control under a democratic form of government.

It is not boastful in this connection to recall to the minds of citizens the constant and successful effort made by Woodrow Wilson and the Democratic Congresses chosen with him to develop and ascertain clear and vigorous public opinion on the issues of the day. We deem it not unfair to ask citizens to study for themselves the contrasting administration of the Republican officials who were chosen under an extraordinary mandate in 1920.

The first active functioning of government in its relation to the people is through taxation, by which the people contribute suitably and ratably to the support and functioning of their government. The really fabulous sums which the expenses of government call for by reason of the world war make taxation a much more vital thing to every citizen than ever before in history. The Democratic party believes that the principles which governed the Republican party's dealing with taxation are radically unsound. It believes that the time has come for the American people to consider the question of taxation from a more fundamental point of view. It will, therefore, propose that the Congress to be elected this year shall give special consideration to the basic principles of taxation and shall formulate legislation by which revenues shall be secured first from the monopolistic wealth which is God-given and which no energy of man can increase and that the next source of revenue should be, in increasing degree, from the accumulated wealth produced by the natural resources and the labor of the people during the whole period of our history.

It is proper in this connection to call attention to the fact that legislation throughout the past has resulted in the accumulation by not more than 1% of the population of a very large percentage of the total unconsumed wealth of the people. Modern practice has developed a conservative, moderate and reasonable recovery of this wealth to the people through the inheritance taxation adopted by nearly all the States as well as by the Federal government. It is proposed that specific study shall be given by the incoming Congress to this source of revenue with a view to having one collection made by the Federal government and a suitable division with the State governments provided, thus doing away with the double levying of taxes in this connection with the increasing hindrances to business and comfort in life. It is also proposed that the Congress shall definitely give consideration to simplifying methods of taxation so that the citizens at large will not be compelled to expend so much money in legal fees to see that they keep within the law and that some do not ignorantly pay more than their due share.

The second most continuous functioning of government in relation to the people is through the control of transportation, which in the highly industrialized life of this vast country is equivalent to the circulatory system of the human body—every hindrance to the free movement of people or commodities is bound to cause a congestion which raises the blood pressure of the body politic. It is, therefore, vital to the normal functioning of the people's government that the utmost assurance of equal, efficient and economic transportation shall be provided by the legislative and executive powers of the government.

This convention recognizes an assumed opposition to government ownership and operation of railroad transportation, but it desires to record its belief that the people have not reached any reasoned conclusion upon this subject. It is manifest to all who know, that the great banking interests and few powerful railroad officials in close affiliation with them have developed a vast and continuous propaganda at great expense, in which the assumption is continually declared of a determination upon the part of the people against government ownership. Many competent to judge from experience and study claim that the facts cited by this propaganda are partial, prejudiced and inconclusive.

The Democratic national convention proposes that the Congress to be elected and the executive shall co-operate in the most thorough study of the entire question of transportation and its relation to every citizen. It promises that all the facts shall be ascertained and that an impartial and unprejudiced summary of these facts shall be prepared and circulated so that every group of citizens shall have the opportunity to be fully informed upon this most vital domestic question.

This question is vital not merely with reference to the economic life of the country but it is forcefully claimed by many that it is essential to the vitality of any democratic republican government. A well-informed citizenship is necessary to the efficient functioning by representatives chosen to carry out the will of the people. No aspect of government can possibly be so related to the daily life and welfare of the people and so informing as to the quality and character of official action as the operation by carefully trained employes of the transportation systems of national extent and, no less, municipal. The foundation of all public transportation is in the public franchise based on the right of eminent domain—an exercise of strictly governmental functions.

This convention urges upon the voters personal consideration of the facts that shall be submitted by the incoming Congress respecting the relation of transportation to the welfare of the whole people of the country, to the functioning of government and whether it may not be that this provides the most effective way for every citizen to learn how his government is operated—whether economically, wisely and unto most efficient production.

With the basic domestic issues rightly adjusted, the circulation of the body politic can approach more nearly to the normal and thus assure the clear brain and the easy co-operation of communities and citizens with the least friction to consistently move forward on the lines of a truly progressive democracy, i.e., a government of the people, by the people and for the people, which thus being truly human and giving continual weight to the major factors in human relations—understanding and sympathy—will develop self-respect and with that a right sense of the obligations which one country owes to all other countries.

Noblesse oblige is an ancient heritage which the people of this land received from their forefathers and which from time to time in periods of crisis they have shown as dominant from north to south and from east to west. During the critical world period occasioned by the war begun in 1914, this country wisely held itself in neutral temper to discover, if possible, a way to aid in bringing to an end the conflict at the earliest possible time. From all of the warring nations there had come great numbers of men and women, who, with their descendants, numbered millions of our citizens. From out this patient waiting with hope deferred the country finally reached the conclusion that the world's future ultimate peace could be assured only by the association of the United States with the allied powers. The leadership of our great President, Woodrow Wilson, was sustained by an extraordinary unanimity of temper and by a spirit of resolve so high that the whole world acknowledged its force. At that time the United States gloriously illustrated noblesse oblige.

The reaction in the temper of the people shown in the election of 1920 was due to many causes but largely, we believe, to the misguided determination of our German citizens and others with intense interest in and racial relations in Europe to rebuke the administration responsible for leading the people into the war, which resulted in victory over the central powers. Following this the United States had lost its prestige through the partisan machinations of members of the U. S. Senate, whose passionate prejudice for the time disorganized the high temper which the people of this country had manifested throughout the seven years of splendid manifestation of a democracy's majesty and power.

While the issues affecting the vote cast in 1922 were varied and due in large part to the unpatriotic and selfish legislation of the Republican Congress, it is still our belief that this action was merely preliminary to a taking stock of the economic and political situation in this country. This convention has faith to believe that the result of such reflection as the country has now undertaken and of such development of basic facts respecting the principles of government will be to recover promptly among the American people their sense of noblesse oblige. They will realize that the entire world—Africa with her 200 millions of earnest seekers for light, India with her 300 millions praying for a way to fuller self-expression, China with her 400 millions eagerly desiring to attain the benefits of republican democracy, and Europe in the welter of war's hellish and unlimited results—all look to the United States of America to not only show them the way to climb up to the heights of human progress and happiness but to extend to them that most valuable of all human expressions—valuable more to the giver than to the recipient—sympathy and help and the willingness and courage to take any risk to help the brother in need.

Therefore, with confident hope of the recovery of moral leadership by the United States for the sake of service to others and not for selfish advantage, this convention records its hope and belief that your votes will elect a Congress in sympathy with the candidates of this convention to accept membership in the League of Nations. It will doubtless be the best method of help, following the demoralization of these years by which this country can exercise in fullest sympathy all its influence, to take advantage of the experience of the years since 1919 in making the League of Nations most completely helpful in its main object to assure the peace of the world.

T MS (WP, DLC).

From Bainbridge Colby

My dear Mr President: New York City November 27, 1922

I beg to acknowledge your letter of the 24th in answer to mine of the 20th. I was not at the office on Saturday, the day of its receipt.

The warm and generous words with which it concludes, I deeply prize and thank you for them.

The opening paragraph of your letter, however, is so unresponsive to my letter of the 20th, that I am in some quandary as to how to accept it. When I wrote you that "I should hate to feel deficient in a promptness of perception that the time had possibly arrived to offer, without waiting for you to ask, the opportunity to re-examine your position with reference to the firm," I also referred to the "complete accord" with which we had imposed upon ourselves certain restrictions in the acceptance of proffered business. I am not aware that there has been any divergence of viewpoint between us on such matters, and I should regret very much to have you think I approached these decisions in a temper different from your own. The truth is that I have declined, without even consulting you, a number of cases many times in excess of the few that I have referred to you for your opinion, so fully did I feel that I understood your views and shared them. And as to the future, I expressed the thought in my letter that I could see no escape for either of us from the operation of these sound restraints.

If you will again glance at my letter of the 20th, you will see that

I brought up the question of the firm's future, with a frank recognition that its results up to the present must be disappointing to you. I was moved by a sensitiveness lest a situation which had possibly become irksome to you should be prolonged through silence or oversight of mine.

Your secretary, Mr Bolling, in a letter which accompanied yours,[1] indicates that it is your thought to issue your letter of the 24th, as a combined announcement and explanation of the firm's dissolution, thereby practically releasing it for publication. This idea deserves further consideration. I should at once be questioned as to the nature of the matters on which we had disagreed. I could only answer that we had had no difference on any matter. The next question would be,—what are the matters to which Mr Wilson refers in his significant opening paragraph. I could only reply truthfully that I did not know. The interrogator would then pass to his next question,—what are the matters as to which this restriction which you have imposed upon yourselves, has arisen. And so on and on, trenching upon professional confidences, until we would find ourselves buffeted by a discussion which should never have been permitted, much less invited.

I would suggest a simple announcement that the firm has been dissolved by mutual consent—nothing more. There is no occasion for a wide distribution of formal notices, and to circulate letters that may have passed between partners is without any precedent that I can recall, and I think in debatable taste.

Would it not be well for me to come down to Washington, and in conference with you, arrange these matters of form, so that you will be quite satisfied with the procedure.

Always with affectionate regard,

Faithfully yours   Bainbridge Colby

TLS (WP, DLC).
[1] JRB to BC, Nov. 24, 1922, TLS (B. Colby Papers, DLC).

To Angus Wilton McLean[1]

My dear Friend,   [Washington] 28th November 1922

It would of course have given me pleasure to send the message you suggested in your telegram[2] if I could have done so consistently with the policy I am now pursuing,—a policy I am sure your own judgment will approve.

The party is still looking to me for leadership, and the country at large gives a good deal of heed to what I have to say. I think, therefore, it is wise not to say what is in my mind in broken and scattered places, but wait until some occasion when I can give careful expression to the whole of my thought about affairs. I have, therefore, refrained from scattered messages here and there. As you will readily believe, requests for messages come with almost every day. I could not in any case comply with all of them, and I have felt it would be invidious and unfair to discriminate. I am sure you will think so yourself when you consider the matter.

The election results in North Carolina were most gratifying and reflect the highest credit upon those loyal and energetic Democrats who, like yourself, steadfastly labour to lift the ideals of the political standards of the country and put our party at the front as the leader in all truly progressive policies. I congratulate you very heartily.

The whole atmosphere in which the National Committee works must have been changed by the facts of November seventh, and I believe that it will now be comparatively easy to give to the party the necessary organization and spirit for the great achiev[e]ment which awaits it in the next Presidential campaign.

With warm regard, and with the hope that it may not be long before I can have the pleasure of greeting you in person,

Cordially and Faithfully Yours,   [Woodrow Wilson]

CCL (WP, DLC).
[1] Public man, businessman, lawyer, and leader of the Democratic party in North Carolina and the country at large. He was Governor of North Carolina, 1925-1929.
[2] A. W. McLean to WW, Nov. 27, 1922, T telegram (WP, DLC), asking Wilson to send a message to the dinner being held in Raleigh "tonight" to celebrate the Democratic party's victory in North Carolina in the recent campaign.

To Bainbridge Colby

My dear Colby,   Washington D C 29th November 1922

I am quite ready and willing to accept the verdict of your taste as to the announcement of the dissolution of our partnership and have no doubt that it adequately meets all the necessities of the case.

The main idea I wished you to get from my letter of November 24th was one which I now repeat: It was that this dissolution of our partnership had come about through no dissatisfaction on the part of either of us by the actions or influence of the other.

It has been a matter of no small gratification to me that your own judgment and preference have so completely coincided with mine in regard to the business we have declined. It reassured me as to the soundness of my own conclusions that they should be yours also.

It seems to me that it would be perfectly easy to answer the impertinent questions of interrogators if we should deem it best to mention business declined. We could say that it was business which directly or indirectly affected the action of the Government. But there need be no mention of business declined, and therefore no interrogations to answer.

I need not tell you, I hope, how much it pains me to dissolve a connection which has been so altogether agreeable and enjoyable to me. You have behaved in every way with the most considerate and ideal friendship and I am sure that nothing you could have done or omitted would have brought us the kind of practice we could accept. It would distress me if you should think there was in my mind the slightest thought of any derelictions or blunders on your part.

If it is your wish to talk matters over before the final announcement, I will of course welcome the opportunity to see and confer with you. I hope that I have made you feel how sincerely glad I have always been to see you and how truly I have enjoyed our personal intercourse as well as our professional association. One of the rewards of that association was that it threw us so much together, and I am glad to believe that a formal partnership is not necessary to the continuance of our close association in thought and action.

If I have left anything unsaid which would adequately express my confidence and affection you can simply deem it said in the form which you would most prefer.

With unalterable affectionate regard,

Faithfully Yours,   Woodrow Wilson

TLS (B. Colby Papers, DLC).

From Bainbridge Colby

New York Dec 1 1922

Your touching letter just received You are the dearest man in the world I want to come down just take you by the hand I like to feel that there is no hurry about the next move I feel all broken up

Colby

T telegram (WP, DLC).

A Draft of "The Document"[1]

[Dec. 2, 1922]

CONFIDENTIAL DOCUMENT.

1. We recognize the fact that the complex, disturbing and for the most part destructive results of the great war have made it necessary that the progressive countries of the world should supply for the reconstruction of its life a programme of law and reform which shall bring it back to health and effective order; and that it lies with the political party which best understands existing conditions, is in most sympathetic touch with the mass of the people, and is ready and best qualified to carry a constructive programme through to take the initiative in making and pressing affirmative proposals of remedy and reform.

2. In this spirit and with this great purpose we, as representatives of the Democratic party of the United States put forth, in deep earnestness, the following declaration of principle and purpose and thereby seek to serve America, and through America, liberal men throughout the world who seek to serve their people.

3. "AMERICA FIRST" is a slogan which does not belong to any one political party; it is merely a concise expression of what is in the heart of every patriotic American. We enthusiastically incorporate it into this our declaration of principles and purposes. But it means different things in different mouths and requires definition. When uttered by the present leaders of the Republican party it means that America must render no service to any other nation or people which she can reserve for her own selfish aggrandizement. When we use it we mean that in every international action or organization for the benefit of mankind America must be foremost; that America, by developing within her own citizenship and acts a sensitive regard for justice in all the relations of men, must lead the world in applying the broadest conceptions of justice and peace, of amity and respect, to the mutual relations of other peoples, and in rendering them material aid in the realization of those ideals.

4. We are suffering in common with other nations of the world from the industrial and commercial prostration which followed the great war. Bound up with world conditions from which we could not extricate ourselves, the Republican Administration nevertheless committed itself to a policy of isolation. It blindly persisted in the delusion that we are unaffected by the world's all-encompassing perils and calamities and that, although we have great accumulated strength and matchless resources, we have no responsi-

---

[1] There are three complete typed drafts of this document in WP, DLC. Wilson made extensive WWhw and WWT changes in the first and second of the drafts, and Mrs. Wilson made two changes in the third draft, which is printed below. A note on the penultimate draft reads: "Revised to Dec. 2, '22."

bility for and need not interest ourselves in efforts to discover and apply safeguards and remedies. It still refuses to take the lead or to cooperate with the Governments of other nations in the adoption of measures which would improve our own situation or that of our customers and debtors.

The Republican Administration has no economic policy, domestic or foreign. In economic matters it is trying to go in several opposite directions at the same time. It declares its desire to stimulate foreign trade and to revive shipping and yet, under pressure of special interests and for their benefit, it erects a high tariff barrier to lessen imports and therefore to limit or destroy foreign trade. It recklessly ignores the fact that we have more than half of the gold of the world; that other nations cannot pay us in gold; that it would not benefit us to receive it if they could and that we cannot sell our surplus products of the farm and factory and collect our debts unless our customers and debtors can produce and sell their goods.

That it would be worse than stupid to try to maintain a merchant fleet by direct and indirect subsidies to carry freight and then to destroy trade by excluding commodities, does not enter the minds of the Old Guard Republican leaders who are in charge of the Government. They assert their eagerness to reduce taxes and the cost of living and yet ought to know, in their hearts, if they had an intelligent conception of the situation that they add to both by their tariff programme, based on greed. They preach economy and yet press legislation for new undertakings and obligations involving hundreds of millions of dollars. They profess to be concerned about the laborers' standard of living, and at a time when the beneficiaries of their tariff policy are omitting nothing to reduce wages they are devising measures to increase the laborers' cost of living. They clamor for the stabilization of trade and exchange and by their course contribute to the conditions which render stabilization impossible. They are blind to the fact that the protection which the American farmers and manufacturers need is that which would be afforded by a great foreign market, and that this can be secured only by measures which will bring peace to the world, stimulate the forces of production everywhere, and make possible through legitimate business ventures this nation's assistance to Europe through loans and investments.

5. We demand the immediate resumption of our international obligations and leadership,—obligations which were shamelessly repudiated and a leadership which was incontinently thrown away by the failure of the Senate to ratify the Treaty of Versailles and the negotiation of separate treaties with the central powers. We heartily approve and endorse the proposal of President Harding that the

United States officially adhere to the permanent international court of justice established under the auspices of the League of Nations, but the proposal is manifestly only a fragment of a policy which is incomplete and which ought to be frankly and courageously rounded out and made self-consistent. We deem it essential to the maintenance of the dignity of the United States, to the vindication of our national honor and to the final confirmation of the good faith of our Government toward the nation[s] with whom we were associated in the recent war that the United States should become a member of the League of Nations, assuming the same responsibilities that the other members assume for the organization and maintenance of peace.

6. We condemn the group of men who brought about these evil results as the most partisan, prejudiced, ignorant and unpatriotic group that ever misled the Senate of the United States.

7. We call attention to the lamentable record of incompetence, evasion and political truckling of the last Congress, dominated in both the Senate and House of Representatives by a commanding Republican majority. No step has been taken toward the redemption of the pledges made by the Republican party. Despite the crying needs of the hour and the hopes of the people, it has not enacted a single piece of constructive or ameliorative legislation, although for the last three years it has controlled both houses of Congress.

8. The demand for a revision of the tax laws, made three years ago by a Democratic President upon the conclusion of the armistice, is still unheeded, and the burdensome and unequal taxes, born of and justified only by a great emergency, still persist, thwarting the normal processes of economic recovery, and robbing the frugality and industry of the people of their just rewards.

9. We believe that the President and the members of his cabinet should be accorded the right to places on the floor of the Senate and the House of Representatives whenever those bodies have under discussion affairs which are entrusted by the Constitution or the laws to the executive branch of the Government; that they should also be accorded the right to take part in such discussions; and that they should be required to answer upon the floor all proper questions addressed to them concerning matters dealt with by the executive.

10. We call attention to the fact that a budget still unbalanced, and distended beyond the requirements of efficient and economical administration in time of peace, shows no sign of contraction, and every day brings the report of some fresh conspiracy against the public treasury. We promise studious and disinterested ap-

proach to the problems of national relief and rehabilitation and condemn the callousness and levity with which the Republican party has subordinated the duty of intelligent attention to these vital problems to petty considerations of partisan politics.

11. We shall use every legitimate means to advance to the utmost the industrial and commerical [commercial] development of the United States. That development has already made the people of the United States the greatest economic force in the world. It is as convincing proof of their practical genius as their free institutions are proof of their political genius. It is their manifest opportunity and destiny to lead the world in these great fields of endeavor and achievement. Our opponents have sought to promote the accumulation of wealth as an instrument of power in the hands of individuals and corporations. It is our object to promote it as a means of diffused prosperity and happiness and of physical and spiritual well being on the part of the great working masses of our people.

12. Without the systematic coordination, cooperation and interchange of services by the railroads the expanding, varying and changeable commerce and industry of the country cannot be properly served. All of these conditions are now lacking because our present laws deal with the railroads without system and altogether by way of interference and restriction. The result is a confusion which is constantly made worse almost to the point of paralysis by the multiplicity and intermittent conflict of regulative authorities, local and national.

13. The Eighteenth Amendment made prohibition the law of the Nation. The Volstead Act prescribed for the Nation what liquor should be deemed intoxicating. But the people, when adopting the Amendment, recognized fully that the law could not be enforced without the cooperation of the States within the Nation. Hence it provided in Section 2 that "The Congress and the several States shall have concurrent power to enforce this article by appropriate legislation." The intention was that each government should perform that part of the task for which it was peculiarly fitted. The Federal Government's part is to protect the United States against illegal importation of liquor from foreign countries and to protect each State from the illegal introduction into it of liquor from another State. To perform that part of the task effectively required centralized, unified action and the employment of the large federal powers and resources. Experience has demonstrated that to perform adequately this part of the task will require all the resources which Congress makes available for enforcement of this law. To this part of the whole task of enforcement the Federal Government

should, therefore, devote its entire energies. The protection of the people of a State against the illegal sale within it of liquor illegally manufactured within it, is a task for which the State Governments are peculiarly fitted, and which they should perform. That part of the task involves diversified governmental action and adaptation to the widely varying conditions in, and the habits and sentiments of the people of, the several States. It is a task for which the Federal Government is not fitted. To relieve the States from the duty of performing it, violates our traditions; and threatens the best interests of our country. The strength of the Nation and its capacity for achievment is, in large measure, due to the federal system with its distribution of powers and duties.

There should be frank recognition of the fact that the prime duty of the Federal Government is to protect the country against illegal importation from abroad and from illegal introduction of liquor from one State into another; that the full performance of this duty will tax the resources of the Federal Government to the uttermost; and that, for the rest, the people of each State must look to their state governments. But the Eighteenth Amendment should remain unchanged. And the Volstead Act should remain unchanged.

14. We need a Secretary of Transpor[t]ation who shall rank with the heads of other great federal cabinet departments and who shall be charged with the formulation and execution of plans for the coordinated use and full development of the transportation systems of the country. He should be associated with a federal Transpor[t]ation Board which should be invested with all the powers now lodged with the Interstate Commerce Commission and, in addition, with the authority to determine the occasions and the conditions of all loans floated and of all securities issued by the several railway and steamship lines. This Board should have the same powers of supervision and regulation over the steamship lines of the United States that are now exercised by the Interstate Commerce Commission over the railways.

15. The present menace to political liberty and peaceful economic prosperity lies, not in the power of kings or irresponsible governments, but in hasty, passionate and irrational programmes of revolution. The world has been made safe for democracy, but democracy has not yet made the world safe against irrational revolution. It is the privilege and duty of ours, the greatest of all democracies, to show the way. It is our purpose to defeat the irrational programmes of revolution beforehand by sober and practical legislative reforms which shall remove the chief provocations to revolution.

16. Among these we hold the following to be indispensable:

A practical plan for a veritable partnership between capital and labor, in which the responsibilities of each to the other, and of both to the nation, shall be stressed quite as much as their respective rights. Our industrial system must command the interest and respect of the wage earners as an avenue to those liberties and opportunities for self-development which it is the nature of free men to desire. Justice must reign over it, and its dignity as one of the foundations of the national vigor and as a great training school for democratic citizenship must be recognized and cultivated.

A plan by which the raw materials of manufacture and the electrical and other motive power not [now] universally necessary to industry shall be made accessible to all upon equitable and equal terms.

Such legal requirements of the manufacturer and the merchant as will serve to bring the cost of production and retail price into a clearly standardized relationship made known to the purchaser.

17. We heartily endorse and believe in the efforts which the farmers and certain other producers are making to set up and administer cooperative organizations for purchase and sale in all the markets which they serve or which serve them, and we earnestly advocate the fullest possible assistance of all our State legislatures in making these efforts successful and effective.

18. We unqualifiedly condemn the action of the Republican administration in interrupting and in large part destroying the work of creating and developing an American merchant marine so intelligently begun and so efficiently carried forward by the Democratic administration, and we demand the immediate rehabilitation of the Shipping Board and such appropriations for its use and such additions to its powers as may be necessary to put its work upon a permanent footing and assure its energetic and successful completion. An efficient and adequate merchant marine is vital to the nation's safety, and indispensable to the life and growth of its commerce.

19. In close relation to the upbuilding of our overseas trade is the development of our inland waterways. We demand therefore the unprejudiced and scientific study of this vastly important filed [field] of national expansion, and the prompt inauguration of adequate and effective measures to bring to the service of our producers in the interior States a systematized, cheap and efficient transportation by inland water routes, including the development of ship canal communication with the Atlantic seaboard.

19 [20]. Inasmuch as access by all upon equitable and equal terms to the fuel supply and to the raw materials of manufacture and also the availability to all upon fair and equal terms of the mo-

tive power supplied by electrical power companies and other similar privately owned and controlled agencies are indispensable to the unhampered development of the industries of the country, we believe that these are matters which should be regulated by federal legislation to the utmost limit of the constitutional powers of the federal government.

CC MS (WP, DLC).

From William Gibbs McAdoo

Dear Governor: Los Angeles, Cal. Dec. 2, 1922.

I send you under separate cover a few photographs of Nell, the children and myself which will give you a very good idea of the present appearance of your daughter and two granddaughters. The little girls are simply splendid, to say nothing of their mother, and I wish very much that you could see them out here. I have never seen two finer children, mentally and physically, than little Ellen Wilson and little Mary Faith. The baby is certainly a headstrong little mite and full of mischief beside being a perfect bundle of energy. As you know, she is now two years and eight months old.

The moving picture is, I think, going to turn out very well. It is not ready yet, but as soon as it is we shall send it to you. We have not yet been able to get a good picture of the house, but I am going to send one to you soon. You can get some idea of the front elevation from picture No. 1, but it does not convey at all a correct impression of the whole.

Nell and I have just returned from an automobile trip to Oroville, in Northern California, where I had to make a speech at the opening of the Northern California Orange and Olive Exposition. It is a small city, population 5,000, in Butte County, one of the richest agricultural, timber and mineral counties in the State. I was surprised to find that oranges and olives and other semi-tropical fruits could be produced so far north of Los Angeles. We had a very pleasant trip except that my chauffeur was "pinched" for speeding at one point on the highway, which gave rise to a lot of ridiculous newspaper stuff to the effect that I had been arrested and was likely to be sent to jail for violating the motor vehicle law.

I have not been able to write to you since the election. I had a very interesting experience, campaigning in twelve states west of the Mississippi. On numerous occasions I alluded to you, and always received a wonderful response from the audience, whether it happened to be largely Democratic or largely Republican. Frequently the audiences were sixty to eighty per cent Republicans, I was told. I wish you could have been present on some of these occasions to see how much you are appreciated by the rank and file of your fellow-countrymen. I gave out a brief statement on the election at the solicitations of the news associations, which you may perhaps have seen.

The Democratic Party has a great opportunity now if it is wisely led in the Senate and the House during the next two years, and if it militantly champions liberalism, progress and righteousness. I am sure that if the Party convinces the people that it is standing for these things, we can elect a President with the South and West in 1924, as we did in 1916.

On Armistice Day I spoke at Fullerton, Cal., under the auspices of the American Legion. I send you a copy of the speech,[1] and hope that you may be able sometime to read it.

Nell and I were delighted to read your speech on Armistice Day. It was bully, and made us very happy too, to know that you had received such a wonderful greeting. What a contrast with the lack of recognition accorded to the White House!

The reports about my being ill on the train were baseless. I am in fine shape—haven't felt better in years. As I said before, Nell and the children are splendid, physically, mentally and in every other way. I hope that you are feeling better every day and that Edith is in perfect health. We think of you and her with constant solicitude and devotion. If we can possibly manage to go East this winter, we shall certainly run down to Washington to see you all.

Nell joins me in deepest love to you and Edith.

Devotedly yours,　W G McAdoo

TLS (WP, DLC).
　[1] It is missing in WP, DLC.

From Tasker Howard Bliss, with Enclosure

My dear Mr. Wilson:　　　　Washington, D. C. December 4, 1922.

The same mail which brought me your most kind note of November 30th[1] also brought me a letter from Mr. House in which he urged me to send you a copy of a letter of mine which he had seen.

After a good deal of hesitation I now take the liberty of doing so, and I attach it hereto.

Some time ago Mr. Mark Sullivan, a political correspondent of the N. Y. Evening Post, sent me a copy of an article which he had written for the November 11th issue of that paper and which, he tells me, was suggested by the anniversary of Armistice day.[2] He also said that he had been advised to elaborate it into a pamphlet or small book.

As the article related almost entirely to the Peace Conference rather than to the Armistice, it suggested the letter of which I inclose a copy. Please note that the stupid remark about "bamboozling, etc." is one attributed by Mr. Sullivan to an Englishman (unnamed)[3] at the time of the Peace Conference. With the highest esteem, I am   Very cordially,   Tasker H Bliss.

TLS (WP, DLC).

[1] WW to T. H. Bliss, Nov. 30, 1922, CCL (WP, DLC), in which Wilson thanked Bliss for sending a copy of his review essay, "The Armistices," *The American Journal of International Law*, XVI (1922), 509-22, a review of Mermeix, pseud. for Gabriel Terrail, *Les Négociations Secrètes et les Quatre Armistices, avec Pièces Justifications*, 5th edn. (Paris, 1921). This review had been published as a pamphlet, a copy of which Bliss sent to Wilson.

Bliss detailed the story of the Pre-Armistice negotiations between the Allied and American leaders and the negotiations over the subsequent renewals of the Armistice of November 11, 1918. He argued that the British and French were solely responsible for an armistice that was fundamentally defective because it did not provide for the complete disarmament and demobilization of Germany, a fact that prolonged the peace conference because it made it difficult for the Allied and Associated Powers to impose peace terms on Germany.

[2] Mark Sullivan, "Hopes of World Still Unfulfilled," New York *Evening Post*, Nov. 11, 1922. Against the background of books on the war and peace conference, including Baker's *Woodrow Wilson and World Settlement*, Sullivan asked why the high hopes of Armistice Day 1918 had not been fulfilled. The central figure of the drama was Woodrow Wilson, who now had to be seen as a tragic figure. He had raised the hopes of the world to new heights in his Fourteen Points and other war addresses. The Germans had taken him at his word, and had quit fighting in the belief that the Allied and Associated Powers would live up to that word. But since the Armistice was signed, the Allies had proceeded to impose peace terms that violated or ignored the Fourteen Points "point by point." Why had Wilson not stood firm behind his peace program? One reason was his "lapse from a constitutional firmness on moral points at precisely the point where firmness was called for and would have been justified." This, Sullivan said, may have been due to Wilson's health. But Wilson also became convinced that the basis of the new world order he was seeking was cooperation, and that it would be fatal for him to refuse to cooperate with the Allied leaders. A Wilson in full intellectual vigor would never have fallen into such self-justification. But he consented too much and permitted himself to be "bamboozled." Another way Wilson used to justify himself was to think that if only he could get the League of Nations into operation, it would undo all the errors and mend all the breaches of faith in the Versailles Treaty. The final step of the tragedy was Wilson's refusal to accept reservations to the treaty, which was his share of responsibility for the failure of the United States to ratify the treaty and join the League.

[3] He of course referred to John Maynard Keynes who had said in his *The Economic Consequences of the Peace* (London, 1919) that Wilson had been "bamboozled" by Lloyd George, Clemenceau, and others at Paris.

E N C L O S U R E

Tasker Howard Bliss to Mark Sullivan

My dear Mr. Sullivan: Washington, D. C. November 28, 1922.

I thank you very cordially for your letter of November 18th, and the inclosed copy of your article suggested by the occasion of the anniversary of Armistice Day. (By the way I inclose one of mine more or less in connection with the same occasion.)[1]

I sincerely hope that you will see your way to elaborate the idea in your article into book form, because there is a lot more than a brief newspaper article can contain on the subject.

Permit me to suggest only this one thing,—that such a book should analyze the subject in a philosophical rather than in the purely historical spirit. A man who looks at facts purely in the historical spirit is apt to say, "Certain facts show that the basic principles of the Peace of Versailles were wrong; these facts were as well known to the makers of that peace at the time, as they are known now; therefore, those makers deliberately did wrong; why did they do it?" In the answer to that question "Why" is where the philosophical spirit comes in.

Why the representatives of other nations did wrong was, and is, obvious. They were dominated by an unthinking, passionate sentiment of the peoples behind them. In their then recent general election campaigns, these men were largely responsible for the creation of this sentiment. But after it was done it made no difference how the evil Afrit came to be released from the bottle. The fact was that it was out and dominated its former masters.

But the main thing is, from your point of view, "why did Mr. Wilson do what he did?"

You say "Why did not Wilson stand firm? Why did he not put his foot down," etc? When the Allies agreed to discuss peace *on the basis* of the fourteen points and subsequent addresses, no one supposed that they meant to empower Mr. Wilson to write the Treaty. He had to negotiate it with men who had just been held in power by national general elections which practically gave a mandate to the negotiators of England and France. You know the doctrines as to reparations, war pensions, etc., which gave Lloyd George an overwhelming victory. It was the same in France. I myself heard speeches by their Minister of Finance[2] in which he promised the people that, if they would keep Clemenceau in power, their taxes would never for all time be increased, but would soon be reduced; that all the past costs of the war and all future expenses incident to it would be paid by the enemy. We may say as much as we please that a negotiator should take no mandate except from his own conscience. In our own country the most able men of a great political party condemned the President because he did not take negotiators who would receive a mandate from that party. Had he done so, would they have supported him in his demand for abso-

[1] That is, a copy of his *The Armistices*.
[2] Louis-Lucien Klotz.

lute adherence to the fourteen Points, even to the point of America's withdrawal from the Conference? I think not. If you will scrutinize the utterances of these very men at the time you will find that they criticized Mr. Wilson for not yielding *in toto* to the wishes of the Allies. Public sentiment here would not have supported him in breaking up the Conference.

It is very likely that public sentiment would support him *now*. But there was no evidence of it at the time, and it was a fearful responsibility to take.

The upshot of it is that in a *negotiation* there comes a time when a man has to say, "Shall I insist on my extreme demand and break off the negotiation, or shall I take what I think is the best I can get, under conditions that give me a hope that in time I will get all I ask?"

I think it a not misleading illustration of Mr. Wilson's attitude of mind to compare him to a business man negotiating with others who are his rivals—but not so much his rivals as they are "cut-throat" rivals of each other. He finds that each man, taking a narrow view of his own interests, is bringing the entire group to the verge of ruin. He himself has very positive views as to what they must do to save themselves. He has written these views out, whether in four or fourteen or forty points. He presents them at a round-table conference. His views are broad, because in reality he is in less danger of ruin than the others. Each of the others is thinking only of saving himself from imminent disaster. While unanimous in the belief that they must have some sort of formal association to control their future actions, each thinks that for the moment he must seize whatever is in sight. Mr. Wilson, as a business man, is in a quandary. He wants his fourteen points. One of them provides for a formal association. If he gets his other thirteen, the association is for the time of lesser importance. As it becomes more evident that, at that moment, he can not get the thirteen *in toto*, the association looms up as more and more important. Mr. Wilson says to himself, "My thirteen points may be absolutely right, or they may be wrong or require modification; to whatever extent any of them is wrong I don't want it enforced; to whatever extent they are right these business men will soon discover that they must be enforced to save them from ruin; in our Articles of Agreement I'll get what I can and trust to their own self interest to eventually agree to the rest."

So he took what he could, including these articles of association. And if the members of that association—one of whom we are not—live half way up to its spirit it will result, very slowly for a good while, in good. Already it has done good. Europe seems in hopeless turmoil. The dogs are snapping and snarling at each other but most of them—unfortunately not all (I don't mean ourselves, but Germany and Russia)—are in a leash and in some slight degree pulling together. If you have ever seen a half-broken dog team, you would think that the only way to have peace is to cut the leash and let each cur "gang his own gait." Even as it is I think that Geneva is already doing well to lessen the chances of a *world* war.

And if it keeps on doing good, however much less than was at first hoped, Geneva will be the eternal glory of Mr. Wilson, whether we are there or not.

And if Geneva fails it will only prove that in 1919 Mr. Wilson was not dealing with business men around a table, but with rogues and tricksters who can chuckle over the idea that they have "bamboozled the old Presbyterian" at the very time their civilization is rocking under their feet. In spite of any mistakes made, Mr. Wilson did what was *practicable* to save that civilization. The ruin would have come quicker if he had broken up the Peace Conference. If it is saved it will be largely to his credit; if it is imperilled it will be entirely to their shame.

Now, as usual in a hasty letter, I have said much, but little to the point. My sole idea is that such a complex subject as the work of the Peace Conference must be analyzed in the light of the limitations of the time,—limitations that become evident when men come together not for the purpose of emphasizing their differences but to make an agreement. If it had been Homer's "Gods in Council" perhaps it would have been different. But even they had their differences. And Olympian Zeus himself had sometimes to yield.

I sincerely hope that you will carry out your idea.

Cordially yours,   (S'g'd) Tasker H Bliss.

TCL (WP, DLC).

A News Report

[*Dec. 6, 1922*]

TIGER AND WILSON RECALL OLD TIMES
IN CORDIAL REUNION
Clemenceau Visits Ex-President and
Says Their Meeting Was "Affectionate."

15-MINUTE CHAT IN LIBRARY
"MENTALLY ALERT AS EVER"

Washington, Dec. 6.—Woodrow Wilson received Georges Clemenceau this afternoon.

The meeting was a fifteen-minute reunion between the two men who were virtual dictators in wartime but who have suffered disappointment since they parted over three years ago. One is making slow recovery from broken health, in virtual seclusion since the rejection by his own country of his ideal for world peace. The other, 81 years old, with an assassin's bullet in his back, was called the "Father of Victory" by the people of his country, who then denied him the one honor he coveted—the Presidency of the French Republic.

The last time these two men saw each other was on the night of June 28, 1919, on the platform of Gare des Invalides, in Paris. The Treaty of Versailles had been signed six hours before. Woodrow Wilson was leaving for Brest to sail for home on the George Washington, taking with him the treaty that had just been signed, together with another treaty that would bind the United States with Great Britain to protect France against invasion.

Only six hours before, in the Hall of Mirrors of the Versailles Palace, Georges Clemenceau, Premier of France and President of the Paris Peace Conference, called the plenipotentiaries of the twenty-nine nations to order and announced: "The Signatures will be given now and they amount to a solemn undertaking to execute the conditions embodied by the Treaty of Peace. I now invite the delegates of the German Reich to sign the treaty."

Three years and five months later M. Clemenceau arrived in this country to plead that Germany was not executing the conditions of peace, and that America in leaving Europe had left France unprotected.

Only two men know what went on in the library on the second floor of No. 2,340 S Street this afternoon.[1] Shortly before 5 o'clock a motor car drew up in front of the house. Some photographers got out and set up their cameras in the driveway. More automobiles arrived carrying newspaper men and more photographers. Passersby stopped and there was a group of some two hundred people in front of the Wilson home. Precisely at 5:30 a squad of motorcycle police, escorting a motor car, turned into S Street. The knot of people parted and a limousine with M. Clemenceau and Colonel Stephen Bonsal drew up at the front door. There was a short cheer, photographers' flares flashed, and the door closed.

John Randolph Bolling, Mr. Wilson's brother-in-law and secretary, conducted M. Clemenceau to the second floor. Here Mrs. Wilson received him, took him to the library and left. The two framers of the Treaty of Versailles were alone. Mr. Wilson was seated in a chair from which he did not rise during the entire interview.

M. Clemenceau later described the meeting as "affectionate, of more than the utmost cordiality, as between old friends."

Old times in Paris were recalled. Mr. Wilson made no reference either to M. Clemenceau's speeches or to his mission to this country. The subject was brought up by the Tiger, who informed Mr. Wilson that the mention of the ex-President's name in his addresses had caused more applause than any point he made. This appeared to please Mr. Wilson.

Finally, M. Clemenceau, fearing that his visit might fatigue his host, arose to leave, and he said that if he could be of any service to Mr. or Mrs. Wilson he was at their disposal.

M. Clemenceau said tonight that he had found Mr. Wilson somewhat stouter, but as "mentally alert as ever." He noticed no difference in the former President's voice and said that he spoke "clearly and with precision of thought." . . .

Printed in the *New York Times*, Dec. 7, 1922.
[1] Clemenceau did not mention this conversation in any of his writings. For the only evidence about it, see Dr. Grayson's memorandum printed at Dec. 28, 1922 (the second of that date).

To Tasker Howard Bliss

My dear General Bliss,   [Washington] 6th December 1922

Thank you very much for sending me a copy of your letter to Mark Sullivan. It rings true like yourself in every paragraph and should give everyone who might have the good fortune to read it a perfectly true conception of the real issues. I am disappointed to see Sullivan go astray. He is I believe at bottom a man of principle and intelligence but has allowed himself to be perverted by the associations which have warped the point of view and morals of so many of our writers. I sincerely hope that your letter may have the effect of swinging him around into the right course again.

It is heartening and reassuring to feel that you are on the lookout to serve the truth in the essential matters in which the country has been so sadly misled, and I thank you with all my heart for having brought me in touch with you again.

With heartfelt regard and good wishes, and my very respectful salutations to Mrs. Bliss,[1]

Cordially and Faithfully Yours,   [Woodrow Wilson]

CCL (WP, DLC).
[1] Eleanora Anderson Bliss.

To Francis Xavier Dercum[1]

My dear Dr. Dercum,   Washington D C 10th December 1922

I heartily wish that I might have the privilege of being personally present on December twenty-seventh at the celebration of the birthday of Louis Pasteur. Since I cannot be I take the means of this letter to express to you, and through you to those who will participate in the celebration, the tribute which I can with genuine enthusiasm pay to the great man of science who undoubtedly contributed as much to the physical welfare and betterment of mankind as any worker in the great realm of science has ever contributed.

My knowledge of the problems and methods of the great field of science in which Pasteur worked is not sufficiently intimate to entitle me to attempt a critical estimate of his achiev[e]ment, but I can see that it is his immortal distinction that he not only broadened the thought and enlightened the practice of the great medical profession in the treatment of certain diseases, but also erected barriers against all disease, and so conferred an inestimable benefit upon mankind. He deserves our most grateful praise and is undoubtedly entitled to stand very high indeed in the roll of honour in which those are entitled to have their names inscribed who have worked with beneficent intelligence for the good of their fellow men.

I join with all my heart in the acclaim which must greet his name and declare his fame.

With much respect,   Sincerely Yours,   Woodrow Wilson

TLS (received from Steven Lomazow).
[1] Wilson sent this letter to be read at a Pasteur Centennial celebration at the Philadelphia Academy of Music on December 27. See F. X. Dercum to WW, Dec. 8, 1922, TLS (WP, DLC).

To William Gibbs McAdoo

My dear Mac,   Washington D C 12th December 1922

It was a pleasure to get your letter.[1] We are always eager for news of you, Nell and the girlies, and the pictures you were kind enough to send seemed to add a vividness and reality to what you tell us of their health and prosperity. One of the pictures gives a charming view of the house of which we have [been] so anxious to see and which Madge and Ed Elliott[2] and all other visitors to you give such an enthusiastic account.

I think you are quite right in saying that the programme our party offers to the country must be radical, though of the intelligent type of radicalism which affords remedies without provoking revolution. Sober, steady judgment and courageous conviction were never more needed than they are now, and with them the party may render our country a service in 1924 which will indirectly benefit all the world which just now stands so much in need of the right sort of liberal guidance.

So far as I can judge from this distance it seems to me that you are in a part of the country in which it will be more difficult than in any other to coordinate opinion in a way to promote what the usual leaders there have no comprehension of; but you may see the way as I do not to effect this.

It is very delightful to know how well you all are. We were not disturbed, though for a day or so anxious, by the statement you had broken down. We never take such things at second hand.

Edith joins me in all loving messages to you all. She agrees with me that the pictures you sent show little Mary Faith to be a truly charming little creature.

With dearest love to all,

Affectionately Yours,   Woodrow Wilson

TLS (W. G. McAdoo Papers, DLC).
    [1] WGM to WW, Dec. 2, 1922.
    [2] That is, Margaret Axson Elliott and Edward Graham Elliott.

To Georges Clemenceau

[Washington] Decr 12th 1922

Allow me to bid you an affectionate farewell and to congratulate you upon the admiration you have won from our people stop All good fortune attend you.   Woodrow Wilson

T telegram (WP, DLC).

From Norman Hezekiah Davis

My dear Mr. Wilson: New York, December 12, 1922.

In obedience to your kind and valuable suggestion, I have made certain alterations in the address on the Democratic Party delivered by me at Philadelphia. Since you indicated the possible desirability of having this printed by the Democratic National Committee, and your willingness to suggest that it be done, I am enclosing a copy in order that you may do so if you think it worth while.

With reference to our last conversation regarding criticisms of the Federal Reserve System and the inadequate measures proposed by the "Farm Bloc" for the relief of the farmers, I have written something which I enclose herewith,[1] in case you might think it advisable to incorporate this in the general statement of policy, etc. If the tariff or the general policies of the Democratic Party are dealt with in some other paragraph of the statement, it might be well to drop off the first paragraph of the enclosed draft.

Mrs. Davis and I enjoyed very much our visit with you and Mrs. Wilson last week, and hope that you are continuing to improve.

With affectionate regards, I am, as ever,

Sincerely yours,   [Norman H. Davis]

CCL (N. H. Davis Papers, DLC).
  [1] This draft is missing in both the Davis and Wilson Papers, DLC. A revised version is printed as an Enclosure with NHD to WW, Dec. 28, 1922.

A Press Release[1]

[c. Dec. 13, 1922]

Announcement was made today at the office of Wilson & Colby in this city that the firm would be dissolved on December 31st, the date of the expiration of the copartnership agreement. Mr Colby when seen at the office of the firm was asked if there was anything to say in supplement of the announcement.

He said: "There is little to add. As a result of the steady gain in Mr Wilson's health during the last few months, which has been so gratifying to his friends, he is turning his energies once more to subjects which have long invited him, and the importance of which cannot be overestimated.

"Of course to me the termination of our professional relationship is a matter of great personal loss and the keenest regret. Mr Wilson's disciplined power and effectiveness as a lawyer have been a veritable revelation, considering the long interruption of his active work at the bar. He has taken a most active interest in the work of the firm and has shown the same effectiveness that he has displayed in every field into which he has turned his energies.

"Our relations are of the most cordial character imaginable, as they have always been."

CC MS (WP, DLC).
  [1] The *New York Times*, December 13, 1922, quoted the words in the following statement attributed to Colby in a front-page news story about the dissolution of Wilson & Colby.

To Cordell Hull

My dear Mr. Chairman,   Washington D C 14th December 1922

The address on the Democratic Party by Mr. Norman H. Davis which I enclose struck me as so interesting and suggestive that I have said to him that I thought it ought to be in the hands of all our campaign speakers in 1924. I write to you to suggest that it be printed in a small pamphlet and distributed among our speakers at that time. It seems to me that it would help them to make many interesting points about the party and its equipment for public service. I sincerely hope that you will agree with me and view it in the same light. I am trying to help to get everything in shape at an early date for the most effective possible campaign.

I hope that you are feeling well and that Christmas will prove a very happy season for you and for all your associates at headquarters.

With very warm regard and cordial assurances of my admiration and support,
Sincerely and Faithfully Yours,   Woodrow Wilson

TLS (C. Hull Papers, DLC).

To Bainbridge Colby

My dear Colby,   Washington D C 14th December 1922

You managed the announcement admirably and with the perfect good taste and good feeling which I have learned to expect of you, but which is none the less gratifying upon every occasion when it is exhibited.

You were more than generous in what you said of me. I wish that it were all true, but true or not I thank you for it with all my heart.

With every grateful acknowledgment,
Affectionately Yours,   Woodrow Wilson

TLS (B. Colby Papers, DLC).

From Ray Stannard Baker

Dear Mr. Wilson: Amherst Massachusetts December 14, 1922.

I have been somewhat under the weather for some days and have not expressed, as I should have done, my real and great appreciation for your letter of November twenty-second with its generous words of approval for the book. I have very greatly desired your approval, as I feel and know that I have had your confidence in the preparation of the work.

It is a pretty formidable book—in size at least—and starts slowly, but it seems now to be really and genuinely started. Doubleday is already, this week, on the second printing of the narrative volumes. It is getting some good notices in quarters that count. Norman Davis, whose judgment I prize above that of almost any other of your advisers at Paris, gave it a fine review in the new *International Book Monthly* of the *Literary Digest*, and one of the editors of the *Atlantic Monthly* showed me, the other day in Boston, a most commendatory review that they are having in their January number. Albert Shaw writes that he has a four-page notice next month in the *Review of Reviews*, and the *Times* called it, the other day, "the one indispensable work to anybody who would deal intelligently with the Paris conference."

Doubleday is, I think, doing his level best and will do more as the reviews begin to come in and to count. I believe the book is already assured the real approval of thoughtful men, and that it will help shape future leadership; but we want and *must have* more than that. We want a real popular reading and discussion, and it would now seem that it would require only a little push to send it over the divide to the broader success. If we can get that—with the discussion that is bound to come with it—it will do much to spread quickly the truth regarding your principles and to bring the public back strongly to the support of them. The American, to be really moved, must have moral sanctions; and here in our book—*your* book!—they are set forth and developed. It is of the deepest importance, it seems to me, to do everything in our power to provoke this wider reading and discussion.

Now the publishers have asked me again and again if I could not get an approving word from you that they could use regarding the book. They have felt that such a word might be just what would give the book the necessary push to carry it across to a big reading, but I have steadily refused to speak to you about it, for I shrank from asking such a favor. And here you have more than generously expressed your approval in your letter of November twenty-second. I know that you have a profounder interest than I have—or anyone!—in having the people understand; and I have wondered if you would let the publishers use your comment in their publicity. I assure you it will be a great thing in spreading the gospel! Nevertheless, if you do not think it best, I will "go way back and sit down" and not say a word. If you are willing and will drop me a line in care of The Century Club (7 West 43d Street, New York City), where I shall be next Monday or Tuesday, it will make me most happy. The paragraph I thought of using from your letter was this:

"Let me congratulate you again on the completion and publication of the book. I feel confident it will fulfill the high mission to which you have so generously dedicated it. It contains the truth, and the truth will prevail."

You may be interested to know that one of my scholarly neighbors here at Amherst, who has been all along a rather bitter critic of yours, said to me earnestly the other day:

"I have read your book from cover to cover and I want to tell you that it has entirely changed my view of Woodrow Wilson and what he did at Paris. I had no conception of the fight he had to make there."

I have received recently several letters of the same tenor. What we want is to see them change—all over this country!

Please remember me warmly to Mrs. Wilson.

Cordially yours,   Ray Stannard Baker

TLS (WP, DLC).

From Georges Clemenceau

New York Dec 14 [1922]

I can be but most grateful for the kind message you have been so good to send me. Your feelings are mine. All your efforts for the best which you did not spare while in our country are those of the French people and can be summed in two words justice and peace to all. These are Frances principles as well as those of America. My best wishes for your health and welfare and kindest regards to Mrs Wilson   Clemenceau.

T telegram (WP, DLC).

To Frank Irving Cobb

My dear Cobb,   [Washington] 15th December 1922

I send you the enclosed editorial from the Washington Evening Star of December 13th[1] in order to advance a step further in our consideration of a programme for the party and the country. It seems to me evident that the object of the editorial is to create as much prejudice and jealousy against me as possible, and I dare say that its theme will be very generally taken up, namely, that I am trying to dictate to the next national convention of the party both with regard to the platform and the candidate. Does this circumstance (if I am right about it) at all alter your judgment that I ought, by some proper process, to give out a programme? Baruch and I together have thought out a method which we think would be less likely to wound susceptibility than any other, but before employing it I am anxious to be fortified by a re-statement of your own judgment with regard to the general policy of my personal action. I rely greatly on your sagacity and insight, and will be very much indebted to you if you will tell me, with your usual frankness, your last thought on the subject. I am very anxious to serve, but I am anxious to do so in the way that will produce fewest complications and obstructions, because party unanimity and hearty cooperation of all elements in it are of course of the greatest importance to the welfare of the country.

I know that you will receive and answer this in the spirit of friendship and confidence in which it is written.

With affectionate regard,

Faithfully Yours,   [Woodrow Wilson]

CCL (WP, DLC).
  ¹ It reads as follows:

"Wilson Concentrates on Politics

"In announcing the termination of the law partnership of Wilson and Colby, Mr. Colby gives as the reason that the former President 'is turning his energies once more to subjects which have long invited him.'

"Not so long maybe, but with great force since the November election.

"Mr. Wilson, there is good reason for saying, sees the democratic party coming back and expects it to arrive in November, 1924.

"Nay, more. It is coming back, as he believes, on a tide of revived Wilsonism. The people have repented of the verdict they gave in 1920, and are preparing to render one in favor of the policies they then unwisely condemned.

"Naturally, Mr. Wilson wants to direct the flowing of this tide—wants to give his whole time to it.

"And then in politics Mr. Wilson will be more at home than in the law. Years ago he met with no success at the bar, and soon left it for a teacher's chair. But in politics he has risen in twelve years to the proportions of a world figure, and today many of the men who followed him while he was in the White House are still in his train.

"There seems no reason to believe that Mr. Wilson has in mind another nomination to the presidency. Improved as his physical condition may be since retiring from office, it is not such as would warrant his assumption as a candidate of the duties and responsibilities of a national campaign, and particularly not of the duties and responsibilities of the presidency for another four years.

"Hence the opinion, widely and strongly entertained, that the object of his activity is control of the next democratic national convention in the interest of a man of his choice and the adoption of a platform of his construction."

From Cordell Hull

My dear Mr. President: Washington, D. C. Dec. 15th, 1922.

I am delighted to get your note of the 14th instant enclosing copy of address of Norman H. Davis, which I have carefully read.

I was deeply impressed with the subject matter contained in this address. It is a most timely utterance and one which, if circulated, will prove of incalculable value in an educational way to Democratic and many other voters. I am in the heartiest accord with all the views which Mr. Davis enunciates in such a logical and impressive manner.

I assure you that I am greatly interested in having the benefit of this production, and shall carefully plan to give it wide circulation at such early stage as the condition of our finances will permit.

I sometime ago had a conference with a rather noted writer, whose name I do not just now recall, in regard to the writing of a history of the Democratic party. This Professor was very enthusiastic upon the subject, but has not been able thus far to procure the necessary financial support. John W. Davis and others have been in conference with him relative to such undertaking.

Wishing for yourself, Mrs. Wilson and the family an enjoyable Christmas and a Happy New Year, I am

Very sincerely yours,   Cordell Hull

TLS (WP, DLC).

John Randolph Bolling to Bernard Mannes Baruch

Dear Mr. Baruch: [Washington] 15th Decr 1922

At my suggestion, Mr. Wilson has allowed me to send you the enclosed copy of a letter which he has to-day written to Mr. Frank I. Cobb.

The general tendency of all the editorials (and we are receiving dozens of them) which have come, is to lay Mr. Wilson on the shelf, politically, and to draw from him if possible a statement of some kind. I recall that when we discussed this matter a few weeks ago, you felt that a statement at this time would be most unwise; and from what I have seen in Mr. Wilson's mail I am inclined to think it even more so now than it was then.

I pass all this along for consideration, that you may keep in touch with the general situation.

Mr. Wilson's improvement continues, and he is more interested in everything today than he has been at any time since his illness.

Cordially yours,   [John Randolph Bolling]

CCL (WP, DLC).

To Norman Hezekiah Davis

My dear Davis,   Washington D C 16th December 1922

I see now that I misled you in advising the character of the paragraph I asked you to prepare for the Statement. I think that such a document must necessarily be dogmatic, stating only conclusions and not setting forth the arguments which establish them. The public will not read arguments, and we must be content I think with stating conclusions very positively. I should have told you too that I consulted Baruch about what was to be said for the farmers, because he has, as you know, been for a long time in intimate consultation with those who most truly represent the farming interests, and I have already embodied in the Statement what I understood to be the conclusions he has arrived at as to the kind of relief which should be afforded the farmers and the method which should be employed in affording it. I should have told you all this before. I wonder if you could re-state these interesting paragraphs which you have written in some simple dogmatic way? I feel guilty that I should have misguided you and made any such additional labour necessary, and I hope you will forgive me.

Please don't forget that you and Houston were to agree upon a paragraph in regard to the tariff and taxation. I shall expect it with the utmost interest and shall attach the greatest importance to it. This is all a very laborious business, but I know how little you begrudge labour spent in such causes, and it would be quite impossible to dispense with your counsel.

It was a great pleasure to get a glimpse of Mrs. Davis and you, and a talk with you always does me the invaluable service of clearing and stimulating my thought, for which I am truly grateful.

I am glad to think that the months immediately ahead of us will bring us into a closer and closer comradeship in affairs, and constantly associate us in counsel in trying to develop a rational and effective policy for the Government.

I constantly think of you most affectionately, and constantly rejoice in, and am strengthened by, your friendship.

Please give our affectionate regards to Mrs. Davis, and please keep for yourself, my dear fellow, all the affection your heart can desire from   Yours Affectionately,   Woodrow Wilson

TLS (N. H. Davis Papers, DLC).

From Bainbridge Colby

My Dear Mr. President.   New York Dec. 16./22

I am carrying your last letter around in my pocket, and reading it and re-reading it with the greatest pleasure and satisfaction.

That was just the impression I hoped you would receive—that the matter had been handled discreetly, and when you say it in such generous words, it makes me feel quite puffed up.

I am coming down to see you in a few days—just to see you. I haven't any reason to, except that I just want to be with you a little while.   Affectionately always   Bainbridge Colby

ALS (WP, DLC).

John Randolph Bolling to Ray Stannard Baker

Dear Mr. Baker: 2340 S Street N W 16th December 1922

Mr. Wilson asks me to thank you for your letter of December 14th and say that he is glad to have such encouraging news about the book.

He further directs me to say that he is entirely willing that the publishers of the book use in their publicity the quotation from his letter to you of November twenty-second as given on the third page of your letter under reply.

With warm regard from us all;
                    Cordially yours,   John Randolph Bolling

TLS (R. S. Baker Papers, DLC).

To Eleanor Randolph Wilson McAdoo

My darling Girlie,   Washington D C 18th December 1922

Please apply the enclosed to any Christmas object you prefer. My course [choice?] would be something for yourself. I need not tell you with what love the gift is freighted.

I am getting on about as usual except that today, which is the anniversary of our wedding, I am especially stimulated by memories of the delightful years of my intimate association with Edith for whom my admiration and love constantly increase. In spite of breakdown and political persecution I realize that I am the most fortunate man in the world.

Please keep well and let us know all about all of you as often as you possibly can.

With dearest love,   Your Devoted   Father

TLS (photostat in RSB Coll., DLC).

From Frank Irving Cobb

Dear Mr. Wilson: New York December 18th, 1922.

Baruch and I went over the memorandum[1] yesterday in detail, and are in thorough agreement. He is going to Washington today I believe. The only question left relates to time. Personally, I think the present situation might be allowed to stew in its own juice for a while, but nothing can be done anyway until the new leadership in Congress is decided. I think your present plan is better than any of the others that have been suggested.

As to editorials such as that which appeared in the Washington Star, I should not take them too seriously. A certain Republican element will inevitably make that line of attack on you, but if we can get the Democratic party reunited again, the attack will be futile. Besides, everybody knows that no Democratic candidate in 1924 will have the ghost of a chance unless he is acceptable to you, and unless the platform is acceptable to you. Without your support and co-operation the ticket would be doomed to defeat.

It seems to me that there need be no great difficulty in getting the Democratic party together on a programme such as you have outlined. Even Jim Reed would probably be glad to sneak in at the back door in the interest of harmony, and the country at large is only waiting for an insistent note of leadership.

Incidentally, I think you have less to worry about than you suspect on the subject of Republican incitement to Democratic jealousy. You are in a unique position in the Democratic party, and what other Democrats will be seeking from you is your support and co-operation.

You have probably seen the dispatches announcing that The Irish Free State had applied for admission to The League of Nations. If France will now change her stupid policy and permit Germany to come in, I am convinced that the entire opposition to the League in the United States will collapse.

With sincerest regards,   As ever yours,   Frank I Cobb.

TLS (WP, DLC).
[1] That is, the confidential document printed at Dec. 2, 1922.

From William Gibbs McAdoo

Dear Governor: Los Angeles, Cal. December 19, 1922.

A few days ago I shipped to you by express the film of the McAdoo home and family. It is a very good picture considering the fact that the glare in the children's eyes makes them squint a bit and that Miss Mary Faith was somewhat on the warpath that day.

For some reason she refused to take her usual nap and then, being a most fascinatingly determined little character, every artifice possible had to be employed to make her perform as well as she did. On the whole, I think she did very well.

My friend Douglas Fairbanks had the titles prepared at his studio and his people made the picture. He was delighted to learn from us that you are still using the moving picture machine which he sent you a few years ago.[1] He is really a very fine fellow. I am not his counsel, nor am I counsel for any moving picture concern, for that matter, but we are friends.

In the picture you will observe a group sitting on the front steps that includes others than Nell, myself and the two babies. These are William G. McAdoo, Jr., and his wife[2] and a little playmate of Ellen's, Miss Gwenn Milner, and Katherine, our nurse.

I was very sorry that the moving picture man did not take a picture of the "back yard" as we call it in the South. It is really a charming garden, although the flowers are nearly all gone at this season of the year. You can get a slight idea of it from the picture of the pergola and of one part of the yard which is shown in the picture. I am sorry, too, that they did not get a full picture of the house. It is somewhat abbreviated as it is, but I think you will get a fair idea of it.

I hope that the picture may reach you in time for Christmas, although the railroad and express services are so rotten that you may not get it before the New Year.

We have had some winter rains for the past ten days, which have made the country look green already, with a decided springtime atmosphere. I really wish you and Edith could be out here this winter to enjoy this wonderful climate. I am sure that it would do you great good. Why don't you get aboard a ship and come out via the Panama Canal? We can put you up and make you thoroughly comfortable. I think the babies alone could make you have a wonderful time, and I am sure that you would be benefited by it. Nothing would make us happier than to receive a visit from you and Edith.

Nell joins me in every kind of loving message to you and Edith. We hope that you may have the happiest kind of Christmas and New Year.   Always your devoted,   W G McAdoo

TLS (WP, DLC).
[1] See WW to D. Fairbanks, Jan. 13, 1919, Vol. 54.
[2] Molly Tackaberry Ferguson McAdoo.

From Norman Hezekiah Davis

My dear Mr. Wilson: [New York] December 21, 1922.

I have read with interest your letter of December 16th.

I am sure it was entirely my fault that I did not understand just the kind of statement you had in mind, and I assure you that it is a pleasure to me to try to prepare just what you do want.

It is, of course, rather difficult to disconnect the tariff and foreign policy from any statement relating to the requirements of the farmer. I realize that Baruch has kept in very close touch with those who are interested in the welfare of the farmer, but I have been impressed with the fact that the farmers have been misled into believing that their ills have come from a lack of credit and a failure on the part of the Federal Reserve Banks to encourage the maintenance of high prices.[1] They have not realized at all that the trouble was world wide. Since one of the most constructive pieces of legislation in our history was the establishment of the Federal Reserve System, and since that was one of the great achievements of your Administration, I think it is important that every endeavor should be made to educate the farmer and show him just what are the causes of his difficulties and from what measures relief may be expected.

The prescriptions which the farm bloc have offered will certainly not give them relief. In substance, the program given out by Senator Capper[2] calls for additional credit, warehousing and transportation facilities. This is important but is not the key to the solution. The farmer is today suffering from over-production, or under-consumption, in that there are surplus farm products which the world needs but which it is unable to buy because of world wide economic prostration—which the Administration refuses to help alleviate. The farmer is also suffering because he is forced to sell his products at prices established in the competitive world market and to buy his goods in the non-competitive American market. Unless measures are taken to restore the purchasing power of the world and to give the farmer an opportunity for an equitable exchange of his products for his requirements, the remedies offered by the farm bloc would merely increase his production, get him further into debt, and increase the disproportion in value between what he sells and what he buys.

While arguments supporting these facts are not appropriate in a condensed statement such as you have in mind, I do feel that it is important that someone should speak out on the subject. I am informed that Senator Robinson[3] has in mind the making of a speech in the Senate on the general policies of the Democratic party and it might be well for him, or someone else, to discuss this particular problem. However, I have endeavored to prepare a more condensed statement, which I enclose, with apologies. If it is not what you want, just throw it away, or—if you think I might be able to do better on another attempt, please do not hesitate to so advise me.

I am very sorry because of absence and my inability to see Houston since my return that it has been impossible to send you the proposed paragraph in regard to the tariff and taxation. I am, however, arranging for us to get together and expect to submit this to you this week.

After my delightful talk with you on my last visit, I made some inquiries about the contest in the Senate and in the House over the Democratic leadership. In my surprise I found that Simmons spoke for Reed[4] on the floor of the Senate before Reed was nominated. This was infinitely worse than what Robinson did, namely, to make a speech in behalf of Reed after he had been nominated in the Democratic Primaries. I understand that even then he made it particularly plain that he did not agree with Reed's views regarding the League of Nations and you.

Do not hesitate to call on me for anything that you think I can do. It is a pleasure to spend any amount of labor on the general cause and it is a great pleasure and a great inspiration to me to work in such close contact and collaboration with you.

I hope to go to Washington some time after the first of the year and to have the pleasure of discussing the situation with you again. In the meantime, I remain, with deep affection,

Yours faithfully,   Norman H. Davis

P.S. After re-reading my attempt to recast the statement which you returned to me, I am not satisfied with it and have decided to wait and send it along with the draft on tariff and taxation.

TLS (WP, DLC).

[1] See Arthur S. Link, "The Federal Reserve Policy and the Agricultural Depression of 1920-1921," in A. S. Link, *The Higher Realism of Woodrow Wilson and Other Essays* (Nashville, Tenn., 1971), pp. 334-35.

[2] That is, Arthur Capper, Republican of Kansas.

[3] That is, Joseph Taylor Robinson, Democrat of Arkansas.

[4] That is Furnifold McLendel Simmons of North Carolina and James Alexander Reed of Missouri, both Democrats.

To Norman Hezekiah Davis

My dear Davis,   Washington D C 24th December 1922

You are quite right in your letter of December twenty-first in what it is necessary for the farmers to have, and I therefore submit this idea to you:

Could you not write a brief pamphlet, elucidating the whole matter, that could be distributed to the speakers in the next campaign and generally circulated along with the admirable address on the party itself. I know of no one who could do this with greater lucidity than yourself, and it would be a most substantial contribution to truth and to the party's success.

It is delightful to feel the spirit of unselfish service which you always manifest, and each evidence of it knits closer the bonds of affection which I feel for you.

I hope that this Christmas and New Year season is bringing to you and yours all sorts of happiness and cheer and that you are all well.

Mrs. Wilson joins with me in affectionate messages to you all and I am as always, my dear Davis,

Affectionately Yours,   Woodrow Wilson

TLS (N. H. Davis Papers, DLC).

To William Gibbs McAdoo

My dear Mac,   Washington D C 26th December 1922

We are delighted to get the film,[1] and it came in time for Christmas. We have not yet put it on the machine but hope to do so sometime this week when I am sure we shall greatly enjoy it. How delightful that friends and dear ones may hope to keep in touch with one another by means of exchanged moving pictures!

You may be sure that your generous invitation to come out to Nell and you is very tempting, but I am sure you will understand I should not attempt such a journey until I get a good deal stronger, and that our hearts constantly cross the continent to greet and enjoy you all.

We unite in all loving messages and in the hope that this Christmas and New Year season has brought to you all what you most desire.

With greetings of heartfelt affection,

Affectionately Yours,   Woodrow Wilson

TLS (W. G. McAdoo Papers, DLC).
[1] Wilson was replying to WGM to WW, Dec. 19, 1922.

To Norman Hezekiah Davis

My dear Davis,   Washington D C 27th December 1922

It occurs to me that the paper by Houston on contrasted policies and performances of the Democratic and Republican parties in the economic field[1] would be an admirable thing to distribute in its entirety to our speakers in 1924, and if Houston will let me have a copy of the paper I will propose such a distribution of it to Chairman Hull. It would no doubt supply the basis for many convincing speeches.

At same time I hope that Houston will be so generous as to prepare a compact "plank" on the subject, though I know how difficult such a task is. As I said in a recent letter to you, the people give little heed to discoursing, but are often impressed by a confident and dogmatic statement.

I am particularly grateful for the cooperation you and Houston are so generously consenting to.

We had a very quiet but very enjoyable Christmas, and are looking to the New Year a good deal refreshed. I am glad to hear of your merry Christmas, and Mrs. Wilson joins me in every affectionate wish for you all.

I am sorry to say that, willing and even anxious as I am to meet Dean Robbins,[2] I can't figure out an appointment before lunch on January sixth. But it would be entirely convenient for me to see you both at five-thirty that afternoon, if you can arrange that. I would suggest five-thirty the day before, the fifth, were it not for the fact that we shall be engrossed in Mrs. Bolling's birthday. Please present my compliments to Dean Robbins and tell him I entertain the pleasantest anticipations of our meeting.

You may be sure that the Wilsons think of the Davises with nothing but deep affection. We hope that the New Year will develop for you all every happy and rewarding circumstance.

Affectionately Yours,   Woodrow Wilson

TLS (N. H. Davis Papers, DLC).
  [1] A revised version is printed as an Enclosure with DFH to WW, Jan. 11, 1923.
  [2] Edwin Clyde Robbins, Dean of the School of Business Administration, University of Oregon.

From David Franklin Houston

Dear Mr. Wilson: New York December 27, 1922.

Norman Davis and I were talking the other day about a statement which we were to prepare for you on taxation. I decided to try my hand on a broader statement. I dictated one which I showed to him. He thought you would be interested in it, and I am therefore sending you a copy. It was dictated hastily. It is not complete and is by no means adequate. It might serve as a basis for discussion. It is, of course, not in platform shape, not being sufficiently dogmatic.

Mrs. Houston and I regretted that we did not have more time when we were in Washington so that we might see you and Mrs. Wilson. It is probable that I shall be in Washington the 13th and 14th of January. I shall hope to see you then if it is convenient for you.

With the greetings of the season to you and Mrs. Wilson from both of us, I am   Faithfully yours,   D. F. Houston.

TLS (WP, DLC).

Three Telegrams from Franklin Delano Roosevelt

New York NY 1922 Dec 27 PM 10

Members of permanent board of trustees executive committee and original organizers of Woodrow Wilson Foundation in assembly here today are happy to be able to advise you that publics loyal allegiance to those fine ideals and principles for which you stand assures the success of the foundation Stop We regard support given foundation by men and women in every state and in all walks of life as a splendid reexpression of faith in you Stop The foundation will live as a permanent tribute to your world services to the cause of human freedom. In this and future generations is destined to render conspicuous public service Stop Please accept our cordial good wishes for the New Year

Franklin D Roosevelt.

New York NY 1922 Dec 27 PM 11 13

Following telegram read at Woodrow Wilson Foundation meeting here today Quote To Woodrow Wilson scholar statesman and patriot many thousands of your fellow countrymen have united to establish a permanent fund or endowment bearing your name the income to be used from time to time to promote in future generations meritorious service to public welfare democracy or peace thru justice. On December twenty eighth your sixty sixth birthday the contributors to this fund with many other thousand of your countrymen desire to express to you their admiration and gratitude for your extraordinary services in the cause of human freedom international cooperation and goodwill among men. May you live to see the full fruition of your strenuous and self-sacrificing labors Charles W Eliot End Quote   Franklin D Roosevelt.

                                        New York NY 1922 Dec 28 AM 12 54
    Following telegram read at Woodrow Wilson Foundation meeting here today Quote To Woodrow Wilson on this your birthday millions of your fellow citizens who have had the high privilege of following your leadership in great affairs rejoice at your steady recovery and affectionately welcome you back to active leadership in our counsels for progressive and helpful national policies. The Woodrow Wilson Foundation now completed has been established by those who believe in the saving quality of your political philosophy and who hope thru it as an agent to broaden the development of those principles and speed their acceptance and application thru it and all other ways. We tender our affection our admiration and our gratitude to you for your services to mankind Respectfully yours Newton D Baker End Quote   Franklin D Roosevelt.

T telegrams (WP, DLC).

To Franklin Delano Roosevelt

                                        Washn DC Dec 28 11:40P
    I feel no less honored by the character and generous friendship of those who like yourself have made the foundation endowment a success than by the remarkable completion of the project which you have brought about Stop Please accept my deep thanks and heartiest good wishes for the New Year Stop Thank you for forwarding the messages from Baker and Eliott
                                        Woodrow Wilson

T telegram (F. D. Roosevelt Papers, NHpR).

A News Report

[*Dec. 28, 1922*]

SENATE FELICITATES WILSON ON BIRTHDAY
Resolution, Offered by a Democrat, Is Put Through Without a Dissenting Vote.

Washington, Dec. 28.—Ex-President Wilson celebrated his sixty-sixth birthday quietly today in his home on S street to which during the day came messages of congratulation and felicitation from all parts of the world. A delegation from the Woodrow Wilson Foundation called during the afternoon and informed him that more than $800,000 had been collected and that the $1,000,000 fund for the perpetuation of his ideals was assured. Later in the day a messenger brought an engrossed copy of a Senate resolution congratulating him on his "rapid recovery to good health." It was accompanied by a friendly note from Vice President Coolidge.

The resolution was introduced in the Senate at noon today by Senator Harris of Georgia, who asked unanimous consent for immediate consideration, to which no objection was raised. Most of the Senators were in their seats, including such opponents of the Versailles Treaty as Senators Lodge, Reed of Missouri, Johnson, Brandegee, Moses, France, Poindexter, Norris and La Follette. There was no debate on it and the resolution was adopted without a roll-call with a chorus of "ayes" from the Democrats, while many of the Republican members were so occupied with other matters that they paid no attention to it.

The text of the resolution is as follows:

Whereas the Senate has heard with great pleasure the announcement of the rapid recovery to good health of former President Hon. Woodrow Wilson; be it

Resolved, That the Vice President be requested to express to Hon. Woodrow Wilson the pleasure and joy of the Senate of the United States because of his rapid recovery to good health.

In presenting his resolution, Senator Harris said:

"From every part of the world, from all classes of people today are coming letters and telegrams congratulating Woodrow Wilson on his birthday and his rapid recovery to health. When all of us are forgotten, the name of Woodrow Wilson will be remembered as the greatest of the century."

In transmitting the resolution, the Vice President wrote:

United States Senate.

Washington, D. C., Dec. 28, 1922.

My dear Mr. Wilson:

It gives me great pleasure to be the medium of transmitting

the enclosed resolution to you. It was unanimously adopted. To it I wish to add my own felicitations on your recovering good health and my congratulations on the return of another anniversary of your natal day.

With the greetings of the season, I am

Cordially yours,   CALVIN COOLIDGE.

Hon. Woodrow Wilson,
Washington, D. C.

All day long messenger boys arrived at the Wilson home with telegrams and cables of good wishes from all parts of the world and there was a very heavy mail also conveying congratulations. Mr. Wilson spent most of the morning reading these expressions of good-will. The text of none of the messages or the names of their authors were given out. Except for immediate members of the family and a few personal friends, the only callers were the delegation representing the Woodrow Wilson Foundation, headed by Hamilton Holt of New York.

A demonstration by Mr. Wilson's admirers had been planned for three o'clock in front of his home this afternoon but this was called off because of a pouring rain. Nevertheless, when Mr. Holt and his committee arrived, there were more than a hundred people, in addition to photographers and newspapermen who shivered in the cold rain, hopeful of catching a glimpse of Mr. Wilson. The curb on both sides of the street for a block was lined with automobiles containing people with similar hopes but with more concern for the weather.

Mr. Holt was accompanied by Mrs. Charles E. Simonson of New York, Mrs. J. Malcolm Forbes of Boston and Miss Caroline Ruuts-Rees of Greenwich, Conn. They were members of a special committee sent to Washington to inform Mr. Wilson of the permanent establishment yesterday of the Woodrow Wilson Foundation, to make awards to those who render "meritorious service to democracy, public welfare, liberal thought or peace through justice." Rabbi Stephen S. Wise and Judge Martin T. Manton,[1] the remaining members of the delegation, were unable to make the trip.

The delegation remained with Mr. Wilson for nearly an hour. None of the members would discuss what went on within on the ground that their call was of an informal character and that there were no set speeches. They said they told Mr. Wilson of their confident expectation that within a few weeks the $1,000,000 of voluntary subscriptions required would be complete, and they bespoke the conviction that never before had a public man been recognized within his lifetime by a foundation designed to perpetuate his ideals. Mr. Wilson, they said, showed himself particularly affected and pleased by their call and the news of the establishment of the foundation that bears his name.

When the delegation emerged there was a rush of people through the rain to the gate at the side of the house behind which Mr. Wilson's closed automobile was waiting at the porte cochere. There was enthusiastic cheering when Mr. Wilson appeared, wearing a soft brown hat and a cape over a Winter overcoat. He hooked his cane over his left arm and stood alone with the hat in his right hand, bowing and smiling. Then he tossed his hat into the car and was assisted to a rear seat.

"Don't catch cold," cried one woman, bobbing up and down under her umbrella, while figures behind her were loud in lamentation over the obstruction in front of their cameras. Mr. Wilson smiled again and put on his hat. Then Mrs. Wilson entered the car and they drove off for an hour's ride around the Potomac speedway.

Those who had not seen Mr. Wilson for several months found him looking heavier and fuller faced, with possibly more color. Although he did not move his left arm and side with freedom, he appeared to depend less upon his cane.

Mr. Holt said that incomplete returns from last week's final appeal for funds showed that more than $800,000 of the $1,000,000 Woodrow Wilson Foundation had been received.[2] The appeal closed yesterday, and he said that he expected final returns would show a collection of $900,000, mainly in small contributions. Members of the committee expressed their satisfaction over the number of contributors rather than the amount of their donations, declaring that the aim of the foundation was to enlist as many founders as possible. They also pointed out that no "drive" for funds had been made, it being the wish of those in charge of the appeal not to solicit but to invite subscriptions. The amount on hand, they said, will be sufficient to establish the foundation as a going concern, and that while the appeal has ended the subscription books have not been closed.

Printed in the *New York Times*, Dec. 29, 1922.
[1] Martin Thomas Manton, judge of the United States Court of Appeals, Second Circuit.
[2] The Woodrow Wilson Foundation was chartered as an educational and charitable foundation by the State of New York on December 14, 1922, "in recognition of the national and international services of Woodrow Wilson." It was to have "for its particular object the promotion of public welfare, the advancement of liberal thought and the furtherance of peace through justice for the benefit of the people of the United States and of other nations." Its trustees were empowered to solicit, receive, and hold funds for the maintenance of an endowment fund, and the foundation was authorized to "award prizes, grant scholarships, to publish reports, to engage in research and to make studies of social, economic, political and industrial problems; and to do and perform any and all

things necessary and appropriate to a corporation created for the purposes hereinabove provided."

The directors named in the charter were E. A. Alderman, General Bliss, Cleveland H. Dodge, Samuel Gompers, Ernest M. Hopkins, William J. Mayo, M.D., Cyrus H. McCormick, Jr., Henry Morgenthau, Roland S. Morris, Franklin D. Roosevelt, Mrs. Simonson, Mrs. Tiffany, Senator Thomas J. Walsh, William Allen White, and Mary E. Woolley. "CERTIFICATE OF INCORPORATION," T MS (WC, NjP).

The foundation was formally organized in Franklin Roosevelt's New York City home on December 27, 1922. Roosevelt was elected chairman of the board of directors, Hamilton Holt, executive director, with offices at 150 Beekman Street, New York. The board elected an executive committee headed by Dodge and including Frank L. Polk, Colonel House, Frank Cobb, Rabbi Wise, and numerous others. After the organizational meeting, the foundation held its first luncheon at the Hotel Biltmore. Herbert S. Houston, Norman Davis, and others spoke. *New York Times*, Dec. 28, 1922.

A Memorandum by Dr. Grayson

[c. Dec. 28, 1922]

It was on the afternoon of Thursday, December 28, 1922,—Mr. Wilson's sixty-sixth birthday anniversary—that I dropped in on S Street to wish him many happy returns of the day. This was, of course, aside from my usual professional visit. I called at two o'clock and spent an hour with him. He was in better spirits and looked better than he had since his great illness. There was a healthy glow to his skin and he spoke with animation. He was dressed in anticipation of meeting a delegation representing the Woodrow Wilson Foundation, which called on him at three o'clock. In the group were Mr. Hamilton Holt and other members of the executive committee of the Foundation.

Mr. Wilson was seated in what he calls his "old Princeton Chair." It is a plain, wooden chair, with arms, and with a high back. The seat is of brown leather and the arms are also mounted in brown leather. The black paint is worn off at places where his elbows have rubbed. It is not a revolving chair. He spoke very affectionately of his old chair, saying—"This chair stood by me through all my days at Princeton; we have encountered stormy weather." It is interesting to note that the President has his old Princeton desk in his bedroom. It is a flat top desk, with drawers at the sides, and in these he keeps his private papers. He used this desk constantly while at "Prospect" in Princeton.

On this afternoon he took delight in showing me through the library and dining room, calling my particular attention to the large number of beautiful bouquets and baskets of flowers that had been sent to him by admiring friends on this natal day. "It is very pleasing to be remembered by my friends in this way," he said. He then pointed to a large pile of cards with all sorts of felicitous remarks indicated on them. There was quite a basket full of these cards which had been left during the day. He said, "I am having quite a card party today, as you see."

He also called my attention to the larger number of letters and telegrams on his desk—perhaps the largest mail he had received in any one day in S Street. He made no comment—simply pointed to the pile. He did refer, however, to one letter which he had received that morning and which was signed by a number of World War veterans, which read in part: "You have been wronged, and, by God, we are going to right it," and as he said this he pounded the arm of his chair with his fist. "That tone and meaning is in nearly every letter that I get from an ex-soldier," he remarked.

During the course of our conversation he said: "I get impatient when people come here and ask me for advice and then do not take it." He continued: "I predict that the next President will be a Democrat and that he will not be elected as Harding was by 7,000,000, but by 10,000,000.

He spoke of Borah as a "fine, sincere fellow," but he said, "the trouble with him is that he does not quite arrive." He then made a pun and referred to him in it in connection with "boric acid."

I told him about the Senate Resolution which was adopted unanimously on this day, and which is contained in the following clipping from the Congressional Record: [blank] He chuckled and said: "Think of them passing it and not meaning it. Of course, I do not mean to say that all who voted for it were not sincere, for I know many were sincere, but I feel sure some of them were not. I would much rather have had three Senators get together and draw up a resolution and have it passed with sincerity than the one that was passed today. That would be worth far more than the one the Senate did pass." He then repeated this limerick:

> "There was an old man of Khartoum who kept two black
>   sheep in his room,
> To remind him, he said, of two friends who were dead,
>   but *he would not tell whom* (?).

It seems that former Justice Clark and Hamilton Holt and others had urged the President to give his endorsement for the raising of a fund to create interest in the League of Nations by a series of lectures on Chautauqua platforms. He told these gentlemen that he was opposed to this idea. He said the League of Nations did not need that kind of advertising; that people got stale hearing about it and being preached to in this way; that they did not want it Chautauquaized. He felt that it was too big a matter to be handled in that way.

He asked me if I had analyzed the face of Mussolini, the Italian

Premier.[1] "I want to get your reaction as to what you think of it," he said. I told him that it was more difficult to judge a man by his picture than by the man himself; that in one picture Mussolini is shaking hands with the King of Italy and is looking at the King's feet. I said, "That's a bad sign." He replied, "Exactly so. It reminds me of some one whom you well know and about whom we have had more than one talk. You will recall he never looks one in the eye while in conversation. You will also recall that he proved to be shifty."

He practiced with the pronunciation of the word "fascisti." He said it was "fas-chees-ti," emphasizing the middle syllable, which, he said, was pronounced the same as "cheese."

He asked me if by any chance I had read the article in the Saturday Evening Post by Dr. John H. Richards, one of Roosevelt's physicians in his last illness. It appeared in the issue of December 9, 1922, and the particular reference is as follows: [blank][2] Mr. Wilson said: "Think of a statement of that kind coming from an ex-President. Just think of that." His tone was by no means bitter, and this is all he said about the article.

T MS (received from James Gordon Grayson and Cary T. Grayson, Jr.).
    [1] Benito Mussolini had taken office as Prime Minister on October 30, 1922.
    [2] Hermann Hagedorn, ed., "Roosevelt's Talks with his Physician," *The Saturday Evening Post*, CXCV (Dec. 9, 1922), 40, 42, 44, 46. Hagedorn edited this memorandum by Dr. Richards who attended Roosevelt at his home, Sagamore Hill, and in Roosevelt Hospital in New York between early October 1918 and early January 1919. It is difficult to know to what indiscreet statement Wilson referred, because the article was replete with very frank comments. Perhaps Wilson referred to Roosevelt's comment about himself: "Wilson reminds me of Cowper, who could write fine English, but who knew nothing of the human nature of which he was writing. If Wilson had known anything of human nature he would not have conducted himself as he did." *Ibid.*, p. 46.

From Norman Hezekiah Davis, with Enclosure

My dear Mr. Wilson: [New York] December 28, 1922.

I am enclosing a statement, intended primarily for the benefit of the farmers, in the hope that this may be of some service later on as indicated by you in your letter of December 24th.

Since this is intended mainly to educate the farmers, I have brought in the question of international cooperation because, according to my information, the fallacy was in some way put over on the farmers that the League of Nations would involve us in another European war.

With best wishes, I am as ever

                              Affectionately yours,   Norman H. Davis

TLS (WP, DLC).

ENCLOSURE

The Democratic Party believes in and adheres to the principle of equal rights as between individuals within the nation. Its domestic policy has accordingly been directed to the maintenance of freedom and equality of rights and opportunities in the economic as well as in the political field of activities within the nation.

Its foreign policy has in effect been to extend and apply these same principles in the relationships between nations.

The Republican Party professes to believe in the same principles but whenever opportunity offers it proceeds to disregard them. Through the imposition of excessive protective tariffs and other preferential legislation, The Republican Party creates inequalities, stifles the economic forces of the country and grants benefits to a few which increase without any compensating benefit the burdens of the people as a whole.

In pursuance of its policy to set free and develop the agricultural and industrial resources of the country, the Democratic Party established the Federal Reserve Banking and Currency System, and the Farm Loan Banks. By these measures our financial resources were decentralized and for the first time in our history stable machinery was set up for the elastic issuance of currency and the mobilization of credit adequate to move and market our agricultural and manufactured products. We were thus enabled to stand, as no other nation has been able to do, the financial strains of the world war and of the trying reconstruction period.

Other measures are required for providing long time credits and better warehousing and transportation facilities to our agriculturalists but this will not cure the principal ills from which they are today suffering. While the farmers need these improved facilities, what they need above all are world markets for their surplus products and an equitable exchange of their products for their requirements.

Experience has amply proven that with the possible exception of sugar and wool, the farmers are not aided by the protective tariff, but on the contrary, are placed at a distinct disadvantage. The prices of all the farm products which we produce in surplus are necessarily fixed by the price obtainable for that surplus in the world market which is competitive. Under the present protective tariff, the purchasing power of the foreign customers is reduced and the foreign market weakened. Nevertheless, the American farmer has to sell his entire product at the price which the surplus brings abroad, and to buy his goods in the local non-competitive market where, on account of the tariff, an artificial price is added to what he buys. As longs [long] as such conditions prevail, there will be no substantial relief for the farmer, and discontent will continue in the agricultural districts. Additional credit and improved warehousing and transportation facilities may enable the farmer to cheapen and increase his production, but that will not get him out of debt and his condition will not improve unless he can get a fair price for what he produces and can buy at a fair price what he consumes.

The foreign market, upon which the welfare of the American farmer is so dependent, will not improve until world conditions improve and the foreign customers have credits and markets which will enable them to produce and exchange their products for their requirements, and world conditions will not improve substantially without appropriate action taken by nations working in concert.

Realizing the economic interdependence of the world and the necessity for justice, law and order between nations, as a prerequisite to peace and healthy trade and commerce, the last Democratic Administration advocated constructive plans for the stabilization of peace by securing through international cooperation-freedom and justice, the only means by which we can hope to banish world wars and escape further serious involvements which obstruct our freedom of action and our economic development. The failure of the present Administration to accept and to cooperate with the other powers in carrying out those plans has been accompanied by continued political instability and industrial depression in Europe, further derangement in foreign exchange, and contraction in the world's purchasing power, all of which destroys confidence, threatens peace, and reacts adversely on our domestic situation.

T MS (WP, DLC).

From Eleanor Randolph Wilson McAdoo
and William Gibbs McAdoo

Los Angeles Cal Dec 28 [1922]

We are thinking of you with devoted love and wishing for you many recurring anniversaries full of happiness You all contributed immensely to our lovely xmas   Nell and Mac

T telegram (WP, DLC).

A Memorandum by Dr. Grayson

(Dec. [c. 28] 1922)

Doctor Axson had two very pleasant visits in S Street—one on Christmas Day, when he dined with the President and Mrs. Wilson, and another on Thursday, December 28th, (Mr. Wilson's 66th birthday anniversary), when he again dined with them in S Street.

They talked about the break between Mussolini (the Italian Premier) and D'Annunzio.[1] Mr. Wilson said: "The Fascisti party is the extreme nationalist party, is it not? This, of course, is what D'Annunzio stood for, but what their belief or creed is, I do not know. I understand, however, that it was organized to resist Bolshevism, and that that is the real start of the whole thing." Reference was made to the King of Italy[2] and some one asked why the King had accepted the party. Mr. Wilson said: "Clemenceau had great contempt for the King for permitting this party to take hold of things. He told me during his recent visit—'Italy has no Government.' Clemenceau, in his characteristic way, threw up his hands while saying this."

At the Christmas day dinner Doctor Axson asked: "What do you make of Borah? What is it that he is doing?" Mr. Wilson said: "I don't know just what to make of him. He is a very interesting man, but the trouble with him is that he never goes far enough."

There was very little public talk at these two dinners and the talk was not fast at all. Everything moved along very leisurely.

Christmas night was awfully sweet, according to Doctor Axson. After dinner the packages were opened and Mr. Wilson showed the greatest interest in the presents. This took about two hours' time, and after the packages had been opened Mr. Wilson showed evidence of being tired, not peevishly tired, no irritation whatever— he just began to be a little more silent.

He handed Doctor Axson some small poems to read saying: "Official reader, read these." In the midst of this reading Mrs. Wilson interrupted by saying: "Is there anything the matter with me?" She was asked, "What do you mean?" She replied, "Why, I have opened nothing but towels, wash-rags and bath soaps." Mr. Wilson was very much amused but did not say a word—simply laughed.

Both on Christmas night and on his birthday he showed emotion each time, Doctor Axson said. Addressing Mr. Wilson, Doctor Axson remarked: "By the way, I spent Tuesday night in Princeton and saw a number of our old friends." Just a little ironically Mr. Wilson said: "Friends." Doctor Axson said: "You bet they were friends." And then Doctor Axson told him how when David Magee,[3] his host, brought out some liquor after dinner, put a table in front of the fire, and placed the bottle and glasses on it, the guests—there were eight or ten—reached over for their glasses, when somebody started to drink. "Don't drink," said Magee, "wait." Every man jumped up, and the interesting thing was that everybody said in chorus: "Woodrow Wilson." That touched Mr. Wilson deeply. A little later wine was served—very little wine was served at Mr. Wilson's table—and Mrs. Wilson said, "We must have a toast." Miss Bertha Bolling (who, with Miss Margaret Wilson and Mr. John Randolph Bolling, was present) said: "Why not the Princeton toast?" Mrs. Wilson said: "Everybody on their feet," and they all said, "Woodrow Wilson." But it was the Princeton incident that caused Mr. Wilson to fill up.

At the birthday dinner he filled up once in the same way. During the dinner he turned to Mrs. Wilson and said: "Dear, what thing in Europe stands out above everything else in your mind today." Mrs. Wilson said: "Oh, I don't know but that I would say Suresnes."[4] Doctor Axson spoke up and said: "That interests me very much; I was not very much with you but that day (Memorial Day—1919) stands out very strongly." Mrs. Wilson very prettily pictured the whole scene, the soldiers in khaki, and the lines of people along the streets. Mr. Wilson did not say anything.

At this point Doctor Axson referred to the burial of the Unknown Soldier and repeated a statement made to him by a friend at the ceremonies. This friend said: "There are only two men who occupied the Presidential chair who could have met this situation (the delivery of the address at Arlington)—Lincoln and Wilson." The last thing in Doctor Axson's mind was to move Mr. Wilson, but he was moved. Mrs. Wilson observed him and putting her hand on his said: "What scene is uppermost in your mind?" Mr. Wilson did not have much control over his voice and pretty near sobbed. He just indicated that it was the blind soldier.[5] It gave Mrs. Wilson the clue and then she painted the picture for Doctor Axson and the other guests.

It was while visiting a French hospital on a Sunday afternoon that the President and Mrs. Wilson saw this *blind* French soldier standing with his back to the wall of a low-ceilinged, smoky, dingy room singing the Marseilles. The soldier was tall, very erect, and had his head resting against the wall singing this national anthem of France in full volume. Mr. Wilson said: "That is the scene. That I remember above everything else." He was very much overcome while Mrs. Wilson was speaking about it.

Mrs. Wilson while the dinner was being served said: "I find it so hard to cultivate the habit of saying, 'Won't you have some turkey?' instead of saying, 'Won't you have some more turkey?' " Doctor Axson said: "This amounts to sarcasm, judging by the amount of turkey I have had." Mr. Wilson looked up and said: "I am going to correct you. Some one in Washington always insisted on correcting the speaker for using the word 'sarcasm' when he meant 'irony.' I always insisted that 'sarcasm' was not 'irony,' and that 'irony' was not 'sarcasm.' "

When they brought in the birthday cake and lighted the candles, a strong light was thrown on Mr. Wilson's face. Doctor Axson was very much struck by the vigor in his face, especially the quietness of his expression, for it was a peaceful face—very ruddy—eyes very bright—and nothing at all that indicated pain or strain or anything of that sort.

On leaving the Wilson home Doctor Axson called on some friends—Admiral and Mrs. Helm[6]—Mrs. Helm was Mrs. Wilson's secretary while in the White House—to pay his respects, and Mrs. Helm in talking about Mr. Wilson said that this Fall is to her a miracle; that it is almost incredible that Mr. Wilson could be as well as he is. Then she said: "I think he is better than he was before he broke down." And to partly prove that she got out some pictures of Mr. Wilson which had been taken in Europe. Pointing to one in her scrap book which had been taken of Mr. Wilson at Suresnes in 1919, where he was assisting a nurse in placing a wreath on the grave of one of our soldiers, she said: "Now look at it, that is perfectly beautiful, but he does not look as well as he does now. He looks much better in the face now than he did then." It must be recalled, of course, that Mr. Wilson had not at that time fully recovered from his attack of the influenza.[7]

During the Christmas dinner reference was made to somebody else and his father, when Mr. Wilson said: "I wish I were like my father." Miss Bertha Bolling said: "Well, I hope it is not irreverent to say it, but you have rather gone beyond your father." He said: "That is where you are very much mistaken." She made some little apologetic remark, and he continued: "Of course, I was wider known than he was, but in the essential hold which he had on the group which he touched, he went beyond me."

Mrs. Wilson gave an intimate glimpse of him. She was looking over a collection of sayings of men and presently in her merry way she looked up and said: "Are you sorry for yourself?" He said, "What do you mean?" She said: "I read here—'I am sorry for the man who does not read his Bible every night.' " He said: "Yes, I am too." Mr. Wilson did read his Bible every night during the war. He has a little book of Bible texts—and these texts he reads every night now.

T MS (received from James Gordon Grayson and Cary T. Grayson, Jr.).
¹ In mid-December, the Mussolini regime had begun a crackdown against rival para-military groups, including Gabriele D'Annunzio's "legionaries." After making a token

protest, D'Annunzio announced on December 20 that he was dissolving his forces. Adrian Lyttelton, *The Seizure of Power: Fascisim in Italy, 1919-1929*, 2d edn. (Princeton, N. J., 1987), p. 104; *New York Times*, Dec. 21, 1922.

  [2] That is, Victor Emmanuel III.

  [3] David Magie, Professor of Classics at Princeton University.

  [4] When Wilson spoke at Memorial Day exercises at Suresnes Cemetery outside Paris. See his remarks and the extract from the Grayson Diary printed at May 30, 1919, Vol. 59.

  [5] About this incident, see the extract from the Grayson Diary printed at Dec. 22, 1918, Vol. 53.

  [6] That is, James Meredith Helm and Edith Benham Helm.

  [7] Wilson had long since recovered from his viral illness of early April 1919. What Grayson probably knew, but did not say, was that Wilson had not fully recovered from the small stroke which afflicted him on April 28, 1919. About this incident, see the Appendixes on that subject in Vol. 58.

From William Edward Dodd

Dear Mr. Wilson: University of Chicago December 29, 1922.

It is hardly necessary for me to indicate to you how deeply I rejoice at every sign of returning good health. My interest and activity for several years must speak for me. But I do wish you to know particularly how glad I am that the Foundation Fund has been completed. Many times I have had occasion to observe the depths of the popular feeling on the subject of your worth to the world, and value especially to this, our own country. Even very wealthy men, who in general have had their mind poisoned by their wealth or by the false estimates of the meaning of wealth, have often been deeply moved when the facts have been stated. I could not, if I were to try, describe many of the demonstrations, say, in Saint Louis or in Columbus, Ohio, where I spoke recently—and above all in North Carolina.

The resolution of the Senate of yesterday both pleases and angers me. How much do they not confess by this resolution? I am glad they had the courage, though to confess their sins, for confession of sin is still a good thing in this world. But the confession by implication that they have done infinite damage to ourselves and the whole world by indulging in personal and party fears and hatreds stirs again some of the feelings of deep resentment of the last few years.

You may never have seen those closing paragraphs of my book upon you and your work[1] in which I endeavor to indicate the kind of place you have earned in history. When I wrote those passages I felt that I was taking time a little by the forelock. But since that day all my observations as I have moved among people of all levels of intelligence, and all my reading of the books and articles of friends and foes alike have confirmed the judgment. At the risk of being personal, I shall now say that it seems to me no man who ever led American political thought and action has ever quite earned so high a place. And this I believe nearly all the thoughtful historians of the country are about to agree to (there are unthoughtful historians as you rather twitted us with last June).

Yesterday I spent in finishing an article on "Wilsonism" for the *American Journal of Political Science*[2] in which I tried to sum up the case and at the same time indicate the value of five or six recent works, such as poor Page's and Baker's invaluable book. It seemed a fit way to spend the day. My friend McLaughlin[3] came in late in the afternoon and remarked that he had been reading *Page*. He added what a pity so good a friend could not keep his head in London and really understand what his great friend in Washington was trying to do! I was glad to hear McLaughlin, long a Republican say that, for he gave a fine son to the cause, the very last day of the war, I believe—a son who had just finished at college and married.

But this letter threatens to be a plague instead of a felicitation. Let me close with a hearty God bless you! And the prayer is the feeling of every member of our household.

Yours sincerely,   William E. Dodd

I must not fail to say how much we honor Mrs. Wilson for her services these years and her fine taste shown on so many occasions.

TLS (WP, DLC).
  [1] William E. Dodd, *Woodrow Wilson and His Work*, rev. edn. (Garden City, N. Y., 1921), pp. 434-37. Among American Presidents, Dodd seemed to think that only Jefferson and Lincoln were Wilson's equals.
  [2] "Wilsonism," *Political Science Quarterly*, XXXVIII (1923), 115-32. This was a review essay of W. F. McCombs and Louis J. Lang, *Making Woodrow Wilson President*; Burton J. Hendrick, *The Life and Letters of Walter Hines Page*; J. P. Tumulty, *Woodrow Wilson As I Know Him*; and R. S. Baker, *Woodrow Wilson and World Settlement*. However, Dodd also surveyed all the important extant literature on Wilson and his political career and policies. The essay is a good evaluation of the early literature on Wilson and his time.
  [3] Andrew Cunningham McLaughlin, Professor of History at the University of Chicago, noted historian of the constitutional history of the United States.

To Calvin Coolidge

My Dear Mr. Vice President: [Washington, Dec. 30, 1922]

The very gracious letter with which you are so kind as to accompany the Resolution of the Senate of 28th December has given me genuine pleasure. It pleases me very greatly to receive so generous an expression of your kind personal sentiments, and I beg to express the hope that the new year will contain for Mrs. Coolidge[1] and you every genuine satisfaction and lasting contentment.

Believe me, my dear Mr. Vice President, with great respect,
        Cordially and sincerely yours,   Woodrow Wilson.

Printed in the *New York Times*, Dec. 31, 1922.
  ¹ Grace Anna Goodhue Coolidge.

To David Franklin Houston

My dear Houston,   [Washington] 30th December 1922

I have read with a great deal of interest your short paper on contrasted policies of the two parties in matters of fiscal and economic
legislation, and if you do not object I shall suggest to Chairman
Hull that the paper be printed preparatory to putting it in the
hands of all our speakers in 1924. They ought to get a lot of good
speeches out of it.

It occurs to me that the paragraphs on page four would not need
a great deal of condensation to convert them into the dogmatic
statements we need for a platform. Will you not be willing so to
transform them?

It is a great satisfaction to be in touch with you again about public questions of first importance, for I have great confidence in your
counsel, and believe that it can be so given as to carry conviction
to the whole country.

I am returning the paper, but only that you may have it before
you when you consider the suggestions which I have made.

I hope with all my heart that the New Year will be for you, Mrs.
Houston and all your family one of unusual blessing and happiness. Mrs. Wilson joins me in that wish, and also in affectionate
messages of every kind to you all.

With affectionate regard,
                    Faithfully Yours,   [Woodrow Wilson]

CCL (WP, DLC).

From William Gibbs McAdoo

Dear Governor,   Los Angeles, Cal. Dec. 30/22

I send you by post today the book I had ordered for your birthday.
It did not arrive until today as the publishers were slow in making
delivery.

The book is by my friend Claude G. Bowers, Editor of the Fort
Wayne (Ind) Journal-Gazette and is called "The Party Battles of
the Jackson Period."¹ It is one of the most fascinating books that I
have read in a long time and I believe you will enjoy it thoroughly.

There is a startling parallel between the Whig venom toward Jackson and the Republican venom toward you in domestic as well as international affairs. I wrote a review of this book for the January International Book review.[2]

It is barely possible that Nell and I may go to New York and Washington in January. We shall let you know definitely as soon as our plans mature.

With affectionate wishes for many happy years of life and health and love for Edith and you all from all of us. I am

Devotedly   Mac

ALS (WP, DLC).
[1] Boston and New York, 1922.
[2] William G. McAdoo, "Party Battles in the Heyday of Democracy," *The Literary Digest International Book Review*, I (Jan. 1923), 23-25.

From Norman Hezekiah Davis

My dear Mr. Wilson: [New York] December 30, 1922.

In case it may be of some interest to you and that you might have some suggestion to make—I may say that I contemplate talking to the Overseas Writers, January 6th, on Reparations, its political and economic aspects, and the relations of the United States to the questions involved. These newspaper men have been after me for months to address them and have now asked me particularly to discuss Reparations.

I propose to show—after reviewing the economic factors, that Reparations, which seems to stand out as the greatest obstacle to European recovery, is a product of the war and not of the Peace Treaty, and that failure to remove this obstacle by a definitive settlement is primarily due to conflicting political policies—which have been nurtured by our failure to play our part by discharging our moral obligation and safeguarding our material interest.

It is pitiful that Hughes and others should still call this a purely economic question when it is primarily political and will never be settled without political settlements which will induce the powers to adopt political policies which accom[m]odate themselves to economic necessities and to a square deal all around.

I feel that it is wrong in principle and also unwise to mix Reparations and Inter-Allied Debts, and may discuss that somewhat. The ability of the Allies to pay us may depend on what they collect from Germany, but their obligation to pay has nothing to do with that. Each question should be dealt with liberally but on its merits—otherwise we will find ourselves jockeyed into the position of subsidizing European wars.

Economic conferences wont get anywhere and it seems to me that we ought to begin to point out that, because of its failure to take the obviously safe course, this cowardly Administration is making a fool of itself at the expense of the world's peace and welfare.

No publicity is to be given of my talk but I think it may do good to try to educate the newspaper men.

Please don't bother to answer this unless you want to "put on the peddle."

As ever,   Affectionately yours,   Norman H. Davis

TLS (WP, DLC).

To Hamilton Holt

My dear Mr. Holt,   Washington D C 31st December 1922

May I not consider it my privilege as a one time historian to ask you for information on a point about which I have come to entertain some doubt. When you were down here with the committee on December 28th you spoke of Mrs. Simonson as the originator of the Foundation. I had previously been told that the project was originated by Mrs. Charles Tiffany, and I will be very much obliged to you if you would recite for me the facts of the case so far as you recall them. You will understand that every point of fact about the Foundation is of very great interest to me.

The visit of the committee was most gratifying, and I feel every day more proud that the Foundation should have been originated and completed by such people and in such a spirit as has been displayed throughout.

Would you not also repeat for me again that wonderful letter from a North Carolinian which you repeated while we were standing in my library?

I hope that the New Year will develop for you every happy circumstance and experience.

Cordially and Sincerely Yours,   Woodrow Wilson

TLS (Woodrow Wilson Coll., NjR).

To Norman Hezekiah Davis

My dear Davis,   [Washington] 1st January 1923

Thank you for your letter of December thirtieth. I am glad you are going to clear up for the Overseas Writers the much befuddled question of Reparations, and in view of Mr. Hughes' recent second-hand proposals I suggest that it might be well to point out that the United States was to have had a controlling hand in the Reparations Commission set up by the Treaty which we were so stupid and dishonourable as to reject. As I remember it, the American member of the Commission was to have the deciding vote in every matter of consequence. Let them have both barrels, and do make clear among other things how the Allied Governments have from the first been trying to make the people of the United States pay the whole cost of the war.

Let me speak for a moment of the little paper you sent me the other day. If you do not object, I shall keep it and put it in the hands of Chairman Hull as I did your address on the party. There are passages in it which seem to me to contain excellent dogmatic matter for the platform.

Hoping that the New Year will contain for you all every satisfying blessing,   Affectionately Yours,   [Woodrow Wilson]

CCL (WP, DLC).

To Francis Klapuš[1]

My dear Friend,   [Washington] 3rd January 1923

Your letter of December 12th, 1922,[2] has given me deep pleasure. It makes me very proud indeed to know that I am thought to have promoted the liberties of the people of Czechoslovakia. My interest in them can never grow less, and I shall always deem the title "friend of Czechoslovakia" as one of the most distinguished I could bear.

May I not also express my deep interest in the Communion to which you belong and to hope that as the years go by both religious and political liberty may constantly increase and be fortified in the stout little Republic over which your President Masaryk so admirably presides. Believe me, my dear sir, your sincere friend and the interested friend also of all who devote themselves to the welfare and happiness of the people of Czechoslovakia.

I thank you warmly for the unusual pictures you have been gracious enough to send me. I shall keep them as highly valued reminders of your friendship and kindness.

I hope the New Year which is just opening will bring you every blessing and your Heart's desire.

Cordially and Faithfully Yours,   [Woodrow Wilson]

CCL (WP, DLC).
[1] Pastor of the Bohemian Brethren Evangelical Church of Přelouč, Czechoslovakia.
[2] F. Klapuš to WW, Dec. 12, 1922, ALS (WP, DLC).

From Hamilton Holt, with Enclosures

My dear Mr. Wilson: New York Jan. 4, 1923.

I can best answer the inquiry contained in your letter of December 31st., by quoting verbatim from the little speech that Mrs. Simonson made at the meeting of the National Committee of the Woodrow Wilson Foundation, when the origin of the Foundation was discussed. While you can see that Mrs. Charles Tiffany played a very important part in originating the Foundation, undoubtedly Mrs. Simonson was the "original" originator. At least that has always been my understanding of the situation. I came into the movement after the ladies had gotten it well organized and can only give you second hand information.

I also enclose to you the telegram from the North Carolinian which has so touched every audience to which I have read it. Of all the fine tributes that have been paid to you since this Foundation has commenced its work, none has a finer ring than this.

I trust that the New Year will be a happy one for you.

Very respectfully yours,   Hamilton Holt

TLS (WP, DLC).

E N C L O S U R E   I

Fellow Friends of Mr. Wilson: December 2, 1921

I questioned very much when Mr. Holt asked me to tell briefly the history of the starting of this movement for the Foundation. I questioned the propriety of my doing it, but Mr. Dodge assured me that this was to be a family party and it is as to a family party that I am speaking.

The women of New York worked hard for their enfranchisement, as most of you know. Some of you helped in it and when we won our vote I think it meant a great deal to all of us. I know it did to me. I learned much about practical politics in my effort to get that vote and I astonished my perfectly good Republican family, Republicans for many generations, by announcing after we had won our vote that I was a Democrat, and a Wilson Democrat at that. They were really quite startled. Some of them have not gotten over it yet. In the 1920 campaign it was my privilege to work with the National Democratic Committee and during the last three weeks of the campaign I spoke at bi-partisan meetings. The propaganda of untruth and the lack of understanding of Mr. Wilson was unbearable to one who felt that Mr. Wilson was the outstanding statesman of his day and generation. This experience crystal-

Greeting women from the Pan-American Conference at his home
on April 28, 1922

Greeting well-wishers at his home on Armistice Day, 1922

Out for a drive with Mrs. Wilson

"The Straphanger," reproduced from the original cartoon by Charles Dana
Gibson

Carter Glass, Joseph Taylor Robinson, and Cordell Hull

Hamilton Holt

On a drive on November 12, 1923

Lost in thought on his sixty-seventh birthday

Wilson's physicians (Sterling Ruffin, Cary T. Grayson, and Harry Atwood Fowler) leave the house on February 2, 1924, after an all-night vigil

On the way to the interment in the Washington Cathedral

ized in my own mind the vital importance of the friends of Mr. Wilson doing something immediately to show their appreciation of him. The day after the Election I happened to meet another ardent friend of Mr. Wilson, Mrs. Tiffany—and my one regret today is that Mrs. Tiffany is not here. When I met her I said: "Can we not do something for Mr. Wilson?" She replied: "That is an awfully nice idea, but what can we do?" "What should we do?" "I did not know, but felt we were going to do something." In the course of the next few months I met many admirers of Mr. Wilson and always made the suggestion to them and the enthusiasm with which they received the idea convinced me that it was not only possible but that many shared with me the desire to pay tribute to this great man.

Through mutual interests Mrs. Tiffany and I often met and we never failed to talk over the possibility of a worthy tribute. We thought of material things but very quickly eliminated anything of that kind. I think we had particularly in mind a house that had been given to one man, a man not quite so famous as Mr. Wilson, but that had not turned out particularly well so we thought it was dangerous, and we gradually came to realize that a tribute to Mr. Wilson, that was worthy of the man we wished to honor was a difficult thing to decide. By chance, Mr[s]. Tiffany and I met at the City Club on the day the papers announced Mr. Wilson had been awarded the Nobel Peace Prize. We lunched together and very naturally rejoiced that their prize had been given to him. Mrs. Tiffany said: "I wish we could do something like that." And I being a born optimist said: "That is what we are going to do; that is the inspiration we have been looking for." And she, in her brilliant way, began to explain what an award of that kind might mean to this country. We both broke engagements to talk it over in the afternoon and within a few days met again, asking Miss Ogden[1] to join us. She was just as enthusiastic as we were. And it was then we decided to call that meeting which was held two days before Christmas last year.

We made out a list of twenty-five women and out of the twenty-five invited, twenty-three came to that meeting, which I think was a test of devotion, for if there is any time that women are busy it is two days before Christmas. Those women took up the idea with perfectly splendid enthusiasm, and they immediately got in touch with the men. Mr. Dodge said the men clamored to come in. I do not know that I agree with him. I do not think we gave them the opportunity to clamor, for we knew from the very beginning that we needed the men and that this could not be a women's movement. It was to be a movement of all the friends of Mr. Wilson; that movement started two days before Christmas last year and it culminated in its launching at the meeting held at the Biltmore Hotel on the 15th of last March. I think we can all be proud to have had a share in that. I think that we were making history. To my mind it is far more important to tell Mr. Wilson while he is with us how much we appreciate him, that [than] to wait for future generations to say how wonderful he was.

¹ Unidentified.

E N C L O S U R E   I I

COPY OF TELEGRAM RECEIVED FROM
JOSEPHUS DANIELS

January 14, 1922.

Today Mrs. Josephus Daniels, State Chairman of the Woodrow Wilson Foundation, received a check for $100 with this brief note "From the family of Frank M. Thompson,¹ who gave his life in the World War in the cause of world peace, in gratitude to Woodrow Wilson for the faith he has kept with the dead." This expresses the feeling of many who are interested in the campaign. Young Thompson was one of the bravest American soldiers who was a star football player.

T MSS (WP, DLC).
    ¹ We have not been able to identify him further. He did not attend the University of North Carolina.

A Toast¹

[Jan. 5, 1923]

The guest of the evening, whose vitality and vigor are equalled only by her gentleness and sweetness of spirit.

May she continue for many more years to bless us with her benign presence and influence.

T MS (WP, DLC).
    ¹ Offered by Wilson to Sallie White (Mrs. William Holcombe) Bolling at a dinner celebrating her eightieth birthday.

To the Chairman of the Nobel Peace Prize Committee¹

Honourable Sir,   [Washington] 7th January 1923

I understand that the name of Miss Jane Addams, my fellow countrywoman, is being presented to your Committee as a recipient of the Nobel Peace prize, and I take pleasure in adding my testimony to her high character and purpose and asking permission to say that I believe that the prize would be most worthily bestowed upon her.

I hope that I am not taking an unwarranted liberty in thus addressing you on behalf of a woman who has enjoyed the highest esteem of thoughtful persons throughout the United States.

With much respect,

Sincerely Yours,   [Woodrow Wilson]

CCL (WP, DLC).

¹ This letter was prompted by William Isaac Hull to WW, Jan. 5, 1923, TLS (WP, DLC), asking Wilson to write on Miss Addams' behalf. She was co-recipient of the Nobel Peace Prize with Nicholas Murray Butler in 1931.

To William Gibbs McAdoo

My dear Mac,   Washington D C 8th January 1923

I am warmly obliged to you for the book. I have often read of the party battles of Jackson's time, of course, but each fresh account shows things at its own angle, and I shall expect to be instructed by Mr. Bowers in things which I had overlooked.

We are delighted to know there is a possibility of seeing you and Nell this month, and hope with all our hearts that the proposed trip will not be forgotten or given up. We have been made happy by repeated reports we have had of the health of your little family, and of the happiness which the new home has brought to you all, and shall be eager to hear your own personal accounts of it all.

Things go as usual with us. I am slowly growing stronger. Even those of us who are in the ranks can now scent the oncoming battle, and take heart for the great contest that will make our opponents wonder why they were ever so blind as to oppose the policies which represent the deepest convictions and highest purposes of our people. It becomes clearer and clearer that the party's plans must comprehend all the great ends of justice, and must serve to lift the nation once more to the high levels upon which it moved during the war. I think that most of the leading men of the party are realizing now, perhaps as they never did before, these compulsions of duty and opportunity. The party is on the eve of its greatest service, and its spirit is rising to the occasion.

We shall impatiently await news of your coming East, and hope that when you do come we shall have a real chance to enjoy you. Edith unites with me in warmest love to you all, and the eager expectation of your visit. In the meantime, take care of yourselves, and I shall try to be more physically fit than even now for the pleasures of our intercourse.

We hope that the opening year, and the years that follow, will prove the happiest and most fortunate that you and Nell have ever known, and that the children will develop in everything except Mary Faith's propensity to dislike Christmas trees.

With every loving greeting to you all,

Affectionately Yours,   Woodrow Wilson

TLS (W. G. McAdoo Papers, DLC).

From Henry Morgenthau

My dear Mr. President: [New York] January 8th, 1923.

Yesterday, when I visited Mr. Ochs[1] who has just returned to his home from the hospital where he had undergone a very serious operation for prostate glands,—he disclosed to me in our conversation that the main worry on his mind was that you had not written him a congratulatory letter on his twenty-fifth anniversary as publisher of the "New York Times."[2]

He looks upon you as the greatest living American and considers his "Silver Book of Testimonials" incomplete without a contribution from you. I thought if you knew how much he desires to hear from you you might be willing to gratify him.

Saturday, I spoke at the Republican Club, following Senator-elect Fess[3] who frankly admitted that America could do nothing to alleviate European conditions. I told him that he had no right to speak for America's expected action unless he distinctly limit-it [limited it] to two years because after that time we Democrats expect to be in control and will carry out our policies. The audience, though they did not approve of my sentiments, evidently admired my courage for bearding them in their own den.

With kindest regards, I am

Very sincerely yours,   [Henry Morgenthau]

CCL (H. Morgenthau Papers, DLC).
    [1] That is, Adolph Simon Ochs, owner and publisher of the *New York Times* and the *Chattanooga Times*.
    [2] See, e.g., WW to B. M. Baruch, June 2, 1921, Vol. 67.
    [3] Simeon Davison Fess, Republican of Ohio.

From David Franklin Houston, with Enclosure

My dear Mr. Wilson:					New York January 11, 1923.

I send you herewith a re-statement of the paragraphs on page 4 to which you refer. I am by no means satisfied with the statement and am sure that you and others can greatly improve it.

I fear that very many of our Democratic leaders are not in accord with my views on taxation and may not be willing to accept them.

I am returning the complete statement. Of course I have no objection to your giving it to Mr. Hull for his own use. If it is published, I would prefer that it be used without any reference to my name.

I expect to be in Washington Saturday and possibly Sunday morning. It would make me very happy if I could see you for a few minutes, but do not let me interfere in the slightest with any of your plans or with your comfort. I shall be with Mr. Brookings,[1] and can be reached through his office at the Institute of Economics, 26 Jackson Place.		Faithfully yours,	D. F. Houston.

TLS (WP, DLC).
[1] That is, Robert Somers Brookings, St. Louis businessman, capitalist, and philanthropist; founder and chairman of the board of directors of two research organizations that were merged into the Brookings Institution of Washington, D. C., in 1928.

E N C L O S U R E

The Republican party was in control of all branches of the Federal Government from 1895 to 1911 and of all except the House of Representatives until 1913. It had developed a singular incapacity to entertain new ideas or to formulate and execute constructive policies. It had become blind to changing social and economic conditions and had failed to enact legislation to remedy evils which had appeared in many directions. Particularly, it had failed to enact legislation to give the nation a sound currency, to release business from the shackles which hampered it, and to promote the welfare of the farmers. It had become bound to a single idea,—that of attempting to promote the welfare of the masses by insuring the prosperity of the rich. It had formed a partnership with its protected favorites under the pretense that they would care for the masses of the people. It permitted these favorites to dictate the terms of legislation. Behind the constituted authorities there had arisen an invisible government of privileged groups which gave the law to the nation. Their all powerful lobbies, always present and unceasingly active, unduly influenced the course of legislation and administration.

Against this party the nation arose in revolt, drove it from power in 1912, and turned to the Democratic party for relief.

In two years, although from the outset the Democratic administration was burdened with a heritage of difficult problems and finally with a world convulsion, it enacted into law more helpful legislation than had been given the nation in a generation.

It reformed the currency. It created the Federal Reserve system which corrected the currency evils from which the nation had suffered for more than half a century, which enabled the country to withstand the shock of war and reconstruction, and which saved us from the demorilization [demoralization] and impotence under which most of the nations of Europe now labor.

It reformed our system of taxation, reducing excessive tariff duties and placing upon the statute books a progressive income tax measure which introduced into our revenue system safety and equity.

It created a non-partisan tariff commission to furnish the Congress and the Executive reliable information upon which sound legislation might be based, and to give the people information upon which they might intelligently form their judgments.

It provided business with a helpful agency in the Federal Trade Commission, which was intended to enable business to discover the rules of the game, to protect legitimate business against unfair practices of dishonest enterprise, and to relieve business leaders from the handicap of attempting to direct their activities under the constant menace of court processes.

It placed upon the statute books a Water Power law, under the terms of which, in all parts of the country the nation's water power may be utilized under private direction with due regard to the public interest.

It enacted more and more important legislation to develop agriculture and to improve rural life than had been placed upon the statute books in more than a generation. It recognized the peculiar needs of the farmer for credit by giving agricultural paper a maturity of 6 months instead of 90 days, and it made it possible for the farmers to get long time credit at low rates of interest through the establishment of the Farm Loan System. It enacted the Agricultural Educational Extension Bill, the most significant extension measure ever passed anywhere; the Cotton Futures Act and the Grain Grades Act to control trading in farm commodities and to enable the farmers to secure fair prices; the Federal Aid Road Act under the stimulation of which the nation is rapidly securing highways which are essential for better production, for better marketing, for better rural schools and for more attractive country life;

and the Federal Warehouse Bill; and created the Bureau of Markets with the view of promoting more orderly and economic distribution of farm products; and it omitted nothing to promote cooperation among the farmers in their own interest and in the interest of the public.

None of these measures has the Republican party seen fit to attempt to set aside. None of them has it substantially modified, and to date it has been able to make no significant additions to them. In fact, it has again shown marked incapacity to develop creative plans. It has no consistent or helpful policy, either domestic or foreign. It has stood in the way of the world's business and economic readjustment, and is responsible for an unnecessarily long continued business depression. Its economic thinking and international inaction have been both opportunist and contradictory. It has tried to go in many directions at the same moment. It has talked economy and projected measures which would entail large additional burdens on the taxpayer. It has at one moment made money available to stimulate foreign trade and at the next moment taken steps to restrict or destroy foreign trade. At a time when the interest of the nation as well as of the world should dictate a freer interchange of commodities, it has enacted a tariff measure with rates higher than any that have heretofore prevailed, and it now proposes to subsidize shipping for the trade which it has restricted. It has carried the nation back to the futile policies that prevailed before the great war.

The Democratic party pledges itself to rescue the nation from the condition into which it has been brought through lack of leadership and confused thinking. It will again undertake to restore the government to the people and to legislate and administer the nation's affairs free from the dictation of groups or of special interests.

It will safe-guard the Federal Reserve System, strengthen the hands of the Inter-state Commerce Commission and the Tariff Commission and the Federal Trade Commission, and will extend the Civil Service System and keep it free from the taint of politics.

It will develop a real budget system and in accordance with its long-established traditions will enforce economy in all Federal expenditures.

It will reduce taxes to the minimum consistent with the efficient and safe handling of the public business. It will resist efforts again to abolish all taxes except consumption taxes which unduly burden the masses of the people. It believes in direct progressive income taxes, but it does not regard it as necessary or desirable under the guise of taxation to confiscate the greater part of large incomes and to hinder initiative thrift and industrial development. Precisely because it believes in direct progressive income taxation, it will undertake to commend such taxation to the public by making it just and reasonable. It will reform the income tax schedules and place them on a permanent peace basis.

It will institute rational consistent measures to expand foreign trade and thereby to furnish, particularly to the farmers, a market for their surplus which is the protection which they so greatly need, and the only real protection which the government can afford them.

It will continue to expand its program for the development of agriculture and rural life. It will provide additional aids to the farmers in the task of marketing their products and will devise helpful plans for financing their operations by additional short term credits.

It will enact legislation and develop agencies cooperating with the states for the improvement of rural health, through sanitary surveys and the eradication or control of preventable disease.

It will undertake to provide generously for the care of disabled sailors and soldiers and sympathetically to administer all provisions for their welfare.

It will cooperate in the establishment of just and reasonable relations between workers in industry and the employers, and pledges itself to work out just relations between the government and the transportation agencies of the nation.

Especially will it again take up the task of leading the nations of the world along the path of peace and economic readjustment. It will again assert America's moral leadership and align this nation with other civilized countries of the world in efforts to restore economic order and to prevent a recurrence of war. It recognizes that this nation cannot isolate itself, that it is entangled with the other nations of the world, and that it should not in cowardly fashion attempt to withdraw itself from all responsibility for the course of the world's business. Therefore, it favors entrance into the League of Nations with acceptance of all proper obligations and responsibilities, and the exercise of its influence to arrive at equitable adjustments of international problems and to make the inevitable entanglements of the world beneficent rather than baneful and menacing.

It asserts its continued adherence to its doctrines of economic and political freedom, of the rule of law and of the whole people as against the rule of blocs, and of equal opportunity for all men and of special privileges for none. It reasserts its conviction of the necessity of strengthening state and local governments, and of promoting individual self reliance and initiative and it expresses its growing faith in humanity and also in democracy as the best assurance for the promotion of social welfare, of justice, and of individual and of national prosperity.

CC MS (WP, DLC).

From Norman Hezekiah Davis

My dear Mr. Wilson: New York January 11, 1923.

There seems to be a tremendous increase in disgust at the cowardly policy, or lack of policy, on the part of the present Administration, and a realization that it is the moral duty, and in the interest of the United States, to help straighten out European affairs. The Administration is now in such a panic that it seems unable even to try to run down any more blind alleys, and I have the impression that if a resolution were introduced in the Senate, authorizing the President to put the United States into the League of Nations, it would receive the immediate and overwhelming support of public opinion.

If such a move were considered wise, it might be well, in order to dispel any lingering doubt in the minds of the people regarding the exact obligation under article X, to stipulate what you have often stated, namely, that our acceptance of the Covenant shall not be construed as a limitation of the rights of Congress which alone has the power to declare war.

Some of the pro-League Republicans are coming out in the open now in favor of entrance into the existing League of Nations. George Wickersham made a speech last night in which he states in substance that the pro-League Republicans had waited patiently for this Administration to get us either into this League upon such terms and conditions as would be consonant with the dignity and the honor of the country, or to offer some other and better form for securing international cooperation, but that the Administration had failed to do either, which was proof that it could devise no other suitable means by which the United States could discharge its moral obligation and play its necessary part in world affairs. He stated in substance that he and his associates had come to the conclusion that it is too late to try to devise another plan, even if it were possible to do so, and that they would work to get this Administration to enter the existing League, and failing in that, to work to get an Administration in the next election that would do so.

If such a resolution were introduced in the Senate, it seems to me that it would place in an impossible position those senators who are on record as having favored our entrance into the League, with or without reservations.

Dean Robbins enjoyed his visit very much indeed, and as always, I enjoyed very much seeing you and Mrs. Wilson again.

With best wishes, I am, as ever,

Affectionately yours,   Norman H. Davis

TLS (WP, DLC).

To Norman Hezekiah Davis

My dear Davis,   [Washington] 12th January 1923

I have your letter of January eleventh and realize the importance of the suggestion it contains. But it is a suggestion which I do not think it would be wise to act upon without mature consultation with the leaders of the Senate, and I am without the opportunity at present of instituting such a consultation. As you know, I do not believe that it is possible to insist upon an interpretation or qualification of the League Covenant without creating the opportunity,—which would certainly be taken advantage of,—to dilute and nullify the portions affected. The country is getting more and more ready for an out and out fight on this subject at the earliest chance we have to turn to the voters. I do not doubt what the result will be, and should not like to go into the fight hampered by any indications that we were ready to compromise or to tone down any provisions of the Covenant.

A little patience and a little watchfulness, and we shall see our opportunity. It will be a great one, and no qualifications will be necessary.

Wickersham was entirely right in this speech, as you report it, and the country will, at the next presidential election, undoubtedly insist upon providing itself with an administration which will carry us into the League under its existing constitution. Such is my confident faith, and I think we must be very careful not to suggest in the meantime any detour from the straight road.

There is a rapidly growing interest in the subject throughout the country, and every month makes its settlement upon unqualified principle easier and more certain.

I need not tell you, my dear Davis, how your hearty comradeship in this great matter cheers and encourages me, or how glad I am that you so often direct your clear mind to the consideration of advisable courses of action.

Mrs. Wilson joins me in warm regard to you all, and I am, as always,   Affectionately Yours,   [Woodrow Wilson]

CCL (WP, DLC).

From John Hessin Clarke

My dear Friend: [New York] Jany 17th 1923

I have delayed writing you of the Biltmore dinner[1] until I could form some notion of the effect of it.

The indications are many that the country will respond to the appeal. Letters yesterday from Texas, Iowa, St Louis, Tenn, Florida, Ohio and Indiana & many from the eastern part of the country asking what the writers can do to help the great cause is one encouraging circumstance. Almost $50,000 has been subscribed within a week—unsolicited. I have at least twenty five invitations to speak at important church, college & business men's meetings. All this indicates that the country is ready. Miss Wilson[2] no doubt wrote you that your sentence—"No party has any right to appropriate this issue & in the long run no party will dare oppose it" called forth the demonstration of the evening. We have 16 of the 31[3] with us & hope to have 20 by Saturday when I speak at a luncheon in Boston.

I shouldn't have accepted the Boston invitation & would not have done so had I not thought I could use the Biltmore speech but it was published in full in two Boston papers & I must write another.

Alas, I am far from well. In bed almost all of yesterday. My heart irregularity is clearly increasing & I must take a rest. At all events I have done what I could for the "Great Cause" & others are eager to carry it forward. No difference how it comes about the honor of the great conception and the part it will fulfill in the service of mankind will always be yours, my dear Friend,—and it will be the supreme distinction of all history.

God bless & keep you,—I must be done. Always

Sincerely your friend   John H. Clarke

ALS (WP, DLC).

[1] This was the organizational dinner of the League of Nations Non-Partisan Association at the Hotel Biltmore in New York on January 10, mentioned in n. 1 to H. Holt to WW, Nov. 5, 1922. Clarke's speech at that dinner is printed in full in the *New York Times*, Jan. 11, 1923. The speech was an eloquent and closely reasoned argument for American membership in the League, but it could not have pleased Wilson if he read it because of its call for nonpartisan action and its lack of maledictions against Republicans.

[2] Margaret Wilson, who was present at the banquet.

[3] To repeat, the thirty-one prominent Republicans who, during the presidential campaign of 1920, came out in a statement saying that the best way to insure American membership in the League of Nations was to vote for Harding. See WGM to WW, Sept. 28, 1922, n. 4.

To John Hessin Clarke

My Dear Friend,   [Washington] 19th January 1923

I am sincerely sorry to hear of your returning ill health, and know in what spirit you are exhausting such strength as you have.

I was a good deal startled by the statement, in your letter of January seventeenth, that you have quoted me as saying "No party has any right to appropriate this issue and in the long run no party will dare oppose it." If I said that, it must have been drawn out by the peculiar circumstance of the moment for,—as I think you know,—it is by far from stating my position now; for the Democratic Party will certainly, with my full cooperation, appropriate the issue and carry it to settlement. As you know, I do not believe there can be any settlement of the question except by party action.

I must say that I am sorry to hear that members of the discredited thirty-one are cooperating with you. The good faith of not one of them can be trusted.

I know by experience how burdensome it is to be obliged to admit physical weakness and spend one's time caring for broken health. But intelligent care will work out the cure in your case, as it is working it out in mine, and we must get fit to quicken and assist the final electoral act by which the voters of the country will vindicate the honour and restore the leadership of the United States.

As I have frankly told you before, I do not believe in non-partisanship in this great matter of international policy, but I honour you personally for the great effort you are making, and shall be most solicitous to see you re-gain your full strength and vigour. I think I can assure you that patience in such circumstances is the most difficult state of mind possible to obtain.

I am steadily getting better, and every day growing stronger in my resolution to bring our party to triumphant action in this greatest of all issues.

With the hope that you will take a complete rest and soon be quite yourself again,

                    Faithfully Yours,   [Woodrow Wilson]

CCL (WP, DLC).

From Louis Dembitz Brandeis

My dear Mr Wilson: Washington, D. C. Jan. 22/23

Some passages in your admirable "What is Progress?" lead me to send you enclosed opinions on the Cave-in law.[1]

Cordially   Louis D. Brandeis

ALS (WP, DLC).
[1] Pennsylvania Coal Company v. Mahon et al., 260 U.S. 393, decided December 11, 1922. Justice Oliver Wendell Holmes ruled in the majority opinion that a Pennsylvania law which prohibited the mining of coal in a manner to endanger the lives or damage the property of persons occupying buildings on the surface soil was unconstitutional in that it was arbitrary and deprived the mining company of its property rights without due process of law. Brandeis in a dissenting opinion maintained that the law in question was a valid exercise of the police power of the state.

To Louis Dembitz Brandeis

My dear Brandeis,   Washington D C 23rd January 1923

I do not happen to remember having published anything under the title: "What is Progress," but I am none the less pleased that you should have been struck by anything I have written, and am sincerely obliged to you for sending me copies of opinions in Pennsylvania Coal Co., Plaintiff in Error, vs. H. J. Mahon and Margaret Craig Mahon.

I hope as the New Year develops it is bringing, and will bring, to Mrs. Brandeis[1] and you the happiest and brightest fortunes.

With warm regard,
Always,   Faithfully Yours,   Woodrow Wilson

TLS (L. D. Brandeis Papers, KyLoU).
[1] Alice Goldmark Brandeis.

From Norman Hezekiah Davis

Dear Mr. Wilson: New York, January 25, 1923.

Newton Baker, who is now President of the Cleveland Chamber of Commerce, has induced me to make an address, and in case you may be in the mood to recall your College days by reading a declamation, I am enclosing draft of the speech which I propose to make in Cleveland on February 6th.[1] Please don't feel that you are called on to read this, but if you do happen to read it and think I am pulling the wrong string, do not hesitate to say so.

I am beginning to believe that sentiment is coming around so rapidly in favor of our taking a man's part in world affairs, that this Administration is going to be forced to change its policy and do something before 1924. Public opinion seemed to have favored Borah's proposal to call an Economic Conference.[2] Such a Conference wouldn't get anywhere, because the first problems to be settled are political, and it would put our Government in a poor strategic position because if it is a purely economic conference, the Allies won't want to discuss anything but cancellation of debts. It might have the advantage, however, of finishing up the Republican Party. The only feather in their cap they got at that religious revival known as the Washington Disarmament Conference, and if they hold one now just to settle economic questions, they won't even have a cap left.

I had rather hoped that the Democrats instead of an Irreconcilable might better take the lead in forcing the issue.

I am not in favor of compromising or toning down any of the provisions of the covenant of the League of Nations, and if the proposal suggested in my recent letter to you[3] would do that, then I am not in favor of it. The more I think about it, the more am I convinced that the League of Nations, without Article X, would develop into a debating society. I have been astonished, however, to find that there are so many people, ardent advocates of the League, who are willing even to eliminate Article X. Since so many people have been misled by misrepresentations, and still believe that adherence by the United States to Article X, as it now stands, would take away from Congress its sole power to declare war, my feeling was that we would not compromise a principle or weaken the League by agreeing to a statement of fact which would help clear that up, namely that while the United States would be morally obligated to proceed under Article X in case there is unanimous opinion in the Council that an occasion has arisen for so doing, we could not and would not go to war without specific Congressional action.

We are on safe ground when we contend that the principles upon which the League of Nations is based are sound, and that we are opposed to any measures which will weaken them. We are not, however, it seems to me, on such firm strategic ground if we contend that the Covenant of the League is impeccable, and that no modifications should ever be made even to strengthen it. As you are aware, the Assembly of the League last September passed a resolution which is to be submitted to the Council which provides in effect that the world will be divided into four territorial regions, and that in case action is required under Article X, only the powers within the region affected will be called upon to enforce its provisions. At the time I had an idea that this was being done with the view of building a bridge over which this Administration might be led to the League. In a recent speech, Judge Clarke indicated his approval of this proposal on the ground that the United States, insofar as concerns any obligation to furnish military forces would merely be confronted with its old friend the Monroe Doctrine. I myself am doubtful of the wisdom of purely regional guarantees, because it might lead to the strongest nations in the region imposing their will upon the weaker nations. I merely cite this, however, as an indication of the way thought is tending on that subject, and to raise the question whether or not it is wise to take the position that no alterations in the Covenant shall be made even to strengthen it, when the Assembly has unanimously voted for certain alterations.

With warmest regards to Mrs. Wilson and yourself, and with apologies for such a long letter, I am, as ever,

Your affectionate friend,　Norman H. Davis

TLS (WP, DLC).

[1] CC MS (WP, DLC).

[2] Borah, on December 21, 1922, had proposed an amendment to the naval appropriation bill which requested the President to call an international conference to consider world economic problems and a further limitation of armaments. For the text of his amendment, see the *New York Times*, Dec. 22, 1922. Borah made it clear in his public comments that he believed that a readjustment of the burden of war debts, the solution of the problem of reparations, and further reductions in armaments were necessary to prevent the insolvency of the European nations heavily involved in the late war and that the United States would have to take a major role achieving these objectives.

Borah's proposed amendment soon ran into strong opposition from senators such as Hiram W. Johnson, Reed Smoot, and Lodge. President Harding on December 27 addressed a public letter to Lodge in which he questioned the usefulness of such a conference at this time and urged that his administration be allowed a free hand to deal with international problems (his letter is printed in *ibid.*, Dec. 29, 1922). Borah abruptly withdrew his amendment on December 29, after receiving assurances from Lodge and Senator James E. Watson, Republican of Indiana, that the administration was holding exploratory talks with European nations looking toward the solution of critical economic problems. For the Senate debates and public comments on Borah's amendment, see *ibid.*, Dec. 22-30, 1922. For a discussion of the background of Borah's proposal and his motives in presenting it, see Robert James Maddox, *William E. Borah and American Foreign Policy* (Baton Rouge, La., 1969), pp. 131-35.

[3] NHD to WW, Jan. 11, 1923.

From Louis Dembitz Brandeis

My dear Mr Wilson:　　　　　　　　Washington, D. C. Jan. 25/23

Herewith—"What is Progress?" Now, will you confess?

Most Cordially　Louis D Brandeis

ALS (WP, DLC).

To Louis Dembitz Brandeis

My dear Brandeis,   Washington D C 28th January 1923

I can't "confess," because I still do not admit having written an essay "What is Progress." I can only conjecture that what you have sent me was extracted or compiled out of some extemporaneous address which I have forgotten. I remember using on several occasions the illustration from "Alice Through the Looking Glass,"[1] but that is all I do remember. Fortunately I subscribe to the sentiments expressed in the paper, and am free to hope that it will at least do nobody any harm.

It was very kind of you to take the trouble to send me the printed sheets,[2] and I have just been reminded by Mr. Bolling of the circumstances which led me to consent to the proposal of the International Pressmen to print these sentences.[3]

With warmest regard and entire contentment that we should have had a new occasion to communicate with each other,
          Cordially and Faithfully Yours,   Woodrow Wilson

TLS (L. D. Brandeis Papers, KyLoU).
  [1] For example, in a speech at Hartford, Connecticut, on September 25, 1912, Vol. 25, p. 235.
  [2] They are missing.
  [3] George Leonard Berry to WW, April 14, 1922, TLS, and JRB to G. L. Berry, April 16, 1922, CCL, both in WP, DLC. Berry, the president of the International Printing Pressmen and Assistants' Union of North America, had asked permission to use a photograph of Wilson and "one of the many fine statements that you have made in the past" in an annual volume published by the union. Bolling in his reply stated that Wilson had given his permission to use a photograph and "one of his statements."

To Franklin Delano Roosevelt

My dear Roosevelt,   Washington D C 29th January 1923

I cannot let tomorrow, your birthday, go by without sending you my heartfelt felicitations and expressing the hope that your health is steadily returning to you, and that with your health will come every other desirable blessing. May each return of your birthday be happier than the last.

Please present my warm regards to Mrs. Roosevelt and believe me,
          Always,   Your Friend,   Woodrow Wilson

TLS (F. D. Roosevelt Papers, NHpR).

From John Hessin Clarke

My dear Friend—   Youngstown, Ohio February 1, 1923

I cannot tell you how it pleases me to have word direct from yourself that you are growing stronger if not "day by day in every way," nevertheless steadily and substantially. You may be sure millions of followers and friends are constantly praying for your complete recovery.

I wish I could make as good a report of my condition. I was in the midst of a "spell" when I 'rose to speak at the Boston luncheon but determined to go on and I got through with it acceptably I think. I, however, found myself so exhausted that I have hurriedly made arrangements to sail for South America next Saturday. I shall be at sea six weeks and with change of scene I hope to be sufficiently rested and restored to speak in several of the large cities of the country before warm weather.

It distresses me deeply that you and I, so entirely at one in our conviction as to the importance of "The Great Cause" to our country, should differ in opinion as to the present method of best promoting it. However, there will not be any important national elections for more than a year and I have hopes that in that time we can test out the value and promise of a non-partisan appeal. I am sure you know you haven't a more devoted admirer or friend in the world than I am and that only a profound conviction and sense of duty could induce me to differ with you even in this matter of method. But you have thought to your conclusions as carefully as I have to mine and I do not wish to disturb you with discussion.

The quotation is from your New York speech in March 1919[1] when you spoke with Ex-President Taft just before returning to Paris—it has been widely reproduced in various publications.

The voyage will decide whether I shall go forward or submit to the advice of the less encouraging of my physicians.

Please remember me to Mrs. Wilson very cordially and believe me always   Sincerely your friend,   John H. Clarke

TLS (WP, DLC).
    [1] It is printed at March 4, 1919, Vol. 55. The quotation from it in Clarke's letter of January 17 is on p. 413.

From Ray Stannard Baker

My dear Mr. Wilson: Amherst, Massachusetts February 1, 1923.

I thought you might care to know how our book is coming on.

Almost all the reviews so far—except one or two in such intensely partisan papers as the Boston *Transcript*—have been excellent and helpful, and there is every evidence that we are reaching and winning the thoughtful readers with whom judgment of those great events in the end must rest. I know the book is having real and immediate influence in several quarters that count. I had a letter recently from Senator Borah[1] saying that he had read the complete volumes carefully, and I think it is certain that his recent change of attitude is due to the more complete knowledge of the truth that he has thus acquired.

The book is not selling, of course, like a popular novel, but there is evidence, even in these dull book-days since Christmas, that it is surely and steadily making its way. It is averaging now about sixty sets a week, and the publishers are going ahead with what seems to me a far-sighted policy of advertising and circularizations. I am impatient, of course, to see these life-giving facts swiftly spread abroad—for the world is surely perishing for the want of your vision—but there seems no good way of hurrying the process.

The book was published last week in England by Heinemann, and already they have cabled for more sets. It will be most interesting to see what reaction comes from the British. I am trying to get A. G. Gardiner to review it for the Manchester *Guardian*.

It has also just been published, in its German edition, in Berlin, and, according to the Associated Press reports I have seen within the last few days, it is being widely commented upon already. All these things, it seems to me, will help to get the American point of view and your principles before the world. It seems to me most fortunate that we could get first into the field with a comprehensive record of what happened.

One cannot look out upon the world today without a profound sense of depression, or at the conduct of America without a sense of black shame. If only we had gone into the League of Nations and had had a representative upon the important Reparations Commission, the present crises in Europe[2] could easily have been averted and America today securely exercising a beneficent world leadership. There is undoubtedly a considerable new turning toward the League, and a newly awakening sense of American responsibility—though it may be too late. I attended the great meeting in New York about two weeks ago, which was addressed by Justice Clark and Mr. Wickersham, and was much impressed with the pro-League feeling. Even here in this old stronghold of Republicanism a petition to President Harding has recently been circulated and signed only by faithful Republicans, asking him to make good on his early promise of doing something to bring the world together or to take steps toward joining the League. But with the utter weakness, cowardice, vacillation, and lack of vision, at Washington, what is to be expected? One blast of *your* bugle horn were worth a thousand men!

I wish there were something *I* could do, or help *you* do. I have been writing and talking wherever I could, but a kind of lethargy and paralysis of emotion and moral purpose seem to have settled down upon the country, and only some great and inspiring word, some wind of vision, will stir the sleepers to action.

I think of you much and often, and know how deeply all these things must weigh upon you. I hope your health steadily continues to improve.

With kindest regards for Mrs. Wilson, I am,

Faithfully yours, Ray Stannard Baker

I am working on a new book and with great pleasure and satisfaction.[3]

TLS (WP, DLC).
  [1] Not found in the Baker and Borah Papers, DLC.
  [2] The latest of which was the French invasion of the Ruhr district in Germany. After much controversy and several meetings of the Reparation Commission and leaders of the former Allied governments, the Reparation Commission, on December 26, 1922, declared Germany in default on reparation payments and in default again on January 9, 1923. Two days later, French and Belgian troops began an invasion and occupation of the Ruhr district.
  [3] It was a novel, *Adventures in Understanding* (New York, 1925).

To Louis Seibold

My dear Seibold, [Washington] 5th February 1923

I learn by this morning's newspaper the sad news of your Father's[1] death, and my heart goes out to you in deepest and warmest sympathy. It grieves me that you should have to suffer this loss. I know only too well by experience what it means, and hope with all my heart that sources of consolation will be opened to you of which you as yet have little conception. I know the steadfastness of your spirit, and it leads me to hope that you will be able to bear this misfortune as you have borne everything that seemed like a reversal of fortune.

Mrs. Wilson joins with me in truest sympathy, and we hope that many years of friendship may assist in softening the sorrow which has come to you. We shall be happy if our friendship is of any service to you in this great matter.

With affectionate regard,

Faithfully Yours, [Woodrow Wilson]

CCL (WP, DLC).
  [1] Louis Philip Seibold.

To Ray Stannard Baker

My dear Baker,   [Washington] 6th February 1923

Thank you for your letter of February first. It gives me what seems to me a most satisfactory account of the impression the book is making. I believe that it will rapidly become widely known, and that there will be new light wherever it is read.

I share your feeling of depression about the present condition of world affairs, but I believe the truth will presently prevail once more and will bring with it its invariable gift of liberty. There is nothing we individually can do at present that would be of much consequence, but forces are working which we need only acquiesce in and follow to be present at the death of the whole drove of foxes who have been spoiling the vineyard.

I warmly appreciate your generous words about myself, and you may be sure that I always think of you with affectionate gratitude.

Mrs. Wilson joins me in every kind message, and I am always,

With affectionate regard,

Faithfully Yours,   [Woodrow Wilson]

CCL (WP, DLC).

From Hamilton Holt

Dear Mr. Wilson: New York February 7, 1923.

The Woodrow Wilson Foundation has decided to hold the formal installation of the fifteen permanent trustees of the Foundation in some appropriate hall in Washington on Saturday afternoon, April 7th, at three o'clock, provided you would try to attend if your health permits.

I have agreed to lecture on the League of Nations at Mt. Vernon Seminary, Washington, next Monday evening, February 12th, and I shall arrive at the Union Station at 2:50 o'clock that afternoon. I shall be free the rest of that afternoon and all of the next day, February 13th, and I should like, if possible, to see you for a few minutes to talk over your participation in the ceremony.

Mr. Schulyer Warren and I are also most anxious to have a conference with you in regard to the future plans of the Woodrow Wilson Democracy as it seems wise now to be considering what we ought to do as soon as the political pot begins to boil which I expect will happen at no distant date. We would esteem it a great privilege if we could counsel with you on this matter. We can come to Washington at any time you desire but possibly it would be advisable if we combine these two meetings as neither one of them will take very much of your time.

It is most gratifying to hear from all sources of your continued improvement in health.   Very truly yours,   Hamilton Holt

TLS (WP, DLC).

From William Cox Redfield

My dear Mr. Wilson: New York February 7, 1923.

I trust you will permit my sending you a copy of the American Federationist for February, in which, on page 122, is a brief address made by me on the subject of America's World.[1] I am so audacious as to venture to hope that it may meet with your approval.

With cordial regards, in which Mrs. Redfield[2] very earnestly joins, to yourself and Mrs. Wilson, I am,
Yours very truly,   William C Redfield

TLS (WP, DLC).
[1] William C. Redfield, "America's World," *American Federationist*, XXX (Feb. 1923), 122-27. Redfield had originally delivered this address before the Conference of Lecturers in Washington on December 9, 1922. His theme was the interdependency of the United States and the rest of the world, especially in economic matters. He maintained that America's close relationship with Europe and other parts of the world had begun in colonial times and continued down to the present. Hence, the idea of American isolation was not "splendid," but rather "a fatuous dream of ignorance."
[2] That is, Elise Mercein Fuller Redfield.

From the Diary of Ray Stannard Baker

Washington Feby 10th [1923]

I lunched yesterday with the Graysons, both of whom look well. Grayson says that W.W. is steadily getting better: much better since the encouraging elections of November. His left leg really shows increasing strength.

Hw bound diary (R. S. Baker Papers, DLC).

To Hamilton Holt

My dear Mr. Holt,   Washington D C 10th February 1923

I am sorry to miss the pleasure of a talk with you, but I should be drawing you by false pretenses if I made as if it might be possible for me to attend the installation of the permanent directors of the Woodrow Wilson Foundation. I must frankly say that whatever

the state of my health at that time I should deem it most inappropriate for me to be present, and must beg that you will have me
excused.[1]

In haste, with sincere good wishes,

Faithfully Yours,   Woodrow Wilson

TLS (DeCoppet Coll., NjP).
  [1] The abruptness and rather cold tone of this letter may have stemmed from the fact
that Wilson was very much out of sorts with Holt because of his organization of the
League of Nations Non-Partisan Association. Bolling wrote a letter to Holt to accompany
Wilson's and tried to soften its impact. JRB to H. Holt, Feb. 10, 1923, CCL (WP, DLC).
But someone, probably Wilson, saw the TLS, and it was not sent.

To William Cox Redfield

My dear Friend,   Washington D C 11th February 1923

Thank you for sending me the article. It is characterized by the
clear thinking and complete information which are characteristic
of you and is calculated I should think to clear other minds as well.
It is just the sort of thing that is needed just now to bring the
thoughts of those who care to think back upon firm ground, and I
am glad that you are interesting yourself in this sort of public education.

My thoughts often go out to you. I was very grateful for your
answer to the Lane letters. What an extraordinary exhibition of secret disloyalty! They made a very painful impression on me. It was
interesting however to have our impressions of the time confirmed,
namely, that the leak in the Cabinet was in the Secretary of the
Interior, for you will remember that nothing we said or did remained long private.

I hope that the year is opening for Mrs. Redfield and you every
happy fortune and many happy prospects, and that you are both
keeping well. I am afraid that when I get my strength back I shall
be a crank on the subject of health. Still a little prudence will not
hurt in one who has never spared himself.

Mrs. Wilson joins me in messages of warm regard to Mrs. Redfield and you, and unites in warmest personal greetings and best
wishes.

With much regard,   Faithfully Yours,   Woodrow Wilson

TLS (W. C. Redfield Papers, DLC).

To Alfred George Gardiner

My dear Friend,   [Washington] 11th February 1923

A friend of mine, Mr. Arthur Krock, is starting for the Ruhr and will of course pass through London on his way. I have taken the liberty of suggesting that he call on you as more likely than any other man I know to make suggestions to him and give him information that will be a light to his path. I am writing this in the hope that you will allow it to serve as my personal introduction to you of Mr. Krock. You will find him altogether frank and straight. I have known him for a long time and think he is likely to prove one of our most brilliant journalists.

I often wish our too brief acquaintance might ripen into something much more intimate. You may be sure that whether it does or not you have permanently won my admiration and friendship.

Mrs. Wilson joins me in warm greetings, and I beg that you will always think of me as

Your Sincere Friend,   [Woodrow Wilson]

CCL (WP, DLC).

To William Gibbs McAdoo

My dear Mac,   [Washington] 14th February 1923

Mr. George Foster Peabody told me the other day that he had advised you to write an account in as summary and popular form as possible of what was accomplished for the railroads by centralized federal administration. I thought the idea so good a one that I am writing to add my counsel to the same effect. Such a brochure would be of great service in the next campaign and might besides prove a very stimulating contribution to public thought on a subject which I believe the country wishes to see thought out on very practical lines. It could be put in the hands of our campaign speakers everywhere and would be of material service. I sincerely hope that you will write it.

There is nothing new with us. Everything goes as usual and goes satisfactorily well.

Edith and I unite in most loving messages to you all.

In haste,   Affectionately,   [Woodrow Wilson]

CCL (WP, DLC).

To Edith Bolling Galt Wilson

My lovely Valentine   [Washington] $\overset{14}{13}$ Feb'y, 1923.

Since I am unable to coin my heart into words adequate to express my admiration and adoration, I must send it to you whole, to do what you will with. It is altogether yours.   W.W.

ALI (WP, DLC).

From Edith Bolling Galt Wilson

Bless your precious heart!   [Washington] Feb. 14, 1923

No one ever thought of a more perfect Valentine, and I cherish the wonderful gift and send you my heart love in return—for you already have my heart!   Always   Edith.

ALS (WP, DLC).

From Hamilton Holt

Dear Mr. Wilson: New York February 16, 1923.

I received your very kind note saying that you would not be able to come to the ceremony in connection with the installation of the trustees of the Woodrow Wilson Foundation as you felt that your presence would be inappropriate.

I did not explain in my letter in any detail just what was in the minds of the trustees but our idea had been that possibly you would come in for a minute or two at the end of the meeting, after the principal addresses had been made and simply let your friends who would be there have the pleasure of seeing you face to face. Even if you had decided to come, we had thought it would probably be better to make no announcement of the fact to those who were going to be there but rather have it come in the way of an agreeable surprise. The whole thing was in our minds an entirely informal affair.

Since returning to town and consulting further the committee, it has seemed wise not to hold the meeting in Washington but in New York on the first day of May, which is the date set for the annual meeting of the Board of Trustees, under the articles of incorporation.

With my very kindest regards,
                    Very respectfully yours,   Hamilton Holt

TLS (WP, DLC).

To Furnifold McLendel Simmons

My dear Senator,   [Washington] 18th February 1923

I am grieved to learn that you have not been well, and I beg that you will take the most assiduous care of yourself now that you know your strength is not without limit.

The close association I have been privileged to have with you has, permit me to say, made me admire your character and abilities alike as a party colleague and as a personal friend.

I hope and believe that many years lie before you in which you can continue to be highly useful to your party and your country, and I trust that the approaching vacation will afford you an abundant opportunity to seek and obtain the necessary rest and strength of which you stand in need.

This little letter is just a heartfelt expression of sympathy and of personal esteem.

I hope that at the next session of Congress I shall see you in full health and vigour again when affairs will once again stand in need of the best guidance and devotion we can devote to them as party colleagues and patriots.

Please, my dear Senator, accept my assurances of warm regard and think of me always as

Your Sincere Friend   [Woodrow Wilson]

CCL (WP, DLC).

From Robert Latham Owen

My dear Mr. President—   Washington, D. C. Feb 18th. 1923.

The French invasion of the Ruhr and the management and conduct of their leaders there and elsewhere confirm the view that militarism is in control.

The World will in due season realize the wisdom of your counsel at Paris. Time will compensate you for the criticism of the last few years. I am glad to hear from time to time of your improving health and I wish you peace and happiness.

Cordially and Sincerely,   Robt. L. Owen

ALS (WP, DLC).

From Bainbridge Colby

My dear Mr President: New York February 19, 1923

I think you can never know just the degree of pleasure you gave me in sending me your autographed picture with its very kind and friendly little inscription. I have always liked that engraving of you and I think it must have been a year ago I bought it, thinking I would ask you to autograph it, and then my courage oozed. I knew how pestered you were with such requests and I hated to voluntarily put myself in the category of your annoyers.

Our young friend Mr Kriz, with a hardihood that made me gasp, apparently thrust the picture before your notice at the time when we were clearing up our Washington office. He knew that I had obtained the picture for that purpose, and probably acted on Ben Franklin's maxim that "Many things which are difficult of design are easy of execution."

I am grateful, deeply grateful to you for it and it is among my most prized possessions.

I hope very soon to find myself in Washington and to have the pleasure of a little visit with you.

With my kindest regards to Mrs Wilson, believe me always

Affectionately   Bainbridge Colby

TLS (WP, DLC).

To Robert Latham Owen

My dear Senator,   [Washington] 20th February 1923

Your letter of February eighteenth has given me a great deal of gratification. Your friendship I highly value and feel complimented by. The world's affairs are in such shape as must give every thoughtful and conscientious man the gravest concern, and I am entertaining the lively hope that our party may presently be instrumental in giving the country again the kind of leadership which will assist the nations of the world to find a rational and healing solution for the multiplying distresses and difficulties of the time.

I hope that Mrs. Owen[1] and you are well and that all goes happily with you both.

Again thanking you for your letter,

With every cordial good wish,

Faithfully Yours,   [Woodrow Wilson]

CCL (WP, DLC).
[1] Daisey Hester Owen.

John Randolph Bolling to John Melton Hudgins[1]

My dear sir: [Washington] 21st February 1923

Mr. Wilson directs me to say that you probably are not aware that he has frequently declared himself as not being in favour of college fraternities, and for this reason he does not feel that he could consistently comply with the request contained in your letter of February 19th, received this morning.

Very truly yours,   [John Randolph Bolling]

CCL (WP, DLC).
[1] A member of the Phi Kappa Psi fraternity and of the Class of 1925 at the University of Virginia, who had written to Wilson as "Dear Brother Wilson" to ask if he would send him a photograph of himself signed "Fraternally Yours," which the university chapter wished to hang in its room. J. M. Hudgins to WW, Feb. 19, 1923, ALS (WP, DLC). Wilson was a member of Phi Kappa Psi during his student days at the University of Virginia.

From William Gibbs McAdoo

Dear Governor: Los Angeles, Cal. February 24, 1923.

Thank you very much for your kind letter of the 14th inst., and for your generous counsel about the railway statement. I agree with you and Mr. Peabody as to its importance. You may, perhaps, recall that I made a very complete statement before the Senate Committee on Interstate Commerce in February, 1922, which is the best document[1] I know of for convenient reference as to the accomplishments of the Federal Railroad Administration. But for general circulation, a brochure of the kind you describe would be much more serviceable. My difficulty is to find the time to write it and again, I have felt that the appropriate or so-called psychological moment had not yet arrived when I could say something on the railroad problem with the most effect. I think that time is coming, however, and I shall try to prepare something for release in the near future.

One difficulty that has constantly confronted me as I have thought of writing about the railroads (and I have been invited frequently, too, to make speeches on the subject) is the matter of constructive suggestions for a solution of the problem. I think that I will be expected to offer such suggestions if I speak on the subject at all. We may have to do something very radical about the railroads in order to get sufficient efficient transportation at reasonable rates to meet the needs of the country, but I doubt if public opinion has arrived at the point yet where it is convinced of the necessity for such drastic treatment.

The problem lies in my mind about as follows:

We shall never get sufficient transportation at reasonable rates until the railroads are operated as a unified national system, or as three or four unified systems covering their respective sections of the country. If so unified, where shall control be placed, in private or in public hands? If the former, the dangers of so great a monopoly will be extremely grave and formidable; if the latter, politics and bureaucracy are a menace. I am afraid that we shall have to decide eventually on a choice of evils. Have you any suggestions on this subject? I shall be very happy to receive them if it will not tax you too much to send them.

I may have to go back to Augusta, Ga., in the latter part of March on that case which called me there in January, in which event I shall try to take in Washington for a few days, going or returning. It will be a great pleasure to see you and Edith again.

We are all well at home. Nell joins me in warmest love to Edith and yourself.   Always affectionately yours,   W G McAdoo

TLS (WP, DLC).
    ¹ *Railroad Revenues and Expenses: Testimony of William G. McAdoo. Extract from Hearings before the Committee on Interstate Commerce, United States Senate, Sixty-Seventh Congress, Second Session, Pursuant to Senate Resolution 23 . . . February 1 and 2, 1922* (Washington, 1922).

From John Sharp Williams

My Dear Mr. Wilson: [Washington] March 1, 1923.

I had in anticipation the pleasure of calling on you as I was leaving town for home. I earnestly hope that this will not be the last time we see one another. If at some time you and Mrs. Wilson want absolute rest cpme [come] down to me at "Cedar Grove" Plantation. I can't promise anything but rest and a lot of good books and some flowers.

I could not resist the temptation before leaving Washington of letting you know that I shall be as faithful and as loyal to you and your cause now, after I retire from office, as when both of us were holding public position. I am such an ultra-states rights man that I voted against your ideas in connection with two or three things, especially Federally declared woman suffrage; but, upon the whole, there is no man I have ever known personally or in political life or known historically with whom I have more nearly agreed in thought and ideal and for whom I have a greater fondness personally.

I am, with every expression of abundantly deserved regard,
                    Very truly yours,   John S Williams

TLS (WP, DLC).

To William Gibbs McAdoo

My dear Mac,   [Washington] 2nd March 1923

I have your letter of February 24th and am greatly pleased that you will undertake, so soon as possible, to write a brief popular statement upon what was accomplished by Federal administration of the railways. I think a statement of that kind will throw such light on the entire question of railroad administration as to make it unnecessary to couple it with any suggestions as to future policy. I believe constructive suggestion is going to arise almost spontaneously in the minds of all who are really acquainted with the fact, and a solution suggested in that way will be sure of the backing of public opinion. I believe the railway men themselves are beginning to see the light, and that they will not long stand in the way of any radical remedy that promises to be effectual.

I am sorry that you are obliged to turn your situation again to the Court in Augusta, but it pleases me very much to think that something will bring you back to Washington soon so that we may have the pleasure of seeing you again.

We join in every loving message to you all. It makes us happy to know you are all so well. Our thoughts turn to you very often.
                    Affectionately Yours,   [Woodrow Wilson]

CCL (WP, DLC).

To John Sharp Williams

My dear Friend,   [Washington] 2nd March 1923

Your letter has gratified me very deeply, and I am sure you must know with what genuine and affectionate regret I see you leave the Senate. I have very much admired your course there, and have shared to the full the universal admiration for your unusual gifts. The Senate will be the poorer without you, both intellectually and morally, and I shall feel so long as I am in Washington the kind of loneliness which only can come from the memory of a friend who has proved indispensable.

Mrs. Wilson permits me to say that our affectionate regards will follow you to your home, and that if we cannot accept the attractive invitation to visit "Cedar Grove" in person, our thoughts will often turn thither, and always with much affection.

I am sure that a man like yourself, whose education and training have so enriched his mind, will find much happiness and refreshment in retirement; and I am happy to reflect that your recollections of your public service must always be full of satisfaction and pride.

I believe that our party is certainly coming back into responsible leadership in affairs of the country and therefore of the world, and I esteem it a most fortunate circumstance that you will always be accessible even in retirement for such counsel as only you can give.

May I not ask you to convey our very warm regards to Mrs. Williams,[1] and to think of us always as your affectionate friends.

Au revoir, and may happiness meet you at every turn of your new experiences.

Cordially and Faithfully Yours,   [Woodrow Wilson]

CCL (WP, DLC).
[1] Elizabeth Dial Webb Williams.

To Bernard Mannes Baruch

My dear Baruch,   Washington D C 4th March 1923

Mrs. Wilson has just had a short talk with you over the long distance wire, and I appreciate your communicating promptly the opinion which you and Cobb have formed about the present situation. But it is a matter of such grave consequences,—and there are so many aspects of the situation to be considered,—that I would appreciate it very much if you and Cobb would come down and give me your reasons. The three of us together might clear one another's thoughts far beyond the clarification which so far has been reached in my own mind; and I should, besides, enjoy such a conference.[1] I beg that you will choose your own day, and let me know by telegraph when to expect you.

I suggest that you and Cobb plan to get here in time to lunch with Mrs. Wilson at half past one. Then after lunch you can both come up to my room (about two thirty) and we can have our confab at leisure. I hope that this plan will suit you both.

In haste, with affectionate regard,
Faithfully Yours,   Woodrow Wilson

TLS (B. M. Baruch Papers, NjP).
[1] As WW to NHD, March 27, 1923, and F. I. Cobb to WW, March 27, 1923, reveal, Wilson wanted to review certain articles of "The Document," or platform for the Democratic party in 1924, with Baruch, Cobb, and, as we will see, Norman Davis.

Two Letters from Bernard Mannes Baruch

My dear Mr. Wilson: New York March 5, 1923.

Cobb, who has been quite under the weather, left Saturday to be gone until the end of the week. Immediately on his return, I will telegraph you when we can come. I am sure that he, like myself, will be delighted to lunch with Mrs. Wilson, and to go over the matter with you afterwards.

Sincerely yours,   Bernard M. Baruch

My dear Mr. Wilson: New York March 10, 1923.

I got in touch with Cobb to-day, and he is still very much under the weather. It seems that he had an attack of influenza, which affected his intestines. He would like, if convenient to you, to make it for luncheon on Tuesday the 20th, but preferable [preferably] on Wednesday the 21st. I hope that this will be satisfactory to you, and if it is not, let me know.

I am, as ever,   Devotedly yours,   Bernard Baruch

TLS (WP, DLC).

To Josephus Daniels

My dear Friend,   Washington D C 11th March 1923

I have heard with real grief of the death of your Mother,[1] and write to express for Mrs. Wilson and myself our heartfelt sympathy. Having been through a similar distress myself, I think I can understand your feeling, and I hope with all my heart that you will find sufficing sources of consolation. I am glad I once had an opportunity of meeting your Mother and forming some conception of her strong character.

I hope that in all other respects life goes happily with Mrs. Daniels and you, and that it will not be very long before I shall again have the pleasure of seeing you and knowing what you are thinking about.

With affectionate regard,
Faithfully Yours,   Woodrow Wilson

TLS (J. Daniels Papers, DLC).
    [1] Mary Cleaves (Mrs. Josephus) Daniels, a widow since January 28, 1865. Mrs. Daniels died on March 7, 1923.

To Bernard Mannes Baruch

My dear Baruch,   Washington D C 12th March 1923

Wednesday, March twenty-first, will suit me perfectly for the visit of Cobb and you, and I shall be delighted to see you both.

I sincerely hope that Cobb is better and that he is taking good care of himself. He is so valuable a soldier that he is missed from the ranks if absent only a day, and we must be careful not to put too much upon him.

Margaret, my daughter, is considering a business proposition about which she shall probably consult you. I shall rely on your judgment as much as she does, and hope you will not be burdened or bothered by going over the matter with her. I would appreciate it very much if you would let me know directly your opinion of her scheme after you have heard about it.

Mrs. Wilson joins me in affectionate regards to you all, and anticipates as gladly as I do having another and early glimpse of you.

As always,

With affectionate regard,

                    Faithfully Yours,   Woodrow Wilson

TLS (B. M. Baruch Papers, NjP).

To Norman Hezekiah Davis

My dear Davis,   [Washington] 12th March 1923

Just agreed with Baruch to see him and Cobb on Wednesday, March twenty-first, at my usual midday hour. It would be a great advantage all around if you too could be present, but I want you to get perfectly well and therefore don't want to interfere with your vacation. Please do as you feel is best in the matter, letting me know your decision.

I hope dear old sleeply Augusta is already giving you the sense of remoteness and rest you hoped to gain. I should dearly love to go over with you my old boyhood haunts down there, but we must reserve that for another season.

Mrs. Wilson joins me in warmest regards to you both and also in thanking you for letting us get a glimpse of you on yesterday,—a visit which we greatly enjoyed.

                    Faithfully Yours,   [Woodrow Wilson]

CCL (WP, DLC).

From Alice Garrigue Masaryk[1]

Dear Mr. Wilson,   Prague, Czechoslovakia, March 20th 1923.

There are no better messengers of sincere thanks than singing children.[2]

Please listen to them sing, and there over the ocean you will hear the expression of our determination to prove worthy of the liberty and the freedom which you helped us win.

This courageous little group is strengthening many of us in decision and faith here at home. May God help them to open the hearts of those in America who will hear them so that they will grasp the truth that there is no distance between those countries who are aiming at the same goal.

In you personally, Mr. Wilson, the songs will fortify the conviction that your ceaseless work, your sleepless nights, and your intense suffering were by no means in vain.

With best wishes, believe me,

Sincerely yours,   A G Masaryková.

TLS (WP, DLC).

[1] Miss Masaryk (1879-1966) was the daughter of Thomas Garrigue Masaryk. She received the Ph.D. in history and economics from Charles University in Prague in 1903 and also studied at the University of Berlin and the University of Leipzig. After spending the years 1904-1906 at the University of Chicago Settlement with Mary McDowell, she returned to Bohemia and taught in lycées there. She was arrested and imprisoned by Austrian authorities in 1915 and was released in 1916 following a campaign on her behalf in the United States led by Charles R. Crane. At the time she wrote the following letter to Wilson, she was her father's hostess in the presidential quarters in the Hrad, the castle in Prague on Hradčany Hill. Ruth Crawford Mitchell, comp., *Alice Garrigue Masaryk, 1879-1966: her life as recorded in her own words and by her friends* (Pittsburgh, Pa., 1980), *passim.*

[2] The Bakule Children's Chorus of Prague, named for their director, Frantisek Bakule, was about to embark on a goodwill tour of the United States under the auspices of the Red Cross organizations of Czechoslovakia and the United States. They arrived in New York on April 7 and sailed from there for home on June 2. The tour included twenty-five cities and covered approximately 5,000 miles. The thirty-five members of the chorus both sang Czech and Slovak folk music and performed folk dances of those ethnic groups. They also sang American popular songs. *New York Times*, April 6, 8, 10, 12, and June 3, 1923.

To Bernard Mannes Baruch, with Enclosure

My dear Baruch,   Washington D C 22nd March 1923

The enclosed is a suggestion that occurred to me just after our little conference broke up on Wednesday. It is a suggestion as to the best procedure when we shall agree the time has come for action. I believe it to be the most effective way of proceeding in its effect upon the party and as certain to keep in line such politicians as might otherwise be inclined to go off on tangents of their own or to try to evade essential issues altogether. I send it that it may form part of your thought, and I hope that it may commend itself to you.

I very much enjoyed and profited by our little conference of the other day and hope it may be frequently repeated with the same personnel.

With affectionate regard,

Faithfully Yours,   Woodrow Wilson

TLS (B. M. Baruch Papers, NjP).

ENCLOSURE

That each leader obtain from his caucus a resolution empower-
ing and directing him to prepare for its consideration a party programme and instructing him to confer with Mr. Wilson in its preparation.[1]

Excuse this poor typewriting. I had to do it with one hand.[2]

W.W.[3]

WWT and WWhw MS (B. M. Baruch Papers, NjP).
   [1] This paragraph WWT.
   [2] This line WWhw.
   [3] Wilson had earlier typed the following: "*RESOLUTION Resolved* that our floor
leader be instructed to prepare for the consideration of this Caucus a programme of
party policy, and that he be requested to consult in its preparation the Democratic
leader of the other House and the Hon. Woodrow Wilson, to whom we look up [to] as
the leader of our party and of the liberal thought of the nation and the world."

To Morris Sheppard

My dear Senator,   [Washington] 22nd March 1923

You are doing admirable work in publicly recording the work of
the League of Nations and in obliging your fellow Senators to realize what is going on about them, and I thank you sincerely for
giving me the privilege of reading your addresses.[1] Your words
about the value of the League, and your generous estimate of my
own public work, give me the greatest pleasure and not a little
pride, and I thank you with all my heart.

I hope that everything goes happily with you and that it is not in
fact true that your new colleague represents in any sense the Ku
Klux Klan.[2] I hoped that was true only in appearance, for no more
obnoxious or harmful organization has ever shown itself in our affairs.

With cordial regard,

Faithfully Yours,   [Woodrow Wilson]

P.S. May I not suggest that the League of Nations Bureau, Wool-
worth Bldg., New York City, would doubtless very much appreciate
it if you would put them in the way of obtaining a number of copies
of the speeches you have been kind enough to send me.

CCL (WP, DLC).
   [1] Wilson was replying to M. Sheppard to WW, March 20, 1923, TLS (WP, DLC).
Sheppard informed Wilson that he was sending under separate cover a "copy of my
recent address on the League of Nations covering its work from October 5, 1921 to July
24, 1922." He also noted that he had delivered an address in the Senate on October 5,
1921, describing the work of the League from its organization up to that date. This
address is printed in *Cong. Record*, 67th Cong., 1st sess., pp. 6005-6058. The Editors
have found no copy of, or printed reference to, the speech that Sheppard sent to Wilson.
   [2] Sheppard's new colleague was Earle Bradford Mayfield, who served only one term

in the Senate, 1923-1929. He was a member of the Klan and had won the Democratic nomination in Texas in 1922 by the direct intervention and manipulations of Dr. Hiram Wesley Evans, then the Imperial Kligrapp (national secretary) and soon to be the Imperial Wizard of the Ku Klux Klan. With overwhelming Klan support, Mayfield defeated Senator Charles Allen Culberson, who was running for a fifth term in the Democratic primary on July 22, 1922. In fact, the elderly and ailing Culberson, one of Wilson's strongest supporters, ran third in the contest. Charles C. Alexander, *The Ku Klux Klan in the Southwest* (Lexington, Ky., 1965), pp. 122-25.

From Alexander Mitchell Palmer

My dear Mr. President: Washington, D. C. March 23, 1923

In the litigation which I discussed with you last week,[1] the main contention of the present administration seems to be that you were ill informed as to the true relation of the development of organic chemistry, and the subject of industrial medical independence and national defense.

Mr. Rogers,[2] Patent Counsel of the Federal Trade Commission during the year 1918, has sent me a copy of his report to Governor Fort[3] in which he finds a memorandum he prepared to be transmitted to you in January, 1918, or over a year before the formation of the The Chemical Foundation. I enclose a copy.[4] I am using your name with Senator Nugent[5] in order to get a copy of this memorandum from the files of the Federal Trade Commission if it was in fact sent to you.

I am also enclosing copy of the report of the Allied Commission appointed to visit the chemical factories in the occupied zone, and report their relation to the subjects before the Peace Conference.[6] This mission was headed by Lord Moulton.[7] Although dated February 26th, and therefore not available to you until you returned to Paris the second time, I find that Lord Moulton had stated the same thing in a public address published in the London Times, and that a copy of that address was sent to you at the steamer. You probably also saw it in the paper itself. I have marked with blue pencil the essential part of this report so that you may not have to try to read the whole thing,—(pages 210 - 211 - 212 - 213 - 214).

But more important than all, I find in Chap. 23 of Ray Stannard Baker's book evidence that you were, before anyone else in the world, fully alive to the importance of the subject, and that on January 25, 1919, you made an address at the conference in which you said: (quoting from page 410 of Volume I of Baker's book)—

"President Wilson had seen the larger aspects of the problem with a prophetic eye. He asked the Peace Conference to 'take a picture of the world' into its mind. 'Is it not,' he said, 'a startling circumstance * * * that the great discoveries of science, that the

quiet studies of men in laboratories ∗ ∗ ∗ have now been turned
to the destruction of civilisation?' "

He sets forth also the method, as he sees it, for meeting this new
problem:

"Only the watchful and continuous cooperation of men can
see to it that science, as well as armed men, is kept within the
harness of civilisation."

Mr. Baker states that the discussion of this great new problem began early in February and continued intermittently until the middle of June.

From what I can understand, it was the policy of England and
France first to take over the German chemical industry on the
same basis that the ships were taken over, or, failing in this, the
Germans were to be compelled to disclose all their chemical secrets
and processes, and that you opposed this on the ground that it was
too grave an interference with the industrial life in peace time of
the German Empire, but apparently showed your determination to
see to it that the problem was met by building up similar industries
and research and chemical personnel in this country. You pursued
this policy by the continuation of the War Trade Board's power of
limiting chemical imports, by your two messages to Congress, by
the establishment of the Textile Alliance, and the creation of The
Chemical Foundation, etc.

I would like very much to obtain access to the minutes so spar-
ingly quoted by Mr. Baker, for I am quite sure that they would
develop a large amount of important material. It becomes of tremendous importance to establish the historical record of your pre-
vision in the matter on the pending legislation. All the more so, as
the industries are now fully established despite the efforts of this
administration to undo your creative work. Over sixty million dollars have been expended or voted by the universities of this country
this year to the further development of the study of chemistry. Millions and millions have been given for research institutions. Our
industries are now supplying ninety-eight per cent of the requirements of the country, and have entered into active competition for
the markets of the world. What your administration set out to do
has been accomplished without aid or assistance, but with the active opposition of the present administration, and it is essential that
the historical picture be drawn in the trial of this case so that it
may be a public record forever.

I also direct your attention to the situation of the Ruhr at the
present time when France has taken over ninety per cent of the
German chemical industry. This makes it all the more important
to demonstrate what we have done in this country to free ourselves

from the power in peace time and in war of the German chemical world control. The relation of this industry to the safety of the world is best expressed in a book which I also send you called "The Riddle of the Rhine."[8] If you do not find time to read it all, the introduction of Marshal Foch to the French edition and the introduction of Brig. General Wilson[9] to the English edition will give you a good idea of its content and purport. This book was written under the direction of the British Government, and with the approval of the French military authorities, and consultation with our own military authorities shows that it is authentic history.

Very respectfully, A Mitchell Palmer

TLS (WP, DLC).

[1] Palmer, as Alien Property Custodian, in early 1919 had sold about 6,000 German chemical patents to the Chemical Foundation, a nonprofit private corporation organized to purchase them. As his biographer says, one of his chief objectives was to break the monopoly of the so-called German dye trust, particularly in the field of coal-tar derivatives. Stanley Coben, *A. Mitchell Palmer: Politician* (New York and London, 1963), pp. 147-50. However, Palmer did not always act with regard to legal and ethical niceties, and there were soon rumors of irregularities and personal favoritism on his part. In response to a plea from the German former owners of the patents, and in an effort to embarrass the Wilson administration and to curry favor with German-American voters, Harding's Attorney General, Harry Micajah Daugherty, brought suit in 1922 in the federal district court in Wilmington, Delaware, for return of the patents to the United States Government, on the ground that the sale of the patents to the Chemical Foundation was invalid. This was the situation when Palmer wrote the following letter to Wilson.

The judge in the district court dismissed the case, whereupon the government appealed his ruling to the circuit court in Philadelphia. The new Attorney General in the Coolidge administration, Harlan Fiske Stone, argued the case himself when it was heard in November 1924. The government lost the case, and lost again when it was heard before the Supreme Court. Alpheus T. Mason, *Harlan Fiske Stone: Pillar of the Law* (New York, 1956), pp. 171-74.

[2] Edward Sidney Rogers.

[3] John Franklin Fort, Governor of New Jersey, 1908-1911, member of the Federal Trade Commission, 1917-1919.

[4] "MEMORANDUM FOR GOVERNOR FORT," CC MS (WP, DLC), which reviewed the problems created by the German monopoly on patents relating to the chemical, pharmaceutical, etc., industry and made certain recommendations concerning them.

[5] John Frost Nugent, Democratic senator from Idaho, 1918-1921, who resigned to accept membership on the Federal Trade Commission.

[6] Undated printed copy (WP, DLC).

[7] John Fletcher Moulton, 1st Baron Moulton (life peer).

[8] Victor Lefebure, *The Riddle of the Rhine: Chemical Strategy in Peace and War* (London, etc., 1921), which has a chapter on the problem of the German dye trust's monopoly of the chemical industry in the United States before the war and on the new German dye cartel and its aggressive policy.

[9] Actually, Field Marshal Sir Henry Wilson.

To William Ellery Sweet[1]

[Washington] 26th March 1923

I trust you will not think it an unwarranted liberty if I express the hope that you will select my friend Huston Thompson for the vacant seat in the Senate.[2] Woodrow Wilson.

T telegram (WP, DLC).
    [1] Governor of Colorado, Democrat.
    [2] To fill the vacancy caused by the death of Samuel Danford Nicholson, Republican, who died on March 24, 1923. Samuel Huston Thompson, Jr., Princeton 1897, was Wilson's former student. He had practiced law in Denver, had long been active in Democratic politics in Colorado, and was at this time a member of the Federal Trade Commission.

From Samuel Huston Thompson, Jr.

My dear Friend: Washington, D. C. Mar. 26. 1923.

I am leaving tonight for Boston where I am to address the Commercial Club of that city.

The newspaper men have called me on the 'phone and informed me that a telegram was given out at the State House this afternoon from you to Governor Sweet in which you asked that he appoint me to fill the senatorial vacancy. While I shall never forget to my dying day your kindness and generosity I am at the same time greatly distressed for fear that the giving out of the telegram at Denver may have embarrassed you.

Please accept the grateful appreciation of Mrs. Thompson[1] and myself.

If Governor Sweet sees fit to appoint me[2] I shall dedicate my whole self to carrying out your policies and forwarding your ideals.
            Cordially and gratefully yours.   Huston Thompson

ALS (WP, DLC).
    [1] Caroline Margaret Cordes Thompson.
    [2] He did not do so.

To Norman Hezekiah Davis

My dear Davis,   [Washington] 27th March 1923

You will recognize the enclosed as extracts from the document[1] to which we gave some consideration at our conference on the twenty-first, and will no doubt recall your comments apropos of the present artificial "prosperity." You will remember we all concurred with you that passages needed revision. Would you feel like revising them now, or prefer to wait until you get back to New York? In any case I feel you are the only one competent to revise them in the spirit of the document as a whole, and shall leave them with you in the hope that when you feel you can you will give me the benefit of your reformulations.

The papers tell us of your arrival with your family at the Springs,[2] and I feel conscience stricken that I should again be trespassing on a period of rest. I hope your daughter and all of you will feel promptly the benefit of the change, and will find at the Springs complete renewal both of health and of spirits.

With warmest regard to you all from both Mrs. Wilson and myself,   Affectionately Yours,   [Woodrow Wilson]

CCL (WP, DLC).
¹ It is printed at Dec. 2, 1922. He enclosed a typescript of Articles 1, 2, and 4 of this document.
² That is, at the Greenbrier at White Sulphur Springs, West Va.

To Alexander Mitchell Palmer

My dear Palmer,   Washington D C 27th March 1923

Your letter of March twenty-second shows that you are assembling material which ought to be very valuable in the approaching trial.

As for minutes to which you refer in connection with the quotation from Ray Stannard Baker's book,—Baker can guide you to them more readily than I can, and I am writing to him today that if you write to him about it I hope he will assist you to the use of the minutes.

I need not say that for every reason I wish you the most complete success before the court.

With much regard,   Faithfully Yours,   Woodrow Wilson

TLS (A. M. Palmer Papers, DLC).

To Ray Stannard Baker

My dear Baker,   [Washington] 27th March 1923

This Aadministration [Administration] is actually trying to pay its political debt to the German-Americans for their support in 1920 by restoring to German ownership much of the alien property which we took possession of during the war and some of which we sold, and has brought action to annul the sales of the chemical patents in particular. Mr. A. Mitchell Palmer, who was Alien Property Custodian, and who will be actively concerned on behalf of the defense in the suit, thinks that the minutes to which you refer in your book will be of great use to the defense. He will probably write to you, and if he does I hope you will be his guide to the minutes he wishes to see, and afford him every assistance in making use of them. He will no doubt give you an idea of the significance of what he wants when he writes.

I sincerely hope this will entail very little trouble for you, and I assure you I ask this cooperation of you with the greatest reluctance, because I would like to feel that your unselfish labours in connection with my peace work were concluded. But I am sure you will understand and will render any public service requested of you.

Mrs. Wilson joins me in warm regard and most cordial greetings, and I am,
    Always,
        Sincerely and Faithfully Yours,   [Woodrow Wilson]

CCL (WP, DLC).

From Frank Irving Cobb

Dear Mr. Wilson: New York March 27th, 1923.

The suggestion I made in regard to Prohibition was this—first, that the Volstead Act be repealed except in respect to foreign and interstate commerce. That the enforcement of the 18th amendment be referred to the several states under the "concurrent power" clause.

All State laws would naturally be subject to the interpretation of the United States Supreme Court in order to prevent nullification of the amendment. The issue would naturally turn on what constitutes "intoxicating beverages" within the meaning of the Constitution—in other words, what is a reasonable percentage of alcohol beyond which a beverage must be regarded as intoxicating, and below which it cannot be fairly so regarded.

The advantage of this arrangement is that it would take the Prohibition question out of the field of national politics, and end all the confusion which it has brought about. It would also restore to the States the police power which has been taken away from them under the Volstead law. It would end the conflict between State and Federal jurisdiction and do away with the double jeopardy which now exists under the recent decision of the United States Supreme Court by which every offender against the prohibition laws can be punished twice for the same act, once by the State and once by the Federal Government.[1]

The only argument that I have heard against this plan is that some of the States might refuse to enact enforcement legislation. I doubt that this is valid because public sentiment would naturally oppose an outright effort to place State responsibility under the amendment. For that matter, Congress itself could refuse, if it wished, to enact legislation to enforce the 18th amendment, as it has done in regard to the 15th amendment. Under this arrangement, however, New York could have beer which it demands, and Kansas could prohibit buttermilk if it wished to.

I am not sure that the Southern and Western Democrats would permit such a compromise, but unless they are willing to make concessions, the East is lost to the Democratic party. If the Democratic attitude toward Prohibition is to be identical with the Republican attitude, the East is likely to remain Republican.

Three years ago I discussed this matter with Hoover.[2] He was very favorable toward it, and then promptly ran away from it, as he always does. Walter Lippmann tells me that Justice Brandeis favors this plan. It might well be worthwhile for you to discuss it with him sometime before you come to a decision. I am submitting it to you with no pride of opinion, but merely for what it may be worth in an attempt to arrive at a general policy which is in accordance with the principles of the Democratic party, and on which the majority of Democrats can get together.

It was a great pleasure to see you, and find that you were looking so well.

With sincerest regards,   As ever yours,   Frank I Cobb.

TLS (WP, DLC).
  [1] United States *v.* Lanza *et al.*, 260 U.S. 377, decided December 11, 1922.
  [2] That is, Herbert Hoover.

To Frank Irving Cobb

My dear Cobb,   [Washington] 28th March 1923

Thank you sincerely for your letter of March twenty-seventh. The suggestion interests me deeply, and I shall take leave to let it fix itself in my mind for meditation. I find that slow thinking is generally the best thinking. I shall of course act upon your suggestion that I discuss the matter with Justice Brandeis. I know of no clearer or more serviceable mind than his in intricate questions of this sort. Hoover has no mind but only an instinct of publicity.

It was a great pleasure to have you down here the other day, and your counsel added greatly as it always does to the advantage of our little conference. I hope that such meetings between us will be often repeated.

With warmest regard and appreciation,
                    Faithfully Yours,   [Woodrow Wilson]

CCL (WP, DLC).

From Lord Robert Cecil

Personal.

Dear Mr Wilson   New York. March 29th 1923.

I hope you will allow me on arriving in the United States to present my warmest respects to you. I shall never forget all your kindness to me at Paris, and much look forward to the pleasure of seeing you again when I get to Washington.

It touched me very much to hear that Mrs Wilson purposes to attend the dinner at which I am speaking on Monday next. Would you express my warmest gratitude to her?

With kind regards,   Yours very sincerely,   Robert Cecil

TLS (WP, DLC).

From Arthur Blythe Rouse[1]

My dear Mr. President: Covington, Ky., March 29, 1923.

Since my return from Washington I have found a growing popular discussion of the proposal by President Harding to have the United States join the Permanent Court of International Justice, established by the League of Nations.[2] There is, moreover, a very deep interest and there are numerous inquiries as to what your views are with respect to the conditional adhesion of the United States to the Court.

Among our Democratic friends, the feeling is somewhat general that the Republicans are coming by steady, even though reluctant, steps to repudiation of their policy which led to the wrecking of the world peace program by the Senate in 1919. There is no mistaking the growth of popular sentiment for genuine American participation in international affairs to re-establish the moral leadership, which the Senate sacrificed. That the Administration, notably Mr. Hughes, is coming to recognize that fact, and that Senator Borah is drawing much of his inspiration from it, are put down as the factors responsible for the World Court concession to the public feeling.

With the Republicans proposing to stage another family row over the issue this summer, it has occurred to me that the Democrats ought to have the benefit of a positive and clearly defined attitude around which they might rally as a unified force; that we certainly ought not to overlook the opportunity of reasserting our own leadership in this whole question. It does seem that little by little the Administration is coming to the course which your vision mapped out for America, though nothing really effective has been done to date.

The proposal to devitalize the project, as far as possible, through the medium of reservations[3] means to some with whom I have talked, that the United States wishes a Court without a sheriff's office, the mere moral influence of which in its readiness to support a decision gives practical effect to the word of the Court. Others say it puts us in a position of never doing a full duty, of seeking benefits of world co-operation while attaching conditions to exempt us from a fair share of the responsibility. The apparent resentment against the French proposal to attach reservations to the Naval Limitation treaty[4] is taken to reflect something of the world opinion to our constantly attaching reservations to every commitment to the general welfare.

If it is possible, I should like very much to have, for the guidance and counsel of your many admiring supporters, some expression of your views. It would be most heartening and invaluable, and, with your permission, I will give wide publicity to your views.

With constant wishes for your improved health, I am

Most sincerely,   A B Rouse

TLS (WP, DLC).

[1] Democratic congressman from Kentucky, chairman of the Democratic National Congressional Committee.

[2] Harding, on February 24, 1923, sent to the Senate with his endorsement a copy of a letter from Secretary of State Charles Evans Hughes advocating American membership in the Permanent Court of International Justice.

[3] Hughes had suggested four reservations to the protocol of adherence. One said that membership in the court did not imply any relationship to the League on the part of the United States; another that the court statute could not be amended without the consent of the United States. Opponents of membership were suggesting other reservations at this time.

[4] It was announced on March 24 that the Foreign Relations Committee of the French Chamber of Deputies had requested Premier Raymond Poincaré to add two "reservations" to the law authorizing the President of the Republic, Alexandre Millerand, to ratify the Five-Power Naval Limitation Treaty. One reservation stipulated that France did not regard the ratio of tonnage in capital ships established by the treaty as permanently binding upon her. The second reservation declared that France regarded the entire treaty as binding upon her only through December 31, 1936. *New York Times*, March 25, 1923. The French government announced on March 28 that Poincaré had agreed to submit to the Chamber of Deputies a bill which combined the two reservations by recommending the ratification of the treaty with the stipulation that France reserved all rights relative to the continuance of the ratio of capital ship tonnage after December 31, 1936. *Ibid.*, March 29, 1923. For an example of the annoyance in the American press over France's proposed use of reservations, see the editorial, "FRANCE AND THE NAVAL TREATY," *ibid.*, March 27, 1923.

To James Thayer Gerould[1]

My dear Mr. Gerould,   [Washington] 30th March 1923

I am heartily obliged to you for your thoughtful kindness is sending me copy of the Bibliography of my work which the Library has issued.[2] I cannot expect to find it thrillingly interesting, for I subscribe to the utterance of Augustin Birrell that he found it more and more necessary for the enjoyment of his own works that they should be written either wholly or in part by somebody else. But I am sure the Bibliography will be of much service to me in keeping track of my past indiscretions.

I am very much interested to see you are Librarian of the University, and I hope you are deriving a great deal of pleasure from your work.

With warm regard,
                    Sincerely Yours,   [Woodrow Wilson]

CCL (WP, DLC).
  [1] Librarian of Princeton University.
  [2] Princeton University Library, *Essays toward a Bibliography of Woodrow Wilson*, 3 vols. in 1 (Princeton, N. J., 1913-1922).

From Frank Irving Cobb

Dear Mr. Wilson: New York March 30th, 1923.

Robert Cecil made his first speech yesterday on The League at a luncheon that Frank Munsey gave to the various newspaper editors of New York. By previous agreement it was not reported, but it was altogether most admirable and expressive. If he sticks to the thesis he maintained yesterday, he is bound to do great good.

He told me that he hopes that you will be able to see him when he goes to Washington, and he spoke of you with great affection.

With sincerest regards,   As ever yours,   Frank I Cobb.

TLS (WP, DLC).

Revisions of The Document

[c. March 31, 1923]

Being aware that it is our duty as representatives of the Democratic Party in the Congress of the United states to do everything in our power to serve the country in the true spirit of the great principles which our Party has professed, we deem it an obligation of good faith to set forth as clearly andfrankly as possible to our constituents and the country at large the means and policies by which we believe that those principles can best be realized and which we mean to do everything we can to establish and develop. We therefore set them forth in the following terms:

Ve consider it our first, immediate, and imperative duty to redeem the country from the dishonourable and therefore ignoble isolation into which a small group of ignorant and partisan Republican leaders in the Senate have drawn it in violation of our manifest moral obligations to the nations with which we were recently associated,—indeed to all civilized nations and to mankind itself.

Not content with making it everywhere known that we would neither consider nor. serve any interest but our own and causing every other nation to look upon us askance, with dislike and suspicion in resp- respect of every matter affecting the public policy or general welfare of the world, the Republican leaders proceeded to put by their tariff legislation the narrowest possible limitations upon upon our trade and are attempting to develop our commerce on the principle of selling as much and buying as little as possible. a discredited policy now abandoned elsewhere except by the ignorant and inexperienced.

AMERICA FIRST

"AMEHICA FIRST" is a slogan which does not belong to any one political party. It is merely a concise expression expression of what is in the heart of ewery patriotic American. But it means different things in different mouths mouths and requires definition.

When uttered by the present leaders of the Republican party it means that America must render no service to any other nation or peoplewhich she can reserve for her own selfish a aggrandizement. When we use it we mean that in every international action or organization for the benefit of mankind America must be foremost; that America, by developing within her own citizenshipand actions a sensitive regard for justice in all the relations of men, must lead the world in applying the briadest conceptions of justice and peace, of amity and respect, to the mutual relations of other peoples, and in rendering them material aid in the realization of those ideals.

World Court.

We applauded and are still ready to approve and support the proposal of President Hardi Harding, that this government give its adherence to the protocol by which the present court of international justice was established; but that proposal is evidently not in itself a policy. It cannot be thought if as more than a fragment of a policy which needs to be rounded out and completed. We regard it as absolutely necessary for the vindication of the honour and good

faith of the United States and the restoration of our government to
its natural leadership in international affairs,—a leadership which
was wantonl wantonly thrown away by the Senate'srejection of the
treaty of Versailles,—that our government should become a
membe member of the League of Nations and assume equal responsibility with the other great powers in the maintenance o of
international order, peace, and justice.

◊

It is our judgment that the prohibition amendment to the Constitution and the soAcalled Volsted Act, passed to enforce its provisions, should remain unaltered as they are, but that the methods
of enforcement should be radically re-considered.

WWT MS (WP, DLC).

To Lord Robert Cecil

My dear Lord Robert,   [Washington] 31st March 1923
It is a great pleasure to know you are in this country and that I
am before long to have the privilege of seeing you again. I look
back to our association in Paris with the liveliest interest and pleasure, and that association created in my heart a genuine affectionate regard for you.
Mrs. Wilson is looking forward to the dinner on Monday evening
with keen interest, and I wish with all my heart that I could hope
to go with her. But getting about for long distances is for the present denied me.
I understand you are the guest of my friend, Mr. Lamont. Please
give him my warm regards.
I hope that you are very well and that every hour of your stay in
the United States will prove satisfying and enjoyable. I think you
can say anything in commendation of the League that you choose
to say, for I believe our public opinion is ripe for a definite movement in the direction of our joining the League. The meaning of
our election of 1920 has been grossly misinterpreted and misrepresented. The voters did not vote against the League; they voted
for the flesh pots which they believed they could get from the Republican Party, and even the flesh pots have not proved as savory
and palatable as they were led to expect.
I am delighted to hear from time to time of the extraordinary
success with which your League of Nations Union is meeting in
Great Britain. It cannot but have a very stimulating and beneficial
influence.

I shall look forward with impatience to seeing you, and I hope you will tell me of some way in which I can contribute to making your stay in the United States completely successful and enjoyable.

Hoping that the dinner on Monday night will be a great success, With warm regard,

Cordially and Faithfully Yours,   [Woodrow Wilson]

CCL (WP, DLC).

To Frank Irving Cobb

My dear Cobb,   Washington D C 31st March 1923

Thank you for your little note of March thirtieth. I hope that you said or will say to Lord Robert Cecil what you say in your note to me about his thesis; it should be of real service to him.

I think of you very often and always with stimulating results, and I read most of your editorials. When we start our paper down here we shall have great fun concocting editorials together.

With warm regard, in which Mrs. Wilson joins,

Faithfully Yours,   Woodrow Wilson

TLS (IEN).

From Norman Hezekiah Davis

White Sulphur Springs

My dear Mr. Wilson: West Virginia March 31/23.

I shall be glad to try my hand at revising the portion of the document which you sent me[1] but since you gave me the choice of revising it here or in New York and since I am going back home Monday and have no stenographer of confidence here I have decided to undertake it on my return home. I am glad however that you sent it to me here because I prefer to have a little time to think it over. My guess is in that about twelve to eighteen months the conditions will be as described in the document but today we are having a false prosperity temporarily caused by accumulated credits and the making up of deferred maintenance. The farmers and clerks on salary are not enjoying this prosperity but nearly every one else is.

I enjoyed—as usual—my last visit with you.

I am going to have a long talk with Lord Robert Cecil next Tuesday. I hope his visit will do some good.

Mrs. Davis joins me in affectionate regards to Mrs. Wilson and yourself.   Faithfully yours,   Norman H. Davis.

ALS (WP, DLC).
  ¹ In WW to NHD, March 27, 1923.

From Ray Stannard Baker

Dear Mr. Wilson: Amherst Massachusetts March 31, 1923.
    I have your letter of the twenty-seventh.
    I shall be glad to help in any way I can. It is somewhat like looking for the proverbial needle in the haystack to try to find any particular discussion in those vast minutes, and be sure of getting everything upon any given subject—as I know from laborious experience. I have made a thorough, and, I think, accurate digest of the records of the Four and Ten for those subjects which I wished especially to treat, as well as many others. Whether this will reach to Mr. Palmer's needs, I do not know; but I will do the best I can.
    Our book continues to be widely and vitally discussed in England and Germany, and it will soon come out in France, where, I have no doubt, it will produce lively fireworks. The French are not going to like it at all!
    Every evidence in the reviews shows clearly that the book is producing a substantial revision, often a complete reversal, of view regarding the Peace Conference, and especially your part in it. And the more it is read and studied, the clearer all this must become. It seems to be helping to keep the fundamental problems—which you saw so clearly—before the world. It is a record that many of the commentators would like to get around and avoid, but cannot.
    The *English Review* for March has a fine commentary entitled "A Terrible Book." Here are two or three of the shorter paragraphs:
    "It is by far the most impartial and sincere account of what took place, based on documents and inner knowledge, and to it future historians will turn for perspective and judgment. It bears no malice, studiously refrains from all sensationalism, undertakes nothing but the plain ungarnished truth about the politicians of the Old World on trial and in trial with the projection of the New World, which formed the basis of the armistices and of President Wilson's peace.
    "Out of this book the figure of President Wilson emerges clearly and nobly. For the first time we learn how splendidly he fought for a world attitude as against the squalid selfishness of the spoils attitude, what terrific forces were opposed to him, how he was beaten down in detail, step by step, stabbed in the stomach by the

French, and eventually in the back by his own people. All, for varied reasons, were determined to smash him."

"The President is here reinstated."

"In this terrible book—terrible is the only word—the story of the peace is told truthfully. Our own part in it is so pitiable one hardly likes to refer to it. We spiked the President. Mr. Lloyd George blew hot or cold, according to circumstances, thwarting the President at every turn. * * *"

"History will speak of all these men with execration, but the lone struggle of President Wilson will go down to posterity as the white light of civilization. His fame will grow; his battle will not have been fought in vain. He has lit a candle which will not go out, as already men are perceiving, as shortly America too will understand, when France has brought Europe to the brink of ruin."

There is plainly a great awakening coming in the country regarding our international obligations—and the League of Nations. It is evident on all sides. The hasty move of Mr. Harding in the last days of the Congress, regarding the World Court, is one of the clear evidences of it. He sees the handwriting on the wall. I was told the other day, by a man who knew, that nineteen out of the famous "Thirty-one" were now committed to a new move for bringing the country into some association of nations. I do not know the exact terms, but something of the sort is in the wind.

I think the best policy now is to sit tight and let the virus work. One thing it will certainly do, and that is, split the Republican Party still more widely asunder, with the Harding wing feebly flapping for some weak international arrangement: and the Johnson-LaFollette wing excitedly demanding a kind of Sinn Fein policy for America "for ourselves alone." My metaphor is not so mixed as this bird of a Republican Party!

With cordial best wishes,   Ray Stannard Baker

Kindly remember me to Mrs. Wilson.

TLS (WP, DLC).

From Gustavus Myers[1]

Dear Mr. Presdient: Bronx, New York City, March 31, 1923

This is from a minor to a major historian—to one who has both written and made notable history.

I often think of you and yet, apart from my great personal esteem for you, reflect that there is really no occasion for any solicitousness. The ideals for which you stood and stand are permeating the hearts of men and women, slowly, it is true, but all the more invincibly. You are too good an historian not to know that the greater the stature the more of a distance it requires for many to get the true perspective of the magnitude. The petty characters who so vindictively opposed your ideals and defamed you are already sinking into ignominy; and the very memory of them would pass into utter oblivion were it not that posterity will hold them up to infamy as a set of moral assassins, all the more cowardly because they assailed one stricken in health by reason of the strain of his services to his country and to mankind. History will tell all this, but, in addition, many a novel, many a drama, will be written around that event, commemorating your life and work and affording inspiration to future generations.

This is my sober opinion, and I do not think myself guilty of any extravagance of judgment. The world has had from time to time its great men renowned for deeds for their country. But you, I think, will rank first of all in having the vision to transcend boundaries and practically plan for the good of humanity.

With my good wishes, Mr. President,

Sincerely,   Gustavus Myers.

ALS (WP, DLC).
    [1] Muckraking journalist, author of *The History of Tammany Hall*, *History of the Great American Fortunes*, *History of the Supreme Court of the United States*, and other books.

To Arthur Blythe Rouse

My dear Mr. Rouse,   [Washington] 1st April 1923

In reply to your letter of March twenty-ninth let me say that I approve not of the "conditional" but of the *unconditional* adhesion of the United States to the World Court set up under the auspices of the League of Nations; though I think it would be more consistent with the fame of the United States for candor and courage to become a member of the League of Nations and share with the other members of the League the full responsibilities which its Covenant involves.

Respectfully Yours,   [Woodrow Wilson]

CCL (WP, DLC).

To Louis Dembitz Brandeis

My dear Mr. Justice,   Washington D C 1st April 1923

A short time ago I was discussing with Mr. Frank I. Cobb, the brilliant editorial writer of the New York World, the question of prohibition in connection with the declaration of principles and purpose, in the preparation of which you and Colby so generously assisted me at the outset, and which Mr. Cobb has read with interest and acquiescence. He made a suggestion which I asked him to send me in writing. He has complied with my request in a letter of which I enclose a copy.[1]

I would like very much to have the privilege and advantage of discussing this matter with you at your convenience, and will be obliged if you will let me know when it would be convenient for you to come to my home for this purpose.

I hope that Mrs. Brandeis and you are are quite well, and that the opening Spring will bring you great refreshment and sufficient relaxation after the confining labors of the winter.

With warm regard,   Faithfully Yours,   Woodrow Wilson

TLS (L. D. Brandeis Papers, KyLoU).
[1] F. I. Cobb to WW, March 27, 1923.

To James Grover McDonald[1]

[Washington] 2nd April 1923

Please convey to Lord Robert for me an affectionate welcome to America stop It is characteristic of him that he should devote himself to strengthening the foundations of peace stop I am glad that Mrs. Wilson is to be one of the guests stop I cannot pretend that she represents me for she is much finer than I am stop But she does represent my extraordinary happy fortune in winning her

Woodrow Wilson

T telegram (WP, DLC).
[1] Wilson addressed this telegram to "Chairman of dinner to Lord Robert Cecil." He was McDonald, a former history professor and at this time chairman of the board of directors of the Foreign Policy Association of New York.

The dinner at which Lord Robert spoke was held on April 2 in the ballroom of the Hotel Astor, which contained, as the *New York Times* put it, "one of the largest and most distinguished gatherings that has ever filled the large ballroom and the boxes above it." It was the first public speech that Lord Robert was scheduled to give in the United States. Two of Wilson's severest editorial opponents in the treaty fight—Herbert Croly and Oswald Garrison Villard—were among the diners. Mrs. Wilson sat at a table in front of the speaker's stand. There was a wave of enthusiasm, which brought the diners to their feet, when it was announced that Woodrow Wilson was listening to the remarks and Cecil's speech at his home by radio. Lord Robert was so fervent in his praise of the League of Nations that he was almost unable to speak at the end and had to be rescued by McDonald before his voice gave out. McDonald did this by interrupting Lord Robert and asking if there were any questions from the floor. McDonald answered the first in order to give Lord Robert an opportunity to recover his voice. *New York Times*, April 3, 1923.

From Louis Dembitz Brandeis

My dear Mr Wilson: Washington, D. C. April 2/23

Replying to yours of yesterday: the Court is in recess this week, and I shall be glad to call on the day and at the hour most convenient for you;—today, if you desire. Awaiting reply

Cordially   Louis D. Brandeis

ALS (WP, DLC).

John Randolph Bolling to Louis Dembitz Brandeis

My dear Mr. Justice: [Washington] 2nd April 1923

Mr. Wilson asks me to thank you for your note and say he will be grateful if you will come in to see him at four o'clock this (Monday, April second) afternoon.

Cordially yours,   John Randolph Bolling

TLS (L. D. Brandeis Papers, KyLoU).

To Gustavus Myers

My dear Mr. Myers,   [Washington] 3rd April 1923

Your letter of March thirty-first is most generous, and has gratified me very deeply. It is very delightful to receive such an expression of your confidence and friendship, and I am sincerely grateful.

Hoping that every happy circumstance will develop in your experience, and with renewed assurances of warm appreciation,

Cordially and Sincerely Yours,   [Woodrow Wilson]

CCL (WP, DLC).

To Ray Stannard Baker

My dear Baker,   [Washington] 3rd April 1923

I enjoyed your letter of March thirty-first very much. It is most heartening to hear what is happening to the book, and I congratulate you with all my heart.

Thank you for your willingness to assist Palmer. It may become an exceedingly important case.

With warm regard and repeated felicitations,

Faithfully Yours,   [Woodrow Wilson]

CCL (WP, DLC).

John Randolph Bolling to Alexander Mitchell Palmer[1]

My dear Mr. Palmer: [Washington] 3rd April 1923

Mr. Wilson promptly wrote to Mr. Ray Stannard Baker about your desire to consult the minutes to which you refer in your letter of March 22d, and asks me to quote his reply:

"I shall be glad to help in any way I can. It is somewhat like looking for the proverbial needle in the haystack to try to find any particular discussion in those vast minutes, and be sure of getting everything upon any given subject—as I know from laborious experience. I have made a thorough, and, I think, accurate digest of the records of the Four and Ten for those subjects which I wished especially to treat, as well as many others. Whether this will reach to Mr. Palmer's needs, I do not know; but I will do the best I can."

Mr. Wilson hopes that preparations for the case are making such progress as satisfies you.

Cordially yours,   [John Randolph Bolling]

CCL (WP, DLC).
[1] There is the following note at the top of this letter: "Dict by WW for me to sign"

From Norman Hezekiah Davis, with Enclosure

My dear Mr. Wilson: New York City, April 4, 1923.

Enclosed you will please find a redraft of that portion of the document which you sent to me.[1] I have merely made a few deductions and a few additions, which I hope will meet with your approval. I gather from the extract which you sent me that Article 3, which was eliminated, defines the principles and purposes of the party. If such is not the case, then I think Article 2 should be somewhat altered.

As you have no doubt noticed, Lord Robert Cecil is expressing very frankly his views about the League of Nations.

It was very nice to see Mrs. Wilson in New York yesterday. I told her that I was going to Washington Sunday night, in which case I should like to call to see you on Monday. There is a possibility that I shall not be able to go, in which case I will let you know. At any rate, I hope to see you some time in the very near future, and remain, as ever,   Affectionately yours,   Norman H. Davis

TLS (WP, DLC).
[1] In WW to NHD, March 27, 1923.

E N C L O S U R E[1]

1. We recognize the fact that the complex, disturbing and for the most part destructive results of the great war have made it necessary that the progressive countries of the world should supply for the reconstruction of its life a programme of law and reform which shall bring it back to health and effective order; and that it lies with the political party which best understands existing conditions, is in most sympathetic touch with the mass of people, is not dominated by any class or interest seeking its own selfish gain, and is ready and best qualified to carry a constructive programme through to take the initiative in asking and pressing affirmative proposals of remedy and reform.

2. In this spirit and with this great purpose we, as representatives of the Democratic party of the United States put forth, in deep earnestness, the following declaration of principle and purpose and thereby seek to serve America and, through America, liberal men throughout the world who seek to serve their people.

— —

4. Our participation in the world war imposed upon us a duty to cooperate with our associates in the solution of problems inherited from the war and in the adoption of measures to prevent the recurrence of such another calamity. Our position as a creditor nation, with a surplus of farm and other products for export, establishes for us a vital interest in the recovery of economic order and the maintenance of peace throughout the world. Ignoring these controlling facts and embracing the *ignorant* fallacy that the progress and welfare of one nation may be advanced by injury to another, the Republican Administration has repudiated our moral obligations and sacrificed our material interests by failing to take any constructive steps to remove sources of international friction which seriously threaten ⟨the⟩ peace and prevent the establishment of international confidence and healthy prosperity.

4. *Although bound* ⟨Bound⟩ up with world conditions from which we could not extricate ourselves, the Republican Administration even committed itself to a policy of isolation. It blindly persisted in the delusion that we are unaffected by the world's all-encompassing perils and calamities and that, although we have great accumulated strength and matchless resources, we have no responsibility and need not interest ourselves in efforts to discover and apply safeguards and remedies. It still refuses to take the lead or to cooperate with the Governments of other nations in the adoption of measures which would improve our own situation or that of our customers and debtors.

The Republican Administration has no economic policy, domestic or foreign. In economic matters it is trying to go in several opposite directions at the same time. It declares its desire to stimulate foreign trade and to revive shipping and then, under pressure of special interests and for their benefit, it erects a high tariff barrier to lessen imports and therefore to limit or destroy foreign trade.

That it would be worse than stupid to try to maintain a merchants fleet by direct and indirect subsidies to carry freight and then to destroy trade by excluding commodities, does not enter the minds of the Old Guard Republican leaders who are in charge of the Government. They assert their eagerness to reduce taxes and the cost of living and yet ought to know, in their hearts, if they had any intelligent conception of the situation, that they add to both by their tariff programme, based on greed. They preach economy and yet press legislation for new undertakings and obligations involving hundreds of millions of dollars. They profess to be concerned about the laborers' standard of living, and at a time when the beneficiaries of their tariff policy are omitting nothing to reduce wages they are devising measures to increase the laborers' cost of living. They clamour for the stabilization of trade and exchange and by their course contribute to the conditions which render stabilization impossible. They are blind to the fact that the protection which the American farmers and manufacturers need is that which would be accorded by a great foreign market, and that this can be secured only by measures which will bring peace to the world, stimulate the forces of production everywhere, and make possible through legitimate business ventures this nation's assistance to Europe through loans and investments.

T MS (WP, DLC).
    [1] Words in italics inserted by Wilson; words in angle brackets deleted by him.

From Franklin Delano Roosevelt

Miami Florida April 4 1923

. Leaving boat after long cruise today Will be in Washington from Friday afternoon to Sunday staying at Adolph Millers Much hope I can come to see you I will telephone after I arrive My warmest regards to you both   Franklin D Roosevelt

T telegram (WP, DLC).

Edith Bolling Galt Wilson to Henry White

My dear Mr. White,   [Washington] April 5, 1923

Your note[1] has just reached me and I am sending an answer at once, knowing how many claims will be made on you for your distinguished guests time. Mr. Wilson asks me to say he will be so happy if Lord Robert will come in on Friday, the 20th at five thirty for a cup of tea with him, and unless we hear to the contrary he will expect him at that hour. He—(Mr. Wilson) said—please tell Mr. White I count him and Mrs. White[2] such good friends that I am asking Lord Robert alone, knowing they always understand, and that I want them another time alone, when we can talk. Of course I will say nothing about your hope to give Lord Robert a quiet Sunday with you.

Did you know that I tried to catch you and Mrs. White Tuesday when you were leaving your house about one oclock.

I had been out with Mrs. Baruch,[3] and we were just returning when I said "I wish I might stop and say a word to Mr. and Mrs. White," and she said, "Well you have 15 minutes,["] when just then you came out and got in the motor with Mrs White and drove off, and we were just too late to catch you. However as you will be here so soon I am looking forward to making up for it. Mr. Wilson gives me his warmest message to you and Mrs White.

                    Faithfully,   Edith Bolling Wilson

ALS (H. White Papers, DLC).
  [1] It is missing in the EBW Papers, DLC.
  [2] Emily Vanderbilt Sloane White.
  [3] Annie Griffen Baruch.

John Randolph Bolling to Franklin Delano Roosevelt

Dear Mr. Roosevelt: 2340 S Street N W 6th April 1923

I have delivered the message of your secretary to Mr. Wilson, and he says that he and Mrs. Wilson will be glad to see you and Mrs. Roosevelt tomorrow afternoon at three o'clock, before he goes for his daily motor ride.

                    Cordially yours,   John Randolph Bolling.

TLS (F. D. Roosevelt Papers, NHpR).

To Marietta Minnegerode Andrews[1]

My dear Mrs. Andrews,   [Washington] 6th April 1923

I wish that it were possible for Mrs. Wilson and me to attend the meeting at Charlottesville in the interest of the purchase of Monticello. And since it is not, I wish to give myself the pleasure of saying how much the project interests me, and I hope it will meet with complete success.

I think that the purchase and preservation of Monticello as a national memorial and place of rendezvous for those who cherish the ideals of Democracy with which Jefferson enriched the thought of this nation ought to meet with universal approval, and I hope and believe that the money will be forthcoming in abundance. The generosity and patriotic feeling of our people would be admirably expressed in such a gift to the nation.

Allow me again to express the hope that the plans of The Thomas Jefferson Memorial Foundation will be realized in full.

Respectfully and Cordially Yours,   [Woodrow Wilson]

CCL (WP, DLC).
¹ Mrs. Eliphalet F. Andrews of Washington, president of the National Monticello Association, which was trying to raise money to acquire and preserve the Jefferson homestead. She had sent the Wilsons an invitation to attend ceremonies there on April 13, 1923, to inaugurate a national drive for funds.

Ray Stannard Baker to John Randolph Bolling

Dear Mr. Bolling: Amherst Massachusetts April 6 1923

It was most kind of you to send me Mr. Brandeis letter with Mr. Wilson's reply.¹ I was quite overcome by such generous and affectionate words. Such things mean more to me than almost anything else: and I wish you would convey to Mr. Wilson my hearty thanks. I have felt all along that it was worthy of every ounce of energy I possessed to help make people understand the importance of Mr. Wilson's vital idea—for upon it rests the future happiness of men—and to be able to do this, and at the same time to win Mr. Wilson's personal confidence and affection is reward indeed.

I have received the Syndicate report for March—now dwindling small, & yet with something still to come. I enclose it.

Total Collection   291.75
Mr. Wilson's share   145.88

I enclose a check for the amount.
With many good wishes

Sincerely   Ray Stannard Baker

I am return[ing] Mr. Brandeis letter with copy of Mr. Wilson's reply: venturing to make a copy of them.

ALS (WP, DLC).
¹ Bolling's letter to Baker, Brandeis' letter to Wilson (undoubtedly an ALS), and Wilson's letter to Brandeis are missing in the Baker, Wilson, and Brandeis Papers.

A Draft of an Essay[1]

[c. April 8, 1923]

THE ROAD AWAY FROM REVOLUTION

In these doubtful and anxious days, when all the world is at unrest and, look which way you will, the road ahead seems darkened
by shadows which portend dangers of many kinds, it is only common prudence that we should look about us and attempt to assess
the causes of distress and the most likely means of removing them.
There must be some real ground for the universal unrest and perturbation. It is not to be found in superficial politics or in mere
economic blunders.

It probably lies deep at the sources of the spiritual life of our
time. It leads to revolution; and perhaps if we take the case of the
Russian revolution, the outstanding event of its kind in our age,
we may find a good deal of instruction for our judgment of critical
situations and circumstances.

What gave rise to the Russian revolution? The answer can only
be that it was the product of a whole social system. It was not in
fact a sudden thing. It had been gathering head for several generations. It was due to the systematic denial to the great body of Russians of the rights and privileges which all normal men desire and
must have if they are to be contented and within reach of happiness. The lives of the great mass of the Russian people contained
no opportunities, but were hemmed in by barriers against which
they were constantly flinging their spirits only to fall back bruised
and dispirited. Only the powerful were suffered to secure their
rights or even to gain access to the means of material success.

It is to be noted as a leading fact of our time that it was against
'capitalism' that the Russian leaders directed their attack. It was
capitalism that made them see red; and it is against capitalism under one name or another that the discontented classes everywhere
draw their indictment.

There are thoughtful and well informed men all over the world
who believe, with much apparently sound reason, that the abstract
thing, the system, which we call "capitalism" is indispensable to
the industrial support and development of modern civilization. And
yet everyone who has an intelligent knowledge of social forces
must know that great and widespread reactions like that which is
unquestionably manifesting itself against capitalism do not occur
without cause or provocation; and before we commit ourselves irreconcilably to an attitude of hostility to this movement of the time
we ought frankly to put to ourselves the question, Is the capitalistic
system unimpeachable, which is another way of asking, Have capitalists generally used their power for the benefit of the countries

in which their capital is employed and for the benefit of their fellow men?

Is it not, on the contrary, too true that capitalists have often seemed to regard the men whom they used as mere instruments of profit whose physical and mental powers it was legitimate to exploit with as slight cost to themselves as possible either of money or of sympathy? Have not many fine men who were actuated by the highest principles in every other relationship of life seemed to hold that generosity and humane feeling were not among the imperative mandates of conscience in the conduct of a banking business or in the development of an industrial or commercial enterprise?

And if these offenses against high morality and true citizenship have been frequently observable, are we to say that the blame for the present discontent and turbulence is wholly on the side of those who are in revolt against them? Ought we not, rather, to seek a way to remove such offenses and make life itself clean for those who will share honourably and cleanly in it?

The world has been made safe for democracy. There need now be no fear that any such mad design as that entertained by the insolent and ignorant Hohenzollerns and their counsellors may prevail against it. But democracy has not yet made the world safe against irrational revolution. That supreme task, which is nothing less than the salvation of civilization, now faces democracy, insistent, imperative. There is no escaping it, unless everything we have built up is presently to fall in ruin about us; and the United States, as the greatest of democracies, must undertake it.

The road that leads away from revolution is clearly marked, for it is defined by the nature of men and of organized society. It therefore behooves us to study very carefully and very candidly the exact nature of the task and the means of its successful accomplishment.

The nature of men and of organized society dictates the maintenance in every field of action of the highest and purest standards of justice and of right dealing; and it is essential to efficacious thinking in this critical matter that we should not entertain a narrow or technical conception of justice. By justice the lawyer generally means the prompt, fair, and open application of impartial rules; but we call ours a Christian civilization and a Christian conception of justice must be much higher. It must include sympathy and helpfulness and a willingness to forego self-interests in order to promote the welfare, happiness, and contentment of others and of the community as a whole. This is what our age is blindly feeling after in its reaction against what it deems the too great selfishness of the capitalistic system.

Many grave and even tragical mistakes have been made, practically all of which have been illustrated in the course of the Russian revolution; but they need not be repeated, and many of them can be retrieved.

A friend of mine, on a visit to the country, was one day standing beside a farmer, his host, leaning on the fence of a pig-sty, watching a number of pigs eat out of a trough. The usual things were happening. The pigs all had their forefeet in the trough; were slopping its contents out on the ground; and were getting as much of the food in their faces and on their hides as into their throats,— making a mess of their performance in every possible way. Presently the farmer turned to my friend, a philosophical light in his eye, and observed "Well, Sir, they're all well named pigs: they *eat* like pigs." I am told that in Russian the word Bolshiviki means the Minority, and I am tempted to echo the farmer's reflection and observe, "Well, Sirs, they are well named the Minority: they *act* like a minority, with the haste, ignorance and passion characteristic of a minority suddenly come into possession of all the machinery of power and free to do as they please, obliged to respect no opposition either of reason or of force from any quarter. But the mistakes which have been made need not be repeated, and we can move on towards right ends by right means, if only we think clearly and act unselfishly.

The sum of the whole matter is, that our civilization cannot survive materially unless it be redeemed spiritually. It can be saved only by becoming permeated with the spirit of Christ and being made free and happy by the practices which spring out of that spirit. Only thus can discontent be driven out and all the shadows lifted from the road ahead.

Here is the final challenge to our churches, to our political organizations, and to our capitalists,—to everyone who fears God or loves his country. Shall we not all earnestly cooperate to bring in the new day?

T MS (WP, DLC).
    [1] A typewritten note by J. R. Bolling attached to this manuscript reads: "1st copy made from W.W.'s typewritten original. Read to me by Edith Sunday, April 8th, 1923, and corrected by WW Sunday night April 8, 1923."

To John Hessin Clarke

My dear Clarke,   Washington D C 8th April 1923

The newspapers report of what you said in New York the other day say you declared that your non-partisan organization had formed, or was forming, organizations in every locality in the United States and were going to make it the main business to commit every candidate for office in the elections next year on the subject of the League of Nations. If this is true it is certainly good work and ought to contribute greatly to making the results of the elections unmistakable and irresistible. I congratulate you on the thoroughness of the work.

I often think of you and always you may be sure with the most sincere regard. I hope that your strength is increasing notwithstanding your strenuous labours, and that every happy circumstance may attend your daily experience.

With warm regard,   Faithfully Yours,   Woodrow Wilson

TLS (J. H. Clarke Papers, OClW-Ar).

To Norman Hezekiah Davis

My dear Davis,   [Washington] 8th April 1923

Thank you very much for the revision. It answers the purpose admirably and I will take an early opportunity to incorporate it in the document.

It is a great disappointment to me that I am not to see you tomorrow as I had hoped. I trust it is a pleasure only postponed,—not foregone,—and that I shall hear soon again you are turning this way.

Mrs. Wilson keenly enjoyed her visit to the Baruchs and found it a great pleasure to get a glimpse of you and many other faithful friends.

Things go as usual with us. My progress I believe continues though its stages it is impossible to mark.

I hope that your visit to the White Sulphur has put the whole family in fine physical shape, and that every kind of happiness is now filling your days.

Mrs. Wilson joins me in very warm regards to you all and I am,

As always,   Affectionately Yours,   [Woodrow Wilson]

CCL (WP, DLC).

To George Creel

My dear Creel,   Washington D C 9th April 1923

Many months ago as you may remember you, with characteristic generosity, suggested your willingness to act as my representative in placing with publishers anything I might write, and since then I have several times presumed on the strength of that generous suggestion to refer publishers to you in matters which concern me. To my great satisfaction you acted as my representative in discussing, along with Ray Stannard Baker, contracts with the publishers for his "World Settlement."

All this, as you have already guessed, is preface to saying I have recently written a short essay entitled "The Road Away from Revolution" which contains I believe one or two vital suggestions, and for those suggestions I am anxious to get as wide a circulation as possible. Would you be willing and would you deem it worth while, to advise me as to the publication of this essay? If you would, I shall send you along a copy at once so you can judge for yourself the best way to handle it. If you would not, I absolutely count on you to say so with all frankness, and you know that I will perfectly understand.

Margaret disturbed us recently by telling us that Mrs. Creel[1] and you had some thought of picking up and moving your whole household to California. We are disturbed because it is a great pleasure to have you near at hand and to know we may often see you and be stimulated by your presence and counsel. But whether you go or stay our affection for you all will continue to grow and to be pressed upon you at every opportunity.

Mrs. Wilson joins me in affectionate regards to you all and in the hope that you are all perfectly well and content.

With warmest greetings,

Affectionately Yours,   Woodrow Wilson

TLS (G. Creel Papers, DLC).
[1] Blanche Bates Creel.

From Norman Hezekiah Davis

My dear Mr. Wilson: New York City, April 9, 1923.

I was sorry I could not be in Washington today, but I hope to go down some time in the near future. I should have liked particularly to discuss with you some of the present activities here in relation to the League.

Determined efforts are being made by certain groups of Republicans to get the Administration to make a move to get in the League next Winter. I heard last week that the strategy would be to show that the League has developed along a different line from what was contemplated; that as the covenant is now interpreted, public opinion is to be the force back of the League, and no nation is to have any sort of obligation to enforce decisions, or to compel obedience to the Covenant, and that Senator Pepper[1] would lead off with a speech along these lines. I was not surprised to read in today's papers an account of Pepper's speech in Philadelphia, in which he is reported as stating that the League of Nations as now functioning and as described by Lord Robert Cecil, is what he and many Republicans have always contended for, and that the time has now come when we should, upon certain conditions, enter the League, the primary object of which shall be that of conferences without binding obligations.

Having had reason to believe that several pro-League Republicans in close touch with Lord Robert Cecil were trying to persuade him that it would not be possible to get the United States into the "Wilson" League of Nations, but that it would be possible to get us into the League provided it is more loosely constructed, I called on Cecil last Tuesday and had a talk with him. I congratulated him on his speech the night before, and told him I was glad to note that he was not offering any concessions to get the United States in, a mistake which Europe has been making from the beginning. I explained that every time a bid had been made for our entrance, the anti-Leaguers took advantage of it to try to prove that Europe cared nothing for the League, but was only interested in getting something out of us. I told him some of my acquaintances, pro-League Republicans, recognizing the trend of sentiment in favor of the League and the danger from a political standpoint of the failure of the Administration to get in in some way, have been taking the position lately that too much had been undertaken under the present Covenant, that public opinion is not yet prepared for binding obligations, and that the wiser course for the time being would be to have the League merely as an instrument for periodical conferences. I told him that some of us feel that unless Europe is prepared to accept certain fundamental principles which are essential for establishing peace and justice between nations, the United States could not serve any useful purpose in trying to settle quarrels there under the old rules of the game, and would better keep out. Cecil said he recognized the force of my views, which he was very glad to have, that he was not in favor of a League so loosely constructed that it merely provided for conferences, and that all previous attempts at world cooperation had failed because machinery had not been established under specific Covenants.

The night following my talk with Cecil I was surprised at a statement which he made in a speech at the Colony Club. In discussing Article X, he said he was afraid he did not agree entirely with the two principal conflicting views; that while he thought Article X was good, he did not feel it is of such vital importance as some contend, nor at all dangerous as others contend, but that he would be willing to recommend its complete elimination from the Covenant if that were the only obstacle which prevents the United States from entering. On the following morning, in a conversation with MacDonald, the President of the Foreign Policy Association, which is acting as Cecil's host here, I told him I was sorry Cecil had seen fit to go so far as to make the above statement. Assuming that Article X is the obstacle to our entrance into the League, and that the present members of the League would be willing to eliminate it to get us in, I said it was a mistake for the proposal to come from Europe, particularly when this Government is not now prepared to take any definite step. I also said that if the position taken by Cecil were construed by the Wilson pro-Leaguers, who after all have been the real friends of the League in this country, as a willingness to sacrifice a fundamental principle in order to curry favor with luke-warm friends of the League, and to assist them in getting over a political obstacle, he might create a situation which would not be promising. MacDonald said he agreed thoroughly with me, and that as he was going to see Cecil that day he would reiterate our views. I did not get to talk with Cecil again, but MacDonald told me he had spoken to Cecil, who recognized the potency of the reasons advanced.

Aside from the fact that he has not, insofar as I know, repeated his willingness to make concessions, I judged that Cecil had been influenced somewhat because Lamont, who had evidently been one of those advising him to bid for us, came to me on Thursday night at the banquet of the Council on Foreign Relations, where Cecil was speaking, and told me he understood I thought it a mistake for Cecil to suggest the elimination of Article X as an inducement to get the United States into the League, and since he did not agree with me, he wished to talk it over. I told him what I thought. In substance, Lamont said it was now out of the question to think of getting us into the League with Article X, and since the important thing was to get us in under any conditions, he thought it was good policy for Cecil to propose the elimination of Article X, and get that out of the discussions. I replied that while the Republicans were of course free to define any conditions under which they would be willing to enter, it was poor tactics to try to get Cecil to build a bridge for them.

While Cecil is thoroughly sincere and honest, and a most ardent advocate of the League as it stands today, I suspect that he thinks it is better to have us in the League, even if that requires certain important concessions, and that he does not see quite clearly yet why he should not offer concessions. Having heard that Ceceil [Cecil] is going to call on you in the near future, I thought I would give you my impressions for whatever they may be worth.

It is undoubtedly true that as a result of our failure to join the League and the failure of the British and French Governments to give it their hearty support, the League has developed upon somewhat different lines from what was contemplated. It is remarkable what the League has been able to accomplish under the circumstances because, due to this lack of support, it has not been able in some cases to do more than try persuasion, and in others it has been unable to intervene, where, according to the Covenant, it could and should have intervened.

In view of the trend of affairs in Europe, and the failure of some of the powers to comply in certain respects with the spirit and the letter of the Treaty of Versailles, I feel that when the time comes for us to enter the front door with our heads up, it will be necessary to survey the situation as it then stands, and stipulate certain conditions which would consider as essential to make our efforts useful. My plan would be the very opposite of what the Republicans evidently have in mind.

With best wishes, I am,

Affectionately yours,   Norman H. Davis

TLS (WP, DLC).
¹ George Wharton Pepper, Republican of Pennsylvania.

John Randolph Bolling to Ray Stannard Baker

Dear Mr. Baker: 2340 S Street N W 9th April 1923

Your good letter of 6th April, with its enclosures, came this morning. Knowing how much Mr. Wilson would appreciate all that you wrote, I read the letter to him—and he was immensely gratified. He often refers to you, and always in the most affectionate manner.

I return herewith the statement of syndicate, and thank you for check for Mr. Wilson's share. I have made a copy of statement as usual for his files.

Mrs. Wilson enjoyed her little trip to New York, and it really did her a lot of good.

With warm regard;

Cordially yours,   John Randolph Bolling

TLS (R. S. Baker Papers, DLC).

From Herbert Sherman Houston

Dear Mr. Wilson: New York April 10, 1923.

You have always been so extremely kind in your disposition toward my publishing enterprise that you are one of the few men that I really want to have informed about my progress. I have recently completed the first year of publication of OUR WORLD and I am now making an edition of 40,000 copies a month. Of course you saw my League of Nations number for March. Your old Princeton classmate, Cyrus McCormick, telegraphed for 100 copies and I had orders for several thousand copies from all parts of the country in addition to my regular normal demand, indicating how the tide is at last flowing our way.

I felt when I began the magazine a year ago that I should stand first for international cooperation and work steadily and surely to the time when I should take a clear-cut and strong position in favor of the League of Nations. This policy, I feel, has justified itself. I now have nailed my flag to the League of Nations mast, and there it will continue to fly.

Some of your staunch friends who are also my friends have the feeling, which I suspect, that I am not making my approach sufficiently on a party basis; but here, again, I feel that a general magazine which is standing broadly for light and knowledge and truth in regard to the world should have a broad national basis and not a party basis. In this view I hope and believe that I have your approval.

I have been wondering, Mr. Wilson, if it would trespass too much on your kindness if I should ask if I might have an appointment to see you if I came to Washington some day soon. There are various matters in regard to policy that I should greatly like to talk over with you. Moreover, my advice as a publisher has been especially sought—probably because I had a good deal to do with Ray Stannard Baker's book—in regard to the publication of a book on the League made up from your addresses,[1] following the literary method that Hale followed in "The New Freedom."[2] I was told, when my advice was sought, that you knew that this book was in preparation.

I have been talking the matter over recently, quite in confidence, with two of our close friends, Bainbridge Colby and Roland Morris, and naturally I should not even presume to offer a positive opinion on the matter without knowing your own wishes. If it should be agreeable to you in every way, I could come to Washington almost any day next week and keep any appointment at your house that it might be convenient for you to make.

You may be sure that when your name was mentioned at the

Lord Robert Cecil dinner at the Astor the other night I was one of the first to come automatically and instantly to my feet—I think Bernard Baruch and I rose from our chairs at the same moment—and it was heartening to your friends to hear the mighty cheer that went up from the two thousand or more people who were present. Time does have its rewards, after all.

With kindest personal regards and assurances of my deep and enduring esteem, I am, as always,

Yours faithfully,   Herbert S. Houston

P.S. I am enclosing a circular that I am just sending out on Irving Fisher's new book[3] in combination with OUR WORLD, merely showing how I am following closely in all my promotion work, the lines of the League of Nations.

TLS (WP, DLC).

[1] That is, Hamilton Foley's *Woodrow Wilson's Case for the League of Nations* (Princeton, N. J., 1923).

[2] That is, William Bayard Hale's edition of Wilson's speeches of 1911-1912 published under the title, *The New Freedom: A Call for the Emancipation of the Generous Energies of a People* (Garden City, N. Y., 1913).

[3] *League or War?* (New York, 1923).

To James Daniel Evans

My dear Mr. Evans,   [Washington] 11th April 1923

Your letter of April tenth[1] has cheered me a great deal. The advocacy of our entrance into the League by a thoughtful and influential man like yourself is of real value to the cause, and I am proud to know that we are associated in a common conviction and a common purpose.

I did not see the article in the Public Ledger to which you refer[2] and can say with regard to it only that it must have been founded on the knowledge that I shall at all times do everything in my power to bring about the redemption of the United States in the view of our recent allies and the rest of the world by the entrance of our Government into the League of Nations. I have no present definite plan of action on my own part, but I am always ready to serve a cause in which I so absolutely believe, and hope with all my heart that opportunities for such service will not be lacking in the near future.

Let me again express my warm thanks for your letter and say how much it has heartened me. There ought to be a concert of all thoughtful and influential men to restore the leadership of the United States in international affairs.

With warm appreciation and regard,

Cordially and Sincerely Yours,   [Woodrow Wilson]

CCL (WP, DLC).
    [1] J. D. Evans to WW, April 10, 1923, ALS (WP, DLC). Evans was vice-president of the Schuylkill Railway Co. of Philadelphia, which owned and operated the electric railways of Schuylkill County, Pa.
    [2] An article in the *Philadelphia Public Ledger*, April 10, 1923, which said that Wilson intended to move at an early date to obtain American membership in the League of Nations.

From John Hessin Clarke

My dear Friend: Youngstown O Apr 11, 1923

I just cannot tell you how your note pleases & strengthens me, on my return from New York this morning,[1] and I feel that I must acknowledge it at once even before my Secretary comes.

Yes we are organized in all the States but three I think & we intend organizing every congressional district if we can manage it. On my return from South America I found what seemed to me amateurish methods prevailing in our office but the greatest enthusiasm—which more than made up for any shortcomings. The truth is the movement is growing so rapidly that it outran our plans. I think now, however, we have plans under-way for thorough systematic organization throughout the entire country.

I shall speak next in the west, probably in Cgo [Chicago], Kansas City & Minneapolis, & shall vary the appeal to suit conditions. I am sure I am not overstating the fact when I say that at last our country is responding in the way in which it would have responded long since had you continued able to present the Great Cause. When the President singles me out by name to say that his party will accept with enthusiasm my challenge for next year & then hurries his strongest woman to Des Moines to head off a declaration in favor of our movement[2] we may be sure the "best minds" are troubled.

I am sorry to say I got little benefit from my voyage. The vicinity of the Equator was most depressingly hot. But the splendid way in which the country is responding to our appeal gives me strength in the appearance of it which impresses me. I wrote the last N. Y. address in bed but I was going strong as twenty years ago when I closed the delivery of it—the cause is inspiring.

I pray God daily that we may both live to see our country deal with this great matter in a manner worthy of our character & dignity & history.

Please remember me cordially to Mrs Wilson & believe me always   Sincerely your friend,   John H. Clarke

P.S. It is not yet published but our Ex Com resolved Monday that it shall be the policy of the Assn to secure a pledge from every del[e]gate to Nat. Convts, & from any candidate for Senate or

House Reps to favor entrance to *existing* League. Of course we do not oppose reservations provided they be "consistent with our Constitution, & consonant with the dignity & honor & history & power of our Republic."

ALS (WP, DLC).
¹ Clarke had spoken at a meeting of the League of Nations Non-Partisan Association to a large audience in the Lexington Opera House. There is a long account of his speech in the *New York Times*, April 7, 1923.
² Harriet Taylor (Mrs. George) Upton, of Warren, Ohio, the Women's Chairman of the Republican National Committee, who was a delegate to the national convention of the League of Women Voters in Des Moines. Mrs. Upton, in a speech on April 10, declared her adherence to the Republican party's "refusal to accept the League of Nations with its suggested supergovernment," thus serving notice that she and her supporters would oppose any resolution that would commit the League of Women Voters to support American entrance into the League. *New York Times*, April 11, 1923. After a long and heated debate, the convention on April 14 passed a resolution which expressed support for Harding's proposal for American participation in the Permanent Court of International Justice. The same resolution was much more vague on the subject of international organization for world peace. "We urge our Government," it said, "to take further steps to eliminate causes of war and to abolish war itself by association with other nations for the maintenance of abiding peace. . . . We call on all citizens of the United States to unite in the support of every constructive effort toward a permanent world organization for peace without regard to party affiliation." *Ibid.*, April 15, 1923.
We have found no evidence on the matter of Harding singling Clarke out by name.

To Norman Hezekiah Davis

My dear Davis,   [Washington] 12th April 1923

Thank you for your letter of April ninth about your little conferences with Lord Robert Cecil. As usual I agree with you and shall do what I can when opportunity offers to reenforce your advice to him.

Hoping you are all well again,
With affectionate regard,
Faithfully Yours,   [Woodrow Wilson]

CCL (WP, DLC).

From Stephen Samuel Wise

My dear President: New York April 12, 1923

You see that Shakespeare is not wholly right. The good does live on and come to light, as more and more will come to light. I am so glad that your part in trying to secure guarantees for Jews in Roumania has come to light through a statement at Bucharest.¹

I am of the hope that the turn in the tide of events, and what is more important, of attitude, of the nation is having a most tonic effect upon you. The Great Refusal is about to be renounced and our country seems to me upon the eve of that Great Affirmation which will bring to your friends and supporters the unlimited joy of knowing that your great battle has not been in vain.

I have been through the Middle West in the last few days and find that Lord Cecil is doing remarkably well. He has made a real impression upon the country. Pepper is not the least of the proofs of what is evidently going to be the rather belated conversion of the anti-Leaguers.

With heartiest greetings,

As ever yours,   Stephen S. Wise

TLS (WP, DLC).
 [1] An anti-Semitic mob had recently done considerable damage in the Jewish quarter of Jassy, and the government had closed all universities on account of anti-Jewish agitation. The government had announced that an investigation of the police of Jassy would be undertaken for alleged negligence during the rioting in that city. *New York Times*, April 5, 1923.

To Herbert Sherman Houston

My dear Friend,   [Washington] 13th April 1923

I heartily congratulate you on the success of OUR WORLD as you report it in your letter of April tenth. It is the more gratifying because it has been altogether deserved.

My feeling about the party aspect of the struggle is merely this:—I do not believe that anything but determined and concerted action of a great organized party can carry this country into the League or make effective any thoroughgoing and constructive policy, and I now confidently believe that the Democratic Party will espouse the cause in dead earnest.

It would be very delightful to see you, and if you can be in Washington on Wednesday next, the eighteenth, it would be entirely convenient for me to see you at the above address at five-thirty P.M. Please let me know if you can come.

With renewed congratulations and very warm regard,

Cordially and Faithfully Yours,   [Woodrow Wilson]

CCL (WP, DLC).

From Louis Dembitz Brandeis, with Enclosure

My dear Mr Wilson: Washington, D. C. April 15/23

I enclose, as you requested, a statement of the propositions which we discussed; also the opinion in the Vigliotti case to which I referred.[1]

The attainment of our American ideals is impossible, unless the States guard jealously this field of Governmental action, and perform zealously their appropriate duties.

Most cordially   Louis D Brandeis

ALS (WP, DLC).

[1] Vigliotti *v.* Commonwealth of Pennsylvania, 258 U.S. 403. The court upheld Vigliotti's conviction under a Pennsylvania prohibition-enforcement law. Brandeis, who wrote the opinion, said that the state enforcement law was a proper exercise of the state's police power.

E N C L O S U R E

The Eighteenth Amendment made prohibition the law of the Nation. The Volstead Act prescribed for the Nation what liquor should be deemed intoxicating. But the people, when adopting the Amendment, recognized fully that the law could not be enforced without the co-operation of the States within the Nation. Hence it provided in Section 2 that "The Congress and the several States shall have concurrent power to enforce this article by appropriate legislation." The intention was that such government should perform that part of the task for which it was peculiarly fitted. The Federal Government's part is to protect the United States against illegal importation of liquor from foreign countries and to protect each State from the illegal introduction into it of liquor from another State. To perform that part of the task effectively required centralized, unified action and the employment of the large federal powers and resources. Experience has demonstrated that to perform adequately this part of the task will require all the resources which Congress makes available for enforcement of this law. To this part of the whole task of enforcement the Federal Government should, therefore, devote its entire energies. The protection of the people of a State against the illegal sale within it of liquor illegally manufactured within it, is a task for which the State Governments are peculiarly fitted, and which they should perform. That part of the task involves diversified governmental action and adaptation to the widely varying conditions in, and the habits and sentiments of the people of, the several States. It is a task for which the Federal Government is not fitted. To relieve the States from the duty of performing it, violates our traditions; and threatens the best interests of our country. The strength of the Nation and its capacity for achievement is, in large measure, due to the federal system with its distribution of powers and duties.

There should be frank recognition of the fact that the prime duty of the Federal Government is to protect the country against illegal importation from abroad and from illegal introduction of liquor from one State into another; that the full performance of this duty will tax the resources of the Federal Government to the uttermost; and that, for the rest, the people of each State must look to their state governments. But the Eighteenth Amendment should remain unchanged. And the Volstead Act should remain unchanged.

T MS (WP, DLC).

From Herbert Sherman Houston

My dear and honored friend: New York April 16th, 1923

I am more than delighted with your extremely cordial letter of April 13th, in which you make some over-generous comments on what I have tried to do with OUR WORLD.

I shall be honored and delighted to keep the appointment at 5:30 Wednesday afternoon at your house in S Street—and I assure you it will give me great personal satisfaction to see you again.

While I dare say it is true that the country's final decision in regard to the League will never be reached except through party action, I've had a feeling that if it were possible to secure a fair and full expression of opinion on the League question it would help matters forward amazingly. Therefore, I was deeply interested in the proposal of one of your staunch friends and supporters, Mr. Alfred Lucking of Detroit,[1] about a national referendum by mail on the question of the League. I asked Mr. Lucking to write an article on the plan for OUR WORLD, for my May number, and I am taking great pleasure in enclosing page proofs of the article with this letter.

With assurances of my enduring and affectionate esteem, I am as always   Yours faithfully,   Herbert S. Houston

TLS (WP, DLC).
    [1] Legal counsel to the Ford Motor Co. and a chief adviser to Henry Ford.

To Louis Dembitz Brandeis

My dear Brandeis,   Washington D C 18th April 1923

Thank you for the statement which you were kind enough to write and send me. It seems to me admirably lucid and just sufficiently elaborate to make the argument clear. It will admirably suit the purpose which I had in mind, and I am deeply obliged to you.

With warm regard,
          Cordially and Faithfully Yours,   Woodrow Wilson

TLS (L. D. Brandeis Papers, KyLoU).

To Frank Irving Cobb

My dear Cobb,   Washington D C 18th April 1923

I took the liberty of drawing Justice Brandeis into conference on the suggestion you made about the way to deal with the liquor question in our statement of principles, and at my request he was kind enough to draw up the enclosed statement of our position.

I hope you will like it as much as I do, and regard it as an adequate formulation of what you had in mind.

With very warm regard,

Faithfully Yours,   Woodrow Wilson

TLS (IEN).

To Alice Garrigue Masaryk

My dear Miss Masaryk,   [Washington] 18th April 1923

I was sincerely distressed that I could not hear the children sing and give them my personal greetings,[1] but my disappointment was entirely due to what seemed to me a wholly unnecessary blunder on the part of the Commercial Attache of the Legation.

You may be sure, in any case, that I did not need the gracious assurances of this special message through the children to assure me of the very generous feeling of the people of Czechoslovakia toward me. What I did to assist that stout little nation to gain independence was done with genuine zest, and I shall always be proud to have it thought I played any part in the Nation's birth and the establishment of its independence.

The flowers were very beautiful and enhanced my pleasure in the message which the children brought. Thank you very warmly for them.

Please present my cordial regards to your distinguished Father and beg of him to always think of me as a genuine friend of the people over whom he so worthily presides. I am hoping I may not be denied the privilege and pleasure of a closer personal acquaintance with him in the years to come, as well as the privilege of cooperating with him in anything that will advance the interests of your people.

Please accept my warmest greetings and assurances of my admiration and regard, and allow me to subscribe myself,

With heartfelt good wishes,

Faithfully Yours,   [Woodrow Wilson]

CCL (WP, DLC).
[1] Wilson was replying to Alice G. Masaryk to WW, March 20, 1923.

From Jessie Woodrow Wilson Sayre

Dearest, darlingest, Father,   [Cambridge, Mass.] April 18, 1923

It was so fine to hear directly from the Moors[1] just how you were looking and it made me more homesick than ever to see you my self. Thanksgiving seems already a long time off.

The children are over their whooping-cough and Francis and Eleanor are back at school. The house seems uncannily quiet without them about.

We have made a daring decision for this summer. Frank is going to teach at summer school in Los Angeles and the children and I are going, too. We have taken a house near where Nell's children will be for the summer and we are promising ourselves very happy times being near her. I have never been across the Mississippi so I am very much excited.

Another interesting question has come up for decision. Frank is very doubtful about it for there are many factors to be considered and they point away from accepting it, *most* of them, that is. This is an invitation to go to Siam for four years as International Law adviser to the Nabob or what ever he is.[2] Can you give us any light as to what kind of a job it would be? Would you consider it worth while in itself? We probably couldn't go even if it were worth while, but we would like any information on the subject we can get!!

Give my dearest love to darling Edith, and to your dear dear adorable self   Devotedly,   Jessie.

ALS (WC, NjP).
   [1] John Farwell Moors, broker and businessman of Boston, and Ethel Lyman Paine Moors.
   [2] About Francis B. Sayre's work for the Siamese government in obtaining full sovereignty for Siam in dealing with foreigners, see FLP to WW, Feb. 28, 1920, n. 1, Vol. 65.

From Frank Irving Cobb

Dear Mr. Wilson: New York April 19th, 1923.

I think the Brandeis statement is excellent. I do not see how it could be improved. Of course I have my own views about the last two sentences, but those views have nothing to do with the matter of defining the policy of the party in the 1924 campaign.

It seems to me that the Justice has made a statement of the case that our friends in the South cannot consistently reject, unless they are prepared to abandon the States and scrap the whole system of local self-government.

Thank you for letting me see the statement,

With sincerest regards,   As ever yours,   Frank I. Cobb.

TLS (WP, DLC).

From Norman Hezekiah Davis, with Enclosure

My dear Mr. Wilson: New York City. April 19, 1923.

Your letter to Congressman Rouse[1] broke the monotony and gave something to talk about. In spite of the fact that some people, including Democrats, misinterpreted your letter, I believe it will do good. Some of the Democrats have expressed a fear that your letter might cement the Republicans, and prevent a rift in their ranks over this question.

To me it seems that if the Irreconcileables interpret your inability to give an unqualified approval as opposition to President Harding's proposal to adhere to the protocol constituting the International Court as opposition to this inadequate step, it will have a tendency to increase the rift between the two Republican factions.

As I foresee it, the principal danger to be guarded against is the creation of the impression on the part of the people that joining the Court is all that is necessary to bring law and order into world affairs. Arguments will of course be advanced that the Republicans have for years favored an International Court of Justice, and that one of the few specific commitments in the last Republican platform was in favor of such a Court. It will also be argued that this is a wonderful way for the United States to assist Europe, and to advance our own prosperity without the assumption of any obligation whatever.

After the Republican factions have definitely lined up on this matter, and made their respective attacks, it may be very advisable for you, some time at the end of Summer, and before Congress reconvenes, to make a statement to the American people, explaining that while the court is one of the necessary instrumentalities for composing controversies between nations, experience has shown that few of the wars have arisen over justiciable questions which could have been disposed of by such a Court. After Congress convenes you can give a more detailed expression of your views for the guidance of the Democrats.

I am enclosing, with apologies, a draft of the general position which in my opinion the Democrats should take later on in reference to the Court, and the general line of thought which might be embodied in such a statement.

Our daughter May is recuperating rather slowly, and Mrs. Davis and I do not feel like leaving for Europe until she is well, so we have postponed our trip, at least for several days, and if we go at all, I do not believe we will get away before the 28th of this month.

I enjoyed very much my last visit with you and Mrs. Wilson, and sincerely hope that you are continuing to improve. It seems that

Spring is here at last, and this weather ought to do you a lot of good.

With most affectionate regards, I am, as ever,

Faithfully yours,   Norman H. Davis

TLS (WP, DLC).
  [1] WW to A. B. Rouse, April 1, 1923. The Rouse-Wilson correspondence was printed, e.g., in the *New York Times*, April 14, 1923, in a front-page story.

E N C L O S U R E

The United States ought to associate with and give its support to the Permanent Court of International Justice, because that Court provides means for the settlement of controversies of a justiciable character between nations that are peacefully inclined. The United State has for years been a foremost advocate of the establishment of such a Court, and adherence to the protocol establishing the present Court would be in harmony with a well settled policy supported by both political parties.

I feel that the Democratic Party should support any steps, even though inadequate, for the settlement of international disputes by peaceful rather than by forceful processes, and should therefore support President Harding's proposal to adhere to the protocol establishing the Court. I cannot give my unqualified endorsement to this proposal because I deem it to be an inadequate step. It would be unfortunate if the impression were created that the International Court of Justice is sufficient to stabilize peace and prevent the recurrence of another world war. History and experience prove that only a small percentage of the wars during the last century or so arose over questions which were of such a character that a court could have dealt with them effectively. The evils and sources of friction which led to the last war, and in fact those which lead to most wars, are too intangible and involve too many questions which are not justiciable and cannot be dealt with by a Court. Nevertheless, a court does aid in the establishment of law and order, and tends to accustom nations to the substitution of peaceful processes for those of force or anarchy.

The International Court will be valuable as one of the instrumentalities for the development and application of international law as exists, and since the League of Nations, which is composed of fifty-two nations, is already making valuable additions to the body of international law every time those nations agree upon some general principle and rule of conduct, the United States ought by all means to be a part of this great body, and assist in this practical way in the advancement of international law.

While the International Court has already rendered valuable services, and while it can dispose of many minor disputes in Europe today, it cannot give a constructive solution to the controversy between France and Germany which is threatening the peace of the world and preventing its economic recovery.

In order to eliminate the major causes of war, it is necessary to have machinery for conference, conciliation and adjustment, such as that provided for under the covenant of the League of Nations, and since the International Court is a direct product of the League of Nations, and is only one of the various instrumentalities provided for under the Covenant of the League for composing controversies between nations, we ought to join the League and thus perform a duty to the community of nations, protect our own material interests, and prevent the recurrence of another world war. It is not in keeping with the dignity and courage of America to shirk a responsibility or shrink from taking the lead in efforts to establish peace and justice between nations.

T MS (WP, DLC).

From Bernard Mannes Baruch

My dear Mr. Wilson: New York April 19, 1923.

Norman Davis told me of the chat he had with you in reference to the new publication and of his preference for a weekly rather than a daily paper. Doubtless a weekly paper would cost less to get out. There is no such thing as a national weekly.

Of course, there will always arise the question of management. With the right kind of man you can have a successful daily; with the wrong kind of man you will have a failure of a weekly. I myself am fitted for neither. However, in addition to making a considerable subscription to such a publication, I should be glad to do whatever I could. So far as you are concerned, it seems to me that you would not get the pleasure out of it, nor would it be of value, unless you were identified directly with it and from time to time wrote things for it. It would not be necessary to sign the articles, but no one could mistake your style. If I could get a good manager to handle it, I could be more definite than I am. A bad manager can sink a great deal of money in a very short while. The next time I come to Washington, we can talk a little more at length about this.

The American Legion is holding a dinner here on the 17th of May for the purpose of raising one hundred to two hundred thousand dollars in cash as a permanent fund with which to buy flowers to decorate the graves of those who lie in France. I was wondering if you would care to come over, say a day or two in advance, and make a speech that night. It need not be over five minutes long. They were your comrades in the great war, the ones whose purposes you spoke for. Just turn this over in your mind. It seems to me that it would have great effect if you spoke of the unfinished work and what we owe to those who were left behind.

With best wishes and affectionate regards, as ever,
                    Sincerely yours,   Bernard M Baruch

TLS (WP, DLC).

George Creel to Edith Bolling Galt Wilson, with Enclosure

                                    New York City April Nineteenth,
My dear Mrs. Wilson: Nineteen Twenty-Three.

Speaking quite frankly, and from the very bottom of my heart, the article is far from being what it should be in view of the significance that will be attached to it as Mr. Wilson's first public writing since his illness and also as the signal of his return to active public life.

I was honest enough when I said that it had all of his old fecility [felicity?] of phrase, and that it proved the return of his ability to write, but as I tried to point out to him as delicately as I could, what the article lacks is *body*.

Under different circumstances I would advise instantly and with all my power against its publication. What we have got to consider, however, is the effect of such advice upon Mr. Wilson. I have the feeling that it would crush the confidence that you have been at such pains to build, restoring all of the old depression with possible effect upon his physical state. I cannot, therefore, gain my own consent to give this advice, even though I appreciate keenly the grave danger that we run in permitting publication.

Mr. Walsh,[1] the editor of Collier's, and a very true friend, feels exactly as I do. What is more, I took up the question of newspaper syndication this morning with certain people that I felt able to trust, and all were flatly opposed to handling it. They felt that a selling campaign to the newspapers would inevitably arouse expectations that the article itself would not fulfill and that there would be a very ugly reaction.

What, then are we to do? As I have said, I feel that the gravest consequence might be entailed by our announcement to Mr. Wilson that we do not regard the article as worthy of publication. The one course, therefore, left open to us, in my opinion, is to print in such manner as to minimize the expectation and to establish the impression that the article is more of a contribution to periodical literature than to political debate.

Collier's stands ready to give $2,000 for the article and they will handle it handsomely and with dignity. Such publication averts the danger of a huckstering campaign by newspaper syndicaties [syndicates] and at the same time gives a fair return and almost the same amount of publicity. Surely you can understand how painful it is for me to have to write this letter. It leaves me sick at heart, and yet I would be less than honest and less than a true friend if I did not lay these opinions before you.

This letter is for your own eyes, to be torn up instantly, and I enclose herewith another letter for you to show to Mr. Wilson.

Believe me,   Always devotedly,   George Creel

[1] Richard John Walsh.

ENCLOSURE

George Creel to Edith Bolling Galt Wilson

                                    New York City April Nineteenth,
My dear Mrs. Wilson: Nineteen Twenty-Three.

I have made the surveys that I promised and these are the results: Collier's is willing to pay $2,000 for the article and will not only handle the publication handsomely and with dignity, but will advertise it in such manner as to gain the widest possible circulation.

Against this we have the alternative of newspaper syndication. Undoubtedly, this will mean at least $1,000 more in money, but it entails a huckstering campaign that will undoubtedly have many disagreeable reactions.

To sell it, any syndicate will have to play it up as Mr. Wilson's return to public life, his first significant utterance, a message of the highest importance, etc., and quite frankly, the nature of the article doesn't lend itself to any such descriptives.

My advice, therefore, is to accept the Collier's offer and give up all idea of syndication. This plan protects dignity and minimizes the danger that lies in expectations based upon over-statements.

Collier's, of course, feels that no time should be lost and is pressing me for immediate decision. Will you, therefore, be kind enough to take this up at once and either wire or write me so that I may have the answer by Saturday morning.

Believe me,   Always devotedly,   George Creel

TLS (WP, DLC).

A News Report

[*April 20, 1923*]

Cecil Visits Wilson: Sees Harding Today.

Washington, April 20.—Lord Robert Cecil, who has been explaining the work of the League of Nations to audiences in this country, arrived in Washington today. He conferred for half an hour or more with Woodrow Wilson at the ex-President's S Street home and will visit President Harding at 11 o'clock tomorrow morning.

Twice in the afternoon Lord Robert met the newspaper correspondents, first at a luncheon of the Overseas Writers Club and subsequently at the home of his host, Henry White, on Crescent Place. He talked freely but carefully, avoided saying anything that might be interpreted as critical of the international or other policies of the United States.

Lord Robert refused to disclose the subjects of his conversation with Mr. Wilson. He said that he had "a very pleasant half hour" with the ex-President.

Pressed to give an opinion as to the health of Mr. Wilson, Lord Robert said that he would be consistent and refuse to discuss the visit in any way.

"You must realize," he said, "that I simply cannot talk about what passed between Mr. Wilson and myself, and that includes all references to his health."

Printed in the *New York Times*, April 21, 1923.

Edith Bolling Galt Wilson to George Creel

Dear Mr. Creel: 2340 S Street N W 20th April 1923

Your letters have just reached me, and before answering the subject matter, let me say how sincerely and deeply I appreciate the friendship represented by your counsel.

I so fully agree with you that his literary reputation must be safeguarded that I am not willing to take my own snap judgment, and feel at the moment that the whole facts should be laid before him.

However, this may be a first impression; so I am going to hold the letters and think over the matter. A short delay can make no real difference.

He has so many appointments for today and tomorrow that I may not submit it to him in any form before the first of the week, when I will write you again.

Have you seen Mr. Herbert S. Houston since he was here on Wednesday? W.W. spoke to him about the article, as he asked the definite question if he would be willing to let his magazine (OUR WORLD) have a chance at anything he wrote, and certainly the first thing. So, he told him you had a short paper he had written, and that he had left it to your judgment as to publication. W. also spoke to him about the Foley business.

Randolph is writing this letter for me, as of course I have no secrets from him, and he agrees with me that a little delay is wise.

It was the greatest pleasure to see you, and I wish you could come down again before you go to California.

Thanking you again, and with warm regards to you both,

Affectionately,   Edith Bolling Wilson

TLS (WP, DLC).

From the Diary of Lord Robert Cecil

April 21st. 1923.[1]

I went to see Wilson and found him and his wife sitting in a smallish house. He is said to be very much better than he has been, but I thought him very feeble. His left side is definitely paralysed and he panted a good deal while he talked to me. I should judge that he was quite incapable of any continued exertion. Mrs Wilson sat with us the whole time and I think that was to prevent any really serious conversation. He asked me after my trip, and I told him I had had very good audiences and so on but he did not seem really very much interested. He said that he was sure that the League was winning, and that the Republicans were trying to take cover and to pretend that they were in favour of the League. I said I was quite prepared to look the other way. "Yes," he said, "and hold your nose now." He told me a number of stories in exactly the same way as he used to in Paris. None of them remarkably good, but some amusing. Mrs Wilson, who seemed to me quite definitely a foolish woman, sat there the whole time interposing banal observations. His daughter came in a little later on, but added nothing to the conversation. I stayed there for over half an hour, and as I left I asked him whether he thought I was doing any harm. He said, "Not at all, you are doing a great deal of good, but remember we are on the winning side and make no concessions." It was a tragic observation. This half paralysed man, the repository of a great idea, who up to a point had done so much to carry it into effect, and then done everything he could to destroy it, having learnt nothing and forgotten nothing, continuing to say "make no concessions." Unfortunately he still wields very great influence in the country and since he knows his own mind and is afraid of nothing he will, I fear, ultimately direct the policy of his party, and if he does it seems most probable that the League will be again defeated in the next Election. Indeed he is quite capable of bringing about the defeat of the Court if he could, in order to force a general engagement on the League issue.[2]

T MS (R. Cecil Papers, PRO).
  [1] This entry covers events of April 20 and 21.
  [2] In this same entry, Cecil writes about conversations at dinner at the Henry Whites with a group of Republican leaders—Senators Pepper, Watson, and Edge, Secretaries Mellon, Weeks, and Hoover, and Elihu Root. On April 21 he had longer conversations with Senator Borah; President Harding, who did not impress him; Hoover; Secretary Hughes; Undersecretary of State William Phillips; and others.

To Bernard Mannes Baruch

My dear Baruch,   Washington D C 22nd April 1923

Thank you for your letter of April nineteenth. I am glad we are soon to have another talk about the publication, for I am greatly interested and think the matter of vital importance. I am inclined to coincide with the views expressed in your letter and believe we can agree on a definite policy.

Unfortunately I can't come over to New York to make a speech on the occasion to which you refer. I am not up to that yet, but am obliged to you for the invitation and shall hope it is only a pleasure deferred.

Mrs. Wilson joins me in warm regards to you all. She greatly enjoyed her visit to you and always looks forward with much pleasure as I do to seeing you here.

With warmest messages of regard to you all,
                    Affectionately Yours,   Woodrow Wilson

P.S. I myself made a small contribution to the fund for putting flowers on graves. Unfortunately all my subscriptions must be small.

TLS (B. M. Baruch Papers, NjP).

George Creel to Edith Bolling Galt Wilson

Dear Mrs. Wilson: New York City April 24, 1923.

The original went to you this morning. When you talked to Mr. Wilson, I do hope you made it clear that my suggestion sprang entirely from the importance that will be attached to this publication. It is impossible to overestimate the scrutiny to which it is going to be subjected. I am going to California on May 7 and unless the matter can be completed before this date I would suggest these courses:

1 - Drop a note to Mr. Richard Walsh, editor of Collier's enclosing the manuscript and telling him that his offer, of $2,000 made to me, has been accepted if Mr. Wilson approves.

2 - Newspaper syndication. McClure's Syndicate is the best and a letter to Mr. P. G. Eastment, 373 Fourth Avenue, will bring him down to Washington to talk terms with Randolph. In this event— the split should be sixty percent for you and forty for him.

As I have explained to you, however, I am very much opposed to newspaper syndication, for it involves an exaggeration of significance and will, in the end, get very little more than what Collier's has agreed to pay.

In event that the matter is concluded before my departure, however, please feel that I am only too happy to carry out the details of any decision that you make.

Believe me,   Always devotedly,   George Creel

TLS (WP, DLC).

Edith Bolling Galt Wilson to George Creel

                                                2340 S Street N W
My dear Mr. Creel: 24th April 1923

I have taken up the matter of the article with the person most concerned and while I deemed it best not to read him either of your letters to me I told him of your suggestion as to further development of the subject and your feeling that it needed amplification to give more body to the article. After we had discussed the matter he wanted me to say that he valued any suggestion from you, but that in this instance he felt you had the point of view that he was writing a newspaper article which should be more developed where, as a matter of fact, it was simply a short essay in the form of a "*challenge*"—to quote from his last paragraph which is the keynote of it all. But to show you how eager he is to make this a clear clarion call, and not cloud that high call he (and you will be surprised at this I know) has decided instead of making it *longer* to make it even *shorter*,—omitting two paragraphs[1] and making it stronger as a "challenge." Randolph will send you with this the revised edition which is the form in which "he" W wants it to appear. So much for that!

Now we come to the publishing part. I did not tell him that you had submitted the article to any one or mention the Collier offer. I want to put this thought before you and say frankly that while the sum mentioned ($2,000) would seem a good price for an obscure author, I personally do not feel it is commensurate with his dignity and all that this article stands for as the first thing he has done in years. I fully agree with you that it must not be "huckstered about," but I think there are many dignified ways of playing up such a thing in a way to attract attention without cheap advertising. A simple announcement of the fact in the previous issue of whatever magazine is to publish it to the effect that "Our next issue will contain a contribution from" &c.—the first thing from his pen since he left public life, &c.&c. That to my mind instead of cheapening it gives it at once dignity and importance, and does not appear as a contribution of no moment as it would without any such announcement.

I do not consider Colliers the proper vehicle to publish this, and in talking the matter over with W he reminded me that the Atlantic Monthly had published nearly all of his essays and said that his personal preference would be for that or some other monthly magazine of equally high standing. I hope therefore that you can get in touch with the editor of the Atlantic Monthly[2] and see if he will not come down to New York to read the article and make an offer for it. I may mention that he has been offered $5,000 each for twelve editorials of 500 words on any subjects that he might care to write upon; so it seems to me that the magazine rights alone (of course reserving the book and foreign publication rights) should be worth that to any magazine.

I have written you at great length because I am so sure of your complete understanding.

With warmest messages from us all,

As always,   E.B.W.

April 25th 1923:
Your letter and the mss. have just come. I know the countless demands on your time, in these days when you are hurrying to get away. So if it will be imposing on you in the least to take the matter up with the Atlantic Monthly, please don't hesitate to say so—and we will take it up directly from here.

TLI (G. Creel Papers, DLC).

¹ Wilson deleted the paragraphs beginning "Many grave and even tragical mistakes have been made" and "A friend of mine" from the draft of the essay printed at April 8, 1920.

Ray Stannard Baker recorded the following interview with Stockton Axson. In the first paragraph, Axson is speaking:

" 'We three [Wilson, Axson, and Mrs. Wilson] were riding through the Park a little later. They were seated on the back seat, and I was seated on one of the seats that unfolded. The conversation could not be heard by the chauffeur.'

"Presently Mrs. Wilson spoke and Dr. Axson believes she had been greatly dreading what she had to say. She said that someone to whom the article had been sent had seen her, personally, and said that the article simply wouldn't do. It didn't do justice to him—it didn't reason out what he had to say, and the old touch wasn't there at all; and just for his own sake they did not want to publish it.

"Mr. Wilson grew very impatient—not with her. He would never be impatient with her, beyond suggesting that she herself had urged him to do it—but with all the people who had been urging him to write something. 'They kept after me to do this thing, and I did it.'

"Mrs. Wilson tried to soothe him—'Now don't get on your high horse about this. I am just telling you that they say that what the article needs is expansion, reasoning out the case more.'

" 'I have done all I can, and all I am going to do,' said Mr. Wilson. 'I don't want those people bothering me any more.'

"After the ride was finished, and Mr. Wilson had been helped upstairs, Dr. Axson lingered in Mr. Bolling's office. Suddenly he became aware that Mrs. Wilson—'that strong woman'—was there in the hallway, sobbing. He went out to her at once.

" 'All I want to do,' she said, 'is just to help in any way I can. I am not urging him to do things he doesn't want to do. I just want to help and I just don't know how to help. I don't know what to do.'

"Dr. Axson urged her not to feel so about it. 'It is the only time I ever saw her break down,' he told Mr. Baker. Finally he said:

" 'Would you mind letting me see the article?'

"She did so, and Dr. Axson read it carefully, two or three times, and finally said:

" 'This doesn't need to be longer, it needs to be shorter. This is not an argument, it is a challenge, and that is all it is. These paragraphs (indicating two or three paragraphs) should come out altogether. Then the earlier and the later paragraphs tie up and it becomes just simply a challenge, and that is what he meant to write.'

"Mrs. Wilson asked him if he would mind saying that to Mr. Wilson.

" 'I would be very glad to.'

"He took the matter up with Mr. Wilson soon after that.

" 'Why you see exactly the point,' said Mr. Wilson. 'Fix it.'

"Dr. Axson replied that there was no fixing to be done except to draw a pencil through the paragraphs indicated. That was done. The article was then re-typed, and was sent off to the *Atlantic Monthly*, where it was published under the title: 'The Road Away From Revolution.' " R. S. Baker, "Memorandum of a Conversation with Stockton Axson, on the evening of September 2, 1931," T MS (RSB Coll., DLC).

² That is, Ellery Sedgwick.

George Creel to John Randolph Bolling

My dear Randolph: New York City April 24, 1923.

Mr. Hamilton Foley came to see me yesterday and we went over his matter with the utmost thoroughness. There is no question as to his sincerity and unselfish devotion, and the thing that he has done is very necessary and bound to result in great good.

He has taken the thirty-seven odd speeches made by the President on his tour and with amazing ability has brought about a sequence of sentences that combines the whole thirty-seven in one smoothly flowing address that covers the League of Nations from a to z. Not one word of his own appears in the manuscript. All are the words of Woodrow Wilson, spoken at different times and at different places, but joined together so admirably that it is as though he had spoken it as an address.

Mr. Foley's idea has been one of service only, and what he has done *is* service. In my opinion, the book ought to be offered to some publisher at once, preferably Harper, Mr. Wilson's publisher—and given widest possible circulation. Mr. Foley stated frankly that the money arrangement was up to me and I am of the opinion that a fifty-fifty split of the royalties is fair. Without Mr. Wilson's approval, the work will not be given its true importance nor will he be able to win the circulation that it ought to have. What I suggest is that he write a letter to Mr. Foley congratulating him upon a very remarkable piece of work, giving it his complete approval, and stamping it as his case for the League of Nations. This can be used as a foreword to the book and also in advertising matter. I cannot overestimate the importance of the work that Mr. Foley has done and I only wish that I had thought of it myself.

Sincerely,   George Creel

TLS (WP, DLC).

John Randolph Bolling to George Creel, with Enclosure

My dear George: [Washington] 26th April 1923

Your letter of the 24th inst. came on yesterday, and I had an opportunity to read it to Mr. Wilson this morning. The enclosed letter to Mr. Foley is the result, and seems to me to give just what is wanted.

I asked Mr. Wilson if he would object to this letter being published in the book, as a sort of foreword, and he said he would not—*if you recommended it*. If you feel that this letter is adequate, I suggest you write me saying you do—and recommending that it appear as indicated. I think it could also be used very effectively on the paper cover of the book.

I am sending the letter to you in the hope that you will be good enough to wire Mr. Foley to come to see you—and close the matter up. As you know he (Foley) has discussed publication with Doubleday, Page—and if they offer more liberal terms than the Harpers—Mr. Wilson would be guided by your recommendation in the matter.   Faithfully yours,   [John Randolph Bolling]

To Hamilton Foley[1]

My dear Mr. Foley,   [Washington] 26th April 1923

I congratulate you upon the completion of a difficult piece of work, and I confidently hope that the book will be of service to all who wish to understand the League of Nations and the vital issues which arise out of the attitude of the United States towards the League.

As I have written you before, I could not consent to have the book appear as my own, but if you will publish it with a frank statement on the title page of what it is and how it was made, it will have my entire approval.[2]

Sincerely Yours,   [Woodrow Wilson]

CCL (WP, DLC).

[1] Typed at the top of this letter: "Revised letter—as outlined by draft attached to Creel's letter Aug. 26, 1923."

[2] To repeat, this book was published by Princeton University Press in 1923 under the title *Woodrow Wilson's Case for the League of Nations. Compiled with His Approval by Hamilton Foley*.

To Jessie Woodrow Wilson Sayre

My darling Jessie,   [Washington] 28th April 1923

I am sorry to say that I know little or nothing about Siam that would be of use to you and Frank in making your decision.[1] But it is undoubtedly one of the most progressive and enlightened of the Oriental countries and much more directly touched and affected by western ideals of civilization than the others. I can easily imagine that it may be very difficult for you either to leave the children in this country for so long an absence or take them with you; but if you can take them with you, I think it would be worth while for Frank to accept the interesting offer that has been made him. I understand the King of Siam[2] (whom I met years ago when he was Prince) is an enlightened and progressive man, and I believe that his court could be influenced to play a very helpful part in the politics of the East. By such an experience Frank could, I should think, gain an outlook upon world affairs that it would not be possible to gain in any other way. And although my heart sinks at the thought of your going so far away for so long a time, my advice would be that Frank should accept.

I hope that he can obtain some sort of assurance from the University authorities that a place will still be open to him on his return. That assurance obtained, I should think that the most serious doubts about the matter were cleared away.

We are so glad the children are well again, and are very much cheered by the general tone of your letter.

Please give my regards to Mr. and Mrs. Moors, whom I greatly enjoyed meeting, and who I hope I shall have an opportunity of knowing well.

We unite in sending to you all more love than you can divide among you. Please let me hear promptly when the decision is made.   Lovingly,   [Father]

CCL (WC, NjP).
    [1] Wilson was replying to Jessie W. W. Sayre to WW, April 18, 1923.
    [2] Rama VI (Vajiravudh).

From Sylvester Woodbridge Beach

Dear Wilson: Princeton, N. J. May 1, 1923

I want you to welcome me into the populous ranks of the Emeriti (if the dreaded word be of the second conjugation), for I have been, or am about to be, initiated into that order. Eighteen years seemed to me long enough for such a pastorate as the First Church, ever growing in importance and involvements. I am pulling up by the roots, for I seem to be rooted deeply in the confidence and love of the people. I might stay too long for this; some have done that. But I am not dropping out of the ranks of honest toilers, on the contrary only seeking to enjoy a curriculum a little more elective.[1] I am venturing to send you a copy of a minute adopted.[2] It was drawn by the hand of our mutual friend, Henry van Dyke, as like him as like can be.

Very often do I think of you, and always with ardent love and loyalty. You can never know to what extent you have influenced my thinking and character, and always for the better.

May God bless you and Mrs. Wilson, and long may you live to hold before the untold multitudes of your friends and followers the ideals with which the name of Woodrow Wilson is synonymous.

I remember with much pleasure the visit I had with you just before I sailed last June. I am afraid I have never written to tell you how ardently you are loved by many of the peoples of eastern and southeastern Europe; and nowhere more than in that sterling and progressive republic of Czechoslovakia.

As ever, affectionately yours,   Sylvester W. Beach

TLS (WP, DLC).
    [1] What Dr. Beach did not say was that the congregation of the First Presbyterian Church of Princeton, on April 10, 1923, had voted to elect Beach pastor-emeritus, at an annual salary of "not less than $2,500." Philadelphia *Presbyterian*, May 3, 1923.
    [2] Printed in *ibid.*, it lauded Beach for his ministry of nearly eighteen years in the First

Church, related the spiritual and material growth of the church during his pastorate, and ended on a sweet note of farewell:

"May he ever be comforted of God with the same comfort which he has imparted so often to us! May his wider ministry to the Church general, in which he has already done such noteworthy service, not deprive us of his beloved genial presence and his ever-ready aid! May his strength remain unabated, his eye undimmed, and his last years be his best! This is the prayer of the grateful people of the First Presbyterian Church of Princeton, for their honored pastor-emeritus Dr. Sylvester W. Beach."

George Creel to Edith Bolling Galt Wilson

Dear Mrs. Wilson: New York City May 1, 1923.

Upon receipt of your letter I saw Herbert Houston. Unless you want to make him a virtual gift of articles, there is no use in considering him, for he is in no position to meet competition in prices. It is not possible for him to pay even $500, if that.

This afternoon I called upon Glenn Frank, editor of the Century, not only because he's our friend, but because the Century is the most important of the monthlies with respect to this sort of article. Mr. Frank offers $750 and guarantees the very best treatment.

With respect to the Atlantic Monthly, I think it best for you to get in touch with Mr. Sedgwick as I am leaving for California next Sunday and would not be able to continue any negotiations. Quite frankly, however, there is not the slightest hope of receiving any offer from him at all commensurate with your expectations. If he offers more than $250 I shall be greatly surprised. The monthly magazine, in the very nature of things, is not able to pay real money for its purchases.

I am sorry to go away at this stage, but I think that after you have seen Mr. Sedgwick you will be able to make your own decisions in the matter. The offer of Collier's—$2,000—still stands. At any time you can write to Mr. Richard J. Walsh, the editor, and have him confirm it. This offer, as I am sure you will find, is the very best obtainable and I have no hesitation in urging its acceptance. Neither the Atlantic Monthly nor the Century, nor any other monthly magainze [magazine] has more than 100,000 circulation. Collier's has 1,200,000.

With respect to your expectation of $5,000, no magazine magazine [sic], either weekly or monthly, can pay any such price. It might be possible to gain such a sum from newspaper syndication, and while I am still convinced that this is a method that should not be employed, I am utterly unwilling to stand in the way of your own approach. If, after securing the offer of the Atlantic and weighing the respective merits of the offers from the Century and from Collier's, you still believe that these offers are inadequate, I suggest to you that you get in touch with Mr. Clinton Brainard, c/o McClure's Syndicate, 373 Fourth Avenue. He is the best of the lot and more to be depended upon.

I will be here until Sunday, and if there is any further way in which I can serve you please feel at complete literty [liberty] to call upon me. With warmest regards, believe me,

Always devotedly,   George Creel

TLS (WP, DLC).

To Ellery Sedgwick

My dear Mr. Editor,   Washington D C 2nd May 1923

In former years, whenever I happened to have produced an essay, it used to be my preference and pleasure to send it to the Atlantic. I have just now quite unexpectedly to myself produced a short essay to which I have given the title, "The Road Away From Revolution," and I am taking pleasure in sending it to you under another cover in the hope that you may find a place for it in the Atlantic.

In case you should accept it, I should wish to reserve the right to publish it separately as a pamphlet as [at] some subsequent date, and I hope that this reservation will not be unacceptable to you. I still continue to feel as I used to feel that the Atlantic is my natural medium of literary expression, and I hope you will find the little essay suitable for your pages.

With cordial good wishes for yourself and for the magazine,

Sincerely Yours,   Woodrow Wilson

TLS (MHi).

To Sylvester Woodbridge Beach

My dear Beach,   [Washington] 2nd May 1923

Thank you for your letter of May first and its enclosure. I know that your retirement from an active pastorate will not mean giving up work, and I warmly felicitate you on the happy circumstances attending your retirement from the active care of a Church in which you have done so much and where you have won so many genuine friends. I hope you will find every source of contentment and satisfaction.

With abiding regard,

Faithfully Yours,   [Woodrow Wilson]

CCL (WP, DLC).

From Herbert Sherman Houston

Dear Mr. Wilson: New York May 2nd, 1923

It would have warmed your heart to have heard the addresses at the meeting of the Woodrow Wilson Foundation yesterday afternoon, when the trustees of the Foundation were installed. I don't know when I have felt a spirit running through a large company of people that was more sympathetic and enthusiastic. Your old friend, Mr. Cleveland Dodge, made an inspiriting address which stirred us mightily; and Miss Wooley,[1] Professor Dodd, Henry Morgenthau and others did likewise.

After it was all over, I said to Mr. Dodge that all the things the Foundation stood for, as representing the cause to which you had devoted your great talent and your life, I was striving to carry out, to the limit of my capacity in my publishing enterprise. He expressed great interest in all that I was doing, as he has done from the beginning.

You will remember that when I had the pleasure of seeing you the other day in Washington I told you that I was coming on in a satisfactory way but that I was going to need a certain amount of financial cooperation; and I venture to suggest that if you could drop a friendly note to Mr. Dodge or Mr. Baruch or Mr. Norman Davis or any of your close friends, that you believe OUR WORLD and its publisher were working in an effective way along the lines of your great principles, this would be of the very greatest service to me and I would be profoundly grateful to you.

As I told you and Mrs. Wilson the other day I would do, I undertook to reach George Creel at the earliest possible moment. Due to various complications, we did not get together until two or three days ago. I then found that he had written you fully about the manuscript for the article that had been sent along to him and also had written you about his conference with Mr. Foley. As this whole matter is in such capable and friendly hands, when they are in the hands of George Creel, I don't know that there is anything in particular that I can do; but, as I said both to you and to Mrs. Wilson, if there is anything that I can do in any way please call upon me by letter, by telephone, or by telegraph. I assure you, my dear Mr. Wilson, that I shall instantly do everything in any direction to serve you personally, or to serve the principles for which you have so splendidly stood, up to the top of my capacity.

The other day Mr. Bolling told me that the last two or three numbers of OUR WORLD had not been received, so I sent forward to you the recent copies when I returned to my office.

With kindest remembrances to you and to Mrs. Wilson, and with every good wish for your steady recovery of your strength, I am as ever   Yours faithfully,   Herbert S. Houston

TLS (WP, DLC).
  ¹ Mary Emma Woolley, President of Mount Holyoke College, 1901-1937.

From the Diary of Ray Stannard Baker

Washington May 2 [1923].

I have been here two days. Mr. Wilson wanted me to help with the documents, to find all references relating to the matter of chemicals & dyes. I thought at first he meant to bring these over to Mitchell Palmer & argued that it might involve him in much difficulty: for I suspect this whole affair of the sale of the German patents. He took my view and will use the facts for himself & not open the records for this doubtful purpose. I lunched with the admirable Graysons & met many old friends. Also lunched with the Wilsons in S. street. Mr. W. is steadily but slowly improving in health.

Edith Bolling Galt Wilson to George Creel

My dear Mr. Creel: [Washington] 3rd May 1923

Your letter with enclosure came yesterday. Let me thank you for what you did in the matter and regret that we troubled you when you were so busy getting off to California. Of course we will handle the rest of it, but I want you to know that it was not the *amount* paid for the article that concerned me but the fact that it should receive the proper respect and appear in a dignified way—in the right channel.

With the hope that you will find refreshment and happiness this summer, and greetings from all of us here;
                    Affectionately,   [Edith Bolling Wilson]

CCL (WP, DLC).

George Creel to Edith Bolling Galt Wilson

Dear Mrs. Wilson: New York City May 3, 1923.

Please do not think for one moment that you troubled me in any degree. I am at your service at *all* times. Nor do I want you to have any idea that I thought you were putting emphasis entirely on remuneration. I am the one who always put this emphasis and I am going to keep it up. Why shouldn't we get the best possible price?

There is no question that you can get $3,000 or $4,000 by syndicating the articles through the newspapers, but as I told you, I don't think that this particular article lends itself to that treatment. Collier's will not only pay twice as much as any other magazine but it will give it better treatment. As a last word, I do hope that you will write to Mr. Walsh and let him have it.

Always devotedly and affectionately,   George Creel

P.S. My address will be c/o The Family Club, San Francisco, Calif. Do not hesitate to write or wire me.

TLS (WP, DLC).

John Randolph Bolling to Herbert Sherman Houston

My dear Mr. Houston: [Washington] 5th May 1923

Mr. Wilson asks me to say that he has very carefully noted the contents of your letter of May second, and greatly appreciates your kindness in telling him of the addresses at the meeting of the Woodrow Wilson Foundation.

With regard to the other matter you mention; he directs me to say that he feels the friends you mention are already under such heavy demands that he could not add to them by doing what you suggest.

It was very kind of you to send the back numbers of your magazine, and they came to hand several days ago.

With sincere appreciation of your many kind offers to be of service;   Cordially yours,   [John Randolph Bolling]

CCL (WP, DLC).

Two Letters from Ray Stannard Baker

My dear Mr. Wilson: Amherst Massachusetts May 7, 1923.

I have reviewed the minutes of the Four, Ten and Five carefully and am enclosing herewith the transcript of all the actual discussion of the subject of poison gas, chemicals and dyes.[1] There were references to the military terms regarding poison gases in earlier sessions but no discussion which would reveal the American position.

Your record here seems absolutely clear and consistent. You were against attempting to force the Germans to reveal their chemical secrets, not only because such a method would be futile ("It could serve no useful purpose to expose oneself to be deceived.") but because you believed that the effort to force the revelation of these secrets was only a device of rival economic interests to discover and exploit German chemical processes, particularly the secrets of dye-making. "Others than military experts," you said, "were interested in the revelation of these secrets," and "the Allies must trust their own inventors to cope with their German rivals." You also said "the Germans could not reveal this information without also revealing trade secrets."

Your clear and strong attitude here prevented the proposals by the British and French for a demand, backed up by powers of inspection, for all the secrets of the German chemical industry. As the minutes quote you: "What he (President Wilson) wanted to avoid was an article which could be used in a round about way for irritating investigation of all possible secrets."

I am confining myself here strictly to what is in the record.

With warm regards and good wishes,

Yours sincerely,   Ray Stannard Baker

¹ He enclosed transcripts of the minutes of the Council of Five, April 15, 1919, 3 p.m., printed in *PPC*, IV, 560-62; of the Council of Ten, April 16, 1919, 4 p.m., printed in *The Papers of Woodrow Wilson*, Vol. 57, pp. 402-404; of the Council of Four, April 26, 1919, 12:15 p.m., *ibid.*, Vol. 58, p. 148; and of the Council of Four, April 28, 1919, printed in *PPC*, V, 310-11.

PERSONAL AND CONFIDENTIAL

Dear Mr. Wilson: Amherst, Massachusetts May 7, 1923.

In this connection I would not feel myself doing right unless I told you that I have felt profoundly uncertain in my own mind about the way in which powerful American economic interests, the Du Ponts among others, have got hold of these German patents, for a low price, and are exploiting the very German processes which you prevented the British from forcing the Germans to reveal at Paris. Apparently our great interests are not willing boldly "to trust their own inventors." It is probable that the transaction is sound enough legally, but I do not like the look—or the smell—of it. It seems like a part of the whole tendency of the great American economic interests, regardless of human rights, or of ultimate peace in the world, to dominate the earth. Your policy at Paris, by leaving the Germans some of their economic resources, tended to make for real future peace in the world: but the policy of some of these great, powerful, and unharmed economic interests, entering the field against a broken and defeated nation with the advantage of possessing their patents, which they have bought for a low price, does not, I submit, make for future peace and good feeling in this world.

More and more, it seems to me, the issue grows clearer in this country: whether we are to have government by and in the interest of property, or government by and in the interest of people. The traditional interest of the Democracy back to Jefferson has been in human rights, and you have been for that. But more and more these great and utterly selfish money machines are coming to control us and warp our ideals: they are represented by the old line Republicans—and I, for one, fear them and abominate their influence upon American life. It sometimes seems as though America, in process of gaining the whole world as a result of this war, is losing her own soul. I cannot see wherein the spirit of rapacity in America, which was at the very heart and center of the opposition to you, is any different in essence from the spirit of rapacity now manifested in the Ruhr by the French.

Won't you pardon these remarks, made because the whole matter is so deeply felt by

Your loyal friend,   Ray Stannard Baker

TLS (WP, DLC).

From John Hessin Clarke

My dear Friend—   Youngstown, Ohio May 8, 1923

I have returned from speaking at Chicago, Minneapolis, Kansas City and St. Louis, and thinking that some account of my experience may be interesting to you, I am writing.

Each of the meetings was all that I could desire in point of attendance and interest. There were no demonstrations because I said at the outstart in each case that almost any experienced public speaker could provoke applause from almost any audience and that the decisison [decision] of the subject to which I was about to speak was so fateful to our country that the question had taken on with me a semi-religious, if not sacred, character, and I therefore requested that the audience should not interrupt my argument with applause. The enclosed letter[1] will indicate perhaps better than I can otherwise the character of the impression made which I believe was quite general although nine-tenths of my address was, I think, a lawyer-like argument in support of the Covenant.

I am enclosing a statement which I made in opening my address at Chicago which may be of interest to you. The last sentence may strike you as discordant, but I think upon second thought you will see what my purpose was in using it.

I have become convinced that the only way to correct the 1920 misrepresentation of the League is by the spoken word. It would be difficult for anyone to get more newspaper publicity than I received everywhere, but after all, few of the articles were long enough to contain the necessary answer to the misrepresentation and this was no doubt because the managers believe that their readers would not read more if it were printed.

It seems to me, therefore, that we can make progress only by addressing conventions, noon-day clubs, churches, labor union meetings, and the like. Unfortunately, we have very few speakers of sufficient prominence to attract good meetings and I am so handicapped by the state of my health that I cannot do what would otherwise be easily possible.

The labor unions are turning strongly our way. I wonder if you saw the April number of "The Locomotive Engineers' Journal" which was devoted wholly to peace publications and contained my January 10th address almost in full. The churches are very much in earnest but they fall short of having a definite policy and in their meetings are content with general resolutions in favor of peace, not greatly different from the one adopted by the women at Des Moines.[2] Of course, this is just about as helpful as a resolution would be approving the Lord's Prayer.

I have great faith that the World Court proposal of the President cannot be discussed without bringing up the whole subject and I am very sure that any serious examination of the subject will change the attitude of the people upon it.

I am sorry to say that I was much exhausted after each address but fortunately I so far have re-acted promptly and do not find myself any the worse for my activities and travel.

Perhaps you have noticed that I speak in Washington with Dr. Lowell on May 23rd at which time I shall call to pay my respects and I hope I may see you if only for a few minutes.

Believe me always

Sincerely your friend,   John H. Clarke

P.S. The above was dictated before Mr Bollings note came.[3] Yes, we are sending out a pamphlet with the covenant in full & a carefully prepared account of what the League has done. I will send a copy to Mr Stevenson.

TLS (WP, DLC).
[1] Bolling returned this enclosure and all others mentioned below in JRB to J. H. Clarke, May 10, 1923, CCL (WP, DLC).
[2] See J. H. Clarke to WW, April 11, 1923, n. 2.
[3] JRB to J. H. Clarke, May 7, 1923, CCL (WP, DLC).

To Ray Stannard Baker

My dear Baker,   [Washington] 9th May 1923

Your personal letter about the chemical patents rings true to what I know you to be, and I thank you with all my heart.

I believe the legal case of the Government to be sound, and it is too late now of course for me to withdraw my consent to the sale of these patents under the power of the Alien Property Custodian.

I am heartily obliged to you for the pains you have taken, and the work you have done, in regard to this patent matter, and assure you it will help to clarify the matter for me very much.

Please accept once more my very warm thanks and affectionate regard.

Faithfully and Affectionately Yours,   [Woodrow Wilson]

CCL (WP, DLC).

To John Hessin Clarke

My dear Friend,   Washington D C 10th May 1923

It is delightful to learn of the progress you are making in the serious work to which you are devoting yourself, and it is undoubtedly the result of your genuineness and your mastery of the subject. I am warmly obliged to you for writing me as you do.

I am greatly pleased to learn that your unusual efforts have not had a permanently serious affect upon your health, and I again beg that you will be careful not to tax your health too far. I can testify that the consequences might be serious.

I am glad I am to have a chance to see you when you come to Washington in the next fortnight, and beg that you will let me know beforehand where I can reach you here so that if possible an appointment can be arranged. I always have to clear a space in the routine of my convalescence.

I need hardly tell you again that with all my heart I wish you Godspeed in what you are doing.

With warmest appreciation and regard,

Faithfully Yours,   Woodrow Wilson

TLS (J. H. Clarke Papers, OCIW-Ar).

From Bernard Mannes Baruch

My dear Mr. Wilson: New York May 11, 1923.

This is just a line to let you know that I think of you often, and that I have not forgotten what you and Norman [Davis] and I talked about. There is a man available for the management, but if I remember correctly, you did not seem to care so much for him. The great difficulty lies in getting the right man, who, of course, must have correct views or able to be kept in line.

Have you determined just what part you yourself want to take in the matter—whether direct or indirect, known or unknown. I want you to know that my interest in it will be continuous and serious, and I will give my best efforts to it when and if you say the word.

Things are, I think, still working in the right direction and really need no stimulation.

It seems to me, now that France is in the Ruhr, she must say what her terms are. She cannot, in seeking security, ask anything that is not in line with the principles of the League and that will not require the League's activities.

I should have been down to see you before this were it not for the illness of my son.[1] A very bad case of jaundice forced him home from college. This disease keeps the sufferer in a very depressed frame of mind. It is such a pleasure to be with him, particularly if I can be helpful to him, as I seem to be in his present distress.

The venom and hatred of our opponents is becoming exhausted. In many instances it seems to have acted as a serum and have cured some of its own authors. It is rather interesting to note the attitude of the Hearst papers. They are opposed to the League and to the World Court; but they say if we are to enter Europe, it is much better to follow the Wilsonites who frankly, courageously, and honestly want to enter the League than to follow the other group who have deceived the American public as to their attitude on the League and who are now trying to fool the public. Taking it all in all, I think we have cause for encouragement.

So far as candidates are concerned, they are bobbing up like pieces of vegetables in boiling soup—now a carrot, now a potato, now a piece of meat, but very frequently onions.

As soon as my boy improves sufficiently, I am going to wire you to let me have the pleasure of seeing you again; not for anything in particular but just to see you.

With affectionate regards to yourself and Mrs. Wilson, in which my whole family join, I am, as ever,

Devotedly yours,   Bernard Baruch

TLS (WP, DLC).
[1] Bernard Mannes Baruch, Jr., Harvard 1923.

To Bernard Mannes Baruch

My dear Baruch,   Washington D C 12th May 1923

I am very much distressed to learn of the illness of your son, but am confident that with your companionship and help he will rapidly improve. I hope it may be very rapid. Please give him my sympathy and regards.

I have been waiting, as in most other things, to have a personal conference with you and Davis again before determining just what sort of part I ought to play in the enterprise we discussed. Your attitude as always is perfectly fine and gratifies me deeply.

I am happy to learn that there is a prospect of your coming down soon to see me. I hope it will be very soon though I must admit there is nothing new which needs immediate discussion.

Mrs. Wilson joins me in warmest regards to all the family and I am,

As always,   Your Devoted Friend,   Woodrow Wilson

TLS (B. M. Baruch Papers, NjP).

From William Gibbs McAdoo

Needles Calif 1923 May 12

I shall have pleasure of seeing you about sixteenth Sorry Nell could not come Love   W G McAdoo.

T telegram (WP, DLC).

From Ellery Sedgwick

Dear Mr. Wilson: Boston 16 May, 1923.

It is an immense satisfaction to me to find, on my return from a journey through South America, a kind note from you, together with an article which, brief as it is, will set the nation thinking. My associates tell me that the manuscript arrived too late to be given a leading place in the issue for July, and so I am planning to hold it until August, and will, of course, send you a proof.

Ever since your Mobile speech,[1] which I read with an enthusiasm which no previous public utterance had, I think, ever awakened, I have sought to guide the editorial conduct of The Atlantic by your utterances, and your letter, saying that you regard this magazine as the natural outlet for your occasional essays, delights me. I am glad to say that during these years the circulation of the magazine has increased more than tenfold; so your paper will be nationally read even before it is reprinted by the newspapers.

Of course, subsequent to its publication in The Atlantic, you are to make such use of the article as you may desire. Should you ever gather your new essays into a volume, you will, I hope, consider the possibilities of our Atlantic Press.

With many thanks, believe me,

Gratefully yours,   Ellery Sedgwick.[2]

TLS (WP, DLC).
   [1] It is printed at Oct. 27, 1913, Vol. 28.
   [2] Sedgwick enclosed a form letter dated May 17, 1923, saying that a check for $200 was enclosed for Wilson's article.

To Ellery Sedgwick

My dear Mr. Sedgwick,   Washington D C 18th May 1923

Your letter of May sixteenth has given me a great deal of pleasure, not only because you accept the essay for publication in the Atlantic but also and chiefly because you accept it with such gracious words of approval. It serves to increase my feeling that my natural association in a literary way is with the Atlantic.

With much appreciation,

Sincerely Yours,   Woodrow Wilson

TLS (MHi).

To Thomas Garrigue Masaryk

My dear Friend,   [Washington] 19th May 1923

Will you not allow me to express to you the genuine grief and very deep sympathy with which I learned of the death of Mrs. Masaryk.[1] My thoughts go out to you in profoundest sympathy, and I wish that there were some touch of friendship by which I could assist in cheering and steadying your spirits in the face of this tragedy.

I very often think of you and always, you may be sure, with the deepest and most genuine interest in your own personal welfare as well as in the welfare of your people.

Please accept assurances of my warm regard and always think of me as   Your Sincere Friend,   [Woodrow Wilson]

CCL (WP, DLC).
   [1] Charlotte Garrigue Masaryk, who had died on May 12, 1923.

From Edgar Odell Lovett

My dear President Wilson: Houston, Texas. 19 May 1923

I have just returned from a journey North on errands for the Rice Institute, and while in New York I had the privilege, in virtue of an invitation I had received before leaving home, of attending the meeting arranged for the installation of the trustees[1] of the permanent foundation which bears your honoured name. You have of course received full accounts of the proceedings, but I should like to tell you, if I may, how lasting an impression the occasion made upon me.

I had never before been enveloped in an atmosphere so charged with loyalty, sincerity, and determination. As an emotional experience, it literally wore me out. All the performances, whether impromptu or prepared, were notable. The presiding officer was altogether happy in his remarks, and I also liked what the newly elected president[2] of the board had to say. Miss Wooley's characterization was worthy of a masculine mind, and Mr. Holt's reminiscences of the early promotion of the enterprise were to me extremely interesting. There was in Professor Dodd's appeal the tempered judgment of the historian, and Mr. Morgenthau's prophecies came straight from the East, with all its fervour filtered through the idealism of the western mind. But Mr. Cleveland H. Dodge's performance was easily the best of all. His unstudied eloquence, and it was real eloquence, lifted us up to the very skyline of present and more distant horizons; and for all of us who heard him, the Tower of the Metropolis took not only the new meaning with which his moving words invested it, but also the personification of his own incomparable loyalty to friend and to principle.

I wish that you could have been there. Indeed I think you must have been there. In any event, to me you were there, and I saw you again as I had seen you on the steps of Nassau Hall, at the Jefferson Day dinner in New York, in the church and auditorium of Dallas, on the veranda at Sea Girt, and in the halls of the White House. And I left the meeting, even as I had always left your presence, in great exaltation of spirit.

Faithfully yours,   Edgar O. Lovett

TLS (WP, DLC).

[1] For their names, see n. 2 to the news report printed at Dec. 28, 1922. The installation of the fifteen "permanent" trustees was held at the Biltmore Hotel in New York on May 1, 1923. Franklin D. Roosevelt, chairman of the national committee, presided and, after the ceremony, turned over "more than" $800,000, which had been subscribed.

[2] Ernest Martin Hopkins, President of Dartmouth College.

To Andrew Bonar Law

[Washington] May 21 1923

Having myself been hampered by ill health I know how to sympathize with you[1] and I do with all my heart stop I trust that your health may steadily return to you   Woodrow Wilson

T telegram (WP, DLC).
[1] Bonar Law had just resigned as Prime Minister due to an inoperable malignancy in his throat. He died on October 30, 1923.

To Edgar Odell Lovett

My dear Lovett,   Washington D C 22nd May 1923

I am sincerely grateful to you for your letter of May nineteenth. It brings me the kind of cheer and the assurance of friendship which hearten me most, and I thank you with all my heart.

I hope that everything goes happily with you.

With warm regard,   Faithfully Yours,   Woodrow Wilson

TLS (E. O. Lovett Papers, TxHR).

From Andrew Bonar Law

London May 23 1923

I thank you for your kind message of sympathy
                                             Bonar Law

T telegram (WP, DLC).

To Jessie Woodrow Wilson Sayre

My dear Little Girlie,   [Washington] 26th May 1923

I was so much obliged to you for telling me about your plans, and am so glad you are going to California.[1] It will I am sure be a delightful experience. I am particularly delighted that you are to come by this way and let us see you. I shall look forward to it with impatient eagerness.

Mac was here the other day and says Nell and the children are models of healthfulness and strength; he gives a most delightful account of them all.

I hope that your little ones are equally as well and that I shall at last have a glimpse of them when you come this way.

I hope that your Siam plan is not entirely abandoned as it would constitute a wonderful experience for Frank.

We are getting along about as usual, and unite in warmest love to you all.   Your devoted,   [Father]

CCL (WC, NjP).
  [1] Jessie's letter, to which Wilson's was a reply, is missing.

Two Letters from Glenn Frank[1]

My dear Mr. Wilson,   New York 26 May 1923

By the gracious courtesy of Miss Bones,[2] I am sending you this note. I shall be in Washington Tuesday, May 29, to deliver the commencement address at The American University. I speak at 2:30 P.M. I hope your day may not be so full but that you can allow me a few moments in which to pay my respects.[3]

I have been holding my breath—hoping against hope that you would let me have your ringing challenge on "The Road Away from Revolution" for The Century.

Respectfully,   Glenn Frank

  [1] Publicist, writer, and advocate of the League of Nations; at this time editor of *The Century Magazine*; President of the University of Wisconsin, 1925-1937.
  [2] That is, Helen Woodrow Bones.
  [3] Wilson was not able to receive him on this day. See JRB to G. Frank, May 28, 1923, CCL (WP, DLC).

My dear Mr. Wilson,   Washington 29 May 1923

As I said in an earlier note, I have been hoping against hope that I might be fortunate enough to have the honor of giving your challenging paper on "The Road Away from Revolution" to the American people through the Century Magazine.

It keys in so admirably with the spirit I have tried to make the Century express. I wonder whether, by any chance, you saw my editorial on "The Lost Spirituality of American Politics"[1] which was my comment on the opening days of the Harding administration? It was my inadequate attempt to pay tribute to the high prophetic quality of your political ministry by which you actually made politics seem to us the supreme spiritual adventure of the race.

I do hope you have not given your paper to any other magazine. When Mr. Creel and I spoke of it my budget was fearfully cramped. Since then I have economized here and there in the hope that you might let me have the paper, despite the inadequate honorarium of $1000 I am able to provide.

I should like to print it in the front of the magazine in special type as a challenge to the American people to find their souls and to pull out of the moral slump into which they allowed partisanship and reaction to plunge them. Of course, I should put it, on the day of my publication, at the disposal of the whole American press, as a national service. It is the first great note that may lead us back from our Great Apostasy.

With expressions of high regard, I am,

Respectfully,   Glenn Frank

ALS (WP, DLC).
¹ Glenn Frank, "The Tide of Affairs: The Lost Spirituality of American Politics . . . ,"
The Century Magazine, CII (May 1921), 153-55. Among other things, Frank wrote:
"Woodrow Wilson's foreign policies now lie in ruins, a dismantled house of cards, but the historian of the future will look back upon the period from 1916 to 1919 as a time when an American President turned the sinister game of diplomacy into a quest for the Holy Grail. For a few fleeting months the moral leadership of world affairs rested in Washington. World politics was a religion, and Woodrow Wilson was its prophet."

Richard John Walsh to Edith Bolling Galt Wilson

My dear Mrs. Wilson: New York May 29, 1923.

Just before George Creel left for the Pacific Coast, he told me that he had returned to you the manuscript which he had shown me and that you had not decided just what to do with it. He suggested that, if I did not hear from you soon, I might write to you again and confirm what I had said to him. This was that I should be very proud to print the article in Collier's and should take the greatest pains to handle it with dignity and force, and that my original offer of $2000 for it still stands. My recollection of the article is that it was about 1000 words and this price, therefore, is about $2.00 a word, which is twenty times our usual rate and ten times what we have paid any other author during my term of editorship. I state these figures merely to indicate that I have a high appreciation of the value of the article.

I earnestly hope that your decision will be to permit its publication in Collier's where it will not only reach thoughtful readers in more than a million homes, but will attract wide attention in the newspapers, which are in the habit of following closely and commenting promptly on material which appears in Collier's.

In any event, I hope you will give Mr. Wilson assurances of my great respect and best wishes.

Sincerely yours,   Richard J. Walsh

TLS (WP, DLC).

To Glenn Frank

My dear Mr. Frank, [Washington] 30th May 1923

I am both gratified and honoured by your note of May twenty-ninth, and I hasten to assure you that the Century Magazine would have seemed to me an entirely appropriate medium for my little essay, "The Road Away from Revolution," which I recently surprised myself by writing.

When I was just a literary man it was my habit to send my essays to the Atlantic Monthly, and when I finished this essay I was moved by some natural impulse, largely sentimental, to resume my old connection. I therefore gave it to Mr. Sedgwick who will print it in the August number of the magazine.

I did not have the good fortune to see the editorial of which you speak, and will be very much indebted to you if you will send me a copy.

I greatly value your comradeship and help in an effort to bring the people back to their elevated view of affairs which I believe is natural to them.

Allow me once again to thank you for your note of yesterday and say how honoured I feel by your confidence.

I hope you had an interesting time at the American University, and that when you come to Washington again I shall be able to enjoy an interview with you from which I am sure I shall derive not a little inspiration.

With warmest appreciation and regard,
Faithfully Yours, [Woodrow Wilson]

CCL (WP, DLC).

John Randolph Bolling to Richard John Walsh

My dear Mr. Walsh: [Washington] 31st May 1923

Mr. Wilson asks me to reply to your letter of 29th May and say that—following a custom of many years—he had arranged for publication of his article in The Atlantic Monthly before the receipt of your communication under reply.

Mr. Wilson desires me to express his warm appreciation of the very friendly spirit of your letter, and convey to you his greetings and best wishes.

Cordially yours, [John Randolph Bolling]

CCL (WP, DLC).

To James Henry Taylor[1]

My dear Friend,   Washington D C 1st June 1923

The beautiful roses were a most welcome and acceptable gift, and it was very gracious of you to send them in the name of the Church. I am greatly cheered and benefited by such evidences of your friendship and am correspondingly grateful to you.

I sometimes get discouraged at the exceedingly slow progress of my recovery, but I am ashamed of myself when I do because God has been so manifestly merciful to me, and I ought to feel much profound gratitude. I believe that it will all turn out well, and that whether well or ill it will turn out right.

With renewed thanks for your generous friendship,

Gratefully Yours,   Woodrow Wilson

TLS (WP, DLC).
[1] Pastor of Central Presbyterian Church of Washington, of which Wilson was a member.

John Randolph Bolling to Ellery Sedgwick

My dear Mr. Sedgwick: [Washington] 3rd June 1923

With Mrs. Wilson's permission, I am writing to know if you would be interested in publishing in book form Mr. Wilson's essay, "The Road Away from Revolution"?

My thought is that if you would write Mr. Wilson, suggesting that you would like to handle this matter on a satisfactory royalty basis for him, that it would secure you the publication of the essay.

If I may be pardoned the suggestion; it seems to me that the essay could be brought out in a book, say about 3 x 5 inches (type size page)—set in a large face of type, with wide margins, to make the pages run about 75 words each. The binding to be of dark material, and the book made up to retail at say 50 Cents.

Should you be in a position to take this matter up—and will write Mr. Wilson a strong letter outlining the entire proposition—I believe it will secure the publication of the book for you. I am sure you feel, as both Mrs. Wilson and I do, that the book should be brought out immediately following publication of the essay in The Atlantic.

You are no doubt familiar with Mr. Wilson's "When a Man Comes To Himself"[1]—and I am sure that the publication of the present essay, in some such similar form, would meet with ready sale to those who will wish to keep the essay in permanent book form.

With high regard,

Cordially yours,   [John Randolph Bolling]

CCL (WP, DLC).
¹ It is printed at Nov. 1, 1899, Vol. 11. Harper & Brothers published this essay in book form in 1915.

From Ellery Sedgwick

Dear Mr. Wilson: Boston 5 June, 1923.

I have just received from your secretary, Mr. Bolling, a friendly note, in which he suggests the possibility of our issuing your essay between boards at the time of its appearance in the magazine, thus rendering it immediately available in permanent form. I welcome the idea, and am writing to ask if you will not allow The Atlantic Monthly Press to carry it out.

True, the essay is short—scarcely over a thousand words—but it is not less effective for that, and, issued in a very small volume, with a page not much more than 3 x 5 inches, it is mechanically practicable. I propose that the price of this book be fifty cents, that it be dignified in format, and that it run, if possible to twenty-four pages.

A small, inexpensive volume is not apt to bring large returns, but our interest is in the book itself, and I shall be glad to have you name such royalty arrangement as may seem to you proper.

I need not add that, if you grant this permission, we shall use our very best efforts to promote the distribution and sale of this book, and, if you can conveniently let us know your wishes soon, it will be possible for us to have it ready for distribution by the 1st of August, when the magazine will carry your message through the country.   Yours very sincerely,   Ellery Sedgwick.

TLS (WP, DLC).

From Louis Seibold¹

My dear Boss: New York June 6, 1923.

In times of perplexity I naturally turn to you for guidance, even though professional exigencies frequently compel the subordination of personal ambitions to the sterner ones of professional obligation.

My perplexity is this: dear old Frank Cobb has been working too hard and is not in good physical shape. Like most of us, he is disregarding the inexorable rules of nature, and sacrificing, I fear, too much to professional responsibilities. I have been greatly alarmed about him, and have been urging him to go out to grass for a time, but he (also like most of us) is stubborn and hesitant. I think if you could find time to drop him a note and tell him he *must* look out for himself it would have more weight with him than any other influence that could be brought to bear, as it would with me.

I have thought of imposing upon your good nature by dropping you a line once in a while regarding information which might be of interest to you, but hesitated because of my appreciation of the exactions on your time and my disinclination to intrude on your well earned privacy. I want you to always know that if I can ever serve you, in any field of personal or professional adventure, I will always be ready to obey a summons or act on any suggestion that you may be good enough to make.

I was informed last night that you had written an article for a magazine, touching on an important subject, and that you had further addressed a letter to the Democratic National Committee, wherein you defined the issues which confront that party. I should, of course, value the privilege of presenting them in as sympathetic and understanding a way as falls within my humble ability and real desires.

I recently made a tour of the country, resulting in the conviction that the utmost confusion prevails in all parties, regular as also in such independent groups as the Socialists, the Non-Partisan League, and other independent branches, which seem to have lost the power to attract or at least hold on to their adherents—or victims.

The paramount impression that I gained in this survey was (1) that it is to you that the largest number of Democrats of the country will listen, and for whose views they will show respect, (2) that unless and until the Democratic party stops wool gathering and chasing rainbows inaccurately painted by detached and not efficiently organized groups such as affected the coalition of hatreds three years ago, the Republican party, with rather less to offer, will win through the faults of the opposition.

I know I am presuming a good deal to even attempt to define to you the situation as I see it, but if there is any particular phase of the matter on which you desire information I will at least be accurate. My affectionate regards to Mrs. Wilson and yourself. I am, with great respect,   Louis Seibold

TLS (WP, DLC).
¹ He was now an editorial writer for the *New York Herald*.

From Bernard Mannes Baruch

My dear Mr. Wilson: New York June 6, 1923.

Yesterday I had a call from Margaret, and we discussed the advisability of her selling bonds, which I approved provided she associated herself with a first-class house. This seems to be the same advice that was given by some one with whom she had previously consulted.

In the course of the conversation she told me of an offer she had from an advertising agency.[1] I believe her success in that business would be quicker and perhaps a bit surer. She told me, however, that you were adverse to her entering the advertising business. While to some extent I share your feeling, at the same time it is a perfectly legitimate business and opens a very wide field. Magazines and newspapers would be unable to live without advertising. Nobody with a good article to sell can do it without advertising. Pursuant to your request that I advise with Margaret, I am going to ask you to suspend judgment as to her entrance into the advertising business until we have had a talk. I shall investigate concerns of that kind with which she could affiliate. I do not believe her difficulties or possibilities for mistake would be greater in the advertising than in the bond business, and I am inclined to think her chances for financial success are greater in the advertising field. But more of this when I see you.

I am glad to say that my son returned to college several days ago. He found that he will have only one more final examination to take, so he is now home with me again, almost fully restored to health. I am expecting a lull in my activities here, and want to go down and have the privilege of seeing you, but I shall ask you in advance over the telephone whether that will be possible.

The sale of the GLOBE here to Munsey,[2] with the consequent merging of it with the SUN, has created a great deal of confusion in journalism here. I was hopeful that out of it we might be able to secure the editor for the enterprise we have discussed; but I regret to say that nothing has come from this that will be helpful to us.

Last Sunday night, with my family, I attended the Lambs "Gambol."[3] At the end of his monologue, J. C. Nugent[4] asked the audience to suggest several subjects for him to discuss in the remaining few minutes of his time. A number of subjects were tendered, all concerning "booze," until one man in the rear of the audience shouted out, "Woodrow Wilson."

So Nugent took for his text Woodrow Wilson. He said something like this: that as one travels away over the plain from a certain range of great mountains, the lesser ones disappear, until they mingle with and are lost in the blue; but Mount Shasta does not merge, but continues to stand out and maintain its place in the vision of the traveler as far as the plain extends. He compared the lesser mountains to little people and their criticisms, which soon are forgotten and vanish; and he likened Mount Shasta to the ideal that you placed before humanity, which will never disappear or merge into the rest of human effort. These are not his exact words, but I maintain his figure of speech.

When he had finished the audience broke out in long and up-roarious applause, which lasted three or four minutes, and the whole performance temporarily had to be suspended.

I neglected to say that one of the things that keeps me here is a subpoena to appear as a witness in one of the suits growing out of my activities as Chairman of the War Industries Board. I am trying to get free so that I can come to Washington at the end of this week, because I have already delayed too long my visit to you. I haven't anything in particular to say, but I should just like to see you and talk with you. As I said before, I shall telephone you in advance as soon as I have wriggled free of my engagements.

With affectionate regards to Mrs. Wilson and you, I am, as ever,

Yours,   [B. M. Baruch]

TL (WP, DLC).

¹ The Biow Co. of New York, for whom she soon went to work.
² Frank Andrew Munsey, owner and publisher of *Munsey's Magazine*.
³ The Lambs, a New York club of actors and other individuals connected with or in-terested in the theater, founded in 1874. The organization was famous for its "Gam-bols": skits on current plays. Its clubhouse, located at 130 West 44th Street, included a complete theater. There is an account of this "Spring Gambol" in the *New York Times*, June 4, 1923.
⁴ John Charles Nugent, actor and playwright of New York.

To Ellery Sedgwick

My dear Mr. Sedgwick,   Washington D C 7th June 1923

I am complimented and pleased that the Atlantic Monthly Press should propose to issue my little essay separately, as a tiny book, and will be glad to have them do so.

I hesitate to take advantage of your kind suggestion that I name the royalty terms because, not knowing the expense to the publish-ing house of such a volume, I do not know what terms would be just and fair. I should think a half and half division of the profits, if there should be any, would be the outside of what I should pro-pose. I am perfectly willing to leave the determination of this mat-ter in your hands, knowing you will be fair and generous.

I am glad to know you feel the little essay is worthy of special attention.

Cordially and Sincerely Yours,   Woodrow Wilson

TLS (MHi).

A News Report

[June 10, 1923]

WILSON, STRONGER PHYSICALLY, TURNING AGAIN TO POLITICS

By R. V. Oulahan.[1]

In Washington every Saturday evening shortly before 11 o'clock a Lieutenant of Police and a squad of patrolmen march into G Street, between Fourteenth and Fifteenth Streets, and take station in any alley leading to the stage entrance of a vaudeville theatre, whose front faces the gloomy but impressive east facade of the Treasury Department Building.

Groups of people begin to gather, and soon a good-sized crowd is assembled, the eyes of all turned alleyward. There is nothing in the alley to attract attention save a large limousine, standing close to the stage entrance. Passing strangers, unfamiliar with the conventional Saturday night ceremonial about to be enacted, pause curiously.

As the exits of the theatre open for the audience to pass out the Lieutenant of Police and his men become active. Some of them rush to the G Street roadway and proceed to divert traffic into Fourteenth Street and Fifteenth Street. Others clear the alley of spectators and see that space is kept where the alley crosses the sidewalk.

Through the open doors of the theatre comes the sound of vigorous handclapping. Members of the audience pass hurriedly to the street and add themselves to the throng lined up along the outer edges of the alley. Others of the audience who have left the theatre by the main entrance in Fifteenth Street scamper around the corner of the theatre building into G Street and press eagerly against the fringes of the crowd.

There is more hand-clapping heard as a little party comes out of the stage entrance. Foremost among them is a man in evening clothes who moves slowly and with obvious difficulty. He walks with a limp. Holding him on one side is a sturdy negro, while another attendant grasps his other arm. Usually in the group behind him are two or three ladies and a man or two who watch carefully and solicitously as the attendants help the man in evening clothes into the waiting motor car.

Then more hand-clapping, this time from the crowd around the alley's entrance. As the man in evening clothes settles himself in the seat of the motor car all appearance of feebleness vanishes. He

[1] Richard Victor Oulahan, Wilson's old friend, chief Washington correspondent of the *New York Times* since 1912.

smiles broadly, touches his hat, waves his hand gayly. One of the ladies, seating herself beside him, smiles gratefully on those who applaud. As the motor car draws slowly out of the alley the other people gathered there give a loud cheer. The man waves his hand again, his smile more beaming. As the car turns into G Street and speeds away the crowd scatters, and G Street settles for another week into its customary prosaic existence.

The man in whose honor this regular weekly demonstration is given is Woodrow Wilson. The demonstration is interesting not only in its visible and vocal aspect, but in its psychological phase. It marks a radical reaction from a few years ago, for Woodrow Wilson was not always popular with Washingtonians. He had to come [sic] to live in the capital as President with a mind suspicious of its spiritual atmosphere, and had shown this suspicion plainly in public utterances and in acts which had been resented by a considerable part of the resident population.

For instance, his virtual acceptance of the truth of an allegation that the Municipal Government was dominated by a triumvirate of selfish business interests, meaning a group of local bankers. He had declined to sanction the traditional inaugural ball in honor of a new President,[2] and the inference of his course was that he looked upon that function as a piece of local graft. And, again, his refusal to accept honorary membership in a fashionable country club,[3] customarily conferred on his predecessors in the Presidential office and accepted by them.

Business Washington had a period of hard times in the Wilson Administration, and many accused the President of responsibility for it by his attitude toward the city. Hand-clapping and cheers were scanty in those days when the President faced a gathering of Washingtonians.

The explanations offered of the reaction are various: Personal sympathy for Mr. Wilson in his ill health, a latent appreciation of his high-minded adherence to idealistic principles, the feeling that he is a disabled soldier of the World War, the passing of bitterness with his relinquishment of office. These are the principal explanatory suggestions offered. Another, less charitably meant, is that the enthusiastic crowds which gather outside the vaudeville theatre on Saturday nights are composed of visitors to Washington from various parts of the country who are actuated by curiosity in the desire to see the former President—which hypothesis, when scrutinized carefully, with the hand-clapping and cheering not overlooked, is capable of the deduction that Wilson is popular with the country, whatever Washington may think of him.

[2] About this incident, see the news report printed at Jan. 17, 1913, Vol. 27.
[3] Wilson had refused membership in the Chevy Chase Country Club.

But all these offered explanations, whether they explain or fail to explain, do not dim or confuse the outstanding fact that Mr. Wilson is a foremost figure in the capital of the nation, a dramatic personality in whom there is intense interest. He lives in virtual retirement, seeking no opportunity to keep himself before the public. Yet whenever some utterance of his, contained in a letter to an inquiring fellow-citizen, finds its way into the newspapers through the medium of his correspondent, widespread discussion is aroused. The character of comment is such that Wilson is made to appear as a living, forceful power to be reckoned with, and not as a stricken man relegated to political and personal oblivion by current indifference to his views on public questions and the feeling that, mentally and physically, his day is done.

It is somewhat difficult to make one visualize his physical state. Most who see him assisted from the theatre to his motor car carry away the impression that he is a hopeless cripple. What they do not realize is that there has been an extraordinary bodily improvement since that time, nearly four years ago, when he suffered a devastating stroke and for weeks lay at the point of death and for months was in a condition that hovered between the precarious and the serious.

From helpless invalidism Mr. Wilson has come back gradually, if very slowly, to the point where his crippled arm and hand are able to resume some of their normal functions, and his powers of locomotion are improved to a degree that must be considered remarkable by comparison with his complete helplessness in the early stages of his affliction.

His painful, shuffling gait has disappeared. While he limps, close observation shows that he lifts his feet and does not drag them. Customarily he uses a cane but can walk without it. He can enter or leave his motor car without assistance and has done so, but for caution's sake he is willing to permit attendants to assist him. He has good color, his eyes are clear, his voice is strong, his cheeks are filled out, and he has lost that emaciated appearance of face and body which shocked those who saw him on his first outings after his long siege of confinement to the White House.

Mentally, from all accounts, he is the Woodrow Wilson of the stirring days prior to September, 1919. The burden of labor which is the portion of a President of the United States has been lifted from his shoulders, but the ability to work is there. If anything, his lack of constant mental occupation and pressing responsibility is a detriment rather than a help in his upbuilding. This lack is compensated for somewhat by the interest he takes in public questions, which necessitates a close reading of the newspapers.

In one respect his returned mental and physical capacity is dem-

onstrated in full measure by his punctilious regard for his episto-
lary correspondence. Many of the letters he receives are answered
by him personally, the responses, as a rule, being dictated to his
secretary. Lately so marked is the improvement in his crippled arm
that he is credited with again using the typewriting machine upon
which he personally wrote many important public papers when he
was President.

Even obscure persons, unknown to him, whose communications
show lack of education, but whose sentiments of loyalty to and admiration for the stricken man are not lost in clumsy literary construction, receive direct responses from Mr. Wilson. The skill of
diction, with that ability to intrigue the popular imagination which
made his World War utterances so stimulating to patriotic endeavor in the allied countries and were effective anti-German propaganda in enemy territory, is still to be observed, apparently un-
impaired, in his brief letters on public affairs which have been
given to the press by the recipients.

Strangers in Washington show widespread interest in the Wilsonian personality by inquiry as to his physical condition. Those
who care to do so may satisfy this interest in part by watching for
the opportunity of seeing Mr. Wilson take his regular afternoon
motor ride. Always he is accompanied by Mrs. Wilson and usually
by some member of her family, or a close friend of the ex-President
in addition. There is testimony that on these occasions he is a
lively, even vivacious, conversationalist. His stories, largely anec-
dotal, are drawn from what seems to be an inexhaustible store.
Something seen along the way will suggest a humorous experience of his own or of one of his acquaintance. Nowadays, there is
little to denote care, disappointment or physical distress in the
bearing of Mr. Wilson as he takes his daily airing.

What manner of life does this man lead? Where does he go?
Who visits him? What are his diversions? These are questions that
the stranger in the capital asks of the resident Washingtonian.

Little of detail is forthcoming in the answers. The life of the Wilson household is not open to the public view. He and the other
members of that household feel that, as he is no longer in official
life, it is his and their privilege to live as quietly and unostenta-
tiously as they please. Even in the White House days a sharp line
was drawn between the President as the head of the Government
and as a citizen. The remoteness of the White House family in its
social aspect was sometimes criticised, but Mr. Wilson—who must
have known of it, for a President hears pretty much of everything
that is being said of him, even privately—was affected not at all.

The house in which he lives may be described as both handsome
and unpretentious. It is a large house, but situated in a street of

large houses and fairly inconspicuous by comparison with its neighbors. The street itself is of the kind usually described as "quiet." The locality saw its beginnings as a fashionable neighborhood only a short time before Mr. Wilson came to Washington to be President, and its vacant spaces have filled slowly in the process of urban expansion. Its front is of plain red brick, in the modern adaptation of the town Colonial style, and there is a central entrance. There is a spacious side yard, and an attractive rear garden which lends itself to terracing by a natural slope.

This house, now one of the sights which rubber-neck wagon guides point out to their patrons, has been the scene of several demonstrations in honor of its occupants. Mr. Wilson seldom makes an appearance on the occasion of a public ceremonial away from his home. Admirers have gone in procession to his residence to acclaim him and have been rewarded by a sight of him in the front doorway or at a window. When the delegates of the Pan-American Conference of women came in a body from Baltimore last year and marched to the former President's house,[4] he responded to their greetings by reciting his favorite limerick, the authorship of which is unknown, but has been erroneously attributed to Richard Burton:

> In good looks I am not a star.
> There are others more lovely by far.
> But my face—I don't mind it,
> Because I'm behind it—
> It's the people in front that I jar.

Few heard the words, but all cheered.

There have been rumors that Mr. Wilson is to deliver a public address somewhere, but he has not translated the rumors into fact. His only appearances at public ceremonials since he was stricken in September, 1919, have been in his ride from the White House to the Capitol with Mr. Harding on the latter's inaugural day, and when he followed, in his motor car, the body of the Unknown Warrior for part of its processional progress from the Capitol to Arlington National Cemetery.

As befitting the solemnity of the occasion, the crowds along the route of that impressive parade were quiet and reverent as the flag-draped casket passed by on an artillery caisson. But the sight of Woodrow Wilson was too much for pent-up patriotism and his progress was a continuous ovation. And that vast throng was composed mainly of Washingtonians.

Periodically Washington is startled by a report that Mr. Wilson is

---

[4] About this incident, see the news report printed at April 28, 1922.

dead. With whom these baseless rumors originate is a mystery. One of the latest came early in the evening from a suburb of the capital. It brought many inquiries to newspaper offices. Only with the greatest difficulty were Washington correspondents able to obtain evidence of its untruth, and this by roundabout methods which consumed much time. There is a telephone in the Wilson home, but it is unlisted. That anxious night made Washington newspaper men realize how isolated they were from communication with the Wilson household.

When the law firm of Wilson & Colby maintained an office in Washington the method of communication with the Wilson residence was through that office, and then only in ordinary business hours. The process was to request the office of Wilson & Colby to convey a message to Mr. Wilson's house. If there was an answer it was telephoned direct to the person making the inquiry. If no answer came it was useless to renew the effort.

With the former President's approach to normalcy in health, the daily family life in the Colonial-type residence in S Street is much the same as it was in the White House when the Wilson family resided there. Mr. Wilson is an early riser. He is up at 7. He bathes and has breakfast and then undergoes a massage treatment which is gradually making headway against the lameness in his arm and leg. The massage serves, too, to take the place of physical exercise. After that he reads newspapers and personally attacks the batch of mail, always heavy, which has been delivered that morning. Many of his answers are dictated to his secretary. Other responses the secretary prepares.

After luncheon Mr. Wilson goes for his daily motor ride, accompanied by Mrs. Wilson. Sometimes a close friend or two will be with them. There may be visitors when the ride is over. Visitors have also been at the Wilson home in the morning and occasionally these take luncheon with the former President and his wife. After dinner Mr. Wilson reads or is read to by Mrs. Wilson, just as in the old days at the White House. By 10 o clock he is ready for bed.

The visitors are close personal or political friends. Members of the Wilson Cabinet who do not live in Washington drop in on their former chief when they are in the capital. Others of them who live here—Senator Carter Glass, A. Mitchell Palmer and Thomas W. Gregory—call more frequently. Senator Robinson of Arkansas, the Democratic leader of the Senate, sees Mr. Wilson occasionally. So do Representative Cordell Hull, Chairman of the Democratic National Committee, and Senator Swanson of Virginia. Mr. and Mrs. Charles Dana Gibson are welcome visitors.

The former President is very fond of some of the men who were associated with him in Washington during American participation in the World War or at Paris while the Peace Conference was on. They find him always glad to see them and to chat over strenuous and bygone days. In this list are Bernard M. Baruch, Norman H. Davis and Henry Morgenthau of New York and Charles R. Crane of Chicago. When Franklin D. Roosevelt was in Washington recently he received a cordial greeting from Mr. Wilson. Distinguished foreigners passing through Washington leave cards at the Wilson residence or pay their respects personally. Among the latest of these received by Mr. Wilson was Lord Robert Cecil, whom he had known during the Peace Conference.

With these callers Mr. Wilson talks politics and public tendencies and from them he learns the latest political news. His callers have noted that he is meticulously careful to avoid saying anything that might appear to be critical of President Harding personally or of the honesty of his motives. He does not hesitate, it is said, to criticise sometimes the judgment of the powers-that-be in Washington, but his remarks do not question his successor's good faith. It is reported that he frequently counters criticism leveled at present public officers by suggesting that it is not well to condemn without an understanding of all the facts upon which these officers act—facts not available to outsiders. His course in this respect suggests a mellow charity born of experience and current ability to take a detached view.

Rumors circulate in Washington that Mr. Wilson is keenly interested in the contest over the Democratic Presidential nomination of 1924. To those best qualified to know the facts these rumors are groundless. There is no evidence to afford credence for any statement that he has committed himself to any aspirant for the party's greatest prize, even his son-in-law, William G. McAdoo.

His conversation on politics shows that he is interested in the principles upon which his party will go before the country next year and not in the man who will lead the party on those principles. The impression obtained by some of his visitors is that he believes if the platform is right there will be no trouble in finding a man to fit its declarations. The League of Nations is naturally accepted as the thing nearest his heart as a party platform plank. That Mr. Wilson expects to take an active part in offering advice concerning the framing of the Democratic platform of 1924 is evident from his attitude.

When Mr. Wilson takes his afternoon motor ride in an open car and attends the Saturday night performance at the vaudeville theatre he is closely observed by spectators. The most striking thing in his appearance to those who remember him in the early days of his convalescence when the afternoon airings were initiated, is that he has overcome the emaciated and drawn appearance of that time. Not only that, but it is obvious to many whose memories are retentive of the Woodrow Wilson prior to his illness that he is even heavier in weight than he was then. As far as the eye is able to judge, he is fifteen or twenty pounds above his normal weight of the days of his strength and vigor.

In the years of his illness he has never traveled on a railroad train. His last railroad journey ended when he returned to Washington a sick man from his country-wide speech-making effort to arouse popular sentiment in behalf of American participation in the League of Nations. Rumors are recurrent that he is to visit this place or that remote from Washington. The fact appears to be that he is better satisfied and more comfortable in his Washington home, even in the heat of Summer, than he would be elsewhere.

It has become apparent that Mr. Wilson does not require constant medical attention, although his friend and physician, Rear Admiral Cary T. Grayson, is a frequent caller at the Wilson residence and is credited with keeping in touch with his patient practically every day. There is no longer a trained nurse in the Wilson household in the daytime. A nurse is there at night, but her presence is attributed to caution rather than to absolute necessity.

He has few excitements. The current of his life flows easily and serenely. Once in a while, something unusual and unexpected occurs that furnishes an intensive diversion, but it is always pleasing and thereby helpful. One Saturday night in the vaudeville theatre when the former President was present, an elderly actor came before the footlights and addressed the audience. What he said made a diversion of the character noted. He spoke somewhat as follows:

"My only boy was killed in the war, and not in words can I express how much I miss him. Today I visited the Walter Reed Army Hospital, and I saw there what were literally pieces of still living men. And when I looked upon this horrible result of war I was glad my boy was not among these poor victims but was sleeping peacefully in France. But one of the greatest casualties this war has produced is the distinguished man who is in this audience tonight."

It was well meant. It came from the heart. Many in the audience were in tears. Then, suddenly, a new spirit came upon them. Men and women rose and, turning toward the rear seat where the former President sat, began to cheer. Some leaped on the chairs, waving handkerchiefs and joining in the cheering. A girl performer walked down from the stage and handed Mr. Wilson a bunch of flowers. There was more cheering. The whole house was in an uproar.

The spontaneity of the proceeding must have reminded the former President of that great demonstration in his honor in Milan, when thousands of Italians broke through thick lines of soldiers into the Piazza del Duomo and, massing under the balcony of the Palazzo Reale, where the then President stood, acclaimed him as "god of peace." The demonstration in the Washington theatre was on a smaller scale, but it carried the suggestion of what had occurred on that rainy January Sunday in the Italian city.

When Lord Robert Cecil arrived in New York, not long ago, the newspapers noted that Mrs. Wilson was in the city. One of her reasons for this trip from Washington was to hear the ardent advocate of the League of Nations tell the story of the League, an experience not denied her husband, for by means of a radio telephone installed at his home, he was able to listen in while the British statesman was delivering his address more than 200 miles away. What probably was overlooked at the time was that this was the first extended separation of Mr. and Mrs. Wilson since he was stricken in September, 1919. She had made occasional shopping excursions to near-by Baltimore, but these kept her from Washington for a portion of the day only. On her visit to New York Mrs. Wilson left Washington one morning and was back in the capital the next evening. That day and a half marked the longest period she had been away from her husband in more than three years.

This devotion of Mrs. Wilson to her husband has produced a profound impression in Washington, not excepting that portion of the city's population which has a lively memory of the attitude the then President of the United States adopted toward the capital when he first came to reside there. It has made her an inspiring and heroic figure.

None of the trained nurses who attended him in the critical and serious periods of his illness worked harder than she to keep life in his stricken body. She is always near him now as she was in those days of danger. Day in and day out, morning and night, through the intervening years, Mrs. Wilson has been her husband's constant attendant.

This devotion has had a large share in winning the battle for the restoration of the former President to his present physical condition, more satisfactory and encouraging than there was reason to hope for until comparatively recently.

Printed in the *New York Times*, June 10, 1923.

To Louis Seibold

My dear Seibold,   [Washington] 10th June 1923

Thank you sincerely for your letter of June sixth, and please never hesitate to write to me. Your letters are always welcome and stimulating and I get more from your analyses of situations than from those of anybody else.

It is true that I have written an essay. It is entitled "The Road Away From Revolution" and is to appear in the August number of the Atlantic Monthly and at about the same time from the Atlantic Monthly Press as a tiny booklet.

But I have not written a letter to the Democratic National Committee of the sort you have heard of, and of course would not think of volunteering to do so.

My whole conviction is that the party will steady down,—and is indeed already steadying down,—in time to make effective use of its numbers next year.

I hope that they are giving you work which affords you some satisfaction.

Mrs. Wilson joins me in very warm regard, and you may be sure that we always think of you as a valued and delightful friend upon whom we can always count for any reasonable service. And that is a great consolation, I can tell you.

With affectionate regard,

Faithfully Yours,   [Woodrow Wilson]

P. S. I shall take real pleasure in writing to Cobb as you suggest.

CCL (WP, DLC).

To Frank Irving Cobb

My dear Cobb,   Washington D C 10th June 1923

I hear through reliable sources that you are sadly overworking yourself, and because the thing is intrinsically probable I must feign [fain] believe it. I write therefore to beg that you will pull up and take the necessary rest and recreation to get yourself back into form, and I beg this not only in my own name as your sincere and warm friend but also for the sake of the great public causes which you so admirably serve from day to day in your editorial work.

Having made the mistake myself of going too far and too fast, I feel that I can advise with some authority in such a matter, and I sincerely hope that you will heed it. Personally I shall count upon you to do so.

Mrs. Wilson joins me in warm regard, and I am always,
With affectionate regard,
                    Faithfully Yours,   Woodrow Wilson

TLS (IEN).

To Bernard Mannes Baruch

My dear Baruch,   [Washington] 10th June 1923

Enclosed you will find the copy which I promised you yesterday in which Justice Brandeis has formulated the idea suggested by Cobb.[1] It seems to me excellently stated and so simple that the man in the street will get the idea at once and be pleased. I hope that you will like it as much as I do.

It was very delightful to see you on yesterday and I shall count upon the pleasure of seeing you again before you sail,—at which time we can have a final round up of our ideas concerning things we are most interested in.

Mrs. Wilson joins me in messages of warmest regard and affectionate salutation to you and all of yours.
                    Affectionately Yours,   [Woodrow Wilson]

CCL (WP, DLC).
    [1] See the Enclosure printed with LDB to WW, April 15, 1923.

From Frank Irving Cobb

Dear Mr. Wilson: New York June 13th, 1923.

I am touched more than I can tell you by your letter. I shall follow your advice and shall leave tomorrow for Maine to fish for a month. Fishing seems to do me more good than anything else.

The specialists have finally hunted down my trouble and find that it comes from infected teeth, which have been poisoning me— a sort of private republican national committee. The doctors tell me, however, that what I need most is rest and that with the source of the poison gone, I ought to be all right in a few months.

I hope in turn that you will have a comfortable and pleasant summer.

Please give my sincerest regards to Mrs. Wilson and thank her for her kind words, and as for you it is unnecessary to tell you again the place you hold in my affection and in my respect.
                    As ever yours,   Frank I Cobb.

TLS (WP, DLC).

To Margaret Woodrow Wilson

My darling Little Girl,   [Washington] 14th June 1923

The result of my recent conversation with Mr. Baruch is that I am willing that you should undertake the business engagement similar to that which Miss McLeod[1] has been working under, and that on the whole that would be preferable to the alternative business which we had discussed and about which I had advised you to talk with Mr. Sheldon.[2]

Before you make any contract, it is important that you show it to Mr. Baruch and get the approval of his judgment concerning it.

I write in haste so as not to keep you in doubt any longer, and I hope that with Mr. Baruch's help you can find the very best connections.

Edith joins me in the very deepest love and in the hope that everything will go well.   Your Devoted,   [Father]

CCL (WC, NjP).
[1] Unidentified.
[2] Edward Wright Sheldon, Wilson's classmate at Princeton, president of the United States Trust Company of New York.

From Thomas Garrigue Masaryk

Dear Mr. Wilson,
My Dear Friend,   Marseille, 15/vi, 23.

Thank you for your very kind letter:[1] I am happy knowing that you feel so friendly towards me & our people. My wife was a real American, living up to the best & loftiest American ideas; I shared her views & accepted her americanism & that brought me to you in 1918. I believed in the American ideals as you expressed them.

With gratitude & in sincere friendship   T. G. Masaryk.

ALS (WP, DLC).
[1] WW to T. G. Masaryk, May 19, 1923.

To Margaret Woodrow Wilson

[Washington] 21st June 1923

I trust the news report is not true that you are promoting a prize fight stop It would bring deserved disrepute upon our names
                                        Woodrow Wilson

T telegram (WC, NjP).

To William Douglas Mackenzie[1]

My dear Dr. Mackenzie,   [Washington] 21st June 1923

It is always a pleasure to receive a letter from you,[2] and nothing cheers me more than to be reminded of your generous friendship. But I must frankly say, in reply to your letter of June eighteenth, that I do not feel qualified to write such a book as you suggest. It ought to be the result of such mature reflection as I have not been able to give the theme.

I have not been unmindful of the stimulating effect of intellectual effort, and have I believe made, and am making, enough to fill the prescription.

In the August number of the Atlantic Monthly will appear a little essay of mine upon which I should be very interested to learn your judgment if you should ever care to express it.

I trust the years ahead of us will give me many opportunities to enjoy the stimulation of more intimate intercourse with you, and that I shall always find you as vigorous and alert as I am accustomed to think of you.

With affectionate regard,

Faithfully Yours,   [Woodrow Wilson]

CCL (WP, DLC).
[1] Wilson's old friend, President of the Hartford Seminary Foundation.
[2] W. D. Mackenzie to WW, June 18, 1923, TLS (WP, DLC). Dr. Mackenzie asked Wilson to contribute a book on the ethics of citizenship to a series in the field of ethics which he was editing.

To Edwin Clinton Wilson[1]

My dear Edwin,   [Washington] 22nd June 1923

Your telegram announcing the death of your Father[2] was all the greater shock to me because I had not heard that he was ill or even indisposed, and I am writing now to beg that you will tell me something of his symptoms and the character of his illness. I hope with all my heart it was not a sort to cause him extreme suffering, and that the end came without any kind of physical agony. I will be very much obliged to you if you will tell me as much about his last days as concerns his general condition and state of mind.

I have already tried to express to your Mother[3] the burden it was to my heart of his taking off. I hope you can report to me that she is bearing up with her usual courage, and finds much to comfort her in the sympathy of friends and the memory of the years of happy association with John.

Where is Alfred[4] now? I hope that you, he and your Mother are all well notwithstanding the trial you have been through, and that the days will soon grow brighter for you in every respect.

    With love to all,

                    Affectionately Yours,   [Woodrow Wilson]

CCL (WP, DLC).
    [1] Son of John Adams Wilson, Wilson's first cousin.
    [2] John Adams Wilson, about whom see n. 1 to J. A. Wilson to WW, Jan. 17, 1894, Vol. 8. The telegram is missing.
    [3] Ida Gordon Wilson. Wilson's letter to her is missing.
    [4] Alfred McCalmont Wilson.

To Cordell Hull

My dear Mr. Chairman: [Washington] 22nd June 1923

    I am taking the liberty of suggesting (no doubt quite unnecessarily) that you make sure of a list of the men calling themselves Democrats who sailed with Lasker on the "Leviathan."[1] It is thoroughly worth while to keep such a list for further reference. But I am no doubt urging what has been in your mind all along, and I beg you will pardon me if my interest in the matter has led me to advise you unnecessarily.

    With cordial regard,

                    Faithfully Yours,   [Woodrow Wilson]

CCL (WP, DLC).
    [1] Albert Davis Lasker, chairman of the United States Shipping Board, took 318 guests on a trial voyage of the former German liner, S.S. *Leviathan*, from Boston Harbor, June 19-24, 1923. Actually, Lasker had resigned his position on the Shipping Board on June 10. Among prominent Democrats aboard were Senator Edwards of New Jersey, Senator Duncan U. Fletcher of Florida, Representative James A. Gallivan of Massachusetts, and Byron R. Newton, former Collector of the Port of New York. The maiden voyage of the refurbished *Leviathan* was condemned as a junket by Hull and others.

To Alexander Meiklejohn

My dear Meiklejohn,   [Washington] 25th June 1923

    I hope you realize that your friends outside of Amherst have been thinking of you since the present trouble began.[1] You have on your side the conviction and enthusiastic support of thousands of thoughtful men of whom I am glad to include myself as one.

    Of course my sympathy may be coloured by my personal knowledge of you which has generated in me a confidence close akin to affection. I could not deny myself the pleasure of writing to you to express that confidence, and also the utter contempt that all thinking men must entertain for the united [benighted?] trustees of the college you are leaving and to which they have now given so fatal a wound,—a college which is one of the finest in the country. I have dealt with similar trustees myself and the experience enhances my contempt.

Please think of me as your fast friend, and please,—if you have an opportunity,—congratulate for me the men in the faculty who have stood by you.

With warmest regard,

Faithfully Yours,   [Woodrow Wilson]

CCL (WP, DLC).

¹ Meiklejohn, trained in philosophy (logic and metaphysics), had been Dean of Brown University, 1901-1912, and President of Amherst College since 1912. He was an ardent advocate of an integrated nonelective curriculum based on the liberal arts and did not hide his contempt for what he regarded as fads and frills in higher education. He was equally strongly opposed to the semiprofessionalization that was invading college athletics in the United States and insisted that coaching staffs be unpaid. He irritated many alumni by his open scorn for the sons of rich men; as he put it, "intellectually, they are nonexistent." He also brought a number of professors to Amherst who shared his views and who, along with their leader, kept the campus in constant turmoil.

The Amherst board of trustees, headed by George Arthur Plimpton, a publisher-scholar of New York, requested Meiklejohn's resignation on June 19, 1923, on the ground that he had lost the confidence of a majority of the faculty and asked him to stay on as professor of logic and metaphysics. Meiklejohn replied that it would be better for the college if he withdrew entirely. *New York Times*, June 20, 1923; "Meiklejohn Stirring Figure in American College Life," *ibid.*, June 24, 1923, Sect. VIII, 3.

Meiklejohn was appointed Professor of Philosophy and chairman of the Experimental College of the University of Wisconsin in 1926. He retired in 1938. During this period and afterward, until his death at ninety-two in 1964, he was a defender of free inquiry and free speech. President Lyndon B. Johnson awarded him the Medal of Freedom in 1963. Obituary, *New York Times*, Dec. 17, 1964.

From Alexander Meiklejohn

Dear Mr. Wilson: Amherst, Massachusetts July 2, 1923

I am sure you can not realise how much pleasure and encouragement your good letter of June 25th has brought me. I have never forgotten our trip together crossing the ocean¹ and the many kindly expressions of your attitude at that time as well as on more recent occasions. It has been a constant source of satisfaction to me to feel that in some measure I knew you and could share in what you have been doing.

In the present situation I find, of course a very keen delight in the realisation that you have been through this sort of thing before and can place it where it belongs. It is not easy to tell just what to say about trustees, but at least one can smile at them. I fear that my chief difficulty with them has always been that I have not been able to take them very seriously.

You speak to me so kindly that I dare to send you expression of the same kindliness of attitude on my own side. I hope that if ever I should come toward Washington you may be able to let me stop in to tell you in person what I say here very haltingly.

On the chance that it may interest you, I send you enclosed page proof of a paper which I have coming out in the September Century.[2] It was written long before our recent crisis developed, but I think perhaps you and I can both feel the influence which brought it to expression, quite apart from their emergence in such crises as do or do not arise in the rush of circumstances. I should be delighted if you could find time to glance through the paper. If, however, you have not the time do not hesitate to throw the proof aside.

With very hearty appreciation of your kindness, I am

Sincerely yours,   Alexander Meiklejohn

TLS (WP, DLC).
  [1] Wilson and Meiklejohn were fellow passengers on S.S. *Furnessia* from New York to Greenock, Scotland, in June 1899.
  [2] Alexander Meiklejohn, "To Whom Are We Responsible?: A Memorandum on the Freedom of Teachers," *Century Magazine*, CVI (Sept. 1923), 643-50.

To Alexander Meiklejohn

My dear Meiklejohn,   [Washington] 5th July 1923

Thank you for your letter of July second, and its enclosure. It has given me real pleasure, and I am sure that I shall read the paper with acquiescence as well as pleasure.

We seem just now to be going through a period of violent intellectual reaction,—made as intense as possible by such extraordinary persons as Mr. William Jennings Bryan,[1] and I fear that many of our colleges will experience the unhappy results. Being a politician myself, I cannot help connecting these phenomena in my thought with the influence of the present reactionary administration. But that is another story which need not receive its full exposition until next year.

I hope that you will find many compensations in your relief from the worries and perplexities of university administration and the harrassment of ignorant trustees. I had myself the unhappy experience of having to deal with one of the most ignorant and prejudiced groups in the country, and am saddened by my every thought of the present situation of my alma mater.

If you should happen to come to Washington, please let me know a few days in advance so that I can adjust the routine of my convalescence in such a way as to give myself the pleasure of seeing you.

With very warm regard, and great pleasure in our friendship,

Faithfully Yours,   [Woodrow Wilson]

CCL (WP, DLC).
  [1] A reference to Bryan's crusade against the teaching of evolution in public schools, colleges, and universities, about which, see F. L. McVey to WW, Jan. 26, 1922, n. 1, Vol. 67.

To Bernard Mannes Baruch

My Dear Friend, [Washington] 6th July 1923

Please regard this letter as a message of deep gratitude to you for the interest you have taken in Margaret's plans and for the indispensable help you gave her in maturing them and making the right start. Your advice and assistance have been invaluable to her and have set my mind at ease with regard to her affairs. I thank you with all my heart.

I hope that this letter will find you somewhere where you are free to enjoy yourself and gain the refreshment you need after such constant devotion to unselfish service. Our thoughts are always with you and are of the sort that I believe would make you glad if I could interpret them.

With enduring regard,

Affectionately Yours, [Woodrow Wilson]

CCL (WP, DLC).

To Cyrus Hall McCormick, Jr.

[Washington] 6th July 1923

I am inexpressibly shocked and grieved to hear of your Mother's[1] death stop I had a real affection for her and always thought of her as one of my most cherished friends stop Our hearts go out to you in deepest sympathy. Woodrow Wilson

T telegram (WP, DLC).
[1] Nancy, or Nettie, Maria Fowler McCormick died on July 5, 1923. Wilson was replying to C. H. McCormick, Jr., to WW, July 5, 1923, T telegram (WP, DLC).

To Margaret Woodrow Wilson

My darling Little Girl, [Washington] 15th July 1923

Your letter[1] and Mr. Baruch's about your beginnings in business have relieved me very much. I hope that you find all the beginnings propitious, and that you will find the business you have undertaken more and more satisfactory to you as your experience develops. I infer that it will bring you into even more closer association with Miss McLeod, and I dare say you will welcome that. I need not tell you that our affectionate sympathy will attend you at every step, and that our hope is that you will succeed even beyond your sanguine expectations.

Things go as usual with me. There is not much to encourage me, but not enough that is discouraging to justify making a bad mouth over.

Edith joins me in warm love to you, and also joins me in all the hopes that I have for your complete success. She says that the handkerchiefs have come and are most satisfactory; that if you will let her know what they cost she will forward you check to cover.

With deepest love,   Your Devoted,   [Father]

CCL (WC, NjP).
[1] It is missing.

To Sir Eric Drummond[1]

My dear Sir Eric,   Washington D C 27th July 1923

I can vouch for the bearer of this note, Mr. James J. Forstall, as an honourable, straight-forward man whose interest in serious things is genuine and intelligent.

In taking the liberty of introducing him to you, may I not extend to you my warm personal greetings, and express also the profound pleasure with which I have witnessed the steady progress of the League in the confidence and admiration of the world.

With sincere regard, and the hope that I may from time to time be able to serve the interests of the League in some practicable way,   Cordially and Sincerely Yours,   Woodrow Wilson

TLS (League of Nations-Ar, Geneva, COL 352/6).
[1] Wilson wrote this letter in response to J. J. Forstall to WW, July 25, 1923, TLS (WP, DLC). James Jackson Forstall, Princeton 1904, was a lawyer with the firm of Butler Lamb Foster & Pope of Chicago. Wilson's reply to Forstall's letter is WW to J. J. Forstall, July 27, 1923, CCL (WP, DLC).

To Thomas Bucklin Wells[1]

My dear Mr. Wells,   [Washington] 27th July 1923

I am very much complimented by your desire that I should contribute something to Harper's Magazine.[2] It has been true of me all my life that it was impossible for me to write to order,—even my own order. I must always wait for the subject and the impulse.

You may be sure that my feeling towards Harper is most cordial. I sent my little essay to the Atlantic because of a sort of loyalty to my old relationship and association in the publication world as well as because I have very much admired the way in which Mr. Sedgwick has handled the long distinguished monthly over which he presides.

Allow me again to thank you for your confidence, and to echo the hope that it may not be long before we may have the pleasure of seeing one another face to face. When you plan a trip to Washington, please let me know some days in advance so that I may plan an interval in the routine of my convalescence which will make a short interview possible.

With much regard and cordial good wishes,

Sincerely Yours,   [Woodrow Wilson]

CCL (WP, DLC).
[1] Editor of *Harper's Magazine*.
[2] Wilson was replying to T. B. Wells to WW, July 26, 1923, TLS (WP, DLC).

An Essay[1]

[c. July 27, 1923]

THE ROAD AWAY FROM REVOLUTION

In these doubtful and anxious days, when all the world is at unrest and, look which way you will, the road ahead seems darkened by shadows which portend dangers of many kinds, it is only common prudence that we should look about us and attempt to assess the causes of distress and the most likely means of removing them.

There must be some real ground for the universal unrest and perturbation. It is not to be found in superficial politics or in mere economic blunders. It probably lies deep at the sources of the spiritual life of our time. It leads to revolution; and perhaps if we take the case of the Russian Revolution, the outstanding event of its kind in our age, we may find a good deal of instruction for our judgment of present critical situations and circumstances.

What gave rise to the Russian Revolution? The answer can only be that it was the product of a whole social system. It was not in fact a sudden thing. It had been gathering head for several generations. It was due to the systematic denial to the great body of Russians of the rights and privileges which all normal men desire and must have if they are to be contented and within reach of happiness. The lives of the great mass of the Russian people contained no opportunities, but were hemmed in by barriers against which they were constantly flinging their spirits, only to fall back bruised and dispirited. Only the powerful were suffered to secure their rights or even to gain access to the means of material success.

It is to be noted as a leading fact of our time that it was against 'capitalism' that the Russian leaders directed their attack. It was capitalism that made them see red; and it is against capitalism under one name or another that the discontented classes everywhere draw their indictment.

There are thoughtful and well-informed men all over the world who believe, with much apparently sound reason, that the abstract thing, the system, which we call capitalism, is indispensable to the industrial support and development of modern civilization. And yet everyone who has an intelligent knowledge of social forces must know that great and widespread reactions like that which is now unquestionably manifesting itself against capitalism do not occur without cause or provocation; and before we commit ourselves irreconcilably to an attitude of hostility to this movement of the time, we ought frankly to put to ourselves the question, Is the capitalistic system unimpeachable? which is another way of asking, Have capitalists generally used their power for the benefit of the countries in which their capital is employed and for the benefit of their fellow men?

Is it not, on the contrary, too true that capitalists have often seemed to regard the men whom they used as mere instruments of profit, whose physical and mental powers it was legitimate to exploit with as slight cost to themselves as possible, either of money or of sympathy? Have not many fine men who were actuated by the highest principles in every other relationship of life seemed to hold that generosity and humane feeling were not among the imperative mandates of conscience in the conduct of a banking business, or in the development of an industrial or commercial enterprise?

And, if these offenses against high morality and true citizenship have been frequently observable, are we to say that the blame for the present discontent and turbulence is wholly on the side of those who are in revolt against them? Ought we not, rather, to seek a way to remove such offenses and make life itself clean for those who will share honorably and cleanly in it?

The world has been made safe for democracy. There need now be no fear that any such mad design as that entertained by the insolent and ignorant Hohenzollerns and their counselors may prevail against it. But democracy has not yet made the world safe against irrational revolution. That supreme task, which is nothing less than the salvation of civilization, now faces democracy, insistent, imperative. There is no escaping it, unless everything we have built up is presently to fall in ruin about us; and the United States, as the greatest of democracies, must undertake it.

The road that leads away from revolution is clearly marked, for it is defined by the nature of men and of organized society. It therefore behooves us to study very carefully and very candidly the exact nature of the task and the means of its accomplishment.

The nature of men and of organized society dictates the maintenance in every field of action of the highest and purest standards of justice and of right dealing; and it is essential to efficacious thinking in this critical matter that we should not entertain a narrow or technical conception of justice. By justice the lawyer generally means the prompt, fair, and open application of impartial rules; but we call ours a Christian civilization, and a Christian conception of justice must be much higher. It must include sympathy and helpfulness and a willingness to forego self-interest in order to promote the welfare, happiness, and contentment of others and of the community as a whole. This is what our age is blindly feeling after in its reaction against what it deems the too great selfishness of the capitalistic system.

The sum of the whole matter is this, that our civilization cannot survive materially unless it be redeemed spiritually. It can be saved only by becoming permeated with the spirit of Christ and being made free and happy by the practices which spring out of that spirit. Only thus can discontent be driven out and all the shadows lifted from the road ahead.

Here is the final challenge to our churches, to our political organizations, and to our capitalists—to everyone who fears God or loves his country. Shall we not all earnestly cooperate to bring in the new day?

Printed in *The Atlantic Monthly*, CXXXII (Aug. 1923), 145-46.
    [1] The final typescript of this essay has not survived.

From James Edward Freeman[1]

My dear Mr. Wilson: Sorrento, Maine, July 27, 1923.

I am inexpressibly grateful to you for your brief but very suggestive article in the current number of the Atlantic Monthly. It is a word "spoken in season," and, coming from you, it ought to produce a widespread influence throughout the country. One of the reasons why I am heartily committed to the building of the great Washington Cathedral is that I believe it may be made a centre from which the great prophets of our age may speak to the people of the country. When I speak of "prophets," I mean prophets—clerical and lay,—without respect to denominational bias or affiliation. You probably know that we are projecting this fall a nation-wide movement to raise funds to complete this great building, and it will be one of the large tasks to which I must commit myself immediately after my consecration.

With reference to the latter service, which I trust may be held on Saturday, Sept. 29, in Epiphany Church, I would esteem it a matter of deep personal satisfaction to have you and Mrs. Wilson present, and in due course I will forward to you an invitation.

Should you be able to come, I would have special seats assigned you.

If, at some time, you feel that you can express to me a word concerning the value and importance of the Cathedral, I am confident it would prove of great value to me in the work of prosecuting the campaign now under way. It may interest you to know that I have secured General Pershing as a member of the Cathedral Chapter.

Again, let me express my gratitude for your noble article. I trust that every day sees a marked improvement in your physical health, and I beg to send to you and Mrs. Wilson my very sincere and affectionate greetings and good wishes.

Always sincerely yours,   James E. Freeman

TLS (WP, DLC).
    [1] Rector of Epiphany Church of Washington; soon to be consecrated Protestant Episcopal Bishop of Washington.

To James Edward Freeman

My dear Dr. Freeman,   [Washington] 30th July 1923

Your note of July twenty-seventh was very welcome and I thank you for it warmly.

I am glad to second you in any way possible in accomplishing the completion of the cathedral here. Its completion will not only add greatly to the stately beauty of our national capitol but will provide a center from which I believe, under your guidance, the most useful and beneficial work can be done for the uplift of the community and stimulation of the nation. I hope with all my heart that your efforts in this matter will be crowned with the most complete success.

I hope that you are having a bit of vacation and are gaining real refreshment from it.

I am interested to learn the date of your consecration. It is impossible for me to judge at this distance whether I can be present or not, but even if I am not physically present you may be sure I shall be there in spirit and with warmest hopes for the sort of success on your part which will satisfy both your heart and your mind.

Mrs. Wilson joins me in warm regards, and I beg to subscribe myself,   Your Sincere Friend,   [Woodrow Wilson]

CCL (WP, DLC).

To Warren Gamaliel Harding[1]

[Washington] 31 July 1923

I have learned with concern of your illness and sincerely hope that you will make a rapid and complete recovery.

Woodrow Wilson.

T telegram (WP, DLC).
[1] This telegram was addressed to Harding at the Palace Hotel in San Francisco.

To Frank Irving Cobb

My dear Cobb,   Washington D C 1st August 1923

Perhaps as I am myself a veteran in the practices of convalescence you will allow me the privilege of making a suggestion with regard to your own recuperation,—which I trust will be as brief as mine has been protracted.

Fishing as I have observed it (and I am no fisherman) can hardly be called active physical exercise, and I beg to suggest that you will do wise to take vigorous exercise. When I was well, I kept well by playing golf every day, and am confident that if I could play it now I could double the rate of my recovery. Why don't you find some golf course where you can stretch your muscles and at the same time enjoy what I think is the most enjoyable game in the world.

I write these things, not as impertinent advice, but as the earnest counsel to a friend whose life and health I know how to value and to be of immense consequence to the country and to the world. Please give the matter full consideration and go to work to get muscular development as well as rest. I am sure that if you do the results will make you bless me for the suggestion I am making. At any rate I cannot attest my sincere solicitude and affection for you in any better way than by pointing out what I believe to be the way to health and strength.

My thoughts go out to you constantly, and always with genuine affection. Be good, get well and come back into the momentous undertaking of lifting the world again to high ideals and noble practices.

This is the earnest advice of

Your Devoted Friend,   Woodrow Wilson

TLS (IEN).

To Florence Mabel Kling DeWolfe Harding

[Washington] Aug. 3 1923

Allow me to express my profound sympathy. I deplore with all my heart the loss which the nation has sustained.   WW.[1]

EBWhw telegram (WP, DLC); printed in the *New York Times*, Aug. 4, 1923.
   [1] Harding had died in San Francisco on August 2.

A News Report

[Aug. 3, 1923]

HARDING KEPT GRAYSON WITHIN WILSON'S CALL
The Former President Did Not Know of an Order Given to the Navy Department.

Washington, Aug. 3—Exactly twenty-nine months ago Warren G. Harding actually helped lift Woodrow Wilson down the steps of the White House portico and into the carriage which took both to the inaugural ceremonies at the Capitol.

No one of the thousands who saw the robust figure in contrast to the waxen, drawn and stooped man beside him ever dreamed that the latter would be living to write a message of condolence on the death of the former. But the tale which moulds men's lives brought a fair measure of returning health to one and exhaustion and death to the other.

Mr. Harding's gentle consideration for his stricken predecessor on that day excited the admiration of the many who saw it and won the warm respect of Mr. Wilson himself. When the crowd along Pennsylvania Avenue cheered and applauded the healthy and robust incoming President, he silenced them with a deprecating gesture, signifying consideration and sympathy for the stricken, almost pathetic figure beside him. At the Capitol during the inaugural ceremonies his considerate attention to the outgoing President was most marked, and it did not stop there. It took practical form. Here follows a bit of hitherto unpublished history:

Rear Admiral Cary T. Grayson had been President Wilson's physician for eight years, as he had been physician to Presidents Taft and Roosevelt before him. He knew Mr. Wilson's case as probably no other physician could know it. Mr. Harding brought Dr. Sawyer,[1] his own physician of years acquaintance. Dr. Sawyer knew equally well the complicated and long-standing illness of Mrs. Harding. Dr. Grayson's White House detail ended and he was subject to assignment elsewhere.

Without a request or suggestion from anybody and without any one knowing of it, President Harding personally gave an order to the Navy Department that Dr. Grayson was to be assigned to duty in Washington, where his services would be available to Mr. Wilson and that in no circumstances was he to be ordered elsewhere without the President's consent.

Woodrow Wilson probably will get his first knowledge of Mr. Harding's action if he reads this dispatch.

Printed in the *New York Times*, Aug. 4, 1923.
  [1] That is, Dr. Charles E. Sawyer.

From Calvin Coolidge

My dear Mr. Wilson: The White House August 4, 1923.

It is with great distress that I have to inform you officially of the death of President Harding. In his death the nation suffers an irreparable loss; to me personally it is the loss of a true friend.

Should you contemplate participating in the funeral services of the late President, which I should greatly appreciate, upon the receipt of an expression of your wishes you will, of course, be duly apprised of the arrangements.

Yours very sincerely,   Calvin Coolidge

TLS (WP, DLC).

A News Report

[*Aug. 4, 1923*]

Wilson Is Unable to Attend Harding Funeral:
He Is Deeply Affected by President's Death

Washington, Aug. 4.—Woodrow Wilson, because of the condition of his health, will be unable to attend the funeral of President Harding in the Capitol Wednesday.

From a source close to the ex-President THE NEW YORK TIMES was informed today that Mr. Wilson was "greatly upset" and deeply affected by the death of President Harding. It is thought likely that Mr. and Mrs. Wilson will call at the White House Wednesday to express their sympathy to Mrs. Harding.

One of President Coolidge's first acts on his arrival in Washington was to communicate with Mr. Wilson to ascertain whether it would be possible for the ex-President to attend the ceremonies.

The result was announced in this statement issued by Colonel Sherrill,[1] military aid to the President:

"President Coolidge has conferred with ex-President Wilson in order to ascertain his wishes in reference to attending the funeral exercises over the remains of the late President Harding and offering to make any arrangements agreeable to Mr. Wilson for his participation in the exercises.

"Mr. Wilson has indicated his appreciation of the courtesy extended by President Coolidge, but regrets his inability to participate on account of the condition of his health.

"Admiral Grayson is in communication with Mr. Wilson and indicates that while the ex-President will not be able to participate in the ceremonies he is in a satisfactory state of health."

It was added that the word "conferred" in the statement simply meant that the President and Mr. Wilson had been in indirect communication through Colonel Sherrill and Rear Admiral Grayson.

Printed in the *New York Times*, Aug. 5, 1923.
    [1] Clarence Osborne Sherrill.

To Calvin Coolidge

My dear Mr. President,   Washington D C 5th August 1923

Thank you sincerely for the gracious courtesy of your note just received. I sincerely grieve as you do over the death of President Harding who had undoubtedly won the esteem of the whole nation by his honourable and conscientious conduct in office.

I shall esteem it an honour to take part in the funeral procession and shall be obliged if you will assign a position in the procession for my car which will be occupied by Mrs. Wilson and myself, and I hope by my friend Admiral Grayson. It will be with feelings of the utmost solemnity and reverence that I will attend. I regret to say my lameness makes it impracticable for me to attend the exercises in the Capitol.

Allow me to express the hope that your administration of the great office to which you have been so unexpectedly called will abound in satisfactions of many kinds.

                    Sincerely Yours,   Woodrow Wilson

TLS (C. Coolidge Coll., MNF).

From Frank Irving Cobb

Dear Mr. Wilson: New York. August 7, 1923.

Your letter was better for me than medicine, and I cannot tell you how much I appreciate it. What you say is all true. For years I have had no exercise in the Winter. This is a damnable town in which to get exercise in any circumstances but I have allowed myself to grow stale and spend my energies like a drunken sailor and now I am paying for it. I am getting better slowly but it will be a long process. I am hoping, however, to be on my feet by Fall.

I was so pleased yesterday with your letter to President Coolidge. It seemed to me perfect.

I have much curiosity in regard to Coolidge, coupled with a good deal of hope. He came from a better political school than Harding but whether he can defend his jugular vein or not from all the Republican senators who will set out to cut his throat is a matter of speculation.

It was so good to hear from you that again I thank you.

Please give my best regards to Mrs. Wilson. I trust you are both having as comfortable a Summer as anyone can have in this heat and drought.   Your sincere friend,   Frank I Cobb.

I don't go to the office, but I manage to make a few Editorial suggestions now and then.

TLS (WP, DLC).

A News Report

[Aug. 8, 1923]

ORDEAL FOR WILSON TO ATTEND FUNERAL

Washington, Aug. 8.—Woodrow Wilson was a dramatic figure in the parade which escorted the body of President Harding to the Capitol this morning. For more than an hour, the former President waited in the hot sunshine outside the White House to take his place in the funeral procession and thus pay his tribute to the man who succeeded him.

The former President, with Mrs. Wilson and Admiral Grayson, his friend and physician, passed down Pennsylvania Avenue in their automobile to the east front of the Capitol, but he did not attempt to enter the building, but drove away to his home in S Street. The former President had a place of honor in the cortege. His car followed that of Chief Justice Taft, which was preceded by the automobile of President Coolidge. Behind Mr. Wilson came the foreign ambassadors.

It appeared that Mr. Wilson was much moved today. When he was waiting in the White House grounds, and the flag-covered coffin was taken from the East Room to the artillery caisson, his eyes were fixed upon it, and on his face was an expression of sadness.

During the slow ride down the avenue he was a silent figure. A few times he spoke in a hushed tone to Mrs. Wilson. Hundreds of the people along the sidewalks bared their heads as he passed.

The effect he left upon observers was that of a man stronger physically than he was when he rode down Pennsylvania Avenue behind the body of the Unknown Soldier on Armistice Day, Nov. 11, 1921. His face was fuller, his eyes were firmer and he held his head more alertly. He still has to be assisted in and out of his automobile, two attendants helping him into it this morning as he left the S Street house.

After the former President returned to his home, Admiral Grayson said his patient had stood the ordeal well. This was taken as an indication that the naval doctor considers that Mr. Wilson is improving, and, in fact, Dr. Grayson confirmed that belief by saying:

"Mr. Wilson is stronger today than he was a year ago. He came through today excellently."

Printed in the *New York Times*, Aug. 9, 1923.

To Frank Irving Cobb

My dear Cobb,   Washington D C 9th August 1923

Your letter of August seventh cheers me for it shows me that you are waking up to the necessity of taking care of one of the most valuable men in the country. You now have an opportunity, it seems to me, to come out of your present indisposition stronger and better than when you went into it,—which God permit.

I hope that you will always remember that you are attended in all you do with the affectionate thoughts of
Your Sincere Friend,   Woodrow Wilson

TLS (IEN).

From Ray Stannard Baker

Dear Mr. Wilson: Amherst Massachusetts August 10 1923

I cannot tell you how greatly pleased I was yesterday to have a copy of the Road away from Revolution with your friendly autograph. I had just read it in the *Atlantic* and was about to write to you expressing my deep sympathy for your point of view. There is, I believe, a genuine revival of interest in spiritual processes in this country, but few have dared, as you have in this essay, to make the target of these forces the evils of the capitalistic system. Many people want a kind of vague spiritual up-lift: few see in it the only cure of the "sickness of an acquisitive society."

This desire for the *feelings* of virtue and of spiritual power without setting them at the grim work we have to do seems to me a disease of the times. We want the engine going hard, but do not throw in the gear. We want freedom—for what? And power—for what?

We have just had an example here at Amherst: in the Meiklejohn case. If I had been in the faculty here and had to make a decision for myself I should have gone out without hesitation with Meiklejohn. The issue of free teaching, unbossed by ignorant trustees and sentimental alumni, would have seemed to me more important than anything else. But never-the-less Meiklejohn's program was most unsatisfying. His whole educational philosophy seemed to consist in knocking down all the former beliefs of the students, asking questions without end, leading nowhere. He seemed to have no philosophy of his own. He left his students vibrating excitedly in a kind of intellectual vacuum. But of what use is it to be free intellectually if you are going nowhere: propose to do nothing with the power so generated? You can make fine pessimists in such a school: but not fighters.

One of the things that always strongly attracted me to you, Mr. Wilson, was the sense I always had that while you were willing to ask the most pointed questions regarding established institutions, you were always in gear—as it were!—you were applying the power: going somewhere.

It was truly encouraging that you were able to ride on Wednesday in the sorrowful procession at Washington. May your health and strength steadily increase!

With many regards to Mrs. Wilson, I am, your friend,

Ray Stannard Baker

Our book has just been translated into Bohemian and is soon, also, to go into the Italian language. I hoped before this it would be in French, but the French publishers have been twisting and turning, trying to get permission to publish only selected parts of the book. But I can see in this only an attempt to warp the truth and to present the material as to make out a case for France.

Postscript.

Pasot is soon to bring out a French translation of our book and Mario Borsa, with the help of Ferrero, is working upon an Italian translation—which I fear they will find to be bitter fruit. I have the most remarkable comments & reviews of the German edition of the book—from all parts of Central Europe. They react to it as though it were the first good breath of truth they had had.   R.S.B.

With this background, I think such an interview as I suggest[1] could be made to echo around the world.

ALS (WP, DLC).
    [1] Baker must have suggested the possibility of his publishing an interview with Wilson during his latest visit to the Wilsons in early May 1923. There is no correspondence between Baker and the Wilsons on this subject to this point.

A News Report

[*Aug. 11, 1923*]

WASHINGTON CROWD GIVES WILSON OVATION

Washington, Aug. 11.—Former President Woodrow Wilson received an unusually hearty greeting tonight both inside and outside of Keith's vaudeville theatre. As usual, he was applauded when he came and took his seat in last row with Mrs. Wilson and Admiral Grayson. The audience seemed unusually interested in him, because, no doubt, of the dramatic circumstances of his appearance in the funeral procession of President Harding.

When Mlle. Diane, a French soprano, made a curtain speech thanking the audience, and in broken English called attention to "our distinguished guests, Mr. and Mrs. Wilson," the audience applauded. Immediately after she left the stage a news reel was thrown on the screen, and when pictures of President Coolidge at work on his father's New England farm were shown there were many handclaps.

After the performance and when Mr. Wilson was leaving the theatre by the stage alley, as he always does, a double quartet surrounded his automobile and sang "Just a Song at Twilight." The music quickly enlarged the customary crowd that waits each Saturday night to see Mr. Wilson go away from the theatre, and when the song was over some 400 or 500 people had gathered.

By this time all of the performers on the bill were in the stage alley near the Wilson car. The former President asked Mlle. Diane to sing "The Marseillaise," and she responded amid cheers from the throng. Mr. Wilson bowed his thanks, taking off his hat and smiling. As his car drove away some one in the crowd cried, "There's the man you can't forget."

Printed in the *New York Times*, Aug. 12, 1923.

From William Procter Gould Harding

My dear Mr. Wilson: Boston 13 August, 1923.

I have undertaken to write an account of "The Administration of the Federal Reserve Act, 1914-1922" to be published by Messrs. Houghton Mifflin Company of this city.[1]

You may remember that in November 1916 an effort was made by a prominent international banking firm to sell an indefinite amount of British Treasury bills to banks and bankers in the United States,[2] and that the Federal Reserve Board submitted to you a draft of a statement which cautioned American bankers to keep themselves in a strong position and warned them against making heavy purchases of obligations of foreign governments. I enclose copy of a letter which you addressed to me on the subject,[3] and ask if I may have your permission to reproduce it in my book. The letter is marked "CONFIDENTIAL" and it has never been made public in any way although at the time the Federal Reserve Board's statement expressing disapproval of the offering as an investment for banks caused a great deal of comment and a good deal of adverse criticism. It was insinuated in some quarters that the statement was made at the behest of a foreign born member of the Board.[4] Although the incident was soon forgotten and the wisdom of the statement fully demonstrated by the events of the succeeding months, it occurs to me that it would be of interest historically to show that before being issued a draft was submitted to you, and was not only approved by you but was made stronger and more pointed at your suggestion.

With great respect, I am
                    Sincerely yours,   W P G Harding.

TLS (WP, DLC).
    [1] It was published as W. P. G. Harding, *The Formative Period of the Federal Reserve System* (Boston and New York, 1925).
    [2] About this affair, see Arthur S. Link, *Wilson: Campaigns for Progressivism and Peace* (Princeton, N. J., 1965), pp. 200-201.
    [3] See WW to W. P. G. Harding, Nov. 26, 1916, with its Enclosure, Vol. 40.
    [4] Paul Moritz Warburg; German-born.

John Randolph Bolling to William Procter Gould Harding

Dear sir: [Washington] 15th August 1923

Mr. Wilson directs me to say, in reply to your letter of 13th August, that he doesn't think the acts of the Board need any such support, and that he would prefer the letter, of which you enclose a copy, *not* be published.
                    Yours very truly,   [John Randolph Bolling]

CCL (WP, DLC).

From Bernard Mannes Baruch

Stonehaven, Kincardineshire.

My dear Mr. Wilson,   Aug. 17th [1923]

Your "Atlantic" article was very timely and is being much commented upon here where things "socially" are in great confusion.

There is a deep-seated feeling that what the great land owners have should somehow be divided and turned over to those who have none. The only way the "have nots" can figure is by just taking it without compensation or due process of law or order.

I saw Clemenceau who is much better than when in America[.] He sent his affectionate regards. He frankly says that he says nothing because he does not know what should be done.

I have seen many people here in the same box.

To my way of thinking they look at it too much from their own selfish national view point instead of as a whole. Each one must 'apparently' give up something for the benefit of all which in the end will improve the position of each one.

I wonder how long this selfish narrow viewpoint lead by America will continue?

The papers here are full of news items and editorials on the League which seems to have a greater hold than last year.

I am trying to impress upon the League's friends here that instead of trying to emasculate it to get America in, they should stand up to Article X for without it the force of our argument and the heart of the thing is gone. The younger men understand it better.

Your remarks keep coming back to me about the people of Europe and America not yet being ready for the League and that perhaps it might be better after all to let them learn through grief and suffering.

If you, my friend, had not been made to suffer so perhaps I could have appreciated your comment.

Do we have to learn thru such great grief? Will the world have to approach the brink of the dissolution of our present social and and [sic] eco[no]mic order before we turn to reason and the League idea?

To me it seems that no where in the world is there any authority to say yes or no. Democracy does not give even a temporary authority to do what should be done in its own behalf. It must be made safe for itself.

We have a fine time here. My boy has not yet recovered, but we are hoping to welcome him here well from his cure in Vichy.

When I return in September I hope to find you better and stronger. We will have need of all you can do or give us.

We send you both our most affectionate regards and best wishes. As always   Devotedly   Baruch.

ALS (WP, DLC).

From Florence Mabel Kling DeWolfe Harding

The White House

My dear Mr Wilson   August seventeenth [1923]

Before leaving Washington I want to express my gratitude for your kind message of sympathy which I received in San Francisco.

Assuring you of my deepest appreciation and with kind regards to you and Mrs Wilson, believe me

Sincerely yours   Florence Kling Harding

ALS (WP, DLC).

From William Jennings Bryan

My Dear Mr President: Miami, Florida Aug 21—1923

Am gratified to read your article in The Atlantic Monthly, first, because of the evidence it gives of improvement in your health and, second, because of the timeliness of the spiritual note that you struck.

Beyond the worlds economic and political needs, great as they are, is its religious need—to get back to God. Mrs Bryan[1] joins me in regards to Mrs Wilson & in good wishes to you both. With assurances of esteem I am, my dear Mr President,

Very truly yours,   W. J. Bryan

ALS (WP, DLC).
[1] Mary Elizabeth Baird Bryan.

John Randolph Bolling to William Jennings Bryan

My dear Mr. Bryan: [Washington] 25th August 1923

Mr. Wilson asks me to thank you for your very kind letter of August twenty-first and say he is gratified to know that you like his little essay which has just appeared in The Atlantic Monthly.

Mr. and Mrs. Wilson join in cordial greetings to Mrs. Bryan and you.   Sincerely yours,   [John Randolph Bolling]

CCL (WP, DLC).

From George Creel

New York City. August Twenty-Seventh,
My dear Mr. Wilson: Nineteen Twenty-Three.

I have been in almost continuous correspondence with Mr. Foley these last few months and the book is now ready for publication by the Princeton University Press. The contract provides for royalties of ten per cent on the first 2,000, fifteen per cent on the next 3,000 and twenty per cent thereafter, one half to go to you and the other half to Mr. Foley.

At every point Mr. Foley has impressed me with his unselfish quality, and I am also of the opinion that he has done a very remarkable piece of work. In looking over the letter you wrote him for a foreword, certain changes seem advisable to me, and I take the liberty of enclosing a draft for another one. As you will notice by comparison with the copy of the original, there are no additions, but only a few elisions. Mr. Foley's other need is an autographed photograph to be used as frontispiece. He does not like the one that is being used by the Atlantic Monthly, and neither do I.

I spent three very happy months in California and had a particularly pleasant visit with the McAdoos. I hope very much to get to Washington in the near future for a visit, for I feel sure that many of the things that I have to tell you will be of interest.

My warm regards to Mrs. Wilson,

Always devotedly,   George Creel

TLS (WP, DLC).

A Telegram and Two Letters
from Edith Bolling Galt Wilson

Providence RI Aug 27 1923

Have just had breakfast and are starting for Mattapoisett thirty mile ride weather fine love[1]   EBW

T telegram (EBW Papers, DLC).
  [1] Mrs. Wilson had just left with Edith Benham Helm for a visit to the Charles Sumner Hamlins at their summer home at Mattapoisett, Mass., on the western shore of Buzzards Bay.

Mattapoisett Massachusetts
Dearest One: 11-40 a.m. August 27, 1923

Here we are—all settled and my thoughts fly to you and I long to have you with me & to know about the night & how you are this morning. The time here is an hour ahead of yours. So it is just time for your Electricity and I picture the Dr. giving it to you, & your telling him stories all through. Be sure to let me know if you want me.

Now to tell you of the trip. The drawing room was most comfortable & we arrived on time. Mr. Hamlin took us across to the new Hotel in Providence where we had a nice breakfast & then started on our motor ride. I sent you a telegram from the Hotel which I hope has already reached you. When we got on the train last night Mr. Hamlin said he had just heard from Mrs Hamlin that some drunken bootleggers had run into their car & smashed it very badly so she would have to borrow a car to meet us.

So it turned out that John & Richard Crane[1] were driving here last night & then going on to Providence to take a night train to N. Y. so they said they would leave their car in Prov. for us, & we found the chauffeur waiting at the gate, and he brought us the 40 miles most comfortably.

We found Mrs. Hamlin & Anne[2] on the porch to welcome us and their house is so wonderfully situated—right out on a point, with the blue waters of the Bay dancing in the sunlight, and back of the house a stretch of pine woods, and further out to the front of the point a picturesque Light House—the whole place is filled with glowing autumn flowers, and I just long for you to share it all. Your picture I brought is on my bureau with a single great pink rose bowing to it from a slender vase.

Edith Benham & I have adjoining rooms. Each with a big bath, and everything to make us comfortable. And the Hamlins are just as thoughtful as anyone could be & have each one asked so much about you

Dear Heart remember how I love you, and that I want to come whenever you want me. Stay out for all the air you can. I do hope the picture tonight will give you pleasure. With all my love

Always,   Edith

[1] John Oliver Crane was the youngest son of Charles Richard Crane. His brother, Richard, was former and first United States Minister to Czechoslovakia.
[2] Huybertie Lansing Pruyn Hamlin and her daughter, Anna, not Anne.

Mattapoisett Massachusetts

Dearest One: 11.45 a.m Tuesday, August 28/1923

I am so eager for the afternoon mail to hear how you are getting on and if every thing is going well. I have followed you all along in my thoughts, and hope they have been so vivid that you have felt them, and they have assured you of my love and tenderness.

I wrote you about this time yesterday & hope the letter reached you this morning

After I finished my letter we sat in the sun parlor, which is just surrounded by a lawn which in turn is surrounded by the water, which was blue and sparkling, and we talked until lunch, with the diversion of several neighbors coming in to get tickets for the play last night. After lunch we all walked over to the woods to see the players put up their stage & tents—it really is very ingenious and I will tell you of it when I come home. Then we came back & got unpacked and took a bath & a good rest before dinner. Then the plays were at 8, and we really enjoyed them. I will enclose one of the "Leaflets." There were about 200 people in the audience & every one I was introduced to said such lovely things about you.

Mrs Hamlin had asked all the players to come here afterwards for ice cream & cake and they asked some of their special friends too. So there were about 20 in all, and the moon being full and a radiant night the whole thing went off beautifully. This afternoon we are going to Mr. Hamlin's sisters'[1] to tea, and then on to see Plymouth Rock. Tomorrow we go to Newport for the Horse Show, & they have just had a message saying Franklin Roosevelt is to be here tomorrow on a yatch with some one

I asked Mr. Hamlin the meaning of the word "Mattapoisett" and he said it means "place of rest" and it seems to me the very embodiment of it for there is not a sound but the gentle lap of the water or the whispering of the wind. I just long for you dear one! and miss you all the time.

Edith Benham is so full of real affection for you that it makes her very dear to me. And in talking of your Essay she said such a pretty thing I must tell you of it. She said she read the Essay four times— once for the Essay itself and the other 3 times for the delight of the English. She said it was so exquisite, and that of course it was the genius like that of a master touching the strings of a violin—to get music, where others got only sound, or a sculptor making with a touch a beautiful statue out of common clay. So it seemed to her you touched words and made a living thing. She said "that is crude but it is what I feel"

Now I must stop for this time but my thoughts and love go on and on.

Give Randolph & the Dr my love, and remember me to Scott and Mary[2] & take precious care of your most precious self.

Always   Edith

Three years and 11 months today since you were taken ill, but the end of the road is in sight and we are going to have lots of lovely times together Goodnight Dear Heart   E.

ALS (WP, DLC).
  [1] Harriet G. Hamlin and Jane Hamlin of Boston.
  [2] Wilson's servant, Isaac Scott, and Mary Scott, Mrs. Wilson's personal servant.

To Edith Bolling Galt Wilson

Adorable Sweetheart,   Washington D C [Aug. 28, 1923]

I've had a bit of a knockout yesterday and to-day, but am on the usual levels to-day and anxious about nothing but interfering with your vacation.   I love you!   Woodrow

ALS (WP, DLC).

To George Creel

My dear Creel,   Washington D C 28th August 1923

I am glad to know that you are back home, and shall look forward with real pleasure to seeing you soon.

I in turn have somewhat altered the letter to Mr. Foley, but I have left it in substantially the form you suggested, and it will go forward to him immediately.[1]

I hope that you find all the family well and that you yourself are feeling benefited from your little run away from business and back again.

I dare say you think as I do that the administration is finding it too easy to rely on promises of the present Mexican Government.[2] It seems to me they are still upon the quicksands.
                    Affectionately Yours,   Woodrow Wilson

P.S. I am sorry to say the photograph Mr. Foley does not like is the only one available. Some day I may have a satisfactory photograph, but it has not been made yet.   W.W.

TLS (WP, DLC).
  [1] Actually, Wilson must have sent Foley a new copy of his letter to Foley of April 26, 1923, printed as an Enclosure with JRB to G. Creel, April 26, 1923. This letter is reproduced in facsimile following the table of contents in *Woodrow Wilson's Case for the League of Nations*.
  [2] A reference to the negotiations before, then, and afterward between the Mexican and American governments over the rights of ownership of American citizens and companies in Mexico, particularly oil companies, under the Mexican Constitution.

To Jessie Woodrow Wilson Sayre

[Washington] 28th August 1923

Many many happy returns of the day stop Am looking forward to seeing you with the keenest pleasure stop Love to all

Father

T telegram (WC, NjP).

To Edith Bolling Galt Wilson

My precious Darling,   Washington D C Wednesday, 29.

For me, not the house inly but the world als also itself has been empty since you left. In spite of everything I am managing things as I think you would wish, but alas the difference! I never before realized so fully how completely my life is intertwined with yours. I keep stead steadyby constantly reminding myself that I am protecting your vacation from interruption. That gives me peace of mind

It makes me very happy to know that you are having a littl little good time, bless you.

These few.lines are a very narrow channel through which to p pour out a heartful of love to you, but they contain nothing less, my darling.   Your own   Woodrow

The proper messages to everybody.   W.

WWTLS (WP, DLC).

From Edith Bolling Galt Wilson

Dearest One: Mattapoisett Massachusetts August 29/1923

We are to go to Newport today for the horse show so I am sending a very hurried note just to bring you my tender love. I could only hear Randolph enough yesterday to learn that you were "okeh," and I am so grateful for that. But Mr. Hamlin says if you send another message to get R. to ask for the Chief Operator & ask that you get a clear line—that otherwise it is almost impossible to hear.

After lunch yesterday we motored over to Plymouth & saw *the* "Rock" and many of the pretty old homes, and then came back through "Marion" & had tea with Mr. Hamlin's sisters—you remember we had them to tea last Winter? and they are wild about you. Then we went by their brother's house¹—for a moment—as we were using his motor

He married one of Mr. Holmes Conrad's daughters, and she, poor thing, is hardly expected to live, as she has cancer & is in Boston in a hospital. They have the most charming house—almost in the water—with only the entrance on land. I will tell you about it when I get back.

Give R. & the Dr my love and keep a heart full for your precious self, from   Edith

R's letter of Monday has just come please thank him for me. We are just starting

ALS (WP, DLC).
¹ Edward Everett Hamlin of Boston. His wife, mentioned below, was Katharine Brooks Conrad Hamlin.

To Edith Bolling Galt Wilson

My Lovely Sweetheart,   Washington D C Thursday, Aug. 30

It turns out that Grayson intends only to sleep and eat here, and expects me to have him summoned from the Dispensary if I need him at any other time. It is.disappointing, but of little practical importance.

THe servants are very gracious and hawe admitted me to an eary intimacy which is without ceremony or formality of any kind.
I am taking my daily drive and behaving with a good deal of sense. My intense loneliness only deepens my love for you. You fill my heart.

With utter devotion,   Your own   Woodrow

Forgive the wretched typewriting

WWTLS (WP, DLC).

From Edith Bolling Galt Wilson

                                    Mattapoisett Massachusetts
My precious One: Thursday Aug. 30, 1923

This is just the most radiant day, and I am hoping that it will be made even brighter by a letter from you. I have Randolph's thoughtful ones of Monday & Tuesday, but not a word from you, and I know you have written, and I so long to hear. Thank you dear Heart, for taking your walk every day. I know how hard it is and that you do it for me, and I love you for it more than you know

Now to tell you of our trip to Newport, it turned out to be a very rainy gray day, but we had a closed car & it was an interesting ride over—through Fair Haven Fall River etc—and we went to Bailley

Beach to see the bathers. There were few people in as it was raining but the place was swarming with people & the one most in evidence was Jimmie Gerard.[1] He wanted us to lunch with him, or come back & let him give a "real party" or "anything in the world" etc etc. We had promised to lunch with a Mrs. Hoppin[2] who is Mrs. Hamlin's sister in law, so we got out of that and went to the lunch—and then afterwards to the Casino to the Horse Show. There were some lovely horses—& I really enjoyed them—but again Mr. Gerard attached himself and introduced everyone he could find—from a pretty little girl of 7 who, he said was the daughter of the Pretender to the throne of Portugal—to all the old dowergers of the 400 Of course it was amusing, for some of them, including the horses has sense!

Who should walk by but Vance McCormick, who wanted to know all about you & sent his love and said he was coming down to "just see you" very soon.

We left at 4:30 and got back about 6:30 where Mr. Hamlin had hot tea waiting for us & we talked over the day, and had dinner at 8. After which I played Pool with him & then he played some music he had written years ago & we all told stories until 12:30

I asked Mr. H. yesterday to see if I could get a reservation home for Monday or Tuesday of next week & he has tried both in Providence & Boston and can get nothing until Wednesday night, which will put me home on Thursday Sept 6th. If this is not too long to stay will you get R. to telegraph me, and I will be home Thursday early morning but if you need or want me sooner I can take a day train & not mind it a bit, so please *be honest and tell me.*

We are going to lunch today with a Mrs Weld,[3] and then go on to Woods Hole to call on the Cranes—John & Mrs Chars R.[4] sailed on last Wed. but Mrs Letterbu [?] & the Richard Cranes[5] are there & I am anxious to see the place

It is time to start so I must stop. Please give Randolph the enclosed. With all my love & a big kiss always   Edith

ALS (WP, DLC).
  [1] James Watson Gerard.
  [2] Eleanor D. Wood (Mrs. Joseph Clark) Hoppin of Boston.
  [3] Probably Sylvia Parsons (Mrs. Rudolph) Weld, who had a summer home at Wareham, Mass.
  [4] Cornelia W. Smith Crane.
  [5] Richard and Ellen Douglas Bruce Crane.

To Edith Bolling Galt Wilson

Dear Love   Washington D C 31st.

I do not feel equal to the typewriter to-day but must send a line
to say *I love you*.   Woodrow.

Everything is as usual.   W.

ALS (WP, DLC).

Two Letters and a Telegram
from Edith Bolling Galt Wilson

                                    Mattapoisett Massachusetts
Precious One: 11:30 a.m. August 31st 1923

Your little note of Tuesday came last night and filled my heart
with joy. How much you managed to convey in those few lines! All
the things that my heart was longing for, and I hope it did not tire
you to write. Please don't do it if it does.

I also had Randolph's letter so I felt quite rich.

Yesterday was Mr. Hamlin's birthday, and we had a birthday
cake and a small dinner party of Hugh Tennent and the aircraft
man from the British Embassy & the wife of the Naval Aid.[1]

Some other young people came in afterwards & we had some
nice music & a very jolly evening. In the morning I wrote to you &
then we went to the lunch with Mrs Weld. She has the loveliest
garden that reminded me of those at Cornish.[2] From there we motored to Woods Hole to find all the Cranes had gone off for the day
to a "Fair," so we looked round the place, which is very lovely, in
many ways, and came home. I will tell you about it when I come.

When we got in we found a Mr. Baker here who is with Franklyn
Roosevelt on the sailing yatch, which was anchored just opposite
Mr. Hamlin's peer—and said he came to see if we would all come
out to the yatch as it was so hard for Mr. R. to come in. So we went
and had a nice little visit and he was so appreciative.

Said please give his love to you and say he would be in Wash.
soon and was coming to see you to tell you all the political gossip
he thought you would be interested in. Said he thought Smith[3] had
admitted he is a candidate & will state he believes in "freedom" on
the wet & dry question, and that as far as he could learn that was
the only thing he would take a definite stand on.

I want to write to Mother so must stop. Let me know if you want
me precious one, and with all my love,   Always   Edith

[1] Hugh Vincent Tennant was secretary to the British Ambassador; the "aircraft man"
was Col. Lionel Evelyn Oswald Charlton, air attaché; the "Naval Aid" was Capt. Francis

Loftus Tottenham, R.N., the naval attaché at the British embassy, who was not married until 1932.
   2 At Harlakenden in Cornish, N. H., Wilson's sometime summer residence, which Mrs. Wilson had visited in 1915.
   3 That is, Gov. Alfred E. Smith of New York.

Mattapoisett Massachusetts
My dearest One: Saturday Sept. 1, 1923

We drove in to the village yesterday for the mail and I was rewarded by your dear note of the day before and I need not tell you with what eagerness I read it. I am sorry if you misunderstood about the Dr. You see I asked him to stay there at night and of course any or all meals, but that you would not want to interfear with his duties and would let him know if you should need him any time during the day. So you see he is doing exactly what I asked, and if you were disappointed it is my fault and not his.

I have just gotten Randolph's telegram to stay until Thursday and want to thank you for sending it so promptly.

Edith Benham goes tonight and I am getting her to take this to you, so there will be no possibility of its not reaching you tomorrow She said she would call up first thing and tell you

Yesterday Mr. Hamlin made a speech on the Federal Reserve, and we all went to hear him. He made the most beautiful tribute to you and the fact that but for you the thing could never have been done.

I hope you will go to Keith's tonight, and that everything will continue to go well.

With all my love,   Always   Edith

ALS (WP, DLC).

Mattapoisett Mass Sep 3 1923

No mail went out yesterday so am writing today Very well and having wonderful time Love   Edith

T telegram (EBW Papers, DLC).

Two Letters from Edith Bolling Galt Wilson

Dearest One: Mattapoisett Massachusetts Sept. 2 [3], 1923

There was no mail out of this post office yesterday, so I have just sent you a telegram to explain why there was no letter from me today. You know it is a tiny place, and they did not even deliver

Randolph's special delivery to me yesterday, but it was left in the office to be called for and came when they got the mail this morning.

Yesterday we went to church in the morning and a number of people dropped in for tea here in the afternoon & Mr. Hamlin's brother & sister came to dinner

This morning we have been walking & went in to see some of the beautiful gardens of various people. And they are perfect riots of color and remind me of the Cornish gardens.

The Hamlins are the dearest people I ever saw, and have done every thing in the world for my pleasure and comfort and they are the most loyal and ardent friends of yours. I will have so much to tell you when I come that I will never stop talking

Only 2 more days and I will be there, and until then I am with tender love, Yours Edith

Mattapoisett Massachusetts

Dearest One: Tuesday [Sept. 4, 1923]

This letter must be the last before I come in person to bring you all my love and thank you for the generous dear way you have made this little visit possible for me. I do hope you have not been too lonely and that the knowledge of what your love was doing for me has brought you happiness. I do feel so refreshed and have a new outlook on the world. And I only hope that you may get some reflex from it when I come back. I have missed, and wished so, for you, and surely you must feel the wave of love and admiration all over the country that is set toward you.

Do you remember the young officer who used to be on the Mayflower—named Dick Bird?[1] He came over to see me yesterday & gave me such a long message to give you of how your ideals & teachings had changed the world for him & how he is seeking some way to help the League, etc that I will have to wait & tell it to you. We are going in now to New Bedford, & Mrs Hamlin is waiting for me so I must hurry. All my love, Edith

ALS (WP, DLC).

[1] Richard Evelyn Byrd, a graduate of the Naval Academy in the Class of 1912. After a retirement for medical reasons in 1916, he entered naval aviation in 1917 and was made commander of U.S. Naval Air Forces in Canada in 1918. By 1923 he was one of the top leaders in aviation in the world.

From Charles Sumner Hamlin

Dear Mr. Wilson: Washington September 4, 1923.

I enclose an editorial from the Waltham, Massachusetts, Free Press Tribune,[1] which I think will interest you. I am not quite sure, but I believe this is a Republican paper.

I want to tell you again what a pleasure it was to us to have Mrs. Wilson as our guest. I carefully explained to her that the word Mattapoisett was an Indian word meaning "Place of Rest," though I greatly fear she will tell you that the name ought to be changed. There was a wonderful outpouring of the people to greet her, and man after man would come up to me, saying "I am a Republican but I have the greatest respect and admiration for President Wilson and I deem it a great honor to be permitted to meet his wife." Mrs. Wilson made a most charming impression. We had a reception one afternoon for the townspeople, and over seventy-five attended. I wish you could have heard the expressions of their impressions of Mrs. Wilson. It would have done you good to have heard it. Among others, Mrs. Hamlin invited the Democratic town committee of three members. They all came up to the door but hesitated to come in; they were so bashful I literally had to drag them into the door, but an hour later I literally had to drag them out, they were so absorbed and delighted to meet Mrs. Wilson. One evening, as I told you this morning, I had planned to go to Rochester to a combined meeting of several of the farmers' granges, of which Mrs. Hamlin and I have been members for many years. I did not expect that Mrs. Wilson or Mrs. Hamlin would think of attending, but on the morning of the day the librarian of the Grange wrote such a charming letter referring to the respect and admiration they all had for you and their keen desire to see Mrs. Wilson that she finally said she regarded this letter as a command, and so we all went over. We found there about a hundred and thirty-five people, some of whom had come from a distance of from ten to fifteen miles. The women were all dressed in white, and they carried through the evening with as much ceremony, yet all in good form, as one would have seen at a European court. I had assured Mrs. Wilson that she would not be called upon for any address, and so told the Grand Master, who assured me that he would not call upon her, and he kept his word. A lady, however, at the other end of the room, put a pebble into the machine by rising and saying that she felt she expressed the feeling of every woman present that they would be terribly disappointed if they could not hear just a word from Mrs. Wilson. I was much embarrassed, but Mrs. Wilson arose to her feet and made a short and charming address. It was an event these people will talk about to their grandchildren. They will never forget it. Yesterday, we had three old maids,—the Misses Howland,[2]—at lunch. They were born and bred in the Democratic party and have fought for you with all their energy. They were more or less isolated, living in a strong Republican community, and Mrs. Hamlin felt they ought to have the opportunity of meeting Mrs. Wilson. I drove them home after the lunch on the way to meet my train at Providence, and I wish you could have heard them. They were in a state of exaltation, and long before we reached their house they had ceased to be able to express their gratification in words. I verily believe that if they had ridden with me a mile further they would have felt obliged to express themselves by bursting into song, as did Beethoven in his Ninth Symphony. I wrote Mrs. Hamlin last night from the University Club that if they had done so, I should have joined with them.

We all trust that this will be the first of many visits, and we are all living in hope that you may be able to come and see us sometime and receive a demonstration similar to that received by Mrs. Wilson.

Believe me,   Very sincerely yours,   Charles S. Hamlin

TLS (WP, DLC).
   [1] It is missing in WP, DLC.
   [2] Two of them might have been Priscilla Howland and Jane Howland of Brookline, Mass.

From James Middleton Cox

New York NY Sep 4 1923

In the present crisis[1] the great moral force of your voice is needed Please consider the suggestion that you speak the duty of the League Its preservation is necessary to the salvation of the world and if it fails now much will be lost to the great cause Cordial good wishes.   James M Cox[2]

T telegram (WP, DLC).
   [1] He referred to the so-called Corfu incident. Relations between Italy and Greece were very strained in 1923, and Mussolini was looking for an excuse to seize the Greek Island of Corfu. It was not long in coming. General Enrico Tellini and four members of his staff, who were members of an Anglo-French-Italian commission appointed by the Conference of Ambassadors to define the boundary between Greece and Albania, were assassinated on August 27, 1923, near the Greek town of Jania. To this day, no one knows for certain who the assassins were, although it is possible that Mussolini himself was implicated. The Italian government sent an ultimatum to Athens demanding certain things; the Greek government refused the demands; and on August 31 Italian warships and men bombarded and occupied Corfu.
   Greece appealed to the League Council, which was then in session, on September 1 for redress. The Italian government claimed that the League had no jurisdiction because the incident had occurred on the Albanian border and ought to be referred to the

Conference of Ambassadors. During the debates in the Council, world opinion turned
sharply against Italy. Even so, the Conference of Ambassadors announced on September 5 that it would handle the Italo-Greek dispute. Without going into further details,
let it be said that the Greek government paid an indemnity and the Italians, in return,
withdrew from Corfu on September 27, 1923. Alan Cassels, *Mussolini's Early Diplomacy* (Princeton, N. J., 1970), pp. 95-126.
  ² "no reply—W.W." (not WWhw) written at the top of this telegram.

To Charles Sumner Hamlin

My dear Friend,   Washington D C 5th September 1923

It was most thoughtful of you to write me the letter of September
fourth, with the added news of Mrs. Wilson, and I thank you with
all my heart.

I am sure that she has had a delightful time, and we shall both
be very grateful to you always.

                    Gratefully Yours,   Woodrow Wilson

TLS (C. S. Hamlin Papers, DLC).

From Sir Eric Drummond

My dear Mr. Wilson,   Geneva. September 7th, 1923.

May I take the opportunity given me by the letter of introduction
which you kindly gave to Mr. Forstall¹ to send you something more
than a mere formal acknowledgment.

Much has happened since the months in Paris during which the
Covenant of the League of Nations was worked out by the Commission which met under your Chairmanship; and I think that
everyone who has closely followed the work of the League since
that time, agrees that the text which emerged from the meetings
of that Commission has stood in a remarkable way the tests of time
and of experience. Some few amendments, it is true, have been
adopted by the Assembly, and may probably come into force before
very long. But they are, for the most part, not concerned with essentials. It has, indeed, been remarkable how, as each question,—
large or small, political or technical,—has come before the different
organisations of the League, the necessary guide and authority are
found in one or other Article of the Covenant.

So long as great and powerful States remain outside, the League
cannot, of course, be altogether what you and your collaborators at
Paris intended to create. Nevertheless, the greater number of the
different nations who at first were outside the list of original Members, have one by one requested, and obtained, their admission.

In the meantime, the League has been able to perform some

great pieces of constructive work; to circumscribe and solve some important, and many unimportant, differences and difficulties before they were able to reach a dangerous development, and to carry out much work in matters of a technical nature in the field of relief and in that of Social questions, which made in the past slow, if any, progress, simply on account of the difficulty of bringing together the various elements whose different views and interests have to be conciliated in order to achieve an advance in common.

It is on the work that it has accomplished that I base my faith in its future and my hope that it may before long include also those nations which, up to now, have stood aside.

Of the great and serious problem with which the League is faced at this moment, I will say nothing. By the time this letter reaches you, it is likely that its outcome will be already known. At least it can be said that the meeting of the Assembly has already provided an unequalled opportunity for the opinion of the world to make itself heard when the moment comes.

It is, therefore, I feel a peculiarly appropriate opportunity to send you these few words as to the present developments here. My own strong belief is that the conception of the League has justified itself many times over and that the seeds sown at Paris are already bearing much fruit. We have experienced many difficulties and shall, no doubt, continue to experience them for many years to come, but personally I believe that the future is already secure.

Please allow me in closing to express to you my very deep gratitude for the personal greetings conveyed in your letter and my most profound appreciation of the confidence which you and the other members of the Peace Conference at Paris shewed in me four years ago. I frequently have news of you from our many American friends, and I can assure you that I follow that news with the deepest interest.

Believe me, my dear Mr. Wilson,

Yours very sincerely,   Eric Drummond

TLS (WP, DLC).
¹ WW to J. E. Drummond, July 27, 1923.

From Lord Riddell's Diary

[Sept. 10, 1923]

September 10th.—Long talk with Barney Baruch, the American, at the Ritz Hotel. . . .

He gave a dramatic account of an interview between him and President Wilson, which took place recently. They are old friends.

Wilson, placing his paralysed arm on the table beside him, said in slow but firm accents, "Perhaps it was providential that I was stricken down when I was. Had I kept my health I should have carried the League. Events have shown that the world was not ready for it. It would have been a failure. Countries like France and Italy are unsympathetic with such an organisation. Time and sinister happenings may eventually convince them that some such scheme is required. It may not be my scheme. It may be some other. I see now, however, that my plan was premature. The world was not ripe for it."

Baruch said that the incident was so pathetic that he could only say in reply, "Well, Mr. Wilson, you did what you thought was for the best!"

R.: I don't know that you could have said anything more appropriate.

Printed in George Allardice Riddell, *Lord Riddell's Intimate Diary of the Peace Conference and After, 1918-1923* (London, 1933), p. 409.

To Jessie Woodrow Wilson Sayre

My darling Jessie,   [Washington] 12th September 1923

I am sorry and ashamed to have overlooked when you were here my usual birthday present, and content myself with the thought that perhaps after all it will be of more immediate service to you now than it would have been in August. Tonight I send it,—with a great deal of pleasure and lo[ve.]   Lovingly,   [Father]

CCL (WC, NjP).

From Margaret Woodrow Wilson[1]

Precious Father,   New York Sept 13th 1923

When I was home I forgot to show you an article by our dreamer friend, Mr Ferguson,[2] that I promised to ask you to look at. He wants your approval of some plan of his with which General Goethals[3] is cooperating. I don't quite understand it but perhaps you will. If General Goethals is really interested, and he must be since he is allowing Mr Ferguson to say he is in print, it must be more practical than most of Mr Ferguson's plans. At any rate I will send you the article and then you can decide whether or not you wish to give him an expression of opinion concerning it.

Well I'm back in harness again having caught up with the little accumulation of mail waiting for me on my return.

The above was written, dear Father, last week and this is the first opportunity I have had since to go on with it.

Friday I drove up to Harmon Sophie Loeb's home, with Mr Nicholson,[4] the Corporation Counsel, (a merry widower) and two of his friends, where we were joined by Emily Smith, the Governor's daughter, Mr Tenant[5] the editor of the Evening World and his wife[6] and others.

We had a very gay party which at times became so deafeningly noisy because of the radio and the victrola and everybody talking at once, that I fled several times and found strength and peace from the woods and the river all by myself. I must say that as I get older I like big parties less and less, especially if they last two days.

I saw Helen[7] the other day. We had dinner together. She looked much better than when she Iwent [sic] away, but was a little tired as she too had been to several big parties and they tire her worse than they do me.

I must run to make my next engagement and I don't want to postpone sending this off, so I'll just send it as it is.

It was such a joy being with you again, darling Father, and didn't we have a good time with the children and Jessie and Frank! Have they written you that they are going to sail from Montreal instead of New York! I am dreadfully sorry not to see them again, but at least I won't have to see the boat carry them off.[8] I dreaded that.

Give my love to beautiful, sweet Edith.

I adore you and love you with all my heart and soul, wonderful, wonderful Father of mine.   Your devoted,   Margaret.

I have just read the article that Mr Ferguson asked me to give you, and how he expects you to give an opinion on it I don't know! I suppose he expected me to explain it to you. While he gave me a much better idea of the scheme than he does in this article, he certainly has not worked out anything definite enough for you to pass an opinion on. Well I'll inclose it, but I'll tell Mr Ferguson that you are not willing to give an opinion on this subject, or something to that effect. M.W.W.

TLS (WC, NjP).
[1] She wrote this letter on the stationery of the Biow Co., advertising and merchandising, 116 W. 32nd St., New York.
[2] Charles Ferguson of New York, sometime Episcopalian priest and Unitarian minister; journalist; served in special missions for the Commerce and State departments, 1914-1915, 1918; prolific author on current affairs. Bolling returned the clipping in WW to Margaret W. Wilson, Sept. 19, 1923.
[3] That is, George Washington Goethals.
[4] George P. Nicholson.
[5] John Hunter Tennant.
[6] Gertrude Ruth Snyder Tennant.

[7] That is, Helen Woodrow Bones.

[8] Frank, Jessie, and their children sailed aboard the Cunard liner R.M.S. *Andania* on October 7, 1923, for Plymouth. After a few days in England, they sailed aboard the S.S. *City of Paris* of the Ellerman City Line for Singapore, and from there went by rail, about November 20, to Bangkok. F. B. Sayre to JRB, Oct. 7, 1923, ALS (EBW Papers, DLC). Jessie and the children returned to the United States, landing at Boston, on April 21, 1924. EBW to Jessie W. W. Sayre, April 20, 1924, T telegram (EBW Papers, DLC).

To Burton Johnson[1]

My dear sir,   [Washington] 14th September 1923

It is a long time since I either saw or heard of the little island which I own in Lake Rosseau, and I am very much obliged for your thoughtful kindness in sending me the little picture of it and telling me of the successful fishing near it. Not being a fisherman myself I never discovered the fishing ground in which the bass were taken. I must reserve that I suppose until the wished for time, which seems never to come, when I can build on and occupy my little estate. I regard the Muskoka Lake region as the most attractive playground in America.

With cordial good wishes and warm appreciation,

Sincerely Yours,   [Woodrow Wilson]

CCL (WP, DLC).

[1] Of Memphis, Tenn. Wilson was replying to B. Johnson to WW, Sept. 11, 1923, ALS (WP, DLC).

To Rudolf Bolling Teusler[1]

My dear Teusler,   [Washington] 16th September 1923

Edith and I wish to make a small contribution to the Japanese relief fund[2] and agree in hoping that it may be more immediately serviceable if we send it to you, as I do now, than if we sent it through the Red Cross. We hope that you will make such use of it as you deem best.

It was a great pleasure to see you, and I hope that the disaster will in fact take on the happy aspect you were brave enough to predict for it.

With warm regard,

Cordially and Faithfully Yours,   [Woodrow Wilson]

CCL (WP, DLC).

[1] Director of St. Luke's International Hospital in Tokyo. He was the son of Rudolf Teusler and Edith Wilson's aunt, Mary Jefferson Bolling Teusler.

[2] A devastating earthquake had struck Tokyo, Yokohama, and other Japanese cities on September 1, 1923. Some 200,000 people were killed by the earthquake and aftershocks. There was an outpouring of relief from the United States and other countries through various organizations. A note at the top of Wilson's letter says that he sent a check for $100. Teusler was at this time in Richmond, Va.

From Charles Sumner Hamlin

Dear Mr. Wilson: Washington Sept. 17, 1923.

You may remember asking me Saturday evening the middle name of Mrs. Blake. Her name is Mrs. Frances Greenough Blake.[1] Her mother, Mrs. Greenough,[2] belonged to one of the old Boston families, and her mother, I believe, came over from England.

I can not tell you how I enjoyed going with you to the theater Saturday evening, and how I appreciated the reception you received from the audience. After you left I walked around and mixed with the people to hear what they were saying, and I found they were not discussing the play as much as they were talking of you. I heard one old lady say that she would not have missed the sight of that grand man for her life.

Looking forward to the pleasure of seeing you again in the near future, and with warm regards to Mrs. Wilson, believe me

Sincerely yours,   Charles S. Hamlin

TLS (WP, DLC).
 [1] Mrs. Arthur Welland Blake of Brookline, Mass.
 [2] It is impossible to give her full name because there are several Mrs. Greenoughs in the Boston social register at this time.

A News Report

[Sept. 19, 1923]

WILSON MAY LEAD DEMOCRATS IN 1924

Ex-President Woodrow Wilson is manifesting a lively interest in next year's Presidential campaign, according to Democratic friends who have been in communication with him. George Brennan of Chicago, Democratic leader in Illinois and one of the most influential men in the party, recently had a three hours' conference with Mr. Wilson in Washington, at which candidates and issues were discussed.

According to friends Mr. Brennan came away convinced that if a situation should arise in which he was needed, and if his health would permit it, Mr. Wilson might even permit himself to be drafted as a candidate for the Presidential nomination. On the other hand, seasoned Democratic politicians do not believe that Mr. Wilson could have said anything to justify the inference made by Mr. Brennan.

Mr. Wilson, it was said, talked at some length about the League of Nations, and compared the benefits that would accrue to America and to the world from full participation in the League with what might be derived through the realization of President Harding's

World Court plan. He is said to have expressed the opinion firmly that sooner or later the United States would have to enter the League, virtually in the form incorporated in the Treaty of Versailles.

Mr. Brennan, according to a friend with whom he has discussed his visit, was greatly surprised when he received word that Mr. Wilson was anxious to see him. The conference took place on one of the hottest days in recent weeks.

It was learned that the candidacy of William G. McAdoo, former Secretary of the United States Treasury and President Wilson's son-in-law, was dwelt upon at some length during the talk. The candidacy of Senator Oscar Underwood of Alabama, of United States Senator Samuel M. Ralston of Indiana, who throughout the Middle West is regarded as a rather formidable figure in the Presidential race, and other Democrats whose names have been mentioned in connection with the nomination came up for discussion and comment. Mr. Wilson, it was learned, did not express any opinion with regard to their availability to lead the Democratic race at any point in the conversation.

Mr. Wilson, it was understood, asked Mr. Brennan to explain why the Irish Democrats had been alienated, and Mr. Brennan told him bluntly how certain acts of the Wilson Administration had led them to believe that the Administration was not friendly to the aspirations of the Irish, then fighting for independence.

News of the Wilson-Brennan conference leaked out after a conference relating to the coming Democratic national fight which was held today in which Thomas F. Ryan,[1] among others, participated. Another participant was Urey Woodson, Democratic National Committeeman from Kentucky and at one time Secretary of the Democratic National Committee. Mr. Woodson is a friend of Mr. Brennan, who has been here recently in conference with Tammany Leader Murphy[2] and other Democrats.

Mr. Brennan suggested to Mr. Wilson that some of the Washington correspondents might ask him about the conference. "What shall I tell them," he asked Mr. Wilson.

"Tell them anything you want to," Mr. Wilson is said to have replied.

Printed in the *New York Times*, Sept. 19, 1923.

[1] Virginia-born Thomas Fortune Ryan, street, railway and utilities magnate, railroad consolidator, and financier of New York. He had long been associated with the conservative, anti-Bryan wing of the Democratic party.

[2] That is, Charles Francis Murphy.

To Margaret Woodrow Wilson

My darling Little Girl,   [Washington] 19th September 1923

I send you this line immediately to say that I do not care to comment upon,—or even to consider,—any scheme that Ferguson has in mind. My experience with him was quite sufficient to show he has no practical gift at all, and that it is a waste of time and effort to try and assist him in the unpractical things which he conceives. I judge from your letter that you have said this already to him in substance.

I am happy to get the impression from your letter that you are settling down to an even pace in your work and are getting hold of it as you hoped to do. You may be sure my loving sympathy is with you all the time.

Let me know as often as possible the little things as well as the big things which are happening to you. I cannot be content without frequent news of you.

Please give my kind regards to Miss McLeod and to Mr. Biow.[1]

Things go as usual with us here, and the weather on the whole is very kind to us.

Edith joins me in all affectionate messages, and I am as always,

Your Loving,   [Father]

CCL (WC, NjP).
[1] Milton H. Biow.

From John Farwell Moors

My dear Mr. Wilson.   Cohasset, Mass Sept 23/23

Let me tell you how much Mrs. Moors & I liked your article in the Atlantic Monthly. It was so self-restrained, so free from present controversies, so eternally true that it was a real comfort to read it. May I not add that it was also good to have again a public utterance from one whose every word was read eagerly for years. Sometimes it has seemed to us that you could, like Cordelia, love & be silent even better & more impressively than you can say what is in many hearts, but is it too much to hope that you will write again?

I enclose a little contribution to the newspapers,[1] written when all about me were asserting that the League of Nations had failed because the Council of Ambassadors, not the League, had brought a settlement between Greece & Italy. Everyday confirms me in my view that it was fortunate indeed that both the Council & the Assembly of the League were in Session & that thus the voice of the world (apart from our own!) could be heard immediately. In the game of chess, as I see it, France might have alienated Italy from England but only at the cost of losing all else—Belgium & Poland & the little entente & what is left of world good-will. Meanwhile the League has proved indeed, as you intended, a citadel for all the little nations & the men who have upheld the League, from Lord Robert [Cecil] down, speak the language which you taught them & speak it with conviction. The forces of good & evil seem, even in these days of bitter disappointment & weariness, to be aligning themselves more clearly. But we miss your voice & your grasp on things eternal.   Always sincerely yours,   John F. Moors.

ALS (WP, DLC).
  [1] It is missing in WP, DLC.

To Emily Chapman Martin Yates[1]

My dear Friend,   Washington D C 23rd September 1923

It was a pleasure and privilege to receive your letter of September eleventh,[2] and to hear what it tells about you all.

We recently had a call from Miss Yates[3] who told us about your son's[4] children, and I was deeply distressed to hear of the painful circumstances of his recent life. I think the children are very fortunate in the home and the guidance which they have found. I am sure that the arrangement you describe would have pleased Fred mightily.

I am truly distressed to learn of the death of Miss Arnold.[5] I had come to entertain the highest opinion of her and was made happy by the thought she was my friend. She was certainly a most valuable woman and her death will prove a great loss to the whole countryside.

Things go very equably with me at present. The building up of a broken-down nervous system is a slow and tedious business, but I am hopeful that the outcome will be a complete renewal.

It is evident from your letter that Mary is developing the splendid qualities we all saw in her from the first, and you are to be most heartily congratulated on such a daughter.

Please give her my love, and accept for yourself once more assurances of my very warm and loyal friendship.

It was thoughtful of you to enclose the little pictures.

I congratulate you and the League of Nations Union on the work you have been doing for it. The results you tell me are most gratifying and remarkble.

I hope that it will not be long before God vouchsafes to you and yours brighter days and happier fortunes. My thoughts will always go out to you with affectionate remembrance and in solicitous good wishes.

With real thanks for your letter,

Affectionately Yours,   Woodrow Wilson

TLS (Yates Coll., NjP).
¹ Of Rydal, Ambleside, England, widow of the painter Frederic Yates.
² It is missing.
³ Probably a sister of Frederic Yates.
⁴ Her son by her first marriage, whose name is unknown to us.
⁵ Frances Bunsen Trevenen Arnold (1833-1923), sister of Matthew Arnold, of Fox How, Ambleside.

From James Edward Freeman

My dear Mr. Wilson: Washington September 24, 1923.

It was a deep personal satisfaction to me to have the little visit with you today.

Pursuant to your suggestion, I am venturing to remind you that it would give me the greatest pleasure, as it would your host of friends throughout the country, if you could find it convenient to dictate a few words that I might read as a message from you, at the great open-air service on Sunday. As you probably know, this service is to mark in some way my consecration as Bishop of the Diocese, and, at the same time, to signalize the beginning of the great nation-wide campaign to complete the Cathedral on Mount Saint Alban. You have very generously expressed to me in a former letter, your feeling concerning this Cathedral,¹ and if you can find it convenient to write me, so that I may receive it before Saturday, a brief message for Sunday, I shall be very grateful to you.

If there is anything I can do to make your visit to Epiphany on Saturday to the consecration, convenient to you, please command me.

With warm personal regards to Mrs. Wilson and your good self, I am,   Faithfully your friend,   James E. Freeman

TLS (WP, DLC).
¹ WW to J. E. Freeman, July 30, 1923.

To James Edward Freeman

My dear Dr. Freeman,   [Washington] 25th September 1923

I cannot in justice to my own feelings let the occasion of your induction into the office of Bishop pass without again expressing my gratification that you should be assuming these new responsibilities, and my constant interest in what I know is very near your heart, namely, the completion of the great cathedral which is to crown Mount Saint Alban.

May I not also express again my confident hope that your service in the office of Bishop will be crowned with the greatest spiritual blessings, and that a great service to the community and to the nation may be opened to you.

With warm esteem,

Faithfully Yours,   [Woodrow Wilson]

CCL (WP, DLC).

From Alexander Meiklejohn

Dear Mr. Wilson,   New York. Sept. 26 [1923]

I cannot refrain from sending a word to tell you of my enjoyment and appreciation of the chance to see you again, and to meet Mrs. Wilson.

I said nothing to you of my admiration for you and your achievement. Scotch blood does hinder the tongue, but you know already how deeply I am committed to the cause which you lead as no other man could have led it.

As for my own affairs, you can appreciate their tones and qualities as no one else can do, I suppose. You must not let me bother you, but I should like to ask for advice perhaps. In any case you have made me feel that you are interested and that gives me much courage and resolution. The college presidents who get kicked seem to be dangerous fellows and I am not downhearted at being in the company.

May I send my respects to Mrs. Wilson, and my very high admiration and affection to you?

Sincerely yours,   Alexander Meiklejohn

ALS (WP, DLC).

To John Farwell Moors

My dear Mr. Moors,   [Washington] 27th September 1923

Thank you for your letter of September twenty-third and its enclosure. I was cheered and gratified to hear from you in such terms, and I beg that you will accept for Mrs. Moors and yourself every cordial assurance of appreciation and friendship.

Faithfully Yours,   [Woodrow Wilson]

CCL (WP, DLC).

To Bernard Mannes Baruch

My dear Baruch,   Washington D C September 28th 1923

The paper is admirable;[1] the argument unanswerable; all that it needs is as much condensation as possible.

Can't you, keeping the argument in tact, state the several parts more briefly? We want the man on the street as well as the student of affairs to read this and take off his coat in our behalf.

I shall be glad to associate myself in any way you think best with this tremendous appeal to General Smuts. I suggest that you let me know when the message goes to General Smuts so that I may, if you think wise, at the same time cable my concurrence.

I am distressed to be obliged to say that at the present time I do not feel physically able to undertake the condensation of the article myself, but that is the less important, because I feel ready to subscribe to the appeal exactly as it stands.

Affectionately Yours,   Woodrow Wilson

P.S. Please tell me General Smuts' present address.

P.S. You might be interested in this letter I have just gotten from Baker.   W.W.

TLS (B. M. Baruch Papers, NjP).
[1] This enclosure is missing. However, see the revised version printed as an Enclosure with BMB to WW, September 29, 1923.

From James Watson Gerard[1]

My dear Mr. Wilson: New York September 28, 1923

I am enclosing herewith a paper against the ratification by the Senate of the Turkish Treaty.[2] I earnestly hope that it may be possible for you to express yourself, for publication, concerning that Treaty.

Consistent with the declaration which you made in 1917, that Armenia must enjoy an unmolested autonomous development, and interpreting the sentiment of the vast majority of Americans, repeatedly pressed upon your attention by leaders of both great political parties, you espoused in Paris the cause of Armenia; and, on your return home, pleaded with your countrymen to lend practical measures of help to her. Later, at the invitation of the Allies, you defined her boundaries.

The present Administration, in recognition of the commitments which many Republican leaders have made to Armenia, and in view of the responsibility which some of them bear for her plight, pledged itself to advocate and defend her rights at Lausanne. It has failed to fulfil that pledge.

Whatever the critics of the Versailles Treaty may say against it, they cannot say that you bartered away the rights of any people or nation for material advantages for this country or any group of favored Americans.

You better than another know that Armenia, at tremendous sacrifice of blood and treasure, had acquired certain elementary rights to existence, the realization of which depended to a very large extent upon the attitude of the American representatives at Lausanne. Millions of Americans, who had contributed over $70,000,000 toward the relief of the stricken Christians of the Near East, had earned the moral right to speak for them. But, at Lausanne, the United States Government bartered away these rights, and the time-honored rights of our missionaries, for economic concessions of dubious value, for the benefit of a few promoters, who subsequently sold them at public auction for $300,000, plus 10% of any possible profits.

Do you, Sir, believe that a Treaty based upon such considerations should be ratified by the Senate of the United States?

Very respectfully and sincerely,   James W. Gerard.

TLS (WP, DLC).
    [1] Gerard wrote again as chairman of the executive committee of the American Committee for the Independence of Armenia, One Madison Ave., New York.
    [2] That is, the treaty of amity and commerce between the United States and Turkey, signed at Lausanne on August 6, 1923, about which, see Laurence Evans, *United States Policy and the Partition of Turkey, 1914-1924* (Baltimore, Md., 1965), pp. 403-12. For the text of the treaty, see *FR 1923*, II, 1153-66. Gerard's paper is missing.

To Newton Diehl Baker

My dear Baker,   [Washington] 29th September 1923

Your letter about your visit to the League of Nations[1] is far and away the most adequate and informative I have received from any quarter. You are one of the few among my correspondents who, when they look at the League in action, really comprehend and is able to interpret what he sees.

I took the liberty of sending your letter to Baruch for his perusal, because he is in correspondence with active supporters of the League on the other side, and I am sure will profit by your observations and reflections.

I thank you very warmly and want you to know as time goes by I more and more value,—and derive more and more pleasure,—from your confidence and friendship. I only hope that our association with one another has been as satisfying to you as it has been to me.

With affectionate regard,

Faithfully Yours,   [Woodrow Wilson]

CCL (WP, DLC).
   [1] NDB to WW, Sept. 25, 1923, TLS (WP, DLC). Baker had just returned from Switzerland and had spent three days in Geneva while the League Council debated the question of referring the Corfu incident (about which, see n. 1 to J. M. Cox to WW, Sept. 4, 1923) to the Conference of Ambassadors. He described the debates in vivid detail and lamented the absence of a United States representative on the Council.

John Randolph Bolling to Alexander Meiklejohn

[Washington]
Dear Dr. Meikeljohn [Meiklejohn]:   29th Sept., 1923

   Mr. Wilson asks me to thank you very warmly for your letter of the 26th inst. and say you may be sure he will be glad to give you whatever assistance his advice from time to time may afford you.

   Both Mrs. and Mr. Wilson enjoyed your little visit and join in warm regard and good wishes.

                    Yours very truly,   [John Randolph Bolling]

CCL (WP, DLC).

From Bernard Mannes Baruch, with Enclosure

My dear Mr. Wilson: New York September 29, 1923.

   Enclosed you will find a copy of the cablegram I am sending to General Smuts, which I have condensed as much as I could. The only address I now have is General Jan Smuts, London; but I will endeavor to get a better one so that if General Smuts makes the cablegram public, you can then, if you wish, endorse it.

   I herewith return Mr. Baker's letter, which I have read with much interest.   Affectionately yours,   Bernard M Baruch

   Your letter[1] made me very proud and happy.   B.

TLS (WP, DLC).
   [1] That is, WW to BMB, Sept. 28, 1923.

                    E N C L O S U R E

General Jan Smuts
London   September 29, 1923

   Your presence in Europe at this critical time in its history impels me to despatch these thoughts for your consideration thus carrying out the promise I made to you to do so Stop The fact is generally recognized that unless peace and order are soon restored in the world we cannot proceed to our fullest development comma maintain our present standards of living or pay the obligations that we have incurred Stop The corollary seems to me just as certain that

if peace and order are restored we shall have an industrial and social renaissance and disperse the financial dangers faced by the
overburdened governments as well as lighten the tax load on
overburdened humanity

Paragraph Conditions in the world have gone from bad to worse
whether we view them financially morally or economically

Paragraph One Stop Financially Stop To any thoughtful observer
it must be quite apparent that through inflation repudiation or
confession of inability to pay many of the governments of the world
are in the position of an insolvent debtor Stop There seems to be
very little idea of working and paying but more of an idea of borrowing and living on borrowed money and the products of the
printing press Stop England is the only country engaged in the war
that has faced the facts and made a sincere effort to pay and this
at a cost almost impossible for others to realize[1]

Paragraph There are still two major questions dash the fixing of
the German reparation and the establishment and maintenance of
peace and order Stop Progress in the settlement of the reparation
question has been slow owing to the intrusion of many other questions growing out of it Stop Whereas the difficulty was originally
limited to the question of French security and the ability and willingness of Germany to pay France has added another issue which
is as complicated as the other two dash the question of the inter-
Allied debts

Paragraph The amount of money that Germany can pay if given
a fair opportunity is generally agreed upon as being about fifty billions of gold marks semicolon but Monsieur Poincare[2] recently
took the position that unless France received twenty-six billions of
gold marks in addition either to the cancellation of debts or the
acceptance of what are generally conceded to be worthless bonds
by the Allies and the United States the reparation problem could
not be decided Stop Despite his brilliant legal argument there is no
just ground upon which he could base any such stand and the
natural sequence would seem to be the repudiation of payment of
the money which France was glad to borrow

Paragraph It would also appear that France insists upon the ful-
fillment of her necessities forgetting the rights and the necessities
of the other nations involved Stop Does any one think that America

[1] Congress, in February 1922, had established a World War Foreign Debt Commission to negotiate long-term funding agreements with America's European debtors. The
British, in January 1923, agreed to refund their short-term obligations into long-term
bonds—$4,600,000,000 in principal and accrued interest over a sixty-two year period at
3 per cent interest for the first ten years and 3½ per cent interest thereafter. However,
the French and Italians up to this point had refused to acknowledge either the moral or
financial validity of their indebtedness to the United States.

[2] Raymond Poincaré, who had become Premier of France on January 15, 1922.

would ever consider cancellation of any part of these loans or contribute anything to the settlement unless the settlement will bring permanent peace between Germany and France Stop Agreeing as we must that Germany should pay all she can comma if knowingly or unknowingly the French policy results in the demoralization of the German people that would be at variance with what America desired to accomplish in the war

Paragraph In this reparation problem there is involved the question which goes to the root of the whole thing dash Shall we have peace based upon justice Stop Shall we have a peace that will give the world an opportunity to look forward with hope and determination to repair damage done to its present civilization resulting in peace and order semicolon or shall we have peace based upon fear and force Stop Instead of the force of the Kaiser and his junkers shall we have the force of prime ministers with chauvinistic and militaristic edicts

Paragraph Two Stop Morally Stop The League of Nations and the whole fabric of new and old international relationships are based on the principle that a treaty is not a scrap of paper to be destroyed at any time it becomes inconvenient to respect Stop If the nations that signed the Treaty of Versailles and the Covenant of the League of Nations do not live up to the spirit of that contract we shall have before us indubitable evidence of the fact that nations remain immoral and that the world is not ready to cooperate in solving its mutual problems and must endure even greater grief and suffering to learn the necessity for cooperation Stop The United States which has not yet advanced to the League idea would certainly reject it on the ground that the nations of Europe continue to sign covenants only to disregard them

Paragraph The fact that it was the Council of Ambassadors and not the League which directly handled the Italian Greek crisis is immaterial in relation to the greater fact that the peaceable outcome demonstrated more emphatically than ever the necessity for having in existence a permanent international association to deal with menaces to the peace of the world Stop Those who believe in that system which necessarily is based on the sanctity of a nation's word must go forward to its accomplishment with greater courage than ever

Paragraph Three Stop Economically Stop An examination of the currencies of Europe will show that the mark ruble et cetera have practically no value Stop The pound sterling is at a discount of about seven per cent the franc sells at about thirty-three and one-third per cent of its normal value and the lire at about twenty-five per cent of its gold value

Paragraph Germany's continuous efforts to escape payment of a just sum in reparations add to the economic instability of the world Stop We have a real interest in seeing that Germany pays her just reparations Stop There seems to be little realization in England and America of what it would mean to them if Germany should escape too lightly Stop In the United States the increased borrowings of the Federal Government as well as those of states counties industries and individuals due to the war have piled up added tax burdens Stop Our Federal budget has risen from one billion to four billion dollars annually Stop While the amount of money we have to raise in taxes because of these increased expenses and borrowings has risen so greatly the taxes of the German Government and the fixed charge on German industries have been practically wiped out owing to the use of the printing press Stop That means that there must be taken from the efforts of our people in taxes for the Federal Government alone four billion dollars a year and nothing from the Germans unless they are compelled to pay some fixed tax in the way of reparations Stop Unless this is done Germany could conquer the world industrially

Paragraph Four Stop Summary Stop If modern civilization with its growing standards of living is to be maintained comma if the world is to pay its indebtedness we must establish the moral responsibility of nations settle reparations and restore the economic balance to enable people to work and save and pay the debts incurred in the war Stop I believe that this cannot be done without a league of nations Stop A league exists which may or may not be in the final form of greatest usefulness Stop It would be very strange if the experience of the past few years should not have taught those who are dealing with this question the wisdom of some changes Stop This we have undoubtedly learned colon that if the signatory members do not respect their agreements there can be no league or any dependable international relations

Paragraph When we talk of the League it is not the League that our enemies make it Stop It is not a superimposed government that will deal with the domestic questions of its members Stop It is an institution which will tend to establish in the world the right of a nation to live its life without fear of a stronger nation seizing its property or putting its people under tribute Stop By a league we mean a central stabilizing force which will establish peace and order in the world which will establish the arbitrament of reason instead of the arbitrament of force which will establish the rule of law and not of war and will give to each nation large and small the right to develop itself without fear of invasion from its neighbors so that nations may treat with one another as individuals do

Paragraph Five Stop Proposal Stop To you in this perilous moment of history I venture to send these thoughts in the hope that you will approve them and the conclusions growing out of them and will lead in the labors which they portend

Paragraph You represent a small nation and in your own person a soldier who has seen the results of the rule of force and a statesman committed to the rule of international peace by cooperation Stop Your hand is in every article of the Covenant of the League Stop Your voice is one of high authority because your motives are unquestioned and your character and attainments eminent in your time Stop You have it in your power to state the world's case and to be heard and heeded Stop If any one can bring about a realization of the facts it is you Stop One clear call at this time from you marshaling behind you men of all nations who stand and think as you do may restore the world's moral and economic balance Stop Beyond and above all that it may save a total loss of all that the young men fought and died for from nineteen fourteen to nineteen nineteen

Paragraph If a strong hand and voice are not now fearlessly and clearly and strongly employed to halt the retrograde movement of mankind all that it spent its blood and property for may be lost again Stop The question before mankind is whether a nation's plighted bond is good Stop It is clear whither we are headed and what the remedy is Stop In earnestness and confidence the friends of peace and progress everywhere look to you to rescue and help render practical the ideals which the world has recently sacrificed so much to attain   BARUCH[3]

CC MS (WP, DLC).

[3] Smuts replied: "Your message. It will be most helpful for me to know whether there is any prospect that United States will be willing to join in reparation and inter-Allied loan settlement which will bring permanent peace to France and Germany. I mean settlement agreed to by France and England and accepted by Germany. Or better still settlement in which United States will take a hand in bringing about. Without moral and financial support of United States it is doubtful whether there is sufficient strength left in Europe to save herself. Great gesture by United States now will have most far-reaching effect. Perhaps you explore ground unofficially or suggest to me other channel through which I could work and let me know result as soon as possible." J. C. Smuts to BMB, Oct. 3, 1923, W. K. Hancock and Jean van der Poel, eds., *Selections from the Smuts Papers* (7 vols., Cambridge, 1966-73), V, 184-85. Baruch could only reply that he could not prophesy what the United States Government would do, and that Smuts would have to get reliable information from some official representative. Baruch added that he favored American participation in the reparation settlement but regarded the matter of an inter-Allied debt settlement as "a matter for the nations of Europe to adjust among themselves." BMB to J. C. Smuts, Oct. 6, 1923, *ibid.*, p. 186.

To Jan Christiaan Smuts

[Washington] 1st October 1923

I beg leave to associate myself with the appeal Baruch is making to you stop I hope with all my heart that you will do what he suggests   Woodrow Wilson[1]

T telegram (WP, DLC).
  [1] There is a WWhw copy of this telegram in WP, DLC.

A Memorandum of an Agreement

[Oct. 1, 1923]

THIS MEMORANDUM is for the purpose of making a record for our private files of an agreement between ourselves to provide an annuity for WOODROW WILSON, and as neither of us ever asked or received political favors from him, we believe he will accept this testimonial in the spirit of affection in which it is offered.

We are doing in part only what we think Congress should do for all retiring presidents, and are prompted by our sense of fairness and justice to this great man for his patriotic and unselfish life, and also by the possibility that in devoting his life to education, statesmanship and politics he may not have laid aside sufficient savings to provide himself properly with the reasonable necessities and comforts which he so richly deserves.

We believe his life and career to be of inestimable value to the world. His fearless and consistent efforts for open dealing in domestic and foreign statesmanship, and his great undertaking to create a new and higher standard of honor between nations, is worthy of the highest praise, and while he may have thought and acted in advance of his time, we doubt if permanent order can be established in the world until the thought of the world catches up with Woodrow Wilson's conceptions and plans. He dared magnificently, and when the verdict of history is rendered we believe he will stand prominent among the greatest men in human records.

The annuity shall be TEN THOUSAND DOLLARS a year, beginning today and payable quarterly on the first days of October, January, April and July, so long as Mr. Wilson lives, and each of us agrees to contribute the proportion of said annuity indicated by our signatures below. This method of procedure has been chosen in order that it may be kept more personal and more private to Mr. Wilson.

WITNESS our hands at New York City this the first day of October, nineteen twenty-three.

Cleveland H Dodge   Five Thousand dollars $5.000.00
    One fourth of the amount each quarter
Jesse H Jones Twenty five hundred dollars $2500 00/xx

T MS (received from Phyllis Boushall Dodge).

To Bernard Mannes Baruch

My dear Baruch,   Washington D C 2nd October 1923

I felt that time was of the essence in the matter we have most recently conferred about, and being perfectly willing to take the terms of the message you cabled to Smuts on faith, I communicated with him as Mr. Bolling's telegram has informed you. I hope with all my heart that Smuts will see the thing as we do, and that what you have so admirably planned will accomplish great results. It is characteristic of your practical ability and your fine loyalty to the highest objects we are seeking to obtain.

Affectionately Yours,   Woodrow Wilson

TLS (B. M. Baruch Papers, NjP).

To Sir Eric Drummond

My dear Sir Eric,   Washington D C 2nd October 1923

Your letter of September seventh was very welcome and has gratified me very much.

I share your satisfaction in the record already made by the League and your confidence that its future is assured. I personally have no doubt that no nation that wishes to play a satisfying part in the affairs of the world will find it possible to remain long outside of the League. The enemies of the League are proving as impotent as they are ignorant and the mills of the gods are proceeding to grind them exceeding fine.

I warmly appreciate your generous assurances of friendship and approval and hope that you may gain increasing satisfaction in the performance of the great duties which have fallen to you. I am sure that you can count upon the confident support of all who have been competent to observe the administration of the General Secretariat.

With sincere personal regard,

Faithfully Yours,   Woodrow Wilson

TLS (League of Nations-Ar).

To James Watson Gerard

My dear Mr. Gerard,   [Washington] 2nd October 1923

I appreciate the efforts that you are assisting in making in behalf of Armenia whose cause is very dear to me.[1] I do not think that an opinion from me would have the least influence with the present Senate of the United States. I must reserve my comment until I believe it will be efficacious.

I hope that you are well and that this new work in which you are engaged will prosper.

Very Truly Yours,   [Woodrow Wilson]

CCL (WP, DLC).
[1] Wilson was replying to J. W. Gerard, Sept. 28, 1923.

From Jan Christiaan Smuts

London October 2 [1923]

Deeply grateful for your message STOP Position most difficult but ground being explored to see what action most advisable STOP My Best Wishes for your health   South [Smuts]

T telegram (WP, DLC).

From Jesse Holman Jones, with Enclosure

My dear Friend: New York City, October 2, 1923.

I have been visiting some this summer at his office with Mr. Cleveland H. Dodge, and both being friends of yours, his friendship of much longer standing but I hope none the less sincere than mine, have talked a great deal about you, and about the great and useful life that you have lived, and of how little in comparison the rest of us contribute to the world welfare.

You have devoted your entire life unstintedly and unselfishly to education and statesmanship, and to politics uninfluenced by and unafraid of the power of gold or greed. No man has done as much. You have been fighting a great battle, and have won a victory of which the world will be increasingly conscious. Because of these things and the innumerable reasons that we might with time set down, and because we want to, we have taken the liberty of forming a very close personal trust as a slight reward and as a slight token of our love and admiration for you. It is not our intention or desire that there be any publicity or public record regarding it, and unless advised to the contrary, payments will be sent to you at your

Washington address quarterly by Mr. Dodge. It is his opinion, however, that Mr. Cyrus McCormick, also a life-long friend of yours, will want the privilege of joining, and he expects to speak to him about it when the occasion presents. I enclose a letter formally setting out our purposes.

With assurance of my great esteem,

Very sincerely yours, Jesse H. Jones

TCL (RSB Coll., DLC).

E N C L O S U R E

From Cleveland Hoadley Dodge and Jesse Holman Jones

Dear Friend: New York City, October 1, 1923.

We have created a trust that will provide an income to you throughout the remainder of your life, of ten thousand dollars a year, and though we are prompted by our love and admiration for you, the trust is in fact intended as a slight material reward for your great service to the world, and while being fully cognizant that in taking this privilege of friendship we are honoring ourselves, we are nevertheless unwilling that you deny it to us, because it is indeed a very great privilege and pleasure.

Yours sincerely, Cleveland H. Dodge

Jesse H. Jones.

TCL (received from Phyllis Boushall Dodge).

From Cleveland Hoadley Dodge

My dear Woodrow: [New York] October 2, 1923.

There are all sorts of memorial funds going around for distinguished old statesmen like Jefferson, and whilst I take more or less interest in those, I would much rather establish a memorial for the biggest man of the bunch whilst he is living.

Aside from my warm personal affection for you, you know how deeply I appreciate the wonderful service which you have done for mankind, which is bearing rich fruit already, and is bound to bear richer in the future. With two or three of your other personal friends, I want to feel that for the rest of your life you are on "Easy Street" and not to have to worry for a moment about financial matters. I have had several talks lately with your personal friend, Mr. Jesse H. Jones, and he has sent you a letter signed by himself and myself, telling you what we propose to do. Cyrus[1] is on his way back from Paris, but has written me that he will be mortally offended if he is not allowed to come in on this fund, and when it is finally arranged, there will be three or possibly four men of our ilk who have no axes to grind, and who are simply establishing this little trust of which Mr. Jones writes you, to show our appreciation of what you have done for mankind, as you might say, a little memorial to the living.

We think it would be better for you to receive this fund in quarterly payments, and I am therefore as,—so to speak,—Treasurer of the fund, sending my check for $2500, which you very likely will find come in handy as the end of the year approaches.

I wish with all my heart that I could get down to Washington to see you, but I am situated somewhat as you are, and cannot very well travel, and I do not know whether I will get down this year or not, but in any event you can be sure that I think of you constantly and am glad to hear that you are getting on so well.

Mrs. Dodge joins with me in warm regards and love to both you and Mrs. Wilson.

Ever affectionately yours,   [C. H. Dodge]

CCL (received from Phyllis Boushall Dodge).
¹ That is, Cyrus H. McCormick, Jr.

Two Letters from Cleveland Hoadley Dodge to Edith Bolling Galt Wilson

My dear Mrs. Wilson: [New York] October 2, 1923.

I was planning to write you this morning when I reached the office, and am therefore particularly glad to find awaiting me, your good letter of September 28th.¹ I certainly wish that I could be in Washington and see you and Woodrow, and have a good talk with you instead of writing, but I fear very much that I will not be able to get to Washington this autumn, as I am in very much the same box that Woodrow is in, and cannot do much travelling or go away from home. Mrs. Dodge and I think of you both, though, very often, and I am particularly pleased that the way is now opening by which I can show my love and affection for you both by doing something concrete.

Admiral Grayson has undoubtedly told you the result of his talk with Mr. Jesse Jones and me. In that talk we all agreed that it would be better to arrange for some annual amount which could be sent directly to you at the beginning of each quarter, so as to relieve the financial strain under which you are laboring. Our only desire is to make the old gentleman perfectly happy for the rest of his life without any care or worry about finances. The amount which we have talked of is at least $10,000, a year, and we may possibly increase it when I have had a talk with Mr. Cyrus Mc-Cormick, who is on his way back from France. You will understand that this fund has not been in any way solicited, but is simply the spontaneous desire of Mr. Jones and myself, in which I am sure Mr. McCormick and probably Mr. Thomas D. Jones will join, for relieving your strain. The only thing that worries me at all is as to how Woodrow will take the matter, and I am sure we can trust you to explain it to him satisfactorily. In any event, I think he ought to be told about it; in case he was not told now he might learn about it in the future, and might think something had been held back from him, and he would have a right to be displeased. The three or four who will give to this fund have, as you well know, no axes to grind, and are simply warm, personal friends to whom it is the greatest joy and pleasure to make this offering of their esteem and affection, so that he ought to have not the slightest hesitancy in accepting it. I know you will be able to explain it to him satisfactorily.

As Admiral Grayson seemed to think that Woodrow should not be worried with financial matters, I am sending you now that a new quarter is beginning, a check to your order for $2500, and I trust that this arrangement will be satisfactory to you. If not, please let me know, and we will try and arrange it some other way.

Admiral Grayson promised to let me know about the automobile, but I suppose he is so excited about his race horse that he has not been able to think of much else. I understand, however, that your brother is looking into the matter, and when I hear from you or the Admiral, I hope that the new Rolls-Royce will make the old gentleman thoroughly comfortable.

I note what you say about Margaret and will not talk to her any more about the matter, although I think she ought to know that her father's friends are helping him out, in view of the fact that she brought the matter up with me herself.

I am glad to know that Woodrow is gaining, even if a little, and sincerely hope he is going to get through the winter most happily and comfortably. Mrs. Dodge joins with me in much love to you both.   Ever cordially and faithfully yours,   [C. H. Dodge]

¹ It is missing.

Dear Mrs. Wilson: [New York] October 2, 1923.

I wrote you a long letter this morning, which goes with this, but after writing it I had a long talk with Mr. Jesse Jones, who told me of a change in the programme. It seems that he has had a talk with Admiral Grayson since I last saw him and the Admiral thinks it is better that Mr. Jones and I should write directly to Woodrow, so that there may be no doubt about the matter in his mind at all. Mr. Jones has sent him a letter, signed by himself and myself, and I have written a personal letter enclosing him check to his order for $2500, which I first intended to send to you. I think perhaps this is a better arrangement, and, in any event, you will be able to talk it over fully with him, and perhaps can show him my original letter, or tell him the substance of it in case you think it is best not to let him see what I wrote about his feelings.

I cannot tell you what a joy it is to make this arrangement, and I only hope that Woodrow will take it as it is meant, and get some comfort out of it.

Again,   Most sincerely yours,   [C. H. Dodge]

CCL (received from Phyllis Boushall Dodge).

To Jesse Holman Jones

My dear Friend,   Washington D C 4th October 1923

I must admit that I am quite overwhelmed by the wonderful kindness and generosity of which the letter signed by you and Dodge informs me. I cannot for a moment consider myself worthy of such friendship or of such benefits. I can only hope that they will inspire me for the services that lie ahead of us in the redemption of the country from the ignoble position into which it has been drawn by ignorant and unprincipled partisans.

I will not attempt to express my gratitude to you and those with whom you are associated in an ideal act of confidence and friendship. I know of no words that would be adequate but let me say at least that I am deeply proud that such men should think me worthy of such benefits.

Mrs. Wilson joins me in messages of warm friendship to Mrs. Jones[1] and you, and I beg to subscribe myself,

Affectionately,   Woodrow Wilson

TLS (J. H. Jones Papers, Barker Texas History Center, TxU).
[1] Mary Gibbs Jones.

To Cleveland Hoadley Dodge

My dear Cleve,   Washington D C 4th October 1923

Surely no other man was ever blessed with so true, so unselfish, so thoughtful, so helpful a friend as you are and always have been to me! My heart is full to overflowing with gratitude and affection.

The letters I have just received from you and Jesse Jones have made me feel very humble indeed because I cannot believe that I have in fact earned or deserved such benefits as you propose. I know of no adequate means of expressing my gratitude or the pride that I feel in having such friends. Thanks of any kind would be thin and pale as compared with the subject of the thanks. I can only pray that God will enable me to prove in some degree worthy of such trust and affection.

It distresses me deeply to learn that you feel that your strength has not entirely returned, and I hope and pray that with care,— such as I am sure you are exercising,—that there may be soon a restoration of the wonderful vigor which has always characterized you.

Please do not try to come to Washington until you feel fully equal to it. It is clear to me it is the duty of both of us to get and keep fully fit for the great tasks awaiting us. As I see it the greatest fight of all lies immediately ahead of the liberal forces of this country and of the world,—the fight to conquer selfishness and greed and establish the rule of justice and fair play and universal cooperation. If I played the part in that fight which I wish to play it would be due in no small measure to the relief from anxiety and unnecessary effort which I have experienced at your hands and at the hands of the other generous friends who have made the provision for my ease of which the letter signed by you and Jesse Jones tells me.

With more affection and gratitude than I know how to express,
Your Devoted Friend,   Woodrow Wilson

TLS (WC, NjP).

To David Lloyd George

[Washington] 5th October 1923

Allow me to bid you a most cordial welcome to the United States stop I am very much gratified that you have come to America and am looking forward with much pleasure to seeing you again.
Woodrow Wilson.

T telegram (WP, DLC).

From David Lloyd George

Montreal Que Oct 8 1923

Greatly touched by your most cordial and kind message which I warmly appreciate Much looking forward to meeting you when I go to Washington   D Lloyd George

T telegram (WP, DLC).

From William Gibbs McAdoo

Dear Governor: Los Angeles, Cal. October 9, 1923

I haven't had a chance to write you sooner and thank you warmly for the photographs you were good enough to autograph for me. They are very much appreciated.

I shall have a chance not long after this letter reaches you to thank you in person for your kindness. Nell and I and the two babies are starting on October 10th for New York where we arrive on the 14th. After a ten days or two weeks stay there, we shall run down to Washington and have the pleasure of seeing you and Edith again.

Nell joins me in warmest love to you and Edith.

Devotedly yours,   W G McAdoo

TLS (WP, DLC).

From Charles Sumner Hamlin

My dear Mr. Wilson: Washington October 9, 1923.

When your article entitled "The Road Away from Revolution," appeared in the August number of the Atlantic Monthly, I read it with great care, and was much impressed with its sound sense and the high principles of conduct it laid down for the preservation of our people from the evils of irrational protest and revolution. Yesterday I re-read it and was not only more deeply impressed with the message it gave, but, as well, I realized what a memorable contribution it was to ethical philosophy.

It brings back vividly to my mind my college days at Harvard when I was studying Ethics under Frederic Palmer. I remember so well the doctrines laid down by the English philosophers Hobbes and Mandeville who could only see a hopeless conflict between man and man and who proclaimed that society was simply an aggregation of individuals who were fighting one another like wild beasts; that only the fittest could survive in the struggle; that in intercourse between man and man the gain of the one was the precise measure of the loss to the other; and that between nations the same principles obtained. I next studied the writings of the Earl of Shaftsbury,—the "gentle" Shaftsbury, so called,—who pointed out, in opposition to the above doctrine, that men and nations were instinctively bound together by sympathy, that the bond of sympathy was far more deeply imbedded in the human breast than the spirit of unruly competition, and that only by this bond could civilization and society be maintained.

When I read Lord Birkenhead's recent address[1] I was at first shocked by his analysis of society and of the conduct of nations as based exclusively upon self-interest,—not to mention his grotesquely inapposite references to you,—but, upon reflection I feel now almost grateful to him for his frankness in throwing aside the mask and revealing his true conception of international relations. He stands precisely where Hobbes and Mandeville stood hundreds of years ago; can see only a hopeless conflict between man and man and nation and nation, and, furthermore, he has not even the sense to realize that if the United States, during the world war, had been guided by the principles of selfish interest which he lays down, his country would now be "hewing wood and drawing water" for the German Emperor. Your article, on the contrary, gives added force, convincing force, to the doctrine of Lord Shaftsbury that sympathy is the underlying bond which alone can save society and civilization. We can at least thank Lord Birkenhead for furnishing the dark forbidding background against which your "idealism," as he calls it, stands forth like a beacon light. It will not be long, in my opinion, before our people will realize,—and signs are not wanting that many have already realized,—that you have been guided not only by a spirit of lofty idealism, but, as well, have blazed out a road and the only road, over which we all must travel to insure the preservation of civilization and humanity.

Very sincerely yours,   Charles S. Hamlin

TLS (WP, DLC).
[1] Frederick Edwin Smith, 1st Earl of Birkenhead, had delivered an address entitled "Problems Left by the Great War" at the Institute of Politics at Williamstown, Massachusetts, on August 24. As Hamlin indicates above, Birkenhead declared that the great mass of individual human beings, and all nations, were, and indeed had to be, ruled by self-interest. Woodrow Wilson, he said, had come to the Paris Peace Conference "with a noble message of hope; but unhappily, in the sequel, hope proved to be his principal equipment." "It is a fascinating speculation," Birkenhead continued, "whether, had he [Wilson] been given health and strength to pursue the campaign which he contemplated, his idealism and personality could have affected the forces of the world. I am bold enough, even at the moment when I pay the highest tribute to his unselfish and courageous motives, to doubt it. For the real truth is that while the whole world requires the encouragement and the light of idealism, the whole world would probably not survive if idealism were given a completely free rein." Wilson, Birkenhead asserted, had misjudged his own countrymen, and "by the error of that judgment," he had become,

paradoxically enough, "the agent of all those post-war developments from which his altruistic mind would most specially have recoiled." The primary, indeed the only, duty of the American government, Birkenhead insisted, was to its own people. If that government could advance the interests of the American people by intervening in the affairs of Europe, it should do so. "But if in cool perspective," he said, "they [the American government] reached the conclusion that no compensating gain to the American people would result from reassuming European and world responsibility, they would be failing in their duty if they embraced an unnecessary responsibility." The full text of Birkenhead's address is printed in F. E. Smith, 1st Earl of Birkenhead, *The Speeches of Lord Birkenhead* (London, 1929), pp. 178-94; the above quotations are from pp. 181-82.

To Charles Sumner Hamlin

My dear Friend,   Washington D C 10th October 1923

Thank you very warmly for your letter of yesterday about my little essay in The Atlantic. I am happy to have it pointed out how remote I am from the point of view of Hobbes and Mandeville, and am content to be associated with the "gentle" Shaftsbury.

Birkenhead is merely negligible like all other crude and insincere intellects. He has long had the reputation in Great Britain of being the egregious ass he is. They smile at him there and pay not the least attention to what he says. The stories of his amazing egotism are innumerable and ought to be collected and published in order that they might add to the gayety of nations.

With grateful appreciation of your generous estimate,
                    Faithfully Yours,   Woodrow Wilson

TLS (C. S. Hamlin Papers, DLC).

To Finis James Garrett

My dear Mr. Garrett,   [Washington] 13th October 1923

Will you not permit me to express the hope that the House Democrats will vigorously follow up Mr. Henry Ford's charges against the present Secretary of War with regard to the disposal of the Government's Muscle Shoals nitrate project.[1] That project is of vital importance to the farmers and it seems to me that every transaction in regard to it should be made a matter of public record by means of a thorough-going investigation by a committee of the Congress.

I hope that this suggestion will commend itself to you; otherwise it is only too likely that the matter will be ignored or covered over by the present administration after the usual manner of Republican administrations.

If this is an intrusion on the field of your own choice and judgment I beg that you will forgive me and believe that I have taken this liberty only because I believed an investigation of this vital matter to be essential to the maintenance of the public interest.

Permit me to say that it has gratified me very much to learn that the Democrats of the House have turned to you as their leader.

If I can, at any time or in any way, be of assistance to you pray feel at liberty to command me.

Cordially and Sincerely Yours,   [Woodrow Wilson]

CCL (WP, DLC).

¹ Henry Ford had offered in July 1921 to purchase from the federal government the nitrate plants built at Muscle Shoals, Alabama, during the wartime emergency. A steam electric-generating plant located at Gorgas, Alabama, was to be part of the purchase. Ford also offered to take a long-term lease on the Wilson Dam and dam no. 3, provided that the government completed the building of these dams and the installation of necessary hydroelectric generating equipment. In return for the government's acceptance of these proposals, Ford promised in vague terms to produce fertilizer for commercial sale at one of the nitrate plants and to make available for sale at least some of the electric power generated by the dams. Ford's offer, with some later modifications, had been hanging fire ever since, as Congress, the Harding administration, and later the Coolidge administration, haggled endlessly both over whether the offer should be accepted at all and what the exact terms of the agreement should be if it was accepted. The offer was widely discussed and debated in the press and in business and political circles, with many Southerners in particular believing that the proposal promised economic salvation to the South in the forms of cheap electric power for its industries and cheap fertilizer for its farmers.

John Wingate Weeks, the Secretary of War, although he had originally encouraged Ford to make his offer, ultimately came to oppose it for various reasons. On September 24, 1923, he dropped a bombshell on the lengthy negotiations by announcing the sale of the Gorgas steam power plant to the Alabama Power Company. In a public statement on October 11, an enraged Henry Ford declared that Weeks by his action had deliberately attempted to torpedo his proposal, and he intimated that Weeks' step had been motivated by private business interests. Ford said, however, that his offer would remain before Congress for final action. See Preston J. Hubbard, *Origins of the TVA: The Muscle Shoals Controversy, 1920-1932* (Nashville, Tenn., 1961), pp. 1-111, especially pp. 28-31, 99-101.

To the Moore-Cottrell Subscription Agencies

Dear sirs: [Washington] 13th October 1923

Enclosed find check for $56.25 for which send me the following magazines for one year, beginning with the November issues, in accordance with your estimate dated Oct. 12, 1923;

Beauty Magazine
Century
Country Life
Garden
International Studio
Life
Midweek Pictorial
National Geographic
Photoplay
Screenland

Theatre Magazine
Vanity Fair
Movie Weekly
Mentor
Town and Country

Yours very truly,   [Woodrow Wilson]

CCL (WP, DLC).

To Lord Robert Cecil

[Washington] Oct 16 1923

Newspaper dispatches say that you have overworked and are not well stop Let me express my grief and affectionate solicitude and the hope that you can reassure me   Woodrow Wilson[1]

T telegram (WP, DLC).
[1] There is a WWhw draft of this telegram in WP, DLC.

To Edith Bolling Galt Wilson

[Washington] Oct. 19th 1923

Everything going well[1] here Stop Please do not feel hurried stop
Love   Woodrow

T telegram (EBW Papers, DLC).
[1] Mrs. Wilson was visiting the Norman Davises in New York over the weekend. They lived at 59 E. 79th St.

From Lord Robert Cecil

London Oct 19 23

Deeply touched by your cable stop Indisposition not serious stop Trust your health continues to improve stop Best wishes
                                                    Robert Cecil

T telegram (WP, DLC).

To Joseph Ramsey Sevier[1]

My dear Dr. Sevier,   [Washington] 20th October 1923

It would indeed be a great pleasure for me if I could accept the kind invitation conveyed by your telegram received on yesterday.[2]

Many of the most delightful recollections of my boyhood center about the Augusta Church of which my Father was pastor, and it would be delightful to take part in the exercises you are planning. But unhappily I am not yet in condition to travel with impunity, and have no choice but to decline.

I hope that all your plans will work out in the happiest manner and that the highest kind of prosperity will always attend the labours of your Church.

Pray accept my most cordial good wishes and assurances of my personal regard.

Cordially and Sincerely Yours,   [Woodrow Wilson]

CCL (WP, DLC).
    [1] Pastor of the First Presbyterian Church of Augusta, Georgia.
    [2] J. R. Sevier to WW, Oct. 19, 1923, T telegram (WP, DLC). Sevier informed Wilson that his church was having a "big home coming day" on October 21. He asked Wilson to send a message to be read at the service on that date.

To Raymond Blaine Fosdick

My dear Fosdick,   Washington D C 22nd October 1923

I am writing to ask if you could make it convenient sometime soon to come down here to see me. Any afternoon next week (week of October 28th) at three thirty would be a feasible time for me to interrupt the routine of my convalescence.

I want to discuss with you not a matter concerning the League of Nations but an educational matter which I shall hope through you to be fortunate enough to interest the Rockefeller Foundation.[1]

I don't want to interfere with your stated duties and shall trust you if it is not convenient for you to come to say so,—counting upon my understanding perfectly.

I hope that you feel encouraged about the impression the League is making in this country, notwithstanding the Greek-Italian mixup and partial miscarriage.

As ever,

With very warm regards,

Faithfully Yours,   Woodrow Wilson

TLS (WP, DLC).
    [1] Fosdick later recalled his visit to Wilson to discuss this matter as follows:
    "I immediately went to Washington, and found him in a reminiscent mood about his days as president of Princeton. 'It was the best period of my life,' he said, 'and I begin to realize that my contribution to my generation, if I have made any, was in connection not so much with my political work as with my activities as a teacher and college administrator.' I remember he told me a story about the Master of Balliol who was asked whether it was not a dreary business to spend twenty years doing the sort of work that the head of any college has to do; to which the Master of Balliol replied: 'Is it dreary business to run the British Empire?'
    "Wilson at this moment was dreaming of the possibility of another chance in educational work, another opportunity, as he expressed it, to help American universities to attain the high standards of scholarship which had been reached by Oxford and Cambridge.

From Evangeline Brewster Johnson[1]

My dear Mr Wilson;   New York City October 23rd, 1923.

In making this request I feel keenly the inadequacy of my words, so intensely do I hope that you may see your way clear to acquiesce.

The New York Telephone and Telegraph Company is anxious to have a message broadcasted by wireless to the people of the United States on the eve of Armistice Day, and naturally turn to you; the creator of that day. You, dear Mr Wilson, are in a position to make this day mean even more both spiritually and materially to the people whom you have so enormously benefited[.] I wonder if you realize what an ever increasing inspiration you are to the public spirited men and women of America. Last Friday evening at a dinner which Mr Bok gave for the heads of the various organizations which are cooperating with the American Peace Award[2] and which represented many millions of citizens, the applause was thunderous when Mr Bok stated the inspiration that Woodrow Wilson had been to him.

We are doing everything we can to urge other wireless stations to have speakers on Armistice Day who will stress the necessity for continued world peace. Of course a message from you on the eve of that day would go straight to the heart of every one who received it. If you will consent to speak for about fifteen minutes, reading from notes if you so desire, on the evening of November tenth, the New York Telephone and Telegraph Company will be glad to install the necessary apparatus in your home, which will transfer your message to their great station in New York from where it will be broadcasted to the United States.

Please forgive me for being repetitous in urging you to speak to your own people, on the eve of your own day.

Respectfully and admiringly,   Evangeline Johnson

ALS (WP, DLC).
  ¹ Daughter of Robert Wood Johnson, cofounder of the medical supply firm of Johnson & Johnson. She was at this time Director of the Speakers' Bureau of the League of Nations Non-Partisan Association. A typewritten note at the top of this letter reads: "Answd. in person to Miss Johnson by WW Oct. 27th 1923."
  ² A "policy committee" appointed by Edward William Bok had announced on July 1, 1923, that Bok had established a prize of $100,000, to be known as the American Peace Award, which was to be given to an American citizen who proposed the most practicable plan by which the United States could cooperate with other nations to achieve and preserve world peace. The prize was to be given in two parts: the first $50,000 to be paid for the winning idea itself; the second to be paid when that idea had demonstrated its practicability either through its adoption by the United States Senate or through its endorsement by "a sufficient popular response." *New York Times*, July 2, 1923. The precise conditions of the contest for the award were announced on July 22. All entries were due by November 15, 1923. It was announced on August 23 that Elihu Root would be chairman of the jury chosen to select the prize-winning plan. The names of the other members of the jury were revealed on October 18 and included Brand Whitlock, Gen. James Guthrie Harbord, Col. House, Roscoe Pound, William Allen White, and Ellen Fitz Pendleton, the President of Wellesley College. The prize contest attracted much attention in the press, and more than 20,000 peace plans were ultimately submitted from all over the United States. On January 7, 1924, the full text of the winning plan was printed, e.g., in the *New York Times*. The author's name was not to be made public until the completion of a nationwide mail ballot of all persons who completed and returned a form printed, e.g., in *ibid*. It was finally announced on February 4, 1924, that the prizewinner was Charles Herbert Levermore of New York, Secretary of the New York Peace Society, former President of Adelphi College, and Wilson's old friend from graduate student days at The Johns Hopkins University. In addition to the issues already cited, see the *New York Times*, July 23, Aug. 24, Oct. 18, Nov. 16, 1923; and Feb. 5, 1924.

From Bernard Mannes Baruch

New York NY Oct 24 1923

Let me call your attention to General Smuts speech yesterday¹ Stop Will you be free next Sunday at usual time

B M Baruch

T telegram (WP, DLC).
  ¹ Smuts spoke to the South Africa Club in London on October 23. He painted a grim picture of a Europe in danger of economic and political collapse. He was especially worried by the possibility of the "disintegration" of Germany. He strongly condemned the French occupation of the Ruhr as totally counterproductive and called for a conference of world leaders, including those of the United States, to discuss the problem of reparations. The full text of his speech is printed in Hancock and Van der Poel, eds., *Selections from the Smuts Papers*, V, 192-205. Extensive excerpts from his remarks appeared in the London *Times* and the *New York Times*, both of October 24, 1923.

To Bernard Mannes Baruch

[Washington] 24th October 1923

Smuts is showing his mettle again and playing vigorously the role you suggested stop Please be so generous as to come on Monday instead of Sunday stop Affectionate messages from us both

Woodrow Wilson

T telegram (WP, DLC).

James Kerney to John Randolph Bolling

My dear Mr. Bolling: Trenton, New Jersey October 24, 1923.

Thanks for your kind note of the 20th.[1] It will be a real delight to see the President Saturday afternoon and meanwhile I am going to ask you to lay before him a very interesting suggestion that came this afternoon from Judge Charles F. Lynch of the United States District Court, whom the President will remember not only as a worth-while appointee to the bench but as a very delightful friend and the law partner of the late Senator Billy Hughes.

Former Senator Frelinghuysen put out today a very savage attack on Senator Edge[2] and in the course of a discussion of the certainty that out of the Republican row would come a Democratic United States Senator from New Jersey next year Judge Lynch expressed the thought that it would be a mighty fine thing for the world, and an especially fine thing for New Jersey if Woodrow Wilson would permit the people to name him. That may appear a bit strange, but the more we discussed it the more I felt that Judge Lynch was on very sound ground. The New Jersey Democracy is unhappily in the dumps about a candidate. Here is a rare opportunity to give the world, in an official way, the benefit of the experience and wisdom of Woodrow Wilson, for whom there is a very decided favorable reaction everywhere. And it would come about, too, with the minimum of effort or personal annoyance on his part. He would not have to leave Washington; in fact he wouldn't have to do anything but permit his friends to support him.

It would be like going back to the early days of his occupancy of the Governorship when the big newspapers of the state rallied to his standard, regardless of previous political leanings. I am sure that the Scudders, the Dears, Matt Ely,[3] the Paterson Press-Guardian, and the publishers and editors of other important papers would welcome a chance to push to the limit a come-back for the President, and there would seem to be no way of a come-back so easy of accomplishment and so hopeful in opportunity and results. Something of that kind would be worth fighting for, particularly in view of the helpless condition existing among a lot of folks who like to be Democrats.

If I felt the matter would tax the President in anyway I would not think of suggesting it. He has already carried burden enough. But I frankly feel that it would be a happy and useful relaxation and that it is well worth thinking over. There has always been a strong feeling among thinking people—if there are such—that the men who had served as President of the United States should occupy a place in the United States Senate in order that the world might have the full benefit of their ripe judgment.

If the President will consider it all, he may do so with the confident understanding that he will not at any time be bothered with petty patronage matters; all he will have to think of will be the big things of the world which are, at this time, in such sad need of intelligent action. He is going to reside in Washington, anyhow, and I am confident that he would find the task not too heavy.

Of course the suggestion will be treated as absolutely sacred.

With warm regard, I am

Faithfully yours,   James Kerney[4]

TLS (WP, DLC).

[1] JRB to J. Kerney, Oct. 20, 1923, CCL (WP, DLC).

[2] Former Senator Joseph Sherman Frelinghuysen announced on October 24 that he had written to President Coolidge demanding the suspension of Adrian Chamberlain, Prohibition Director for New Jersey, and the appointment of a special United States attorney to investigate what he asserted was the total failure to enforce the Eighteenth Amendment in New Jersey. He also made public a lengthy letter to Roy Asa Haynes, the national Commissioner of Prohibition, in which he charged that high officials of both political parties were involved in a corrupt conspiracy to nullify prohibition in New Jersey. This letter included an obvious reference to Senator Edward I. Edwards but no clear mention of Senator Walter E. Edge. However, the newspapers immediately pointed out that it was widely understood that Chamberlain had been appointed by the Harding administration chiefly on Edge's recommendation. Edge refused to comment on the Frelinghuysen charges on October 25, except to say that he believed that Chamberlain was an able official and would probably vindicate himself against the accusations. *New York Times*, Oct. 25 and 26, 1923.

[3] Edward Wallace Scudder and Wallace McIlvaine Scudder, Joseph Albert Dear, Jr., and Walter Moore Dear, and Matthias Cowell Ely, all newspapermen of New Jersey. See the index references under their names in Vol. 26.

[4] Typed at the top of this letter: "Read to W.W. Oct. 26th; said would reply in person, when he saw him Oct. 27th."

From a News Report

[*Oct. 25, 1923*]

LLOYD GEORGE SEES WASHINGTON CHIEFS
PAYS LONG VISIT TO WILSON

Washington, Oct. 25.—An "unofficial Ambassador" from the people of his own country to the people of the United States, David Lloyd George, Great Britain's War Premier, arrived here today to find official Washington intently watching and seriously concerned over a situation in Europe which throughout his speechmaking tour in this country and Canada he had pictured as so grave as to demand the aid of America if a catastrophe is to be averted. . . .

During the late afternoon Mr. Lloyd George rested and received some visitors at his suite in the New Willard, among whom were Rear Admiral Cary T. Grayson and General Tasker H. Bliss. General Bliss, as American member of the Supreme War Council, came into close contact with the British War Premier while the Versailles Peace Conference was in the making. Lloyd George has singled him out for eulogistic praise in his public addresses in America upon more than one occasion. Admiral Grayson discussed the prospective trip over the Civil War battlefields in Virginia, which is included in the itinerary of the British visitor.

Both accompanied Mr. Lloyd George to the home of ex-President Wilson in S Street, where they were joined by Dame Margaret and Miss Megan Lloyd George.[1] Here they were entertained at tea. They remained for three-quarters of an hour. Part of the time was spent by Mr. Wilson and his visitor in the study of his host, where in seclusion they talked over mutual experiences while the peace negotiations were on and discussed the present European situation. It was learned that the British War Premier found his former associate on the "Big Four" alert of mind and displaying the most vivid interest in the European situation, which he has been following closely in all its recent developments.

Mr. Lloyd George expressed keen delight over his talk with Mr. Wilson.

Printed in the *New York Times*, Oct. 26, 1923.
   [1] His wife, Margaret Owen Lloyd George, and his daughter, Megan Arvon Lloyd George.

From Ambrose White Vernon[1]

My dear Mr. Wilson: Northfield, Minn. October 25, 1923

Germany is constantly in my thoughts and the way in which, notwithstanding your noble asseveration in your call to war against her *government*, we have left her to her cruel fate. Must we wait for further manifestations of French vengeance before sluggish public opinion rises in condemnation? You know better than I and you are so superbly patient. But your voice is the only personal one which can now stir the country into some sort of protest—for who can hope for any courageous initiative from Mr Coolidge?

Will you tell me what you think should be done? Do you think it unwise to write to me or simply to the public (which might be far better) a ringing word of protest? We did not fight to put a ruthless France into the place of an imperialistic and heartless Germany, and I know that you did not summon us to any such cause.

Forgive me for this note which comes from a lacerated and impotent heart.

Every faithfully and loyally yours   Ambrose W. Vernon

ALS (WP, DLC).
   [1] Former Congregationalist minister and an old acquaintance of Wilson; at this time Professor of Biography at Carleton College.

To David Lloyd George, with Enclosure

My dear Friend,   [Washington] 27th October 1923

Grayson tells me that you were interested in the rhyme about the sheep, and I hasten to send you a copy of that important literary production.

It has been a great pleasure to see you, and I hope that your visit to Washington has not been spoiled by too many exactions upon you.

With warm regard,

Faithfully Yours,   [Woodrow Wilson]

CCL (WP, DLC).

ENCLOSURE

There was an old man of Khartoum
Who kept two black sheep in his room
    To remind him, he said,
    Of two friends who were dead;
But he never would tell us of whom.

CC MS (WP, DLC).

From Finis James Garrett

My Dear Mr. Wilson: Dresden, Tenn. Oct 27, 1923.

I have been absent from home and hence the delay in responding to your greatly appreciated letter of Oct 14, which was forwarded from my Washington office.

Replying now I beg to state that I am in full sympathy with your suggestion of a Congressional inquiry into the sale of the Gorgas power plant to the Alabama power company, and I shall bend every effort to bring one about.

I thank you most sincerely for your letter. It is deeply gratifying to feel that in the discharge of the duties awaiting me I may turn freely to you for advice and counsel. I shall take advantage of your generous offer I assure you. With all good wishes, I am,

Sincerely yours,   Finis J Garrett.

ALS (WP, DLC).

To Bernard Mannes Baruch

My dear Friend,   Washington D C 28th October, 1923.

I took the liberty on yesterday of referring Mr. James Kerney, of Trenton, N. J. to you, to discuss a political matter of some importance which he had recently brought to my attention. I think you will like him. He is editor and proprietor of the Trenton Evening Times,—was a staunch friend of mine when I was Governor of New Jersey,—and has remained a friend who can be trusted. I hope that it will not prove burdensome to you to consult him.[1]

We greatly enjoyed having your daughter[2] with us last evening, and hope that the pleasure may be often repeated. I had not before recognized her extraordinary resemblance to you. She is very handsome and striking, and seems full of the right kind of spirit. She and Miss Johnson are getting me in for an exceedingly difficult stunt on the eve of Armistice Day, but I can easily forgive them on account of the fine, disinterested work they are doing.

It cheers me that I am to see you before very long. I hope that you are taking care of yourself, and keep perfectly well. There is too much work to be done for any of us to indulge in any kind of incapacitation.

Mrs. Wilson joins me in affectionate messages to you all, and I am, as always,   Affectionately Yours,   Woodrow Wilson

TLS (B. M. Baruch Papers, NjP).
  [1] WW to NHD, Oct. 28, 1923, CCL (WP, DLC), repeats this paragraph.
  [2] That is, Belle Baruch.

To Ambrose White Vernon[1]

My dear Vernon,   [Washington] 28th October 1923

I have studied the European situation as best I might at this distance and am convinced that there is a madness in the French mind at this time against which it is useless to protest. Providence has, I believe, a great and painful awakening in store for the French, but I know of no way in which I or anyone else can hasten the inevitable day of their great reckoning. They are bringing upon themselves an irreparable disaster far more fatal to their national interests than the damage which Germany sought to inflict upon them in the war. But I say nothing about it except privately to my friends, because I know the futility of anything else. If I would say anything publicly about their policy, it would only make Poincare a little more reckless and outrageous. He learned while I was in Paris to hate me as much as I despised him. He was a sneak and a liar, and nothing can be done now to correct his errors. I am sure that God will attend to that in the usual thorough manner which will leave nothing to be desired.

Please present my respects to Mrs. Vernon,[2] and always think of me as Your Sincere Friend, [Woodrow Wilson]

CCL (WP, DLC).
[1] This letter is marked not sent. J. R. Bolling to A. W. Vernon, Oct. 28, 1923, CCL (WP, DLC), said that Wilson did not think it would be wise for him to make any public expression about the European situation at this time.
[2] Katharina Tappe Vernon.

To James Kerney

My dear Kerney, Washington 30th October 1923

Since you were here I have been thinking over the matter we have discussed, and a man has occurred to me whose qualifications I think you and your associates would do well to consider very seriously, Mr. Winthrop M. Daniels. He won the reputation here of being by far the ablest member of the Interstate Commerce Commission, and is unusually conversant with public questions in many fields. I have known him a great many years and can vouch for his being able, conscientiousness and fearless. My own judgment is that he would make a most serviceable member of the Senate.

Let me say also that when you are canvassing the field as a whole I do not think you ought to overlook Tumulty, whose political training has been more varied than that of any other man I know, and who,—when he was in the New Jersey Assembly,—proved himself a redoubtable debater. He would make some of the reactionary Senators sit up and take notice of the arrival of modern times and circumstances.

I felt it my duty to make these suggestions. It was a real pleasure to see you.

Cordially and Faithfully Yours, Woodrow Wilson

TLS (received from Holt A. Murray).

From Henry van Dyke

My dear Wilson, Princeton, N. J. Oct. 30, 1923

This is only a line to thank you for a book sent me by y'r publishers—"The Road away from Revolution"—a bit of true Gospel!

Thinking of you steadily with sympathetic love, backing your horse every time, I've kept away from you only to spare you from the burden of another straw. You are winning out; and thank God you'll live to see the triumph of your *idea* over other men's plots.

I hope that you understand, and that you won't think of answering this, and that you'll believe me,

Ever faithfully yours   Henry van Dyke

ALS (WP, DLC).

From William Gibbs McAdoo

New York Oct 31 23

Warmest thanks and dearest love to you and Edith We arrive four fifteen PM tomorrow and shall see you soon

W G McAdoo

T telegram (WP, DLC).

From James Kerney

My dear Governor: Trenton, New Jersey October 31st, 1923

Those are very admirable names that you so generously suggest. I have an engagement with Mr Baruch and Norman Davis for tomorrow, Thursday, afternoon, and we will go over the situation from all angles. Frelinghuysen's smashing attacks on Edge are daily improving the Democratic chances for success in New Jersey.

It was a real joy to find you so well and your mind so freshly alive to what is happening. I only hope that I did not weary you too much.   Faithfully yours,   James Kerney

TLS (WP, DLC).

From John Spencer Bassett[1]

Dear Mr. Wilson: Northampton, Mass. October 31, 1923

In a few weeks there will be a meeting of the council of the American Historical Association and one of the subjects discussed will be the place and the conditions for the meeting of 1924 which will probably fall within your presidency. Two years ago, it was decided to accept an invitation from Richmond, Va. with the understand[ing] that if it would suit your convenience better, one meeting would be held in Washington at which we should certainly hope you would be the leading participant. I am writing this letter on my own personal responsibility and to inquire if you have any preference in the matter so that I may speak about it when the council meets. I am quite certain that the council will wish to know your views in the matter and I hope that you will not think my request presuming.

With best wishes, I am

Yours sincerely,   John S. Bassett

TLS (WP, DLC).
[1] Professor of History at Smith College and Secretary of the American Historical Association.

From Norman Hezekiah Davis

59 East 79th St.

My dear Mr. Wilson: New York November 1, 1923.

I shall be delighted to see Mr. James Kearney of Trenton. He has already gotten in touch with Baruch, and evidently told him that he wished to consult with both of us, for Baruch called me by telephone today, and arranged to come with him to see me tomorrow afternoon.

It was such a pleasure to have Mrs. Wilson with us, even for a short period, and we appreciate your loaning her to us for that time. Mrs. Davis joins me in affectionate regards to you both, and I remain, as ever,

Affectionately yours,   Norman H. Davis

TLS (WP, DLC).

To Norman Hezekiah Davis

My dear Friend,   [Washington] 2nd November 1923

It has greatly distressed us to learn that you are not well and have had to resort to a hospital, and we shall await with affectionate solicitude to hear of your recovery. I know that your spirit will sustain any trial that comes to you. I hope with all my heart that you will very soon indeed be entirely free of any malady or apprehension of one.

Mrs. Wilson joins me in affectionate messages to Mrs. Davis and you, and I am,

As always,   Affectionately Yours,   [Woodrow Wilson]

CCL (WP, DLC).

To Henry van Dyke

My dear van Dyke,   [Washington] 2nd November 1923
    I am glad you liked The Road Away From Revolution. I can truly
say of it that it came from my heart.
    Hoping that your family are all well,
                                Sincerely Yours,   [Woodrow Wilson]

CCL (WP, DLC).

From James Kerney

My dear Governor: Trenton, New Jersey November 2, 1923
    Mr. Baruch and I went to the home of Mr. Davis yesterday after-
noon and we spent a couple of hours frankly canvassing the entire
situation. At the finish I suggested that, inasmuch as the final decision must rest with you, it would be well to give twenty-four
hours additional thought to the matter and then write you with the
utmost freedom and candor. They are expecting to send their ideas
to you today, and, after you have had opportunity to weigh their
views, I would like to run down and have a short chat. Anytime
that fits in with your plans will be agreeable to me. I could leave
Trenton in the morning and return in the afternoon and one day
would answer as well as another.
    Anyhow I want to briefly recount the very amusing time some of
us had at the Nassau Club luncheon Wednesday when President
Meikeljohn [Meiklejohn] gave the faculty of Princeton his refreshing notions of the relationship of educators to trustees and alumni.
It kept President Hibben a trifle on the jump to soften the work
[words?] of his good friend from Amherst.
                        Always faithfully yours,   James Kerney[1]

TLS (WP, DLC).
    [1] Typed at the top of this letter: "No reply WW"

John Randolph Bolling to John Spencer Bassett

My dear Mr. Bassett: [Washington] 3rd November 1923
    Mr. Wilson asks me to reply to your very kind letter of October
thirty-first, and thank you for consulting him about the meeting to
which you refer. He wishes me to say that Richmond, Virginia, will

suit him as well as any other place, though he can't foresee whether or not he will be able to attend.

With sincere good wishes;

Cordially yours,   [John Randolph Bolling]

CCL (WP, DLC).

From Norman Hezekiah Davis

My dear Mr. Wilson: New York. Nov. 3/23.

Mr. Kearney came up with Baruch to see me yesterday afternoon and we discussed the political matter he had taken up with you. It is difficult to advise you on such a matter as so much depends upon how you feel about it. I think it would do you a lot of good to have some active responsibility and work in keeping with a certain dignity that is imposed upon you but I doubt if what Mr. Kearney proposes is just the thing. You could of course add enough to the dignity of such a post itself to make that allright but I doubt if any contact with Lodge and his crowd would be particularly agreeable. If you should however consider this you should in my opinion count upon the necessity or expediency of going to the State for at least once. You could do it of course and it would no doubt do you good but if you don't feel like it then in my judgment you would better drop it. I hope to get down to see you sometime within a week or so and we can then discuss this further as well as other matters of interest.

Affectionately yours   Norman H. Davis

ALS (WP, DLC).

To Claude Augustus Swanson

My dear Senator,   [Washington] 4th November 1923

You certainly know how to adapt your kindnesses to the tastes and preferences of your friends. Nothing could have been more acceptable to me than the gift of partridges you so generously sent on yesterday. I had been wishing earlier in the day that I might have some, for I am of course exceedingly fond of them,—and they constitute ideal food for me in the present sensitive state of my digestive organs. Thank you with all my heart.

I have not had an earlier opportunity to congratulate you on your marriage. I had the pleasure at Hot Springs of meeting Miss Lulie Lyons and know how attractive and delightful she is.[1] Please present her my warm regards and cordial felicitations. I beg you to believe that everything that concerns your welfare is of deep and genuine interest to me, and you may be sure that Mrs. Wilson joins me in these sentiments.

With warm regard,

Faithfully Yours,   [Woodrow Wilson]

CCL (WP, DLC).
[1] See the extract from Wilson's diary printed at Aug. 6, 1897, Vol. 10; n. 4 to WW to EAW, Feb. 9, 1898 (second letter of that date), *ibid.*; WW to EAW, Feb. 12, 1898, *ibid.*; WW to EAW, Oct. 28, 1898, Vol. 11; and WW to EAW, Oct. 31, 1898, *ibid.*

From Sir Horace Plunkett

London, S.W.

Dear President (as you must ever be to me),   Nov. 7, 1923.

I am enclosing a letter to The Times of today which may possibly be of some slight interest to you.[1] I wrote it under the deep conviction that Western civilization is in the gravest peril, to be averted, if at all, by a gradual reversion of the American Republic and the British Commonwealth to the fundamentals of your peace policy.

In common with many others who know your country, I am always watching for news of your steady progress to the health and vigor of which you were so suddenly deprived when you were carrying the heaviest burden ever imposed upon an individual statesman. About Christmas time I expect to cross the Atlantic, and when in Washington may ask Mrs. Wilson if I may again call and pay my respects.   Very sincerely yours,   Horace Plunkett

TLS (WP, DLC).
[1] H. Plunkett to the Editor, London *Times*, Nov. 5, 1923, printed in *ibid.*, Nov. 7, 1923. Plunkett insisted that, if Theodore Roosevelt had been President of the United States from 1913 to 1917, even he would not have been able to gain the support of the American people, especially those of the Middle West, for American participation in the war until sometime well after the *Lusitania* crisis. Plunkett also told about an exchange of letters between himself and Roosevelt in 1917.

To Alice Starke Hotchkiss[1]

My dear Mrs. Hotchkiss,   [Washington] 9th November 1923

Having learned[2] of the group of devoted Virginians who are assisting in the national movement to purchase Monticello, the home of Thomas Jefferson, I am writing to ask if I may not express to you my very deep and earnest interest in the enterprise both as an American citizen and a Virginian. I feel very deeply concerned that the project should succeed, and I hope that all who love Virginia and adequately appreciate the character of Jefferson are lending a hand to help you in the work. I believe that when it is in the hands of trustees Monticello will become one of the most resorted to shrines in the country. No other shrine could so adequately represent the aspirations and abiding principles of our people. I wish that my means were as large as my enthusiasm in this matter. If they were, the purchase would be made in short order. There are men in America who have the means and who truly reverence the principles associated with the great name of Jefferson. I trust that they will help you with open-handed generosity.

I felicitate you on the progress already made, and venture to wish you Godspeed in its conclusion.

With sincere admiration and regard,

Faithfully Yours,   [Woodrow Wilson]

CCL (WP, DLC).
[1] She was Mrs. Elmore D. Hotchkiss, "Virginia chairman" of the "Virginia Board" of the Thomas Jefferson Memorial Foundation, Inc.
[2] From Alice S. Hotchkiss to EBW, Nov. 3, 1923, ALS (WP, DLC).

From Cleveland Hoadley Dodge

My dear Woodrow: New York November 9, 1923.

When I sent you that rather formal note last week, signed by myself as Treasurer of the Near East Relief,[1] I was a little worried for fear you might be bored by it, but now comes your wonderful reply, through Mr. Bolling,[2] not only stating you have signed the Golden Rule card, but sending your check of $25.00.

It is needless to say that everybody connected with the Near East Relief is thrilled with delight and excitement, and I want to thank you personally for what you have done.

The Golden Rule Sunday idea is taking like hot cakes, and I think will not only bring in a good deal of money but have a splendid effect upon the morale of the country.

With warm regards to Mrs. Wilson,

Yours affectionately,   C H Dodge

TLS (WP, DLC).
[1] C. H. Dodge to WW, Oct. 30, 1923, printed form letter (WP, DLC).
[2] JRB to CHD, Nov. 4, 1923, CCL (WP, DLC).

A Radio Address[1]

[*Nov. 10, 1923*]

The anniversary of Armistice Day should stir us to great exaltation of spirit because of the proud recollection that it was our day, a day above those early days of that never-to-be-forgotten November which lifted the world to the high levels of vision and achievement upon which the great war for democracy and right was fought and won; although the stimulating memories of that happy time of triumph are forever marred and embittered for us by the shameful fact that when the victory was won—won, be it remembered—chiefly by the indomitable spirit and ungrudging sacrifices of our incomparable soldiers—we turned our backs upon our associates and refused to bear any responsible part in the administration of peace, or the firm and permanent establishment of the results of the war—won at so terrible a cost of life and treasure—and withdrew into a sullen and selfish isolation which is deeply ignoble because manifestly cowardly and dishonorable.

This must always be a source of deep mortification to us and we shall inevitably be forced by the moral obligations of freedom and honor to retrieve that fatal error and assume once more the role of courage, self-respect and helpfulness which every true American must wish to regard as our natural part in the affairs of the world.

That we should have thus done a great wrong to civilization at one of the most critical turning points in the history of the world is the more to be deplored because every anxious year that has followed has made the exceeding need for such services as we might have rendered more and more evident and more and more pressing, as demoralizing circumstances which we might have controlled have gone from bad to worse.

And now, as if to furnish a sort of sinister climax, France and Italy between them have made waste paper of the Treaty of Versailles and the whole field of international relationship is in perilous confusion.

The affairs of the world can be set straight only by the firmest and most determined exhibition of the will to lead and make the right prevail.

Happily, the present situation in the world of affairs affords us the opportunity to retrieve the past and to render mankind the inestimable service of proving that there is at least one great and powerful nation which can turn away from programs of self-interest and devote itself to practising and establishing the highest ideals of disinterested service and the consistent maintenance of exalted standards of conscience and of right.

The only way in which we can worthily give proof of our appreciation of the high significance of Armistice Day is by resolving to put self-interest away and once more formulate and act upon the highest ideals and purposes of international policy.

Thus, and only thus, can we return to the true traditions of America.

Printed in the *New York Times*, Nov. 11, 1923.
¹ There is a WWT draft and three other T and CC drafts of this address in WP, DLC. The text printed below varies from all of them and reprints what Wilson actually said.

Wilson delivered his speech from the library of his home. He was introduced at 8:28 p.m. and began to speak three minutes later. Stations WEAF in New York, WCAP in Washington, and WJAR in Providence, Rhode Island, carried his speech across most of the continental United States, and the *New York Times*, Nov. 11, 1923, said that millions of people may have heard it. WCAP was advised that speakers had been installed in auditoriums in various towns in Texas so that audiences there could listen to Wilson's speech.

From Fridtjof Nansen

Dear Mr. Wilson,   Washington Nov. 10th 1923

I deeply regret that circumstances do not permit me to pay my respects to you during my present visit to Washington.

I think perhaps it will comfort you to know that the great work for Humanity which was so nobly given to the world by you, is in spite of all difficulties and adversities actually progressing. It seems to me that in the present desperate plight of Europe, it is more needed than ever. In my opinion the only hope of the world today lies in universal co-operation of all peoples through the League of Nations.

I feel it an honour and it gives me satisfaction to have been allowed to add any little share to this work. I shall always be deeply grateful for the inspiration and encouragement which you gave me in Paris in 1919.

With best wishes for the continued improvement of your health
I am   sincerely yours   Fridtjof Nansen

ALS (WP, DLC).

A News Report

[*Nov. 11, 1923*]

WILSON OVERCOME GREETING PILGRIMS;
PREDICTS TRIUMPH

Washington, Nov. 11.—Three times former President Wilson broke down with emotion as he addressed the third Armistice Day pilgrimage that greeted him this afternoon at his S Street home. But, visibly suffering physical pain and bent with four years of illness, the great war President showed that his spirit was unbowed when, at the close of a two minutes' speech, he declared he "was not one of those who have the least anxiety about the triumph of the principles" he had stood for.

"I have seen fools resist Providence before," he said, "and I have seen their destruction, as will come upon these again—utter destruction and contempt. That we shall prevail is as sure as that God reigns."

The gathering, the largest since his friends and admirers started the annual visits to the war President, was greatly touched as the few faltering words fell from the lips of the ex-President.

Fully 20,000 persons, many of them devout League of Nations adherents, sought the Wilson home, and at least 5,000, including disabled war veterans, stood before its portals, from which the ex-President responded briefly, feelingly and with great hesitation to a speech of greeting delivered by Senator Carter Glass.

Mr. Wilson, standing unassisted, apparently under a severe strain, paused for a perceptible time before he began speaking. He proceeded slowly and with difficulty, and then his voice broke and his face twitched as he raised his eyes to the disabled soldiers and paid tribute to them and General Pershing. His emotion was so great that he abruptly stopped speaking, and the band began to play, but it had proceeded with but a few bars of the hymn "How Firm a Foundation" when Mr. Wilson raised his hand and concluded with his affirmation of faith before quoted.

"Senator Glass, ladies and gentlemen," began Mr. Wilson, after the great applause had subsided when he appeared on the balcony of his home. "I am indeed deeply touched and honored by this extraordinary exhibition of your friendship and confidence.

"And yet, I can say without affectation that I wish you would transfer your homage from me to the men who made the armistice possible. It was possible because our boys had beaten the enemy to a standstill. You know, if you will allow me to be didactic for a moment, 'armistice' merely means 'standstill of arms.' Our late enemies, the Germans, call an armistice 'Waffenstillstand'—an armed standstill—and it was the boys that made them stand still (Laughter and applause). If they had not, they would not have listened to proposals of armistice.

"I am proud to remember that I had the honor of being the commander in chief—(A Voice—The best one on earth) of the most ideal army that was ever thrown together—pardon my emotion—

though the real fighting commander in chief was my honored friend Pershing, whom I gladly hand the laurels of victory.

"Thank you with all my heart for your kindness."

One standing near the former President heard him murmur: "That's about all I can do," as he finished his speech.

Great applause followed, and the band began playing when Mr. Wilson raised his hand and said:

"Just one word more. I cannot refrain from saying it:

"I am not one of those that have the least anxiety about the triumph of the principles I have stood for. I have seen fools resist Providence before and I have seen the destruction, as will come upon these again—utter destruction and contempt. That we shall prevail is as sure as that God reigns. Thank you. (Great and long-continued applause.)"[1]

When the ex-President appeared at his front door at about 2:30 the street was filled from Massachusetts Avenue to Connecticut Avenue, a distance of five blocks. Fully 5,000 persons lined both sides of the street in the vicinity of the house. It was the largest pilgrimage and the most impressive tribute that has been paid to Mr. Wilson in the Armistice Day ceremonies.

Senator Glass stood to the left of the portal as Mr. Wilson, assisted by a negro servant and followed by Mrs. Wilson and Ellen McAdoo, his grandchild, came from the house. A great cheer went up and the band played "Over There."

Mr. Wilson listened, with head bowed and uncovered, while Senator Glass delivered an address praising his record and his efforts in behalf of the League of Nations. Senator Glass spoke five minutes, while the former President stood unassisted, his cane hanging from the top pocket of his overcoat, while in his right hand he held his top hat.

Not once did he lift his eyes as cheer after cheer went up in tribute to him. The applause affected him visibly, and when he began his response he was plainly laboring under deep emotion. He moved slightly from his position, looked first at the line of disabled veterans directly in front of him, and then scanned the sympathetic faces of the women. He raised his head and moved his right arm as in gesture. But no word came from his mouth. It was at least thirty seconds before he could control his emotions and begin to speak.

As he spoke, the crowd was hushed, visibly touched by the stricken appearance of the man who had broken physically in the

---

[1] We have made a few minor corrections and additions from the T transcript of these remarks in WP, DLC.

midst of his fight for a principle. The scene was described by pilgrims who have made all the trips as the most affecting of the three marches to the shrine of the apostle of universal peace.

In voicing the sentiments of the pilgrims in his address to Mr. Wilson, Senator Glass said:

"I need not tell you, Mr. Wilson, what a happy privilege it is to make the salutation of this great throng of your friends and fellow-citizens.

"You will readily understand that we were prompted in large measure to come here by the genuine affection we feel for you and by our admiration of your achievements as President of the United States and commander in chief of the nation's forces in the supremest crisis of its existence.

"But above and beyond this we are here to renew our faith and to signify the unabated loyalty of millions of Americans to that immutable cause which you, more than any other man on earth, so impressively personify. (Great applause.)

"To you, sir, it must be a source of infinite satisfaction to observe on each recurring anniversary of Armistice Day that the American people of all persuasions are coming more and more to realize what a shocking mistake it was to have permitted a conspiracy of racial animosities and selfish politics to cheat the nation of honorably participating in that permanent guarantee of peace for which our boys died and the country sacrificed. (Applause.) . . ."[2]

Mrs. Wilson, wearing an American red rose hat and a moleskin cape with a sable collar, stood directly behind her husband. The ceremony lasted eleven minutes. As the band played "Onward Christian Soldiers" and "Dixie" the former President lingered a moment longer on the portal after he had finished speaking. Then Mrs. Wilson and a servant came to his assistance and he went within doors.

It was announced, when the crowd showed no disposition to leave the scene, that Mr. and Mrs. Wilson would leave for their afternoon drive within a few minutes. The band played and there was singing along the densely filled street until the car appeared, with Mr. and Mrs. Wilson and Mrs. Bolling, Mrs. Wilson's mother.

The man who had just thrilled his auditors by proclaiming that his principles would yet prevail received continuous tribute as the car moved slowly through the packed street.

Among the pilgrims in the demonstration were former Senator Hitchcock of Nebraska, Mrs. Borden Harriman, former Attorney

---

[2] Here follow Glass's further remarks.

General Gregory, Joseph E. Davies, former Federal Trade Commissioner, Judge Siddons,[3] Louis Brownlow, Representative McReynolds of Tennessee,[4] Representative Connally[5] of Texas and Vance McCormick.

Guests of Mr. and Mrs. Wilson included Senator and Mrs. Swanson, Mr. and Mrs. William G. McAdoo, Mrs. Bolling, Mr. and Mrs. Hunter Galt and Mr. and Mrs. Ralph Bolling.

Former Secretary Daniels, who was unable to make the pilgrimage, sent this telegram:

"There are millions of Americans who will be with you in spirit and go with you on Armistice Day on the pilgrimage to the home of Woodrow Wilson. For the absent ones, please assure him that every passing day has strengthened their conviction that he rightly evolved the true plan. The world staggers because the junkers in the United States Senate in 1919 lacked wisdom to follow where Wilson led."

Printed in the *New York Times*, Nov. 12, 1923.

[3] Frederick Lincoln Siddons, Associate Justice of the Supreme Court of the District of Columbia.

[4] Samuel Davis McReynolds, Democrat.

[5] Tom (Thomas Terry) Connally, Democrat.

From Margaret Woodrow Wilson

New York NY 1923 Nov 11

Love and congratulations. Your speech was a wonder. Every word was clear and easily heard. There were no statics to mar it. A group of us who heard it together were deeply stirred and I was so happy. How I wish I could be with you tomorrow. Love to all

Margaret.

T telegram (WC, NjP).

From Norman Hezekiah Davis

My dear Mr. Wilson: New York Nov. 11/23.

Today I found among some papers a note I had written to you a week ago—thanking you for your kind letter of Nov. 2nd. Some stupid person evidently could not distinguish between a stamped addressed letter ready for the mail—and blank papers. My operation was not serious but sufficiently disagreeable and I am glad to have it over and to be about well again.

I enjoyed very much your message on the Armistice sent over

the radio. I believe the people are ready for such a message and that they will soon realize that we have just as vital an interest and even a stronger moral obligation to settle post war problems and make peace than we had to wage war. It is certainly time to stop all the stupid chatter about the obligations of the vanquished and to force a consideration of the obligations of the victors. I think I can arrange to be in Washington next Friday, the 16th, and if it will be convenient for you to see me sometime then I shall endeavor to arrange my plans accordingly. Mrs. Davis joins me in love to Mrs. Wilson & yourself—and I remain as ever

Faithfully yours   Norman H. Davis

ALS (WP, DLC).

To Carter Glass

My dear Glass,   Washington D C 12th November 1923

In the confusion and haste of yesterday I did not have the opportunity (or the voice) to tell you how much I appreciated and admired the speech you made. It seemed to me uncommonly elevated in style and effective in diction,—altogether a literary gem worth preserving quite irrespective of the sentiments and opinions which it embodied. I thank you with all my heart for its generosity towards me, and congratulate you on a very difficult thing done to perfection. Let me add that your gentleness and sympathy when I broke down touched me very deeply and made me very grateful.

With affectionate regard,

Faithfully Yours,   Woodrow Wilson

TLS (C. Glass Papers, ViU).

To Fridtjof Nansen

My dear Dr. Nansen,   [Washington] 12th November 1923

I was sincerely grieved that the conditions of my convalescence were such at the time you were in Washington that we could not arrange to see one another. I warmly applaud the work you have been doing, and believe that your addresses in the United States have made a deep impression on our people and turned the hearts of a great many of them towards Geneva and the great services that are being rendered there.

I hope that health and good fortune will attend you now and always, and that your work will so prosper as to make your heart glad.

    With cordial regard,

                Your Sincere Friend,   [Woodrow Wilson]

CCL (WP, DLC).

From James Middleton Cox

My dear Mr. President: Dayton, Ohio November 13, 1923

    Let me congratulate you with all my heart on the success of your address on Saturday and the few words spoken Sunday. There was tremendous interest on the part of the radio audiences, and the reaction following the publication in the newspapers has been wonderful. The real crack to the whip came with your conclusion that you have seen fools resist providence before.

    Little by little the conviction is making its way into the hearts of hide-bound Republicans who have up until very recently resisted the voice of their own conscience. The churches on Armistice Day in the main inveighed against the policy of isolation. I heard an Episcopalian clergyman, a Republican, but an independent thinking one, Sunday, who made a text of the errors of the Jews, which resulted in Christ's visiting Jerusalem. As He looked upon it He wept. The minister's thought as expressed then turned to the affairs of the world, and his conclusion was, "If Jesus wept over Jerusalem, so He must now be weeping over Washington."

    You have not the slightest idea what your words mean to the cause. A few of us have been endeavoring to preach the gospel, but we constantly run into the so-called practical politician who speaks discouragement. Every statement from you is heartening. What you said within the last day or two will ring and echo in the minds and hearts of our people. You will doubtless be surprised when I tell you that when I went into the Kentucky campaign three weeks ago, the committee asked me to make no reference to the League of Nations nor to the international text. Of course I paid no attention to this sort of advice. Nothing was discussed except the policy of isolation, political and economic, and the crowds were not interested in anything else. The meeting in Louisville took on the size and enthusiasm of presidential years; in fact in lesser degree, it was the same all over the state.

    We painted the picture as best we could of world-wide desolation and then showed that things came from the senatorial conspiracy prompted not by conviction, but by spite. This moved us to say:

"The deeds of traitors cling to history for a long time, but centuries after the name of Henry Cabot Lodge has passed into mere historic nothingness, the children of republics all over the world will gratefully acclaim the name of Woodrow Wilson."

This led to a demonstration the like of which I did not see in the presidential campaign. Fortunately the members of the campaign committee were on the stage. It must be said for them that they came to me and admitted their error and thanked me for paying no attention to their suggestions.

I submit this in the belief that it will be cheering both to your thought and labors.

With every good wish for yourself and Mrs. Wilson, I am

Very sincerely yours,   James M Cox.

TLS (WP, DLC).

To Frank Nelson Doubleday

My dear Mr. Doubleday,   [Washington] 14th November 1923

I am greatly gratified that you should have liked my little speech of Saturday night.[1] It was certainly an utterance of my deep convictions and would gratify me very deeply if its sentiments should have a widespread effect. Certainly a great world crisis finds us very much below the horizon. A drop or two of acid might bring the little fool who now dominates France[2] to his senses though,—having dealt with him in Paris,—I really doubt if there is anything useful in him to awaken. He is one of the narrowest little provincials I have ever known.

With warm appreciation of your generous letter.

Faithfully Yours,   [Woodrow Wilson][3]

CCL (WP, DLC).
    [1] Wilson was replying to F. N. Doubleday to WW, Nov. 12, 1923, TLS (WP, DLC).
    [2] That is, Poincaré.
    [3] This letter was probably not sent, since JRB to F. N. Doubleday, Nov. 14, 1923, CCL (WP, DLC), is an acknowledgment on Wilson's behalf.

To Harry Augustus Garfield

My dear Friend,   Washington D C 14th November 1923

I am heartily glad that you liked my little speech of Saturday night,[1] and must say that it was a relief once more to speak my mind; and God knows that that much and more too sadly needs to be said.

Please present my cordial salutations to Mrs. Garfield[2] and believe me, always,   Faithfully Yours,   Woodrow Wilson

TLS (H. A. Garfield Papers, DLC).
  [1] Wilson was replying to H. A. Garfield to WW, Nov. 12, 1923, TLS (WP, DLC).
  [2] Belle Hartford Mason Garfield.

From William Elliott Gonzales

My dear Friend: Columbia, S. C. November 14, 1923.

I hope you realize to some degree the pleasure it gives your friends who are at a distance to hear of you and actually *hear* you, to know of your continuous, keen interest in the country's welfare, to see the trend of that country's thought coming back to the course you charted; and to know you hold high place in the affection and respect of millions.

I wish it were so that I could have the benefit of a talk with you; of getting your views on men and policies. The East likes to regard the people down here as Bourbons, but they better typify the characteristics attributed to us. And the wirepulling politicians are not original; they are now following the same policy as twelve years ago, in trying to split up the South by encouraging "favorite sons." Harvey and others hoodwinked Colonel Watterson, and he went with them into that campaign.[1] When he came to Columbia and I showed him some letters, he said: "It looks as if they have been lying to me."

Mr. Bryan has recently returned to Florida and has communicated with me. He is openly and vigorously assailing Underwood on several counts—including his wet status and as being the choice of "the interests" that dominate Wall Street. I have no idea whom he regards as the most available candidate for the Democrats next year, but as he often lets one policy dominate his views, his judgment is not always sound. For instance, as he would now make prohibition an outstanding policy to stress, he speaks of our good friend Daniels[2] as a presidential possibility, while I am convinced that even could Daniels be nominated, the election can be won only by a man possessed of unusual force and with striking personality. A fighter with magnetism as a leader will be, in my opinion, almost as important a factor for success next year as a wise platform. Moreover, whatever the more educated and broadminded people of the North may say, I am not prepared to believe any Southern man, wholly identified with the South, whatever his qualifications may be, could enter the race for president without carrying a handicap, for that fact alone, of between one and two million votes. Even in the state of Washington, so remote from Civil War sentiment, many, as I happen to know, yet speak of Southerners as "rebels."

A year ago I did not think of McAdoo as outstanding among the mentioned possibilities, but have now come to so regard him; not so much as a candidate for the nomination, as in the final contest. But Mark Sullivan, who does not take sides or seem to have favorites, wrote me the other day that he estimated McAdoo would go to the Convention with nearly or quite half the delegates. That will not assure nomination, for a tremendous effort by shrewd players to tire out and wear away his following will be made. I must say that the prospect of "a dark horse" being brought to the front as a compromise has no appeal to me. The country should now know him.

I sense an effort being made in South Carolina—already publicly in small weekly papers—to assume that the recent article in Collier's Weekly, to the effect that you were unalterably opposed to McAdoo,[3] is an unquestioned fact. If this continues it will of course hurt McAdoo's prospects. Sooner or later it will be threshed out, but I wish it were possible now to put a spoke in the opposition's wheel.

When we went away in 1913 we sold our home—to disadvantage. On returning here I found it a real problem to get any sort of home to live in, but I finally purchased one and Mrs. Gonzales and my seventeen year old daughter have found happiness, even in the shadow of our great grief of nearly seven years ago,[4] in making again a "home"—not so externally fine as the old one, but a pretty "home."

With very warm regards, from

Your devoted friend,   William E. Gonzales

TLS (WP, DLC).

[1] A reference to the Harvey-Wilson-Watterson affair, about which see Arthur S. Link, *Wilson: The Road to the White House* (Princeton, N. J., 1947), pp. 359-78.

[2] That is, Josephus Daniels.

[3] Edmund G. Lowry, "The Outs Who Want to Get In: How They Are Lining Up to Get a Man to Beat Coolidge," *Collier's, The National Weekly*, LXXII (Nov. 3, 1923), 5-6. Lowry, after speculating that Wilson might favor David F. Houston for the Democratic presidential nomination in 1924, went on to make the following comments about Wilson's attitude toward McAdoo: "While nobody knows whether Mr. Wilson is actively *for* anybody for president at this time, there has leaked out of his tightly sealed house on S Street in Washington the names of two men [he] is *not* for. One of them is his son-in-law, McAdoo, and the other the 1920 candidate, James M. Cox. Wilson opposition to McAdoo (at that time only surmised) was the real explanation of the peculiar candidacy of McAdoo at San Francisco in 1920. . . . Mr. Wilson is still opposed to McAdoo, who is actually a candidate right now. . . . Democratic chieftains make all sorts of guesses why Wilson is not for McAdoo, but admit they are only guesses. Everybody is agreed on one point: That something happened between Wilson and McAdoo that caused the latter's sudden resignation from the Cabinet, but that that something, for family reasons, has been kept secret." *Ibid.*, p. 5.

To James Middleton Cox

My dear Friend,   [Washington] 16th November 1923

Your kind letter of November thirteenth which I have just greatly enjoyed, affords me the opportunity to express my very sincere admiration (which I am sure is shared by all true Democrats) for your steadfast advocacy of the League of Nations. It constitutes the great and only issue worth fighting for, and I know of no one who has been more true to the faith than you have. May I not,— both as a Democrat and as a private individual,—thank you from the bottom of my heart.

It may interest you, as it has interested me, to reflect that the only nations associated with us in our refusal to take part in sustaining civilization are Turkey, Liberia, Mexico and Germany.

With warm regard,

Cordially and Faithfully Yours,   [Woodrow Wilson]

CCL (WP, DLC).

To Varnum Lansing Collins[1]

My dear Collins,   Washington D C 16th November 1923

Have you in your files a copy of my report to the Trustees on the social reorganization of the University[2] which you can spare for my use. My own files are so carefully packed away that I would not be able to get the copy which I am sure I preserved.

The subject matter of the report still interests me if for no other reason than because it led the Trustees in their sagacity to kick me upstairs into the Governorship and Presidency.

I hope that you will have a copy to spare, and that this request will not put you to too much trouble.[3]

Cordially and Faithfully Yours,   Woodrow Wilson

TLS (NjP-Ar).
[1] Secretary of Princeton University.
[2] It is printed at June 6, 1907, Vol. 17.
[3] Collins replied that he had found no copy of the report except as spread on the minutes of the Board of Trustees. However, he sent under separate cover a copy of the *Princeton Alumni Weekly*, VII (June 12, 1907), which printed the report on pp. 606-11. V. L. Collins to WW, Nov. 20, 1923, TLS (WP, DLC).

From Carter Glass

My dear Mr. President: Washington, D. C. November 16, 1923

Passing through on my way from Cleveland to Virginia I have your most gratifying note about Armistice Day,[1] and am sending this word of thanks for your characteristic kindness. If the restrained expression by me of what was in my heart and mind was pleasing to you I am sure it could not have been displeasing to any one whom I would not cheerfully make mad.

May I venture to add, in the exact words of that idolatrous sister of mine:[2] "and Mr. Wilson made a fine speech, *too!*"

With steadfast devotion,   Sincerely yours,   Carter Glass.

TLS (WP, DLC).
    [1] WW to C. Glass, Nov. 12, 1923.
    [2] She was perhaps Meta Glass, Assistant Professor of Latin and Greek, Columbia University, 1920-1925; President of Sweet Briar College, 1925-1946. Glass also had four other half sisters at this time.

To Sir Horace Plunkett

My dear Sir Horace,   [Washington] 17th November 1923

I am glad that your letter of seventh November holds out to us the hope of seeing you so soon again, and I thank you most sincerely for the enclosure in your letter. As usual, I find myself in warm agreement with the views you have expressed, and I cannot but believe that the voters of Great Britain and the United States will very soon oblige their governments to follow the manifest path of duty.

With warm regard and cordial appreciation,
                    Faithfully Yours,   [Woodrow Wilson]

CCL (WP, DLC).

To Margaret Woodrow Wilson

My dear Miss Chairman,   [Washington] 17th November 1923

I wish to give myself the privilege of expressing my very deep interest in the efforts Miss Loeb is making to stimulate interest and action in the all-important matter of child welfare.[1] I hope that her efforts will be crowned with complete success and that all who have at heart the well-being of their several communities will effectively rally to her support.

I wish that I might be present in person at the dinner over which you are to preside to express more fully my concern that public spirited and disinterested services such as Miss Loeb is rendering should meet with the support and cooperation which they so abundantly merit.

Cordially and Faithfully Yours,   [Woodrow Wilson]

CCL (WC, NjP).
    [1] This letter was inspired by Margaret W. Wilson to WW [c. Nov. 16, 1923], TLS (WC, NjP). She reminded her father that she was the "chairman" of a committee to arrange a dinner in honor of Sophie Irene Simon Loeb, a New York journalist, president of the Child Welfare Board of New York City, and a leading sponsor of the pioneering New York State Child Welfare Law of 1915. Margaret suggested that Wilson write a letter or telegram paying tribute to Miss Loeb's work. She also noted that Miss Loeb proposed to use the dinner as the occasion to launch a campaign to promote local child welfare departments nationwide.
    Wilson's letter was read at the testimonial dinner which took place at the Biltmore Hotel in New York on November 19. *New York Times*, Nov. 20, 1923.

To William Elliott Gonzales

My dear Gonzales,   [Washington] 18th November 1923

I entirely share your wish that we might have a talk on public affairs,[1] for I have always valued your counsel and admired your principles.

The question of the nomination next year has not reached such a stage as to make me sure what judgment should be formed, but of course I am watching the whole movement of affairs with the keenest interest and should very much like to be of service in the final determination of the course the party is to pursue.

It is a pleasure always to think of your friendship and of the many intellectual and spiritual ties which unite us. I am glad to learn that you and yours have found a suitable home again, and I hope that every sort of happiness will come to you all in it.

Please present my respects to Mrs. Gonzales and your daughter, and think of me always as

Your Sincere Friend,   [Woodrow Wilson]

CCL (WP, DLC).
    [1] Wilson was replying to W. E. Gonzales to WW, Nov. 14, 1923.

To Ellen Duane Davis

My dear Friend,   [Washington] 18th November 1923

It distressed us very much to hear[1] that you are not well, and we hope most earnestly that the days are bringing back your strength and steadying your heart beat.

You make me ashamed when you speak of my patience. I have been anything but patient, and have repeatedly thrown myself against the bars of my cage. I wish the doctors could tell me what is going to happen to me, but they do not seem to know, and I have to grope along in the dark.

It is delightful to have the prospect of a visit from E.P. between Thanksgiving and Christmas. I hope he knows we are always glad to see him.

Mrs. Wilson joins me in kind regards to you both.

With affectionate regard, and love to E.P.,

Faithfully Yours,   [Woodrow Wilson]

CCL (WP, DLC).
    [1] From Ellen D. Davis to WW, Nov. 16, 1923, ALS (WP, DLC).

Edith Bolling Galt Wilson to Ray Stannard Baker

My dear Mr. Baker: 2340 S Street, N W [c. Nov. 21, 1923]

I was so happy to find a letter from you[1] in my mail two weeks ago, and wanted to answer at once to tell you how eager we always are for news of you, but we had a ten day visit from the McAdoos, in which there was such a constant demand on my time that I have just now caught my breath and settled down to normal life.

Nell and Mac are the most delightful people in the world, but they live under forced draft (!!) and the world reels 'round them. The two little McAdoo girls are charming, and we hated having them leave.

I was deeply interested in the review of "our book" (as you so generously call it) and thank you for letting me see it. I think you must be increasingly content with the splendid work you put on the book, for it is being more and more read and commented on.

I am anxious to see the new things you are at work on, and of course I need not tell you with what personal pride we watch your success.

We had a nice call from the Lloyd George's and he was in great form. They seemed genuinely delighted with their American tour. It is after midnight, so I must say goodnight. Let us know when you will be down. Mr. Wilson and Randolph would have messages if they knew I was writing.   Faithfully,   Edith B. Wilson

TCL (R. S. Baker Papers, DLC).
    [1] It is missing in both the Baker and EBW Papers, DLC.

From Edith Benham Helm

Dear Mr President   Washington, D. C. November 22nd [1923]

The Helms never have a party, be it all lady or lady and gentleman variety, that we do not miss you and at times the missing becomes so acute that this noisy member of the family has to vocifer-
ate on paper!

It is such a real regret that you are not strong enough to come
with our beautiful lady and I know our other guests miss you just
as we do. We all love you so dearly. Then too as a hostess I cant
help but mourn the absence of one who is not only our greatest
living American, but one whose charm is so great that he makes
the success of a dinner assured in advance.

Sincerely yours   Edith Benham Helm

ALS (WP, DLC).

To Thomas Garrigue Masaryk

My dear President Masaryk,   [Washington] 23rd November 1923

I yesterday received at the hands of the Chargé[1] of the Czecho-
slovak legation here the really magnificent volumes in which you
have so thoughtfully had bound photographs of places and objects
which citizens of Czechoslovakia have been so gracious as to name
for me. I feel highly honoured at such evidences of their confidence and friendship, and shall treasure the albums as among my
most valuable possessions.

I hope that everything goes happily with yourself and the admirable little republic over which you preside. It is a matter of intense
pride with me to have had some part in bringing it into the family
of nations.

With very warm regard,
Cordially and Gratefully Yours,   [Woodrow Wilson]

CCL (WP, DLC).
[1] Bohuslav Bartošovky.

To Edith Benham Helm

My dear Mrs. Helm,   [Washington] 23rd November 1923

Your exceedingly gracious and generous letter of November
twenty-second has warmed my heart, and I very gratefully thank
you for the cheer that it has brought to me.

Mrs. Wilson joins me in affectionate regards. Please also present my very warm salutations to Admiral Helm.

Gratefully Yours,   [Woodrow Wilson]

CCL (WP, DLC).

From Ray Stannard Baker

Amherst Massachusetts
My dear Mr. Wilson: November 23 1923.

It is as plain as the nose on one's face that the people are beginning to see—though many of them don't like it—that you told them the truth in 1917, '18 and '19: and that you are telling them the truth now.

I wish you would let me write a first-class interview with you. I think I could thus help along the principles you have at heart—in which I also believe deeply.

Mr. Wilson, I think I understand (perhaps better than other writers) what your spiritual and ethical message truly is—the message by which you will be ultimately judged: and I believe the time is ripe again to set it out—in this way.

I have written an article for the *Current History Magazine* to appear January 1[1] (and I am also making some addresses along the same line) showing the utter failure of American leadership in world affairs and the inevitability of a return to your principles. I think this could be driven home still more forcibly by a careful (and vivid) interview to be widely published in the newspapers.

You have put certain ideas and issues into world politics that were not there before: issues that the world cannot get around, or over, or through, that will plague us until they are settled, and settled correctly. I should like to show this, with all the power of your own words, and a vivid picture of our present position.

I am going to be in Washington about December 5 for a few days and could do it then if you are willing. If not, there is at least no harm in the suggestion and you will feel it, as I mean it, as any [an] expression of my thorough belief in you—and my affection.

Sincerely yours,   Ray Stannard Baker.

We could, I am sure, put the article (or articles) in a syndicate to some advantage and though this is not the important thing (and not large) yet the same arrangement could be made as with the book.

ALS (WP, DLC).
    [1] Ray Stannard Baker, "The Versailles Treaty and After," *Current History*, XIX (Jan. 1924), 547-59.

John Randolph Bolling to Richard Gillmore Knott,[1] with Enclosure

Dear Mr. Knott: [Washington] 23rd November 1923

Dr. Axson has not been at all well, and only last evening brought up to us a draft of the letter which he thinks it will be advisable for you to write Mr. Wilson concerning the matter we have had under discussion. Mrs. Wilson and I have been very carefully over the matter, and feel that the letter as Dr. Axson has written it will receive consideration—if Mr. Wilson is willing to take up the question at all.

Please go over the draft and, if you feel it embodies your ideas of the proposal, put it on one of your letterheads and send it to Mr. Wilson at your convenience.[2] I will then await an opportune time to bring it before him, and Mrs. Wilson and I will do what we can to secure his consideration of it.

Very sincerely yours,   [John Randloph Bolling]

CCL (WP, DLC).
    [1] Publisher of the *Louisville Post*.
    [2] Knott sent this draft *verbatim* as R. G. Knott to WW, Dec. 1, 1923, TLS (WP, DLC).

E N C L O S U R E

Dear Mr. Wilson:

Several years ago I had some correspondence with Dr. Stockton Axson[1] concerning the possibility of entering into some arrangement with you for publication in the Louisville Post of such articles concerning current topics, or expressions of opinion concerning current affairs, as you might care to write. It was my cherishe[d] hope that my paper might become the medium through which you would communicate with your fellow-countrymen, but naturally I refrained from pressing the matter out of respect for your wishes.

I am wondering if a lapse of years and a different sort of plan might possibly induce you to consider a proposal now. I was under the impression that one of your objections to the original suggestion sprang from your high sense of honor, which all your friends and acquaintances so admire, a reluctance to accept a retainer which might result in financial loss to others, no matter how willing they were to take the risk.

My present idea involves no retaining fee, but a definite payment for each article, brief or longer, with which you might favor us. It would be distinctly understood that under such an arrangement there would be no obligation on your part to write a line unless you felt so inclined. We should pay you an agreed sum for each article, and ask nothing, in addition to the articles themselves, except the privilege of publishing everything political, or by way of comment on current affairs, which you wrote within say a year. We would syndicate the articles for simultaneous publication in other newspapers, first submitting the list to you in order that you might know, and advise us, if there were any papers on the list in which you would not care to have your writings appear.

The actual financial details could not be arranged until I could make arrangement for syndication in afternoon papers, and of course I cannot make such arrangements until I can secure your permission to proceed.

My object is not to make money (though of course I must not undertake financial obligations which I cannot fulfill) but is to win the honor of having you contribute to the Louisville Post, and of acting as the medium throu[gh] which you would utter to your fellow beings fresh expressions of those lofty principles for which you stand and have stood with superlative courage and consistency.

The purpose of this letter is to find out whether you will be willing to consider discussing with me the possibility of entering into an arrangement to write for some one paper or group of papers at such times, and only at such times, as you would feel that you would care to write.   Cordially yours,

CC MS (WP, DLC).
    [1] R. G. Knott to S. Axson, Aug. 19, 1920, TLS (WP, DLC).

From Newton Diehl Baker

My dear Mr President: Cleveland November 23, 1923

You will be interested in the enclosed clippings[1] sent me by an English friend. One newspaper account of the behavior of the students says they filled the hall of the University[2] singing "Landlord fill the flowing bowl"! Evidently the boys knew what an impudent drunkard Birkenhead is.
                    Affectionately,   Newton D. Baker

ALS (WP, DLC).
    [1] They are missing.
    [2] Birkenhead held the honorary title of Lord Rector of Glasgow University.

From Albert Kaufman

Wilkes Barre Penn 1923 Nov 24

Honored sir mindful of your valued service you have rendered to the cause of the Jewish people during your two terms as President of the United States and since and cognizant of your great and never to be forgotten service in sponsoring the Balfour Declaration through which your name will be linked in the history of the Jewish people Stop Therefore as President of the Zionist district of Wilkes Barre and vicinity representing American citizens throughout the historic Wyoming Valley on the eve of the first annual convention of the Zionist Council of the middle district of Pennsylvania I extend to you our deep sense of gratitude Stop We also express sincere prayer for your long life and health that you may be spared for many years to serve the cause of humanity and social justice   Dr Albert Kaufman

T telegram (WP, DLC).

To Newton Diehl Baker

My dear Baker,   [Washington] 25th November 1923

Thank you very much for your letter of November twenty-third and its enclosures. The English have long known from close-hand observation what an egregious ass and impossible person Birkenhead is. Many stories are current in Great Britain of his quite absurd vanity and empty-headedness. Such men, when dispassionately looked at, merely add to the gayety of nations. They are harmless in all matters of moment.

I wish I had a good verbal memory and could repeat to you the warm praise of you which Mr. Lloyd George uttered when he called on me here. He was quite enthusiastic about you, as are also of course all who really know you.

It was a pleasure to hear from you, and is always a pleasure to think about you.

With affectionate regard,

Faithfully Yours,   [Woodrow Wilson]

CCL (WP, DLC).

To Albert Kaufman

My dear Dr. Kaufman,   [Washington] 25th November 1923

Your telegraphic message of November twenty-fourth has gratified me very much, and you may be sure that the few services I
have been able to render the Jewish people have redound[ed] more
to my pleasure than to their benefit. I hope that as the years go by
the fortunes of that great people may grow constantly, and the
foundations of their success become constantly more and more
steadfast and solid.

Pray accept assurances of my personal regard, and believe me,
with heartfelt good wishes,

Faithfully Yours,   [Woodrow Wilson]

CCL (WP, DLC).

From Norman Hezekiah Davis

My dear Mr. Wilson: New York November 26, 1923.

I shall endeavor to outline to you a plan which I have in mind,
which I think you could carry out with great success. You of course
know the psychological value of a well planned suspense before
the discharge of a volley, and that the suspense is intensified if it
is known when the broadside will be discharged.

The first thing is to spread the idea or find some appropriate way
of announcement that you are preparing a message to the American people which you will give out on a certain date. That could be
arranged by selecting someone to write you an open letter inquiring what you consider to be the vital issues confronting the American people, and how they can best be solved. In reply to that my
idea is that you should make the following points:

1. Having twice led the Democratic Party to victory, having twice
won the vote of the people to the highest position in the Republic,
and having been in such close relationship to the developments
which carried us into the world war and to the problems which
grew out of that war and remain still unsettled, you are glad to
render a still further service to your country in advising them upon
these vital questions with which you have had such close contact.
Because of your unique position, you should in my judgment assume an attitude of dignified detachment from rough and tumble
conflicts of the political campaign and disclaim any desire to mix
in the details of party organization.

2. Since leaving the White House you have endeavored to turn
away from personalities that come and go in the life of a political

policy to those fundamental principles of political action which
abide. While expressing the conviction of the need of organized
political parties in a Democracy, you could take the position that
your attention is centered more on principles and policies than on
candidates, and that while you are convinced that the Democratic
Party offers the greatest hope, in order to render the service which
must be done the party must abide by its fundimental [fundamen-
tal] principles and ideals, it must have the support of all forward
looking people, and must nominate a man with the experience and
ability necessary to carry forward the program.

3. Call attention to the set-backs which democracy has suffered,
particularly in Europe, because the aspirations of the people have
not been satisfied, and politics have fallen into disrepute because
it has substituted the ambitions of individuals and the interests of
classes for its primary dignity of principles. Parties lose their meaning if they fail to stand courageously for real issues. When political
parties avoid the issues of the day, and allow selfish personal ambitions to take the place of fighting programmes, the whole machinery is destroyed and the menace of a dictatorship threatens.

4. Indicate the need for clear-cut issues which will appeal to the
idealism for which the Democratic Party must stand if it hopes to
win in 1924. "Regular" voters have already made up their minds
how they will vote next November irrespective of what program
their party adopts, or what candidate it chooses. Of such there are
probably more Republicans than Democrats, and if the Democrats
hope to win they must secure the support of the independent voters which they can only do by standing for clear-cut issues.

5. With the confusion which still exists at home because of the
misrepresentations in 1920 and with European civilization slipping
downward, it appears that you can best serve your party, your
country and humanity by concentrating attention on the fundamentals of present day politics which must determine the issues
on which the next election must be fought, and attempt to clarify
them.

6. With this purpose in view, it is your intention to concentrate
your attention on these fundamental problems during the Winter,
in the hope that you may, at a coming day, say May 1st, have ready
for publication a message to your fellow citizens.

— — —

The curiosity aroused by such an announcement and the mystery as to what you are going to say would be kept alive. The Republican campaign managers would be perplexed and the Democratic organization leaders who have not the courage or the vision
to stand up for your principles would be still more disturbed. You

of course are the best judge as to what you should say in the forth-coming message. My idea is that it would receive greater attention and would soak in more deeply if you should divide this into, say, six short messages which would appear daily until completed.

With apologies, I make the following suggestions as a basis for future consideration:

1. General—On the far-reaching importance of the present crisis in political and economic affairs. This could be emphasized by ref-erence to the farewell addresses of Washington, Jefferson and Jackson, demonstrating that the present crisis is more serious than those which confused the country when they summed up their ex-perience for the benefit of their fellow-citizens. Denunciation of the blind, selfish policy that refuses to look at the danger, and of those who play the fiddle of party intrigue while Rome burns. The need of today is clear issues and men who will stand for them cou-rageously.

2. Foreign policy.—Arraignment of the Republican Administra-tion for its inaction. The only possible justification for the repudia-tion of the League of Nations would have been the substitution of something better suited to serve the interests of the American peo-ple. The most vital interest of America beyond its frontiers is the maintenance of peace. The war demonstrated that Europe alone is not capable of maintaining peace, but that if left alone they will breed wars which spread until we become involved morally and materially. It is therefore only the part of wisdom, to say nothing of moral duty, for us to prevent the creation of a situation which leads to war and which now would destroy civilization. After our experi-ence we cannot afford any longer to be absent at any meeting or conference where our vital interest, peace, is being dealt with, and we cannot afford any longer to leave such a vital interest in the hands of those who have proved their incompetency to deal with it. The Republicans have destroyed, or have failed to build up. They have surrendered the position of proud and useful moral leadership which we had secured, and have ignored our duty and sacrificed the interests of this country in order to avoid disruption of the Republican Party, in which there was such a divided opinion on the great issue.

Although worried about the Reparations question, which is a post-war problem threatening the peace of the world and obstruct-ing its economic recovery, the Republican party has admitted its impotence. America having been a party to the Armistice which terminated armed hostilities and provided for the surrender of the vanquished upon certain terms, they have felt no responsibility to see that advantage should not be taken of the defeated enemy because of the defenseless position in which we had helped to place them, nor have they indicated any feeling of responsibility towards those who were associated with us in winning the war. The issue has become clear—ignominious and unconsidered isolation in the world, drifting towards new wars, or effective cooperation with the other nations in organizing peace based upon the traditional principles and policies of the United States.

3. The tariff—Re-state the traditional Democratic policy and point out how the change in our status from debtor to a creditor nation has accentuated the absurdity of the position of the protectionists. Call attention to the most vicious abuse of the rights of the people which the Republican Party has ever attempted through the passage of the Fordney McCumber Tariff bill. This increased to a great extent the inequalities and injustices which had heretofore prevailed, and was a radical departure from their former alleged policy of giving protection to "infant industries." It is time for some of our industries to reach manhood, but they will never reach manhood as long as the Republican Party remains in power.

4. Internal prosperity—Point out that it is impossible to work out any wise programme in regard to our internal economy until we have settled our relations with foreign countries, and have definitely made up our minds about the tariff. For instance, take the railroad problem. If we are going to build our tariff walls so high as to prevent importations, our railroad system will have to be developed in accordance with such a plan, and we will have to restrict our agricultural and manufactured products primarily to home consumption. If on the other hand we are going to have incoming and outgoing traffic, the railroads may develop on natural and more economic lines. Relief to the agricultural interests and a solution of the railroad problem must come from expansion and development rather than from contraction. This requires policies which accommodate themselves to unalterable economic laws. The economic forces must be set free and they cannot be free as long as the existing artificial barrier erected by the Fordney McCumber bill remains. It is well to recall what the Democratic Party has done for the country, and how it has fought the special interests. It was under Jackson that the man who tills the soil first secured an influence in the Government. The first credit relief for the farmers was given during your Administration. The consumers have only received aid through the Democratic Party. Organized labor has for many years found that its just petitions were more sympathetically received by the Democratic Party of the people than by the vested interests that have dominated the Republican Party. The Democratic Party has done more to advance the inter-

ests of legitimate business; a striking instance of which was the establishment of the Federal Reserve Banking system. While unwilling to give special protection to special interests, the Democratic Party has stood for the interests of the people as a whole.

The above questions form the roof structure of national prosperity, which cannot, however, be erected on a foundation of do-nothingness in foreign affairs, or upon the artificial tariff wall which has been erected at the demand of selfish minority interests.

5. Foreign Affairs—Return to this subject and force the League issue. Explain how the Republican Party has misrepresented the League and how it led so many people to the erronious [erroneous] belief that Article X obligated the United States to go to war. Fortunately most of the fallacies and misrepresentations advanced have died of exposure. One of the misrepresentations about the League is that it is an Alliance. Every honest man who has been able to give this question proper consideration knows perfectly well that membership in the League is not in any sense of the word an alliance, but on the contrary, one of the principal objects of the League is to do away with alliances, and that the only way we can hope to escape the baneful influence of the results of alliances, or to avoid being dragged into another war caused by such practices is through the association of all the nations pledged to cooperate upon the principle of the equality of nations and the settlement of disputes by orderly legal processes rather than by force. Our failure to enter the League and make it what it was intended to be has not only militated against its success, and retarded the stabilization of peace in Europe, but it has at least indirectly contributed to the failure of some of the nations that joined the League to abide by the principles to which they pledged themselves, and a situation has been created by which we are threatened with greater entanglements than any heretofore experienced.

It might be well to suggest that as a result of the experience of five years and certain developments which would not have taken place had we played our part, it may be advisable to survey the situation in view of conditions as they exist at the time the incoming administration takes office, and to clarify certain questions and make certain stipulations which would strengthen the League and insure a more strict adherence to the principles upon which it is based.

Then state again the fact that America's paramount interest beyond her frontiers is the maintenance of peace. We cannot afford any longer to entrust such a vital interest to the good will or incapacity of others. Wherever the nations of the world assemble to discuss the affairs of peace, or to deal with problems which threaten peace, America must be present since a war may now spread until it becomes every nation's war, and the maintenance of peace and the prevention of such a situation has become every nation's business.

6. Candidates—While you are interested primarily in a proper solution of the vital questions which confront the American people and the world, and in having the Democratic Party take the proper course, you are only interested in candidates to the extent that the Party shall be assured of nominating a man as to whose position on these questions and his ability to solve them there can be no doubt. Since the predominating issue is our proper relationship to international questions, because upon that depends so much the solution of our most pressing domestic problems, it is important to select a man who is well versed in foreign and domestic affairs, and who has had adequate experience and preparation.

You could develop this last section in such a way that certain people would be eliminated from consideration. The Convention would not dare nominate anyone who does not meet these requirements, and by a process of elimination I think the desired result would be obtained. At any rate you will have forced the Democratic Party to stay on the right line, and by the detached position which you take you will mobilize public opinion and obtain support for the Democratic Party which is essential in order to win, no matter who is nominated by the Party. Most of the material which you have already prepared will serve admirably for such a plan as I have indicated.

With affectionate regards to Mrs. Wilson and yourself, I am, as ever,				Faithfully yours, Norman H. Davis

P.S. I am leaving tonight for a hurried trip to Tennessee. It now looks as I will have to be back here on Tuesday of next week, in which case I shall not be able to stop off in Washington on my way back as I had hoped to do. If, however, I do not have to rush back here quickly, I shall advise you in the hope that I can stop off and see you.

TLS (WP, DLC).

From Ambrose White Vernon

My dear Mr. Wilson:			Northfield, Minn. Nov. 27, 1923

May I take my place in the multitude of those who pay you their grateful and reverent thanks for your Armistice Day address?

I read it to my class on Great Americans amid a noble stillness.

Even college seniors were detected with tears in their eyes. I hope they had tears in their hearts.

God bless you always and keep you with us many years. This is one of the colleges which is behind the League. Its faculty voted in a very considerable majority even for Mr Cox. And the great idea is making visible conquest all about in our student body. I wish your faith "may vanish into sight."

                            Ever loyally yours   A. W. Vernon

ALS (WP, DLC).

From Sophie Irene Simon Loeb

My dear Mr. Wilson: New York City November 27th, 1923.

How can I thank you for the beautiful words you sent me on the occasion of the dinner tendered to me? All I can say is that I will try to live up to them. Great enthusiasm was manifested by those who heard your message—nearly a thousand representative people of this City and State—and from the many clippings, great good has been sent forward in the interest of Child Welfare.

Doubtless it will interest you to know that the one thing that gave me personally the keenest joy at the dinner was the splendid way in which Margaret opened the meeting. It was done with such charm and simplicity and honesty of purpose, pertaining to the cause in which we are both so interested, the children, that she won a place in the heart of each one present, I am sure.

I just wish you could have heard it and the comments about her following the dinner. Never before did she so strongly show the inherent qualities in her of being truly a good and great woman, and I who have seen considerable of her in the past few years am looking forward to some really splendid things and feel she will find her own place in the Sun.

I trust you will pardon my writing so personally to you, but I cannot help it for that is the way I feel about her.

Again thanking you, and with every good wish, I am,

                    Sincerely yours,   Sophie Irene Loeb.

TLS (WP, DLC).

From Raymond Blaine Fosdick

My dear Mr. Wilson: New York November 27, 1923.

I have been giving a great deal of thought to the subject which we discussed at your house two weeks ago, and I have had several conferences bearing on it. There is, as far as I can make out, a very strong feeling as to the soundness of your position regarding the necessity of personal contact between instructors and small groups of students—students who will work under such direction, but on their own responsibility, and with a good deal of personal freedom. The difficulty at this end of the line arises from the fact that the boards with which I happen to be associated are necessarily reluctant to initiate enterprises of an experimental character in education. They have found that they can generally be effective only to the extent that they are able to cooperate with institutions in the financing of policies upon which the institutions have independently determined. To take any other course would be to give color to the charge so often made that educational policies in this country are purchasable.

Just how this difficulty can be avoided, I do not yet see. Two or three institutions, I understand, are now making the beginnings of an experiment along the line you suggested, but their plans are still too immature for practical consideration.

I shall not, of course, let the matter drop, and it is the hope of all those with whom I have talked that some opportunity may shortly arise which will permit practical experimentation in this field. Whether the idea can be accelerated, and in what form, is a question to which earnest consideration will be given.

I shall hope to be in touch with you about this matter later on as new plans develop.

It was a great pleasure to talk with you the other day, and I appreciate more than I can tell you the opportunity which you so kindly made possible.

With warm best wishes,

Ever faithfully yours,   Raymond B. Fosdick

TLS (WP, DLC).

To Raymond Blaine Fosdick

My dear Fosdick,   Washington D C 28th November 1923

Please do not let the idea get rooted in the minds of the Rockefeller Trustees that what I have in mind is experimental. It is in fact in full operation and realization at Oxford University, and what they have matured there can be transplanted to this country. I believe that if the Trustees cannot aid me in this matter a great opportunity will be lost forever. I can honestly say that my plans are so thoroughly thought out in detail that there is nothing experimental about them.

I thank you warmly for what you have attempted, and for your generous promise not to let the matter drop. I believe it would prove a crowning honour to the great Foundation which Mr. Rockefeller so generously and wisely founded.

With affectionate regard,

Faithfully Yours,   Woodrow Wilson

TLS (WP, DLC).

To Ray Stannard Baker

My dear Baker,   [Washington] 1st December 1923

Both my affection for you and utter confidence in you prompts me to agree to the interview you propose;[1] but my judgment is against it. That has never been for me a successful method of utterance.

In any case you must let me know when you get here, and we must see each other if only for a few minutes. Let me know a few days in advance of your arrival when you will get here and what your address will be so that I may have an opportunity to arrange an interval in the somewhat exacting routine of my convalescence.

With affectionate regard,

Faithfully Yours,   [Woodrow Wilson]

CCL (WP, DLC).
    [1] Wilson was replying to RSB to WW, Nov. 23, 1923.

To Norman Hezekiah Davis

My dear Davis,   [Washington] 4th December 1923

Since I have read your last letter[1] I must warn you that if ever again you tell me you can't write I will laugh in your face. That letter is, in my opinion, a model of lucidity and force, and yet that was not my main thought in reading it but rather that it exhibited an extraordinary range of vision and an ideal spirit of disinterested friendship.

In spite of the deep impression it made on me, I must say, after long and conscientious consideration, I was not convinced by its arguments. I believe that the plan you propose would generate more heat than light, and besides that it involves a kind of writing which I have never done and which I would attempt in direct contravention of my whole intellectual and literary habit and practice. I would do it with misgiving and without zest, and that would be ruinous to it. I could not be myself in executing so uncongenial a task, and that is another way of saying that it would be folly for me to undertake it. The worst part of this conclusion to my mind is that it will disappoint you. But it is a conclusion which I find I cannot escape, and I can only beg that you will forgive me for not seeing the thing as you do.

I dare say that your judgment in these matters is as good as mine, and probably better than mine; but you will expect of me what I have now given you,—my candid and conscious judgment.

Mrs. Wilson joins me in affectionate messages to you all, and I am, as always,   Your Devoted Friend,   [Woodrow Wilson]

CCL (WP, DLC).
  ¹ That is, NHD to WW, Nov. 26, 1923.

From Ray Stannard Baker

Dear Mr. Wilson: Amherst Massachusetts December 10, 1923

I was sorry indeed not to see you when I was in Washington, for I had a budget of news I thought would hearten you; but I know and appreciate the difficulties of your convalescence and would not put a thing in the way of your recovery, which is more needed than almost anything else I know of. I also understand perfectly your position regarding the published interview which I proposed. During my trip in New York and Washington I met quite a number of men who feel as I do—that a "Back to Wilson" movement is essential to the country. At the Century Club, for example, I met George Foster Peabody and Thomas Mott Osborne, who see the situation clearly. Such men, also, as Arthur Bullard, Manley Hudson and Herbert Houston are strong for the high and true position. I saw William Allen White in New York and he wished to be warmly remembered to you; and Mark Sullivan in Washington, who spoke most enthusiastically about the reception on Armistice Day.

These men, like all truly thoughtful men who have the genuine interests of the country at heart, see the need now, as never before, of a true moral and ideal leadership—and no one in sight to take up the torch. When one puts the formula in some such guise as this he gets a surprising response:

"The principles of Mr. Wilson were true when he put them forth in 1917-18; and they are true still; the world cannot be healed without getting back to them."

I am having an article in *Current History* for January, reviewing "America's Part in the Peace of Europe" and setting forth anew your policies. Several friends have read it and think it good (among them Mr. Peabody) and are talking of having a reprint made and widely distributed throughout the country. One friend suggested that some senator, like Mr. Glass, might possibly be willing to put it in the *Congressional Review* and have a separate brought out. I will try the article on Mr. Glass after it comes out, and see what he thinks.

I am sure you have this whole situation in mind far better than I have or could have, but you will forgive a friend if he is bold enough to give you his views. You have a tremendous following in the country, and these elements—which are strong among quiet people back in the country, especially the church people—can be used to peg up the platform of the Democratic Party to the high-road of service and cooperation in international affairs. We see now the policy of the Republicans. The danger is that the Democrats will not be bold enough to take high enough ground. I believe the American people will do almost anything if you ask of them the *hard, great task*, not the little, trimming, politically-minded things. If the Democrats ask enough in 1924, they will win; if not, the "safe and sane" Republicans will win.

If you could intimate in some letter soon—some letter that is certain to be published—that you propose at some later time to say definitely what you think the Democrats should do in 1924, you would provide that element of suspense so potent in publicity, and exert a most salutary influence upon the cogitations of Murphy, Brennen and Taggart[1]—who are afraid of you. But you ought to withhold your real fire until you can see the whites of the enemies eyes. Toward the last of the winter, or in the early spring, if you could come out with two or three short articles or interviews setting forth the whole situation, it seems clear to me that you would force the Democrats to take the high ground. I have some ideas of what should go into such articles to make them most effective from the point of view of publicity (which is the point I am stressing) and I could help, I am sure, if you cared for it in this matter, or, when the time comes, in getting the article, or articles, a wide showing in some syndicate. There is a great opportunity here, as I see it, and I hope you will not think me presumptuous in speaking of it.

I have just had a letter from our London representatives with this observation, "I am glad to say our foreign department has just sold the Polish translation rights to the Woodrow Wilson book. The cash receipts, of course, are microscopic, but it is good to have the book done in the Polish language."

I am enclosing a leaflet sent out by the German publishers,[2] which contains quotations from quite a number of the German reviews of the book, which are most remarkable both as to the extent and quality. I think the book has helped a great deal in correcting the views in central Europe. I should be glad if Mr. Bolling could return this German circular to me.

Cordially yours,   Ray Stannard Baker

TLS (WP, DLC).
¹ That is, Charles Francis Murphy, George E. Brennan, and Thomas Taggart.
² Bolling returned this leaflet in WW to RSB, Dec. 13, 1923. We did not find it in the Baker Papers, DLC.

From Norman Hezekiah Davis

My dear Mr. Wilson: [New York] December 10, 1923.

On my return today from Tennessee I find your letter of December 4th. Your reasons against attempting to follow the plan indicated by me are quite controlling. It is not always possible to perform a congenial task, and I quite recognize the futility of deliberately attempting an uncongenial one. We must do things our own way. I am at least glad to know that I succeeded in expressing myself clearly. A duty which my friendship for you imposed upon me has thus been discharged, and since you are the only one who can properly judge of the wisdom of undertaking the task suggested, I cannot say that I am disappointed, or that I think you are wrong in declining it.

I had hoped to stop by Washington on my way from Tennessee, but found it impossible because I was delayed there longer than expected, and had to be here today. Mrs. Davis joins me in affectionate regards to you all and I remain as ever,

Affectionately yours,   [Norman H. Davis]

CCL (N. H. Davis Papers, DLC).

From Cleveland Hoadley Dodge

Riverdale-on-Hudson
Dear Woodrow   New York Dec 10th 1923

If you have not heard it already, you will be interested.

One of the 2200 plans submitted for the Bok Peace prize is the one that I shall vote for if there is a referendum. It consists of only two words

"Assassinate Lodge"
Brilliant inspiration!

Wish I could go to Washington this month but I cannot travel very well & will have to give it up.

Wishing you all a very Merry Christmas & Happy New Year

Yrs' affly   C H Dodge

ALS (WP, DLC).

To Cleveland Hoadley Dodge

My dear Cleve,   Washington D C 11th December 1923

Thank you for your letter of tenth December. It distresses me very much that you still feel unequal to travel, because I had hoped that you were fast regaining your strength and would soon be your old splendid self again.

Mrs. Wilson joins me in most affectionate messages to you all, and I earnestly hope and pray that the New Year may bring you complete health and every other blessing.

Gratefully and Affectionately Yours,   Woodrow Wilson

TLS (WC, NjP).

From James Kerney

My dear Governor: Trenton, New Jersey December 12, 1923

Upon more mature reflection, I feel it would be better for you to write a few smashing articles for magazine publication, to be followed perhaps by a series of expressions that might be put out through one of the big newspaper syndicates. I realize that you are not concerned about the remuneration; yet, frankly, I see no reason why you should not accept something, and at the same time do the forward looking people of the world endless good. If you do not take a good crack or two at the situation, it will not, in my judgment, be possible for the voice of the liberals to get much of a hearing. There's too much of the sordid and too much of the Bok and other bunk schemes afloat and the people are apt to be fooled.

What would you think of an article or two for World's Work, to be followed by several articles put out through the McClure or some other big newspaper syndicate? If you cared to have me do it, I would gladly look after the business details, as I know most of the concerns and their ways. I do not personally particularly favor one crowd above another; what I am anxious to see happen is genuine liberal leadership assert itself. It was fine to see both yourself and Mrs. Wilson looking so well.

Faithfully yours,   James Kerney.

TLS (WP, DLC).

To James Kerney

My dear Kerney,   Washington D C 13th December 1923

Thank you for your thoughtful letter of December twelfth and for the generous purpose of what it proposes. But the kind of writing you suggest for me is the particular kind in which I have had no practice, and the kind least suited to what I believe to be my best literary method. I shall have to find,—and no doubt I shall find,—other means of assisting liberal thought. I am none the less obliged to you for your disinterested counsel.

It was a real pleasure to see you the other day, and I hope that we shall be frequently thrown together.

With most earnest good wishes for you and yours, and with very warm regard,   Faithfully Yours,   Woodrow Wilson

TLS (WC, NjP).

To Ray Stannard Baker

My dear Baker,   [Washington] 13th December 1923

You may be sure that you were not more disappointed than I was in our unavoidable failure to make connections when you were down here. I could have arranged,—and would have been happy to arrange,—a call from you, but knew that I could not give you the interview which you suggested, and therefore thought it most frank to say so. Please come this way soon again and let us have one of our old confabs.

You may be sure that I will keep my eye out for every opportunity to guide the Democrats, and I hope and believe that that opportunity will not now be long deferred.

It was a pleasure to hear from you, and I congratulate you on the deserved progress the book is making.

I shall await with great interest your article in "Current History" for January.

With affectionate regard,

                    Faithfully Yours,   [Woodrow Wilson]

CCL (WP, DLC).

To James Watson Gerard

My dear Mr. Gerard,   [Washington] 13th December 1923

I had already seen the paper about the Lausanne Treaty[1] which you were so kind as to send me in your letter of December eleventh,[2] and was very glad indeed that you and those associated with you had undertaken to show the Senate the iniquity of that treaty. It is indeed iniquitous, and I sincerely hope (though I cannot confidently expect) that your protest will be effectual. The Republicans are not thinking just now of justice but only of partisan advantage. But God is in His Heaven, and they will yet come into their own.

With every good wish for the Holiday season,

Faithfully Yours,   [Woodrow Wilson]

CCL (WP, DLC).
[1] About which, see J. W. Gerard to WW, Sept. 28, 1923, n. 2.
[2] J. W. Gerard to WW, Dec. 11, 1923, TLS (WP, DLC). Its enclosure is missing.

From John Joseph Pershing

Dear Mr. Wilson: Paris, December 13, 1923.

It happens that I am in France for the first real rest I have had since the beginning of the war, and as the Holiday Season approaches, my thoughts naturally flow back to the trying days of the war when you stood so firmly behind me in our earnest efforts to build up a fighting force worthy of the nation and the cause; therefore I can do no less than to extend to you at this time my warmest greetings and my most heartfelt good wishes, not only for your happiness at this moment, but for your complete restoration to health and strength.

Believe me, dear Mr. President, with kind remembrances to Mrs. Wilson,

Your affectionate and devoted friend,   John J Pershing

TLS (WP, DLC).

From Vernon Allen Crawford[1]

Dear Mr. Wilson: Columbia, S. C. Dec. 17, 1923.

Will you please consider a somewhat audacious request?

"A History of Columbia Theological Seminary" is the subject of my Master's thesis which I am now working on at the University of South Carolina. This subject is of peculiar interest at this time as the question of the removal of this Seminary will probably be fought out within the next month or two. The question at issue concerns the removal of our Seminary to a new location, Atlanta, Ga., perhaps; its retention here in Columbia; or its consolidation with some other Presbyterian Seminary. When completed the thesis will probably be published as a bulletin by the University.

Knowing that you once were familiar with the Seminary and its library, I realize that a statement from you with reference to any influence the environment of, or reading in, the Seminary may have had upon your life would be of peculiar interest and value in the above thesis and at this particular time. If you can and will take the time to write a few words or lines relating to your connection with the Seminary it will be more deeply appreciated than I can express without become [becoming] very extravagant in my language.

May I also at this time congratulate you, and our country, upon your increasing health and vigor, and express the hope that you may be spared many years yet to receive the homage which we feel you so well deserve. A joyous, peaceful Christmas to you and yours; and a very happy birthday—mine is on the same day, the twenty-eighth; I've been glad of it ever since I learned it! God bless you, Mr. Wilson—and your loved ones. I Corinthians 1:3.

Respectfully,   Vernon Allen Crawford

TLS (WP, DLC).
  ¹ Crawford was also at this time a student at Columbia Theological Seminary. He received a B.D. from that institution in 1925. He later served as a Presbyterian minister in Brevard, N. C., and as a missionary in Japan. He apparently never completed the work for his master's degree at the University of South Carolina, and there is no evidence that he ever published anything about Columbia Theological Seminary. The seminary was removed to Decatur, Ga., in 1927.

John Randolph Bolling to Richard Gillmore Knott

My dear Mr. Knott: [Washington] 18th Decr 1923

Mr. Wilson has had under consideration your letter of December first, and has told me on one or two occasions that he was not yet ready to reply to it. As we are just now entering upon the Holiday season—when his mail is mountain high—Mrs. Wilson agrees with me that we had better not urge a decision, but rather let the matter drift until after the first of the year—unless he takes it up again. We are encouraged that he is willing to consider it, and I will keep you posted.

With the season's kindliest greetings;

Cordially yours,   [John Randolph Bolling]

CCL (WP, DLC).

John R. Mott's Notes of a Conversation

[Dec. 19, 1923]

Wilson 3 30 P.M.

After JRM tht of leadship still his, he said, I must get well and help them.

— Abt Turkish treaty. It's disgraceful. They care more for oil than religion. Worst of it is I can't feel like a Xn toward those who did it (Lausanne Treaty &tc) I want to get their scalps, and I will.

— Germany. I am sorry for her.

— France. I hope Germany will wipe her off the map.
That skunk Poincare.
He is a sneak also.
Style—b[o]t[h] skunk & sneak—a white streak on back.
He was a liar.

— Lloyd George.
He will prob. come back.
Trouble w him is that you never know where to find him.
Even his friends [?] Philip Carr [Kerr] & Hankey had to apologize for him.

— Amazing this trust of them. We will never get over it.

Hw MS (J. R. Mott Papers, CtY-D).

To Vernon Allen Crawford

My dear Mr. Crawford,   [Washington] 20th December 1923

My only connection with the Columbia Seminary was through my Father during his professorship there. But I spent many interesting hours in its library and should very much regret to see the environment with which I became so familiar in any way altered. I am a firm believer in the wisdom of letting institutions, which have become a part of the history of education, remain untouched so as to in no way lose their identity. I should very much regret to feel that Columbia Seminary no longer stood where I had known it and loved it.

Cordially and Sincerely Yours,   [Woodrow Wilson]

CCL (WP, DLC).

From William Gibbs McAdoo

Dear Governor: Los Angeles, California December 20, 1923

Nell and I took a hurried trip the other day through the Imperial Valley and made it a point to stop at Indio and inquire about the 61 acres of land you own there.

I find that this land is not under the canal and that irrigation can only be secured by drilling a well and putting in the necessary apparatus. It is estimated that to get water on the land and to level it so that it may be irrigated properly will cost about $65 per acre. The best real estate man at Indio, Mr. King, tells me that the land as it stands now is worth $75 to $100 per acre but that sales are slow. The Southern Pacific Railroad has a great deal of property there through the original land grants it received, which it is constantly offering on the market. The[re]fore, the opportunity of disposing of the property is not as good as it might be.

Mr. King says that if $65 per acre were spent on the land to level and irrigate it, it would be worth probably $200 an acre. In other words, the present value of $75 an acre would be increased to approximately $135 an acre by spending $65 for grading and watering.

There is a project, as you know, for an all American canal around the Imperial Valley Basin and I have no doubt that this canal will some day be built. Just when, nobody knows, of course, but the people of the Imperial Valley are urging it strenuously before the Congress and may some day succeed in getting the necessary appropriation. If this canal should be built, your land will be very favorably situated under the canal so that ample water for irrigation purposes will be provided and without the large expenditure involved in drilling private wells.

This is good date land. Date culture is going to be a very large business in the Imperial Valley. It is one of the most profitable crops but it takes from five to eight years to mature a good orchard. The expense of planting, cultivating and maturing an orchard of this character is very great and then again, the difficulty of getting the necessary care and supervision of such property when one doesn't live on it is almost insuperable.

I am sorry I can not give you a more favorable report. We had a delightful trip, covering three days and carrying us through the Imperial Valley almost to the Mexican border, thence to San Diego and back to Los Angeles.

Nell and the babies are well and the latter, of course, are looking forward with keen joy to Santa Claus. We hope you may have a very happy Christmas and that the New Year may bring you nearer to the realization of all that you have so nobly and wonderfully fought for.

With dearest love to Edith and yourself, in which Nell joins, I am, as always,   Devotedly,   W G McAdoo

TLS (WP, DLC).

To Margaret Hubbard Ayer Cobb

[Washington] 21st Decr 1923

It gives me the deepest grief to learn of the death of your gifted husband[1] stop I had learned both to admire and to love him stop Pray accept my heartfelt sympathy   Woodrow Wilson

T telegram (WP, DLC).
    [1] Frank I. Cobb died in the afternoon of December 21.

From James Watson Gerard

My dear Mr. Wilson: New York 21st December 1923

We are deeply grateful to you for your heartening letter of December thirteenth. Will you authorize us to furnish copies of it, confidentially, if you so direct, to those Democratic Senators, who supported you during your Administration? We feel that, with your moral support, it should not be difficult to secure 32 votes to beat the Treaty. Senators Robinson, Borah, King and Ralston have already expressed themselves against it. I am informed that the President and the Secretary of State do not regard the treaty as 'wholly' satisfactory. The so-called Chester concession[1] is reported to have been already annulled by Angora.

We do not surrender to the Soviets nor do we fight them. Should we not pursue a similar policy toward Turkey?

Most Respectfully,   James W Gerard

TLS (WP, DLC).
    [1] Rear Adm. Colby Mitchel Chester, U.S.N., Ret., had initiated a scheme in 1908 in which an American company under his leadership would build railroads and exploit mineral resources in Ottoman Turkey. He and his associates had negotiated extensively for a concession from the Ottoman regime from 1909 to 1914 but never succeeded in obtaining it. The project was dormant during the war but was revived by Chester and others in 1920. Following lengthy negotiations with the postwar Turkish government, an agreement for the concession was reached and was actually ratified by the Turkish National Assembly on April 23, 1923. However, the inability of Chester's organization, the Ottoman-American Development Co., to raise the necessary funds to begin operations in Turkey led the Turkish government to announce the annulment of the concession on December 18, 1923. On the complex history of the Chester project, see John A. DeNovo, *American Interests and Policies in the Middle East, 1900-1939* (Minneapolis, Minn., 1963), pp. 58-87, 210-228.
    The so-called Chester concession was not mentioned in the Treaty of Lausanne.

John Randolph Bolling to James Watson Gerard

My dear Mr. Gerard: [Washington] 22nd December 1923

Mr. Wilson directs me to reply to your letter of 21st December and say that—as his letter of 13th December was not written with the thought that it would be seen by anyone other than yourself—he would prefer that it not be used in the way you suggest.

Cordially yours,   [John Randolph Bolling]

CCL (WP, DLC).

From Newton Diehl Baker

My dear Mr President: Cleveland December 22, 1923

Mrs Baker and I beg you and Mrs Wilson to accept our warmest greetings and good wishes for a merry Christmas [and] a happy New Year.

I hope to be in Washington within a few days and will try to find from Mr Bolling a time when you will be free to see me. I must report to you every now and then of my doings and observations. In a general way I think Cleveland is becoming more and more intelligent about our foreign relations and though I have made at least a hundred speeches on the League in the last two years I find people still come to hear about it,—so the interest seems to grow.

Betty[1] is, as I think I wrote you, at Lausanne at school this year and Mrs Baker and I have been made quite happy by fine reports of her health and progress from her teachers. In a letter received from her yesterday she says that she cut a picture of you out of the Times and put it on the wall of her room alongside of Mrs Baker's picture—whence she boasts quite proudly of the company she keeps—and well she may!

With high regard and every good wish believe me always respectfully and   Affectionately yours,   Newton D. Baker

ALS (WP, DLC).
[1] His daughter, Elizabeth Baker.

To Eleanor Randolph Wilson McAdoo

My darling Nell,   [Washington] 23rd December 1923

We very much appreciated the thoughtfulness which prompted you and Mac to send us the box of fruits and nuts.

We think a great deal about you, and are hoping that the New Year will be rich in the experiences which you most desire.

We are jogging along as usual, and are just now greatly cheered by having Margaret and Helen[1] with us. Their presence will give Christmas an added flavour, and we shall keep them as long as they can stay.

Give our dearest love to the children (excluding Jackie Coogan),[2] and keep for yourselves whatever sentiments you most desire from

Your loving,   [Father]

CCL (WP, DLC).
    [1] That is, Helen Woodrow Bones.
    [2] John Leslie Coogan, born 1914, a child motion-picture star.

To Frank Ernest Ghiselli[1]

My dear Mr. Ghiselli,   [Washington] 26th December 1923

It was most generous and thoughtful of you to send me the bottle of Scotch which Mr. Bolling brought me last night. It is a tonic which the doctors consider necessary for me in my convalescence, and I am sure that its value as a medicine will be enhanced by the consciousness that it is the gift of a friend.

With every good wish for the New Year,

Gratefully Yours,   [Woodrow Wilson]

CCL (WP, DLC).
    [1] Investment banker of Washington.

From Ray Stannard Baker

Amherst Massachusetts
My dear Mr. Wilson: December 26, 1923

I have just had an interesting letter from Dr. Mario Borsa of Milan, Italy, with whom I became well acquainted during the War. He is one of the strong liberals of Italy, was editor of the *Secolo* of Milan which was recently bought out from under him by the Fascisti. He has read our book, and I am rather surprised to have even a liberal Italian take the view that he does in regard to it. I thought you would be interested in what he says, since it also expresses the view of Ferrero and Count Sforza.[1] I quote below from his letter:

"I need hardly say that I have read it with the greatest interest, and found it, as I expected, full of significant disclosures and thoughtful considerations. It is a faithful, powerful, suggestive and authoritative reconstruction of a great historical event, and at the same time an honest, sincere, luminous, and much deserved vindication of Mr. Wilson, whose motives and acts were so malignantly interpreted, and so vulgarly abused in Europe, and, I am sorry to say, particularly in Italy. Both Ferrero and Count Sforza (the ex-foreign minister) with whom I was talking about it recently, agreed that it is the best document we have on the Peace Conference; and, I wish to add on my part, it reveals in the writer one of those men of vision and ideals whose type is so rarely found nowadays."

I thought you might be interested in this reaction, but please do not bother to reply.

I hope you and Mrs. Wilson enjoyed a truly happy Christmas. We had our children at home and our house full of merriment that was altogether delightful.

With many warm regards,

Sincerely yours, Ray Stannard Baker

TLS (WP, DLC).
[1] Guglielmo Ferrero, historian and liberal leader, an opponent of the Fascist regime. Count Carlo Sforza had most recently been the Italian Ambassador in Paris but had resigned when the Fascists came to power.

To John Joseph Pershing

Washington D C
My dear General Pershing, 27th December 1923

You may be sure that it was always a matter of pleasure as well as pride with me to support you in the distinguished services you rendered in the war, and the greeting you have just been so kind as to send me gratifies me deeply.

You may always be sure of my admiration and affection. I am happy to think of our association in the great world crisis of the war.

I hope that the New Year may bring you the happiest fortunes and every circumstance of contentment.

With affectionate regard,

Faithfully Yours, Woodrow Wilson

TLS (J. J. Pershing Papers, DLC).

From Ignace Jan Paderewski

New York NY Dec 27 1923
Always remembering your great and noble deeds, always aware of my country's unredeemable indebtedness to your generosity, always thanking God for the priceless privilege of knowing you, I beg

today to be allowed to renew with the expression of profound reverence and everlasting gratitude my warmest and most affectionate wishes   Paderewski

T telegram (WP, DLC).

From William Cox Redfield

My dear Mr. Wilson   Brooklyn Heights Dec. 27 '23
  Although I am to have the high privilege of speaking briefly tomorrow at the meeting of the Woodrow Wilson Foundation in
honor of your birthday I must send you directly a more personal
word of memory and appreciation.
  This, then, expresses anew my faith in you, in your principles
and in your ideals. You have experienced the loneliness of leadership but the country, though unconsciously in part, is none the
less truly following after you. In a real sense you are leader still. I
trust you may see the day which shall bring your plans and purposes into full and fruitful realities.
  I wish I could feel as sure that our party will follow your hopes
as I am that the country will do so. But this thought may arise from
my own deep desire that the day of fruition may soon come.
  Meanwhile congratulations and high hopes to you and the assurance of undiminished faith.
  Mrs. Redfield joins in best regards to you and to Mrs. Wilson
                          Cordially   William C. Redfield

ALS (WP, DLC).

From Margaret Hubbard Ayer Cobb

My dear Mr Wilson—   [New York] Dec. 27th, 1923.
  Thank you for your kind message. Thank you especially for the
cheering letters you wrote Frank during his illness, letters which
he reread and cherished and which made him happier than anything else could have done.
  Aside from his admiration of you as a leader, Frank's love for you
was strong, unswerving and personal. Speaking of you a few days
before he died, he end[ed] up triumphantly—"*He* never lowered
his Standard."
  I think you will like to know that he did not suffer any pain and
never at any time realized his condition. My regards to you and
Mrs Wilson—   Sincerely yours,   Margaret Ayer Cobb.

ALS (WP, DLC).

A News Report

[*Dec. 28, 1923*]

WILSON IS HONORED ON 67TH BIRTHDAY:
FRIENDS GIVE AUTO

Washington, Dec. 28—Friends of former President Wilson presented him today with a specially constructed Rolls-Royce automobile in celebration of his sixty-seventh birthday.

The gift came as a surprise and Mr. Wilson first saw the car when he left his home in S Street soon after 3 o'clock with Mrs. Wilson and Miss Margaret Wilson to go for a drive.

It was said that the machine was built at a cost of $15,000. The donors withheld their names, and the car was presented to the former President simply as a gift from admirers. Several of those who joined in making the gift, it is reported, were associated with the Wilson Administration.

The automobile has two bodies, one for touring and the other of the closed limousine type. The chassis is standard, but both bodies were planned on special lines to care for Mr. Wilson's comfort.

The touring car body has a higher top, to permit the former President to enter without stooping, wide doors to admit him with ease, and high deep cushions on the wide back seat.

The closed body has a still higher top than the touring body. Both bodies are of dark blue, trimmed with a fine orange stripe, bearing on both rear doors the monogram "W.W." The car is said to be the finest special auto ever turned out by the company.

Admiral Grayson was out of the city today and could not be reached with inquiries concerning the health of his patient on the latter's birthday anniversary. Aside from the special gift of the automobile, plans for the birthday anniversary were for a generally quiet observation at home.

The former President, since leaving the White House, has used continuously one of the White House machines he used during his Administration which he purchased from the Government.

Franklin D. Roosevelt, former Secretary of the Navy, announced yesterday at the luncheon of the Woodrow Wilson Foundation, held at the Hotel Biltmore, that nominations are open for the annual prize of $25,000, which will be offered by the Foundation to the individual who has rendered within the year the most unselfish public service of enduring value.

The award is to be made for specific work recently done, and will be adjudged by a jury of nine men, with Charles W. Eliot, President Emeritus of Harvard University, as Chairman.

The luncheon was in celebration of ex-President Wilson's 67th birthday, which was yesterday.

Norman H. Davis, Under-Secretary of State during the Wilson Administration, told how he had lunched with the ex-President at his home in Washington ten days ago. Mr. Davis said that Mr. Wilson is interested in all public affairs as keenly as ever. "His mind," he said, "is very active, and he seems to have considerably more endurance, although he would be unable to stand such terrific strains as were placed upon him during his tenure of office." . . .[1]

Mr. Roosevelt, who presided at the luncheon, announced that a banquet would be held by the Foundation on Dec. 28, 1924, at which the name of the first recipient of the service award would be announced. No candidate for a prize will be permitted to hand in his own recommendation. Proposals must be handed to the Secretary of the Foundation before June 1, 1924. Every work, in order to qualify, must be written in the English language.

Mrs. Charles L. Tiffany, Secretary of the Foundation, said that already more than $800,000 has been collected toward the goal of $1,000,000.

Printed in the *New York Times*, Dec. 29, 1923.
  [1] Here follow remarks by Redfield and further remarks by Norman Davis.

To William Gibbs McAdoo

My dear Mac,   Washington D C 28th December 1923

I am sincerely obliged to Nell and you for going to see my remote land and sending me a report about it. It is evident I shall have to take my chances on the future development of the region. It would be out of the question for me to irrigate the land at my own expense just now.

The photographs of Ellen and Mary Faith came safely in their pretty frames, and I am very glad indeed to have them. The photograph of Mary Faith makes her look many times her age, but she is nevertheless lovely, and I shall prize it. The very ingenious and unusual rest for a newspaper interests me very much, and I have no doubt will prove very useful to me. Thank you for sending it.

Edith joins me in loving messages to you all, and in the hope that the New Year may be rich in most satisfying experiences for you all.

In unavoidable haste,

           Affectionately Yours,   Woodrow Wilson

TLS (W. G. McAdoo Papers, DLC).

To Ignace Jan Paderewski

[Washington] 28th Dec 1923

Thank you with all my heart for your message stop I am proud to have won your friendship and to have rendered some service to your native country for whom and for you I wish every enduring good fortune.   Woodrow Wilson.

T telegram (WP, DLC).

From Franklin Delano Roosevelt

New York, NY Dec 28 1923

Trustees of the Woodrow Wilson Foundation and the many friends present here today comma your birthday comma desire to express to you our joy at your steady recovery and our gratitude for your extraordinary services in the cause of human freedom international cooperation and good will among men through the Woodrow Wilson Foundation. We tender our affection to you and our heartiest wishes that we may long be guided by your self sacrificing example   Franklin D Roosevelt   Vice President

T telegram (WP, DLC).

From Charles Sumner Hamlin

My dear Mr. Wilson: Washington December 28, 1923.

I write this note to wish you many happy returns of the day, and to congratulate you upon your wonderful physical improvement which is impressed upon me every time I have the privilege of seeing you. There is much work yet ahead for you to do. While we see foreign nations drifting back into a grim sullen isolation your work for international peace has steadily gained ground with our people. I am glad to see that the churches have at last been aroused to a realization of the fact that international isolation is Antichrist and imperils civilization itself. This has been brought about through the inspiration of your leadership. May you live many years to enjoy the fruits of your wonderful work, which in my opinion, was never more appreciated by the American people than at the present time.

Sincerely yours,   Charles S. Hamlin
Approved.
Huybertie Lansing Pruyn Hamlin

TLS (WP, DLC).

From Samuel Huston Thompson, Jr.

My dear friend: Washington December 28, 1923.

Mrs. Thompson joins me in congratulating you on your 67th Birthday.

As time goes on you must be having the pleasurable realization of knowing that the world is coming back to that for which you fought, and those in America who opposed you are gradually being forced to their knees or driven out of public life. Either condition can not occur too soon for me.

There was one thing which constantly recurred to me on my trip abroad last summer in the many Northern countries where the peoples are for the first time having the stimulus of "self-determination" for their races and governments. It was that phrase "peace without victory" which you used in one of your speeches and which caused so much discussion.

In the countries to which I refer, while the farmers underwent many privations during the war and after, they were victors. In Finland and the Baltic Republics agrarian groups are in control of the governments and the peasants for the first time in two hundred years are having their spiritual and land hunger satisfied. It seemed to me that the farmers of these countries obtained peace and also victory, and that there is a more hopeful outlook for their countries than for most of the others that I was in.

As I went further south, through Poland, Germany and France, and even England, where among the artisans I found much suffering, it seemed to me that your prophetic phrase "peace without victory" had come to pass. It was not the kind of peace, however, that I imagined you had in mind when you used the phrase, for while there is a cessation of arms, there is not that kind of peace "which passeth all understanding."

I would deeply appreciate it if sometime you could let me know whether that much-debated phrase was one which occurred to you while you were speaking or whether it was a fully designed expression meant to convey a future condition that you were aiming for.

I have just returned from a trip to Denver where all of your old-time friends were keen to know how you were and gave forth many expressions of affectionate regard.

With best wishes from Mrs. Thompson and myself, I am
                    Cordially yours,   Huston Thompson

TLS (WP, DLC).

Thomas Davies Jones to Cleveland Hoadley Dodge

My dear Mr. Dodge: Chicago December 29, 1923.

Cyrus McCormick has submitted to me the matter of joining in the annuity agreement for Mr. Wilson, and also contributing toward the purchase of an automobile for him. I am very glad to have a part in both of these matters, and I enclose to you herewith my check for $1,625, of which $1,000 goes to you on account of the purchase of the automobile. I think it is quite likely that on the first of October last you advanced the entire amount of the annuity, namely $2,500, and if that be the case, then $312.50 out of the proceeds of this check should reimburse you for that amount of your advance for the October 1st insallment of the annuity, and the remaining $312.50 will be for the January annuity.

Wishing you a very happy New Year, I am

Faithfully yours,   Thomas D Jones

TLS (received from Phyllis Boushall Dodge).

To Franklin Delano Roosevelt

Washington Dec 30 1923

The birthday message which you sent me on behalf of the Foundation has given me the greatest pleasure and I am glad to detect in its phrasing the warmth of your own personal feeling.

Woodrow Wilson

T telegram (F. D. Roosevelt Papers, NHpR).

To Cleveland Hoadley Dodge

My dear Cleve,   Washington D C 30th December 1923

The Rolls Royce is a joy. I had for a long time been wishing that I might have a car of that make but had never dreamed that the wish could be gratified; so that it took my breath away to receive a fully equipped Rolls Royce on my birthday as a gift from a friend whose generosity knows no bounds. I shall greatly enjoy the use of the car. If the Democratic party had the perfect coordination and harmonious force which that car has it might alter and dominate the political action of the whole world. Surely no other man ever had such friends as you and Jesse Jones have been to me, and I hope with all my heart that in the years to come I may have the strength and opportunity to show some proof of my gratitude.

I hope, my dear fellow, that you can presently send me word that you are yourself much better and stronger, and that before very long you will be able to travel at least far enough to come within hand grasping distance of me.

Mrs. Wilson joins me in affectionate messages to Mrs. Dodge and you and I am and shall be always, with devoted affection,

Your Grateful Friend,   Woodrow Wilson

TLS (WC, NjP).

From John Spencer Bassett

Dear Mr. Wilson: Northampton, Mass. December 30, 1923

It gives me much pleasure to inform you that on Friday, the 28th, you were unanimously elected president of the American Historical Association at the annual meeting in Columbus, Ohio. May I express to you my personal gratification and my sense of the high value to the Association of your services in the position during the year just beginning? Miss Washington,[1] the assistant secretary, at 1140 Woodward Building, will be glad to hold herself at your commands for the execution of your desires in the course of your official duties. Anything I can do will be done with great pleasure.

In announcing your election Mr. Cheyney[2] used words, as nearly as I can remember, them like these:

"I have heard our presidents called 'our greatest his[t]orians' and I confess I do not like the terms used in that sense. It is hard to know what one means by it. But that aside, I have the honor to assure you that you have elected a great man."

The quick and vigorous burst of applause that followed was gratify[ing] to those of us who have given you our gratitude and love in all your course of service to this country and to the world.

Yours sincerely,   John S. Bassett

TLS (WP, DLC).
    [1] Patty W. Washington.
    [2] Edward Potts Cheyney, Professor of European History at the University of Pennsylvania and President of the American Historical Association for 1923.

To Ray Stannard Baker

My dear Baker,   [Washington] 31st December 1923

It is not often that a book is assessed at its true value so early and so universally as yours has been, and I felicitate you on its success the more heartily because the verdict is so just and true.[1]

I was greatly interested in your quotation from Dr. Borsa.

I am glad to learn that you have had a merry Holiday season, and I hope that the New Year will fulfill your every hope.

With affectionate regard,

Faithfully Yours,   [Woodrow Wilson]

CCL (WP, DLC).
¹ Wilson was replying to RSB to WW, Dec. 26, 1923.

To Samuel Huston Thompson, Jr.

My dear Thompson,   Washington D C 31st December 1923

Thank you for your letter of 28th December. It is full of interest for me.

The phrase, "peace without victory," was intended by me as a warning against a vindictive triumph such as too many seemed at that time to desire as an outcome of the war. The idea was to punish the Germans and not merely to put a final check upon the reckless and arrogant German government. What I meant to say therefore was we must beat them for the sake of the principles involved but not in order to humiliate and destroy them.

Thank you again for your letter. I hope that the New Year will be a peculiarly happy one for Mrs. Thompson and you, and that we shall enjoy together the impending triumph of the great party which we serve.

Cordially and Faithfully Yours,   Woodrow Wilson

TLS (RSB Coll., DLC).

To William Cox Redfield

My dear Redfield,   Washington D C 31st December 1923

I am truly grateful to you for your letter of December twenty-seventh. I prize your confidence and friendship more highly than I know how to say. It cheers me to recall our close association in the past and to look forward to the hope of constant comradeship in the affairs of the future.

Mrs. Wilson joins with me in warmest messages of friendship to Mrs. Redfield and you, and in the hope that the New Year may realize for you both your dearest hopes.

With affectionate regard,

Faithfully Yours,   Woodrow Wilson

TLS (W. C. Redfield Papers, DLC).

From Joseph Tyrone Derry

Jacksonville Florida
Dear Friend and former Pupil,   Monday, Dec. 31st 1923.

I congratulate you on your recent birthday and thank God that
He has spared your life and given you much happiness during the
year just closed. May you remain on earth many more years to
gladden the hearts of all that love you and to be a blessing to the
world even more than you have been in the past. With much love
to you and all your loved ones
     Your devoted friend and admirer,   Joseph T. Derry.

Mrs Derry joins in all these good wishes. The health of us both
has been precious in the sight of our God.   J.T.D.

ALS (WP, DLC).

To John Spencer Bassett

My dear Bassett,   [Washington] 2nd January 1924

It rather startles me to learn that the American Historical Association has elected me its president, because I cannot be sure that
I shall be fit for the duties that fall to the occupant of that office.
But I feel highly honoured, and shall do my best to live up to the
obligations involved.

It was a real pleasure to be reminded of your generous friendship, and I beg to express the hope that the New Year will contain
for you blessings of the sort you most desire.
     Cordially and Sincerely Yours,   [Woodrow Wilson]

CCL (WP, DLC).

Cleveland Hoadley Dodge to Jesse Holman Jones

My dear Mr. Jones: [New York] January 2, 1924.

I received, this morning, Mr. Thomas Jones' check to cover
$1000 for the automobile, and $625 for his share of the October
and January payments, and Mr. McCormick promises to send me
his check after the first of January. He has also returned the agreement, duly signed by both Mr. McCormick and Mr. Jones, which I
am enclosing herewith to you.

I have also had a beautiful letter from our friend in Washington,
thanking me for the car and I have taken great pleasure in writing
to him and telling him that it is a gift from the four members of the
"W W Trust," so that he will know exactly who the car is from.

The account of the car in the New York papers was certainly wonderful, and I think we did right in giving him the very best that could be obtained. I understand that you propose to make a contribution to the car, too, and you also told me that the bill was to be sent to you, so when you get the bill if you will let me know how much you want me to send you, I shall be greatly obliged.

I am planning to leave New York on January 25, to be gone about six weeks but will be back before the April first payment is due. Wishing you a very "Happy New Year"

Yours sincerely, [C. H. Dodge]

CCL (received from Phyllis Boushall Dodge).

Raymond Blaine Fosdick to John Randolph Bolling

Dear Mr. Bolling: New York January 3, 1924.

I expect to be in Washington some day next week, and while I have no progress to report in regard to the matter which the President and I discussed when I saw him a month or six weeks ago, it occurs to me that I might be able to tell him something of the situation that confronts the various Boards with which I am associated. I do not want to impose upon his time when he is so pressed with other matters, but if you think that any report I might make might be of service to him, please do not hesitate to let me know.

My present plan is to be in Washington on Wednesday, the ninth. Ever cordially yours, Raymond B. Fosdick

TLS (WP, DLC).

To Jesse Holman Jones

My dear Friend, Washington D C 4th January 1924

The check which I have just received from Cleve Dodge again makes me vividly conscious of the extraordinary privilege I enjoy in having such friends as you and he and the others of the little group who have so generously and so thoughtfully relieved Mrs. Wilson and me of pecuniary anxieties. He also writes me that you have joined with the others in the gift of the beautiful car which I received on my birthday.

There are no adequate words in which I can express my feeling in this matter. I can only trust that as the years go by I may have many opportunities of making you conscious of my deep affection, trust and gratitude.

Mrs. Wilson joins with me in the hope that Mrs. Jones and you

may find the New Year a time of peculiar happiness and contentment.

Please do not fail to let me have a glimpse of you whenever it is
possible for you to come this way.

With most affectionate regard,

Gratefully Yours,   Woodrow Wilson

TLS (J. H. Jones Papers, Barker Texas History Center, TxU).

To Thomas Davies Jones

My dear Friend,   Washington D C 4th January 1924

I do not believe that any other man is so wonderfully blessed in
the character of his friends, or in the tact and unlimited liberality
of their generosity towards him.

It pleases me particularly that you should have wished to be one
of the group who have relieved Mrs. Wilson and me of pecuniary
anxiety. I have long felt that your friendship and confidence was
the chief evidence that I have some kind of substantial worth. It
has meant and always will mean a great deal to me that a man of
such a character and of such powers of judgment as yours should
have complete confidence in me.

I have just heard from Cleve that you have also joined the others
of the "celebrated Trust" in the gift of the beautiful car, and I am
deeply grateful for this additional evidence of your kindness and
generosity.

I hope that the New Year will in many ways bring you the happiness of knowing how you are admired and how much you have
done to sustain those who were trying to do their duty.

My heart goes out to you in deep gratitude, and with the hope
that in the years to come, as in those which have passed, we may
be closely associated with one another in the task which the extraordinary condition of affairs throughout the world makes imperative upon those who mean to render such service as they can to
the country and to mankind.

With most affectionate regard,

Gratefully Yours,   Woodrow Wilson

TLS (WP, DLC).

From James Kerney

My dear Governor: Trenton, New Jersey January 4, 1924

Princeton just now is quite excited by Dr. van Dyke's pleasant little letter giving up his pew in the First Church.[1] I know you have seen the letter, but felt that you might be interested in Dr. Machen's sermon, and send herewith today's report of it in the Times.[2]

I sincerely hope that the Rolls-Royce is bringing comfort and pleasure to Mrs. Wilson and yourself, and that you continue to improve in health. Henry Ford may be a good business man, but I don't think he has affected the flivver vote very greatly.

With every good wish, I am,

Faithfully yours,   James Kerney.

TLS (WP, DLC).

[1] Henry van Dyke had attended divine service on December 30, 1923, at the First Presbyterian Church of Princeton. The service was conducted by the Rev. Dr. John Gresham Machen, Assistant Professor of New Testament Literature and Exegesis at Princeton Theological Seminary, who was the interim pastor of the church and an old friend of Wilson. On January 3, 1924, Van Dyke wrote a letter to Howard E. Eldridge, the treasurer of the church, and released it to the Associated Press on the same day. It read as follows: "Having had another Sunday spoiled by the bitter, schismatic and unscriptural preaching of the stated supply of the First Presbyterian Church of Princeton (directly contrary to the spirit of His beautiful text), I desire to give up my pew in the church. The few Sundays that I have free from evangelical work to spend with my family are too precious to be wasted in listening to such a dismal, bilious travesty of the gospel. We want to hear about Christ, the Son of God and the Son of Man, not about the Fundamentalists and Modernists, the only subject on which your stated supply seems to have anything to say and on which most of what he says is untrue and malicious. Until he is done, count me out and give up my pew in the church. We want to worship Christ, our Saviour." *New York Times*, Jan. 4, 1924.

Machen was the leader of the extreme conservatives, both in the seminary and in the Presbyterian Church at large, but the controversy between the so-called liberals and the conservatives centered in and was focused upon the seminary faculty, a majority of whom were extreme conservatives on such questions as Biblical inerrancy. The General Assembly of the Presbyterian Church in the United States of America in 1927 reorganized the board of trustees of the seminary and postponed Dr. Machen's election to the chair of apologetics and ethics. Further discussions and actions led to the defeat of the conservatives in 1929, whereupon, led by Machen, they withdrew, founded Westminster Seminary in Philadelphia, the Independent Board for Presbyterian Foreign Missions, and the Presbyterian Church of America from 1929 to 1936. See Lefferts A. Loetscher, *The Broadening Church: a study of theological issues in the presbyterian church since 1869* (Philadelphia, 1954), pp. 136-55.

[2] It is missing in WP, DLC.

To James Kerney

My dear Kerney,   [Washington] 5th January 1924

I had seen Van Dyke's letter in the paper and regard it as petulant and childish.

Thank you for sending me the copy of Dr. Machen's sermon. I may have occasion to turn to it. It is delightful and heartening to know you are thinking of me.

I hope that the New Year will bring you many kinds of enduring happiness.

With warm regard,

Faithfully Yours,   [Woodrow Wilson]

CCL (WP, DLC).

John Randolph Bolling to Raymond Blaine Fosdick

Dear Mr. Fosdick: [Washington] 5th January 1924

I have brought to Mr. Wilson's attention the contents of your letter to me of January third, and he hopes that you can find it convenient to run in and see him for a few minutes at three-thirty o'clock on next Wednesday afternoon, January ninth. I need not tell you how glad I shall be for the opportunity of another little visit with you.   Cordially yours,   [John Randolph Bolling]

CCL (WP, DLC).

A Tribute[1]

[Jan. 6, 1924]

I have known no man whose sturdiness of character and clear vision of duty impressed me more than those of Frank I Cobb. He completely won my confidence and affection and I recognized in him a peculiar genius for giving direct and effective expression to the enlightened opinions which he held. I consider his death an irreparable loss to journalism and to the liberal political policies which are necessary to liberate mankind from the errors of the past and the partisan selfishness of the present. His death leaves a vacancy in the ranks of liberal thinkers which some one should press forward to fill if the impulse of progress is not to be stayed.

CC MS (WP, DLC).
    [1] The following statement, dictated January 6, 1924, was printed as the foreword to John L. Heaton, compiler, *Cobb of "The World": A Leader in Liberalism* (New York, 1924), p. v. Wilson wrote the tribute in response to L. Seibold to WW, Jan. 4, 1924, TLS (WP, DLC).

From Norman Hezekiah Davis

My dear Mr. Wilson: New York January 7, 1924.

I am going to bother you again over the question of whether or not I should accept the invitation from the Council of the League of Nations to act as President of the Committee of Three to make an investigation and propose to the Council a plan to settle the controversy over Memel.[1]

The view held by you, which Mrs. Wilson kindly communicated to me by telephone, to the effect that the importance of the issue involved and the probable service that might be rendered would not justify me in dropping everything here and being absent for three months, was entirely in accordance with my own reaction and impulse.

There is nothing in the task that appeals to me, but somehow I cannot get away from the feeling that since the League of Nations has felt that the problem to be solved is of sufficient importance to justify them in asking me to undertake it, I cannot conscientiously refuse to do so without a good alibi. I also have a feeling that if the friends of the League do not come to its aid when called upon, its task will become impossible of solution.

Raymond Fosdick, to whom Drummond has cabled requesting that he prevail upon me to accept the invitation, and who as you know has worked so valiantly for the League, is firmly convinced that I not only should do this but that I can render a most valuable service. He says that in all of the speeches which he has made on the League, he finds that one of the things which makes the greatest impression is that an American acted as Chairman of the Committee which settled the dispute over the Aaland Islands[2] and averted a war, and that the more practical illustrations we can give of what influence an impartial American can exercise in settling disputes between the nations in Europe, it will add to the evidence of how much more our Government could do if it threw all of the weight of its influence into the settlement of all such questions.

In the despatch from the League, it is stated that the Council of the League, at its last meeting, considered the question of Memel of urgent importance, affecting not only the good relations of Poland and Lithuania, but general international relations throughout the Baltic, and that a settlement would undoubtedly remove a serious European difficulty which becomes more aggravated the longer it remains open. In the desire to be especially fair and make a fresh start towards a settlement, the Council decided to name an impartial Committee of Three to propose a solution, and it resolved to invite Whitlock,[3] who was in Europe, or former Ambassador Warren,[4] or me to serve as the President. It was desirous that the Commission should meet in January, if possible, in order to report to the Council by the first of March, and that what is desired is an impartial American of commanding prestige, whose personal authority can bridge the relatively small differences which are blocking a solution.

I must admit that it would have been difficult for the League to hand me a more unpalatable package, but since Whitlock has refused to act, because as I am told of illness, and because Warren has refused to act, probably because this Administration, not wishing to help the League, advised him not to accept, I am afraid that if I now refuse it might give the League a black eye. Probably my conscience may be a little too active, and probably I am exaggerating the harm that may result if the League fails to get me or some other American who could do this to undertake it, but since I have been unable to get away from the feeling above indicated, in spite of my personal desire to stay at home, I have written you thus frankly in the hope that if you do not agree with my line of reasoning you can furnish me with an adequate alibi.

If I should decide to go, it would now seem that I ought to be able to leave here about the 20th or 25th of this month, and be back by the 15th of March. In any event, I may be able to run down to Washington some day this week and have a chat with you at your convenience. I must make a final decision and give an answer to the League, and I may therefore call Mrs. Wilson by telephone tomorrow, in order to get your views without delay.

With warmest personal regards, I am, as ever,

Affectionately yours,   Norman H. Davis[5]

TLS (WP, DLC).
[1] That is, the long-standing dispute over the ultimate disposition of the territory of Memel (now Klaipeda), the control over which, by Article 99 of the Treaty of Versailles, had been transferred by Germany to the Allied and Associated Powers. *PPC*, XIII, 237. Lithuania had occupied the territory by military force in January 1923, and the Conference of Ambassadors in Paris, bowing to a *fait accompli*, had agreed in principle to the transfer of the territory to Lithuania in February of that year. However, the Conference of Ambassadors and the Lithuanian government had been unable to agree on the details of the incorporation of Memel into Lithuania in such matters as the degree of political and economic autonomy which the territory was to enjoy and the status and rights of its inhabitants. Therefore, the Conference of Ambassadors had referred the matter to the League of Nations in September 1923, and the Council of the League had decided on December 17 to appoint a committee of three to study the entire issue and produce a draft convention embodying its recommendations. For a detailed history of the Memel question, see Thorsten V. Kalijarvi, *The Memel Statute: Its Origin, Legal Nature, and Observation to the Present Day* (London, 1937), pp. 9-115.
[2] That is, Abram I. Elkus.
[3] That is, Brand Whitlock.
[4] Charles Beecher Warren, Ambassador to Japan, June 1921 to March 1923; appointed Ambassador to Mexico in February 1924.
[5] Typed at the top of this letter: "Answered by 'phone Jany 8 1924—EBW."

From Ray Stannard Baker

Dear Mr. Wilson: New York January 7, 1924

The more I think and write about you and your work the more interested and fascinated I grow: and the more important to the country and to the world seem the correct interpretation of your message and of the things you represent. You have a vision essential to the safety of the world: one that ought to be made thoroughly clear.

I spoke to you once—as poorly as only I know how to speak!—about going forward with a further and more complete study of your whole career. I have a great ambition to do this and do it thoroughly: but I do not wish to undertake it unless I can feel behind me as complete a confidence upon your part as I felt in the utilization of the Peace Conference material: unless I can also, at some later time, as you may think wise and proper, have full and first access to all of your other personal material—letters, memoranda, and documents, so that what I should write would have full authority.

I had also a plan, which I think I suggested before, of beginning soon—so that I could do the work in a leisurely and thorough way—of visiting the places where you have lived, and of talking with men who have, through the years, known you best, and thus getting together a mass of foundation material. On such a work I should want much more time than I had on the Peace Conference book—to give it a quality and unity not possible there. It ought to be done without any pressure for publication—and appear when it was truly ready. I should wish to do it, as I could find time, along with my other work.

Of course my association with you and my study of your work at the critical period have given me a great deal of vital material which no one else has—much indeed that I could not use in "Woodrow Wilson and World Settlement"—but it has only whetted my appetite for more. I have a vision of a book that will be a kind of handbook of Americanism!

Someone, at some future time, will do this work—well or poorly. If there is anyone who can do it better than I can, with a clearer understanding or a better background of knowledge, he ought to be the man—and I'll help him! For the work itself is the important thing. But you will not misinterpret me when I say I think I'm the man.

I thought the best way of presenting this subject was the direct way. I thought, knowing you, that you would like this best. And I will not argue it at all—for if it does not of itself, impress you as desirable, why that's the answer! If you do like the plan and are willing to have me tackle it I shall be glad to know it. If not, it will not in the least change my feeling toward you.

Cordially yours   Ray Stannard Baker

P.S. I am going back to Amherst probably Wednesday.
I presided at a large meeting the other night addressed by Jus-

tice Clark on the League of Nations. He makes a fine & convincing speech: and it was clear—and rather surprising to me—how fully he seemed to have his audience with him. The sentiment is there if it can have leadership

ALS (WP, DLC).

From Louis Wiley

Dear Mr. Wilson: [New York] January 7th, 1924.

On the twenty-fifth anniversary of Adolph S. Ochs' direction of The New York Times, I prepared a volume with tributes to The Times from distinguished men, which was presented to Mr. Ochs by our staff.

While you have not always agreed with The Times, it is gratifying to recall your letters to me commending its course on a number of public questions.

I shall be deeply grateful if you will send in my care a short letter to Mr. Ochs for inclusion in the anniversary volume saying a word on the subject of The Times and its qualities. Without an expression from you the book is incomplete. Its contents are not to be published.

With every good wish to you and Mrs. Wilson for the New Year,
                    Always sincerely yours,   Louis Wiley

TLS (WP, DLC).

To Ray Stannard Baker

My dear Baker,   [Washington] 8th January 1924

I think that there is no man who could do what you propose in your letter of January seventh so well as you could. But unhappily the papers and other sources upon which alone you could build a solid structure are so scattered and inaccessible that the task would, at the present moment, be next to impossible. I could not myself assemble the material because I do not know where it is.

I have my doubts whether it is wise to endeavor to promote the great general cause in which we are interested by making too much of a single man and his activities and influence. Such a method would encounter a great body of prejudice and animosity which there will be no means, so far as I can see, of removing.

But the main obstacle is that I myself do not know where the materials are that you would have to have. I have never been in the least systematic about the preservation of my own personal papers, and they are by now widely scattered, or packed away in storage with household effects.

It grieves me to put the least obstacle in your way in the disinterested and generous work which you desire to undertake; but when I ask myself the question how I would go about giving you "full and first access," I realize that I would not know how to do it; and it is only right and frank that I should tell you so. I have had an active and varied career, but I have had no thought of keeping memoranda of it, or records of any kind; so that I am obliged in candor to make this disclosure to you.

It may be that as the years go by I shall come upon material of the kind you desire, but even that is a matter of conjecture and depends upon whether I spend the rest of my life in one place or not. I have not preserved even the original manuscripts of the books I have published.

I think that you will agree with me that, the circumstances being what I have described them, no systematic progress could be hoped for in the development of the work you so generously suggest.

My confidence in your impartiality and justice is absolute, but even your high qualities do not involve the power to create material as well as to interpret it.

I feel almost guilty of disloyalty to you in making this reply to your persuasive letter, but it is the only reply that I can make which would be consistent with the facts as I know them, and I am sure I can depend upon your intuition to put the true interpretation upon it.

With affectionate regard, in which Mrs. Wilson joins me,

Faithfully Yours,   [Woodrow Wilson]

CCL (WP, DLC).

John Randolph Bolling to Louis Wiley

Dear sir: [Washington] 8th January 1924

Mr. Wilson directs me to say, in reply to your letter of seventh January to him, that he doesn't feel he has followed Mr. Ochs's career closely enough to be prepared to write an intelligent estimate of him, such as you suggest.

Cordially yours,   [John Randolph Bolling]

CCL (WP, DLC).

A Letter of Introduction

TO WHOM IT MAY CONCERN:		Washington D C 9th January 1924

The bearer of this letter is Dr. John R. Mott. Dr. Mott is a trusted friend of mine. He is traveling upon a mission which concerns nothing except the spiritual interest of Christians throughout the world. He is associated with men active in religious matters throughout the world, and is seeking to cooperate with them in matters which concern only religious and personal conduct. He is seeking in this time of general anxiety and disturbance to confer with such men wherever it is possible to do so. In his work with the students and other classes of young men he is doing much to promote friendly and cooperative relations among those who to-morrow are to become the leaders of nations.

I commend him to the courtesy and highest consideration of all with whom he may come in contact.
				Sincerely Yours, Woodrow Wilson

TLS (J. R. Mott Coll., CtY-D).

From Jesse Holman Jones

My dear Friend:			Houston, Texas, January 9, 1924.

Permit me to acknowledge your letter of the fourth instant, and to assure you that I have never done anything that gives me the enjoyment and satisfaction I get and shall always have from my participation in the "Woodrow Wilson Personal Trust." It is a rare privilege you have given me and the other three gentlemen with whom I have the honor to be associated in this matter, and I am perfectly sure that neither of us will ever again have an opportunity to do a thing that will afford us as much pleasure, or that we will take as much pride in doing.

In dedicating your life to teaching and political leadership without thought of your own welfare you have rendered a service to mankind impossible to measure, and I am proud beyond expression of having so large a share of your friendship. I value the distinction, and wish you many years of health, happiness and usefulness. Mrs. Jones joins in these felicitations, which extend to and include Mrs. Wilson.		Your friend, Jesse H. Jones

TCL (RSB Coll., DLC).

From the Diary of Breckinridge Long

[Jan. 11, 1924]

Cary[1] and I have several points in interest of mutual nature—horses and Woodrow Wilson. We soon got on the subject of Wilson and he told me—briefly—of several incidents I did not know much about. "Mrs. Peck" was the subject of one. It seems W.W. has talked to Cary several times about her. He used to write her letters—many of them. Mrs. Wilson—the first—also talked about her to Cary and among other things said that the "Peck" affair was the only unhappiness he had caused her during their whole married life—not that there was anything wrong—or improper—about it, for there was not, but just that a brilliant mind and an attractive woman had some-how fascinated—temporarily—Mr. Wilson's mind—and she (Mrs Wilson) did not want to share his confidence or his inner mind with any one.

I have met Mrs. Hurlburt [Hulbert] (the real name of Mrs. Peck) and can testify to her considerable attraction. She was at Nantucket one summer—down on Beach side—near the bathing beach, under the cliff and I think she stayed in the old Hurlburt house there, but about that I may be mistaken. She visited the White House several times, so Cary says, once for several days and once from 7 a.m. till the afternoon of the same day.[2] I got the distinct impression from Cary that he believed the relationship had been quite innocent—but indiscreet for a public man. The last time he saw her it seems was at lunch with the present Mrs Wilson in Los Angeles at the hotel on his ill fated trip,[3] and just shortly before he was stricken.

The Admiral told of the scene Tumulty made in the fall of 1916 when Wilson called him in to discharge him as Secretary, having decided to let Tumulty go and to secure Vance McCormick.[4] It seems Tumulty cried, and prayed and beseeched, and implored, told the story of his life and used his old father, his children, the little old house and every conceivable argument which would appeal to the sentiment of a sentimental man. Mr Wilson was much touched, almost cried himself and walked out of the room without saying a word. And Joe stayed on.

Cary has kept diaries, memoranda of conversations with the President, long accounts of his opinions of men and measures. Once Mr Wilson said to him, "I am glad you do not keep a diary, because if you did I would not be able to talk to you as freely as I do." Cary said nothing, felt very sheepish,—and went on keeping his diary. It will not be published for many years, of course. Mr Wilson will have to have died and so will most of the men of that generation before it would be right to publish it. But he will write a book some-day, not in the immediate future, and will include in it a lot of the things from his diary. The unexpurgated work I hope to live to see. Strangely enough Cary has very few letters from Mr Wilson, but then he was constantly with him and there was no opportunity to write letters.

One interesting thing—and about the only other we spoke of, except the pedigree of my new mare, was Wilsons first impression of Leonard Wood, way back about April 1913. They went for a ride one day and Mr Wilson said to Cary "I have had a great disappointment. I had a half hour's talk with General Wood. He spent his whole time damning Roosevelt. It had only one possible purpose— to curry favor with me, naturally antipathetic to Roosevelt. But Roosevelt made Leonard Wood and if Wood will criticize and condemn the man who made him just to increase his own standing in my eyes—then he would do the same thing to me—and I can't trust him. I am sorely disappointed."

That is the back-ground behind the reason that John J. Pershing and not Leonard Wood was selected to head the army in the World War.

Had Wood been honest with himself and honest with his chief— and loyal to a former chief—it is quite possible the world would have known General Wood instead of General Pershing.

Bound diary (B. Long Papers, DLC).
   [1] That is, Dr. Grayson.
   [2] Mrs. Hulbert visited the White House on May 9-16, 1913 (at Ellen Axson Wilson's invitation), and during the morning and afternoon of May 31, 1915. About the first visit, see Frances Wright Saunders, *First Lady Between Two Worlds: Ellen Axson Wilson* (Chapel Hill, N. C., 1985), p. 240.
   [3] About this meeting, see WW to Mary A. Hulbert, Sept. 20, 1919, n. 1, Vol. 63.
   [4] About the attempt to remove Tumulty from the secretaryship in November 1916, see JPT to WW, Nov. 18, 1916, Vol. 38, and the secondary works cited in the notes thereto. None of these accounts of the affair mentions either Vance C. McCormick as the likely successor to Tumulty or the emotional interview which Long describes just below.

Cyrus Hall McCormick, Jr., to Edith Bolling Galt Wilson

Washington Sunday morning
My dear Mrs. Wilson: [Jan. 13, 1924].

I have just arrived from New York and am looking forward with pleasure to seeing you and Woodrow. May I ask your advice as to whether I come today or tomorrow to lunch?[1]

Before seeing Woodrow I want your counsel—and perhaps that of Mr. Bolling—on a very important question. When I was here last I spoke with you regarding the personal relations between Woodrow and Colonel House. I did not then know Col House's attitude.

I do now, I think. I am most anxious to *try* and remove the misunderstanding and have these two resume, as far as possible, a basis of cordial cooperation. The issue is of great moment not only to the two but to the cause of Democracy generally. We must make no mistakes and therefore I feel that a conference with you before I see Woodrow would be helpful and important. Can it be managed? If there is opportunity from your standpoint I can come any time this morning and then return to your house for luncheon today. If there is no opportunity of seeing you this morning—or if this afternoon or evening is better—I can see you today and put off my luncheon till tomorrow. My train goes at 3:30 pm tomorrow which would give me time for luncheon and a little talk with Woodrow before I went to my train.

Please let me know your preference. I can suit myself to your wishes. You can tell Woodrow that I found it better to come tomorrow, if you so decide.

I assume that your luncheon hour is one oclock

I think half an hour with you and Mr Bolling or with you alone as you prefer will give you the situation as I see it. Perhaps you would wish a little time for reflection before giving me your opinion
Cordially yours   Cyrus H. McCormick.

Cleve Dodge is earnestly hoping that we may find a way to secure the renewal of a basis of cooperation between Woodrow and Col House. No one else knows I have any thot about it
C H McC

ALS (WP, DLC).
¹ Mrs. Wilson had invited McCormick to lunch on January 14. Alice Hoit to EBW, Jan. 7, 1924, TLS (WP, DLC).

Edith Bolling Galt Wilson to Cyrus Hall McCormick, Jr.

2340 S Street N W
Dear Mr. McCormick: 13th January 1924

I am deeply distressed that after getting the note from your secretary I made other plans for today which preclude me asking you to come up for lunch or dinner. But I hope tomorrow you will come at twelve-thirty, when we can have the talk you suggest before luncheon.

Of course I shall keep an open mind for whatever you have to say on the subject you mention; but since seeing you I also have learned things which do not incline me to change my opinion in regard to the present status being the only one possible. However, we will talk it out.

I cannot tell you how deeply sorry I am for the complications which prevent our seeing you today.

Faithfully yours,   Edith Bolling Wilson

Please excuse typed letter.

TLS (C. H. McCormick, Jr., Papers, WHi).

From Norman Hezekiah Davis

My dear Mr. Wilson: New York January 14, 1924.

I have definitely decided to go to Europe, and am sailing Wednesday on the "Paris." Apparently after thinking the matter over, Mr. Hughes realized that there was no ground on which he could offer any official objections, and since I told him that no matter how much I esteemed his personal opinion, it did not influence me in this particular case, because I had not sought it, and it was contrary to my own view as to my duty.

I hope that all will go well with you and Mrs. Wilson during my absence, and that you will be able to help keep the Democrats on the track.

With kindest regards to you both, believe me, as ever,

Affectionately yours,   Norman H. Davis

TLS (WP, DLC).

To Norman Hezekiah Davis

My dear Davis,   [Washington] 15th January 1924

I am sure that you decided right about going to Europe, and I do not believe you will ever regret it. A fine piece of diplomatic work awaits you there.

Mrs. Wilson joins me in affectionate messages to you all, and I am, as always,   Affectionately Yours,   [Woodrow Wilson]

CCL (WP, DLC).

From Ray Stannard Baker

Dear Mr. Wilson: Amherst Massachusetts January 15, 1924

I need not pretend that I am not disappointed by the reading of your letter of the eighth. I had not, of course, thought of asking any immediate access to your papers, but only the reasonable assurance that at some time, as long in the future as you thought best, I could feel sure of a chance to see what I could do with them; and in the meantime be at the business of getting together basic material from other sources.

However, I am with you either way!

The article in *Current History* is getting quite a response. I have had numerous and excellent letters. I enclose two of them[1] (not to burden you with more) that I thought you might care to see. One is from a Swiss. The proposal to republish in pamphlet form by the Federal Council of Churches seems to me excellent. We can thus get a tremendous circulation among church people, who are the sincerest supporters of your principles. I would rather have it done by them than by anybody else. I am going ahead with this anyway.

Please remember me kindly to Mrs. Wilson and to Mr. Bolling.

With cordial regards,   Ray Stannard Baker

TLS (WP, DLC).
[1] The enclosures are missing. The citation to the article appears in RSB to WW, Nov. 23, 1923, n. 1.

A News Report

[Jan. 16, 1924]

WILSON RECEIVES PARTY COMMITTEE

Washington, Jan. 16.—The Democratic National Committee closed its sessions today, after endorsing the "incomparable achievements" of Woodrow Wilson's "great Administration" and made a pilgrimage to the "shrine of peace" in S Street, where the former President and Mrs. Wilson received the members.

Fully two hundred men and women made the pilgrimage in the rain. They were received by the former President, seated in his library. As they passed up the stairway they were met by Mrs. Wilson, before they entered the library. Cordell Hull, Chairman of the committee, introduced the visitors to Mr. Wilson, who, in shaking hands, passed a pleasant word with those whom he had known. He was in the best of spirits and his handshake was strong and cordial.

Chairman Hull briefly informed Mr. Wilson of the action of the committee and presented the resolutions beautifully engrossed. This seemed to give the former President much pleasure as the evidence of admiration and respect expressed by the men and women who had fought under him as Democratic leader and as advocates of the League of Nations.

Mrs. Wilson had a personal word for nearly everyone and thanked the women for the word of cheer they had brought to her husband, whose health appears in many ways to be improving, certainly in his ability to move around with greater freedom.

After exchanging greetings, Mr. Wilson told Chairman Hull that he was to be congratulated upon his work as Chairman, as well as the personnel at the office of the National Committee.

"I am glad that the convention went to New York," Mr. Wilson said.

The last thing the National Committee did was to adopt the resolution endorsing the Administration of Woodrow Wilson, which read:

"Resolved: That the Democratic National Committee hereby extends its cordial greetings to Woodrow Wilson, and assures him that the party is preparing to enter the approaching Presidential campaign inspired by the incomparable achievements of his great Administration and confident of the compelling power of the high ideals which he brought to the service of his country. It wishes for him an early restoration to complete health."

Printed in the *New York Times*, Jan. 17, 1924.

From William Gibbs McAdoo

Dear Governor: Los Angeles, California January 18, 1924.

At last I have gotten a letter from Charles W. King[1] of Indio, California, about your land, which gives some additional information about it, particularly as to the cost of water and grading, that is more favorable than my first report. Of course you may not want to develop water for the land, but it is just as well to have this information for your file. I have made proper acknowledgment to Mr. King, so you don't have to give his letter further attention.

We are all well out here, except for an occasional cold. We have had no rain this winter, which is really very sad for California. Unless we get some soon, irremediable damage may be done to agriculture in various parts of the State, and the question of water for next year will be serious in some localities.

Nell joins me in devoted love to you and Edith. We hope that you are enjoying the new motor. It is a delightful gift and we rejoice with you in such wonderful friends.

Affectionately yours,   W G McAdoo

TLS (WP, DLC).
[1] King's letter is missing.

John Randolph Bolling to Cyrus Hall McCormick, Jr., with Enclosure

Dear Mr. McCormick: [Washington] 18th January 1924

It gives me a great deal of pleasure to send you herewith five limericks which I think can be safely regarded as Mr. Wilson's favorites. His *favorite* one is, I believe, the first—"There was an old man of Khartoum" &c.; at least that is the one most in favor just now.

It was a great pleasure to all of us to see you the other day, and I hope you can arrange to stop by for a few hours whenever you are east.

With warm regard;

Faithfully yours, [John Randolph Bolling]

CCL (WP, DLC).

E N C L O S U R E

There was an old man of Khartoum
Who kept two black sheep in his room
To remind him he said
Of two friends who were dead
But he never would tell us of whom.

There was a young lady of Siam
Who said to her lover named Pryam
You can kiss me of course
But you'll have to use force
And God knows you are stronger than I am

There was an old monk of Siberia
Whose life grew drearier and drearier
Till he broke from his cell
With a Hell of a yell
And eloped with the Mother Superior

There was a young woman named Tucker
Who rushed at her mother and struck her
Her mother said Damn—
Don't you know who I am?
You act like a regular mucker.

There was a young man of Siam
Spent his nights reading Omar Khyam

Said he to old Omar,
Oh you are my Homer—
Said Omar Khyam, So I am.

CC MS (WP, DLC).

To Cleveland Hoadley Dodge and Others

To   Washington D C 20th January 1924

Cleveland H. Dodge, Jesse H. Jones, Thomas D. Jones
and Cyrus H. McCormick:

To this group of incomparable friends I owe a debt of inexpress-
ible gratitude for having lifted Mrs. Wilson and me out of the mists
of pecuniary anxiety and placed us on firm ground of ease and confidence. More than that, they have blessed me with the knowledge
that I have won the affection and loyalty of the finest and most
ideal body of friends that ever gave a man reason to believe himself
worth while. I can offer them in return only deep affection, but I
do offer that by the heart full. They have afforded me the most
powerful additional reasons for continuing to try to be what they
have in their generosity believed me to be.

Woodrow Wilson[1]

TLS (WP, DLC).
[1] There are signed copies of this letter in the Jesse H. Jones and McCormick Papers.

To Newton Diehl Baker

My dear Baker,   Washington D C 20th January 1924

You and I have generally consulted before a national convention
about what should be the terms of the platform.

Presuming on this precedent, I am sending you a document
which is only a part of my own.[1] It is the result (I hope correctly
compounded) of the views of many men,—Justice Brandeis, Mr.
Thomas Chadbourne, Mr. David Houston, Mr. Norman H. Davis
and Mr. Frank I. Cobb. These views have been, I must admit,
rather casually collected but with an attempt at systematic comparison; and I think that you will find the result coherent and in-
telligible. Much of the phraseology is my own, but I have attempted to be a true interpreter of the opinions I was restating.

If you will be so generous, please let me know what you think of
the document and of its prospects of favourable consideration.

I hope with all my heart that the meeting of the convention will result in as complete harmony and good spirits as resulted from the recent meeting of the National Committee here.

When I know that you have won your deserved place on the Committee on Resolutions my mind will be more at rest, and I hope that the Committee will have the good sense to heed your advice, particularly about the greatest issue of all.

The statement drawn from you by Milton Young's unpardonable impudence was admirable.[2]

With warmly affectionate regard,

Faithfully Yours,   Woodrow Wilson

TLS (RSB Coll., DLC).

[1] As the next letter reveals, Bolling did not send the enclosure with this letter.

[2] Young, who had been Baker's secretary when the latter was Mayor of Cleveland, was reported in a dispatch datelined St. Petersburg, Florida, January 18, as saying that Baker would be a candidate for the Democratic presidential nomination in 1924. Baker was reported on the same date to have laughed when he read the dispatch. "Mr. Young," he said, "was my secretary when I was Mayor of Cleveland. He and I are warm personal friends, but I have had no communication with him of any kind for a year. Nothing is further from my thoughts than a candidacy for any political office. My chief interest in the next campaign is for a sound foreign policy, and I am giving all my time to advocacy of entrance by the United States into the League of Nations." *New York Times*, Jan. 19, 1924.

The Final Draft of "The Document"

[c. Jan. 20, 1924]

CONFIDENTIAL DOCUMENT

1. We recognize the fact that the complex, disturbing and for the most part destructive results of the great war have made it necessary that the progressive countries of the world should supply for the reconstruction of its life a programme of law and reform which shall bring it back to health and effective order; and that it lies with the political party which best understands existing conditions, is in most sympathetic touch with the mass of the people, and is ready and best qualified to carry a constructive programme through to take the initiative in making and pressing affirmative proposals of remedy and reform.

2. In this spirit and with this great purpose we, as representatives of the Democratic party of the United States put forth, in deep earnestness, the following declaration of principle and purpose and thereby seek to serve America and, through America, liberal men throughout the world who seek to serve their people.

3. "AMERICA FIRST" is a slogan which does not belong to any one political party; it is merely a concise expression of what is in the heart of every patriotic American. We enthusiastically incorporate it into this our declaration of principles and purposes. But it means

different things in different mouths and requires definition. When uttered by the present leaders of the Republican party it means that America must render no service to any other nation or people which she can reserve for her own selfish aggrandizement. When we use it we mean that in every international action or organization for the benefit of mankind America must be foremost; that America, by developing within her own citizenship and acts a sensitive regard for justice in all the relations of men, must lead the world in applying the broadest conceptions of justice and peace, of amity and respect, to the mutual relations of other peoples, and in rendering them material aid in the realization of those ideals.

4. We are suffering in common with other nations of the world from the industrial and commercial prostration which followed the great war. Bound up with world conditions from which we could not extricate ourselves, the Republican Administration nevertheless committed itself to a policy of isolation. It blindly persisted in the delusion that we are unaffected by the world's all-encompassing perils and calamities and that, although we have great accumulated strength and matchless resources, we have no responsibility for and need not interest ourselves in efforts to discover and apply safeguards and remedies. It still refuses to take the lead or to cooperate with the Governments of other nations in the adoption of measures which would improve our own situation or that of our customers and debtors.

The Republican Administration has no economic policy, domestic or foreign. In economic matters it is trying to go in several opposite directions at the same time. It declares its desire to stimulate foreign trade and to revive shipping and yet, under pressure of special interests and for their benefit, it erects a high tariff barrier to lessen imports and therefore to limit or destroy foreign trade. It recklessly ignores the fact that we have more than half of the gold of the world; that other nations cannot pay us in gold, that it would not benefit us to receive it if they could, and that we cannot sell our surplus products of the farm and factory and collect our debts unless our customers and debtors can produce and sell their goods.

That it would be worse than stupid to try to maintain a merchant fleet by direct and indirect subsidies to carry freight and then to destroy trade by excluding commodities, does not enter the minds of the Old Guard Republican leaders who are in charge of the Government. They assert their eagerness to reduce taxes and the cost of living and yet ought to know, in their hearts, if they had any intelligent conception of the situation that they add to both by the tariff programme, based on greed. They preach economy and yet press legislation for new undertakings and obligations involving hundreds of millions of dollars. They profess to be concerned about the laborers' standard of living, and at a time when the beneficiaries of their tariff policy are omitting nothing to reduce wages they are devising measures to increase the laborers' cost of living. They clamour for the stabilization of trade and exchange and by their course contribute to the conditions which render stabilization impossible. They are blind to the fact that the protection which the American farmers and manufacturers need is that which would be afforded by a great foreign market, and that this can be secured only by measures which will bring peace to the world, stimulate the forces of production everywhere, and make possible through legitimate business ventures this nation's assistance to Europe through loans and investments.

5. We demand the immediate resumption of our international obligations and leadership—obligations which were shamelessly repudiated and a leadership which was incontinently thrown away by the failure of the Senate to ratify the Treaty of Versailles and the negotiation of separate treaties with the central powers. We heartily approve and endorse the proposal of President Harding that the United States officially adhere to the permanent international court of justice established under the auspices of the League of Nations, but the proposal is manifestly only a fragment of a policy which is incomplete and which ought to be frankly and courageously rounded out and made self-consistent. We deem it essential to the maintenance of the dignity of the United States, to the vindication of our national honour and to the final confirmation of the good faith of our Government towards the nations with whom we were associated in the recent war that the United States should become a member of the League of Nations, assuming the same responsibilities that the other members assume for the organization and maintenance of peace.

6. We condemn the group of men who brought about these evil results as the most partisan, prejudiced, ignorant and unpatriotic group that ever misled the Senate of the United States.

7. We call attention to the lamentable record of incompetence, evasion and political truckling of the last Congress, dominated in both the Senate and House of Representatives by a commanding Republican majority. No step has been taken toward the redemption of the pledges made by the Republican party. Despite the crying needs of the hour and the hopes of the people, it has not enacted a single piece of constructive or ameliorative legislation, although for the last three years it has controlled both houses of Congress.

8. The demand for a revision of the tax laws, made three years

ago by a Democratic President upon the conclusion of the armistice, is still unheeded, and the burdensome and unequal taxes, born of and justified only by a great emergency, still persist, thwarting the normal processes of economic recovery, and robbing the frugality and industry of the people of their just rewards.

9. We believe that the President and the members of his cabinet should be accorded the right to places on the floor of the Senate and the House of Representatives whenever those bodies have under discussion affairs which are entrusted by the Constitution or the laws to the executive branch of the Government; that they should also be accorded the right to take part in such discussions; and that they should be required to answer upon the floor all proper questions addressed to them concerning matters dealt with by the Executive.

10. We call attention to the fact that a budget still unbalanced, and distended beyond the requirements of efficient and economical administration in time of peace, shows no sign of contraction, and every day brings the report of some fresh conspiracy against the public treasury. We promise studious and disinterested approach to the problems of national relief and rehabilitation and condemn the callousness and levity with which the Republican party has subordinated the duty of intelligent attention to these vital problems to petty considerations of partisan politics.

11. We shall use every legitimate means to advance to the utmost the industrial and commercial development of the United States. That development has already made the people of the United States the greatest economic force in the world. It is as convincing proof of their practical genius as their free institutions are proof of their political genius. It is their manifest opportunity and destiny to lead the world in these great fields of endeavor and achiev[e]ment. Our opponents have sought to promote the accumulation of wealth as an instrument of power in the hands of individuals and corporations. It is our object to promote it as a means of diffused prosperity and happiness and of physical and spiritual well being on the part of the great working masses of our people.

12. Without the systematic coordination, cooperation and interchange of services by the railroads the expanding, varying and changeable commerce and industry of the country cannot be properly served. All of these conditions are now lacking because our present laws deal with the railroads without system and altogether by way of interference and restriction. The result is a confusion which is constantly made worse almost to the point of paralysis by the multiplicity and intermittent conflict of regulative authorities, local and national.

13. The Eighteenth Amendment made prohibition the law of the Nation. The Volstead Act prescribed for the Nation what liquor should be deemed intoxicating. But the people, when adopting the Amendment, recognized fully that the law could not be enforced without the co-operation of the States within the Nation. Hence it provided in Section 2 that "The Congress and the several States shall have concurrent power to enforce this article by appropriate legislation." The intention was that such government should perform that part of the task for which it was peculiarly fitted. The Federal Government's part is to protect the United States against illegal importation of liquor from foreign countries and to protect each State from the illegal introduction into it of liquor from another State. To perform that part of the task effectively required centralized, unified action and the employment of the large federal powers and resources. Experience has demonstrated that to perform adequately this part of the task will require all the resources which Congress makes available for enforcement of this law. To this part of the whole task of enforcement the Federal Government should, therefore, devote its entire energies. The protection of the people of a State against the illegal sale within it of liquor illegally manufactured within it, is a task for which the State Governments are peculiarly fitted, and which they should perform. That part of the task involves diversified governmental action and adaptation to the widely varying conditions in, and the habits and sentiments of the people of, the several States. It is a task for which the Federal Government is not fitted. To relieve the States from the duty of performing it, violates our traditions; and threatens the best interests of our country. The strength of the Nation and its capacity for achiev[e]ment is, in large measure, due to the federal system with its distribution of powers and duties.

There should be frank recognition of the fact that the prime duty of the Federal Government is to protect the country against illegal importation from abroad and from illegal introduction of liquor from one State into another; that the full performance of this duty will tax the resources of the Federal Government to the uttermost; and that, for the rest, the people of each State must look to their state governments. But the Eighteenth Amendment should remain unchanged. And the Volstead Act should remain unchanged.

14. We need a Secretary of Transportation who shall rank with the heads of other great federal cabinet departments and who shall be charged with the formulation and execution of plans for the co-ordinated use and full development of the transportation systems of the country. He should be associated with a federal Transportation Board which should be invested with all the powers now

lodged with the Interstate Commerce Commission and, in addition, with the authority to determine the occasions and the conditions of all loans floated and of all securities issued by the several railway and steamship lines. This Board should have the same powers of supervision and regulation over the steamship lines of the United States that are now exercised by the Interstate Commerce Commission over the railways.

15. The present menace to political liberty and peaceful economic prosperity lies, not in the power of kings or irresponsible governments, but in hasty, passionate and irrational programmes of revolution. The world has been made safe for democracy, but democracy has not yet made the world safe against irrational revolution. It is the privilege and duty of ours, the greatest of all democracies, to show the way. It is our purpose to defeat the irrational programmes of revolution beforehand by sober and practical legislative reforms which shall remove the chief provocations to revolution.

16. Among these we hold the following to be indispensable:

A practical plan for a veritable partnership between capital and labour, in which the responsibilities of each to the other, and of both to the nation, shall be stressed quite as much as their respective rights. Our industrial system must command the interest and respect of the wage earners as an avenue to those liberties and opportunities for self-development which it is the nature of free men to desire. Justice must reign over it, and its dignity as one of the foundations of the national vigour and as a great training school for democratic citizenship must be recognized and cultivated.

A plan by which the raw materials of manufacture and the electrical and other motive power now universally necessary to industry shall be made accessible to all upon equitable and equal terms.

Such legal requirements of the manufacturer and the merchant as will serve to bring cost of production and retail price into a clearly standardized relationship made known to the purchaser.

17. We heartily endorse and believe in the efforts which the farmers and certain other producers are making to set up and administer cooperative organizations for purchase and sale in all the markets which they serve or which serve them, and we earnestly advocate the fullest possible assistance of all our State legislatures in making these efforts successful and effective.

18. We unqualifiedly condemn the action of the Republican administration in interrupting and in large part destroying the work of creating and developing an American merchant marine so intelligently begun and so efficiently carried forward by the Democratic

administration, and we demand the immediate rehabilitation of the Shipping Board and such appropriations for its use and such additions to its powers as may be necessary to put its work upon a permanent footing and assure its energetic and successful completion. An efficient and adequate merchant marine is vital to the nation's safety, and indispensable to the life and growth of its commerce.

19. In close relation to the upbuilding of our overseas trade is the development of our inland waterways. We demand therefore the unprejudiced and scientific study of this vastly important field of national expansion, and the prompt inauguration of adequate and effective measures to bring to the service of our producers in the interior States a systemized, cheap and efficient transportation by inland water routes, including the development of ship canal communication with the Atlantic seaboard.

19. Inasmuch as access by all upon equitable and equal terms to the fuel supply and to the raw materials of manufacture and also the availability to all upon fair and equal terms of the motive power supplied by electrical power companies and other similar privately owned and controlled agencies are indispensable to the unhampered development of the industries of the country, we believe that these are matters which should be regulated by federal legislation to the utmost limit of the constitutional powers of the federal government.

CC MS (WP, DLC).

Notes and Passages for an Acceptance Speech

[c. Jan. 21, 1924]

Analysis.
  Overwhelming honour.
  Why should it be offered?
Because the Democratic party has proved an effective instrument of public service by its close integration and its frank acceptance of leadership and does not wish to change its organization or its habit and spirit of action. (See Burke on party)
  We wish greatly to add to the services it has already rendered.
  It is a united body devoted to definite principles and purposes.
  It has by practiced association and action qualified itself to fulfil that famous and now classical definition of a political party which I shall take the loberty of quoting in the incomparable English of Edmund Burke (I., 530)

◇

The failure of the Republican party&:

Began by forecasts of policy; ended in inanition, neglect, and mere drift

High time that its place should be taken by a party of well defined purposes and practiced action.

THE United States were at the front of the new forces of diplomacy wh. united and liberated the world. The Republican administration has transferred them to the old forces, which enslaved free peoples and kept governments at loggerheads.

◇

The complete and disastrous failure of the Republicans ca cannot be a proper subject of gratification to any thoughtful man. It has in fact been a great disappointment to the Republicn party not only but also to thinking men of every party throughout the country. It was sinister in origin and sinister in issue. It came at perhaps the most critical juncture in the social and political history of mankind, when, therefore, it was sure to b be most harmful and most dispiriting to the whole world; and by it the world has lost at least a generation of progress

◇

I am sure that in the High Court of Honour and true Loyalty it must be held to be as deep and heinous a treason that a great and holy cause whose success has been bought by the blood of thousands of your fellow countrymen should be betrayed in the moment od its triumph as that the armies of the nation should be betrayed on the field of battle.

WWT MSS (WP, DLC).

Notes and Passages for a Third Inaugural Address

[c. Jan. 21, 1924]

3rd Inaugural

Yearning of peoples the world over for Liberty, Justice, Brotherhood.

The duty of the U. S.—to lead

(1) By example of moderation and constructive plan

and

(2) To fight and defeat all—aggression—all Reaction and thus bring light and hope back into the world of affairs whence they have fled.

◊

Our fathers lighted a torch and placed it at the front of the nations wh. shall never thr. any fault of mine be extinguished or removed from its place There

America, the champion of Right and Justice, the "nearest friend" of free peoples

◊

Putting all partisanship and self-interest firmly aside, let us address ourselves with true singleness of mind and sincerity of devotion to the high and sacred task of Justice

◊

Objects and motives of the nation in the great wa war: Our entrance was an unexampled instance of heroic disinterestedness on the part of a great free people, who wished to. serve, not to profit,—devoting the lives of its men and the whole body of its resources to save the peoples of Europe from an arrogant and odious dominion which would have been destructive of their liberties and of their happiness.

◊

Present objects and motives: to establish an order in which labour shall have assumed the greater dignity and capital acquired the greater vigour and advantage by the practice of justice

◊

I summon to my side andbeg the counsel and suppo support of every man and every woman who loves justice and believes no sacrifice too great which promises to set it up as the rule of life in the community, whether local or national. We can have it so if we will but sincerely turn our purpose to it.

JUSTICE.
Closing passage of third inaugural

Bustice is the only, certain insurance against revolution and the only invariable stimulant to any kind of successful action in any field of human activity. Without justice labour must be disheartened and industry unfruitful. Without justice society must break up into hostile groups,—even into hostile individuals, and go utterly to pieces.

WWsh, WWhw, and WWT MSS (WP, DLC).

John Randolph Bolling to Newton Diehl Baker

My dear Mr. Baker: [Washington] 21st January 1924

Mr. Wilson has written you a letter, with an enclosure—both of which I feel are of such a confidential nature that it is not wise to trust them to the mails.

I recall that you said, when you were here the other day, that you would probably be this way more frequently in the future. The next time you are coming to Washington, please try and stop in for a few minutes and see me. We can then go over the matter together, and arrange for you to see Mr. Wilson about it.[1]

Let me say that there is no hurry about this—as it touches a matter that will not come up for several months; so I hope you will just include it in your next trip east, and not think of coming here on a special trip—as you so generously offered to do.

With warm regard;

Cordially yours,   [John Randolph Bolling]

CCL (WP, DLC).
[1] Bolling handed a copy of the new platform to Baker on January 29, 1924. Baker returned it to Mrs. Wilson on July 11, 1924. R. S. Baker sent it to the Library of Congress with the rest of the Wilson Papers in 1939. Katharine E. Brand, T memorandum (WP, DLC). See also the note at the top of JRB to NDB, Jan. 25, 1924, CCL (WP, DLC).

John Randolph Bolling to William Edward Dodd

My dear Professor Dodd: [Washington] 22nd January 1924

I have just read to Mr. Wilson your letter to me of 20th January,[1] and he wishes me to say that he is deeply pleased that your book has had so much attention. With regard to the additional matter which you will put in new edition; he says that he has several times thought of putting his correspondence in such shape that it could be intelligently consulted, but that at the present time it is not available for the purpose you have in mind.

It was a great pleasure to hear from you again, and I hope all the family keep well. Mrs. Wilson has been in bed since last Friday with an attack of grippe, but is pretty well over it now, and expects to be up tomorrow.

With warm regard from us all to you all;

Faithfully yours,   John Randolph Bolling

TLS (W. E. Dodd Papers, DLC).
[1] W. E. Dodd to JRB, Jan. 20, 1924, TLS (WP, DLC).

John Randolph Bolling to William Gibbs McAdoo

Dear Mac: [Washington] 23rd January 1924

The Governor asks me to thank you very warmly for your kind letter of eighteenth January, with its interesting enclosures relative to his property in California. He does not feel that he has any money to put into irrigation at this time, but has requested me to file all the data carefully—so he can have it quickly if any matter in connection with the property comes up.

We have had one of the mildest winters here I have ever known; practically no snow, and very little cold.

With much love from all of us for you, Nell and the babies;
          Affectionately yours,   [John Randolph Bolling]

CCL (WP, DLC).

From Thomas Davies Jones

My dear Mr. Wilson: Chicago January 23, 1924.

I was deeply gratified to receive your kind letter of the 4th of January. I considered it a privilege to be allowed to join with Cleve Dodge and others in an expression of continuance not only of our friendship for you and our confidence in you, but our warm and enduring affection for you.

I have followed with deep solicitude the varying accounts of your health during the past four or five years. I have not been in Washington since the meeting of the first Industrial Conference in 1919, else I would have made an endeavor to see you. When and if I get to Washington I shall of course call upon you.

I do not know whether you have heard of my brother's death.[1] He died last August. I am sure if he had been living he would claim the right to be one of "the celebrated trust."

With most cordial remembrances to Mrs. Wilson, I am
          Ever affectionately yours,   Thomas D. Jones.

TLS (WP, DLC).
[1] David Benton Jones, who had died on August 22, 1923.

From Charles R. Webster

Hon Dear Mr. Wilson   Atlanta Ga Jan. 23 1924

On May 15th the year of 1920 through Mr. Ralph A Hayes,[1] you commuted my sentence from death to a term of life in Atlanta Penitentiary. I wish to thank you from the bottom of my heart for sparing my life. And hope you will forgive me for waiting so long to show my appreciation. I have so far made a good record. I would willingly be bound under any conditions the balance of my life if only I were given a chance to prove to the world I want to live an honest life. And return to my home in Ohio and help make a living for my dear good wife who is waiting for me. I have nothing but dearest friendship to offer you, for your advice to what steps I may take to reduce my sentence. I have always voted the democrat ticket and all of my people. I am enclosing letter from Mr Hayes.[2]

With best wishes always believe me
                    Sincerely Yours,   Charles. R. Webster.

ALS (WP, DLC).
    [1] Hayes in 1920 had been an administrative assistant to Newton D. Baker. In R. A. Hayes to WW, May 13, 1920, CCL (WP, DLC), he had recommended that Webster's sentence be commuted from death to life imprisonment on the grounds that several psychiatric evaluations of Webster had placed his mental development as that of a child of between nine-and-a-half and eleven years of age and that he became violent only under the influence of alcohol. Neither Hayes's letter nor any of the several other documents in Webster's case file (no. 5235) in WP, DLC, reveal the exact nature of the "shocking crime" for which he had been convicted. Webster's case must have been tried before a court martial.
    [2] It is missing in WP, DLC.

To Thomas Davies Jones

My dear Friend,   Washington D C 25th January 1924

I had intended in my last letter to you to say a few words about the death of your brother. I had learned to have a very real and strong affection for him. His interesting character and his singularly vivid personality made him a marked man, and a man in high degree adapted for executive business leadership of a body of friends. It impoverishes life that he should have gone out of it, and there never was a time when our country stood in greater need of such characters and powers as his.

I hope that you will not think me intruding upon your grief if I express my profound sympathy.   Affectionately Yours,[1]

TL (WP, DLC).
    [1] Typed at top of the CC of this letter in WP, DLC: "Orig. never signed or sent."

To Charles R. Webster

My dear Mr. Webster,   Washington D C 25th January 1924

I was glad to get your letter of January 23rd, and you may be sure that you will have my entire sympathy in every effort you make to prove the entire change in your life and motives. Unhappily I am without authority or influence in the matter of the length of your service, but I believe that your new way of life will accomplish a great deal.

With warmest and sincerest good wishes,

Very truly yours,

TL (WP, DLC).

To Ray Stannard Baker

My dear Baker,   Washington D C 25th January 1924

Every time that you disclose your mind to me you increase my admiration and affection for you.

I always dislike to make, or even intimate, a promise until I have at least taken some step to facilitate my keeping it. I am glad to promise you that with regard to my personal correspondence and other similar papers I shall regard you as my preferred creditor, and shall expect to afford you the first,—and if necessary exclusive,—access to those papers. But I have it on my conscience that you should know that I have not made the smallest beginning towards accumulating and making accessible the letters and papers we have in mind. I would rather have your interpretation of them than that of anybody else I know, and I trust that you will not think it unreasonable that I should ask you to accept these promises in lieu of others which would be more satisfactory but which, for the present, would be without practical value.

Pray accept assurances of my unqualified confidence and affectionate regard.   Faithfully Yours,[1]

TL (R. S. Baker Coll., NjP).

[1] Typed note on the carbon copy of this letter in WP, DLC: "(One of last three letters dictated; too ill to sign) Orig. delivered to Mr. Baker"

From James Watson Gerard

Dear Sir: New York January 29, 1924.

Reports of recently returned American Relief investigators confirm the intense suffering among the German professional classes,—teachers, scientists, doctors, lawyers, ministers, musicians, artists, etc. The collapse of Germany has thrown this intelligent class into abject poverty accompanied by a staggering increase of deaths from starvation and suicide.

Urgent appeals on behalf of the perishing intellectual classes to individuals and American institutions have necessitated the formation of an American Relief Committee in order to preclude the far-reaching destructive effect upon civilization, which in the past has been enriched by German Science and Art.

The American Committee, under whose auspices an appeal for funds shall be made, will in no way duplicate the work of the Committee for the relief of starving German children which has been organized under the splendid leadership of Major General Allen, with whom we are in full accord.

The distribution of the American funds in Germany will be done under American direction and supervision, aided by a highly representative German advisory committee, without political and religious discrimination.

Mr. Edward R. Stettinius of J. P. Morgan & Company has consented to serve as Treasurer of the Committee and among others who have joined in this worthy cause are:

Hon. Loring E. Dresel	Otto H. Kahn
Hon. John W. Davis	Frank A. Vanderlip
Chancellor Elmer E. Brown	Magnus W. Alexander
Dr. Stephen P. Duggan	Samuel Untermeyer
Thomas W. Lamont	Alvin W. Krech, etc.

In behalf of myself and my associates, I urgently request that you consent to serve on the Committee. This does not involve any financial obligation on your part.

Anticipating your early and favorable reply, I am

Faithfully and sincerely yours,   James W. Gerard

TLS (WP, DLC).

A Memorandum by John Randolph Bolling

A BRIEF HISTORY OF THE LAST ILLNESS OF HONORABLE WOODROW WILSON.

Saturday, January 26, 1924: Admiral Cary T. Grayson, Mr. Wilson's physician, left for South Carolina on a shooting trip. Before he left, it was understood between him and the writer that if Mr. Wilson became ill I was to telegraph him that *my* cold was worse and ask him to return.

Sunday, January 27, 1924: Mr. Wilson went over his mail as usual in the morning, and appeared fairly well, but very tired.

Monday, January 28, 1924: Mr. Wilson was not as well as on yesterday. Went over his mail, but seemed very languid and tired.

Tuesday, January 29, 1924: Mr. Wilson went over his mail in the morning. Mrs. Wilson went out to dinner in the evening. When I went upstairs about ten P.M., Miss Hulett, Mr. Wilson's nurse, asked me if Dr. Grayson was in town, saying she thought "Mr. Wilson a very sick man." I told her Dr. Grayson was in South Carolina, and she replied: "Oh, I wish he were here." I went to bed, and about 12.30 A.M. Mrs. Wilson came to my room, woke me up and said when she came in she found Mr. Wilson very sick, and that she thought we had better telegraph Dr. Grayson to come back. I went to the telephone, and sent the telegram in accordance with the arrangement made, asking that the message be charged to a younger brother's telephone. Dr. Grayson was out shooting when the message reached South Carolina, so did not get it until about noon on Wednesday, January 30, 1924. He then called Mrs. Wilson on the long-distance telephone, saying he was leaving for Washington immediately, and would come directly from the train on Thursday morning; believed from symptoms described by Mrs. Wilson that it was only another indigestive attack.

Wednesday, January 30, 1924: In spite of the precaution taken in sending telegram to Dr. Grayson, there was evidently a "leak" somewhere; for very early in the morning newspaper men began coming to the house, saying they had heard Mr. Wilson was ill, and wanted to know just what his condition was. To these inquiries, reply was made that Mr. Wilson had had a slight indigestive attack but he was not "ill." Mr. Wilson went over his mail with me at ten in the morning. He was in bed, and seemed far from well; he did not dictate replies to any letters, but indicated answers to several that he wished me to make.

Thursday, January 31, 1924: Dr. Grayson arrived from South Carolina about ten in the morning, and came directly to the house. When he came down-stairs after seeing Mr. Wilson I asked him what he thought of his condition; he replied that Mr. Wilson was suffering with "one of his old indigestion attacks" and that, while he seemed very unwell, he did not regard his condition as alarming. Mr. Wilson sent word to me that unless there was something important in the mail he would let it go until the following day. Dr. Grayson was at the house late in the afternoon to see Mr. Wilson, and was asked by Mrs. Wilson if he thought his condition was such that his children should be notified. He said he did not; that it would only alarm the children, and start a lot of wild reports from the newspapers, &c. After dinner that evening Mrs. Wilson suggested to Dr. Grayson that he have Dr. Sterling Ruffin come in for consultation—which he did, about 9.30 P.M. When Dr. Ruffin came down-stairs I asked him what he thought of Mr. Wilson's condition and he said: "He is a very sick man, and I want Grayson to spend the night here." This Dr. Grayson did.

Friday, February 1, 1924: While I was at breakfast, about eight o'clock, Mrs. Wilson came down-stairs and said she believed Mr. Wilson was dying, and that his children should be notified to come. While we were talking Dr. Grayson came in and said Mr. Wilson had had a sudden turn for the worse in the early morning hours; and he agreed with Mrs. Wilson that he was sinking. I then telephoned Miss Margaret Wilson in New York to come at once; and telegraphed Mrs. Wm. G. McAdoo in Mrs. Wilson's name. Mrs. Francis B. Sayre, the other daughter, was in Siam; and a cablegram was sent her (through the Siamese Embassy here). Dr. Grayson also advised that a bulletin be given to the newspaper men, as they were already in front of the house and begging for news. It was then that the first Bulletin of the series from February 1 to 3, 1924, was given out. Miss Margaret Wilson arrived from New York in the early afternoon. As Mrs. McAdoo was in California she was unable to reach Washington until the morning of Wednesday, February 6, 1924—the day Mr. Wilson was buried.

The Bulletins which appear in regular chronological insertion give an accurate account of the progress of Mr. Wilson's illness beginning with the first issued on February 1st, 1924, at 9 A.M., and ending with the last of "11.20 A.M., Feb. 3, 1924."

John Randolph Bolling
Acting Secretary to Mr. Wilson from March 4, 1921,
to February 3, 1924).

(The above account read by Mrs. Woodrow Wilson and considered correct by her according to her recollection of the incidents stated.)

T MS (WP, DLC).

A News Report

[Jan. 30, 1924]
Woodrow Wilson Indisposed; Not Serious, Says Doctor

Washington, Jan. 30.—Woodrow Wilson has been indisposed for two days it became known tonight, but Dr. Sterling Ruffin, who was summoned in the absence from the city of Dr. Cary T. Grayson, declared tonight he did "not consider the former President's illness serious.

"The illness for which I was called in," Dr. Ruffin added, "had nothing to do with the former grave illness of Mr. Wilson."

Dr. Grayson, who has attended Mr. Wilson during and since his administration, is on a hunting trip in North Carolina,[1] and is not expected to return to Washington until tomorrow, as he had planned.

Printed in the *New York Times*, Jan. 31, 1924.
¹ Actually, at Baruch's estate, Hobcaw, in South Carolina.

John Randolph Bolling to James Watson Gerard

My dear Mr. Gerard: [Washington] 31st January 1924

Mr. Wilson asks me to reply to your letter of the 29th inst. and say he will be very glad to have you use his name as a member of the Committee to which you refer—provided he will be excused from taking any active part.

Cordially yours,   [John Randolph Bolling]

CCL (WP, DLC).

A News Report

[*Jan. 31, 1924*]

WILSON'S CONDITION IS CAUSING ANXIETY

Washington, Jan. 31.—Former President Wilson suffered a digestive disorder a couple of days ago, it became known today, and while Rear Admiral Grayson, his physician, reports that his condition is yielding to treatment, Mr. Wilson's relatives and friends are quite anxious concerning him.

Dr. Grayson said tonight he hoped the former President would be all right again within a few days.

Dr. Grayson went South three days ago on a hunting trip. During his absence, it is learned, Mr. Wilson's stomach became upset and he was quite sick yesterday. Dr. Sterling Ruffin, a specialist on internal medicine, who was in consultation during the illness of Mr. Wilson in the White House in 1920, was summoned yesterday. Admiral Grayson was notified and returned to Washington this morning.

Mr. Wilson was reported to be better tonight, though confined to his bedroom. Although he has been up several times, it is learned that he had a very uncomfortable day, and it will be necessary to keep him confined to his room for several more days.

For the present Mr. Wilson's daily afternoon automobile rides with Mrs. Wilson through the streets and suburbs of Washington have been abandoned.

Both physicians, Admiral Grayson and Dr. Ruffin, called at the Wilson residence again tonight after visits earlier in the day. They are taking no chances in case of an emergency. Dr. Ruffin is one of the three physicians chosen by the Senate Teapot Dome investigating committee to make an independent examination and report on the condition of ex-Secretary Fall. He confirmed Admiral Grayson's diagnosis of the case of Mr. Wilson as a digestive upset.

Mrs. Wilson has been in close attendance upon her husband. The only other member of the Wilson household is his secretary, John Randolph Bolling.

Except for automobile rides, Mr. Wilson has not been away from Washington during the nearly three years that have passed since he relinquished the reins of office.

Admiral Grayson issued this statement at 10:30 o'clock tonight after he and Dr. Ruffin had made a night call at the residence of Mr. Wilson:

"Mr. Wilson's digestive disturbance has been less acute today, but he is somewhat prostrated by his illness of the past two days and has not been allowed to be up since the earlier part of the day."

The two doctors were with Mr. Wilson between 9:30 and 10:30 P.M.

Printed in the *New York Times*, Feb. 1, 1924.

Calvin Coolidge to Edith Bolling Galt Wilson

My dear Mrs. Wilson: The White House February 1, 1924.

The news of Mr. Wilson's acute illness, and this morning's bulletin indicating its very grave character, have been a great shock to the nation. The whole people will await with deep concern the hoped-for assurance of a turn for the better. I wish to express my sorrow and deepest sympathy for him and also for your devoted self. I join in the universal prayer that there may very soon be a change for the better. If it is possible to do so, I hope you will let your husband know of my great interest in his behalf. Mrs. Coolidge[1] joins me in extending all sympathy, and in the wish that we may be privileged to lend any possible assistance in this time. We shall await further report of Mr. Wilson's condition with the profoundest concern.

Most sincerely yours,   [Calvin Coolidge]

CCL (C. Coolidge Coll., MNF).
   [1] That is, Grace Anna Goodhue Coolidge.

The White House Staff to Calvin Coolidge

The White House,
Memorandum for the President: February 2, 1924.

Admiral Grayson just telephoned to say that both President Wilson and Mrs. Wilson wanted the President to know how much they were touched by and appreciative of the President's letter. The Admiral stated that President Wilson was too weak to talk but whispered when the letter was read to him—"He is a fine man."

T MS (C. Coolidge Coll., MNF).

Four News Reports

[Feb. 2, 1924]

EX-PRESIDENT WOODROW WILSON DYING; TOLD END IS NEAR, HE REPLIES, 'I AM READY'; OXYGEN KEEPS HIM ALIVE IN EARLY MORNING

Washington, D. C., Saturday, Feb. 2.—Woodrow Wilson, wartime President and great advocate of peace, is dying this morning from the illness which overtook him in September, 1919, when he began his fight to stimulate public opinion in support of the League of Nations.

In his S Street home, in the very room from which he gazed thoughtfully over the Capitol in the days of his convalescence, the former President is sleeping away, only partly conscious, his life being sustained by opiates. Death is hourly expected, as his vitality is lessening as the hours pass.

At 10:25 o'clock last night the physicians issued the following bulletin:

Mr. Wilson's temperature is normal. Respiration is 20, pulse 96. He has gradually lost ground. He has no pain. Our chief present concern is to insure a restful night.

(Signed) DR. GRAYSON,
DR. STERLING RUFFIN,
DR. A. H. FOWLER.[1]

A previous bulletin issued at 4:30 o'clock in the afternoon by Dr. Grayson read as follows:

Mr. Wilson's condition is practically unchanged. During the day he has had some sleep and took a little nourishment. He is resting comfortably, but his vitality is very low. All we can do is to hope for the best.

[1] Actually, Harry Atwood Fowler, M.D.

Toward midnight the former President became weaker. His vitality is sinking with the morning hours. The physicians say that he is very weak, and while he may pass the morning crisis, death is only a matter of hours.

The former President has been unconscious most of the evening. He is kept alive by oxygen and morphine, which are being administered to ease his pain. The kidneys have not been functioning properly and uraemic poisoning is slowly deadening the vital functions. The ex-President, however, is showing greater sustaining powers than his physicians thought was possible.

At midnight the double wooden doors of the Wilson home had been closed and bolted, making it impossible to enter the vestibule. At that time the throngs that had gathered all day before the house had thinned out.

But across the street a lone woman paced up and down. She refused to talk to any one or say why she remained at her vigil.

She spoke brokenly and appeared to be foreign born. Beneath her eyes were dark rings and she appeared to be in deep grief. This woman, who probably had been befriended by the former President, came early in the day and remained.

At 2 o'clock in the morning there was no change in Mr. Wilson's condition, judging by the signs. All was quiet at the house.

Since 2 o'clock Thursday morning, when a stomach disorder developed, which caused a grave turn in his illness, the former President's condition has been dangerous.

Throughout all of Thursday night his vitality decreased, and some of the troubles incident to his early disease developed. The kidneys refused to function properly. When the three physicians—Drs. Fowler, Ruffin and Grayson—were unable to overcome this, because of the patient's weakened condition, it was apparent that the end was approaching.

Long before yesterday noon when the patient's pulse became weaker and he refused food, the physicians saw the beginning of the end.

Bulletins issued at that hour indicated the gravity of Mr. Wilson's condition and reports flashed over Washington and the country that the former President had died.

All the afternoon, while hundreds called at the home and sought news from the sick bed, the former President was getting weaker and weaker. He refused nourishment and was delirious at times.

The immediate family was summoned. Miss Margaret Wilson, his eldest daughter, who came from New York, accompanied by Joseph Wilson, the ex-President's brother, entered the sick room and were recognized.

Mrs. Wilson, who has been her husband's constant companion since he was laid low in the West early in September, 1919, remained in the sick room all day save for a few minutes, when she saw ministers who called to offer consolation.

Early in the morning it had become manifest to his physicians that the last fight of the valiant spirit of the former President was about to be lost. And the first alarming bulletin to reach the world as to his condition was given out by Rear Admiral Cary T. Grayson.

"He has taken a sudden turn for the worse," the physician said, "and I regard his condition as very serious."

Other physicians were summoned and they confirmed the conviction of Dr. Grayson that the patient's early death seemed inevitable.

After confiding this melancholy news to the world, Admiral Grayson returned to prepare his patient for it. Mr. Wilson was fully conscious. He understood. But he did not flinch.

"I am ready," he replied. "I am a broken piece of machinery. When the machinery is broken"—the feeble voice failed for a moment. The sentence remained unfinished. Then, recovering, he whispered:

"I am ready."

When he stirred again the patient laid a hand on the arm of the man who for more than twelve years has been daily at his side.

"You have been good to me," the dying man said. "You have done everything you could."

Tears came to the eyes of the physician as he turned away. He left the house and stood with tears in his eyes and a choked voice as he tried to tell a group of newspaper men what he had seen.

"He knows his condition," the Admiral finally said. "He is the gamest man I ever knew."

Admiral Grayson's voice trembled as he read the official bulletin last evening to several hundred people who crowded around the door. Some of them mounted the steps and the copy which Admiral Grayson attempted to retain was torn in two, as various persons attempted to seize it from his hand.

Behind Admiral Grayson, who stood a step from the house with his hat and overcoat on, were Drs. Ruffin and Fowler, who had been in consultation with him for 45 minutes. Admiral Grayson explained they were leaving for the night but that he would remain beside the bedside throughout the night.

Asked as to what was being done to give the former President as restful a night as possible, he said he would not discuss the course of treatment.

To an inquiry as to the truth of the report that Mr. Wilson in his delirious moments pictured himself to be still President of the United States and leader in the lone fight, Admiral Grayson said there was no truth in that rumor. He deprecated the circulation of such stories and said Mr. Wilson was not delirious then, but conscious.

Asked as to how Mrs. Wilson was standing the ordeal, Admiral Grayson said:

"Mrs. Wilson is as wonderful as any one could be under the circumstances. She has been at the bedside practically the entire day. She is there now."

Mr. Wilson, he added, had taken a little light nourishment three or four times.

"Does he recognize people?" the Admiral was asked.

"Yes, but no one has been admitted to his room except his daughter and Mrs. Wilson."

The doctors have been the only other visitors to the sick room.

"Once during the day the former President showed a flash of old-time wit and brilliancy," said Dr. Grayson. "When he saw the other doctors standing there with me he looked at me with a trace of a smile and said: 'Sometimes too many cooks spoil the broth.' He is as game as can be. He is fighting like a man to the very end."

Dr. Grayson said in response to questions:

"Mr. Wilson is not suffering any pain, but he is gradually growing weaker. No one has seen him today except Mrs. Wilson, who is constantly at his bedside, and Miss Margaret, who arrived this afternoon.

"He recognized his daughter immediately on her entrance into the room, and his eyes lighted up with a flash of their oldtime brilliancy and affection. He was not able to talk much with her but seemed to understand easily what she said, with pressures of his hand and slight noddings of the head.

Those present in the Wilson house tonight when the last bulletin was issued were: Carter Glass, ex-Secretary of the Treasury; B. M. Baruch, Fitz William Woodrow, a nephew;[2] Joseph Wilson, a brother; Mrs. Edward Brown, wife of Mr. Wilson's first cousin,[3] a resident of Atlanta; Mrs. Helm, a former secretary to Mrs. Wilson; Miss Margaret Wilson, John Randolph Bolling and the three doctors who had been in constant attendance.

Just before midnight a second-story window in the Wilson home was raised and the head of the colored butler appeared. To the newspaper correspondents who were prepared to remain all the night he called:

[2] Actually, a cousin.
[3] First cousin-in-law of Ellen Axson Wilson.

"Mrs. Wilson asks you to please go away. She is trying to sleep."

By midnight the house was in darkness except for a dim light burning in Mrs. Wilson's room at the rear of the house.

Hope for the recovery of Mr. Wilson was practically abandoned early in the day, when Admiral Grayson and the other attending physicians, after an all-night vigil Thursday night, found their patient so weak that his words were scarcely more audible than a whisper.

Meanwhile word was flashing back and forth during the early morning hours that his death had occurred, and twice during the day Mr. Wilson was reported to have died when he was yet alive in his quiet S Street home, making a gallant fight for his life, under the care of three physicians, two nurses and Mrs. Wilson, who was constantly at his bedside.

Admiral Grayson was summoned to the Wilson residence during the night, and found the condition of his patient such that it became necessary to summon Dr. Sterling Ruffin also and to call into consultation Dr. H. A. Fowler, specialist on kidney and internal diseases, who was consulted several years ago when Mr. Wilson was ill in the White House.

At 10 o'clock in the morning Dr. Grayson made this statement to a NEW YORK TIMES representative:

"Mr. Wilson passed a restful night and has lost strength. He has suddenly taken a turn for the worse and I regard his condition as very serious."

Just before noon Admiral Grayson, looking white and stricken and with tears streaming from his eyes, emerged from the Wilson residence and told the waiting newspaper men that Mr. Wilson was very low.

Dr. Grayson was much affected while endeavoring to relate what took place in the sickroom he had just left. Tears streamed from his eyes and his voice again choked while he said:

"Boys, I'm sorry to choke-up this way. But I have been with him so long and he was so fine a friend I just cannot help it. He knows the situation and is ready. He's the gamest man I ever saw."

Admiral Grayson stated that everything possible was being done for the comfort of Mr. Wilson and in an endeavor to save his life, but that death seemed inevitable. He said that, while Mr. Wilson might die at any hour, he might also linger a day or two.

Vance McCormick, former Chairman of the Democratic National Committee and one of the intimates of Mr. Wilson; Bernard M. Baruch, another close friend of the ex-President, and Joseph P. Tumulty were among the early morning callers, and were grief-stricken when they emerged from the Wilson residence.

"The death of Mr. Wilson seems inevitable, I regret to say," asserted Mr. McCormick. "The end may come today or he may linger into tomorrow. But he is so weak and ill that it does not appear possible for him to recover."

The Rev. Dr. James E. Freeman, Bishop of the Protestant Episcopal Diocese of Washington, called at the Wilson home soon after 3 o'clock. He saw Mrs. Wilson and consoled her and made a brief prayer. He was followed by the Rev. Dr. Johnston[4] of St. John's Episcopal Church, who also offered prayer. Neither of the ministers entered the sickroom.

When the ex-President's condition became grave, Mrs. Wilson summoned his daughters. Mrs. Francis B. Sayre, who was Miss Jessie Wilson, was notified of her father's condition by cable. She is in Bangkok, Siam, with her husband, who is on duty there in connection with the work of the Rockefeller Foundation.[5]

Mrs. William G. McAdoo, who was the President's youngest daughter, Eleanor, was notified at her home in California. Word was also sent to Miss Margaret Wilson of 134 West Fourth Street, New York, the other daughter of Mr. Wilson, who arrived at 3:30 o'clock, and, with Joseph Wilson, the President's brother, immediately went to the sickroom.

Vance McCormick and Bernard Baruch returned at 4 o'clock and remained in the Wilson home half an hour, when they emerged with Admiral Grayson. As each caller left the Wilson residence, he reported there was no hope.

The ex-President received an opiate early in the afternoon. This induced sleep and tended to strengthen him slightly. He had been conscious most of the time, but the physicians reported that in the afternoon he manifested little interest in those about his bedside. He seemed to be semi-conscious, awaiting the end.

After Mr. Wilson fell asleep early in the afternoon, Dr. Grayson, after noting that Mr. Wilson's respiration and temperature were normal, emerged from the S Street residence to walk to his own residence, several blocks distant, on Sixteenth Street.

Surrounded by a group of waiting newspaper men, who moved up the hill with him from the Wilson home, Dr. Grayson, scarcely able to restrain his own emotion, replied briefly to inquiries.

Asked if Mr. Wilson might come out of the sleep sufficiently refreshed to rally, Dr. Grayson hesitated a second, and then said, "Yes," that he was hopeful there might be a turn for the better.

Mr. Wilson might sleep for several hours, he thought, and it was

---

[4] Robert Johnston.
[5] Actually, Francis B. Sayre was serving as an adviser on foreign affairs to the government of Siam.

the doctor's intention to return after a short visit at his own home.

So the former President slept into the afternoon, his life seemingly hanging by a thread, while a nurse kept watch and Mrs. Wilson went in and out of the silent room.

The crisis in Mr. Wilsons' condition dated back to Tuesday, when he suffered a digestive disturbance, which at first was regarded as slight. Dr. Grayson had gone South on a hunting trip in the Carolinas the first part of the week. Mr. Wilson experienced discomfort Wednesday, and Dr. Sterling Ruffin, who was one of the consulting physicians during Mr. Wilson's illness in the White House, was summoned. Dr. Grayson was notified, and returned to Washington Thursday morning.

It first became known that night that Mr. Wilson had taken to his bed. This word followed announcement that for the time being his daily automobile rides with Mrs. Wilson were suspended.

Late Thursday night Dr. Grayson was clearly worried, but was of the opinion that Mr. Wilson's condition was yielding to treatment and that the former President would be all right within a few days.

Despite the moderate tone of the physician's statement that evening, inquiries came plying into Washington from remote parts of the country as to reports that Mr. Wilson had died.

A bulletin issued during that evening said:

"Mr. Wilson's digestive disturbance has been less acute, but he has been somewhat prostrated by his illness of the last two days and has not been allowed to be up since the earlier part of the day."

Sometime between then and Friday morning Mr. Wilson suffered what his physicians described as a "crash."

Dr. Grayson and Mrs. Wilson, in constant attendance at the former President's side, noticed alarming symptoms of collapse. Dr. Grayson summoned Dr. Ruffin and Dr. Fowler and there were reports that there might be an operation, and that it was necessary to tap the patient's kidneys, but these were denied later by the doctors.

"Mr. Wilson had a restless night and has lost strength," said Dr. Grayson in his first statement in the morning as to the changes of the night. "During the night he took a sudden and decided turn for the worse. I regard his condition as very serious."

At about 11 o'clock in the morning Dr. Grayson stepped out of the front door; his white and drawn face was wet with tears.

"Mr. Wilson is very low," he said brokenly. The steadfast friend of the former President, physician and companion in the hours of Mr. Wilson's triumphs when at the pinnacle of world fame, and still his physician and companion in retirement and illness, mastered his emotion as best he could to tell how Mr. Wilson, in full possession of his faculties, had leaned over and patted him on the shoulder. In a whisper Mr. Wilson said he knew that Grayson had done the best he could.

When Dr. Ruffin left the Wilson home just after noon today, and a few minutes later Dr. Fowler, who Dr. Grayson said was summoned by way of precaution, followed him, both said Mr. Wilson's condition was unchanged and most serious. Subsequently, about 1 o'clock, Dr. Grayson announced that his patient was asleep—his first real sleep in twenty-four hours.

At 6:15 o'clock in the evening Admiral Grayson left the sick room for a brief walk. He indicated that the former President was slowly sinking, that his pulse was getting lower and that the patient was then being kept alive with opiates.

"Woodrow Wilson's condition is unchanged. He is conscious only part of the time," he said.

Admiral Grayson was then the only physician in attendance at the bedside, the two specialists having left after approving of the treatment.

All the afternoon the former President had been slowly growing weaker. He took some broth, but so little as to aid little in the final struggle. The nurses and those at the bedside awaited the end, unable to do anything, it was said, except to give relief to the former President. Opiates were being administered frequently to ease the pain.

Speaker and Mrs. Gillett[6] called at the house and left cards about 8:30 o'clock. Joseph P. Tumulty, who has shown the greatest anxiety about the illness of his late chief and called at the Wilson home several times during the afternoon, went again at night. He saw Admiral Grayson at 8:30 o'clock and came away from the house feeling that the end of Mr. Wilson was approaching.

"Mr. Wilson will go down in history as one of the greatest of our Presidents," he said. "His place in history will become greater as time passes. He has never written anything about himself. He will leave no autobiography. He said once that no man could properly write about himself. Lincoln never wrote any autobiography."

Printed in the *New York Times*, Feb. 2, 1924.
   [6] Frederick Huntington Gillett and Christine Rice Hoar Gillett.

[Feb. 3, 1924]

WOODROW WILSON'S LIFE SLOWLY EBBS AS NIGHT PASSES; DOCTORS NOW REPORT HIM IN COMPLETE PROSTRATION; HEART ACTION FAILING, CONSCIOUS ONLY PART OF THE TIME

Washington, Sunday, Feb. 3.—Woodrow Wilson, twenty-eighth President of the United States, bravely fought off death which had been hourly expected throughout last night with his vitality steadily growing weaker and the end nearer at hand. At 1 o'clock this morning he was alive, but very weak.

At 10:15 o'clock last night Dr. Grayson said Mr. Wilson was in a state of unconsciousness, with his eyes closed. But his heart still beat.

Throughout the day it was evident to his physicians that Mr. Wilson was losing his great battle.

"He is making a game fight, but realizes the great battle is over," said Admiral Grayson, his medical adviser for eleven years and his most intimate personal friend.

At 8:30 o'clock last night Dr. Grayson issued a bulletin in which he said that ex-President Wilson was "now profoundly prostrated." There had been no radical change in Mr. Wilson's condition during the day, it said, but rather a gradual wearing-away process. Mr. Wilson slept the greater part of the day, it added, and, while his heart action was feeble, it was regular and not unduly rapid.

At 10 o'clock Dr. Grayson emerged from the front door of the Wilson residence. In answer to questions he said there was nothing to report about the ex-President's condition supplementary to what had been contained in the bulletin of 8:30 o'clock.

He was asked whether the indications were that Mr. Wilson would live the night through. He replied that at the moment the conditions seemed favorable to that end, but that he might have to change that opinion in half an hour should there be any changes in the patient's condition.

"When Woodrow Wilson was stricken before," said Dr. Grayson, "I always believed I would be able to pull him through, but now the old machine has broken down completely. His present illness cannot be attributed to any one malady; his whole physical being is broken. When this is over I will attempt to write out a complete report of his case. I think I will do that tonight.

"At the time Woodrow Wilson went to Paris he was in excellent shape. He had built himself up from the days of 1913 by proper eating, proper exercise and rest. He was an excellent patient."

Dr. Grayson walked two blocks after 10 o'clock with newspaper men and chatted with them as he went along.

"Is Mrs. Wilson still at the President's bedside?" he was asked.

"Yes, she has been there all day and is still there," he replied.

Dr. Grayson said Mr. Wilson "was a mighty lucky man to have lived four years after his breakdown following his return from the peace treaty fight in France."

Dr. Grayson explained that the armistice conferences, the negotiations over the Treaty of Versailles and the Covenant of the League of Nations had greatly taxed his patient's strength before he ever attempted his transcontinental speaking tour in behalf of the ratification of those documents by the United States Senate.

Dr. Grayson in talking to Senator Carter Glass was heard to say: "I told him you sent your love, and he smiled."

The Senator grapsed the Admiral's hand emotionally, but remained silent.

At 4:45 o'clock in the afternoon the following official bulletin was issued:

Mr. Wilson's general condition is the same as it was this morning. He grows steadily weaker.   CARY T. GRAYSON,
STERLING RUFFIN,
H. A. FOWLER.

Dr. Grayson at that time answered the many eager inquiries as to how the day had passed for his distinguished patient as follows:

"Mr. Wilson had a restful day. He is calm. The bedroom is quiet and peaceful.

"Mrs. Wilson had a good night's sleep and spent the day sitting by the bedside, holding Mr. Wilson's hand."

When asked whether Mr. Wilson was able to talk much, he said:

"No, he only says 'Yes' or 'No.' He hasn't the strength to talk. Sometimes he only shakes his head in approval or disapproval of the things suggested to him for his comfort.

When asked if Mr. Wilson was able to recognize visitors, Dr. Grayson replied:

"No one sees him outside of the doctors and nurses, except his wife and daughter."

Many rumors have gone out to the effect that opiates were being given to keep the patient quiet. Dr. Grayson denied this, saying:

"Opiates haven't been used to any considerable extent. Mr. Wilson is not in pain."

Dr. Grayson stated that his patient had been able to take little nourishment today, and the uncertainty he himself feels was shown by his final statement:

"The 8:30 o'clock bulletin tonight will be the last unless something happens."

The indications early yesterday were that Mr. Wilson was gradually losing his fight for life. The first definite information concerning his condition came at 8:30 o'clock in the morning, when Dr. Grayson issued the following bulletin:

Mr. Wilson had a fairly restful night, but continues to gradually lose ground.   CARY T. GRAYSON.

Dr. Grayson added that he had insisted that Mrs. Wilson, who had been almost constantly at the bedside of her husband, get some sleep.

"I noticed a steady dropping down in Mr. Wilson's condition, as shown by the chart," he said in reply to a question. "His life is slowly ebbing away. He is a fighting man and he is making a game fight, but I think he realizes his fight is over. He is as brave as a man could be. It breaks one all up to see the fight he is making."

Dr. Grayson's eyes filled with tears, and he paused for a moment. He was then asked if Mr. Wilson had been informed of the many messages and telegrams received. He replied that he believed Mrs. Wilson had talked to him about some of them, but did not know what either she or Mr. Wilson had said. "I considered that sacred," he said.

Dr. Sterling Ruffin and Dr. H. A. Fowler arrived at the Wilson home at 11 o'clock, and at 11:30 o'clock in the morning the physicians issued the following bulletin:

Mr. Wilson is growing steadily weaker. He has been able to take very little nourishment. He has had some sleep, and has no pain. He recognizes those about him, but is too exhausted to talk. Our efforts in the main are directed toward keeping him comfortable.   CARY T. GRAYSON,
STERLING RUFFIN,
H. A. FOWLER.

Dr. Grayson said there was nothing of public interest in the few remarks that Mr. Wilson had been able to make.

Dr. Grayson was questioned concerning the last sentence of the official bulletin.

"Does that mean that you are trying to make his death easy?" he was asked.

Dr. Grayson's voice choked, and for a moment he was unable to answer.

"Yes," he finally replied with grave face.

Mr. Wilson made no effort to aid the physicians. Apparently he recognized that his end was near at hand. Before the illness took such a decisive turn for the worst the ex-President had what might be described as his last connected talk with his physicians and

Mrs. Wilson. During Friday night he said but little, and asked in mere whispers that he be made more comfortable from time to time.

Despite the fact that her husband was unable to speak much to her, Mrs. Wilson, who has been the constant companion of the former President since the day he was stricken in September, 1919, remained most of the night at the bedside. She took a brief sleep, but returned to the sick-room and in the morning hours Dr. Grayson found her at the bedside when dawn broke over the capital. There she sat and watched her husband's life slowly ebbing away.

Soon after 8 o'clock in the morning Miss Margaret Wilson and Joseph Wilson, brother of the ex-President, entered the sick room and remained at the bedside for a short time. Mr. Wilson apparently recognized them, raising his eyes, but he did not speak.

Mr. Wilson in his illness displayed the same indomitable will that marked his fight for the League of Nations. Many peace advocates who admired this great apostle of peace remarked that he was struggling against death with the greatest courage. They could not understand that a man so long ill, with his sustained powers weakened, was able to survive so long. They said that it was the Wilson will which kept him alive after the body had surrendered.

Mr. Wilson's calm resignation and acceptance of the fact that death is inevitable after more than four years of serious illness has impressed all who have been admitted to the sick room.

Following the morning bulletin there was no further incident until the arrival of some of the relatives. Mrs. Edward Brown, wife of Colonel Brown, a cousin of the former President, arrived before noon and went into the house and Joseph Wilson, brother of the dying man, arrived in the Wilson automobile with Miss Wilson.

Soon afterward Dr. Grayson, who had gone for a walk after the consultation of physicians, returned slowly up S Street. To reporters who expressed sympathy for his position as at once personal friend and official physician of Mr. Wilson, he replied:

"If I could only do something for him, but there is nothing to do but make him comfortable and see he suffers no pain. It makes you feel pretty helpless."

At 1:15 o'clock in the afternoon Dr. and Mrs. Grayson came out of the Wilson home with Bernard M. Baruch. Dr. Grayson said he was going home to luncheon and to get a few moments rest. He said the patient was fairly comfortable and was conscious of what was going on around him. He said Mr. Wilson had understood him when he told him he was going away for a short time to get luncheon. He added that the former President was lying quietly and looking around him to observe what was taking place.

A steady procession of callers has invaded the quiet street. Most of these merely inquire concerning Mr. Wilson's condition of the negro butler who opens the door, and leave their cards. Intimate friends are admitted to the house and see Mrs. Wilson, Miss Margaret Wilson, the only one of the former President's three daughters who has so far been able to reach here, or some other members of the family.

Joseph P. Tumulty, secretary to Mr. Wilson when he was President, was an early morning caller. Mr. Tumulty did not see Mr. Wilson, but talked with Miss Wilson and Dr. Grayson. Questioned by reporters, Mr. Tumulty said the members of the family had not entirely abandoned hope, but realized the seriousness of his condition.

Secretary of Commerce Herbert Hoover, a neighbor of Mr. Wilson; Cordell Hull, Democratic National Chairman and Senator Carter Glass of Virginia, were other early morning callers. Senator Glass, a close friend of the former President, shook his head sadly when asked about Mr. Wilson's condition and walked away without any other reply.

Toward 3 o'clock cards of the various foreign embassies and legations began arriving in increasing numbers, but few of the diplomats entered the Wilson residence. Most of them simply left their cards and inquired about Mr. Wilson's condition and departed. Across the street from the residence the crowd of sympathetic friends increased.

A number of children, some of them little girls dressed in knickerbockers, with roller skates thrown over their shoulders, stood there for hours awaiting word from the sick room.

Early in the afternoon a colored servant wearing a white linen coat emerged from the house and entered the side yard. The great iron gates were swung open and the car recently given to Mr. Wilson by a group of his friends departed. After a half-hour it returned but carried no passengers. Huston Thompson, Federal Trade Commissioner, who initiated the Armistice Day pilgrimage to the S Street shrine and stood at the ex-President's side along with Senator Glass on the last occasion the peace advocates called upon Mr. Wilson, visited the residence this afternoon. He was permitted to enter and remained some time.

The Washington populace, hundreds of whom kept vigil in the street in front of the Wilson home until midnight, returned early this morning to inquire how the former President had passed the night. They expressed surprise after having learned of his dangerous condition, and that death might come at any moment, that he showed such remarkable resistance to the progress of the disease which has gripped him for nearly five years.

Officials, men of affairs, society women and others called at the house, while messenger boys kept calling all through the night with messages of hope sent from foreign countries and the thousands of friends who had looked upon Mr. Wilson as one of the nation's greatest Presidents and as its foremost advocate of a program to prevent war and advance the interests of international peace and friendship. Some of these telegrams expressed the hope that the spirit of Mr. Wilson, the thing for which he was dying, would live after him and that the League of Nations with the United States a member would become a reality and be his monument.

Just before the physicians left the residence at the conclusion of the 6 o'clock consultation tonight a basket of flowers arrived, bearing a message of sympathy and the cards of Mrs. George Vanderbilt and Miss Cornelia Vanderbilt. From early this morning, when the seven-year-old son of Dean Caldwell, a Washington real estate man, and two of his tiny boy chums, arrived at the Wilson door bearing one long-stemmed American Beauty rose, until late tonight, flowers arrived almost momentarily.

Printed in the *New York Times*, Feb. 3, 1924.

[*Feb. 3, 1924*]
WOODROW WILSON PASSES AWAY IN SLEEP

Washington, Feb. 3.—Woodrow Wilson, twenty-eighth President of the United States, a commanding world figure and chief advocate of the League of Nations, is dead. He died at 11:15 o'clock this morning, after being unconscious for nearly twelve hours.

Mrs. Wilson, Miss Margaret Wilson, Joseph Wilson, a brother, and Admiral Grayson, his physician, were at the bedside.

Just before death the war President opened his eyes. His wife and daughter spoke to him, but he did not respond. Ten minutes later he passed quietly away. No word was uttered.

All day yesterday and last night he had been sinking rapidly, his pulse becoming fainter and fainter, until finally it ceased to beat. His "broken machinery" had collapsed.

Washington and the nation were prepared for death. The morning papers had carried the news that he had been "profoundly prostrated." The waiting groups, numbering many hundreds, outside of the Wilson home were silent when Admiral Grayson, five minutes after his patient and friend had expired, opened the door and made the announcement.

Dr. Grayson read the following bulletin:

11:20 A. M., Feb. 3, 1924.

Mr. Wilson died at 11:15 o'clock this morning. His heart action became feebler and feebler, and the heart muscle was so fatigued that it refused to act any longer. The end came peacefully. The remote causes of death lie in his ill-health, which began more than four years ago, namely arteriosclerosis and hemiplegia. The immediate cause of death was exhaustion following a digestive disturbance which began in the early part of last week, but did not reach an acute stage until the early morning hours of Feb. 1.

CARY T. GRAYSON.

Arteriosclerosis is a thickening and hardening of the walls of the arteries, and hemiplegia is a paralysis of one side of the body, the limbs on that side losing the power of voluntary motion. Mr. Wilson's left side was so stricken, the outward manifestation being the helpless drop of his left arm and the dragging of the left foot.

Mr. Wilson died in a room on the third floor of his home, where for so many months, since his retirement, he sat and looked over Washington, the scene of his greatest achievement. He expired on a large four-poster bed, a replica of the Lincoln bed in the White House.

Mr. Wilson's last word was "Edith," his wife's name. In a faint voice he called for her yesterday afternoon when she had left his bedside for a moment.

His last sentence was spoken on Friday, when he said:

"I am a broken piece of machinery. When the machinery is broken—

"I am ready."

Mrs. Wilson held his right hand as his life slowly ebbed away. Admiral Grayson remained in the death room for a few minutes and then went down stairs leaving Mrs. Wilson and Margaret the only mourners at the bedside.

There had been signs during the morning that the end was a matter of minutes. The first bulletin issued by Dr. Grayson at 8:55 o'clock said:

"Mr. Wilson is unconscious and his pulse is very weak."

His 10:30 bulletin read:

"After a quiet night Mr. Wilson is very low and the end may be expected at any time."

When, therefore, Dr. Grayson appeared on the steps of the house at 11:20 it was realized that he was probably there to announce the end.

Dr. Grayson was making a strong effort to keep himself under control. In his hand he held some of the yellow slips on which the bulletins were typewritten. He came toward the newspaper men, who quickly gathered about him near the steps of the house.

"The end came at 11:15," he said in a low tone.

Immediately there was a commotion in the crowd as the newspaper men assigned to flash the news of death which would speed all over the world, broke through their comrades and rushed off.

The crowd across the street, now grown to large proportions, surged forward in an effort to hear Dr. Grayson, but the police lines held and there was nothing for them to do but to listen with strained attention.

Meanwhile Dr. Grayson had begun to read the bulletin. This was the climax of the emotional strain he has been under, and it was only with difficulty that he could force himself to go ahead.

He read slowly. His voice trembled, but did not break. But as he read, very slowly, tears kept rolling down his cheeks and he used his handkerchief.

This action, more than what they could hear, showed the spectators across the street that he was actually announcing Mr. Wilson's death. Here and there in the crowd men began to take off their hats. Soon almost all were uncovered. The women stood with lowered heads, many of them weeping.

Finally, Dr. Grayson finished reading the bulletin. The newspaper men expressed a few words of sympathy and then hurried off to send the detailed news. Dr. Grayson was left standing with only one or two before him.

The physician and friend of the former President, who has been the only link between the sick room and the outside world, was asked whether, now that Mr. Wilson was dead, he would not give a detailed account of his last hours. He demurred, saying he did not believe there was anything more to be added to what had been said.

He was urged to undertake the task as a duty to the memory of his friend and patient. On this ground he assented. He said he would take an automobile ride for the purpose of resting, and that during its course he would endeavor to get his mind together. Then he turned slowly and went indoors.

In ten minutes after the death bulletin had been issued the news was flashed around the world.

The radios which were sending sermons suddenly ceased and then announced:

"Mr. Wilson died at 11:15."

This news was read from many pulpits. It was read from the pulpit of the First Congregational Church, where President and Mrs. Coolidge were attending the service. Almost immediately Mr. and Mrs. Coolidge left the service and called at the Wilson home.

The President and Mrs. Coolidge expressed sympathy for Mrs. Wilson and the members of the family and told Joseph Wilson, a brother, and John Randolph Bolling that the Government wished to be advised as to the desires of the family with respect to the funeral.

President Coolidge told the family that the Administration would be guided entirely by the family's desires as to whether there should be an official funeral or simple private ceremonies.

President Coolidge issued a proclamation announcing Mr. Wilson's death. This was sent to all American embassies and legations in foreign countries.

The White House flag, which had been flying all night, was lowered to half-mast, and this was the signal which told downtown Washington that the former occupant of the historic home had passed away. The flags of other Government buildings were lowered. Foreign embassies showed the same respect for the dead, and the gloom of death settled over Washington.

Washington tonight is in mourning for the only President in recent history who has made this city his home upon retiring from public life. Mr. Wilson was always popular in Washington, but after retiring, broken in health, he seemed to touch their hearts more than ever. Everywhere Mr. Wilson went he was cheered by the Washington people, and this seemed to give him courage to keep up the fight for the League of Nations.

Tonight a hush of affectionate respect rested over S Street and about his home. Traffic moved along other ways, but automobiles by hundreds stopped in nearby streets as passengers descended to walk past the home which would show no light tonight in the third-floor room at the south.

This home, which thousands of his countrymen had looked upon in the last several years as a shrine of world idealism, was visited tonight by the people of Washington who loved him.

Mrs. McAdoo was notified of her father's death while traveling with her husband to Washington, for which they started Thursday from the Pacific Coast. They will arrive Wednesday morning, and the funeral will probably not be held until that day. Mrs. Francis B. Sayre, another daughter of Mr. Wilson's, is in Siam, and will not be here for the funeral.

Official Washington, including Chief Justice Taft, Senators and Cabinet members, called at the Wilson home and left cards.

Tomorrow the House and Senate will adjourn, and may remain

in adjournment until after the funeral. When the Senate meets, Senator Robinson, Democratic leader, will offer a motion that the Senate adjourn, out of respect to Mr. Wilson. This will be seconded by Senator Lodge, who is expected to pay respect to the dead President on the floor tommorrow.

THRONG IN PRAYER AT WILSON HOME

Washington, Feb. 3.—At about 10 o'clock this morning it was noticed that a group in the crowd that stood opposite the Wilson home in S Street were distributing little cards, on which were the words: "Peace on earth, good will to men." When these had been given out a well-dressed woman in a fur coat stepped from the curb a few feet into the roadway, knelt on both knees, and bowed her head in prayer.

Immediately the group of fifty or so persons who had been with her followed her example. All knelt in silent prayer. Others of the crowd looked at them, startled, for a moment, and then here and there in the crowd others followed suit. There were those, especially among the men, who did not kneel, but with scarcely an exception the waiting spectators took off their hats and bowed their heads, if they were men, or, if they were women, assumed a reverent attitude.

The lips of the kneeling men and women moved in silent prayer. Not a person stirred. The silence was so deep that there could be heard for the first time the noise made by a dog scurrying among the dry leaves in a wooded lot opposite the Wilson home.

A crippled girl came up the hill from the direction of Massachusetts Avenue. As she saw the silent kneeling group she shifted one of her crutches and tried to bring her brace-supported limbs to the kneeling position, but could not do it. So, bracing herself against the crutch, she folded her hands and looked upwards to the third floor room, where it was known that Woodrow Wilson was dying, and her lips could be seen moving.

For three minutes the kneeling men and women held their positions. Then they arose and the spell they had cast on the crowd was broken. They mingled with the other spectators and finally left.

The leader of the group was Mrs. Minnegerode Andrews, a prominent club-woman of Washington and a friend of the Wilsons. She said the project to kneel in silent prayer before the Wilson home had been agreed upon the night before among many of the friends of the family.

"We did it not so much for Woodrow Wilson," she said, "as for the people who believe in the ideals he stood for."

Most of those who took part in the demonstration, of whom about one-third were men, were personal friends of the Wilson family, who had left their cards at the house and then gathered opposite to await the time they had agreed upon for the silent prayer.

S Street was still the street of waiting when it awoke this morning. It knew only that Woodrow Wilson had lived the night through. The hundreds of persons who had waited until midnight had gone home and the newspaper men who maintained their vigil until 5 A.M. had left and others had taken their places. Still there was nothing to do but wait in front of the silent house for word of the tragedy within.

It seemed somehow out of place when a negro porter left the house and with broom and pan began to tidy up the street. And when ice and milk were delivered to the house and to others nearby, it came with a sort of a shock that such commonplace incidents of daily life should be taking their customary course.

By 9 o'clock a crowd of about 500 persons had gathered on the sidewalk opposite the house. Profiting by their experience of the day before, the District police put an extra force of six men on the street, bringing the total up to a dozen. The best sort of order was maintained. As before, automobiles were deflected on streets at each end of the block and no cars were allowed to go through except those whose occupants wished to leave cards.

The street again was, as it had been yesterday, strangely quiet. In place of the warming sunlight of yesterday, there was a haze and a slight rawness in the air, which seemed to lend a sinister effect, fitting as a preparation for the sad news spectators looked for at any moment.

About 10:30 o'clock a White House messenger arrived on a motorcycle. Word came to the effect that he brought a message from the President and Mrs. Coolidge to Mrs. Wilson.

Soon afterward an erect and elderly man with white hair passed the house. He removed his hat and held it in a military position of uncover as he walked by the house, not donning it again until he was well past.

At about 10:30 o'clock Dr. Ruffin left the house, accompanied by Dr. Grayson. The two talked in low tones as they walked to Dr. Ruffin's car. Just before he got in Dr. Ruffin was heard to say to his companion, "Too bad, doctor." Those who heard were confirmed in their belief that the end was only a matter of moments, and the feeling spread through the crowd.

When Dr. Grayson appeared on the steps to read the bulletin which announced the death, the crowd across the street had grown to more than a thousand. The spectators could not hear Dr.

Grayson, but they grasped the general import of his words immediately and a murmur swept through the crowd.

Then S Street changed from a street of waiting to a street of mourning.

News of the death spread rapidly through Washington and soon after it was generally known a flood of visits of condolence began. There were notables of all degree who came to assure the family of their sympathy. President and Mrs. Coolidge were among the first callers after the death was known. Then followed Cabinet members, high Government officials, important figures in the embassies of all nations—and there were others whose station was not exalted.

Moving slowly and somewhat feebly a little aged woman who seemed to have stepped out of a story book, came to the steps of the Wilson house. She made no effort to ring the door bell or send in her card. She simply paused there a moment and then came slowly down the steps and moved off toward Massachusetts Avenue.

Reporters asked her who she was and why she came. She said she was Mrs. A. R. Furman of Washington, and that she was 75 years old.

"I only wanted to stand on the threshold of Woodrow Wilson's home," she explained. "I think he is one of the greatest men that ever lived. I have prayed for his recovery every day since he was first stricken. Next to my son, I love him better than any man. If I could give my life now to save his, I would gladly do it."

There was also a boy bringing a flower this morning, as there had been yesterday. This boy was smaller than yesterday's visitor, hardly more than a toddler, yet he came quite alone. He brought a single pink rose. He said his name was Sam White, that he was 5 years old and that his father was a wounded service man undergoing treatment at the Walter Reed Hospital. He did not seem to have any grown-up explanation of why he had come bringing his tribute. It was for Mr. Wilson, and he had brought it, and that was all there was to it.

The first sign of mourning color about the house came soon after the President's visit, when Mrs. Grayson arrived with Miss Helen Bones, secretary to the first Mrs. Wilson and a relative of Mr. Wilson. Mrs. Grayson was dressed in black. Miss Bones, attired in the same color, wore a heavy black veil pushed back from her face.

At about the same time the first funeral flowers appeared. A florist's delivery man appeared bearing over his arm a flat floral piece made of three palm leaves on which were three red roses tied with a white silk sash. It was not learned who had sent them.

Some concern was felt when Dr. Ruffin arrived and spent some time in the house. It was thought Mrs. Wilson might have broken down. When he came out, however, Dr. Ruffin said both Mrs. Wilson and Miss Wilson were in excellent condition. He denied that he had given medical attention to either, and said neither needed it.

Through all the occurrences, the stream of callers continued unabated. J. Butler Wright, Third Assistant Secretary of State, was among the first after the announcement of the death. His call was the first official link between the death and action on it by the Government. He was at the house twice within a short period. The first call was a formal event, made necessary by his official duties, which required that he should receive authoritative confirmation of the death. Later he returned to offer his personal condolences and those of the State Department and to inform the family that the department had notified all American embassies and consulates of the death and directed them to lower their flags to half-staff at once and to fly them that way for thirty days. . . .

Printed in the *New York Times*, Feb. 4, 1924.

Calvin Coolidge to Cary Travers Grayson

My dear Admiral Grayson: [The White House] February 4, 1924.

This is to confirm the message delivered to you by my Secretary, Mr. Slemp, and myself. I trust that you and Mrs. Wilson will know that my entire desire is not to intrude, but to offer every possible assistance. While I have no jurisdiction over the Capitol, I should be pleased to use my good offices in arranging to have the body of President Wilson lie in state there for any period that might be desired. I wish you also to know that Arlington is open as a place for interment, or for using the vault connected with the amphitheatre. Anything that the State, War and Navy Departments can do, I should be glad to have done, if you will let me know. My desire is to assure you of every possible facility of the Government for anything that you may want, without intruding in any way upon your grief or making suggestions of my own.

Whatever I can provide officially or personally is at your disposal.

With kindest regards, I am

Cordially yours,   [Calvin Coolidge]

CCL (C. Coolidge Coll., MNF).

Edith Bolling Galt Wilson to Calvin Coolidge

My dear Mr. President: 2340 S Street N W Feb. 4—1924

On Wednesday afternoon at three oclock I am having a short service here at the house, before leaving for the Cathedral where Mr. Wilson's body will be laid to rest in the vault

At three thirty, there, we will have the regular service and I am writing to assure both you and Mrs Coolidge that should you wish to come to either or both of these, it will be a pleasure to have you, and every provision will be made for your comfort and protection

Assuring you again of my deep appreciation of your personal sympathy and your official tribute to my husband[1] and with messages to Mrs Coolidge

believe me—   Faithfully yours   Edith Bolling Wilson

ALS (C. Coolidge Coll., MNF).
    [1] This very generous tribute, in the format of a presidential proclamation, appears on the front page, e.g., of the *New York Times*, Feb. 4, 1924.

Calvin Coolidge to Edith Bolling Galt Wilson

My dear Mrs. Wilson: [The White House] February 4, 1924.

Your very thoughtful note has been received, and I beg to assure you that Mrs. Coolidge and I desire to attend the ceremony at the house and at the Cathedral.

May I reiterate that whatever you may wish from me or the Government is at your disposal, if you will communicate with me.

Mrs. Coolidge joins me in again extending to you every sympathy.   Very cordially yours,   [Calvin Coolidge]

CCL (C. Coolidge Coll., MNF).

Edith Bolling Galt Wilson to Henry Cabot Lodge

Dear Sir: [Washington] February fourth, 1924.

I note in the papers that you have been designated by the Senate of the United States as one of those to attend the funeral service of Mr. Wilson.

As the funeral is a private, and not an official one, and realizing that your presence there would be embarrassing to you and unwelcome to me I write to request that you do not attend.[1]

Very truly yours,   Edith Bolling Wilson.

TCL (WP, DLC).
    [1] The *New York Times*, Feb. 7, 1924, reported that Lodge, who was to be a member of the delegation to the funeral from the Senate, had been unable to attend because of a severe cold. He had stayed at home at his doctor's orders.

Two News Reports

[*Feb. 6, 1924*]

SIMPLICITY MARKS SERVICE IN THE HOME
A Scripture Lesson, Prayer and Selections From
Mr. Wilson's Private Devotional Book Read.

Washington, Feb. 6.—Three hours and a half before the hour scheduled for Woodrow Wilson's funeral, enormous crowds from the Government buildings, which had closed in respect to the former President, and from the downtown business districts began thronging their way to the Wilson home and out Massachusetts Avenue to the cathedral where the public services were to be held.

By 1 o'clock the assemblage outside the S Street house had grown so large that two companies of soldiers and marines were required to assist the police in making a throughfare for the relatives and friends assembling for the services in the home.

During the morning army trucks had taken away many loads of the flowers which had filled the two lower floors of the residence. Thousands of these were conveyed, at Mrs. Wilson's request, to the army hospitals where they would brighten the lives of her husband's erstwhile "comrades," as he liked to call them.

This distribution of the floral offerings to hospitals and to the cathedral was necessary in order to make room for the 200 invited guests, many of whom had come from long distances or crossed the continent to pay their final respects to Woodrow Wilson.

The weather was chilly and raw, with a hint of threatening storm. The sky was heavily overcast, and the observers most familiar with official Washington found it difficult to identify all those who arrived in heavy wraps and deep mourning.

Every available inch of ground that would give a view of the home was occupied. Corps of photographers and motion-picture men were intrenched on neighboring lawns. Across the street small boys were perched in all the trees, and a steep clay bank was filled with warmly dressed women.

Promptly at ten minutes to 3 o'clock President and Mrs. Coolidge, followed by Secret Service attendants, drew up at the doorway and were saluted by the heavy police guard under Inspector Sullivan[1] and the mixed assignment of soldiers, sailors and marines under General Drum[2] of the War Department.

The actual pallbearers, a selected octette of service men, each of whom had distinguished himself by bravery overseas, had already

[1] Daniel Sullivan, Major and Superintendent of the Metropolitan Police Department of the District of Columbia.
[2] Brig. Gen. Hugh Aloysius Drum, U.S.A., Assistant Chief of Staff for Operations and Training.

entered the house, bareheaded, and taken up their position inside near the casket.

Chief Justice William H. Taft, who had been a frequent caller at the Wilson home during the last days of sickness, when news of the bedroom was so eagerly sought, was unable to attend the funeral, where he expected to serve as an honorary pallbearer, on account of a sudden and serious attack of indigestion which confined him to bed.

Early arrivals for the home service included Newton D. Baker, former Secretary of War under Mr. Wilson, and the following members of his Cabinet: William B. Wilson, former Secretary of Labor; William C. Redfield, former Secretary of Commerce; David F. Houston, former Secretary of the Treasury; Edwin T. Meredith, former Secretary of Agriculture; Josephus Daniels, former Secretary of the Navy, and Joseph Tumulty, Mr. Wilson's secretary throughout his administration.

Bernard M. Baruch, an intimate and trusted associate of the former President in wartime, also came early with his son, Mrs. Baruch and their daughter in deep mourning.

The Rev. James H. Taylor, pastor of the Central Presbyterian Church, which was Mr. Wilson's church, and Dr. Sylvester W. Beach, who was the Wilson family minister at Princeton, N. J., arrived together at 2:45 P.M., and soon after were followed by Bishop James E. Freeman, Episcopal Bishop of Washington, who entered the house with a negro attendant carrying the Bishop's vestments.

Colonel Edward T. Brown of Atlanta, a cousin of the first Mrs. Wilson, with Mrs. Brown and three other members of the family, came soon after, all garbed in deep mourning. Colonel and Mrs. Brown have been frequent guests at the various Wilson homes for over forty years.

Fitzwilliam Woodrow, a nephew and employe of the Interstate Commerce Commission, was a member of this party. Others who arrived in rapid succession were ex-Governor James M. Cox of Ohio, with a group of friends, including White House attachés such as Rudolph Forster, Isaac Hoover Foster,[3] Patrick McKenna and Edward Starling.[4]

These men who worked so closely with the wartime President showed the deepest attachment to Mr. Wilson throughout his long illness. Then came Mrs. J. Borden Harriman with five ladies; Vance McCormick and Frank L. Polk, former Under Secretary of State; Senators Glass and Swanson of Virginia, with Judge John

[3] That is, Irving ("Ike") Hood Hoover.
[4] Edmund William Starling of the White House Secret Service detail. Patrick E. McKenna was a clerk at the White House.

Barton Payne and former Attorney General Thomas W. Gregory; Finis J. Garrett, Democratic leader of the House, and Cordell Hull, Democratic National Committee Chairman.

Mrs. Galt,[5] mother of Mrs. Wilson, arrived in the Wilson automobile with her daughter and Mrs. Wilson's two brothers, Alexander and Ralph Galt.[6] Major Gen. Tasker H. Bliss, a member of the Peace Commission which went to Paris with President Wilson, came alone in full army uniform.

George Creel, who supervised the Government's publicity and propaganda work in the Committee of Public Information during the war, and his wife, Blanche Bates, the actress, arrived with Ray Stannard Baker, who was Mr. Wilson's press representative at the Paris conference, and Mrs. Baker.[7]

Other arrivals included Robert W. Woolley, George White, former Chairman of the Democratic National Committee; the Rev. Dr. Robert Johnston, rector of St. John's Episcopal Church; Admiral and Mrs. Cary T. Grayson, Joseph Wilson, brother of Mr. Wilson, and his wife;[8] Cyrus McCormick of the International Harvester Corporation and a life long friend of Mr. Wilson; former Ambassador Charles R. Crane, a Princeton classmate;[9] Dr. Stockton Axson, a brother of the first Mrs. Wilson and his wife[10] and sister;[11] Charles Lee Swem, the former confidential stenographer and secretary to President Wilson; Dr. Leo S. Rowe of the Pan American Union.

The simple home service began promptly at 3 o'clock, and at that moment the sun, which had been masked by angry looking snow clouds, burst forth upon the scene.

At the same moment the military guard of honor, soldiers, sailors and marines distinguished for exceptional bravery during the World War, took their places in a double line before the doorway to form a lane through which the casket would be carried to the large limousine hearse.

There was no military form or ceremony, except for the presence of this one guard in the simple wartime uniforms. All the pride and panoply of military burial had been omitted by special request of the dead statesman when he laid down the title of "Commander-in-Chief."

[5] An error. She was Sallie White (Mrs. William Holcombe) Bolling. Her daughter, soon mentioned, was Bertha Bolling.

[6] Another error. They were Richard Wilmer Bolling and Rolfe E. Bolling. Corrections from the news report in the New York *World*, Feb. 7, 1924.

[7] Jessie Irene Beal Baker.

[8] Kate Wilson Wilson.

[9] An error; Crane's higher education consisted of a few weeks at the Stevens Institute of Technology, after which he withdrew on account of illness.

[10] Of course Stockton Axson never married. Helen Woodrow Bones accompanied him.

[11] Presumably Margaret Axson Elliott.

Then, in the simplest manner, Woodrow Wilson came forth for the last time to public view, on the shoulders of his former comrades, and started on his last earthly ride, without a blast of bugle or a rifle shot.

His simple casket, which was of copper, covered with black broadcloth, bore the simplest of inscriptions on its silver plate:

WOODROW WILSON.

1856-1924.

The only flowers out of the thousands of floral offerings from friends far and wide was a small and simple wreath of lavender orchids on the casket—a wreath sent by men who had served under him in France.

The guard of honor was a smaller one than would make up the funeral train of the lowest ranking officer of the army or navy.

Even the funeral service in the house, consisting of a reading of the Twenty-third Psalm, a short prayer by his Princeton minister consigning him to the bosom of the Almighty, and a few short Bible verses, was over in fifteen minutes.

The tribute in the prayer by Dr. Sylvester W. Beach, his close friend and intimate for over twenty-five years, was one to catch the imagination of thousands of Mr. Wilson's followers, who will long remember and treasure them:

"For the wondrous vision Thou didst give him of universal peace and good will; for his zeal with the Parliament of Man; for his unswerving devotion to duty; for his courage in the right as God gave him to see the right; for his unflinching integrity; for the fervor of his patriotism, we thank Thee.

"The God of Peace which passeth all understanding keep our hearts and minds in the love and knowledge of God."

The final feature of the simple service was the reading of some Bible verses, selected from a well-thumbed little book of devotional daily readings which had been a favorite with Mr. Wilson for many years.

Bishop James E. Freeman, the Episcopal Bishop of Washington, had seen this little leather-bound volume which always lay on Mr. Wilson's study table, and from which he read almost daily some extracts to hearten and strengthen him for the duty in hand.

The Bishop's first selection, read in the hush of the great room where the books, the easy chairs, the open fireplace all spoke so eloquently of the departed, was taken from the thirty-third chapter of Deuteronomy, the twenty-seventh verse:

"The Eternal God is thy refuge, and underneath are the everlasting arms: And He shall thrust out the enemy from before Thee: And shall say, 'Destroy them.' "

Then, after a brief silence, in which the minds of many went back to the stormy war-time periods and the strenuous fight for "a just and a lasting peace" which Woodrow Wilson made against heavy odds, the Bishop read a passage of humblest submission from the Epistle of Jude, the twenty-fourth and twenty-fifth verses:

"Now unto Him that is able to keep you from falling and to present you faultless before the presence of His glory with exceeding joy:

"To the only wise God, our Saviour, be glory and majesty, dominion and power, both now and forever. Amen."

WILSON BURIED IN CATHEDRAL CRYPT
WITH SIMPLE RITES AS NATION MOURNS

Washington, Feb. 6.—Woodrow Wilson was laid to rest today in the quiet peace of subterranean vaults in the National Cathedral.

The passing of the war-time President, the leading figure in probably the most stirring scenes history has recorded, was without pomp of state, or military trappings.

Down winding corridors into the subterranean chapel there floated the voice of a clergyman in the sacristy, intoning the benediction, and the choir's long-drawn "amen." There was the sound of many feet shuffling over a stone floor in exit. The studded doors of the chapel clanged shut.

The outside world was done with what was mortal of a great President. He belonged now only to the mourning family that remained alone in the chapel. The great stone slab in the centre of the floor was swung aside. Into the crypt entrance which its removal disclosed, the soldier, sailor and marine body-bearers lowered the casket.

At that moment in the Cathedral grounds outside a bugler sounded "taps." The great crowd bared heads and stood in silence as the notes of this most plaintive of all service calls, "lights out," hung about the hillside which dominates Washington and looks out into the hills of Virginia, where Woodrow Wilson was born.

Almost as if it were an echo of the bugle from St. Alban's Hill, another bugle spoke in the same notes from the great white amphitheatre at Arlington, where lies the tomb of the Unknown Soldier.

Outside, the bugle calls dwindled to a close and the crowd breathed again. Inside, the great stone slab was moved to its position, sealing the entrance to the crypt. The visitors began to depart. The funeral honors for the departed President were at an end. Simple dignity had marked the obsequies. To those who witnessed the event it seemed as though a page of history was being read, such a page as tells of the passing of a Napoleon or a Charlemagne.

The attitude of the crowds that surrounded the house in S Street, that lined the avenue of the funeral procession and thronged the Cathedral grounds was that of a people honoring a great chieftain.

Nowhere was the impelling force of the simplicity that has marked the passing of Woodrow Wilson more apparent than in the moments that marked the climax of the day, the interment service in the Bethlehem Chapel at the National Cathedral.

The chapel lies below the main floor level of the great apse, the only portion of the Cathedral finished to its full height. It is entered by a flight of temporary wooden stairs leading down from the ground level. Over the door by which the congregation entered, and which later admitted the funeral procession, is the inscription, "The Way of Peace."

Here the great of the land began to gather about 2 o'clock this afternoon. Long before the funeral procession arrived the 500 seats in the chapel were filled and every niche of space was occupied. It was announced that the chairs were to be removed, but they were in place when the congregation began to arrive, and thereafter it would have been impossible to remove them.

Among the first to arrive were members of the Cabinet and their wives. Secretary and Mrs. Hughes appeared and the Hoovers and Secretary Mellon. The Cabinet members were shown to places down front on the right hand side. Later, when the chapel was more crowded, something was apparently detected to be wrong with the Cabinet seating, and under direction of Third Assistant Secretary of State J. Butler Wright, who had charge of the arrangements, they were all asked to move to a section of seats near the chancel.

The Cabinet seating was without regard to any question of precedence or favored positions. It was so with the other guests. While there was a general plan by which certain divisions of the guests were seated in certain places, it was left to their own discretion and the order of their arrival as to what seats they occupied within these sections, and the order was by no means always carried out.

The absence of special attempt at formality in the seating arrangements was characteristic of all that went on. Always it was borne in mind that this was the funeral of a private citizen, prominent, it is true, but still a private citizen, for whom no official honors were expected or desired.

Diplomacy was represented by Ambassador Jusserand of France and Mme. Jusserand, the former the Dean of the Diplomatic

Corps; the British Chargé, Henry Getty Chilton; Ambassador Hanihara of Japan,[1] and Ambassador Riano of Spain.[2]

A touch of color was added by the uniforms of Major Gen. John L. Hines, Army Chief of Staff, just returned from Panama; Admiral Edward W. Eberle, Chief of Naval Operations, and Major Gen. John A. Lejeune, Commandant of the Marine Corps.

Slowly the chapel filled as guest after guest entered and was escorted to a seat. Finally the seats were exhausted and others had to stand in the rear and at the sides.

Mrs. Harding, wife of the former President, who was veiled, entered between Postmaster General Harry S. New and Mrs. New. Samuel Gompers, President of the American Federal of Labor, came in and took a seat in the back row, where he was later joined by Frank Morrison, Secretary of the national labor organization. Robert Underwood Johnson, the poet, who was present with others, representing the American Academy of Arts and Letters, stood for a while and then was seated down front on the right.

Dr. John H. Finley, Secretary of the American Institute of Arts and Letters, and representing that body, came in at the same time as Judge Alton B. Parker, and the two were seated together. In the back row was A. Mitchell Palmer, Attorney General in the Wilson Cabinet.

By 3 o'clock they had all arrived and the chapel doors were closed. After the confusion of seating was over, the assemblage settled into quiet and waiting.

At 3:15 the silence was suddenly broken by the first notes of the organ. At the keyboard was Warren Johnson, who had been a stenographer to Woodrow Wilson at Trenton in 1919 [1911?], when he was Governor of New Jersey. The first music was a hymn, which opened with three repeated notes that came almost with the effect of a trumpet call, so silent was the chapel.

At intervals the organist played other numbers. First was one of Mendelssohn's "Songs Without Words," known popularly as "Confidence." Then came Chopin's "Funeral March," which had been listed on the order of service. Next was Handel's "Largo." Then came "I Know That My Redeemer Liveth."

The organist was playing the latter number when, at five minutes of 4, the doors of the chapel were opened. From another door in the rear came the Very Rev. G. C. F. Bratenahl,[3] Dean of the cathedral, with attending clergymen. Then the choir, led by a crucifer.

[1] Masanao Hanihara.
[2] Juan Riaño y Gayangos.
[3] George Carl Fitch Bratenahl.

The choir proceeded up the main aisle toward the chancel, the crucifer halting at a point near the foot of the slab which covers the crypt. The organist was playing the hymn "Oh, Rest in the Lord."

Then Bishop Freeman, with Drs. Taylor and Beach, appeared in the doorway which leads in from "the way of peace." Behind them was the casket, borne by the service men. The choir moved slowly down the aisle, followed by the funeral procession. The former pastor of President Wilson's church in Princeton, the Rev. Sylvester W. Beach, read the first words of the service:

"I am the resurrection and the life."

The choir and the clergymen proceeded to the chancel and the chief mourners were seated, while the service men placed the casket on supports in front of the chancel. Mrs. Wilson, Mrs. McAdoo and Miss Margaret Wilson were heavily veiled.

Then came an antiphonal reading from the Thirty-ninth Psalm, in which the Rev. James H. Taylor, pastor of the Central Presbyterian Church, Mr. Wilson's Church in Washington, read the first verse and the congregation responded.

Bishop Freeman, his robes contrasting with the black of the Geneva gowns of the two Presbyterian clergymen, read with solemn effect the lesson from the Order for the Burial of the Dead. His voice resounded through the little chapel.

"There is one glory of the sun, and another glory of the moon, and another glory of the stars; for one star differeth from another star in glory. So also is the resurrection of the dead. It is sown in corruption, it is raised in incorruption; it is sown in dishonor, it is raised in glory; it is sown in weakness, it is raised in power; it is sown a natural body, it is raised a spiritual body."

The faces of trained diplomats, schooled to conceal their feelings, softened. There were others for whom tears were not far away.

"For the trumpet shall sound, and the dead shall be raised incorruptible, and we shall be changed. For this corruptible must put on incorruption, and this mortal must put on immortality. So when this corruptible shall have put on incorruption, and this mortal shall have put on immortality, then shall be brought to pass the saying that is written, death is swallowed up in victory. O death! where is thy sting? O grave! where is thy victory?"

With telling effect the male voices of the choir then sang the hymn "Day Is Dying in the West," a tenor voice rising a moment above the rest in "Holy, Holy, Holy, Lord God of Hosts."

This was followed by the recitation of the Apostles' Creed and the reading of the Lord's Prayer and other prayers from the Episcopalian ritual. At the end there was the benediction, pronounced by the Bishop, and the singing of the recessional hymn, "The Strife Is O'er, the Battle Done."

This concluded the service. A note on the order of service said that after the singing of the hymn, "the members of the congregation are requested to leave the chapel, first permitting the family and the President of the United States to make their departure."

The chapel was emptied from the front. Mrs. Wilson and the members of the family passed out through the door into the north vestibule, where they remained in the sacristy. The President and Mrs. Coolidge were the first to follow them, turning out through the south vestibule. The Cabinet members, the honorary pallbearers, the diplomats and other guests went next in order.

Soon the chapel was almost empty except for the casket that stood near the chancel. It was black, with silver handles, and bore on its face a plaque of sterling silver, on which was inscribed:

WOODROW WILSON.

1856-1924.

It was unornamented. On its top lay a spray of orchids, the flowers chosen and placed there by Mrs. Wilson. As he passed it the Rev. Robert E. Browning, assistant at the Church of the Epiphany when Bishop Freeman was its rector, laid near the orchids two pink roses.

While the family waited in the north vestibule workmen entered and raised the marble slab, three inches thick, that covers the entrance to the crypt. After the marble slab another slab of concrete, six inches thick, was raised, uncovering a vault fifteen feet square and eight feet deep. Into the crypt the workmen descended with ladders, carrying candles to light the interior.

A temporary wooden platform four feet high had been built on the south side of the crypt. There are eight catacombs in the vault, four in the west end and four in the east. The one in which Mr. Wilson's body rests is the upper catacomb on the south side of the west end group. Directly underneath lies Henry Vaughan, first architect of the Cathedral.

In the meantime every one had withdrawn except the members of the family. The description of what followed is furnished by one who was present.

When all was ready for the reception of the coffin, Bishop Freeman and the attending clergymen entered and took their positions. Silently the soldier and sailor bearers carried the coffin and placed it directly over the vault on supporting beams, returning to their positions near the altar.

Mrs. Wilson entered on the arm of William G. McAdoo, and the other members of the family gathered near. The space in which they stood was marked off by wreaths stretched between the columns immediately surrounding the crypt. Candles flickered in the vault immediately beneath the coffin.

The regular Episcopal committal service was then read. Through its lines the Bishop's voice proceeded, "earth to earth, ashes to ashes, dust to dust," until the small gathering joined in the Lord's prayer. The benediction which Bishop Freeman pronounced was:

"Unto God's gracious mercy and protection we commit thee. The Lord bless thee and keep thee. The Lord make his face to shine upon thee and be gracious unto thee. The Lord lift up his countenance upon thee and give thee peace, both now and ever more. Amen."

The only other change from the usual service was made at the request of Mrs. Wilson. As soon as the benediction was concluded Bishop Freeman recited Tennyson's "Crossing the Bar."

Again the soldiers and sailors gathered around the coffin. As the notes of "taps" sounded through the windows of the chapel, the coffin was lowered to the temporary platform underneath and moved forward into the catacomb set aside for it.

A few moments of silent devotion by the family, a few moments in which dim eyes looked into the vault where the workmen sealed up the catacomb by the flickering light of their candles and then the family moved out of the chapel and away.

A slab of white Alabama marble was placed over the mouth of the catacomb and sealed. The workmen left the vault. The slabs covering the opening were put back into their places. Soldiers and sailors took their places on guard around the crypt. Woodrow Wilson lies in peace.

Printed in the *New York Times*, Feb. 7, 1924.

ADDENDUM

Thomas Gedney Patten[1] to Joseph Patrick Tumulty

My dear Joe: New York, N. Y. April 11, 1921.

Excuse my not having answered your letter before, but I have been busy with a lot of things here in New York.

I have a very vivid recollection of the inception of the Federal Reserve Act, as the whole circumstance nearly put me into an untimely grave.

The President summoned the Democratic Members of the newly formed Banking and Currency Committee of the House of Representatives to an evening conference at the White House.[2] This Committee had been recently appointed and had never met. I knew Glass[3] casually from having seen him in the House, but had not spoken to him.

We all went to the White House; met the President, and were invited to the Cabinet Room, where, as it was found that there were not a sufficient number of seats to accommodate the fourteen, or including the President, the fifteen Members, the President suggested bringing in of other seats. I remember distinctly seeing him lugging in a large arm chair, and, when I offered to relieve him of it, he very practically suggested that I secure one for myself. He placed Glass at the head of the table, and so really organized the first session of the Committee.

The bill was read, and the President made a ten minute speech, in which he touched upon the inability of Congress to legislate in this direction for the last twenty years, and expressed an earnest hope that we would be able promptly to report the required legislation to the House, either by the bill under consideration, with such modifications and amendments as we saw fit to add to it, or by some other appropriate legislation.

It was perfectly apparent during the reading of the bill that it was not agreeable to certain Members of the Committee, this disagreement coming principally from the south and west.[4] New York, which I represented, was discreetly silent, although appeared later in the controversy. The disagreement of the men of the south and the west and the discussion which ensued were unequivocal, and the remarks to the effect that certain phases of the bill would be unexceptable [unacceptable] in these localities were very distinctly pointed out. I think that the President, and I know that Glass was quite seriously disturbed by the lack of harmony which developed in the Committee, and the men themselves, in leaving the conference, were quite plain in expressing their dissatisfaction of the bill.

It is difficult to conceive of any projected legislation being born with less promise than this bill upon which the future financial stability of the United States really rested.

I was one of the last to leave, and I think I have already narrated my interview with Glass under the big elm tree in front of the Executive Offices. He was extremely discouraged and quite hopeless as to the future of the legislation. Although New York had been silent, he had, from the known attitude of the New York bankers, classified me with the critics of the legislation, and was surprised and I think delighted when I told him that New York would stand unequivocally behind the bill, and, more than that, that, representing the State, I would at the proper moment call up the bill in Committee with a recommendation that it be discussed, amended and reported to the House, and that all other bills be placed upon the table.

With the period of gestation of this bill, you are of course familiar. It was months in the Committee. We arrived at a condition in which we hardly spoke to one another. I had, without knowing it, walking typhoid, and told both Glass and Underwood[5] that I was sick physically and wanted to go home. I remember distinctly one day Underwood carrying me back to the Committee Room, and telling me I had to sit there until the bill was reported out, which, I am glad to say, I did, and after reporting it into the House, immediately left for home. How I got there, I never distinctly remember. I remember telling my wife that I was sick and going to bed and waking up several days later with a trained nurse at my side.

You, from your position in the White House, are familiar with the difficulties which the friends of the legislation encountered in the Committee, and the difficulties of the task in wearing down the virulence, for it was nothing else, of the objectors. Underwood's tact and patience should not be overlooked. There were other contributing facts of which you have a special knowledge.

I was approached a dozen times to modify my attitude, and if the State of New York had waivered at any time, the prospect of the bill would have been greatly in danger.

I have always been profoundly thankful for the intuition which impelled me to pledge New York to Glass at the night of the conference.

Whatever pressure might have been brought by the President in the Committee Room, I was never aware of. In fact during my time in Congress, I always found the President, while properly insistent upon the prerogatives of the Executive, keenly sensitive to the particular rights of the legislative branch of the Government. His letter to the Chairman of the Committee on Rules in regard to the McLemore Resolution[6] is an instance in point, and is, I think, a model communication.

I expect to be in Washington in the course of a week or so, and will be sure to look you up.

With best regards, believe me,

Yours sincerely, T. G. Patten

TLS (received from Holt A. Murray).

[1] Democratic representative from New York, 1911-1917; Postmaster of New York City, 1917-1921.

[2] On June 20, 1913.

[3] Carter Glass, chairman of the committee.

[4] For the controversy over this version of the Federal Reserve bill, see Link, *Wilson: The New Freedom*, pp. 206-22.

[5] Oscar Wilder Underwood, majority leader in the House of Representatives.

[6] About this resolution and the controversy over it, see Arthur S. Link, *Wilson: Confusions and Crises* (Princeton, N. J., 1964), pp. 167-93.

APPENDIX

A Report of Two Interviews

[c. March 29, 1924]

Last Talks With Woodrow Wilson
By JAMES KERNEY

To the zero hour Woodrow Wilson regarded himself as the spiritual leader of a cause only temporarily lost. Despite his shattered health, he never completely abandoned the hope that he might again become the standard bearer of his party. Under no circumstance would he permit his intimates to commit him to any other candidacy. And he confidently expected to dictate the paramount issues in the coming presidential campaign, which explains much of the nervous anxiety of the past fall and early winter among Democratic candidates and chieftains, particularly those practical folks who felt that the debacle of 1920 had provided a right decent burial for the League of Nations.

It was my privilege to spend the afternoons of October twenty-third[1] and December seventh last with Mr. Wilson at his Washington home. On the occasion of these visits he made clear his belief that the liberals of the world were looking to him to lead them. Whatever historians may do, there can never be a doubt of his own intense conviction that his place was to fight what he was fond of terming the spiritual battles of humanity and democracy. It was a passion with him. I had suggested that, in view of his physical breakdown, he might find an easy way to emerge from his retirement and give effectual voice to his ideas by standing for the United States Senate from New Jersey—not a particularly new thought.

We talked the situation over from all angles—the fact that Governor Silzer,[2] strongest vote getter among New Jersey Democrats, did not want to run for senator; the possibility that the independent newspapers and state forces that had put over Wilson's first political program, and stood by him in his later fights, would line up again; the chance that even the solidly intrenched party machine would accept him. At our meeting on October twenty-third he asked me to go to New York and canvass the ground with his two confidential advisers—Bernard M. Baruch and Norman Davis.

But while appearing ready to consider the Senate as a remotely

[1] Actually, October 27, 1923.
[2] That is, George Sebastian Silzer.

possible outlet for leadership, his thoughts seemed plainly elsewhere. He was bitter in his expressions of contempt for the Senate
itself, and at one point he said, with a flash of the old-time vigor,
"There is only one place, you know, where I could be sure of effectively asserting that leadership." That was the nearest I ever heard
him come to a declaration of candidacy, but he did repeatedly emphasize his determination to prevent any temporizing with his
League policies. The Democratic candidate, he declared, would
not be agreed upon until the national convention was two or three
days old; meanwhile he expected to lay before the delegates a program of principles that would bring vindication at the polls. There
was to be no backing down. He was full of hope about giving his
views to the world. It was impossible to pin him down to writing
anything, however. Frequently he spoke of finding a way of assisting liberal thought; but, aside from the November radio speech,[3]
he apparently did nothing.

Upon leaving the S Street home in the afternoon of October
twenty-third, I promptly put into written form the substance of
what the former President had said. He had been exceedingly generous in his expressions of friendship and declared that he was
baring his soul to me.

"I am going to try to look at myself as though I did not exist," he
added; "to consider the whole thing in an impersonal way. From
the messages I get I realize that I am everywhere regarded as the
foremost leader of the liberal thought of the world, and the hopes
and aspirations of that liberal thought should find some better
place of expression than in the Senate. There is only one place, you
know, where I could be sure of effectively asserting that leadership. Outside of the United States, the Senate does not amount to
a damn; and inside the United States the Senate is mostly despised; they haven't had a thought down there in fifty years."

"You know and I know that I have a temper, and if I was to go
to the Senate I should get into a row with that old Lodge, who no
longer counts for anything. As I have remarked before of him, I'd
rather be a dead dead man than a dead live man. The Senate would
hardly provide the place for liberal leadership that the world is
seeking so sadly. Think of the people of Poland and of Czecho-
Slovakia and the other countries to whom we gave freedom—they
know that they owe their very national existence to me, and they
are looking to me to lead them. When I think of that fine old fellow,
Jan Smuts, for whom I have the greatest affection, and the others
of liberal tendencies who are looking to me, I feel that I should do

---

[3] It is printed at Nov. 10, 1923.

my part. My present political advisers are Bernard Baruch and Norman Davis, and I am going to ask you to see them in New York and talk the situation over and get the benefit of their views. Try to see them together. Perhaps we can yet find some way out."

We talked of many other things. When I entered the library he was seated in a big chair by the fireside. He was most cordial in his words of welcome, but remarked sadly, "I'm helpless, Kerney; this left side is going." His spirit appeared to be badly shot that day. The morning papers had printed official denials of one of those periodical news-ticker rumors of his death. I think the visit of David Lloyd George, on the previous afternoon, had been a bit of a disappointment too. According to the former President, about all that Lloyd George appeared to want to hear was a repetition of some of the limericks with which Wilson had regaled the European statesmen at Paris and Versailles. When I shifted the conversation to old times in New Jersey, his mood mellowed a bit and he got a smile out of the news that James R. Nugent,[4] master mechanic of the steam roller that had nominated him for governor back in 1910, had once again captured the Essex County Democratic organization.

"Nugent is a strange fellow, and though we had some powerful disagreements I always had a feeling of regard for him," Mr. Wilson declared.

He was keenly interested in the coal and road and public utility fights that Silzer, as governer [governor], had been making in New Jersey.

"Silzer is splendidly equipped for public service; he has vision and courage, and those veto messages of last winter were models," he added.

When it came time for his afternoon automobile ride I took my leave, assuring him that I would go to New York at an early date and talk over the senatorship, as well as the situation in general, with Baruch and Davis.

"I hope God will bless you and your family with good health and every happiness," he said as we shook hands in parting.

During the thirteen years since Wilson had come conspicuously into public life, I had as editor of the Trenton Times—from a friendly seat on the side lines—been given an occasional glimpse of most of the confidential advisers. I doubt if any ever had his complete confidence; it was not the Wilson way. Not that there was no affectionate warmth for those with whom he came into personal relationship. At Princeton he had been both the best loved

---

[4] That is, James Richard Nugent.

and best hated member of the faculty. In his public career it was the same.

By nature Wilson was a lonely man, a dreamer, with the type of intellect that found it difficult to tolerate ordinary mortals. His supreme self-confidence was perhaps his biggest handicap, as well as his most outstanding virtue. His habit was to rely upon his own dominating personality and power of persuasion to put things across. It was his lack of flexibility, of accommodation of mind, that led to much of the bitterness and disappointment that came to him in life.

Few, if any, public men thrown into intimate association with Wilson made the whole political distance with him. Harvey, Watterson, Smith,[5] Nugent, House, Lansing—all fell by the wayside. Joseph P. Tumulty, worshipful secretary, seeing no blemish in his idol, retained the favor longest and, outside of the immediate family and one or two old university friends like Cleveland Dodge and Stockton Axson, was best loved. Doctor Grayson of course became a part of the family life.

Tumulty, the play boy, reveling in the dramatics of it all, had given a dozen years of practical political experience, unstinted devotion and joyous laughter to the great mind that so often found itself impatiently battling with a world that would not see freedom the Wilson way. But the ill-starred Tumulty book,[6] about which Wilson appeared to be quite informed even if he had never read it, coupled with the seemingly harmless, if unauthorized message of felicitation that Tumulty carried to the testimonial dinner to James M. Cox in New York,[7] completely barred all further personal contact. Friends vainly tried to patch it up.

The thought that the complimentary message might be regarded throughout the country as an indorsement of Cox was too much for Wilson. He was not for Cox, and was very definitely not ready even to appear to be committing himself to any of the candidates for the presidency, although he frankly told me that "Cox was a very brave man to take up the League of Nations fight in 1920." Despite the estrangement, Wilson never lost his admiration for Tumulty's public experience and service. A few days after he had asked me to go to New York and talk with Baruch and Davis about the wisdom of his considering the Senate possibility, I received a

---

[5] That is, George B. M. Harvey, Henry Watterson, and James Smith, Jr.

[6] That is, *Woodrow Wilson As I Know Him.*

[7] About this contretemps, see JPT to WW, April 5, 1922, and WW to JPT, April 6, 1922, both in Vol. 67; the news report printed at April 8, 1922; WW to JPT, April 10, 1922; JRB to L. Wiley, April 10, 1922; the news report printed at April 11, 1922; WW to the Editor, *New York Times*, April 12, 1922; JPT to WW, April 12, 1922; and JPT to WW, April 13, 1922.

letter suggesting Tumulty for the senatorship as a man "whose political training has been more varied than that of any other man I
know," and one who "would make some of the reactionary senators
sit up and take notice of the arrival of modern times and circumstances." Here is the remarkable letter:

30th October, 1923.

My dear Kerney: Since you were here I have been thinking
over the matter we have discussed, and a man has occurred to
me whose qualifications I think you and your associates would
do well to consider very seriously, Mr. Winthrop M. Daniels.
He won the reputation here of being by far the ablest member
of the Interstate Commerce Commission, and is unusually
conversant with public questions in many fields. I have known
him a great many years and can vouch for his being able, conscientious and fearless. My own judgment is that he would
make a most serviceable member of the Senate.

Let me say also that when you are canvassing the field as a
whole I do not think you ought to overlook Tumulty, whose
political training has been more varied than that of any other
man I know, and who—when he was in the New Jersey Assembly—proved himself a redoubtable debater. He would
make some of the reactionary senators sit up and take notice
of the arrival of modern times and circumstances.

I felt it my duty to make these suggestions. It was a real
pleasure to see you.

Cordially and faithfully yours,   WOODROW WILSON.
Mr. James Kerney,
Trenton, N. J.

November first, on the day following my receipt of the foregoing
letter, Mr. Baruch took me to the home of Mr. Davis in New York,
where we spent several hours in discussing the whole situation.
The feeling of both men was that the former President would be
merely hurrying his death in becoming a candidate for any office.
That had been my own feeling as I walked downtown from the
Wilson home in Washington. It was finally agreed that Baruch and
Davis should each write frankly to Wilson, and that, after the lapse
of a period of time, I should go back and see him. The suggestion
of the names of Tumulty and Daniels was of course not practical.
Neither had lived in New Jersey for a decade. President Wilson had
named Professor Daniels, a Princeton man, to the Interstate Commerce Commission.

When I went back to see Mr. Wilson, December seventh, he was
in excellent spirits. His eye was bright, his mind fairly flashed with
sharp things, and altogether he was full of that snap and pep that

characterized the earlier days at Trenton and Washington. He re-clined on a big steamer chair, wrapped comfortably in a blanket, on the upper sun porch of his home. It was balmy as springtime in Paris and we chatted for nearly an hour. He felt that the reception that had been given to his Armistice Day radio speech showed the swing of the pendulum back in his direction—and he did not hes-itate to say so. When I reminded him that there was quite an inter-national furor over his radio reference to the "sinister climax" of France and Italy having "made waste paper of the treaty of Ver-sailles," he fired back in a spirited voice, "I should like to see Ger-many clean up France and I should like to meet Jusserand,[8] and tell him that to his face." He was plainly irritated at the French politicians; none among them, save Loucheur,[9] he felt had told him the entire truth. Stanley Baldwin's defeat[10] was a good thing not only for England but for its effect on Poincaré,[11] "who is a bully," he added.

"His master's voice has spoken," was his breezy comment on President Coolidge's message to Congress.

The message did not breathe one human hope, he said, but it would insure the nomination of Coolidge by the big-business crowd. The American farmer was not going to be fooled again on the European question; the farmer, he felt, was now fully aware that our unsettled foreign relations were playing havoc with busi-ness at home.

Of the Administration's World Court idea, he said, "They don't know where they're drifting; Hughes is at sea and they have no program." The Republican stupidity, he declared, would give the Democrats their great chance and he meant to see to it that there was no surrender to "the pocketbook brigade."

He was much disappointed at the enthusiastic way so many Democrats appeared to be abandoning principles and ideals in their anxiety to get their income taxes reduced.

"Wealth has its place," he said; "but it should not be the master; it should be made to serve the same as the rest of us."

[8] That is, Ambassador Jean Jules Jusserand.

[9] That is, Louis Loucheur, at this time a member of the Chamber of Deputies.

[10] Stanley Baldwin had succeeded Andrew Bonar Law as Prime Minister of Great Brit-ain on May 22, 1923. In October, Baldwin suddenly decided to request the dissolution of Parliament and a national election on the issue of increasing tariff protection for British industry. As a result of the election held on December 6, Baldwin's Conservative party still held 258 seats in Parliament, but the Labour party increased its total to 191, while the Liberals held 158. It was widely assumed that the Liberals would support a Labour government. As it turned out, Baldwin's cabinet lost a vote of no confidence on January 21, 1924; Baldwin resigned on the twenty-second; and the King asked Ramsey MacDonald to form the first Labour government in British history. Charles Loch Mo-wat, *Britain Between the Wars, 1918-1940* (Chicago and London, 1955), pp. 162-71.

[11] That is, Raymond Poincaré, at this time Premier of France.

And he proceeded to express his complete disgust at the public indifference toward low moral standards in Government. He always despised the traffic in prestige by those who had won the great prizes of governmental office. There is no secret about the resentment he felt at officials who resigned before their time was out to go after the big fees. Though such procedure might be within the law, he was strongly opposed to it on ethical grounds. He would not yield even to the pressure of those who felt he might with absolute propriety accept some adequate compensation for his writings, as Roosevelt had done. His prestige was not for sale in any market.

It was an impossible task to pin him down to writing for publication. He did practically none of it after he got into official life. There was a great deal of discussion between us, on that last December afternoon, regarding the method by which he was going to put over his program for political regeneration, but he reached no decision. When I returned to Trenton I wrote, suggesting that it would be desirable for him to get an article shaped up for some friendly magazine, to be followed by others that might be broadcast through one of the syndicates, and here is the reply I received:

Washington, D. C.

13th December, 1923.

My dear Kerney: Thank you for your thoughtful letter of December twelfth and for the generous purpose of what it proposes. But the kind of writing you suggest for me is the particular kind in which I have had no practice, and the kind least suited to what I believe to be my best literary method. I shall have to find—and no doubt I shall find—other means of assisting liberal thought. I am none the less obliged to you for your disinterested counsel.

It was a real pleasure to see you the other day, and I hope that we shall be frequently thrown together.

With most earnest good wishes for you and yours, and with very warm regards,   Faithfully yours,

WOODROW WILSON.

And then came the Christmas holidays and the January visit of the national committee[12]—and the end. He never got a chance to find the way of putting into concrete form the great dreams he was dreaming in his closing years. He died fully convinced that the whole world was shifting his way.

For me, who had seen him start so buoyantly on his political career, following his battle to democratize Princeton, the recollection

---

[12] About which, see the news report printed at Jan. 16, 1924.

of his cheerful spirit on that December afternoon is especially pleasant. And when the eye of Joe Tumulty falls on this for the first time it will bring pleasure to him.

"That was a very handsome thing, governor, you said about Tumulty in your letter," I told Mr. Wilson, after we had discussed the impracticability of his being a candidate himself for the United States senatorship.

"It's the way I felt; Tumulty would make them all sit up and take notice; he could render the country fine service in the Senate," was the gracious reply.

We talked, too, of other days in New Jersey, and he laughingly repeated an oft-expressed belief that anyone who was in politics and couldn't learn all the tricks of the game in short order in New Jersey had better seek some other field of activity.

He was much interested in a recent speech that I had heard Alexander Meiklejohn, former president of Amherst, deliver at the Nassau Club, at Princeton, in which the faculty of his old university got some rather refreshingly frank views on the relationship of alumni and trustees to educators.

"There are many splendid fellows in the Princeton faculty; but they are allowed no freedom of thought," Mr. Wilson remarked with a tone of bitter sadness in his voice. And be [he] added: "Candidly, Kerney, if I had a son I wouldn't know where to send him for a liberal education in America."

Before I retired he recited a dozen or more limericks. This one of his own, that he had put together to amuse—or perhaps shock—a rather prim woman friend, he repeated with considerable glee:

"There was a young girl from Missouri
Who took her case to the jury;
She said, 'Car ninety-three
Ran over my knee.'
But the jury said, 'We're from Missouri!' "

And he got a lot of fun out of repeating the revised version of the old Massachusetts limerick about where the "Lodges speak only to the Cabots and the Cabots speak only to God."

"You recall," he said, "how that family of Kabotskis in Philadelphia tried to change the name to Cabot, and how the Cabots went to court for an injunction, and so the limerick had to be made over."

And then, with a merry twinkle, he repeated the revision:

"Here's to Massachusetts,
The land of the bean and the cod,
Where the Lodges can't speak to the Cabots
Because the Cabots speak Yiddish, begob."

There was some yarning, and when I rose to go he cordially urged me to "come back soon." It was my good fortune to have enjoyed a most happy relationship with him from the beginning. His letters always had a great charm of expression, and in matters of etiquette he was most punctilious. A couple of years ago, in response to a hastily scribbled birthday greeting that had evidently been mislaid in his correspondence, he sent me this letter:

WASHINGTON, D. C.
13th January, 1922.

My dear Kerney: I am sorry to be belated in replying to your generous birthday letter; but I am sure you will understand and will believe me when I say that the letter gave me the greatest pleasure. After all, the thought and approval of old friends gives the deepest assurance to the heart.

You and I have been within sight of each other for so long that we can be sure of the genuineness of our comradeship.

I am sure that you are looking forward with confidence, as I am, to the early return of our people to their true ideals and of the policies which will restore the moral leadership of the United States in the world. We must spend all that is best in us when that time comes.

Hoping that the New Year will bring you everything that is worth having of satisfaction and success.

Cordially,
Your sincere friend,
WOODROW WILSON.

Though his mind never appeared to dim, he was necessarily a cloistered shut-in during the last years of his life. His days were prolonged by the devoted sheltering from the public provided by Mrs. Wilson and her brother, John Randolph Bolling, who gave up his personal business to act as secretary. Everything was done to guard Woodrow Wilson against the least possible irritation or annoyance, and to conserve his strength. All mail was carefully sorted and resorted, and only such letters as were not calculated to disturb him actually reached him, and on such days as his spirits were low no mail went to him. As was his custom at the White House, he spent Sunday mornings in his study, going over his personal mail and dictating answers. Only one person a day was permitted to visit him. The whole thought of the household was of saving him. He never got over his love for the daily automobile ride and for the vaudeville theater, and despite the pathos of his wrecked body he kept up his Saturday-night visits to the Washington shows. When he quit the White House he expressed distaste for the title "former President." The man who had served as head of the nation was no different from the humblest citizen after he retired from office. And so he was always spoken of as "Mr. Wilson," and formal letters were always signed by Captain Bolling as "Secretary to Mr. Wilson." No man ever ended his days in more considerate and loving surroundings.

Printed in *The Saturday Evening Post*, CXCVI (March 29, 1924), 3-4, 77.

INDEX

NOTE ON THE INDEX

THE alphabetically arranged analytical table of contents at the front of the volume eliminates duplication, in both contents and index, of references to certain documents, such as letters. Letters are listed in the contents alphabetically by name, and chronologically within each name by page. The subject matter of all letters is, of course, indexed. The Editorial Notes and Wilson's writings are listed in the contents chronologically by page. In addition, the subject matter of both categories is indexed. The index covers all references to books and articles mentioned in text or notes. Footnotes are indexed. Page references to footnotes which place a comma between the page number and "n" cite both text and footnote, thus: "418,n1." On the other hand, absence of the comma indicates reference to the footnote only, thus: "59n1"—the page number denoting where the footnote appears.

The index supplies the fullest known form of names and, for the Wilson and Axson families, relationships as far down as cousins. Persons referred to by nicknames or shortened forms of names can be identified by reference to entries for these forms of the names.

All entries consisting of page numbers only and which refer to concepts, issues, and opinions (such as democracy, the tariff, money trust, leadership, and labor problems), are references to Wilson's speeches and writings.

Four cumulative contents-index volumes are now in print: Volume 13, which covers Volumes 1-12, Volume 26, which covers Volumes 14-25, Volume 39, which covers Volumes 27-38, and Volume 52, which covers Volumes 40-49 and 51.

INDEX

Charles University (Prague), 296n1
Charlton, Lionel Evelyn Oswald, 415,n1
Chase, Olive, 188
Chattanooga Times, 268n1
Chemical Foundation, 299,n1
chemical industry: and Palmer's case and
  Germany, 299-301,n1,4,8, 303, 303-304,
  356, 357-58, 361
Chester, Colby Mitchel, 504,n1
Chevy Chase Country Club, 376,n3
Cheyney, Edward Potts, 514,n2
Chicago Nipple Manufacturing Company,
  149n6
Chicago, University of, 259n3
Child Labor Tax Case, 131,n3
child welfare, 492; WW on, 478-79,n1
Child Welfare Board of New York City,
  478n1
Chilton, Henry Getty, 581
Christian, George Busby, Jr., 48n6
Christian Science, 68-69,n1
Chronicle of a Generation: An Autobiogra-
  phy (Fosdick), 451n1
Church Peace Union, 160
Civil Service System: Houston on, 271
Clarke, Alice, 130,n1, 138, 139
Clarke, Ida, 130,n1, 138, 139
Clarke, John Hessin, 164, 184-85, 188-89,
  282; WW on resignation of, 127-28,n1; on
  Supreme Court situation, 130-31; on
  League of Nations, 131-32,n1,n10; WW's
  condolences to, 138; on formation of independent nonpartisan organization for
  League of Nations, 139-40, 140, 143-44,
  157, 158-62, 162, 171, 173, 174-75,
  178n1, 251, 275, 324-25; on his younger
  sister, 139; WW on League of Nations
  plans of, 144, 145, 166-67; health of, 171,
  174, 179, 184, 188-89, 196, 198, 275, 276,
  281; WW on urging unconditional acceptance of League of Nations Covenant, 179;
  WW against nonpartisan action on League
  of Nations, 276; on Article X and League
  of Nations, 279; on difference with WW on
  League of Nations approach, 281; on principles of League of Nations Non-Partisan
  Association, 332-33; on his speaking tour
  for League of Nations, 359-60; WW
  thanks, 361; R. S. Baker on support for
  League of Nations plan of, 524
Clemenceau (Duroselle), 190n3
Clemenceau, Georges, 201, 223n3; mention
  of visit to U. S., 109, 116, 190,n3; WW's
  welcome to and response of, 197, 198;
  Bliss on peace negotiations and, 224;
  meets with WW, 226-28; WW's farewell
  to, 230; good wishes to WW, 234; on Italian situation, 255; Baruch on, 406
Cleveland, Ohio, 505
Cleveland Chamber of Commerce, 277
coal industry: Peabody on federal ownership,
  203; Peabody on coal transport, 205; Brandeis on mining case, 277,n1
Cobb, Frank Irving, 141, 190, 191-92, 197,
  311, 337, 402; on U. S. entry into League
  of Nations and WW's response, 99, 100;

on WW preparing Democratic program,
  100-101, 101; on Democratic party program and Missouri primary, 104; suggests
  WW announce Democratic party program,
  195-96; WW asks advice on party leadership and on critical editorial, 234; on
  League of Nations, 239; on The Document
  and WW's position as party leader, 239;
  and WW Foundation, 249n2; WW to review The Document with, 294, 295, 295-
  96, 534; on development of Brandeis' prohibition statement, 304-305, 305, 315,
  338, 385; on Lord Robert Cecil's speech on
  League of Nations, 308; Seibold on, 371-
  72; WW advises to take a rest, 384-85; to
  follow WW's advice and take vacation,
  385; WW's offers medical advice on exercise, 397, 400-401; death of, 504,n1; love
  for WW, 508; WW's tribute to, 520
Cobb, Margaret Hubbard Ayer (Mrs. Frank
  Irving): WW's condolences to, 504; thanks
  WW, 508
Cobb of "The World": A Leader in Liberalism
  (Heaton, comp.), 520n1
Coben, Stanley, 299n1
Colby, Bainbridge, 13, 4,n1, 118, 118-19, 330; and
  The Document, 4,n1, 10-11, 17-19, 26-27,
  34, 315; on Chadbourne's personal and legal dilemma, 16; and Marshal Joffre, 26;
  on Jefferson Day message brouhaha, 28;
  on loan to Ecuador, 56-57, 74, 111-12,
  114, 118; on Flatt-Badger publishing case,
  81-83, 83; on Western Ukraine Republic
  hearing, 110-11, 118, 119, 125, 134, 140-
  41; WW's advice on Western Ukraine Republic, 113-14, 135-36, 142; Bolling's personal advice on specific issues, 114-15; on
  defending Sinclair Consolidated Oil Corporation, 119, 125; visits WW, 121; off to
  London for Western Ukraine Republic
  hearing, 152; concern over law practice
  leads to dissolution of law partnership,
  199-200, 211-12, 231, 238; WW on dissolution of law partnership, 202, 213-14,
  232; touched by WW's praise, 214; thanks
  WW for autographed photograph, 290; *see
  also* Wilson & Colby
Colby, Everett: and League of Nations Non-
  Partisan Association, 162,n1, 178n1; WW
  on, 163
Colby, Frances Bainbridge, 114,n1, 118, 142
Colby, Katherine Sedgwick, 114,n1, 118,
  142
Colby, Nathalie Sedgwick, 114,n1, 118, 142
Colby, Nathalie Sedgwick Washburn (Mrs.
  Bainbridge), 114,n1, 118, 142, 152
Collier's, 476,n3; and WW's essay, 342, 343-
  44, 353, 357, 368
Collins, Varnum Lansing, 477,n1,3
Colorado: Democratic party in, 301n2, 302
Columbia (S. C.) Theological Seminary, 500-
  501,n1
Columbia University, 478n2
Columbus, Christopher, 92
Conference of Ambassadors: and Corfu inci-
  dent, 419n1, 435; and Memel, 521n1; *see*